Handbook of Transportation Policy and Administration

PUBLIC ADMINISTRATION AND PUBLIC POLICY

A Comprehensive Publication Program

Executive Editor

JACK RABIN
Professor of Public Administration and Public Policy
School of Public Affairs
The Capital College
The Pennsylvania State University–Harrisburg
Middletown, Pennsylvania

Assistant to the Executive Editor
T. Aaron Wachhaus, Jr.

Handbook of Transportation Policy and Administration

Edited by

Jeremy F. Plant
The Pennsylvania State University–Harrisburg
Middletown, Pennsylvania, U.S.A.

Associate Editor
Van R. Johnston
University of Denver
Denver, Colorado, U.S.A.

Assistant Editor
Cristina E. Ciocirlan
Elizabethtown College
Elizabethtown, Pennsylvania, U.S.A.

CRC Press
Taylor & Francis Group
Boca Raton   London   New York

CRC Press is an imprint of the
Taylor & Francis Group, an informa business

CRC Press
Taylor & Francis Group
6000 Broken Sound Parkway NW, Suite 300
Boca Raton, FL 33487-2742

International Standard Book Number-10: 1-57444-565-0 (Hardcover)
International Standard Book Number-13: 978-1-57444-565-7 (Hardcover)

Library of Congress Cataloging-in-Publication Data

Handbook of transportation policy and administration / edited by Jeremy Plant, Van R. Johnston, and Cristina Ciocirlan.
    p. cm. -- (Public administration and public policy ; 127)
    Includes bibliographical references and index.
    ISBN-13: 978-1-57444-565-7 (alk. paper)
    ISBN-10: 1-57444-565-0 (alk. paper)
    1. Transportation and state. I. Plant, Jeremy F., 1945- II. Johnston, Van R. III. Ciocirlan, Cristina. IV. Title. V. Series.

HE193.H33 2007
388.0973--dc22
    2006031908

Visit the Taylor & Francis Web site at
http://www.taylorandfrancis.com

and the CRC Press Web site at
http://www.crcpress.com

To our friends and colleagues in the Section on Transportation Policy and Administration of the American Society for Public Administration.

Contributors

John A. Anderson Ph.D., associate professor, and director of administration and leadership studies research, department of sociology, Indiana University of Pennsylvania, Dixon University Center, Harrisburg, Pennsylvania.

Simon P. Anderson commonwealth professor, department of economics, University of Virginia, Charlottesville, Virginia.

Michael T. Behney instructor of public affairs, School of Public Affairs, and director, Institute of State and Regional Affairs, the Pennsylvania State University–Harrisburg, Middletown, Pennsylvania.

David Connelly assistant professor, department of political science, Western Illinois University, Macomb, Illinois.

Eric T. Donnell assistant professor, department of civil and environmental engineering, the Pennsylvania State University, University Park, Pennsylvania.

Z. Andrew Farkas professor, Institute for Transportation, Morgan State University, Baltimore, Maryland.

Mary Beth Farquahr Ph.D. candidate, School of Public and International Affairs, Virginia Polytechnic Institution and State University, Alexandria, Virginia.

Patrick Fisher department of political science, Seton Hall University, South Orange, New Jersey.

Johnathan Gerber Ph.D. candidate and teaching assistant, department of political science, Washington State University, Pullman, Washington.

Andrew R. Goetz professor, department of geography, Intermodal Transportation Institute, University of Denver, Denver, Colorado.

Steve G. Green professor, department of management, United States Air Force Academy, Colorado Springs, Colorado.

John J. Gruidl professor of agricultural economics, Illinois Institute for Rural Affairs, Western Illinois University, Macomb, Illinois.

R. John Hansman professor, department of aeronautics and astronautics, Massachusetts Institute of Technology, Cambridge, Massachusetts.

Kevin E. Henrickson Ph.D. candidate, Gonzaga University, Jepson School of Business, Eugene, Oregon.

Kurt A. Heppard associate professor, department of management, United States Air Force Academy, Colorado Springs, Colorado.

Pannapa Herabat assistant professor, department of construction management and engineering, North Dakota State University, Fargo, North Dakota.

Paul Hubler MPA, University of La Verne, La Verne, California.

Erik W. Johnston Ph.D. candidate, School of Information, Center for the Study of Complex Systems, University of Michigan, Ann Arbor, Michigan.

Van R. Johnston professor of public policy and business, Daniels College of Business, University of Denver, Denver, Colorado.

Bassel El-Kasaby instructor, Aviation Institute, School of Public Administration, University of Nebraska at Omaha, Omaha, Nebraska.

Wendell C. Lawther associate professor, department of public administration, University of Central Florida, Orlando, Florida.

Joanne L. Lubart assistant counsel, office of chief counsel, Pennsylvania Department of Transportation, Harrisburg, Pennsylvania.

Daniel Madar professor, department of political science, Brock University, St. Catharines, Ontario.

Sarmistha Rina Majumdar assistant professor, department of political science, Sam Houston State University, Huntsville, Texas.

John M. Mason, Jr. associate dean and professor, College of Engineering, The Pennsylvania State University, University Park, Pennsylvania.

Sue McNeil professor, department of civil and environmental engineering, University of Delaware, Newark, Delaware.

Jack W. Meek professor, College of Business and Public Management, University of La Verne, La Verne, California.

Christopher D. Merrett director and professor of geography, Illinois Institute for Rural Affairs, Western Illinois University, Macomb, Illinois.

Göktuğ Morçöl associate professor, School of Public Affairs, the Pennsylvania State University–Harrisburg, Middletown, Pennsylvania.

Margaret Morrow business educator, business department, Frederick High School, Frederick, Colorado.

Aleksandra Mozdzanowska Ph.D. candidate, School of Engineering, Massachusetts Institute of Technology, Cambridge, Massachusetts.

David C. Nice professor, department of political science, Washington State University, Pullman, Washington.

Patrick D. O'Neil graduate assistant, Aviation Institute, School of Public Administration, University of Nebraska at Omaha, Omaha, Nebraska.

Sock-Yong Phang associate professor, School of Economics and Social Sciences, Singapore Management University, Singapore.

Jeremy F. Plant professor of public administration and public policy, the Pennsylvania State University–Harrisburg, Middletown, Pennsylvania.

Theodore H. Poister professor, fepartment of public administration and urban studies, Andrew Young School of Policy Studies, Georgia State University, Atlanta, Georgia.

Willard Price professor of operations and engineering management, Eberhardt School of Business, University of the Pacific, Stockton, California.

Thomas W. Sanchez associate professor, urban affairs and planning program, Virginia Tech, Alexandria, Virginia.

Paul Seidenstat associate professor of economics, Fox School of Business, Temple University, Philadelphia, Pennsylvania.

Aileen Switzer multi-modal planning supervisor, Wisconsin Department of Transportation, Transportation District Office 2, Madison, Wisconsin.

Joseph S. Szyliowicz professor, Graduate School of International Studies, Denver University, Denver, Colorado.

Scott E. Tarry professor, Aviation Institute, School of Public Administration, University of Nebraska at Omaha, Omaha, Nebraska.

Mary M. Timney professor, department of public administration, Pace University, White Plains, New York.

François Vaillancourt professor, economics department, Université de Montréal, Montréal, Québec, Canada.

William L. Waugh, Jr. professor, Andrew Young School of Policy Studies, Georgia State University, Atlanta, Georgia.

Wesley W. Wilson professor, department of economics, University of Oregon, Eugene, Oregon.

Philippe Wingender Ph.D. candidate, University of California, Berkeley, California.

James Wolf professor, School of Public and International Affairs, Virginia Polytechnic Institution and State University, Alexandria, Virginia.

Richard R. Young associate professor of supply chain management, School of Business Administration, the Pennsylvania State University–Harrisburg, Middletown, Pennsylvania.

Ulf Zimmermann associate professor, Kennesaw State University, Kennesaw, Georgia.

Contents

Part I. Transportation Systems in the Twenty-First Century

Part II. Transportation and Federalism

Acknowledgments

The idea of developing the *Handbook* began with discussions I had with my colleagues from the Section on Transportation Policy and Administration (STPA) of the American Society for Public Administration. STPA was formed in 1992, shortly after the passage of the landmark Intermodal Surface Transportation Efficiency Act (know by its acronym, ISTEA) a short time earlier. STPA is an organization dedicated to advancing the knowledge and practice of transportation policy and administration and bringing transportation-related issues to the attention of public administrators and scholars whose primary focus in on general policy and management questions. Three current or former chairs of STPA—Van Johnston, Scott Tarry, and Jeremy Plant—are among the authors represented in the in this volume, along with STPA executive committee members Willard Price and Wendell Lawther.

I also wish to thank a number of individuals whose help has been critical in moving the project forward. The Associate Editor, Dr. Van Johnston of the University of Denver, took the lead in developing the section on Transportation Security and provided overall guidance as the project developed. The Assistant Editor, Cristina Ciocirlan of Elizabethtown College, took time away from her young family and doctoral studies at Penn State Harrisburg to work with authors in developing their chapters and bringing them to closure. Dr. Jack Rabin, the *Handbook* series editor and my colleague at Penn State Harrisburg, supported the idea of the volume and helped answer many of the questions we encountered as the project proceeded. Rich O'Hanley at Auerbach Books provided timely encouragement and guidance, and the staff at Taylor & Francis oversaw the final production of the volume.

It goes without saying that the greatest contribution has been made by the authors of the chapters; without them, there would be no *Handbook of Transportation Policy and Administration*.

Preface

The past three decades have brought sweeping changes to the field of transportation. In the United States and other developed nations, deregulation and greater reliance on markets and the private sector has helped to reconfigure the transport industries. The rise of intermodal goods movements and global commerce has produced efficiencies of operation and a greater interdependence among transport modes. The fundamental importance of transportation in the modern society has been examined by rigorous analysis from a variety of disciplines: engineering, economics, geography, political science, information science, and sociology. Tradeoffs between competing values such as mobility, safety, efficiency, equity, conservation, aesthetics, and historic preservation have helped to heighten our understanding of the critical position transportation—and policies and management guiding transportation—plays in contemporary life. In the post-September 11 era, transportation security issues have moved to center stage as we grapple with the challenge of protecting our vast transportation system while maintaining its operational efficiencies and effectiveness.

The *Handbook of Transportation Policy and Administration* represents an effort to bring together under one cover the work of a number of leading experts in the emerging and interdisciplinary field we call "transportation studies." It is by no means complete—that would require a multi-volume treatment. However, it is intended to provide professionals in the field of transportation, students, scholars, public officials, and informed citizens knowledge of the basic organization of the transportation field, the policies guiding its operations and development, case examples of transportation planning, operations and management, connections between the transportation system and other policy arenas, and a picture of how transportation modes and systems are changing under the pressure to remain safe and secure under new types of threats.

The volume has been developed under what might be called an "open-ended" approach. The various authors were not expected to test any particular thesis or vision of transportation, but rather to contribute their best thinking on major aspects of transportation policy and administration. The *Handbook* takes no stand on the contentious issues that often arise in discussions of transportation: which mode of transport should be preferred, should the public or private sector take the lead in making fundamental decisions or running transportation operations, or what discipline holds the key to understanding transportation issues. The reader is provided a broad range of insights, beginning with overviews of many of the major transportation modes and moving through discussions of transportation policy and transportation management to the final section on transportation security. Authors include practitioners, current and former, as well as scholars and policy analysts. The focus is primarily on the United States and almost entirely on transportation in the developed world: a weakness, no doubt, and one that we hope will be corrected in a future examination of transportation in other settings.

Part I

Transportation Systems in the Twenty-First Century

1 The Big Questions of Transportation Policy and Administration in the Twenty-First Century

Jeremy F. Plant

INTRODUCTION

The past few decades have seen profound changes in transportation systems in the United States and around the world. In the United States, and in much of the developed world, these changes have included at least the following:

- Deregulation or privatization of major modes of transportation and increasing reliance on market forces to produce an efficient and productive transportation sector. Deregulation has affected all modes of transportation and has led to the disestablishment of much of the regulatory regime and shake-ups in the private sectors of the economy providing transportation services along with generally greater choice for consumers and users of transportation services.
- A movement away from narrowly focused transportation programs in favor of more broadly based programs with greater opportunities for stakeholder input and managerial discretion. In the United States, a major milestone in this direction was the passage of the Intermodal Surface Transportation Efficiency Act (ISTEA) in 1991, which broke away from the tradition of specific, functionally based highway and transit programs in favor of a more comprehensive approach to planning and implementing national surface transportation programs.
- A growing tendency to see transportation policy as a clash of competing values—of "wicked problems" (Harmon and Mayer 1986)—rather than as an exercise in technical expertise. Wicked problems, according to Harmon and Mayer, "have no definitive formulation and hence no agreed-upon criteria to tell when a solution has been found; the choice of a definition of a problem, in fact, typically determines its 'solution'" (p. 10). Transportation systems according to this view have to be seen not simply as ways to move people and goods, but as contributors to social values such as equity and access for various groups and individuals in society, historic and cultural preservation, rational land use, energy independence, environmental quality, even aesthetics.

- Globalization of the world economy has led to major changes in goods movement and global commerce, but also has increased the risks of terrorist attacks and other threats to transportation systems worldwide. Transportation facilities and operations have been major targets of world-wide terrorist activities and will presumably remain inviting opportunities for terrorism into the foreseeable future.

Some see such changes as transformational: in their view, we are witnessing the beginning of a new era in transport. Some see transformation in the transportation systems and services; others see a sea change in the way we think about transportation, craft transportation policy, and manage transportation operations. Others see change as more incremental in nature, moving in a more partial or evolutionary manner from the past to the present. The incrementalists point out that we are still an automobile society (and more broadly, a fossil-fuel driven transportation system); that commuting times and distances show a continued preference for suburban living and automobile commuting; that air, rail, truck, and water transport seem to have found functions and market niches that are relatively stable; that major policy initiatives in surface transportation policy, beginning with the ISTEA 1991, have not led to wholesale change in roles, processes or outcomes.

Regardless of how fundamental the nature of change is perceived to be, all observers of transportation agree that change will continue and will not be simple or without costs. One way of focusing attention to the most significant issues raised by the changing nature of transportation is to employ an introspective method commonly known as the "big questions" approach. In the next section we sketch out the big questions that have informed the organization and content of this volume.

BIG QUESTIONS OF TRANSPORTATION POLICY AND ADMINISTRATION

In recent years, a popular theme of the public policy and administration literature has been identifying the big questions of public management (Behn 1995), public policy, ethics, specific policy areas, and the like. Robert Behn has been a pioneer in establishing the big questions approach in the social sciences, and explains it as fundamental to any academic discipline:

> Get any group of scientists from any branch of science together, and they will start talking about the big questions in their field, the latest research published about those questions, and how they, through their own research, are attempting to tackle those same big questions. Any field of science is defined by the big questions it asks. (p. 314)

What are the big questions of transportation policy and administration? Not even the most confident pundit would imagine unanimous support for a list derived from introspection and speculation, but perhaps the approach has merit in stimulating thought and discussion. In such a loosely coupled field as transportation policy, it may be a good way to bring experts from a wide variety of backgrounds together to think holistically about transportation matters. I offer the following "big questions" as among the most fundamental and significant:

- How can transportation systems of different sizes, scope of operations, and means of delivery be considered as part of an all-encompassing system of transportation, while still understood as having unique characteristics of value? How can we consider both the forest and the trees within the individual modes of transport and the overall system of moving people and goods to which they contribute?
- On what basis, and by whom, should the most important decisions on transportation policy be made? By government, by the private sector, through market preference, public-private collaboration, or command-and-control methods? According to economic logic or crafted through political means? What government roles can we assign to the different levels of the federal system?
- How best can transportation systems be managed? How is *performance* defined, made operational, and measured in transportation? What values compete to define good and bad performance—mobility, efficiency, equity, access, environmental protection, energy conservation, security and safety, and economic stimulation—and how are these values weighed?
- How can we deal most effectively with the needs of today's transportation system while securing transportation systems for the future? What is the nature of the obligation transportation decision makers have to future generations as well as today's stakeholders to secure and improve transportation systems?

Today's big questions did not arrive overnight; each, to some degree, is a combination of the constraints and opportunities present today and a pattern of development that stretches well back into history. Thus, a strong case can be made that understanding the nature of today's big questions requires knowing the history of transportation policy and administration. As Chandler (1977, 1979) has famously pointed out, modern organization and management functions can be dated to the rise of the railroads in the first half of the nineteenth century. Today's favored approaches to management bear little resemblance to those of the early railroad companies, steeped as they were in command-and-control orientations, but cannot be understood without a sense of the pattern of development that has led through the era of regulation to today's market-driven and performance-based preferences. Federal transportation policy, since the passage of ISTEA, needs to be seen in light of the devolution of authority from the federal government to the states and the recognition of the need to bring more flexibility into a surface transportation system that was being transformed by the forces of intermodalism, competing values in transportation, and the end of a highway-building approach as the panacea for the federal-state partnership (Dilger 1992; Gage and McDowell 1995). The expanding role of economic logic in policy making and management was stimulated in part by the failure of the regime of regulation to show clearly why it was superior to market-based and rational-actor alternatives. The past is still relevant to understanding the present, even when change has apparently washed away the structures and organizations that failed the test of time.

The four big questions—how to integrate modes, how and by whom important transportation decisions are made, how best to manage transportation system, and how to secure transportation from threats—form the basis of the organization of this book. Section 1 consists of six chapters that describe and analyze major modes of transportation and components of the contemporary transportation system: trucking, air transport, ports, intelligent transportation systems, inland waterways, and toll roads, in addition to this introductory chapter on the major issues facing transportation professionals. The authors raise issues that are also dealt with in remaining sections and chapters: how can we move from a modal emphasis to a more holistic approach? What policies and management approaches seem most appropriate for specific modes? How has the new requirement of security from terrorism changed the way we operate transportation systems?

Sections 2 and 3 consider how decisions on transportation policy and administration are, and should be, made. Section 2 looks at transportation issues through the lens of American federalism: what is being done by the various levels and units of subnational government. The answer, the authors find, is a great deal, ranging from the transformation of state transportation agencies from highway departments to full multi-modal, strategic-thinking organizations to the role of metropolitan planning organizations, urban-based transportation management associations; the issues addressed by states and cities range from questions of economic development and urban revitalization to environmental safeguarding, promotion of passenger rail travel, and the needs of rural residents for adequate transportation options.

Section 3 looks at decision making in transportation from a variety of analytical frameworks. Through case examples and more theoretical essays we find a variety of disciplinary and theory-based approaches that transportation professionals can use to deal with the complex issues of transportation planning and management. Authors from the fields of law, economics, geography, political science, civil engineering, and public administration offer insights into transportation policy issues and the connection of transportation to other policy domains.

Section 4 focuses on the managing of transportation systems and assets. The authors of the four chapters that comprise this grouping touch on such critical management issues as managing supply chains; transportation asset management; performance measurement in transportation agencies; and the development of public-private partnerships in transportation projects. The chapters point to a new reality for transportation professionals regardless of sector or level of government: performance and efficiency matter, requiring thoughtful innovations based on the best thinking of management theorists and practitioners.

Section 5 concludes the volume with six chapters that examine the most recent of the big questions to emerge: the security and protection of transportation systems that has become so problematic after September 11, 2001. Although some earlier chapters touch on security issues within the context of particular modes or policy domains, the chapters in this section combine considerations of the fundamental issues of transportation security after September 11 with assessments of the role of governance institutions and transportation modes and organizations in pursuit of the goal of security while retaining the efficiency, accountability, and adaptability we value in transportation systems.

The *Handbook* has been undertaken with the belief that there is a new profession of transportation policy and management that is emerging—or perhaps has emerged—that holds as an article of faith the need to transcend modal thinking, disciplinary boundaries, the artificial barriers of public and private sector, policy and administration, strategy and implementation. It sees transportation as a subject of great importance in and of itself, and even more so as a contributor to the fundamental needs of society: as an agent of economic prosperity, of individual mobility, of global interconnectedness. The new transportation professional needs to see transportation in the broadest possible light, asking the big questions that help to define it and proposing answers to improve it. It is in this spirit that we offer this *Handbook*.

REFERENCES

Behn, Robert. 1995. The Big Questions of Public Management. *Public Administration Review,* *55*, No. 4 (July/August): 313–324.

Chandler, Alfred D. 1977. *The Visible Hand: The Managerial Revolution in American Business.* Cambridge, MA: Belknap Press.

Chandler, Alfred D. 1979. *The Railroads, Pioneers in Modern Management.* New York: Arno Press.

Dilger, Robert J. 1992. "ISTEA: A New Direction for Transportation Policy," *Publius: The Journal of Federalism 22* (Summer): 67–78.

Gage, Robert W. and Bruce D. McDowell. 1995. "ISTEA and the Role of MPOs in the New Transportation Environment: A Midterm Assessment," *Publius: The Journal of Federalism 25* (Summer): 133–154.

Harmon, Michael M. and Mayer, Richard T. 1986. *Organization Theory for Public Administration.* Burke, VA: Chatelaine Press.

2 The U.S. Air Transportation System

Aleksandra Mozdzanowska and R. John Hansman

INTRODUCTION

Since its formal inception with the passage of the Air Mail Act in 1925, the air transportation system has experienced tremendous growth. Air transportation has evolved from a luxury to an important and necessary part of the economy and of daily life. Air transportation influences how business is conducted, companies are run, and vacations are taken. Because of air transportation, it is possible to travel or deliver products to almost anywhere in the United States within 24 hours. This ability, coupled with advances in communication technology, has increased the business and social clock cycle. Figure 2.1 shows the significant growth of cargo shipments and passenger travel since 1935. Revenue passenger miles (RPMs) is the number of paying passengers multiplied by the number of miles traveled and revenue ton miles (RTMs) is the amount of cargo paid to be shipped multiplied by the distance traveled. In 2004, the air transportation system handled over 70 thousand flights and 146 billion pounds of cargo per day [1].

The health of the air transportation system and the national economy is highly interdependent. Figure 2.2 shows that the gross domestic product (GDP) and the demand for air transportation have been closely coupled for the past 50 years. To understand this connection it is necessary to consider the interactions of the air transportation system with the economy, shown in Figure 2.3. The transportation system takes as input the demand for travel and movement of goods and supplies services to meet these demands. The ability of the system to meet these demands depends on the development of capabilities in the transportation infrastructure as well as the financial status of the transportation providers (airlines) and their ability to acquire appropriate aircraft. Thus, while the air transportation system needs the economy to supply demand and revenue, a healthy air transportation system is also vital for maintaining economic growth and competing in the global market.

HISTORICAL OVERVIEW

The modern air transportation system originates from developments in the post-World War I period that began the commercialization of air transportation. The use of aircraft during the war proved the utility and feasibility of flight, and resulted in technical improvements and a supply of pilots. After the war, these factors combined to produce

9

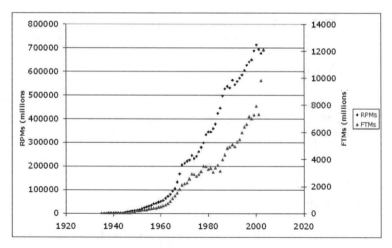

FIGURE 2.1   Growth in number of revenue-passenger-miles and freight ton miles flown in the United States since 1935. [2]

a growing desire for the commercialization of air transportation. Individuals used surplus planes for jobs like crop dusting, aerial photography, or providing rides at fairs. During this time, there was not yet any regulatory body governing commercial and private flight.

Air mail was the first real and steady non-war use for air transportation. The first mail was carried by aircraft in 1911, but routine service did not start until end of the war in 1918. In 1925 the Air Mail Act was passed allowing the post master general to contract with private corporations and pilots to transport mail. Once private corporations received contracts to carry mail, passenger transport also become a reality. The money from carrying mail provided the steady income that airlines needed to form regular schedules and expand service.

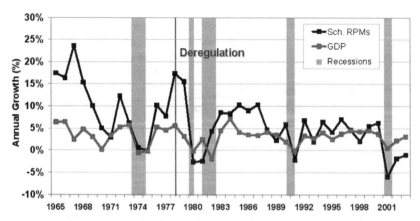

FIGURE 2.2   Annual percentage change in GDP and scheduled domestic revenue traffic, 1954–2000 with economic recession. [3]

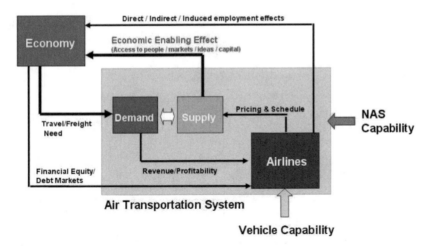

FIGURE 2.3　Schematic diagram of connection between air transportation and the economy. [3]

After the Air Mail Act was passed, the need for government regulation in aviation received more attention. As traffic increased, fears over aviation safety began to grow, resulting in an effort to develop infrastructure and regulations aimed toward improving safety. A federal commission investigated the state of the industry and produced recommendations for the extent and form of government involvement. This investigation resulted in the passage of the Air Commerce Act, which became law on May 20, 1926. The act designated responsibility for promoting the growth of the aviation industry to the Secretary of Commerce. In particular, the act tasked the secretary with safely growing air transportation through the development of airways and navigation aids, regulation when necessary, and increasing public awareness of air transportation as a safe mode of transportation. These developments began with lighted beacons to improve night time safety but soon advanced to using radio and other technologies that would allow safer operation during inclement weather.

Recognizing the importance of nurturing the growing industry, the federal government took an active role in managing the airlines and their growth. The government established routes which were bid for by or given to specific airlines. Cross-subsidies were established so that major routes could help less-profitable ones. This regulation allowed for the expansion of service to more places and prevented excessive competition from killing the young industry.

World War II spurred significant additional improvements in terms of capability and infrastructure, as well as pilot training. In the years following the war, these innovations and the additional labor force were absorbed by the air transportation industry—international flights were offered, aided by the introduction of the jet engine. The introduction of "coach class" helped make air travel an increasingly common mode of transportation, soon overtaking trains in popularity. To sustain this growth, however, reliability and safety needed to improve.

In the 1950s, air traffic control started taking more responsibility for collision and terrain avoidance in high traffic airspace. This was enabled by improvements in

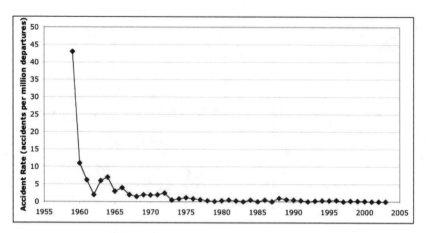

FIGURE 2.4   Commercial aircraft accident rate since 1959. [4]

technology and motivated by an increasing number of collisions. In some cases, large accidents provided the impetus for specific changes: the widespread deployment of radar tracking was catalyzed by the 1956 mid-air collision over the Grand Canyon.

As the air transportation system grew in the 1950s and 1960s, more technology to aid controllers and pilots was implemented. In addition, safety and security regulations were increased and changed to deal with the new jet aircraft, the increase in traffic (and accidents), and a wave of aircraft hijackings that stared in the mid-1960s. The efforts to improve safety have continued until the present day. Improvements of regulations, procedures and technology have led to a significant increase in the safety of commercial operations, as can be seen in Figure 2.4.

In 1973 Federal Express began operations, hoping to solve the problem of how to reliably deliver time-sensitive air freight. Federal Express succeeded. By 1983 the company was earning US$1 billion in revenues. Because of FedEx and its competitors, businesses are now able to ship packages around the globe in 24 hours, an ability that has enabled the growth of Internet companies and on-demand inventory delivery.

The 1970s also saw one of the most important changes in aviation history: the market deregulation of the air transportation system which, in 1978, opened up the system to additional market competition. Deregulation meant that airlines could now choose their routes and compete with each other for passengers. Airlines moved to streamline route structures and developed the hub and spoke airline networks. The network structures of many current operators were shaped during this time period.

OUTLINE OF THE AIR TRANSPORTATION SYSTEM

The air transportation system is comprised of operators and a supporting infrastructure. Operators use aircraft to transport people and cargo within the system. The supporting infrastructure includes airport facilities, air traffic control, communication, navigation, and surveillance technologies, as well as weather tracking and prediction systems.

The many different operators and their flights interact with each other and the support infrastructure in a well-defined manner in order to operate successfully in the same airspace. Integrating these different flights is a challenge since they require different degrees of support and planning. Thus, in order to operate safely and efficiently, operators must follow agreed upon regulations and standards. In the United States, the Federal Aviation Administration (FAA) provides regulatory oversight of aviation. In addition, the Federal Code contains the Federal Aviation Regulations (FARs) that govern the operation of aircraft in the air transportation system. The FARs have evolved over time and regulate many aspects of air transportation. These include air worthiness requirements, standards for pilot schools, certification standards for equipment, emission and noise requirements, as well as specific regulations for the operation of different types of carriers and vehicles.

OPERATORS

SCHEDULED PASSENGER OPERATIONS

Scheduled operations are those that fly according to a regular predetermined schedule. A majority of passengers and cargo in the United States are carried via scheduled operations, which are governed by the rules outlined in Part 121 of the FARs. Carriers who conduct scheduled operations can be subdivided into the major carriers, the national carriers, and the regional carriers.

The major airlines are characterized by a large number of heavily connected operations, the availability of international service, and in most cases have existed since before deregulation. For this reason, they are also called traditional and legacy carriers. In 2005, these airlines included United, American, Delta, Continental, and US Airways. To expand the reach of their networks, these airlines fly hub and spoke operations and often dominate one or more hub airports. By consolidating flights at hubs, majors can provide access to smaller cities that do not offer enough demand to fill a large aircraft. These carriers have large varied fleets, ranging from small to large aircraft. The different types of aircraft allow them to serve various markets. For example, international markets and flights connecting major cities require larger aircraft than flights servicing small out of the way locations.

The national carriers are very similar to the major carriers but do not provide international service and tend to be younger. The networks of these carriers are not as extensive as those of the majors but still provide service throughout the United States. Some of the major carriers are also referred to as low cost carriers because of their lower cost of operations. Examples of national airlines in 2005 included America West, Southwest, Alaska Air, JetBlue, and AirTran.

Regional carriers operate on a smaller scale. In 2005 examples of regional carriers included: American Eagle, Mesa, Mesaba, ExpressJet, Horizon, and many more. Regional carriers tend to fly regional jets and turbo prop aircraft. These aircraft are small and can seat between 30 and 80 passengers. Regional carriers do not operate the large aircraft that appear in the fleets of major carriers. These smaller planes are

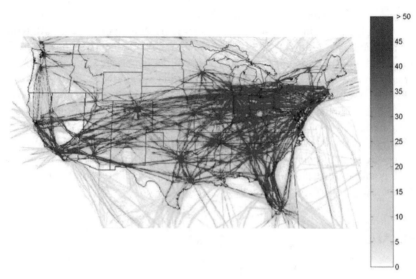

FIGURE 2.5   Density map of 24 hours of scheduled flights over the United States. [5]

ideal for allowing the carriers to serve smaller areas of the United States and to feed passengers to the larger networks of the national and major carriers. Regional carriers can be categorized also by their relationship to the major and national carriers. Some regional carriers are independent companies; they often feed airports that are hubs for larger airlines. However, some major and national airlines have subsidiary airlines that feed only their own hubs. An example of such an airline is American Eagle, which is a subsidiary of American Airlines.

The density map in Figure 2.5 shows the coverage of flights by scheduled carriers. It can be seen that most of the United States is covered with flights and that there is a large concentration of flights in the northeastern part of the United States and along both coasts of the country.

NON-SCHEDULED PASSENGER OPERATIONS

The system also supports non-scheduled passenger flights. Charter operators fly paying customers to a specified destination at a time of the customer's choosing. In addition, businesses and companies own planes that can be flown for meetings or events. Finally, general aviation (GA) includes all flights not flown for compensation. These operations are regulated by Part 135 of the FARs. In addition, Part 91 applies to all non-scheduled flights that are not carrying passengers or freight.

Operators providing non-scheduled service typically fly to smaller airports and often provide access to destinations that are not served by scheduled flights. Business aircraft are usually jet aircraft and GA aircraft are usually propeller aircraft; propeller aircraft are typically smaller than jet aircraft and fly at lower altitudes and slower speeds.

CARGO

The existence of passenger carriers was in part enabled by the Mail Act that made it possible for them to carry mail. Today, many airlines still carry mail and even some cargo as part of their operations. In addition, a number of operators carry mail and cargo exclusively. Cargo operators have routes and schedules that are different from operators that focus on transporting passengers. Flights tend to operate during the night so that pick ups and deliveries can be made to correspond with the day time business cycle. The ability to transport goods in the United States within 24 hours has facilitated the development of just-in-time inventory delivery. Cargo operators use hubs for the same purpose as regular operators—to bring packages into a single point and give the appearance of a large point-to-point network. However, they can place these hubs further away from major cities and require fewer of them. Cargo carriers also tend to have a single bank time during the night, when incoming planes are reloaded and sent back out.

Part 121 of the FARs applies to air carriers, such as major airlines and cargo haulers that fly large transport aircraft. In 2005, the major examples of cargo carriers were FedEx, UPS, and DHL, all of which provide scheduled mail and cargo operations. However there are also small non-scheduled cargo operators that provide on demand service for urgent shipments that cannot wait for an overnight flight. Specialized cargo carriers, such as air ambulances, also provide on demand service.

INFRASTRUCTURE

AIRPORTS

The United States is served by a rich network of over 19,000 airports, of which over 5,000 are open to the public. FAA divides airports into four categories. The commercial service airports service at least 2,500 revenue passenger boardings a year and must have scheduled passenger service. Commercial service airports can be further subdivided into primary and non-primary airports. The primary airports have over 10,000 revenue boardings a year, and the non-primary airports have revenue boardings ranging between 2,500 and 10,000. Cargo service airports, in addition to other traffic, service aircraft that carry only cargo and receive over 100 million pounds of cargo each year. Reliever airports are designated by the FAA to relieve congestion at commercial service airports. The last category does not have an official name, but contains those private airports that do not fit in the above three categories. In most cases, these airports are called "general aviation airports."

The distribution of traffic to airports is highly uneven: in fact, most of the traffic in the United States occurs at a small fraction of the total airports as shown in Figure 2.6. Population centers typically determine the placement of airports. A large population center can provide the demand needed to support a large commercial service airport. Figures 2.7 and 2.8 show how areas of dense airports correspond to areas of dense population. This naturally results in a high density of flights near these cities, as shown

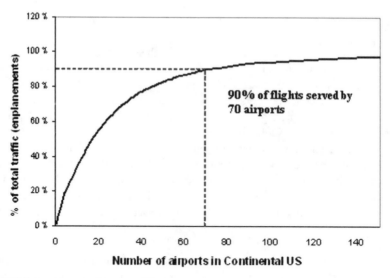

FIGURE 2.6   Airport utilization. [6]

in the density map in Figure 2.5. The density of flights tends to be correlated with the size of the population center; however, the amount of traffic at a particular airport is also related to the size of the airport and the capabilities it offers in terms of runways and instrumentation.

Different categories of airports support different classes of aircraft. Larger aircraft require stronger and longer runways that can support the weight of the aircraft and provide enough space for acceleration and deceleration during take-off and landing. These aircraft also require different support services such as fueling equipment or gates. This means that larger aircraft are restricted in their choice of airports. As a result, the

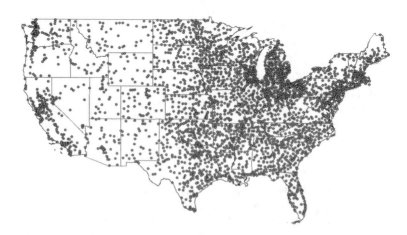

FIGURE 2.7   Locations of airports in the United States. [7]

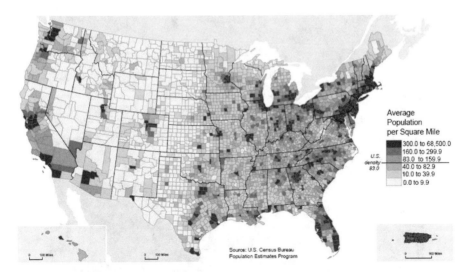

FIGURE 2.8   United States population density. [8]

operators that own large aircraft must fly to airports that can support them, typically the commercial service airports. Operators with smaller aircraft have greater flexibility in terms of airports from which to operate.

The large airports where most of the traffic in the United States is concentrated are also the limiting point in allowing traffic growth. Some of these key airports receive more flights than they can handle resulting in delays and disruptions in service. Some plans exist to add additional runway space to alleviate this problem, but building runways is a long process. Furthermore, many of the congested airports are located so close to cities that all the land around them is used and there is no space available for expansion. The problem of congestion is an important issue that will need to be dealt with in the coming years if air transportation is to continue growing and providing services.

AIR TRAFFIC CONTROL

The purpose of air traffic control (ATC) is to ensure that aircraft are separated from each other and local terrain. By issuing instructions to pilots, controllers maintain a safe and orderly flow of traffic.

Pilots can operate under two different rules that affect how they are handled by air traffic control. Under visual flight rules (VFR), pilots are responsible for maintaining separation and are not managed by ATC. However, VFR is only allowed under weather conditions that provide appropriate visibility and below 18,000 feet. In contrast, under instrument flight rules (IFR), controllers have responsibility for maintaining separation. Pilots flying under IFR must file a flight plan and accept instructions from controllers during flight. However, because aircraft flying IFR may have to share airspace with VFR aircraft not controlled by ATC, IFR pilots must be alert and maintain clearance from VRF flights. Transponders are installed in all major aircraft and broadcast their

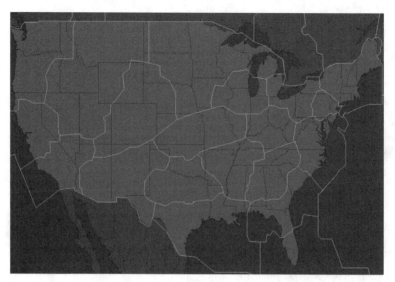

FIGURE 2.9   Air traffic control centers. [9]

identity (e.g., flight number), altitude, and speed to help IFR aircraft detect and avoid
VFR aircraft. Transponders also respond to queries from ATC radar.

Airspace is divided into nested regions: controllers are responsible for aircraft
flying within their region. At the highest level are the 21 control centers, as shown in
Figure 2.9. Each center is divided into sectors. In addition, in each center there are
Terminal Radar Approach Control (TRACON) areas that are about 50 miles in diam-
eter and surround major airports or groups of airports. Finally, each airport also has a
control area that is about five miles in radius. Within the airport, different controllers
manage aircraft as they land, take-off and taxi.

When an aircraft pulls back from the gate and taxis to the runway it is in contact
and receiving instructions from the airport control tower. This continues until the
aircraft leaves the five mile radius around the airport and enters the TRACON. At this
point the airport control hands the aircraft off to the TRACON controller who com-
municates and issues instructions to the aircraft pilots. Once the aircraft leaves the
TRACON area and enters a sector, another hand off occurs. These hand offs continue
as the aircraft flies through sectors and centers eventually into another TRACON and
then an airport area to land.

In addition to the hierarchical division of space, the system has also evolved an
operational structure for traffic to keep the system manageable despite high traffic
volume. For example, aircraft fly along designated airways. This allows controllers to
think of aircraft as flows rather than having each individual plane going in a different
direction. In addition, aircraft are grouped by altitudes depending on the direction in
which they are flying. There are also specific points along which aircraft merge into a
single flow or separate into multiple flows. This structure allows controllers to simplify
the complexity of the situation that they are dealing with.

The Air Traffic Control System Command Center (ATCSCC) manages traffic and coordinates system level changes. They can intervene more directly if there are problems caused by bad weather, traffic overloads, or closed runways. The traffic in each center is monitored and managed by the Air Route Traffic Control Center (ARTCC). The ARTCC is responsible for monitoring and handling traffic in all of the sectors included in the center, but not in the TRACON or airport areas. The TRACON handles all departing and approaching aircraft within its radius, but not in the airport area. The air traffic control tower (ATCT) handles the arriving, departing, and ground traffic within the airport control area.

COMMUNICATION, NAVIGATION, AND SURVEILLANCE

Communication, navigation, and surveillance (CNS) are critical for supporting air traffic control. In order to maintain separation between aircraft and issue clearances, air traffic controllers need to be able to communicate with pilots and see the positions of aircraft they are controlling. Pilots need navigation equipment to know where they are and follow the instructions given to them by controllers. Figure 2.10 shows a schematic of the components of CNS, ATC, and their interactions.

Currently air traffic control is conducted from the ground and all communications go between ground and air. Most navigation and surveillance infrastructure is ground-based as well. This focus on ground-based technologies is a result of the historical evolution of the air transportation system and is now slowly changing to include more satellite-based technologies.

The earliest and most basic technologies implemented in the system involved navigation, which allows pilots to identify their positions and plan how to get to their destinations. Navigation was originally based on following roads. Pilots flew at low

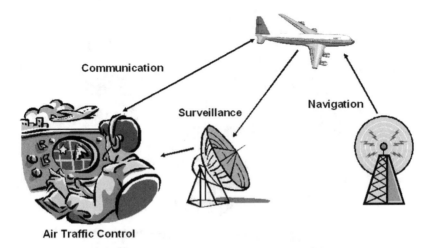

FIGURE 2.10 Communication, navigation, and surveillance facilities are shown interacting with aircraft and providing information to ATC.

altitudes and only when visibility was clear. When air transportation began to develop into a commercial industry, a need for night and all weather flying became apparent and better navigation systems were needed. Bonfires were initially used to mark routes during the night. These were gradually replaced with radio-based beacons that provided more accuracy and reliability. Simultaneously better cockpit equipment was developed to allow pilots to contact these beacons and monitor their position.

Pilots make regular use of navigation aids such as beacons and position markers to allow them to assess their position and heading relative to their desired and assigned flight plan. These technologies form a large infrastructure of beacons located throughout the country that help aircraft fly along precise airways. Figure 2.11 shows an example of a navigational chart used by pilots to determine their position relative to detected beacons. The chart contains information about navigational aids, communication frequencies, airways, and airports.

In addition to the en route navigation aids described above, a separate set of instruments aid pilots during approach and landing. These instruments give pilots precise positioning information, relative to the correct approach path for landing. Such navigational aids are particularly important for use in poor visibility conditions where the pilot may not be able to see the runway itself until seconds before landing. The most common technology used today for approach positioning is the Instrument Landing System (ILS). For appropriately equipped aircraft landing at ILS-enabled airports, a series of beacons guide the pilot into and through the optimal approach corridor and help maintain vertical and lateral alignment during landing.

FIGURE 2.11   Example navigation chart showing region around Portland, Oregon. [10]

Air traffic control was introduced when the growth in traffic started to cause dangerous conditions at some airports where too many aircraft were landing without any control or coordination. In response to this problem, controllers began working near the runways to give instructions to pilots using flags and later colored lights. Both of these methods required that visibility was good. Over time, radio communications replaced these early methods and allowed for control in more weather conditions.

Today, controllers are linked to pilots through radio voice communications. Controllers issue commands and clearances and pilots request routing and acknowledge instructions mostly using radio. There are two types of radio signals used for communication. Most domestic communication occurs over very high frequency radio or VHF. VHF provides reliable and rapid communication capability but it cannot be used when the two parties are not within a line of sight. As a result, high frequency or HF radio communication is used for oceanic flights that cannot stay within line of sight. However, HF radio signals are not as reliable and have a higher latency period. In fact, this type of communication is cumbersome enough that a third party relays messages between aircraft and controllers. In addition to voice communication, there is also the ability to communicate data, such as weather updates.

In addition to communication, controllers need to be able to know the position of aircraft that are moving through theirs airspace; this knowledge enables them to ensure that all aircraft are a separated by a safe distance and correctly following instructions. To meet this need, surveillance technology was deployed. Surveillance is mainly conducted with the use of radar, initially developed during WWII. There are two types of radar used in the air transportation system. Primary radar provides a 60-mile radius of coverage and reports data on range and bearing for all en route sectors and TRACONs. This type of radar is also called independent radar because it does not require any intervention on the part of the pilot or aircraft. Secondary radar or beacon radar transmits an interrogation pulse. A transponder on board equipped aircraft receives the pulse and replies. The reply message contains the aircraft ID as well as altitude data. This radar is referred to as dependent radar because it requires a reaction from the aircraft.

Controllers require timely and accurate data on aircraft location, heading, speed, and altitude but do not have time to look at data provided by multiple radar sources. Thus, data from multiple radars is first collected and post-processed by computers. The data is then presented to controllers as visual information, typically overlaid on a map. Given the safety critical nature of controller tasks, a number of back up channels exist to ensure that radar data is always available. There are redundant radar stations providing overlapping coverage, as well as redundant lines of data transmission and display services.

The structure of today's ATC and support systems grew gradually as the need emerged, with technology improving on existing practices and expanding the ground-air operating pattern to cover most aspects of operation. While current CNS technology relies heavily on radio and radar, plans for the future recommend that the system move toward utilizing satellite based technologies. Satellite technologies would allow for a global system that would increase the reliability and speed of communication, as well as the accuracy of navigation and surveillance. Such a change has the potential to shift ATC and other support systems into new patterns where control is not always done from the ground and where communication does not always go only between ground and aircraft.

WEATHER SERVICES

Adverse weather has been a major cause of air transportation delays and accidents. It is critical that pilots, controllers, and planners have access to timely, accurate and detailed weather information in order to avoid operating in dangerous conditions. Ceiling and visibility at airports govern whether or not an aircraft can safely land using visual flight rules or whether an instrumented landing is necessary. Information on hazardous weather such as convection, icing, or lightning is needed to help guide en route flight. Inaccurate information can lead to operating in conditions that result in decreased aircraft and pilot performance or control. In the worst cases, these factors exceed the capabilities of the aircraft or the pilots and result in incidents and accidents. With accurate and localized weather information, traffic can be directed away from dangerous operating conditions with minimal disruption.

Weather information at airports is provided to pilots in the form of Terminal Area Forecasts (TAFs) and updated with Aviation Routine Weather Reports (METARs). The forecasts cover weather for up to a 24-hour period within a five nautical mile radius of a given terminal area. They are generated by branches of the National Weather Service (NWS); new forecasts are produced every six hours and are updated as necessary. Forecasts are based on known terrain use and characteristics as well as measured conditions. Pilots flying aircraft operating under Part 121 of the FARs are required to use NWS generated or NWS approved reports for making weather-related control decisions, such as estimating the amount of fuel needed or selecting alternate airports.

In flight, many commercial aircraft have radar capable of detecting local convective weather and wind shear. In the vicinity of airports, the Terminal Doppler Weather Radar (TDWR) provides this capability. There is also a nationwide network of 150 NEXRAD stations that monitor for convective weather and are used for non-aviation meteorology as well. These radar facilities are supplemented by other sensors and satellite imagery.

As with terrain avoidance and aircraft separation, control centers (from towers to ARTCCs) help direct aircraft away from adverse weather conditions. Higher level facilities tend to prefer access to longer term forecasts, as their decisions affect more aircraft and system-wide patterns. In addition to relying on controllers pilots also have access to weather data. Pilots receive weather updates both before and during a flight. Finally, pilots can also report weather to controllers who will then pass the new information on to others.

THE FUTURE OF AIR TRANSPORTATION

The air transportation system is currently facing a serious capacity problem: factors such as the lack of runway capacity at major airports limit the number of operations

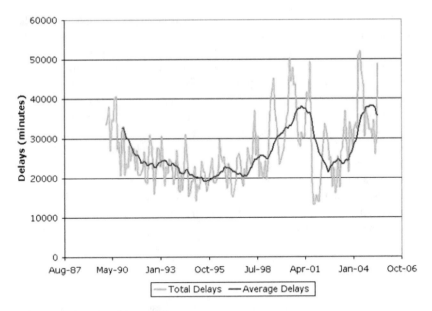

FIGURE 2.12   Growing delays. [12]

that can be handled by the system. Limited capacity, when combined with increasing demand, will result in congestion that could lead to a collapse of operations due to a propagation of delays through the system [11]. Such a collapse would have significant impact on the economy given the close coupling between the economy and the air transportation system. The trend towards increasing delays can be seen in Figure 2.12; prior to September 11, 2001, delays had been steadily growing and drew significant public outcry and attention in the summer of 2000. It can be seen that peak delays have exceeded 2000 levels and average delays have returned.

Unfortunately, it will not be easy to expand runway capacity. Most airports have no land upon which to build new runways and those that do often face local opposition. This opposition comes from communities near the airport that are opposed to the increased noise and emissions that would come from added traffic. The growing environmental consciousness adds another constraint to an already difficult problem.

Compounding this problem are numerous other issues. Financial difficulties of airlines and the FAA are threatening stability and raising the question of who will fund system modernization and transition efforts [13]. New vehicle classes, such as unmanned aerial vehicles and very light jets, will change the national fleet mix and will increase the number and diversity of daily operations. Finally, the United States has been losing its leadership role in setting world standards and regulations for aviation. Such a loss could threaten the ability of the United States to compete effectively in global markets and restrict U.S. options for dealing with domestic aviation problems. The importance of the air transportation system to the national economy, both in its direct impacts and its enabling effects, makes it critical that these challenges be addressed so that the system can continue to function and grow.

Solving these problems appears to be more difficult than solving those of the past. Most problems from the twentieth century were safety problems, which the stakeholders in the system have learned to deal with effectively. Such problems tend to be highly visible with clear stakes and need for solution. In contrast, the problems resulting from emissions or growing delays have broad system-wide impacts but manifest slowly and have low public visibility. There is not yet agreement about the nature and scope of the problem and thus planning solutions is difficult. For example, existing plans for system modernization, as reflected in the FAA's Operational Evolution Plan, will only provide marginal improvements in capacity at the critical locations [14]. However, the potential capacity problem is so large that localized changes may not be sufficient and the current air traffic control system will not be able to expand to meet the growing demand. Significant new changes—technological or procedural—will be needed to respond to this challenge. Meeting this challenge will be the focus of air transportation efforts in the coming years.

BIBLIOGRAPHY

1. U.S. Federal Aviation Administration. Cy 2003 passenger boarding and all-cargo data. http://www.faa.gov/arp/planning/stats/#cy03data, 2005. Accessed May 7, 2005.
2. Air transport association: Economics. http://www.airlines.org/econ/d.aspx?nid=1032, 2005. Accessed September 12, 2005.
3. Ryan Tam and R. John Hansman. An analysis of the dynamics of the U.S. commercial air transportation system. Master's thesis, Massachusetts Institute of Technology, Cambridge, MA, November 2003.
4. Statistical summary of commercial jet airplane accidents. http://www.boeing.com/news/techissues/statsum.pdf. Accessed September 29, 2005.
5. Aleksandra Mozdzanowska and R. John Hansman. Growth and operating patterns of regional jets in the United States. *AIAA Journal of Aircraft*, 42(4):858–864, 2005.
6. Philippe Bonnefoy and R. John Hansman. Emergence of secondary airports and dynamics of regional airport systems in the United States. Master's thesis, Massachusetts Institute of Technology, Cambridge, MA, 2005.
7. U.S. Federal Aviation Administration. National plan for integrated airport system, 2002.
8. U.S. Census Bureau. Population density maps. http://www.census.gov/popest/gallery/maps/PopDensCounties_2004.pdf. Accessed May 10, 2005.
9. Jonathan Histon and R. John Hansman. The impact of structure on cognitive complexity in air traffic control. Technical Report ICAT-2002-4, MIT International Center for Air Transportation, Cambridge, MA, June 2002.
10. U.S. National Aeronautical Charting Office. Seattle sectional aeronautical chart (FAA Product ID: SSEA), December 2005.
11. Gerald L. Dillingham and Randall B. Williamson. National airspace system: Long-term capacity planning needed despite recent reduction in flight delays. Technical Report GAO-02-185, U.S. General Accounting Office, December, 2005.
12. U.S. Federal Aviation Administration. Operational networks (OPSNET) database: Delays by cause updated daily. http://www.apo.data.faa.gov/opsnet/entryOPSNET.asp. Accessed September 15, 2005.
13. Gerald L. Dillingham. National airspace system: Experts views on improving the USAir

Traffic Control Modernization Program. Technical Report GAO-05-333SP, U.S. General Accounting Office, April 2005.

14. U.S. Federal Aviation Administration. Operation evolution plan 7.0. http://www.faa. gov/programs/oep/.

15. Robert M. Kane and Allan D. Vose. *Air transportation*. Kendall/Hunt Pub. Co., Dubuque, Iowa, 1979. Robert M. Kane, Allan D. Vose; Appendices (p. A1–A187): A. Federal Aviation Act of 1958. B. Airline Deregulation Act of 1978; Includes index.

16. Nick A. Komons. *Bonfires to beacons: Federal civil aviation policy under the Air Commerce Act, 1926–1938.* U.S. Dept. of Transportation, Federal Administration. Includes bibliographical references and index. Available from the Supt. of Docs., U.S. Govt. Print. Off., Washington, D.C., 1978.

17. Scenario-economic demand forecast study. Technical report, NASA and FAA, 2003.

18. Michael S. Nolan. *Fundamentals of air traffic control*. Thomson–Brooks/Cole, Belmont, CA, 2004. Michael S. Nolan. Includes bibliographical references and index.

19. Stuart I. Rochester. *Takeoff at mid-century: Federal civil aviation policy in the Eisenhower years, 1953–1961.* U.S. Dept. of Transportation, Federal Aviation Administration. Includes bibliographical references and index. Available from the Supt. of Docs., U.S. Govt. Print Off., Washington, D.C., 1976.

20. Carl Solberg. *Conquest of the skies: A history of commercial aviation in America.* Little, Brown, Boston, 1979. Includes bibliographical material and index.

21. Christopher D. Wickens, Anne S. Mavor, J. McGee, and National Research Council. Panel on Human Factors in Air Traffic Control Automation. *Flight to the future:Human factors in air traffic control.* National Academy Press, Washington, D.C., 1997. Includes bibliographical references and index.

22. Christopher D. Wickens and National Research Council Panel on Human Factors in Air Traffic Control Automation, Commission on Behavioral and Social Sciences and Education, National Research Council. *The future of air traffic control: Human operators and automation.* National Academy Press, Washington, D.C., 1998. Includes bibliographical references and index.

23. Vincent P. Galotti. *The future air navigation system (FANS: Communication navigation surveillance air traffic management).* Ashgate, Aldershot, England, 1997. Includes bibliographical references and index.

24. Laurence Vigeant-Langlois and R. John Hansman. Human-centered systems analysis of aircraft separation from adverse weather. Technical Report ICAT-2004-02, MIT International Center for Air Transportation, Cambridge, MA, June 2004.

3 Trucking

Daniel Madar

The trucking industry uses the public roads to move goods between shippers and receivers. In contrast to railroads, which operate on their private trackage, use of the public roads separates vehicle ownership from right of way, allowing multiple carrier operations on a single network[1] That provides three important advantages. The first is the public roads' comprehensive coverage that provides uninterrupted movement between any set of points in the country, even the smallest and most obscure. The railroads' mobility and point coverage are limited by ownership and by a half century of route consolidation. Although the railroads may grant paid use of their tracks to each other, they still operate within bounded domains, and achieving the public roads' unified network would require a national rail monopoly. The second advantage is that multiple operations encourage structural diversity in trucking and the ability to serve all places where demand exists. The third advantage is that funding for highway construction provides trucking with a subsidized network.[2] Because trucking's right of way is a public good, capital costs are low and are represented mainly by the trucks themselves. Terminals are an additional capital expense, but only one of trucking's sectors uses them. Low capital costs mean low fixed costs and linear rates.

Rates are linear because the largest costs in trucking are variable.[3] These rise and fall according to output, and in trucking represent primarily labor and fuel. Road use is mainly a variable cost because of fuel taxes. Linear rates increase with distance and directly reflect the cost of service. Rail rates, in comparison, are much less linear because of the large fixed costs that must be covered and, under rate regulation, because of requirements that were not directly related to the cost of service. As trucking began establishing itself as a transportation mode, the railroads' rates became a serious disadvantage, and they partly account for the steady diversion during the last century of freight traffic from rail to highway. Reflecting trucking's dominant position is the fact that its revenues are triple those of the rail, water carrier, and pipeline industries combined.[4]

Transportation costs, along with economies of scale in production, strongly influence the spatial distribution of industry.[5] Because almost all intermediate and final goods travel by truck, and because transportation costs are included in final prices, trucking rates directly affect the location of production.[6] That is so because, "in economic geography, the most useful measure of distance is not time or miles but dollars."[7] Because trucking's linear rates reflect the actual cost of movement, the arbitrary regional advantages that were built into regulated rail rates no longer prevail, and the cost of a particular location respective to others is the cost of highway transportation. While rail rates had favored large urban centers, the effect of trucking's linear rates has allowed manufacturing to disperse into previously rural and nonindustrial regions and to close previously wide logistical distances.[8]

Low capital costs in trucking also mean low barriers to entry. Because trucks are the main capital item, investment is not concentrated in a few expensive components but is spread over a set of inexpensive ones. Although economists have sought to identify economies of scale in trucking, most surveys show that they are generally modest, nonexistent or limited to specific sectors of operation.[9] One reason is that capacity is increased not by raising the volume of individual vehicles but by adding more vehicles of the same size.[10] Since scale economies also create entry barriers, their absence, together with low capital costs, means that individuals can enter trucking with a modest outlay. That fact accounts for the growth of trucking historically and, since deregulation in 1980, for the emergence of truckload (TL) carriers. TL carriers serve shippers door to door and move only full-trailer consignments. In smaller operations especially, that business carries moderate capital and organizational requirements, and it is in this sector that low entry barriers have most strongly affected the industry's composition. A related capital characteristic is flexibility. Some truck trailers are limited to particular bulk commodities, but standard dry vans are very versatile. That versatility, together with the mobility provided by the road network, enables trucking to respond quickly to demand generated by both commodity and locale. Fleet size itself is adaptable because trucks have relatively brief service lives, there is an active used truck market, and equipment is readily available through leasing.

Compared to railroads, water carriers, and pipelines, trucks move small individual volumes. Although that concedes most bulk commodity traffic to the other surface modes, it is a decisive advantage with processed and manufactured goods. That advantage had always been present, but recent developments in industrial logistics have magnified it. Just-In-Time (JIT) production cuts costs by eliminating inbound and outbound inventories and scheduling deliveries to the exact time when they are needed. That creates a demand for small volumes in a steady and dependable flow. Outsourcing parts and components produces tightly integrated supply chains and multiplies the demand. Moving small consignments and matching deliveries to customers' timetables represents an optimal application of trucking's resources. It also poses in more complex form the utilization and scheduling tasks that are central to any trucking operation. To stay in business, a carrier must optimize vehicle time and capacity, avoid lapses and backups in cargo, deliver on time, match continually moving vehicles with changeable demand, and select the most efficient routes.[11]

These basic advantages became apparent during the First World War when heavy volumes of military traffic on the railroads created commercial opportunities for the infant trucking industry.[12] Its speed, flexibility and door-to-door convenience pleased shippers, and demand grew rapidly. Also appreciated were cheaper prices. On the railroads, less-than-carload and express freight traveled under the highest rates. These were especially high in regional and short-haul markets because regulation used the returns to cross-subsidize less profitable operations.[13] Short-haul markets, because of poor intercity roads, were the truckers' prime domain, and success there cost the railroads very lucrative business. The Federal Road Act of 1916 authorized using federal funds for highway construction. Use of state gasoline taxes to fund public roads began in 1919 and by 1929 had been adopted by all the states.[14] Assisted by postwar highway construction, the industry grew rapidly, and the railroads began demanding federal regulation.[15]

In 1913 Maine and Massachusetts were the first states to place size and weight restrictions on public road use, and in the following year Pennsylvania was the first state to impose economic regulation on trucking. By 1925 thirty five states were regulating their motor carriers.[16] Although provisions differed among states, regulation in general was intended to promote safety and proper use of the roads. Railroad interests were behind almost all state-level regulation, and their influence was reflected in the states that applied entry restrictions.[17] The federal government became involved when complaints arose over the treatment of out-of-state truckers. In two important decisions in 1925, the Supreme Court ruled that refusing to issue operating permits to applicants from other states interfered with interstate commerce.[18] That ruling created a federal jurisdiction for trucking regulation, which was filled by the Motor Carrier Act of 1935.

Under pressure from the railroads, regulatory legislation was introduced in Congress in 1925 and in every following year. Other supporters were state regulators, who favored a uniform set of national controls, and unions, who hoped to stabilize the industry for better wages and working conditions. Opposing regulation was a coalition of shippers, vehicle manufacturers, farmers and, initially, most truckers.[19] In the advocates' favor were deteriorating conditions caused by the Great Depression. As traffic levels dropped, rail revenues fell. Although trucking at the time carried only 5 percent of intercity freight, the railroads blamed them for unfair competition.[20] The same traffic decline produced turbulence and failure in the trucking industry, giving advocates the argument that controls were needed to restore stability. That fitted well with the Interstate Commerce Commission's philosophy for regulating the railroads, which under the Transportation Act of 1920 was to keep that vital industry dependable and prosperous. The same rationale extended to trucking when the Motor Carrier Act of 1935 placed it under ICC control.

The Commission's view was that trucking's problems were due to excessive competition. Since entry barriers are naturally low, and since at the time there was little differentiation among carrier offerings except price, the task of regulation was to restrict entry and control rates. Doing so would prevent excess supply and maintain adequate earnings.[21] It would also protect truckers from their own inexperience, which led them to underestimate their full costs and to cut rates to ruinous levels.[22] Joseph Eastman, appointed by President Franklin Roosevelt in 1933 to propose remedies, believed that railroad regulation provided the proper model. Even though he agreed that the trucking industry's problems were due to low entry barriers and small operations, his experience as a railroad regulator led him also to expect monopolies to arise naturally in transportation industries.[23] When Eastman's office prepared draft motor carrier legislation, it simply copied the Interstate Commerce Act's principal provisions, which were written for railroads.[24] Although excessive competition and monopoly are opposite conditions, regulating both suited the ICC's mandate and philosophy. In a slightly different interpretation, Thomas Gale Moore argues that railroad regulation had created a cartel, and that regulation was intended to control its natural monopolies in short-haul markets. Trucks were regulated because they provided competition in those markets.[25]

By then the trucking industry had evolved into three main sectors: common carriers that served the general public, contract carriers that served individual shippers on negotiated terms, and private carriers, in-house trucking operations of manufacturers, distributors, and retailers that were not for hire. To some extent that division reflected three different ways of matching the same basic transportation technology to particular requirements. To some extent also it reflected the influence of regulation, which enforced the division by treating each sector differently.[26] Eastman saw this division as a source of instability requiring regulatory control.[27] The sectoral division had emerged in state-level regulation, where a particular point of contention was treatment of contract carriers. Because they do not serve the general public, early court decisions held that states could not regulate them. Texas regulators solved the problem by subjecting contract carriers to a lower entry standard, a policy that was upheld by the U.S. Supreme Court in 1932.[28] That same division was continued in the federal Motor Carrier Act. The most important exemptions from regulation were for private carriers that do not serve the public, and for carriers of agricultural commodities, which farm organizations insisted on keeping unregulated.

The Motor Carrier Act of 1935 applied strict entry controls to common carriers. Those in business at the time of the Act's passage could apply for authorities under a grandfather clause, although the ICC granted less than a third and attached many restrictions.[29] New applicants faced significant barriers. The standard for awarding new authorities was public convenience and necessity, a test in common law. According to the standard, authorization of service should be granted only if it serves an actual public need. The practical meaning of public convenience and necessity was established in an early ICC ruling, the Pan American Bus Lines Operation.[30] Applicants were required to show that certificated carriers were unwilling or unable to provide the proposed service themselves, or that existing service was so unsatisfactory that the situation could be remedied only by granting the application. Applicants also had to show that granting operating authority would not harm the other carriers' business. One form of harm was price competition, and in *Wellspeak Common Carrier Application* in 1937, the ICC held as inadmissible an applicant's showing of lower rates.[31] The ICC allowed existing carriers to protest applications even if the competitive effects were not immediate. The certainty of that happening meant poor prospects. Existing carriers, for their part, were allowed all the business they could handle.[32] Known as the Pan American standard, this set of rules and practices guided the ICC's treatment of common carriers until in-house reform began in the late 1970s.[33]

Common carrier authorities were very specific. Route provisions stated exactly which public roads could be used, along with intermediate points, access roads, and terminals. Commodity provisions stated exactly which among hundreds of finely differentiated items could be hauled on which roads and in which direction. Expanding or modifying an authority required the same procedure for even minor changes and faced the same certainty of protest. As a result, common carrier authorities of any size were incremental creations, won through years of expensive proceedings in the face of opposition. Once obtained, they were very valuable, a reflection of the excess profits possible in tightly restricted markets. Acquiring another carrier's authority was estimated to cost some fifteen per cent of expected earnings, and for some carriers their operating authorities were worth more than their fleet.[34]

The ICC, following its practice with the railroads, encouraged motor carrier rate bureaus to set prices. This was done consensually among the bureaus' member carriers according to an elaborate category of goods. Bureau rates were required to be filed with the ICC, but in practice the commission spent most of its time on entry regulation. That placed effective control of rates in the bureaus. Because this activity was collusive, exposure to antitrust prosecution was removed with the Reed-Bulwinkle Act of 1948.[35] Individual truckers could file lower rates individually, but these could be protested, making it a rarely exercised option. In keeping with its belief that the public interest required a prosperous trucking industry, the ICC pegged its rate approvals to an operating ratio of 93. Operating ratios are the percentage of revenues that are claimed by costs. Because of trucking's low fixed costs, a ratio of 95 is regarded as sustainable.

Under deregulation, ratios in the high 90s are not uncommon, and only a handful of the most efficient carriers have ratios below 90. In that light, the ICC's figure of 93 provided comfortable profits.

Owner-operators buy and maintain their own trucks and lease their services to certificated carriers. ICC rules allowed owner-operators to haul exempt commodities, primarily unprocessed agricultural and forest products, but handling regulated commodities could only be done under lease. Since owner-operators pay their own benefits and operating costs and are non-union, carriers may find them an attractive alternative to purchasing their own equipment and hiring their own drivers, although some large carriers find their own drivers more reliable.[36] Owner-operators are a flexible resource that allows fleet managers to adjust to demand without changing carrier-owned capacity. Since owner-operators are paid a negotiated portion of trip revenues, they are very vulnerable to slack periods and to employers who fail to provide enough work. They have been depicted as colorful and independent figures, but their life is demanding and difficult.[37]

Contract carriers were awarded ICC permits on a showing that their service would be in the public interest. That requirement was much less exclusionary than the Pan American Standard. Even so, contract carriers operated at the margins of the industry. In 1955, for example, there were only 2,646 ICC-certificated contract carriers compared to 15,686 common carriers.[38] They accounted for only 7 percent of ICC-regulated motor freight.[39] One reason for their small market share was that the dedicated services they provided could often be handled much more conveniently by in-house private carriage. The ICC did tighten restrictions in 1962 with the Rule of Eight, which limited contract carriers to that number of clients.[40] Although that rule was widely understood as a flat prohibition, it actually said that serving more than that number might attract the ICC's scrutiny.[41] Even so, it put contract carriers in the position of filling their quotas with shippers who were most able to provide steady volumes and who either had backhaul loads themselves or were located close to another shipper who had them and who was willing to use the contract carrier's services. Balanced traffic is crucial to vehicle utilization in all branches of trucking, and getting a return load near the point of delivery is important enough to turn down a shipment that requires many empty miles. That meant that contract carriers had to be selective. Shippers with small or uneven traffic, or shippers whose cargoes could not balance a contract carrier's trips, were unattractive customers. For shippers unable to buy their own private fleet, common carriers were the only alternative, for whom critics saw the Rule of Eight as a regulatory bonus.[42]

Many shippers did opt for private carriage, and their trucks hauled around half of all intercity freight. Private fleets represent a capital expense and consume managerial talent, but on the positive side they are flexible and adaptive. With no regulatory restrictions on their use, provided they carry cargo owned by the carrier, private fleets can be an integral part of a firm's logistics and deployed entirely according to company requirements and timetables. A related advantage is freedom from dealing with for-hire carriers. It was widely assumed, in fact, that firms opted for private carriage because common carrier rates and service were so unattractive. An interesting Canadian study found that to be true. In comparing the incidence of private carriage in heavily regulated provinces and in the unregulated province of Alberta, the study found a direct relationship: private carriage use was highest in the most regulated provinces.[43] In the United States, the 1960s and 1970s saw a steady erosion of the common carriers' market share to private carriage, a situation that was seen by advocates of regulatory reform as evidence of overpriced and inadequate service. Together with contract carriers, private carriers advocated reform. Contract carriers desired the freedom to serve as many clients as they wish, and private carriers desired the freedom to fill empty trailer space with for-hire cargo.

One of the earliest critics of the Motor Carrier Act was economist James C. Nelson, an important contributor to the literature on trucking regulation. Doubts about the Motor Carrier Act, he asserted, began appearing as early as 1938, and in 1942 he published an article advocating deregulation of transportation. He credited a report he prepared in 1944 for the federal government with establishing the basic ideas that would frame later critiques in the 1950s and 1960s. Nelson's basic objection was that applying railroad regulation to trucking was using the wrong model. It was clear in 1935, he asserted, that motor carriers "were organized as many-firm competitive industries, not as monopolies or oligopolies."[44] Economist Dudley Pegrum elaborated the theme of natural competition in 1952. The industry's structure of many small producers, he argued, assures competitive prices. Allowing competition would reward efficient carriers and provide the public with lower rates. Inefficient carriers exiting the industry would not lead to oligopolistic abuses because low entry barriers and the prospect of earnings would maintain an adequate supply of carriers and competitive rates. By restricting entry and price competition, regulation hobbled a naturally flexible and adaptive industry, saddling the public with inefficient and expensive transportation.[45]

Interest in regulation entered the wider sphere of public policy in 1968 when the Ford Foundation gave the Brookings Institution $1.8 million to fund a research program on regulation. The yield was twenty-two books, sixty-five journal articles, and thirty-eight doctoral dissertations.[46] On the conservative side, the American Enterprise Institute also made regulation a research priority. As this research entered the public policy mainstream, the 1973 energy crisis and stagflation focused political attention. By then there was a professional consensus that economic regulation created and preserved inefficiency and favored the interests of the regulated industries over those of the public.[47] The economic climate made these pertinent critiques. Unnecessarily high freight rates hindered the fight against inflation, and the inefficiencies built into route and commodity restrictions wasted energy. Also important was the deteriorating condition of the railroads, dramatized by the collapse of the Penn Central in 1970. In the eyes of some economists, that could be seen as a result of the government's unnecessary intervention in trucking. By treating the industry as a monopoly and controlling entry and rates, regulation had enabled trucking to prosper at the expense of the railroads.[48] These issues were prominent in President Gerald Ford's 1974 summit conference on inflation, which included a broad spectrum of professional economic opinion. A consensus emerging from the conference was that trucking should be completely deregulated.[49]

During the same time, federal courts, which had previously avoided challenging the ICC's restrictive practices, began doing so. In 1964, a federal appeals court, in *Nashua Motor Express, Inc. v. United States*, ruled in favor of a carrier against an ICC denial of application.

In holding that the ICC should consider the benefits of competition, the decision challenged central tenets of public convenience and necessity.[50] Partly in response to the implications of the *Nashua* decision, the ICC had been reconsidering its entry policy, and in a 1969 policy statement, *Motor Service on Interstate Highways: Passengers*, it asserted that existing carriers "have no inherent right to be protected from merely new, as opposed to destructive competition."[51] In 1974, the Supreme Court, in *Bowman Transportation v. Arkansas-Best Freight System*, ruled that the ICC has no special obligation to protect carriers from competition.[52] As an index of changing attitudes at the ICC, the *Bowman* ruling actually upheld an ICC review in which it had reversed on appeal its previous denial the Bowman application. The ICC justified its reversal on the grounds that the protestants' showing of business loss was not sufficient reason to refuse entry. The case is worth reading as an illustration of the legal workings of public convenience and necessity.

Presidents Ford and Carter appointed pro-deregulation commissioners to the ICC, and in-house review of trucking policy began in 1977. With the implications of the *Bowman* decision in mind, and in light of a second federal appeals court ruling that the ICC, in rejecting an application, had not given enough merit to improved competition, the ICC began revising basic policies through administrative rulemakings.[53] Major changes included removing the Rule of Eight on contract carriers and relaxing the restriction on private carriers on hauling goods for hire.[54] The key development was an ICC ruling that equated competition with the public interest, which reversed the protective effect of the Pan American standard. The same ruling also reversed the onus for protesting new applications from showing harm to existing carriers to showing harm to the public interest.[55] These changes opened the regulatory gates, and carriers began applying for authorities in such number that the ICC issued special guidelines to expedite the process. These changes were administrative modifications of the governing Motor Carrier Act of 1935 and still required legislative removal of public convenience and necessity.

By then Congress was concerned that the ICC was getting ahead of legislative action, and the ICC agreed to refrain from further changes until a new law was passed. Thoroughly alarmed were the American Trucking Associations and the International Brotherhood of Teamsters. These were trucking regulation's beneficiaries, and working as a powerful coalition they had been successful in thwarting occasional reform initiatives in the 1950s and 1960s. In the face of the ICC's speed and thoroughness, the ATA and Teamsters hoped to overturn its rulings or, if legislative change was inevitable, at least to limit the damage. Congress had become interested in transportation regulation with Senator Edward Kennedy's judiciary committee hearings on airline regulation in 1978. The favorable response and resulting legislation directed his committee's attention to trucking. Comprehensive deregulatory legislation was proposed, but by that time the ATA and Teamsters had lobbied sufficiently to force a compromise bill. The draft Motor Carrier Act of 1980 retained the key element of public convenience and necessity but also included the reverse onus provision of presuming competition to be in the public interest. An engaging study by Dorothy Robyn analyzes the legislative politics.[56] One comprehensive assessment regards the deregulation of intercity transportation as the "start of one of the most important experiments in economic policy of our time," partly because of its substantive effects and partly because of its opening the way for deregulation in other industries.[57]

At the time of the Motor Carrier Act's passage there were 18,045 certificated common carriers, and in the first year of the act the ICC processed 28,700 applications. The commission was persuaded that competition and efficiency would best be served by giving carriers the widest operational latitude possible. Transport economics supports that position. Economies of scope can be realized by expanding areas of service and multiplying points of connection.[58] The ICC soon made it clear that it did not intend to be limited by public convenience and necessity. To open the market fully, the ICC granted applications on a showing of fitness. "Fit, willing and able" had been part of previous regulation and, when interpreted strictly, could have exclusionary effect, but the ICC's policy was to presume in favor of entry. When the ICC began awarding authorities for more territory than applicants had sought, the ATA saw the opportunity for a court challenge. The decision upheld the ATA and was followed five months later by a writ of mandamus ordering the ICC to comply, but by that time the initial flood of applicants had already been admitted.[59] Modifying its procedures to agree with the strict terms of the decision, the ICC proceeded with its open entry policy without further intrusion.

The states continued to regulate intrastate trucking, and by 1994 only nine had deregulated. About half continued to apply strict entry and rate controls. Beginning in 1992 a series of ICC rulemakings began circumscribing areas of state jurisdiction in cases where the meaning of interstate commerce was ambiguous.[60] In the meantime, the air package carrier Federal Express, which uses trucks to consolidate cargoes and for pickups and deliveries, was caught in a regulatory conflict. Although the Airline Deregulation Act of 1978 prohibits state regulation of air cargo carriers, states held that ground operations fall under their jurisdiction. The multitude of individual regulations complicated operations for Federal Express. It challenged California's state regulations in court and won, with the Federal Appeals Court of the Ninth Circuit ruling in 1991 that Federal Express's truck operations were outside state jurisdiction.[61] Joined by other express carriers and by major interstate trucking firms, Federal Express began pressing Congress for legislation. The Trucking Industry Regulatory Reform Act of 1994 eliminated the states' power to impose entry, rate and service controls on motor carriers. Together with eliminating rate filing with the ICC, which left rates freely negotiable between carriers and shippers, the act completed the economic deregulation of the industry. Under the new regime, the function of rate bureaus was reduced to keeping official rate records to safeguard carriers from litigation.[62] States continue to have jurisdiction over safety, taxation, registration, and hazardous materials. By then, the Interstate Commerce Commission's authority had become vestigial, and it was sunsetted in 1995.[63]

State-level regulation still affects interstate commerce. The most important restriction is on vehicle length. Truck tractors can pull trailers in five combinations: one 48- or 53-foot trailer, two 28-foot trailers, three 28-foot trailers (triples), one 48-foot trailer, and one 28-foot trailer (Rocky Mountain doubles), and two 48- or 53-foot trailers (turnpike doubles). The last three are longer-combination vehicles (LCV). Triples and Rocky Mountain doubles are permitted in some western states, and turnpike doubles in some states in the northeast. They are desirable for truckers because they greatly improve productivity, and the few studies of their highway safety record have found them to have no greater frequency of accidents than other large trucks. Operationally, these state-level regulations impose barriers at state borders, where the extra trailer on LCVs must be dropped. Differing axle weight limits and varying hazardous materials regulations impose multiple compliances on interstate carriers. States have simplified truck registration under the International Registration Plan. The arrangement allows interstate truckers to pay fees by mileage driven in each jurisdiction and the states to share registration revenues. The same arrangement prevails with fuel taxes under the International Fuel Tax Agreement.[64]

The Motor Carrier Act of 1980 had several important effects on the structure of the industry. First, common carriers began to specialize in less-than-truckload shipments, and the sector since then has been known as LTL. Previously, the ICC had awarded carriers both TL and LTL authorities, and before deregulation common carriers earned some thirty percent of their revenues from TL.[65] Since then they have tended to concentrate on LTL, partly because TL carriers compete very effectively for full-trailer traffic. For their part, LTLs are the only carriers that handle small consignments (under 10,000 lbs.) and offer pickup and delivery service. Terminals are required to assemble full-trailer loads and to separate them at intermediate points and at destinations. These impose capital costs and entry barriers that are not present in the other sectors, and for that reason few new LTLs entered the market after 1980. To rationalize their terminal networks, the largest carriers have organized them into hub-and-spoke systems to preserve local point coverage while promoting full loadings on the trunk routes. To compensate for the delays of moving consignments through intermediate points, some LTLs have adopted direct through service for selected markets.

Under regulation, management was relatively uncomplicated because rates were set by bureaus, and entry, commodity and route controls provided limited and predictable competition. LTL carriers inhabit a much more difficult market, which one survey typifies as an unstable environment.[66] The LTL sector operates on thin margins, partly because it is the only sector that is unionized, partly because of the overhead costs of its terminal system, and partly because competition from other modes makes it difficult to impose rate increases. There are indeed alternatives to LTL. A survey of shippers found them to use on average 5.6 different transportation options for their LTL freight. The alternatives are package carriers such as UPS and FedEx, freight forwarders, pool consolidators and brokers, who assemble small consignments into full-trailer loads and rent transportation from TL carriers, and private carriage.[67] Between the time of deregulation and 1995, LTL carriers lost one third of their traffic to package carriers alone.[68] Because of bankruptcies and mergers, the sector has seen considerable concentration but no increase in market power because of competition. To cope, LTL carriers have cut costs by some 35 percent since deregulation and have sought to tailor services for shippers whose logistics require increasingly small and frequent shipments. That service is very expensive to provide, and the costs have offset genuine gains in efficiency.[69] Intense price competition from the alternative modes remains an unremitting condition.[70]

Deregulation's second effect was the advent of TL carriers. Between 1979 and 1994 the number of interstate TL carriers rose from 13,337 to 54,000. Because of the naturally low entry barriers in this sector, most of the new carriers were small Class III operations.[71] Some were capitalized as new businesses, and others were formerly intrastate carriers. Because TL carriers only handle full-trailer consignments and use the shippers' and receivers' dock facilities, they have much lower costs than LTL carriers and potentially unlimited mobility to serve demand wherever it exists. The main constraint is having a new load near the point of delivery. This sector fits especially well with integrated logistics operations. It also benefits from the work of freight forwarders, who assemble TL loads from smaller consignments, performing the terminal operations themselves. That activity also lends itself to intermodal movement in which railroads provide the linehaul. The TL sector has seen the growth of several very large carriers who operate nationwide and have annual revenues over $1 billion. These firms have large fleets in constant circulation, and to match available units with the nearest available load have employed elaborate computerized scheduling systems and satellite-linked dispatcher-driver communication. Because of that technology, they achieve impressive efficiency.

The challenge for the TL sector comes from shipper expectations, particularly those operating on JIT. To manage the complex and exact movements involved, shippers expect carriers to link with their electronic data systems and use computer-based dispatching. These allow shippers to know the exact location of their goods. Despite the uncertainties caused by highway congestion, both shippers and carriers treat late deliveries as a major service failure. A related pressure is the incentive for shippers to simplify their logistics by reducing the number of carriers they use and giving the ones remaining a more central role in their operations. Being dropped by a large client can mean a devastating loss of traffic that may be difficult to replace given the number of TL carriers in the market. Partly because of these pressures and partly because of non-union wages, the TL sector has a serious problem of driver retention, with some fleets having annual turnovers of 100 percent. A driver shortage has been one reason for TL carriers using railroads for long-haul movement of their trailers.[72] Some firms have addressed the situation with improved wages, but the conditions of work remain demanding.

Deregulation's third important effect was on contract carriage. At the time of deregulation, many common carriers quickly applied for contract carrier permits. One motive was to gain an alternative to regular LTL business. Since existing contract carriers were often small, many of the new entrants were better able to provide attractive service, and marginal contract carriers were faced with very difficult conditions. The ICC no longer required contracts to be filed, and the nature of carrier-shipper relations changed from one of personal relationships to a quest for the lowest prices. Instead of documenting a standing business arrangement, contracts became a way of tendering for cheap transportation. Under the previous regime, it was understood that a shipper under contract would provide an expected amount of freight, but new contracts left shippers free of such obligations. Instead of being concerned about an adequate volume for a contract partner, shippers entered into multiple contracts. The effect was that work under contract became adventitious and situational, and the business came increasingly to resemble regular for-hire trucking. Although firms, including several large ones, still operate primarily as contract carriers, the distinctions between it and other for-hire trucking have largely disappeared.[73]

The number of private carriers declined in the years immediately following deregulation as some shippers abandoned their fleets in favor of contract and TL, although private carriage still handles about half of intercity motor freight. Deregulation had allowed private carriers to apply for authorities to operate for hire and to trip-lease their vehicles. These changes were intended to enable private carriers to fill empty backhauls with revenue-producing cargo. These were significant changes, since the incidence of empty miles is high in supply and distribution operations, which are one of private fleets' primary uses. A recent survey of private carriers found empty miles still to be a problem. The fleets that were most successful in eliminating them did so not so much by using their new ICC authorities or trip leasing as by arranging backhauls within their own firm and through compensated intercorporate hauling. The firms that were most likely to keep their fleets were those that had been most successful in securing full loads. The firms with the fewest empty miles were manufacturers, partly because of the ability to route trucks on continuous circuits between installations. Even so, the most frequent operational pattern was taking a TL load to a customer and returning.[74] The private fleets that remain are those that are needed to meet highly specialized requirements, although empty miles in their operations still make brokerage and for-hire alternatives attractive.

Coordinating transportation in complex supply chains has created a market for third-party logistics services.[75] Using those services spares shippers the work of coordinating transportation among themselves and allows them to focus on their main businesses. The prime benefits are improved logistics—a key consideration in finely-scheduled supply chains—lower costs and more formal integration among the participating firms. A survey of Fortune 500 companies showed that 83 percent reported using third-party services. The most heavily used services were freight payment, shipment consolidation, arranging direct transportation, freight forwarding, and selecting carriers.[76] Large carriers, using their experience in designing customized transportation, offer some of these services themselves.

This sectoral diversity is reflected in the industry's trade associations. The largest and longest-standing is the American Trucking Associations. Before deregulation it was an omnibus organization, as reflected in the plural form of its name, but as interests and concerns diverged following deregulation two of the conferences became independent. They are the Truckload Carriers Association and the National Private Truck Council.

Independent truckers are represented by the Owner Operator Independent Drivers Association. The American Independent Truckers' Association provides small carriers with volume purchasing. In addition, each state has its own trucking association. Shippers associations are the National Industrial Transportation League and the National Small Shipments Traffic Conference. Representing third-party firms is the Brokers and Third Parties Transportation Intermediaries Association, and for intermodal shipping there is the Intermodal Association of North America. Truck suppliers are represented by the Truck Manufacturers Association, the Truck Renting and Leasing Association, and the National Truck Equipment Association. State-level regulators are represented by the American Association of State Highway Transportation Officials. Unionized drivers are represented by the International Brotherhood of Teamsters, whose largest employer is UPS. All have Web sites. The major industry publications are *Transport Topics,* published weekly by the American Trucking Associations, and *Traffic World*, a weekly publication for shippers. The general newspaper of transportation and logistics is the *Journal of Commerce*.

Transborder trucking with Canada is a significant activity. The United States and Canada exchange the world's highest volume of bilateral trade, of which trucks transport nearly 70 percent. The busiest border crossings are at Detroit and Buffalo, and a main logistical corridor is Interstate 75. The two countries previously had virtually symmetrical trucking regulatory regimes. Canada deregulated in 1989 and since then carriers from both countries are free to apply for operating authorities in either jurisdiction. As an index of traffic, the Ambassador Bridge between Detroit and Windsor has well over one million truck crossings annually. Border controls since September 11, 2001 have had to reconcile the need for increased security with the need to avoid backups and delays in very busy traffic lanes. Cabotage, using a foreign carrier to haul shipments between domestic points, is restricted in both countries by customs and immigration rules on equipment and drivers. The rules can be circumvented by opening a place of business and using domestic equipment and drivers.[77]

Until passage of the North American Free Trade Agreement in 1993, Mexico had been completely exclusionary to foreign carriers. Under the agreement, the two countries were to allow each other's motor carriers to operate within adjoining commercial zones in their border states beginning in 1995 and to have complete access to their national markets by 2001. American immigration laws would continue to prohibit cabotage by Mexican carriers. On the day that NAFTA would have opened the border, Transportation Secretary Federico Pena and U.S. Trade Representative Mickey Kantor announced a moratorium on Mexican entry until Mexican carriers could meet American safety standards under the Motor Carrier Safety Act of 1984.[78] President George W. Bush moved to lift the moratorium in November 2002 and was challenged in court on the environmental grounds that Mexican trucks would create pollution. That position was upheld by the Ninth Circuit Court of Appeals in January 2003, but was reversed by the U.S. Supreme Court in June 2004, leaving the terms of NAFTA to take effect.[79]

Several factors affect the future of trucking. The most important is infrastructure. Use of the highways is running well ahead of highway construction. Although almost all the users are private cars, congestion is increasing, particularly in urban areas. The most congested cities are Los Angeles, San Francisco, Denver, Miami, Phoenix, Chicago, and San Jose. Congestion creates delays for motor carriers and makes it necessary to schedule transits through those areas in off-hours. Increasing use of automobiles will worsen the situation. A related factor is energy use. Railroads are more energy-efficient than trucks in moving freight, and although both modes, along with airlines, are affected by rising fuel costs immediately, trucking's thin margins make it particularly vulnerable. If world petroleum supply continues to tighten and prices continue to rise, transportation policy will confront the question of optimizing energy use. One option is to encourage much more intermodal operation between truckers and the railroads. Trucking is likely to retain its central place in transportation, however, because no other mode provides the same speed and flexibility. Current logistics rely on it heavily.

NOTES

1. John Richard Felton, "Inherent Structure, Behavior and Performance," in *Regulation and Deregulation of the Motor Carrier Industry,* ed. by John Richard Felton and Dale G. Anderson, Ames: Iowa State University Press, 1989, 43.
2. B. Starr McMullen, "The U.S. Motor Carrier Industry at the Millennium," *Transportation Quarterly* 39 (Fall 2000) 141.
3. Kenneth Button, *Transport Economics,* 2nd ed., Aldershot: Edward Elgar, 1993, 93.
4. Kenneth Boyer, "NAFTA and the Cost of Distance," *Annals of the American Academy of Political and Social Science* 553 (September 1997) 59.
5. Paul R. Krugman, *Geography and Trade,* Leuven, Belgium and Cambridge, MA: Leuven University Press and MIT Press, 1991, 4–6.
6. Karsten Junius, *The Economic Geography of Production, Trade, and Development,* Tübingen: Mohr Siebeck, 1999, 138–41.
7. Boyer, "NAFTA and the Cost of Distance," 62.
8. Ibid., 63.
9. Garland Chow, *Economics of the Trucking Industry in Transborder Markets,* Ottawa: Hickling Corporation, Division of Economics and Policy, 1991, 2–8; Button, *Transport Economics,* 70.
10. Felton, "Inherent Structure, Behavior and Performance," 44.
11. Theodor Gabriel Crainic, "Long-Haul Freight Transportation," in *Handbook of Transportation Science,* 2nd ed., ed. by Randolph W. Hall, Boston: Kluwer, 2003, 454.
12. John T. Jones, *The Economic Impact of Transborder Trucking Regulations,* New York: Garland Press, 1999, 15.
13. Alexander Morton, "Is There An Alternative to Regulation for the Railroads?" in *Perspectives on Federal Transportation Policy,* ed. by James Miller, Washington, D.C.: American Enterprise Institute, 1975, 28.
14. Paul Teske, Samuel Best, Michael Mintrom, *Deregulating Freight Transportation: Delivering the Goods,* Washington, D.C.: AEI Press, 1995, 28.
15. William Childs, *Trucking and the Public Interest: The Emergence of Federal Regulation 1914–1940,* Knoxville, TN: University of Tennessee Press, 1985, 70–81.
16. Teske, Best, Minstrom, *Deregulating Freight Transportation,* 28.
17. Thomas Gale Moore, "Rail and Trucking Deregulation," in *Regulatory Reform: What Actually Happened,* ed. by Leonard W. Weiss and Michael W. Klass, Boston: Little, Brown, 1986, 16.
18. The decisions are *Buck v. Kuykendall* 267 U.S. 307 (1925) and *George W. Bush and Sons v.*

Maloy, 267 U.S. 317 (1925). The decisions can be read on http://www.caselaw.lp.findlaw.com.

19. Thomas Gale Moore, *Freight Transportation Regulation,* Washington, D.C.: American Enterprise Institute, 1972, 25–26.
20. John Richard Felton, "Background of the Motor Carrier Act of 1935," in Felton and Anderson, eds., *Regulation and Deregulation of the Motor Carrier Industry,* 5.
21. Roger Noll, *Reforming Regulation: An Evaluation of the Ash Council Proposals,* Washington, D.C.: Brookings Institution, 1971, pp. 37, 38; Childs, *Trucking and the Public Interest,* 84–89.
22. Felton, "Background of the Motor Carrier Act of 1935," 5.
23. Childs, *Trucking and the Public Interest,* 124.
24. Eugene D. Anderson, "The Motor Carrier Authorities Game," *ICC Practitioners Journal* 47 (November/December 1979) 27.
25. Moore, "Rail and Trucking Deregulation," 17.
25. Teske, Best, Mintrom, *Deregulating Freight Transportation*, 57.
27. Felton, "Background of the Motor Carrier Act of 1935," 5.
28. *Stephenson v. Binford* 287 U.S. 251 (1932).
29. Moore, "Rail and Trucking Deregulation," p. 16.
30. Interstate Commerce Commission, 1 M.C.C. 190, 202-03 (1936).
31. Interstate Commerce Commission, 1 M.C.C., 712, 715-16 (1937).
32. Dale G. Anderson and Ray C. Huttsell, Jr., "Trucking Regulation 1935–1980," in Felton and Anderson, eds., *Regulation and Deregulation of the Motor Carrier Industry,* 17.
33. A comprehensive survey of the ICC's treatment of trucking can be found in Lawrence S. Rothenberg, *Regulation, Organizations and Politics: Motor Freight Policy at the Interstate Commerce Commission,* Ann Arbor: University of Michigan Press, 1994.
34. Jones, *The Economic Impact of Transborder Trucking Regulations*, 20.
35. James C. Johnson and James P. Rakowski, "The Reed-Bulwinkle Act (1948): A Thirty Year Perspective," in *Proceedings of the Nineteenth Annual Meeting of the Transportation Research Forum,* Oxford, IN: Cross, 1978, 24.
36. Thomas M. Corsi and Joseph R. Stowers, "Effects of a Deregulated Environment on Motor Carriers: A Systematic, Multi-Segment Analysis," *Transportation Journal* 30 (Spring 1991) 11.
37. For a vivid interview-based study of independent truckers, see Michael H. Agar, *Independents Declared: The Dilemmas of Independent Trucking,* Washington, D.C.: Smithsonian Institution Press, 1986.
39. Charles A. Taff, *Commercial Motor Transportation,* Homewood, IL: Irwin, 1955, 108–9.
39. Dorothy Robyn, *Braking the Special Interests: Trucking Deregulation and the Politics of Policy Reform,* Chicago: University of Chicago Press, 1987, 18, 34.
40. Interstate Commerce Commission, 91 M.C.C. 696 (1962).
41. James Hardman, "Motor Contract Carriage in the 1980s and 1990s," *Transportation Practitioners Journal* 58 (Spring 1991) 209–10.
42. Richard Fellmeth, *The Interstate Commerce Omission: The Public Interest and the ICC,* New York: Grossman, 1970, 60.
43. Andrew Klymchuk, *Private Trucking: Analysis and Implications. Research Monograph 15,* Ottawa: Research Branch, Bureau of Competition Policy, Consumer and Corporate Affairs Canada, 1983, 70.
44. James C. Nelson, "Politics and Economics in Transport Regulation and Deregulation: A Century Perspective on the ICC's Role," *Logistics and Transportation Journal* 23 (March 1987) 14–15, 18.

45. Dudley F. Pegrum, "The Economic Basis for Public Policy for Motor Transport," *Land Economics* 28 (1952) 244–63.
46. Martha Derthick and Paul J. Quirk, *The Politics of Deregulation,* Washington, D.C.: Brookings Institution, 1985, 36.
47. Noll, *Reforming Regulation,* pp. 99–100.
48. McMullen, "The U.S. Motor Carrier Industry at the Millennium," 142.
49. Fred Thompson, "Regulatory Reform and Deregulation in the United States," in *Government Regulation: Scope, Growth, Process,* ed. by W. T. Stanbury and Fred Thompson, Montreal: Institute for Research on Public Policy, 1980, 193.
50. 230 F. Supp. 646 (D.N.H. 1964).
51. 110 M.C.C. 514 (1969).
52. 419 U.S. 281 (1974). As an index of the detail and complexity possible under the Pan American standard, transcripts of hearings related to the case cover 23,423 pages.
53. The case is *P.C. White Truck Lines v. ICC,* 551 F. 2nd 1326 (D.C. Cir. 1977).
54. Anderson and Huttsell, "Trucking Regulation 1935–1980," 21–22.
55. *Liberty Trucking Co., Extension*: *General Commodities*, 130 MCC 243 (1978), 131 MCC 573, 575–76 (1979).
56. Robyn, *Braking the Special Interests.*
57. Steven A. Morrison and Clifford Winston, "Regulatory Reform of U.S. Intercity Transportation," in *Essays in Transportation Economics and Policy: A Handbook in Honor of John R. Meyer,* ed. by Jose A. Gomez-Ibanez, William B. Tye, and Clifford Winston, Washington, D.C.: Brookings Institution Press, 1999, 471.
58. Button, *Transport Economics*, 78.
59. *American Trucking Associations v. Interstate Commerce Commission,* 659 F. 2nd 452 (5th Cir. 1981); 659 F. 2nd 957 (5th Cir. 1982). A legal history can be found in *Highway Common Carrier Newsletter* 16 (November 1983) 8–10.
60. For coverage of state-level regulations, see Teske, Best, Mintrom, *Deregulating Freight Transportation,* 92–124. A chart summarizing studies of intrastate trucking appears on pp. 146–54.
61. *Federal Express Corp. v. California Public Utilities Commission*, 936 F. 2nd 1075 (9th Cir. 1991).
62. For legal advice to carriers see Mark J. Ayotte, "The Trucking Industry Regulatory Reform Act of 1994: Understanding the Fine Print"on http://www.library.findlaw.com.
63. Daniel Madar, *Heavy Traffic: Deregulation, Trade, and Transformation in North American Trucking,* Vancouver: UBC Press, 2000 and East Lansing, MI: Michigan State University Press, 2001, 61–64.
64. Teske, Best, Mintrom, *Deregulating Freight Transportation,* 159, 163, 171–79.
65. Jane N. Feitler, Thomas M. Corsi, Curtis M. Grimm, "Strategic and Performance Changes among LTL Motor Carriers: 1976–1993," *Transportation Journal* 37 (Summer 1998) 6.
66. Thomas M. Corsi, Curtis M. Grimm, Jane Feitler, "The Impact of Deregulation on LTL Motor Carriers: Size, Structure, and Organization," *Transportation Journal* 32 (October 1992) 25.
67. Kenneth G. Elzinga, "The Relevant Market for Less-Than-Truckload Freight: Deregulation's Consequences," *Transportation Journal* 34 (Winter 1994) 30, 32.
68. Morrison, Winston, "Regulatory Reform of U.S. Intercity Transportation," 477.
69. McMullen, "The US Motor Carrier Industry at the Millennium," 142–43.
70. For a first-hand view of life and operations in a large regional LTL, see David Rounds, *Perfecting a Piece of the World: Arthur Imperatore and the Blue-Collar Aristocrats of A-P-A,* Reading, MA: Addison-Wesley, 1993.

71. Frederick Stephenson and Theodore Stank, "Truckload Carrier Profitability Strategies," *Transportation Journal* 34 (Winter 1994) 6.

72. McMullen, "The US Motor Carrier Industry at the Millennium," 144–45.

73. Hardman, "Motor Contract Carriage in the 1980s and 1990s," 212–13.

74. Terence A. Brown and Janet Greenlee, "Private Trucking after Deregulation: Managers" Perceptions," *Transportation Journal* 35 (Fall 1995) 6–8.

75. For an introduction to supply chains, see Randolph W. Hall, "Supply Chains," in Hall, ed., *Handbook of Transportation Science.*

76. Robert C. Lieb and Brooks A. Bentz, "Use of Third-Party Logistics Services by Large American Manufacturers: The 2003 Survey," *Transportation Journal* 43 (Summer 2004) 24–27.

77. On deregulation and Canada-U.S. trade, see Madar, *Heavy Traffic.*

78. Jones, *The Economic Impact of Transborder Trucking Regulations,* 21–26.

79. For a brief regulatory history see Cassandra Chrones Moore, "US Supreme Court Finally Removes Decade-Long Roadblock to US-Mexican Trucking," *Free Trade Bulletin* 13 (July 8, 2004) available at http://www.freetrade.org.pubs/ftbs. The case is *United States Department of Transportation v. Public Citizen* 316 F. 3d. 1002 (9th Cir. 2003). The Supreme Court decision is 541 U.S. 752 (2004).

4 Beyond the Waterfront: Ports as Leaders of Intermodal Trade

Paul Hubler and Jack W. Meek

INTRODUCTION

The standardized cargo container, first popularized in the United States in the 1950s and 1960s, has facilitated worldwide intermodal trade, the relatively rapid and cost-efficient transfer of standardized cargo containers among ships, trains, trucks, and jetliners. The intermodal transportation system has brought new efficiencies to the global cargo system, contributing to rapid growth in worldwide seaborne trade. However, the growth in freight volumes has also thrown a spotlight on the weaknesses of intermodal connectors among ships, rail, and road. As gateways for cargo, ports have often been confronted not only by shore-side but also by in-land bottlenecks beyond their marine terminals. This challenge has required ports to coordinate with public and private stakeholders to strengthen the rail and road systems outside their traditional jurisdictions. Coordinative efforts and solutions have ranged from mega-infrastructure projects to logistical changes to achieve greater efficiencies from the existing system. This chapter reviews: (1) the rather significant impact advances in intermodalism have had in creating efficiencies in shipping; (2) how national policy has supported the advancement of intermodalism; and (3) one example of a mega-infrastructure project as an illustration of the significant impact of intermodalism in a major metropolitan arena. The chapter concludes by listing future issues that are central to the continued advancement of intermodalism. The focus of the chapter is on how our ports have become leaders in intermodalism trade and how this leadership is supported by national policy. Such advancement, however, is not achieved without confronting very significant issues that need to be addressed.

THE ADVENT OF INTERMODALISM AND GROWTH IN TRADE

Prior to the advent of widespread containerization, the shipment of goods was comparatively inefficient and slow. Goods to be shipped were packed into non-uniform containers or strapped together on wooden pallets. Cargo moved far more slowly and was subject to far higher labor costs, primarily on the docks. Though there were precursors dating back to the early nineteenth century, standard cargo containers as we know them today were introduced in the 1950s in the United States, with the shipping industry leading the way and the trucking and rail industries subsequently adapting to the new uniform containers (Rosenstein 2000). By the 1960s, containerization was widespread, and emerged as the dominant form of worldwide freight movement by the 1970s. Containerization meant that goods had to be packed and unpacked only once, permitting faster and cheaper loading of ships, trucks, and trains. Ships that formerly had to be berthed for up to a week to be loaded or unloaded by three teams of 26 long-shoremen could be turned around by eight workers in as short as an eight hour shift, reducing port handling costs from $24 per ton to $6 per ton (Rosenstein 2000, 2, 32). As Rosenstein notes, "A labor intensive, piece-by-piece, break-bulk method of load-ing and unloading cargo was replaced by a capital intensive industrialization process: containerization" (2000, ii).

To be sure, containerization facilitated intermodal trade but relatively low-value, bulk freight continues to be carried by and transferred between ship, rail and truck by traditional modes. Nonetheless, containerization has had a profound impact on intermodalism, with the shipping, trucking and rail carrier industries required to conform to uniform cargo container specifications. This standardization resulted in significant growth in world trade by lowering shipping costs and facilitating the rise of multinational production and global supply chain logistics (Erie 2004, 22–23). The containerization revolution, coupled with a post-World War II trade regime aimed at reducing tariffs, contributed to drive up demand for consumer goods. Trade has made the world increasingly economically interdependent and fundamentally altered the U.S. economy. Trade has become as important to the United States as it has to the traditionally export-led economies of Germany and Japan, with imports and exports now accounting for nearly 23.9 percent of gross national product, compared to 12.9 percent just two decades ago (Miles 1994).

BEYOND THE WATERFRONT: PORTS AS LEADERS OF INTERMODALISM

The shipping industry instigated modern containerization and worked closely with key ports on ensuring that investments in new capital, such as cranes to lift containers to and from ships, docks sufficiently sturdy to accommodate the stresses and weight of the new cranes and large expanses of nearby space to stage and store the containers. Containerization also favored ports which had good existing intermodal connectors to highway and railroads. Finally, the significant labor savings of containerization altered the traditional labor relations between ports and the shore-side stevedore and longshore-man unions (Rosenstein 2000). Containerization continues to exert pressures for change on the players in the intermodal system. In the competitive world of global logistics and trade, ports are under constant pressure from shippers to increase the pace of ship turnaround time by easing bottlenecks and accelerating the transfer of containers among ship, truck and train (Peters 2001; Miles 1994). Ports in the United States have been forced to cope with the cargo onslaught by planning and constructing larger facilities designed to ease intermodal transfers. Erie notes that "(t)he watchword of the global logistics revolution is intermodalism: efficient connections between different modes of transportation....Regional competitiveness for places such as Southern California increasingly depends on providing a seamless intermodal transportation network that efficiently links shippers, carriers, ports and airports, highway and rail systems, and ultimately customers" (Erie 2004, 23–24).

With bottlenecks in their backyards and facing increasing competition to accommodate gargantuan and ever-larger ocean-going container vessels, ports have sought to the lead the way in meeting the challenges of intermodalism. To remain competitive in the ever-changing world of intermodal trade, American ports have had to make significant and ongoing investments in dockside facilities as well as in intermodal connectors (U.S. Department of Transportation 2000).

On the West Coast of the United States, the Port of Oakland, California has recently expanded into a defunct naval base for storage and in order build a near-dock intermodal terminal operated by Burlington Northern and Santa Fe Railroad Company (Port of Oakland 2004). The facility eliminates twenty thousand truck trips a year on a twelve-mile journey to the inland rail yard in Richmond, California. Farther north, the Port of Portland, Oregon is proposing a laundry list of truck-rail freight mobility projects, including construction of rail facilities near the docks, roadway improvements and grade separations—in some cases improvements to infrastructure quite distant from the docks and outside the jurisdictional reach of the port (Port of Portland 2005). The Port of Tacoma opened a mega-terminal in 2005, the largest construction project in the history of the port and included a dedicated intermodal yard to permit ship to rail transfers (Port of Tacoma 2005).

New Orleans, competing for trade on the Gulf of Mexico, opened a $101 million container terminal in January 2004 on a cramped seventy-acre site requiring containers to be stacked five high (Port of New Orleans 2005). The port's location on the Mississippi River permits intermodal transfers among trains, trucks, and river barges.

On the East Coast of the United States, seaports jostle for position in the trans-Atlantic trade. More than five thousand ships arrive each year at the busiest East Coast port, the Port of New York and New Jersey, with most arriving from the Atlantic but a growing number from the Pacific via the Panama Canal (Richardson 2005). Approximately 87 percent of the ship-borne cargo at the Port of New York and New Jersey leaves or arrives in a truck, with the remainder traveling by rail. Some five thousand trucks a day arrive at one shipping terminal alone (Larrabee 2002). With increased highway congestion in urban areas, ports and shippers look to rail to carry greater volumes of cargo. Indeed, the Port Authority of New York and New Jersey is engaged in what is touted as the largest port development program in the history of the port, with a primary goal of supporting ship-to-rail connections to ease the flow of cargo to and from the shipping terminals (Port of New York and New Jersey 2005).

Ports have been forced to make investments to their own benefit and to the benefit of their partners in the intermodal freight system. Ports, as well as cargo carriers and transportation planners, appear to have recognized the challenge, and are investing resources in fostering intermodalism. The American Association of Port Authorities (2005) notes, "Like a pipeline, the nation's intermodal transportation system is only as efficient as its narrowest, most congested point, which is often the landside connection at ports."

As container ships have grown in size, and the volume of trade has increased, goods movement infrastructure in the United States has been under severe stress. According to Smith, "Arranging efficient intermodal transport across North America is among the world economy's most pressing and complex logistics problems. Of the ten million trailers and containers moved annually across the country by intermodal, half are associated with international trade. These cargo movements are expected to double or triple by 2020 without corresponding improvements in existing infrastructure" (Smith 2004, p. 16.).

NATIONAL POLICY CONFRONTS CHALLENGE OF INTERMODALISM

American policy makers began confronting the challenges of intermodalism on a national scale with the passage of the Intermodal Surface Transportation Efficiency Act (ISTEA) of 1991. Pedersen notes that with advent of ISTEA, "access to major intermodal transfer facilities, such as airports, ports and rail terminals has been a focus of many statewide planning efforts, particularly with a view to the National Highway System's intermodal connectors" (Pedersen 1999, 4). ISTEA marked a dramatic (some have called it revolutionary) policy shift for the federal government away from traditional highway planning and toward developing a national intermodal transportation system—for freight and passengers—as a cornerstone of federal policy, linking highway, rail, marine, and air transportation. ISTEA sought to overcome traditional barriers to intermodal transportation and marked the first time that freight planning was required by the federal government, calling for state and local transportation plans to consider freight and intermodal issues (Humphrey 1995). Specifically, the regulations called for planners to consider improvements to intermodal terminal access and to safety by separating vehicular and train traffic with the construction of grade separations. ISTEA called for an inclusionary approach to freight planning and sought to engage the port, railroad, and trucking industries to work together in ensuring that transportation plans adequately address freight movement issues such as terminal access, highway-rail grade crossings, and other intermodal issues (Molitoris, Slater, and Linton 2005).

ISTEA was followed by the Transportation Equity Act for the 21st Century (TEA-21) in 1998 which maintained the commitment to funding intermodal improvements along with the traditional highway and transit system improvements (Pedersen 1999). TEA-21 expanded the intermodal emphasis to include the Borders and Corridors Program to fund infrastructure projects near the borders with Mexico and Canada and along high priority international trade corridors leading inland. Congress funded the program at $140 million over five years, an amount that freight stakeholders maintained was not sufficient to meet infrastructure needs, and, as the reauthorization of TEA-21 was being debated by Congress, port advocates called for increasing funding to $2 billion (American Association of Port Authorities, 2005). TEA-21 also called for a report to Congress regarding the state of connector highways to freight facilities, the so-called last mile to the terminus. The report found that "last mile" pavement tended to be in poor condition, that freight projects tended to be overlooked during planning and programming, and that there was little incentive to fund freight projects given the larger and direct public benefit from funding mass transit projects.

Based on the shift of emphasis discussed above, together, ISTEA and TEA-21 represent a paradigm shift away from a highway-dominant transportation arena and toward intermodalism. Heavily dependent on federal transportation funding, state departments of transportation have moved beyond paving highways and adopted the new emphasis on planning for freight intermodalism. Nonetheless, intermodalism has been hampered by the fact that freight rail often competes for funding at a disadvantage with passenger rail and the continuing dilemma of whether and how to appropriately invest public funds in infrastructure projects that benefit private freight rail carriers.

THE ALAMEDA CORRIDOR: MODEL FOR INTERMODAL INFRASTRUCTURE MEGA-PROJECTS?

The Alameda Corridor project in Southern California, a twenty-mile rail cargo expressway from the ports to the transcontinental rail yards near downtown Los Angeles, offers a potential model for financing and building a mega-infrastructure project aimed at easing a bottleneck in the intermodal transportation system. The project is often cited as an example of successful private-public partnership and innovative financing that resulted in the construction of one of the largest public works projects in the United States at a cost of $2.4 billion.

The Ports of Los Angeles and Long Beach together constitute the busiest ports in the nation and the third busiest in the world. The ports serve the Southern California consumer market and economy and are critical gateways for imports and exports to and from the rest of the nation. One-third of the nation's seaborne trade travels through the two ports sited on San Pedro Bay. About half of the in-bound cargo containers are transported by rail out of the Southern California and to the rest of the nation. For instance, 60 percent of the goods shipped into the Chicago region arrived on American shores at the two ports (Erie 2004, 218).

The Alameda Corridor began as a study of freight movement in Southern California, initiated by the Southern California Association of Governments, the metropolitan planning organization for the region. With the backing of the ports, which had cargo bottlenecks on the landside of their marine terminals, the Alameda Corridor became a proposal for consolidating multiple, meandering rail lines out of the ports into a single dedicated rail expressway paralleling Alameda Street. The dedicated rail corridor permits freight trains to travel at speeds of up to forty miles per hour. Trips from the ports to downtown Los Angeles, which used to take up to three hours, now take as little as thirty minutes (Alameda Corridor Transportation Authority 2005). The centerpiece of the Alameda Corridor project is a ten-mile long trench in the middle portion of the corridor, which separates roadway traffic from the trains, eliminating traffic congestion at two hundred crossings. At both ends of the trench, the Alameda Corridor project includes railway bridges and grade separations to ease the passage of trains without impeding the flow of roadway traffic (Alameda Corridor Transportation Authority 2005).

The idea for the Alameda Corridor was first proposed to the Southern California Association of Governments in the 1980s by the ports. Gill Hicks, former general manager of the Alameda Corridor Transportation Authority (ACTA), has noted in his Congressional testimony that the project was initially excluded from government funding because railway infrastructure improvements did not fit in any of the existing categories, such as light rail or highway projects typically funded by the regional transportation planning agencies (Hicks 2001). Such projects were expected to be undertaken by the railroads themselves. Another complicating aspect of the Alameda Corridor financing involved a federal loan to the project which required the project officials to work closely with the White House, the Office of Management and Budget, the U.S. Department of Transportation and members of Congress. However, the bulk of funding was secured via bonds issued against anticipated future revenues based on container fees paid by the railroads.

As in an automated toll booth on a highway, electronic toll collection devices are attached to each railcar and revenues from the user fees paid by the railroads are being used to pay off the project debt. (Railroads also pay a fee for each container that is trucked to inland rail yards, avoiding the Alameda Corridor.) ACTA's financing sources include $1.160 billion in revenue bonds, a $400 million federal loan, $394 million from the ports, $347 million in Metropolitan Transportation Authority grants, and $130 million from other sources (ACTA 2005). The revenue bonds are paid off by the railroad fees. At a dedication ceremony, U.S. Transportation Secretary Norm Mineta called the Alameda Corridor "a national model of innovative financing and public-private cooperation, demonstrating the kind of creativity and resourcefulness we will need in answering our intermodal transportation challenges in the future" (ACTA 2005). Fortner (2002) notes, "This major engineering and construction feat took only five years to complete, came in under budget, and provides an object lesson in how a large-scale transportation project can be completed in the heart of a major metropolitan area."

The Alameda Corridor has not been an unmitigated success. For instance, of the 11.1 million containers handled by the ports in 2002–2003, approximately three million traveled via the Alameda Corridor while another one million were trucked from the ports to inland rail yards. While this volume of containers has met projections and permitted revenue bonds to be paid, proponents had projected that fully half of all containers arriving at the ports would be transported via the Alameda Corridor. Instead, 36 percent has traveled via the Corridor, leaving the rest to be trucked out on already congested freeways. While the Alameda Corridor has operated within expectations as a financing mechanism for a mega-infrastructure project, it has failed to meet popular expectations as a congestion relief project (Agarwal, Giuliano, and Redfearn 2004).

ISSUES FOR THE FUTURE

Clearly, advances in intermodal transportation, led by the dominant ports, and supported by national policy, have had enormous impact on our metropolitan regions. The significant growth in world trade, and the continued significant role world trade plays in the American economy means that the demand for improved support of the free flow of goods and services will continue. As these demands increase, several major issues will be of concern in the future. Here we identify four major issues for the future.

BETTER USE OF EXISTING INFRASTRUCTURE

As congestion forces freight costs upward, previously unused or underutilized modes of transit may become cost-effective. For instance, the rising costs of highway congestion have resulted in returning non-road modes to economic competitiveness: shorter trips inland by rail and by barge on inland waterways or along coastal areas. The Ports of New York and New Jersey, for instance, are seeking to reduce to 57 percent from 87 percent the number of containers carried by truck by growing the numbers of containers carried by rail and barge (Larrabee 2002). Likewise, in the Los Angeles region, freeway congestion slowing convoys of trucks to a crawl has motivated a proposal to develop "inland ports" and distribution centers some fifty to seventy-five miles inland that would be served by shuttle trains that are shorter and more frequent than long-haul trains. Other proposals to reduce congestion and air pollution include truck-only lanes on highways, restricted freight delivery during rush hours and extended port operational hours and peak hour congestion pricing (White 2005; Mongelluzzo 2005).

BUILDING MEGA-PROJECTS AND INTERMODAL INFRASTRUCTURE VIA CONTAINER FEES

The Alameda Corridor project illustrates an effective use of container fee revenue bonds coupled with governmental grants and loans to finance the construction of a mega-infrastructure project. However, in Southern California, at least, infrastructure proponents have been unable to depend on container fees as a financing mechanism. A consortium of municipalities east of downtown Los Angeles have sought to extend the Alameda Corridor improvements through the financing and construction of grade separations but have depended on traditional government transportation grants in the absence of authority to levy container fees. However, the continuing impact of trade on congested transportation infrastructure and worsening air quality has led to the introduction of legislation in the statehouse to impose a per-container fee to benefit clean air programs and congestion relief infrastructure projects (Lowenthal 2005).

MORE AND BIGGER SHIPS

To achieve ever greater economies of scale, container ships have evolved into Panamax size, the maximum ship size permitted in the locks of the Panama Canal, and post-Panamax size, too large even to traverse the canal. The deployment of larger ships with deeper drafts has forced the dredging of ship channels to accommodate those ships. In the case of the Port of Oakland, dredging, coupled with the effects of filling operations to create more port land, raised the ire of environmentalists as early as the mid-1960s (Rosenstein 2000, 71–74).

MITIGATING PUBLIC HEALTH AND ENVIRONMENTAL IMPACTS

To be sure, the growth of world trade means that more products and services will be transferred and facilitated through existing crowded ports and harbors. The impact of increased shipping, expanded harbors, increased use of trains and trucks means higher levels of pollution and an enormous pressure on existing railways and highways. Significant issues with regard to environmental hazards and community health need to be addressed as the expansion of trade continues. The Ports of Los Angeles and Long Beach, for instance, account for the single greatest source of emissions in the smog-ridden Los Angeles Basin, and, port emissions have increased by 60 percent since 2001 due to the boom in Asian imports, leading port oversight board officials to call for rollbacks in emissions (Schoch 2005).

SUMMARY

This chapter offers a review of a significant advancement in world trade: the advent of intermodalism. Through various technological advances and the support of national policy, intermodal strategies have successfully supported the mobility of goods and services. With this success has come the challenges of coordinating ships, rail, and road connectivity. The impact on metropolitan arenas includes the adoption of mega-infrastructure projects that call upon unprecedented levels of coordination and cooperation. The future of continued expansion will call upon even more coordination and collaboration, and there will be very significant challenges ahead that will challenge our social, economic, and political capacities.

REFERENCES

Agarwal, A., Guiliano, G., Redfearn, C. The Alameda Corridor: A White Paper. Proceedings of the Alameda Corridor: A Blueprint for the Future? Conference, University of Southern California: Los Angeles, CA, February 10, 2004.

American Association of Port Authorities. Legislative Priorities: TEA 21 Reauthorization, 2005. http://www.aapa-ports.org/govrelations/TEA21.pdf (accessed August 2005).

Erie, S.P. *Globalizing L.A.: Trade, infrastructure and regional development.* Stanford University Press, Stanford, CA, 2004.

Fortner, B. The Train Lane. *Civil Engineering Magazine,* 2002, 52–59.

Hicks, G.V. Testimony before the House Subcommittee on Government Efficiency, Financial Management, and Intergovernmental Relations. April 16, 2001.

Humphrey, T.F. NCHRP Synthesis of Highway Practice 217: Consideration of the 15 Factors in the Metropolitan Planning Process. Transportation Research Board, National Research Council, Washington, D.C., 1995, 61.

Larrabee, R. Statement of the Port Authority of New York and New Jersey on Intermodal Freight Transportation before a Joint Hearing of the Senate Committees on Commerce, Science and Transportation and Environment and Public Works, Washington, D.C., September 9, 2002. http://epw.senate.gov/107th/Larrabee_090902.htm (accessed July 2005).

Lowenthal, A.S. Senate Bill 760, introduced February 22,2005. http://info.sen.ca.gov/pub/bill/sen/sb_0751-800/sb_760_bill_20050527_amended_sen.pdf (accessed July 2005).

Luberoff, D., Walder, J. U.S. Ports and the Funding of Intermodal Facilities: An Overview of Key Issues. *Transportation Quarterly,* 2000, 54 (4), 23–46.

Miles, G.L. The War of the Ports. *International Business,* 1994, 7 (3), 70–79.

Molitoris, J.M., Slater, R.E., Linton, G.J. ISTEA Regulation and Railroads. Bureau of Transportation Statistics, National Transportation Library, undated letter. http://ntl.bts.gov/DOCS/395ISTEA.html (accessed August 2005).

Mongelluzzo, Bill. Breaking Point. *Journal of Commerce.* September 19, 2005.

Pedersen, Neal J. Multimodal Transportation Planning at the State Level: State of the Practice and Future Issues. Transportation Research Board Committee on Statewide Multimodal Transportation Planning,Washington, D.C., July 1999. http://gulliver.trb.org/publications/millennium/00076.pdf (accessed November 2005).

Peters, H., J.F. Developments in Global Seatrade and Container Shipping Markets: Their Effects on the Port Industry and Private Sector Involvement. *International Journal of Maritime Economics,* 2001, 3 (1), 3–26. http://www.palgrave-journals.com/cgi-taf/DynaPage.taf?file=/ijme/journal/v3/n1/abs/9100003a.html (accessed June 2005).

Port of New Orleans. Port Record: The Worldwide Publication of the Port of New Orleans 2005. http://www.portno.com/PortRecord.pdf (accessed August 2005).

Port of New York and New Jersey, Press Release No. 28-2005, Port of New York and New Jersey Sets Cargo Records in 2004; Announces Plans to Handle Future Growth. March 16, 2005. http://www.panynj.gov/ (accessed July 2005).

Port of Oakland, Joint Intermodal Terminal Overview. 2004 "Media Kit." http://www.portofoakland.com/pdf/news_medi_04.pdf (accessed June 2005).

Port of Portland. 2005 Port Transportation Improvement Program. Business Development Department, Transportation Planning Section, 2005. http://www.portofportland.com/PDFPOP/Trade_Trans_Studies_PTIP_2005_Final.pdf (accessed June 2005).

Port of Tacoma, Expansion Projects. 2005. http://www.portoftacoma.com/whatsnew.cfm?sub=105 (accessed August 2005).

Richardson, M. Panama Canal's Value on the Rise Again. Institute of South East Asian Studies, Singapore, originally published in the *Straits Times,* February 14, 2005. http://www.iseas.edu.sg/viewpoint/mr14feb05.pdf (accessed May 2005).

Rosenstein, M. The Rise of Maritime Containerization in the Port of Oakland, 1950 to 1970. Self-published thesis, Morristown, New Jersey, 2000. http://www.apparent-wind.com/mbr/maritime-writings/thesis.pdf (accessed June 2005).

Schoch, Deborah. New Harbor Panel Aims to Cut Pollution While Expanding Port. *Los Angeles Times.* September 29, 2005.

Smith, J.N. Breaking Through Bottlenecks at the Port. *World Trade*, 2004, 17 (6), 16.
U.S. Department of Transportation. NHS Intermodal Freight Connectors: A Report to Congress: 2000. http://ops.fhwa.dot.gov/freight/documents/2001REPT.DOC (accessed July 2005).
White, Ronald D. Ports to Work Long Hours in Effort to Cut Congestion. *Los Angeles Times*. July 11, 2005.

5 A Description of the Inland Waterway System and Planning Models

Kevin E. Henrickson and Wesley W. Wilson

INTRODUCTION

A critical element of any economy is its transportation infrastructure. The rivers, locks, dams, ports, and the like that make up the inland waterway system are of particular important to the U.S. transportation infrastructure. For many commodities and locations, transportation by barge via the inland waterway system is a cheaper, and more economically sound form of transporting goods than either rail or truck. This is especially true of low-value bulk commodities. In this chapter, we provide an overview of the system in the United States. The overview consists of a description of the major waterways in terms of size, traffic, and trends. We then provide a snapshot of the suppliers of barge transportation in terms of the structure of industry and performance measures. In the final section of the chapter, we describe methods that are used to evaluate improvements in the navigation infrastructure. This description is accompanied by recent criticisms of the modeling and recent research designed to address these criticisms.

The term "inland waterway" is a generic label given to the system of rivers on which commerce, both foreign and domestic, is transported. The three largest components of the U.S. inland waterway system, in terms of ton-miles transported, are the Mississippi, Ohio, and Illinois rivers. However, the Mississippi River is the backbone of this system. Stretching over eighteen hundred miles from Minnesota to Louisiana, the Mississippi River provides access to coastal port facilities for many of the rivers in the United States, including the Illinois, Missouri, and Ohio River systems, and this access is critical to the importation and exportation of goods to and from the U.S.

Transportation in the system is supplied by approximately nine hundred vessel operators. This number has increased over time as traffic has grown and there are relatively minor barriers to enter the industry. Total capacity in terms of tonnages has also increased. From 1995 to 2002, total capacity increased by approximately 8 percent. However, while both firm numbers and capacity has generally increased, the industry has become more consolidated. In the near future, the largest impact on the barge transportation industry will be in the area of technological development both in terms of vessels and in the waterway itself.

To make the navigation service offered by these vessel operators possible, many parts of the inland waterway system use a series of locks and dams. In particular there are currently approximately 230 lock sites are maintained by the U.S. Army Corps of Engineers (USACE). However, many of these lock sites were built more than fifty years ago and are much smaller in size than the "tows" (a term used to describe a configuration of vessel and barges). Many of these locks have been and are being considered for major rehabilitation and/or redesign. For example, there are currently only three locks located on the Upper Mississippi River that are over 600 feet in length; however, most of the current barge tows using the waterway system are nearly 1,200 feet in length (U.S. Army Corps of Engineers 2004). Tows larger than the lock require two or more passes ("cuts") through a lock and take more than twice the time to traverse a lock than a single cut tow. The increase in traffic, the age of locks, and the larger tow sizes have led to increased transit times and growing congestion at the locks on the inland waterway system.

In an attempt to improve this situation, the Army Corps of Engineers have proposed updating several locks in an attempt to reduce the congestion caused by the smaller locks. Prior to receiving funding for such projects, studies are conducted to evaluate the costs and the benefits of such improvements. To accomplish this task, the Army Corps of Engineers uses simulation models and forecasts that are designed to estimate the benefits of potential waterway improvements. These techniques have been the source of considerable scrutiny as of late by, among others, the National Research Council (NRC) of the National Academy of Sciences. Generally, it is held that the forecasts and the assumptions of the models used tend to overstate the benefits of waterway improvements. The two main sources of this criticism relate to the forecasting of future barge transportation demand, and to the demand models used to evaluate the effects of rate reductions occurring from improvements.

The organization of this overview will be first to describe the waterway system in terms of its size, major rivers and the characteristics of each river in terms of commodities shipped, levels of traffic and trends in the traffic over time. Following this general overview of the U.S. inland waterway system, the supply of waterway traffic is examined. Specifically, topics pertinent to the supply of waterway transportation are explored, issues such as: the number and size distribution of firms, product differentiation, ownership, profit rates, and technological change. This overview is then concluded with a description of the techniques used by the U.S. Army Corps of Engineers (ACE) to evaluate waterway improvements. These techniques have been reviewed by the National Research Council and others, and the description contains a synopsis of their comments on ACE planning.

AN OVERVIEW

The focus of this section is to provide a general overview of the inland waterway system and its component parts. To this end, the system is described in terms of geography, size, major rivers, commodities shipped, levels of traffic, and trends in commodity flows. Following this description, each of the major rivers within the system are described.

These rivers include: the Mississippi River, the Ohio River, the Columbia-Snake River system and the Gulf Intracoastal Waterway.

THE INLAND WATERWAY SYSTEM

The inland waterway system is a major component of the United States transportation network. The waterway network competes with other alternative transportation networks, primarily railroads and highways. Over time, as illustrated by, Figures 5.1 and 5.2, the trends in output measured by ton-miles hauled by each of these transportation modes has changed in both absolute and relative terms. Of the four modes, clearly rail carries the largest number of ton-miles of freight, with truck and water ranking second and third. Overall, traffic levels have risen from 1990–2001, but most of the increase has been for rail and to a lesser extent motor carriage. Indeed, waterway traffic has exhibited a slight decline over this time period. Figure 5.1 indicates a slight downward trend in the ton-miles hauled by the inland waterway network. However, Figure 5.2 indicates that the tons of waterborne commerce hauled from 1964–2003 over the entire waterway system, not just the inland waterway system, have been increasing, even over the period of 1990–2001.

Figure 5.2 further decomposes this traffic into foreign and domestic, with increases in foreign traffic clearly being responsible for the increase in tons shipped via the waterway over the period 1964–2003. Of this foreign traffic, Figure 5.3 shows that the increase has been largely because of increased inbound shipments of commerce, i.e., imports. While the United States imports many different commodities from many different regions of the world, the primary waterborne import responsible for the

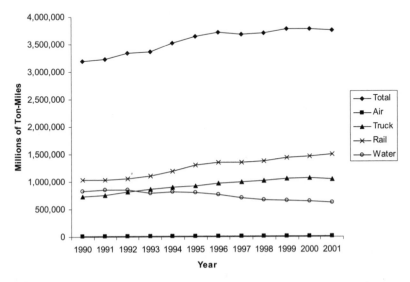

FIGURE 5.1   United States ton-miles of freight by mode 1990–2001. Source: U.S. Transportation Statistics 2004, Bureau of Transportation Statistics, January 2005, Table 1-46.

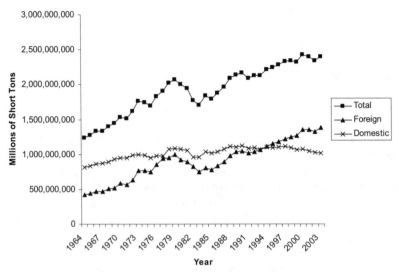

FIGURE 5.2   Total waterborne commerce of the United States 1964–2003. Source: Waterborne Commerce of the United States, Calendar Year 2003, Part 5—National Summaries, U.S. Army Corps of Engineers (2004), Figure 1-2.

increase in waterborne imports, and the primary product transported via water in the country, is petroleum and petroleum related products as illustrated in Figure 5.4. In 2003, petroleum accounted for 45.1 percent of waterborne commerce in the United States, followed by coal (11.7%) and food & farm products (11.1%). However, as we demonstrate latter, there are considerable differences in commodities shipped across the components of the waterway system, i.e., the rivers in the system.

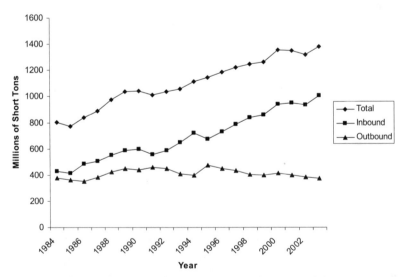

FIGURE 5.3   Foreign waterborne commerce inbound and outbound traffic of the United States 1984–2003. Source: Waterborne Commerce of the United States, Calendar Year 2003, Part 5—National Summaries, U.S. Army Corps of Engineers (2004), Figure 1-4.

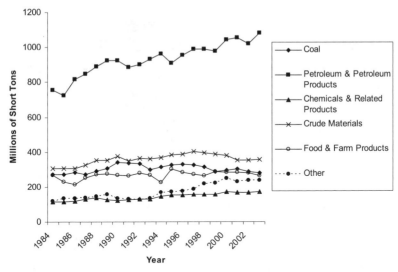

FIGURE 5.4 Principle commodites in waterborne commerce of the United States 1964–2003 (millions of short tons). Source: Waterborne Commerce of the United States, Calendar Year 2003, Part 5—National Summaries, U.S. Army Corps of Engineers (2004), Figure 1-3.

The inland waterway system consists of nearly twelve thousand navigable miles of waterway and offers direct access to ocean ports from the nation's interior, often without seasonal difficulties (the Great Lakes and the Upper Mississippi regions excluded). Geographically, the inland waterway system connects all but nine of the fifty states, with a majority of those nine falling within the southwest (Arizona, Colorado, Utah, Wyoming). Table 5.1 lists the length, tons shipped in 2003 and ton-miles shipped

TABLE 5.1
Domestic U.S. Waterborne Traffic for Rivers with Over Five Million Tons Transported in 2003

Waterway	Length	Tons in 2003 (Millions)	Ton-Miles in 2003 (Billions)
Mississippi River	1,814	308.2	167.5
Ohio River	981	228.8	54.2
Tennessee River	652	49.8	6.7
Illinois River	357	45.0	8.5
Monongahela River	129	27.6	1.1
Columbia-Snake River System	855	23.1	2.9
Big Sandy River	27	22.6	0.1
Cumberland River	381	20.6	2.2
Kanawha River	91	19.4	1.3
McClellan-Kerr Arkansas River System	462	13.0	2.7
Atachafalaya River	121	9.8	0.6
Missouri River	732	8.1	0.3
Green and Barren Rivers	109	7.9	0.5

Source: Waterborne Commerce of the United States, Calendar Year 2003, Part 5—National Summaries, U.S. Army Corps of Engineers (2004), Table 3-21.

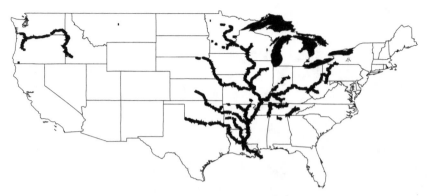

FIGURE 5.5 The major rivers of the inland waterway system.

in 2003 for the thirteen largest rivers (in terms of tons shipped) in the nation. Figure 5.5 provides the locations of these rivers.

Clearly, in terms of length, tons shipped, and ton-miles shipped, the Mississippi River dominates the entire inland waterway system. Add to this the fact that most of the other rivers listed in Table 5.1 flow through the Mississippi River to form the Mississippi River system, and the Mississippi River becomes invaluable to commerce within the United States. Equally important are the ports located on the inland waterway system, which are responsible for loading and unloading commerce on the river. The top fifteen of these ports (in terms of ton-miles shipped) on the inland waterway system are shown in Figure 5.6.

The entire inland waterway system, falls under the jurisdiction of the USACE, whose responsibility is to operate and maintain all waterway infrastructure needs including construction, operation and maintenance. Currently, this entails the upkeep of 230 lock sites, incorporating 275 lock chambers; all of which support a wider private

FIGURE 5.6 The 15 largest ports (in ton-miles shipped) on the inland waterway system. Source: National Waterway Network, U.S. Army Corps of Engineers Navigation Data Center.

infrastructure of over nine thousand commercial waterway facilities. These navigable waterways are also utilized for means other than the transportation of goods; namely for municipal and agricultural irrigation, hydropower (dams), recreation, and flood control along with general regional development.

THE MISSISSIPPI RIVER

The Mississippi River accounts for the bulk of tonnages moved on the waterway. Indeed, most of the other navigable rivers flow into the Mississippi making it the central river in the system. The navigable part of the Mississippi begins in Minneapolis and flows for over eighteen hundred miles to the Gulf of Mexico. The Missouri and Illinois rivers join the Mississippi near St. Louis and the Ohio River near Cairo, Illinois. Before reaching the Gulf of Mexico, the Arkansas and Ouachita rivers also join the Mississippi. Thus, the Mississippi River can be thought of as the backbone of a larger set of interconnected waterways.

Figure 5.7 indicates that traffic on the Mississippi River system has been increasing over the period 1984–2003 and is largely dominated by internal domestic traffic. Of the commodities shipped on the Mississippi River system, coal, food and farm products, petroleum, and crude materials are, in order, the four largest (in terms of tons shipped) as shown in Figure 5.8, an ordering that has been consistent over the period 1984–2003.

The Mississippi River "Main Stem" is a term used to refer to the Mississippi River separate and apart from the rivers that flow into it. Figure 5.9 indicates that tons shipped have been increasing, and that internal domestic shipments are the largest type of shipments as they were with the Mississippi River system. However, because of

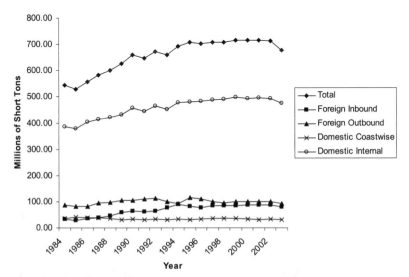

FIGURE 5.7   Types of traffic on the Mississippi River system 1984–2003. Source: Waterborne Commerce of the United States, Calendar Year 2003, Part 5—National Summaries, U.S. Army Corps of Engineers (2004), Figure 3-1.

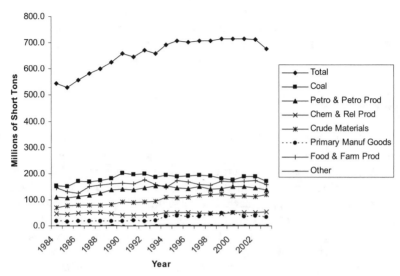

FIGURE 5.8 Principle commodites in waterborne commerce for the Mississippi River system 1984–2003 (millions of short tons). Source: Waterborne Commerce of the United States, Calendar Year 2003, Part 5—National Summaries, U.S. Army Corps of Engineers (2004), Figure 3-2.

its proximity to the farming region of the United States, the main commodity shipped on Mississippi River is food and farm products accounting for 32.7 percent of total commerce on the Mississippi River in 2003 (Figure 5.10).

The Mississippi River is often further separated between the Upper and Lower portions. The Upper Mississippi (UMISS) stretches from Minneapolis, Minnesota, to

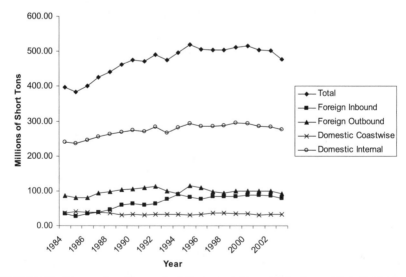

FIGURE 5.9 Types of traffic on the Mississippi River Main Stem 1984–2003. Source: Waterborne Commerce of the United States, Calendar Year 2003, Part 5—National Summaries, U.S. Army Corps of Engineers (2004), Figure 3-5.

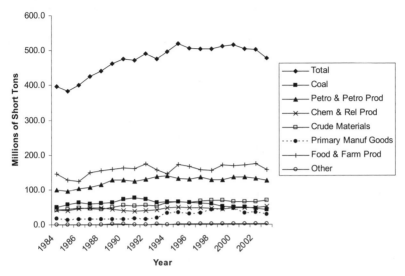

FIGURE 5.10 Principle commodites in waterborne commerce for the Mississippi River Main Stem 1984–2003 (millions of short tons). Source: Waterborne Commerce of the United States, Calendar Year 2003, Part 5—National Summaries, U.S. Army Corps of Engineers (2004), Figure 3-6.

Cairo, Illinois, where the Ohio joins the Mississippi. The Lower Mississippi (LMISS) runs from Cairo to the Gulf of Mexico. The UMISS is made navigable through the use of twenty-nine locks and dams. Meanwhile, the LMISS requires no locks to remain navigable.

To illustrate the geographic differences in the Mississippi River Main Stem, consider Table 5.2, which contains figures on the total waterborne commerce on the Mississippi River. Note that Table 5.2 divides the Mississippi River Main Stem into not just the UMISS and LMISS, but into three distinct sections. The "Upper Mississippi" is the section of the river between Minneapolis, Minnesota and the mouth of the Missouri River, the "Middle Mississippi" is the section of river between the mouth of the Missouri River and the mouth of the Ohio River, and the "Lower Mississippi" is everything below the mouth of the Ohio River. A key factor for navigation on the Mississippi River, illustrated in this table, is that traffic levels increase southward. This simply reflects the nature of networks and a dominate node (i.e., the Gulf of Mexico). In particular, traffic on the Lower Mississippi is more than double that on the Upper Mississippi, and traffic in the Middle Mississippi is approximately 50 percent larger than that on the Upper Mississippi. Further, as indicated in Table 5.2, the UMISS traffic is dominated by farm products. While this is true of the lower segments as well, the proportion is much smaller. In the UMISS, about 55 percent of tonnages are farm products but in the LMISS, the proportion falls to about 40 percent. In the LMISS, about 11 percent of traffic is coal, while in the UMISS only about 5 percent is coal. Finally, there is virtually no crude petroleum moved on the UMISS, while on the LMISS about 11 percent of the tonnages moved are of crude petroleum. Most of these differences are, of course, determined by differences in the economic activity across the regions.

TABLE 5.2
Total Waterborne Commerce on the Mississippi River by Section 1993–2002 (millions of short tons)

Upper Mississippi	1993	1994	1995	1996	1997	1998	1999	2000	2001	2002
Farm Products	39.1	37.9	46.8	45.7	41.1	40.8	47.8	43.9	41.0	46.8
Metals	3.3	6.1	5.0	3.9	4.7	5.5	4.9	6.0	4.2	5.2
Coal	8.4	10.3	9.0	8.6	7.5	8.8	8.6	7.9	7.6	7.4
Crude Petroleum	0.0	0.0	0.2	0.1	0.0	0.0	0.0	0.0	0.0	0.0
Nonmetallic Minerals	7.3	8.8	8.6	8.0	9.5	8.5	9.7	10.2	10.4	10.0
Forest Products	0.1	0.2	0.3	0.3	0.2	0.3	0.3	0.4	0.3	0.4
Industrial Chemicals	3.6	4.3	4.0	3.8	4.1	4.2	3.9	3.9	3.4	3.5
Agricultural Chemicals	3.8	4.5	3.7	3.3	3.0	3.4	3.2	3.4	3.5	3.5
Petroleum Products	6.4	7.4	6.8	6.7	7.7	8.0	7.3	7.5	8.2	7.2
Other	0.1	0.0	0.1	0.1	0.1	0.1	0.0	0.0	0.1	0.0
Total	72.2	79.4	84.4	80.4	77.8	79.6	85.7	83.3	78.8	84.1

Middle Mississippi	1993	1994	1995	1996	1997	1998	1999	2000	2001	2002
Farm Products	48.8	46.6	56.0	54.6	51.9	51.6	59.8	55.3	52.5	57.4
Metals	4.3	7.5	6.6	5.2	6.1	7.2	6.2	7.9	5.6	6.3
Coal	19.5	22.1	22.7	23.1	22.2	23.1	22.9	23.4	24.2	23.8
Crude Petroleum	0.0	0.0	0.2	0.1	0.0	0.0	0.0	0.1	0.0	0.0
Nonmetallic Minerals	12.2	15.8	17.4	14.8	16.7	16.9	20.0	18.5	19.2	17.4
Forest Products	0.2	0.3	0.3	0.4	0.3	0.4	0.5	0.7	0.4	0.4
Industrial Chemicals	3.9	4.6	4.4	4.3	4.5	4.7	4.5	4.4	3.9	4.0
Agricultural Chemicals	4.6	5.2	4.4	4.0	3.8	4.1	3.7	3.9	4.3	4.2
Petroleum Products	5.6	6.7	6.2	6.6	6.9	7.7	7.0	7.4	8.8	7.9
Other	0.1	0.1	0.1	0.1	0.1	0.1	0.1	0.0	0.1	0.0
Total	99.1	108.9	118.3	113.0	112.5	115.8	124.7	121.6	119.1	121.5

Lower Mississippi	1993	1994	1995	1996	1997	1998	1999	2000	2001	2002
Farm Products	73.3	68.0	79.1	75.6	71.8	69.7	79.1	77.3	78.1	80.6
Metals	14.7	20.9	20.8	19.7	20.6	22.9	23.3	26.9	21.0	24.1
Coal	34.2	35.4	32.8	30.7	29.3	28.4	23.7	23.8	25.0	22.5
Crude Petroleum	1.1	1.9	2.2	2.0	2.2	2.2	2.4	2.1	1.6	1.3
Nonmetallic Minerals	23.3	30.0	31.1	29.3	31.2	31.6	36.7	33.4	31.8	29.7
Forest Products	0.8	0.9	0.8	1.3	1.5	1.3	1.1	1.3	0.7	0.7
Industrial Chemicals	10.4	11.1	11.1	11.0	11.2	10.9	10.7	10.7	10.0	10.0
Agricultural Chemicals	8.7	9.5	8.9	8.0	7.9	8.5	8.2	8.4	9.5	8.6
Petroleum Products	17.1	18.7	17.9	18.1	18.1	19.8	19.3	20.2	22.8	20.9
Other	0.2	0.2	0.3	0.2	0.2	0.3	0.3	0.3	0.2	0.1
Total	183.8	196.8	205.1	195.9	193.9	195.9	204.9	204.3	200.6	198.3

Source: Waterborne Commerce of the United States, Calendar Year 2002, Part 2—Waterways and Harbors Gulf Coast, Mississippi River System and Antilles, U.S. Army Corps of Engineers (2003).

THE OHIO RIVER

Of the rivers presented previously in Table 5.1, the second largest river is the Ohio River, and as with the Mississippi the Ohio River can be considered part of a larger waterway system. Geographically, the Ohio River is the central river for the Ohio River system. In terms of navigation, it stretches westward from Pittsburgh towards Cairo, Illinois, near its convergence with the Mississippi River. Across the twenty-eight hundred miles of navigable waterway constituting the Ohio River system, coal is the primary commodity moved. In particular, of the approximately 275 million tons moved on the system, over one-half of the traffic was of coal.

In addition to the Ohio River, the system includes seven other rivers: the Tennessee, the Cumberland, the Monongahela, the Allegheny, the Green, the Kanawha, and the Big Sandy. These waterways all flow into the Ohio River itself, and allow this system to access nine states: Alabama, Illinois, Indiana, Kentucky, Mississippi, Ohio, Pennsylvania, Tennessee, and West Virginia.

To facilitate commerce, the Ohio River system has an infrastructure of approximately 1,000 facilities, docks, and terminals, with many serving large metropolitan areas with accompanying ports. The five largest of these ports are: Pittsburgh, Huntington, West Virginia, Cincinnati, Louisville, and Nashville. As with the Upper Mississippi River, the Ohio River system uses a series of sixty lock and dam facilities to facilitate navigation. Of these sixty locales, twenty are on the Ohio River itself, there are nine each upon the Monongahela and Tennessee rivers, the Allegheny has eight, the Cumberland four, and the Kanawha and Green rivers each have three. The remaining five facilities are located on the Kentucky and Clinch rivers, which are non-navigable but nonetheless require control mechanisms.

Figure 5.11 indicates that of the commodities carried on the Ohio River system, coal is the dominant product accounting for 54 percent of total barge traffic in 2003. The dominance of coal on the Ohio River system is due to high level of coal deposits in the area and the large number of coal-fired power plants located along the Ohio River system. This relation of high coal deposits and a large number of coal fired power plants also makes the Ohio River system unique in that, of the shipments on the river, 66 percent had both their destination and termination points within the Ohio River system. Put differently, more than half of the commerce on the Ohio River system is intersystem commerce, not commerce destined for the Mississippi and other markets.

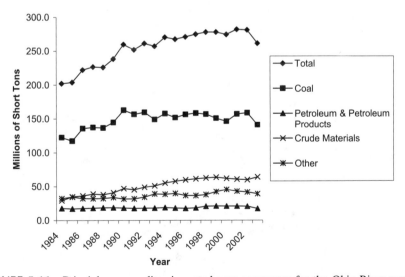

FIGURE 5.11 Principle commodites in waterborne commerce for the Ohio River system 1984–2003 (millions of short tons). Source: Waterborne Commerce of the United States, Calendar Year 2003, Part 5—National Summaries, U.S. Army Corps of Engineers (2004), Figure 3-8.

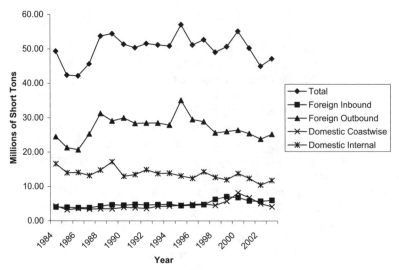

FIGURE 5.12   Types of traffic on the Columbia River 1984–2003. Source: Waterborne Commerce of the United States, Calendar Year 2003, Part 5—National Summaries, U.S. Army Corps of Engineers (2004), Figure 3-16.

THE COLUMBIA-SNAKE RIVER SYSTEM

Unlike the Mississippi River system and the Ohio River system that flow together and terminate in the Gulf of Mexico, the Columbia-Snake river system is completely independent of any other waterway except for the Pacific Ocean through Portland, Oregon. Composed of three rivers, the Columbia, the Snake, and the Willamette, the entire system consists of 596 navigable miles of waterway.

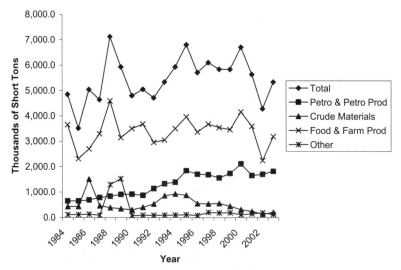

FIGURE 5.13   Principle commodites in waterborne commerce for the Columbia River 1984–2003 (thousands of short tons). Source: Waterborne Commerce of the United States, Calendar Year 2003, Part 5—National Summaries, U.S. Army Corps of Engineers (2004), Figure 3-17.

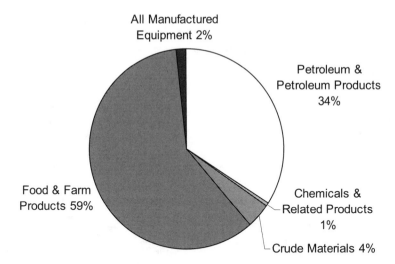

FIGURE 5.14 Principle commodites in waterborne commerce for the Snake River in 2003. Source: Waterborne Commerce of the United States, Calendar Year 2003, Part 5—National Summaries, U.S. Army Corps of Engineers (2004), Figure 3-20.

As demonstrated by Figure 5.12, this waterway system is also different from the other systems in that the dominant type of traffic on the Columbia-Snake system is foreign outbound shipments, i.e., exports, with the second most common type of traffic being shipments to coastal facilities. In terms of commodities shipped, agricultural products for the Columbia-Snake system dominate (Figures 5.13 and 5.14).

THE GULF INTRACOASTAL WATERWAY

The Gulf Intracoastal Waterway (GIWW) spans 1,109 miles along the Gulf of Mexico, and provides waterway connections from Texas to Florida as well as to the Mississippi River system.

Figure 5.15 provides a snapshot of the GIWW over time and across commodities. Generally, traffic has remained relatively stable along this system since the late 1980s. More than any other system, traffic is dominated by internal domestic traffic. And, as indicated by Figure 5.16, the primary commodities are petroleum and petroleum products, a finding that is consistent with the regional economic base.

Supply of Barge Transportation

This section of the chapter provides a description of the supply of transportation services on the inland waterway system. The description loosely follows the structure-conduct-performance (SCP) paradigm of industrial organization. The original paradigm holds that the structure of the industry impacts conduct which in turn impacts the performance of an industry. The development of modern theory has pointed to a

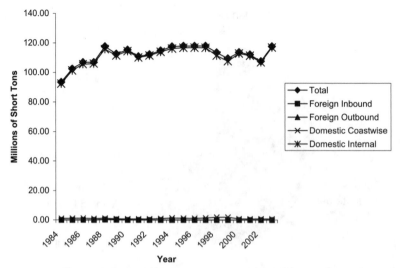

FIGURE 5.15 Types of traffic on the Gulf Intracoastal Waterway 1984–2003. Source: Waterborne Commerce of the United States, Calendar Year 2003, Part 5—National Summaries, U.S. Army Corps of Engineers (2004), Figure 3-13.

number of important effects that run from conduct to structure and from performance to both conduct and performance. The tools of modern theory and econometrics have largely displaced the empirical methods of the SCP paradigm, but it remains useful as a descriptive model for an industry.

The structure of an industry is typically described in terms of the number and size distribution of firms as well as the conditions of entry and product differentiation. To

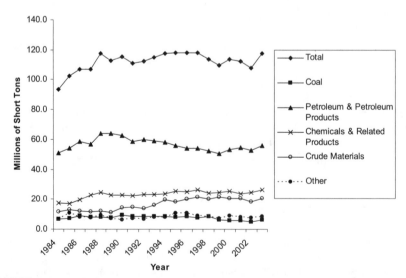

FIGURE 5.16 Principle commodites in waterborne commerce for the Gulf Intracoastal Waterway 1984–2003 (millions of short tons). Source: Waterborne Commerce of the United States, Calendar Year 2003, Part 5—National Summaries, U.S. Army Corps of Engineers (2004), Figure 3-14.

TABLE 5.3
Number of Vessels and Vessel Capacity on the Mississippi River and Gulf Intracoastal Waterway 1995 and 2002

	1995		2002		Change in
Vessel Type	Count	Capacity	Count	Capacity	Capacity
Deck Barges	3,054	3,258,422	3,129	3,844,567	18%
Covered Dry Cargo Barges	11,433	18,487,891	13,224	22,048,334	19%
Open Dry Cargo Barges	8,647	12,696,429	7,791	11,787,260	−7%
Other Dry Cargo Barges	804	426,191	386	156,489	−63%
Self-Propelled Vessels	1,473	545,616	1,263	257,484	−53%
Tank Barges	3,182	7,138,425	3,416	7,854,351	10%

Source: Vessel Data Series, U.S. Army Corps of Engineers Navigation Data Center.

this end, there are about 900 operators that handle traffic on the inland waterway system. Over time, the number of vessel operators has been increasing both in terms of the number of firms and the tonnage capacity (U.S. Army Corps of Engineers Vessel Data Series). Table 5.3 illustrates this point showing that between 1995 and 2002 both the number of barges and tonnage capacity on the Mississippi River system and the Gulf Intracoastal Waterway increased by approximately 8 percent. The number of barges and related capacity is dominated by covered and open dry cargo barges, reflecting the fact that traffic is dominated by dry bulk commodities (primarily, farm products and coal). Over time, the number and related capacity of barges has been increasing with the primary source of increase related to covered dry and deck barges.

In terms of the number and size distribution of firms, there are about nine hundred firms that provide services. The largest four firms in 2002 were ACL, Ingram, American River and Aep Memco. These four firms together have a combined market share of about 43 percent (Table 5.4). Over time, the capacity of barge vessels has increased. However, ownership has become more concentrated. That is, in 1995 the combined share of the largest four firms was about 38 percent. The difference from 1995 to 2002 was largely due to a merger between Ingram Barge and Midland Enterprises (the second and fourth highest capacity firms in 1995).

This increase in concentration is more dramatic when considering vessels with a draft of nine feet or less. This is a particularly important distinction as only vessels with such shallow drafts can navigate the upper stretches of the Mississippi River. Considering vessels with a draft of nine feet or less, the five firm concentration (again, in terms of capacity) increased from 51 percent in 1995 to 71 percent in 2002 (U.S. Army Corps of Engineers Vessel Data Series).

In terms of conditions of entry, the barge transportation industry is a network industry similar to air and rail. As with other network industries, there are large costs to starting a barge transportation company over the entire network. However, operations over part of the network do not require sizable investments. Perhaps, the largest investment is that of purchasing vessels; however, once up and running, the basic service provided, barge transportation, is a relatively homogeneous product in that all

TABLE 5.4

Number of Vessels, Capacity and Market Share of the Leading Vessel Operators on the Mississippi River and Gulf Intracoastal Waterway 1995 and 2002

Company	1995			Company	2002		
	Vessels	Capacity	Market Share		Vessels	Capacity	Market Share
American Commercial Lines	4,474	7,224,340	15.6%	American Commercial Lines	4,300	6,950,609	15.1%
Midland Enterprises	2,405	3,730,923	8%	Ingram Barge	4,209	6,821,142	14.8%
American River Transportation	2,197	3,654,189	7.9%	American River Transportation	2,199	3,656,469	8%
Ingram Barge	1,900	3,145,994	6.8%	Aep Memco	1,592	2,534,694	5.5%
Memco Barge Line	1,104	1,748,656	3.8%	Kirby Inland Marine	860	2,129,120	4.6%
Mcdonough Marine Service	797	1,336,854	2.9%	Crounse Corporation	805	1,207,500	2.6%
Cargill Marine & Terminal	734	1,173,026	2.5%	Cargill Marine & Terminal	744	1,186,958	2.6%
Mid-south Towing Co.	663	1,109,859	2.4%	Teco Barge	616	1,024,921	2.2%
Crounse Corporation	722	1,083,000	2.3%				
American Electric Power River	617	958,415	2.1%				

Source: Vessel Data Series, U.S. Army Corps of Engineers Navigation Data Center.

vessel operators offer a service with little possibility for differentiation. This lack of product differentiation on a network makes it relatively easy for any firm to serve any part of the inland waterway system, which in turn implies that this industry should be characterized by high levels of competition and firm bankruptcies.

Barge companies must also compete with railroads and to a lesser extent motor carriage. The payload capacity of a typical barge hopper is about 1,750 tons, a hopper rail car is about 90 tons, and a truckload about 25 tons. Thus, it takes about twenty railroad cars and about seventy truckloads to move the payload of one barge. These translate into sizable fuel efficiencies and, it is attested, lower emissions per ton moved. However, barge transportation, is a slower mode of transportation relative to rail and motor carriage. Given the operating costs are lower and the service attributes of the mode are lower than for the other modes, the primary goods carried tend to be low value bulk commodities.

Most argue that in terms of conduct, the barge transportation industry is competitive. Thus, the industrial organization focal point on allocative efficiency in this market is relatively moot. However, policy does impact welfare losses from allocative inefficiency in other markets. Specifically, recent survey evidence presented by Train and Wilson (2004) as well as previous research has demonstrated that an important role of the inland waterways is to provide a competitive insulating alternative to railroad pricing. Over the last twenty-five years, the railroad industry has become highly consolidated with only a few major railroads operating in the east and west portion of the United States. Survey respondents and research suggests that even if shippers do not use the waterway, it is an important factor in keeping rail rates in check.

There has been little research on the performance of firms in the waterway industry. However, as noted above, this network industry is characterized by relatively high fixed costs, low marginal costs, and relatively low incremental costs of shifting capacity across network links. The implication is that the industry should be characterized by highly competitive rates, low profits and bankruptcies. As evidence of this, Vachal, Hough, and Griffin (2005) examine the financial health of the industry. Examining various financial indicators for the thirteen largest barge companies as of 2004, Vachal et al. (2005) conclude that the barge industry is indeed characterized by relatively easy entry and exit with a large number of existing carriers offering homogeneous services. Further, Vachal et al. point to the recent bankruptcy of American Commercial Barge Lines LLC as evidence of this high level of competition.

Another element of firm performance is found by Wilson (2005) who examines both vessel and firm efficiency in lock performance. Wilson (2005) finds that firm differences can cause tremendous differences in the time it takes firms to transit a lock. Specifically, Wilson (2005) finds that the time to pass through a single lock can be as much as three times larger than the time of the most efficient firm. These differences are explained by differences in the vessels that each firm operates, the size of the firm, and the diversity of the firm (e.g., some firms specialize at a single lock while others traverse the entire waterway). While most of the time vessels are "in-transit," this research does point to important differences across firms which likely also point to cost differences across firms especially if such differences transcend into transit time differences as well.

Going forward, perhaps the most important factor impacting the supply of barge transportation will be technological development both in terms of vessels and in the waterway itself. In the next section, potential waterway improvements will be discussed in greater detail; however, from the perspective of a barge carrier, any improvements to the waterway system resulting in reduced transit times should increase efficiency and improve profitability in the short run. In the long run, given the ease of entry and exit and the homogeneous service as discussed previously, economic theory would suggest that the short run profits should attract new entrants which will drive any economic profits back down. Of course, improvements lower costs and increase short-run profits. However, given the ease of entry and of shifting capacity, new entrants and/or capacities will be attracted to market. Such changes theoretically, would increase congestion along the waterway, perhaps, negating the initial waterway improvements.

Mitigating his effect, however, will be a greater ability to compete with other modes. Indeed, with improvements, there should be a traffic shift from other modes, i.e., truck and rail to barge.

Another way in which technological change impacts the market is through the development of vessel technologies. Two technological changes mandated by law, and currently underway are: converting to double hulled barges and updating diesel engines to meet emissions standards (Vachal et al. 2005). Both of these changes have direct costs associated with converting to the new technology. These are short-run in nature, and, in the long run may eventually lead to more efficient operation post-implementation due to greater fuel efficiency, speed, and so forth.

In addition to double hulls and diesel engines, a technological change that may have larger effects on efficiency is the use of navigation software. Such improvements will reduce transit times and improve firm performance. This type of technology can do everything from improving logistics to tracking vessel progress. Given that barges on the inland waterway system carry different commodities with different values, one could also imagine a software program whereby barges with high value shipments could pay to bypass the queue, decreasing their transit times.

INFRASTRUCTURE IMPROVEMENTS AND PLANNING

With the 1927 River and Harbors Act, Congress authorized the study of the Mississippi River between Minneapolis, Minnesota, and the mouth of the Missouri River. Based on this study, Congress passed the River and Harbors Act of 1930, which resulted in the construction of twenty-six locks and dams on the Upper Mississippi River by the Army Corps of Engineers (NRC 2001). These locks and dams created a nine-foot channel on the Upper Mississippi River through which commerce could flow from the Minneapolis area down to the Gulf of Mexico. As pointed out previously, the amount of traffic on the inland waterway system has been increasing steadily overtime, increases that would not have occurred without the existing infrastructure of locks and dams provided by the USACE.

However, this increased traffic has caused high levels of congestion on the waterway system which can often amount to several days' worth of transit delays. Compounding these congestion problems is the inadequacy of lock systems built some forty to sixty years ago to handle current barges. Currently, there are only three locks located on the Upper Mississippi River that are over six hundred feet in length; however, most of the current barge tows using the waterway system are well over this length (U.S. Army Corps of Engineers 2004). Because of this discrepancy in length, barges are required to approach the lock, de-couple, bring their tow through the lock one 600 foot section at a time and then re-couple their tow once through the lock.

Due to the increasing congestion on the inland waterway system, the USACE began looking into extending several locks in 1988. With the passage of the Flood Control Act of 1936, Congress required the U.S. Army Corps of Engineers to conduct benefit-cost analysis for any proposed program to improve the waterway system, requiring that the benefits of the proposed plan outweigh the costs before approval would be granted

(NRC 2001). The estimation of the benefits of waterway improvements has been the source of both some of the harshest criticisms of the U.S. Army Corps of Engineers' benefit-cost study as well as much recent advancement in the estimation of benefits (NRC 2004). Perhaps the two biggest criticisms of the USACE benefit-cost study are the estimation of barge demand and the forecasting of future demand.

Currently, the USACE uses two models to estimate the benefits of waterway improvements: the ESSENCE Model and the Tow-Cost/Equilibrium Model (TCM/EQ). Curlee provides a detailed overview of each of these models and their limitations which are well recognized by both their creators and the NRC committee.

According to TCM/EQ, the demand for barge transportation is based on assumptions regarding shippers' choices. First, it is assumed that, so long as the barge rate is lower than the rail rate, all commerce from the shipper will be transported via barge. Alternatively, if the barge rate increases above the rail rate, all commerce from the shipper will switch from barge to rail. This assumption on the shippers' behavior implies a demand curve similar to that pictured in Figure 5.17. Notice that in Figure 5.17 quantity Q0 is shipped by barge so long as the barge rate is less than R0; however, once the barge rate increases past R0, no commerce is shipped via barge and all commerce is handled by rail service.

Given the demand curve implied by the TCM/EQ Model, Figure 5.18 shows the estimated benefits of waterway improvement. Without the waterway improvement, congestion would lead to a barge rate of C1 and a barge quantity of Q0. With the improvement, congestion would lead to a smaller increase of barge rates to C2 and a barge quantity of Q0. Therefore, the benefits of the waterway project are the difference between the costs of transporting Q0 at C1 versus Q0 at C2 (the shaded area in Figure 5.18). Notice that if the barge rate were to increase such that all traffic switched from barge to rail (C1 > R0), then the estimated benefits of the improvement to the waterway project would be the entire area (R0-C1) × Q0.

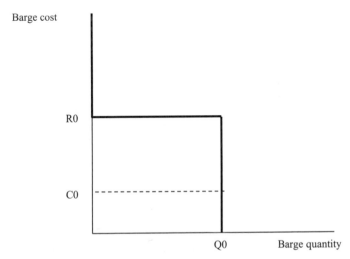

FIGURE 5.17   Barge demand according to the TCM/EQ Model.

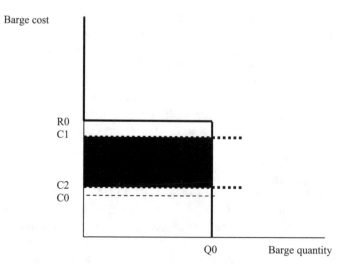

FIGURE 5.18   Estimated benefits using the TCM/EQ Model.

The main shortcoming of the TCM/EQ Model is the assumptions that there is no price responsiveness of shippers until the barge rate increases past the rail rate at which point all traffic switches from barge to rail. The ESSENCE Model recognizes this and attempts to correct for the assumption of no price responsiveness of shippers to changes in the barge rate by assuming that the quantity of barge demanded decreases as the barge rate increases. However, the assumption of complete switching from barge to rail once the barge rate increases past the rail rate is maintained implying a demand curve as depicted in Figure 5.19.

Notice that in Figure 5.19, as in Figure 5.17, at a barge rate of C0, the shipper chooses to ship Q0 by barge. However, at any rate above C0 the shipper ships less via

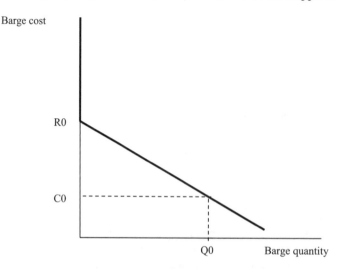

FIGURE 5.19   Barge demand according to the ESSENCE Model.

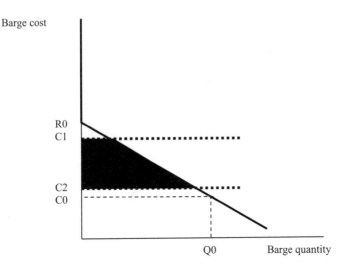

FIGURE 5.20   Estimated benefits using the ESSENCE Model.

barge and at any rate less than C0 the shipper ships more via barge. Using the same procedure to measure the benefits of a waterway improvement, Figure 5.20 shows how the ESSENCE Model will always lead to lower estimated benefits from waterway improvements as compared to the TCM/EQ Model due to the price responsiveness of shippers. While the ESSENCE Model improves upon the TCM/EQ Model in allowing barge demand to be elastic below the least cost rail rate, numerical implementation has drawn some criticism. In particular, the elasticity of demand is determined by a parameter N which is unknown and not estimated. As the NRC points out, with no way of knowing the appropriate value of N and the associated elasticity of barge demand, the ESSENCE Model cannot be assumed to accurately measure the benefits of a waterway improvement. Specifically, the NRC believes that "Price responsiveness is so important to estimating the benefits of waterway improvements that informed judgments about the merit of waterway improvements cannot be made without careful study of these demand and supply elasticities" (2004).

The criticisms of both the TCM/EQ and ESSENCE Models have spurred recent economic research regarding the measurement of the elasticity of demand. What these studies have attempted to estimate is a more traditional demand curve with no restrictive assumptions placed on it, such as the demand curve pictured in Figure 5.21. Notice that with a more traditional demand curve, the estimated benefits of waterway improvements are bounded on the lower end by the ESSENCE Model, but could actually be larger than those estimated by the TCM/EQ Model.

To see how the estimated benefits could be larger than those estimated by the TCM/EQ Model, two cases must be considered. Figure 5.22 shows the case where barge costs without the improvement would be less than the rail rate R0 as was the case when examining the TCM/EQ and ESSENCE Models. According to Figure 5.22, the estimated benefits of a waterway improvement are bounded on the upper end by the estimated benefits of the TCM/EQ Model. However, recall that under the assumptions of the TCM/EQ Model if C1 were larger than R0 all traffic would switch to rail

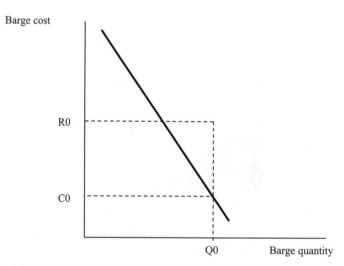

FIGURE 5.21 Barge demand under traditional demand assumptions.

meaning that the estimated benefits would be (R0-C1) × Q0. Using a more traditional demand curve, if C1 were larger than R0 not all traffic would switch to rail implying that the benefits to a waterway improvement could be larger than those predicted by the TCM/EQ Model as illustrated in Figure 5.23.

Recent examples of work being done on the estimation of the elasticity of barge demand are Train and Wilson (2005) and Henrickson and Wilson (2005a,b). Train and Wilson (2005) use both stated and revealed choice methodology to estimate the responsiveness of shippers to both changes in the barge rate and changes in transit times. Alternatively, Henrickson and Wilson (2005a,b) developed a model of transportation

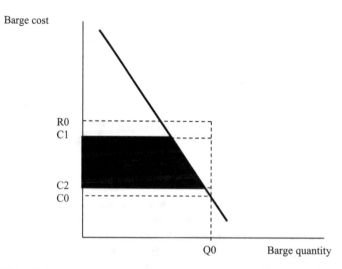

FIGURE 5.22 Estimated benefits using traditional demand assumptions if C1<R0.

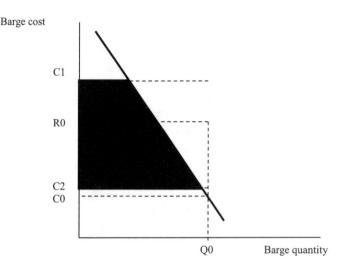

FIGURE 5.23   Estimated benefits using traditional demand assumptions if C1>R0.

demand taking into account comments by the NRC (2004) that attention should be given to the spatial nature of transportation demand, particularly the work by Samuelson (1956), Enke (1951), Takayama and Judge (1971), and Fuller et al. (2000).

Train and Wilson (2005) employ survey data comprised of both stated and revealed preference questions to estimate the responsiveness of shippers to changes in both barge rates and barge transportation times. Using surveys to collect their data, Train and Wilson are further able to examine changes in the choice of mode and origin-destination as the barge rate and/or time fluctuate. Using stated and revealed choice methods, Train and Wilson find that many shippers respond to even small changes in the current barge rate by changing either their mode of transportation or their origin-destination. Further, Train and Wilson find that shippers are responsive to changes in barge transit time, but less so than to changes in the barge rate. Overall, Train and Wilson (2005) find estimates of barge demand elasticity between −.7 and −1.4 depending on the level of the rate change.

Henrickson and Wilson (2005a) develop a theoretical model of spatial transportation demand. They model the output decisions of port grain elevators located on the waterway. Specifically, to enter the waterway all grain must pass through one of the elevators. If the quantity each elevator ships can be modeled, then the demand for barge transportation at the port level can be easily aggregated to the pool model which is the basis for the planning models. In their model, elevators compete with other modes and with each other. They find in this and related research (Henrickson and Wilson (2005b) barge demand elasticity estimates between −1.448 and −1.987 for the Upper Mississippi River and −1.869 and −1.874 for the Illinois River.

The second major criticism of the USACE's benefit-cost study for improving the inland waterway system was in the way forecasts were formed for future barge demand. These forecasts are particularly important for project such as the proposed improvement of the inland waterway infrastructure. This is because any improvements are intended to impact the waterway system for a long period of time, and therefore, the benefits of the improvements accrue over this long period of time. Historically, tonnages of commodities transported were forecasted by fitting trends. The total tonnage forecasted was then allocated to pools on the waterway based on historical patterns. Criticisms of this methodology were that there were important structural breaks that were not taken into account, and that the methodology was not equilibrium based. In the revised Upper Mississippi analysis, a scenario-based methodology where multiple scenarios of future events were developed and used to predict future barge transportation demand. However, of the five scenarios developed during this forecasts assumed that grain production and exportation would increase in the future even though these factors have been steady for the last twenty-five years (NRC 2004).

There is recent work on developing a long-run spatially based equilibrium model of forecasting. This work is more completely described in Wilson et al. (2004). Generally, demands and supplies of grain are forecasted for multiple countries and regions within the United States. These forecasts are then translated into flows between foreign countries and regions in the United States through a least cost algorithm that depends on not just the levels of regional supplies and demands, but also transportation rates, the planting decisions of suppliers, and the level of congestion on the waterways. The method is also combined with various scenarios of future possibilities. Thus, it adds both spatial and equilibrium concepts into the planning models.

SUMMARY AND FUTURE DIRECTIONS

This chapter provided a broad overview of the inland waterway system. Section 2, described the system in terms of its size, location, commodities, and trends was provided. It is a massive system complete with enormous investment and linkages that point to interdependencies in the system between rivers. The primary commodities handled on the system tend to be low-value bulk commodities. The specific commodities vary across rivers owing largely to the economic base of the regions through which the rivers run. Over time, traffic levels in the entire U.S. system have risen, but the increase is largely rail and truck traffic.

In section 3, we provided an overview of the supply of inland waterway transportation services. This overview was developed using the structure-conduct-performance paradigm. The industry is a network industry. There are entry costs, but once those costs are realized the operating costs tend to be relatively low. The supply is provided by approximately 900 firms most of which are relatively small; however, there are several sizable firms in this industry which has a four firm concentration level of nearly 50 percent. However, profit rates and bankruptcies do not point to sizable market power concerns. An important aspect and one that is commonly not discussed is that of tempering rail market power. This is an extremely important aspect of the industry not present in the models, but widely recognized by shippers.

The final section covered, an overview of the role of the USACE. Major changes in the waterway network require a study of project costs and benefits. Over the last ten years or so, their methodology has been routinely criticized. We first described the methodology and its criticisms and then pointed to recent research and attempts to evaluate and improve on the methodology. The primary focus is on the development of planning models that have equilibrium-based forecasting methods and realistic representations of the spatial environment through which transportation decisions are made.

There is tremendous opportunity in the modeling of networks and, in particular, the modeling of the waterway component of the network. This research should continue to include the development of theoretical models that are grounded in the realities of transportation decision-making and are, or fit directly into, equilibrium-based models. Given the recent development of equilibrium-based theory that grounded in the reality of transportation decision making, the next step is the development of both data and empirical methods that allow the theories to be applied to evaluating the costs and benefits of alternative policies to improve the performance of the industry.

ACKNOWLEDGMENTS

Much of this research was made possible by the Navigation and Economics Technologies (NETS) program of the Army Corps of Engineers. We sincerely acknowledge their support and numerous discussions with Keith Hofseth.

REFERENCES

Bureau of Transportation Statistics. "U.S. Transportation Statistics 2004" (2005).

Curlee, T. Randall. "The Restructured Upper Mississippi River-Illinois Waterway Navigation Feasibility Study: Overview of Key Economic Modeling Considerations." Oak Ridge National Laboratory Report, Prepared for the Mississippi Valley Division, U.S. Army Corps of Engineers.

Enke, S. "Equilibrium Among Spatially Separated Markets: Solutions by Electric Analogue." *Econometrica* 19, (1951): 40–48.

Fuller S., L. Fellin, and K. Eriksen. "Panama Canal: How Critical to U.S. Grain Exports?" *Agribusiness: An International Journal* 16(4), (2000): 435–455.

Henrickson, Kevin E. and Wesley W. Wilson. "A Model of Spatial Market Areas and Transportation Demand." In *The Transportation Research Record: Journal of the Transportation Research Board* (2005a).

Henrickson, Kevin E. and Wesley W. Wilson. "Patterns in Geographic Elasticity Estimates of Barge Demand on the Upper Mississippi and Illinois Rivers." In *The Transportation Research Record: Journal of the Transportation Research Board* (2005b).

National Research Council. 2001. "Inland Navigation System Planning: The Upper Mississippi River Illinois Waterway." Washington, D.C.: National Academy Press.

National Research Council. 2004. "Review of the U.S. Army Corps of Engineers Upper Mississippi-Illinois Waterway Restructured Feasibility Study: Second Report." Washington, D.C.: National Academy Press.

Samuelson, P. "Spatial Price Equilibrium and Linear Programming." *American Economic Review* 38, (1956): 496–509.

Takayama, T. and G. Judge. *Spatial and Temporal Price and Allocation Models*. North Holland Publishing Company: Amsterdam (1971).

Train, Kenneth and Wesley W. Wilson. "Transportation Demand for Grain Shipments: A Revealed and Stated Preference Approach." Working paper (2005).

U.S. Army Corps of Engineers. "Waterborne Commerce of the United States, Calendar Year 2003, Part 5—National Summaries." (2004).

U.S. Army Corps of Engineers Navigation Data Center. "National Waterway Network." (1999).

U.S. Army Corps of Engineers Navigation Data Center. "Vessel Data Series." (2002).

U.S. Army Corps of Engineers Navigation Data Center. "Vessel Data Series." (1995).

U.S. Army Corps of Engineers Navigation Data Center. "Lock Characteristics." (2004).

Vachal, K., J. Hough and Gene Griffin. "U.S. Waterways A Barge Sector Industrial Organization Analysis." Working paper (2005).

Wilson, Wesley W. "Vessel, Firm and Lock Efficiency Measures in Lock Performance." Working paper (2005).

Wilson, William, Won W. Koo, Richard Taylor, and Bruce Dahl, "Long-Term Forecasting of US Grain Trade and Gulf Exports," *The Transportation Research Record* (2004).

6 Intelligent Transportation Systems: Evolution and Impact

Wendell C. Lawther

INTRODUCTION

Intelligent Transportation Systems (ITS) can be characterized as:

> Encompass[ing] a broad range of wireless and wire line communications-based information and electronics technologies. When integrated into the transportation system's infrastructure, and in vehicles themselves, these technologies relieve congestion, improve safety and enhance American productivity. (http://www.itsdocs.fhwa.dot.gov/its_overview.htm)

ITS also enhances the capacity of surface transportation. ITS has been recognized as a viable—even preferred—alternative to adding capacity to existing roadways and dealing with growing traffic congestion. In the last two decades, vehicle travel has increased over 70 percent while roadway capacity has increased 1 percent. Much of the needed additional capacity is in metropolitan areas. Adding roads in these areas are the most expensive and least popular politically.

ITS offers a wide range of technology-based solutions to deal with congestion. Advanced Traveler Information Systems, known most recently by the 511 phone number, provide information about specific highways that may be affected by accidents, weather, and construction. The traveler accessing this information can choose to travel by an alternative route or delay travel plans, thereby lessening congestion.

Incident Management Programs, built upon cooperative efforts among transportation, law enforcement and fire personnel, rely upon faster identification, response, and clearance times to further reduce the impact of nonrecurring congestion. Advanced Traffic Management Systems can provide coordinated traffic signal control efforts across jurisdictional boundaries, especially when accidents significantly increase traffic flow on alterative roadways. Commercial weigh-in-motion sensors mean that trucks traveling across state lines do not have to experience inspection delays since they can be weighed while traveling past inspection points. Electronic toll collection systems permit vehicles to make payments without stopping at a toll collection booth, thereby reducing pollution and lowering travel times.

In addition to adding capacity and dealing more effectively with congestion, ITS based technology can improve safety. In-vehicle collision avoidance systems can signal drivers when other vehicles are traveling too closely. Cameras installed at intersections can reduce the number of vehicles that run red lights. Freeway management systems that employ ramp metering reduce the number of crashes.

ITS technologies have been adopted through demonstration projects and experiments, which lead to the purchase and deployment of technology over time. A transit agency, for example, may deploy AVL equipment on only 12 percent of its buses in a given year, hoping to use the experience with limited deployment to gain support for more extensive deployment (Hammerle 2005).

ITS provides incentives to foster a regional approach that was not possible prior to the technology application. Traffic Incident Management programs, for example, rely on cameras to more quickly identify accidents and foster greater coordination among law enforcement, fire officials and transportation managers. ITS has acted as a catalyst to encourage adoption and deployment of non-ITS efforts, such as freeway service patrols. The use of the technology has increased understanding of innovative ways to solve problems and provide better service quality.

This chapter reviews the impacts of these and other ITS components, describing deployment efforts, reviewing intended goals, and discussing impacts. First, though, a brief review of the evolution of ITS policy will be provided. The conclusion will provide an overall assessment, identifying deployment challenges that remain.

HISTORY AND EVOLUTION

In 1986, a group of academicians, transportation industry representatives, and federal and state transportation officials began to meet to discuss ways of promoting the application of advanced technologies to the field of surface transportation. They were concerned about growing traffic congestion as well as the need to improve safety while safeguarding the environment. They recognized that the conventional means of adding to surface transportation capacity—adding lanes of roadway—were limited in the scope of what could be accomplished both in terms of cost and political acceptance. They also were looking ahead to the passage of the next major transportation legislation—the Intermodal Surface Transportation Efficiency Act (ISTEA) of 1991—and wanted to include an emphasis on advanced technology application as a significant part of this legislation (Sussman 1996).

Other concurrent efforts were pointing the way toward what would become known as Intelligent Vehicle Highway System (IVHS) and subsequently ITS. The California Department of Transportation (Caltrans) and the University of California at Berkley established the California Program on the Advanced Technology for the Highway (PATH) in 1986. Along with the University Transportation Centers Program, established in 1987 by the U.S. Department of Transportation, PATH and other researchers began research-ing and experimenting with advanced technology applications (Whelan 1995).

International applications of advanced technology were also seen in Europe—Proj-ect Prometheus—and in Japan, with the AMTICS and RAC projects. They provided examples of what could occur in the United States, and gave impetus to efforts here. From 1988 to 1990, the informal group called themselves Mobility 2000, and issued a report at their annual meeting in Dallas in March 1990 (Sussman 1996). One of the Mobility 2000's goals was to create a formal organization, comprised of members from the public and the private sector, to further the cause of intelligent vehicle systems. With the creation of the Intelligent Vehicle Society of America in 1990, this goal was achieved (Mobility 2000, 1990).

In many respects, the goals and vision outlined in 1990 were an accurate forecast of what has taken place since then. There was the expectation that an IVHS program would be established, one that would involve public and private sector cooperation, and one that would:

> develop, test and deploy advanced electronics technology and systems to meet the increasingly critical operational needs of the highwaytransportation system.... The program contains four broad, interrelated areas: advanced traffic management systems, advanced traveler information systems, com-mercial vehicle operations, and advanced vehicle control systems. (Mobility 2000, 1990, 3)

Significant federal support for IVHS/ITS began with the passage of the Intermodal Surface Transportation Efficiency Act (ISTEA) in 1991. The Department of Trans-portation's Intelligent Transportation Systems program received federal funding of $1.3 billion from 1991 through 1997 (USGAO 1997). The Transportation Equity Act of the 21st Century (TEA-21), passed in 1998, continued the support and funding at similar levels.

Recognizing that the greatest impact of ITS could occur with increased regional cooperation, initial federal efforts provided stimulus to state and local transportation planning and deployment efforts. Field Operational Tests, begun even before 1991 (Little and Wooster 1994), were designed as demonstration projects to provide examples of ITS application effectiveness. The TravTek project (1991–94) in Orlando, Florida, for example, was an early test of in-vehicle navigation systems (Inman and Peters 1996). By 1996, eighty-three field operational tests had been funded, with twenty-eight com-pleted (ITS Joint Program Office 1996). Early deployment grants, designed to bring stakeholders together in a metropolitan area to plan ITS applications were made to over eighty areas in the early to mid-1990s (Lockwood 2000). In total, over three hundred grants were made to metropolitan regions in the early 1990s (USGAO 1997).

The Metropolitan Model Deployment Initiative served to further illustrate the goal and impacts of federal funding. Four metropolitan areas were chosen in the mid-1990s—Seattle, Phoenix, San Antonio, and New York/New Jersey—to demonstrate the value of integrating ITS technologies. Of the nineteen metropolitan areas who responded to the Request for Proposal issued in 1995, a subsequent study indicated

TABLE 6.1
ITS Program Funding in TEA-21 (in $millions)[1]

Year	1998	1999	2000	2001	2002	2003	Total
Deployment	101	105	113	118	120	122	679
R&D	95	95	98.2	100	105	110	603
Total	196	200	211	218	225	232	1,282

that 90 percent of these had deployed part of what they had proposed, finding support for these efforts from other sources (Pederson 1998).

ISTEA focused on the building of ITS infrastructure components, helping to put into place the basic building blocks of ITS. TEA-21 changed the focus to ITS Deployment, funding the integration of existing or legacy systems with ITS. As indicated above, funding of almost $1.3 billion was about the same as for ISTEA (see Table 6.1).

TEA-21 lists several requirements for project funding. Projects must:

- Contribute to national deployment goals and objectives;
- Demonstrate strong commitment among stakeholders;
- Maximize private sector involvement;
- Demonstrate conformity to the National ITS Architecture and use approved ITS standards and protocols;
- Be included in statewide or metropolitan transportation plans;
- Ensure continued long-term operations and maintenance; and
- Demonstrate that personnel have necessary technical skills.

TEA-21 went one step further by mainstreaming ITS planning and funding into the regular federal aid transportation planning and programming processes. In doing so, it clarified the eligibility for state and local governments to access over $70 billion in federal aid funding for ITS projects, including funds from the National Highway System, State Transportation Planning, and Congestion Mitigation and Air Quality (ITS Joint Program Office, http://www.itsdocs.fhwa.gov).

The emphasis on integration of ITS systems is reflected in the projects presently funded. One example, the Surface Transportation Security and Reliable Information System Model Deployment of 2003, more commonly known as "iFlorida," is to provide a highly integrated system of information concerning traffic congestion that draws upon several sources, including cameras along the major interstate highway, transponders placed on vehicles that are used for electronic toll collection, the computer aided dispatch system of the Florida Highway Patrol, transit information, and weather data (www.iflorida.net).

Other examples also reflect the integration of different ITS components. Arlington, Virginia, is deploying the traffic adaptive control systems with bus signal priority systems. Baltimore, Maryland, is combining planned and existing ITS systems into a coordinated regional evacuation plan. The City of Charlotte, North Carolina, and the North Carolina Department of Transportation will connect the city traffic operations center and the state traffic management center to achieve greater regional coordination. Albany, New York, has received funds to deploy cameras and other monitoring devices to support the creation of a regional incident management program (US DOT 2005).

In addition to supporting on-going activities in each of the component areas discussed below, several new ITS application projects focus on increasing safety and reducing accidents, injuries and deaths on United States highways. Cooperative Intersection Avoidance Collision Systems will assist drivers who enter an intersection to more fully understand relevant traffic conditions and avoid collisions. The Emergency Transportation Operations Initiative will assist transportation officials in more closely coordinating regional efforts to respond more effectively if hurricanes and other natural disasters occur. Integrated Vehicle Based Safety Systems will assist drivers to avoid the three most common causes of crashes: rear-end, road departure, or lane change (http://www.itsdocs.fhwa.dot.gov/newinit_index.htm).

ITS COMPONENTS

As ITS has evolved, the names of system components have changed as well. The following components will be discussed, representing the major areas of ITS application emphasis:

- Advanced Traffic Management Systems
  - Advanced Traffic Control
  - Ramp Metering
  - Incident Management Systems
- Advanced Traveler Information Systems
- Electronic Toll and Traffic Management Systems
- Commercial Vehicle Operations and Information System Networks
- Advanced Public Transportation Systems

There is a great deal of overlap or "cross cutting applications" among ITS components. Advanced traffic management systems, for example, make use of a variety of technologies such as closed circuit television cameras that can also provide information applicable to advanced traveler information systems. Given that ITS represents a series of technological innovations that continue to evolve as technology is able to provide more resources and applications, it is also true that most ITS components build upon legacy systems and earlier technologies.

The deployment of ITS is not uniformly accepted, as issues of cost and technical capability among public staff may prevent some municipalities from fully adopting ITS technologies in a given area. For some components, such as ATIS, only freeways or interstate highways are instrumented, while information from arterial roadways has yet to be collected in a systematic fashion.

Institutional barriers, that have existed among jurisdictions in a pre ITS era, also have to be overcome in many instances to allow for transportation systems to fully experience to benefits of ITS. Incident Management teams, for example, may not include all municipal law enforcement, fire and emergency personnel in a given region because there may have been a long standing history that limits interaction with each other. Furthermore, the deployment of ITS technologies has permitted levels of cooperation and coordination among municipal transportation officials that has been unprecedented.

In the following discussion of selected ITS components, a brief description of the major aspects of each component is presented. The major deployment issues and potential benefits are discussed throughout. Examples provided are only meant to be representative of much greater deployment throughout states and municipalities in the United States.

ADVANCED TRAFFIC MANAGEMENT SYSTEMS

Advanced Traffic Management Systems (ATMS) provides an overarching system of control and coordination that is designed to maximize three basic goals: improve the safety, capacity, and predictability of the transportation system (Smith 2000). The basic organizational or structural component of ATMS is the traffic management or operations center. These units are housed in rooms that contain arrays of television monitors, linked by fiber optic cable to cameras strategically placed along major roadways, as well as several computer workstations that are also linked to incident management teams, ramp meters, and traffic signal systems. Stationed in these rooms may be employees of a variety of jurisdictions and organizations.

ATMS integrates several applications of ITS technologies, as ideally they should collect data dealing with traffic flow and use this data "to make real time changes to traffic signals [and] ramp meters" (USGAO 1994, 3) as well as initiate responses to traffic accidents. More specifically, these components of ATMS are:

- Advanced Traffic Control—the use of adaptive signal systems that adjust signal cycles in real time in response to traffic flow
- Ramp Metering—allowing vehicles to enter major freeways at a rate designed to maximize the efficiency of traffic flow
- Incident Management—creating teams of professionals cutting across organizations that can respond quickly and efficiently to clear accidents and incidents from major roadways (Chen and Miles 2000)

Although not fully deployed in every jurisdiction, these three have the greatest impact on achieving ATMS goals.

ADVANCED TRAFFIC CONTROL

There are many benefits of an efficient, synchronized traffic signal system deployed along a corridor or roadway. These systems reduce traffic congestion by reducing the number of stops at traffic signals, and thereby save travel time, reduce fuel costs, and lower pollution (NTOC 2005). Studies throughout the 1980s and more recently have consistently documented a high benefit to cost ratio, as much as 40:1 (USGAO 1994; ITS Joint Office). In addition, the creation of new highways and expansion of highways means that the arterial roadway network will have to handle some of the increased traffic. With an efficient system, the negative impacts of increased congestion can be limited (Skabardonis 2001).

There are severe institutional and financial barriers, however, that have prevented deploying an ideal advanced traffic control system. A recent national survey of state and municipal transportation agencies found the following problems:

- A lack of proactive management (grade F)
- Few signal operations exist in coordinated systems (grade D–)
- A lack of review of signals at intersections (grade C–) and
- A lack of adaptive signal controllers that respond to real-time traffic conditions (grade F)
- A lack of consistent maintenance of control equipment (grade D+)

Traffic signals are often controlled in isolation from each other. The timing is set in a pre-determined Time of Day fashion (Hadi 2002), and often not revisited for three years or more. A lack of staffing and resources for many communities means that signals are not updated unless there is a history of accidents or concerns at a given intersection (NTOC 2005).

Traffic signal systems have two primary components: detectors and controllers. Controllers are of two types: pretimed and traffic actuated. A pretimed sensor cycles through traffic signals in a predetermined, constant manner. It is best for traffic flow that is predictable and stable at a given intersection. Several timing sequences may be present during the day to accommodate differences in traffic flow.

Traffic actuated controllers do not fix the length of the signal cycle, but—controlled by a computer—change in response to differences in traffic flow and speed. Although computerized systems were first installed in Toronto, Canada in 1963, these systems were not widely adopted until the 1970s (Bullock and Urbanik 2000). There are three types: semi actuated—a continuous green light is given to a major street unless a detector signals the presence of a vehicle on a minor street; full actuated—detectors are needed at each road entering an intersection and can respond to changing traffic patterns during a day; and volume density controllers—they record and store records of traffic volumes, and use this information to adjust signals, along with present traffic patterns (ITE 1995).

It is the latter type that is most appropriate for ITS and the support of other components. Two of the most advanced volume density controllers are SCOOT (Split, Cycle-time and Offset Optimization Technique) and SCATS (Sydney Coordinated Adaptive Traffic System). Evidence from a telephone survey of eight metropolitan areas in the United States found a high degree of satisfaction with the system performance of these controllers. The need to maintain trained staff and the requirement of cooperation and coordination with involved agencies were found to be worth the additional resources required (Hadi 2002).

RAMP METERING

With the advent of ITS, ramp metering has become an integral part of ATMS. Ramp meters are traffic signals that are placed at the entrance to (or exit from) major freeways. The goal of ramp metering is to transfer delays experienced by congestion on the freeways to wait time at the ramps. Traffic flow is less congested, resulting in less traffic delay and increased speeds on the freeways and fewer accidents or crashes (Kang and Gillen 1999).

The use of ramp meters predates ITS, with the first function meters deployed in Chicago in 1963. By 1995, over 2,300 meters were in operation throughout the United States (Piotrowicz and Robinson 1995). The variability of ramp metering systems and resulting issues are similar to those discussed for traffic signal controls. Although fixed, pre-timed cycle meters exist, they can not respond to unexpected changes in traffic flow due to non-recurrent caused congestion. Real-time adaptive systems are much more preferable, and can be controlled with a centralized computer system. (Lee et al. 2005).

Studies reflecting greater benefits than costs are plentiful. Ramp meters installed on a roadway leading into Portland, Oregon, showed an increased in peak rush hour speed from 26 mph to 66 mph in the northbound lane in a study performed 14 months after deployment. Accidents were reduced by 43 percent as well (Piotrowicz and Robinson 1995). In a study of a 14 km section of a freeway near Hayward, California, crash potential due to ramp meters was reduced from 5 percent to 37 percent depending upon factors such as time of day and degree of congestion (Lee et al. 2005).

Ramp metering has costs. In addition to capital and maintenance costs, the queue at a ramp can back up into arterial streets, adversely affecting traffic flow. Pollution increases from the stop and go traffic at the top of the ramps. Ramp metering implementation difficulties can occur, as public support for these meters is crucial. Overall, however, all studies have shown that benefits far outweigh the costs (Kang and Gillen 1999).

The most publicized evaluation of ramp metering in recent times was a study of the system in Minneapolis-St. Paul. Originally installed in the 1980s in certain segments of the freeway, in 2000 the state legislature insisted that the meters be turned off and their impact assessed. The resulting study, completed in February 2001, found the total benefits outweighed costs by more than $40 million annually. The study assessed expected travel times/delay due to recurrent traffic; unexpected delay due to accidents; safety/number of crashes; emissions; and fuel consumption. All but the latter was positively impacted by the existence of meters, with an estimated annual reduction in the number of crashes of 1,041. For example:

> On average, the reliability of freeway travel time was found to be degraded by 91 percent (1.9 minutes for a nine-mile freeway segment) without ramp metering. The largest declines in freeway travel time reliability were observed on I-494 southbound a.m. (180 percent), on I-94 westbound p.m. (154 percent), and on I-94 eastbound p.m. (153 percent). This finding is supported

by the increased number of crashes, the reported increase in the duration of incidents, and by state trooper reports that it took longer to get to the accident scene. (Cambridge Systematics 2001, 24)

INCIDENT MANAGEMENT

The impact of ITS technologies on existing institutional relationships is perhaps the greatest in the area of incident management. Where traffic incident management (TIM) programs have been created, they have met with overwhelming customer support and appreciation. Freeway service patrols (FSPs), a key component of TIMs, have provided assistance in ways that help law enforcement and fire personnel perform their jobs more effectively. Countless studies have demonstrated positive impacts in terms of reduced delays and time/money saved as a result of TIM programs. Locally based programs have been bolstered by state and national efforts.

TIM programs have existed in metropolitan areas since the 1960s (Fenno and Ogden 1998). Traffic Incident Management can be defined as

An operational strategy for a transportation network that involves a coordinated and planned inter-jurisdictional, cross-functional, multidisciplinary, and ongoing approach to restore traffic to normal conditions after an incident occurs, and to minimize delay caused by the resulting disruption to traffic flow. (USDOT 2001)

Participants in a TIM Program for a given region include:

- State Department of Transportation officials
- Local transportation agency officials
- Freeway service patrols
- Law enforcement officials
- Fire agency officials
- Emergency medical organizations—if separate from fire departments
- Towing companies
- Asset management contractors

The Incident Management process is coordinated most often as part of an ATMS. It involves the following steps:

1. Detection
2. Verification
3. Response/incident classification
4. Site management
5. Clearance
6. Communication to motorists

DETECTION: ISSUES INFLUENCING ACCURACY

As identified by P. B. Farradyne (2000), there are several ways that an incident can be detected. The most frequent of these are:

1. Motorist calls via cellular telephone
2. Motorist aid telephones or call boxes
3. Police patrols
4. Closed circuit TV cameras viewed by operators in a Traffic Management Center
5. Electronic measuring devices such as loop detectors combined with algorithms that measure traffic abnormalities
6. Roaming freeway service patrols

The first two would constitute the majority of detections under a response that does not include traffic management. The latter three are contributed by transportation agencies.

Each means of detection faces challenges in terms of accuracy and reliability, no matter what type of incident occurs. Cellular phone calls may have problems in identifying exactly where the incident has occurred, especially if there are no nearby road markers. Travelers passing by an accident may call 911, overloading the switchboard with redundant calls or with calls providing conflicting information. Call boxes provide the exact location, but may not be available, especially on arterial roads. The probability of a police patrol passing by an accident may be remote, especially if law enforcement agencies are understaffed and busy with other activities.

Potentially, using closed circuit television (CCTV) and loop detectors, traffic management operators can detect an incident faster than by any other means. This information can then be communicated to law enforcement and other agencies. CCTVs also have the value of accurately communicating the nature of the incident, thereby ensuring that the responding agencies are the most appropriate. If there is an accident with injuries, emergency medical services need to be called immediately. If traffic is delayed because a vehicle has become disabled, a service patrol may be the only response necessary.

VERIFICATION

Verification, the next step, best reflects the significant value of IM partnerships. With CCTV, detection and verification by traffic operators is simultaneous. The location of the incident can be specified. Since accidents comprise only 10 percent of all incidents (USDOT 2001), the value of traffic operator verification is greatest in preventing law enforcement from responding to an incident that can be more appropriately handled by service patrols. Also, verification can assist law enforcement in prioritizing responses when there are several incidents reported within a short timeframe, such as may occur during peak hour traffic.

RESPONSE

Effective response means reaching the scene of the incident as quickly as possible, both in terms of first arrivals as well as the most appropriate response units. Response time depends upon a number of operational factors, many of them also relevant to detection and verification. Without verification from transportation operators, law enforcement personnel may send vehicles that are inappropriate for an incident. If a large trailer has overturned, towing companies need to send the appropriate vehicles to remove it.

For both detection and verification, the role of the service patrol may be significant. For example, an evaluation of the Bay Area Service Patrol (San Francisco) in 1996 reported that 92 percent of all incidents were detected by service patrols (Farradyne 2000).

SITE MANAGEMENT

Proper site management depends upon the first respondent and the nature of the incident. If the FSP is the first respondent, and there is no accident, the vehicle can be pushed to the side of the road and tow companies called. Site management remains in the hands of the FSP under this scenario. If an accident is involved, and the FSP is the first at the scene, then the driver can place flares, cones, and other traffic directional devices on the roadway and begin to direct traffic while waiting the arrival of the police or emergency management.

Once all participants have arrived at the scene of an accident, there is a need for a site management or command structure. As stated by USDOT (2001): "the purpose of establishing a predefined structure is to ensure a coordinated and decisive reaction to the clearance of an incident" (19) while at the same time recognize "the need to balance the safety of motorists, responders, and victims with the need to restore traffic flow" (Allred 2004, 7).

CLEARANCE

The site should be cleared as quickly as possible in line with decisions made by the response units in charge of the site. If the FSP arrives and can push the disabled vehicle to the side of the road, he or she should be trained to do so. If the site requires tow trucks, these should be called as soon as possible. If the site requires public works crews, these must be part of the IM team and trained to respond appropriately.

MOTORIST INFORMATION

Getting information to motorists should occur throughout the management of an incident. Through the efforts of the traffic operator, information can be posted on variable message signs; disseminated via advanced traveler information systems; and broadcasted through highway advisory radio (HAR), and commercial radio and television reports, (Farradyne 2000).

ASSESSMENT AND EVALUATION

Many of the TIM evaluations have assessed the operation of FSPs as part of the TIM. The 1995 evaluation of the Bay Area Service Patrol on a highway north of San Francisco, a true before and after study, found the response time for incidents dropped from thirty-three to eighteen minutes with concurrent declines in fuel consumption and vehicle emissions (Skabardonis et al. 1998). A review of cost benefit studies in 1997 found that benefits uniformly outweighed costs from 3:1 to over 36:1 (Fenno and Ogden 1998). More recently, the annual evaluation of Maryland's CHART FSP program concluded that in 2004 travelers saved over $141 million in reduced delay, fuel consumption, and emissions (http://chartinput.umd.edu).

As TIMs have evolved, the need for different goals and priorities has become apparent. The primary goal of a TIM is to provide rapid response to an incident or accident, ensuring quick appropriate medical attention to travelers if needed and clearing the lane(s) blockage as quickly as possible. The use of Traffic Management Centers and FSPs in providing timely information to law enforcement and emergency personnel has demonstrated the value of TIMs to all participants, thereby overcoming doubts and increasing agency support.

Other goals are necessary as well. Secondary incidents are common, as travelers on a freeway have to stop suddenly because of a major accident ahead of them. These must be prevented, often with greater use of FSPs. Those who respond to incidents must be protected from bodily injury, as efforts must be made to lessen the speed of those who pass by the scene of an accident. Finally, the respondents must be returned to other duties as quickly as possible (Helman 2004).

Assessment of the extent to which all goals are met is challenging. Although specific studies have documented benefits in isolated cases, evaluations of these programs (e.g., Maas et al. 2001) focus on the reduction of delay due to TIM efforts that restore traffic to a normal flow after the clearance of an incident. The overall measurement and documentation of TIM benefits and goal achievement is hampered by:

- A lack of agreement about what measures are appropriate for all agencies
- The lack of data collection by all agencies
- The lack of packaging or marketing the results to gain additional support for TIM efforts (Marigiotta et al. 2004)

A survey of eight metropolitan TIM programs found few that collected information about the type and severity of an incident, or of managing an incident, recording the time taken for detection, verification, and other details. For those agencies that do collect data, there is no consistency or agreement in what performance measures are used and what data is collected. Furthermore, benefits are not measured by every agency with regard to delay reduction, reliability and safety improvements, or fuel savings (Margiotta et al. 2004).

If agreement can be reached on collecting and using this data in the context of a national effort, regional institutional barriers can be overcome and greater acceptance of TIM programs are a natural result. The creation of a National Traffic Incident Management Coalition on June 23, 2004 recognizes the weaknesses in the current TIM operations and identifies nationally supported goals (http://timcoalition.org). The creation of a "community of practice" (see Snyder and de Souza Briggs 2004) in which TIM participants can share best practices, lessons learned and research problems will further increase support for and strengthen TIM efforts.

ADVANCED TRAVELER INFORMATION SYSTEMS

Advanced Traveler Information Systems (ATIS) provide information to travelers about traffic conditions on given roadways. On the basis of this information, travelers can make decisions about route choice prior to traveling that will lead to lower congestion.

There are essentially four parts to an ATIS:

1. The content of the information collected and passed along to the public
2. The information collection processes and devices
3. The data collection or fusion hardware/software
4. The information dissemination means (Hallenbeck 1998)

Data relevant to traffic congestion can be collected from several sources, including police accident reports, both via radio or on a Web site, inductive loops embedded in the highways, traffic cameras feeding visible images to traffic management or operations centers, 911 centers, service patrols, travelers using cellular telephones, and traffic helicopters and airplanes. The ATIS may collect and provide information on a region wide basis. If so, then data will be furnished from local traffic management centers that are under the jurisdiction of a local government or special district.

All of the information will be sent to one data fusion operations center. This data is categorized using software and hardware, translated into a readily understandable format, such as voice messages, and transmitted to the traveling public using a variety of means. These messages contain information about accidents, road construction, bad weather conditions and other reasons for delay. In some cases, the messages may suggest the motorist take alternative routes.

These messages can be sent out via several means. A traveler calls 511, indicates for what roadways information is desired, and listens to a voice message. Other means include highway advisory radio, variable message signs posted along the highways, and Web site information (McQueen, Schuman, and Chen 2002).

ATIS Evolution

ATIS services were a key aspect of ITS development. The field operation tests of the early 1990s included deployment of these services in many metropolitan areas. The Model Metropolitan Deployment Initiative of the mid 1990s, representing a major federal, state, and local effort in four metropolitan areas, was designed to showcase successful ATIS programs that could serve as model deployments for other urban areas (Perez and Carter 2003).

Throughout this time period it was widely assumed that public private partnerships would act to generate awareness and acceptance of ATIS. In many areas, publicly provided data would be combined with similar collection efforts by private vendors, fused and then disseminated by private vendors in a format that would be customized or personalized for subscribers. The revenue generated by this arrangement would be sufficient to subsidize the public deployment costs, and provide income to public agencies that could be invested in further deployment.

The assumption of ATIS self-sufficiency proved decidedly incorrect (Schuman and Sherer 2001). Both public and private officials vastly underestimated the marketing effort that would be necessary to gain public acceptance. For those areas that had deployed ATIS, initial evaluations indicated the average traveler was very much unaware of their existence (Aultman-Hall et al. 2000; Schintler 1999). Efforts by several private vendors to create revenue generation failed in places such as Seattle, Phoenix, San Francisco, and Washington, D.C. (Jensen et al. 2000; Zimmerman et al. 2000; Miller 1998; Shaver 2002).

Public agencies realized that much of the information provided to travelers must be provided without charge. The adoption of the 511 telephone number by the Federal Communications Commission in July 2000 has catalyzed the deployment of ATIS services nationwide.

BENEFITS AND ASSESSMENT

The goal of ATIS is to provide the traveler with timely information related to congestion along a route that he/she plans to travel or is traveling. Given the information received, the traveler can then choose to drive on the preferred route, travel an alternative route, or delay/postpone travel plans to a time at which the preferred route will be experiencing lower congestion. Ideally, the traveler will change modes of travel, choosing public transportation. The result of this decision will be lower congestion on the preferred route if an alternative is chosen or travel plans are delayed. The resulting benefits are those associated with lower congestion: time savings, increased safety, dollar savings, lower pollution, and increased traveler satisfaction.

Assessing the degree to which these benefits occur for a given ATIS service is difficult, as the impact of each contributing factor to congestion cannot be easily identified (Khattak et al. 2003). Linking greater amounts of non-recurring congestion along a route to rising recurring congestion along the same route is also difficult to demonstrate with certainty. Measuring traveler satisfaction may be challenging as well, as viable alternative routes may be limited, thereby limiting the amount of possible time saved. Also, a traveler will not know how much time was saved, only that an incident was cleared so that the normal travel time along a preferred route will be experienced.

Given the limitations of ATIS assessment, two measures are widely used: the number of calls to ATIS services, and traveler satisfaction measured by surveys. Prior to travelers making changes to their travel plans, they must seek information. There are at least four factors that influence the decision to access information:

- The degree of likely congestion in a given metropolitan area
- The reliability and accuracy of the travel information obtained
- Trip characteristics, such as the reason for the trip, the existence of viable alternatives, and the flexibility of travel start times
- Traveler attitudes and experiences, including how much travel time is valued (Lappin 2000)

The combination of the 511 phone number plus a growing acceptance and familiarity with services provide via a Web site have contributed to increased usage. The widespread use of ATIS has improved dramatically in five years since the approval of 511. For example, a survey of a random sample of over three thousand Seattle residents in 2000 indicated that information was sought in only 3.2 percent of trips (Pierce and Lappin 2003). In contrast, a 2003 survey of ATIS users in South Florida found that travelers accessed ATIS/511 an average of once per day (Lawther and Berman 2004).

Overall usage of 511 has shown the same increase. As of May 2005, over eighty million people have access to ATIS in twenty-three states and metropolitan areas, approximately 28 percent of the population. Over thirty million calls have been made, with fourteen million of these occurring in 2004. Satisfaction surveys consistently show high satisfaction of users, with all studies reporting an over 90 percent satisfaction rate (511 Deployment Coalition 2005).

ATIS/511 deployment continues to provide major challenges to public transportation officials. As it is an innovative service, many travelers have not heard of 511. Even though technological advances have drastically increased the number of roadway miles for which information is available, most of these roadways are freeways and interstate highways, and not arterial roadways. Data must be extremely accurate and reliable, since if a traveler calls 511 and receives information that is incorrect, that traveler is less likely to use the service in the future.

Organizational and managerial challenges remain the most daunting. Making sure that the organizational structure of the PPP produces the most effective results for the traveler is a task that not every ATIS/511 PPP has been successful in meeting. Identifying the appropriate roles and responsibilities of each of the public and private partners, as well as ensuring that each partner is fully accountable for his/her actions, has been a task made more difficult by the assumption of roles more appropriate for traditional contracting out relationships. Furthermore, the innovative nature of the service has added complexity and demands changed roles from all partners to achieve maximum success or effectiveness.

ELECTRONIC TOLL AND TRAFFIC MANAGEMENT

Electronic toll and traffic management (ETTM) systems are composed of:

- Electronic Toll Collection
- Automatic Vehicle Identification
- Automatic Vehicle Classification
- Video Enforcement Systems

In addition, ETTMs may also include manual toll collection lanes.

Electronic Toll Collection (ETC) is based upon the use of automatic vehicle identification (AVI) devices, often known as transponders or tags. These are placed in a vehicle, usually affixed to the front windshield. These transponders identify ownership of the vehicle, allowing the correct toll to be charged to the corresponding account. As a vehicle passes through a toll collection point, a stationary electronics unit known as a reader transmits a radio signal to the tag. The tag reflects the signal back to the reader, changing it slightly to identify the unique tag. The toll is thereby collected, as a prepaid account is debited the amount of the toll (Yermack et al. 2000; Smith 2002).

The amount of the toll is determined by the automatic vehicle classification (AVC) system. AVCs consist of in-lane loop induction devices that determine the vehicle presence; treadles that identify the number of axles and wheels, and weigh in motion technology that determines the weight of the vehicle. The AVC system must be closely linked to the AVI system so that the correct toll, assessed by the vehicle characteristics or class, is charged to the correct account (Smith 2002).

The Video Enforcement System identifies those vehicles that do not have a tag or transponder, and travel past the toll collection point without paying the appropriate toll. A camera takes a picture of the license plate of every vehicle, and immediately discards those pictures if the toll is paid. If the toll is not paid, the license number is checked against information obtained from the state's department of motor vehicles. According to established procedures created by the toll agency, violators will be sent warning letters and eventually will be issued traffic citations if tolls are not paid.

BENEFITS OF ETTM

For those who travel a toll road frequently, ETC offers many benefits. The number of vehicles processed per lane per hour with ETC can reach 2,000 without a toll booth, compared to 350 vehicles per hour if vehicles travel through a lane manned by a collector who makes change. Since vehicles do not stop to pay a toll, travelers will save significant travel time. The use of pre-paid accounts increases customer convenience, and provides an easily accessible record of travel if needed for business purposes.

The toll agency and the surrounding communities can also benefit. There is less need for construction to handle available traffic, especially relevant to areas of increased population growth. The agency saves the cost of the construction as smaller toll stations and fewer tollbooths are required, and the community benefits from lower pollution levels and less need to add lanes to existing toll roads (Yermack et al. 2000). Revenue security is greater, and there are lower costs to the agency as the cost of manning toll booths, collecting revenue, transporting coins and dollars to a financial institution, and relevant processing fees are all less.

Congestion or road pricing is facilitated with ETC. One way to slow the growth of the use of private vehicles is through time of day or peak period pricing of travel. The advancement of ETC technology, as seen along SR-91 in California, allows variable pricing depending on the time of day. Motorists—only those with AVI equipment in their vehicles—have the choice of traveling in express tolled lanes or in the non-tolled lanes, paying a toll that ranges from $1.10 from 11 p.m. to 6 a.m. to $7.75 during peak hours on weekday afternoons (www.91expresslanes.com).

Prior to the deployment of congestion tolls for drivers on SR-91 in California, it was largely assumed that the public was strongly adverse to congestion pricing, viewing it as another regressive tax that would unfairly affect the poor (Harrington et al., 2001; Colgan and Quinlin 1997). Initial assessments of the SR-91 experience, however, reported a high degree of traveler satisfaction with the congestion pricing, as travelers of all income levels chose to use the express lanes. Efforts to provide discounts to frequent users may have also helped to lessen opposition (Sullivan 2000)

The use of ETC has proved very popular wherever it has been introduced, as the convenience of prepaying and not having to stop at toll booths has met with universal acceptance. In turn, the introduction of ETTM systems has acted as catalysts to increase public private partnerships in building transportation infrastructure on an international basis. The greater ease and security by which tolls are collected and paid by travelers using ETTM have helped to spawn greater private sector involvement in building and operating toll roads. Highway 407 in Toronto, Canada, is but one example of increased usage due in large part to the use of ETC technology (Mylvaganam and Borins 2004).

COMMERCIAL VEHICLE OPERATIONS AND INFORMATION SYSTEMS NETWORK

By 2020, it is estimated that freight traffic will grow by 40 percent in the United States, due in part to international trade. States such as Texas are experiencing inadequate funding for the increased enforcement personnel that will be needed to regulate this increased traffic. As a result, weigh stations are not operated on a full-time basis. Without consistent monitoring, there is inadequate identification of overweight and unsafe vehicles (Conway and Walton 2005).

ITS technologies have the capability of increasing the safety and productivity of commercial vehicle operations (CVO). The ITS Program supports three basic areas:

- Safety information exchange
- Electronic screening systems
- Electronic credentialing systems

SAFETY INFORMATION EXCHANGE

The USDOT has been developing key aspects of the technology that comprises this component. SAFER (Safety and Fitness Electronic Record) contains safety and recent inspection reports about motor carriers throughout the United States. ASPEN is a software system that allows law enforcement personnel to access SAFER from roadside laptops. Data created by one state is thus immediately accessible by inspectors from another state (ITS Joint Program Office 2004a).

The goal of these programs is to reduce accidents and injuries caused by crashes involving motor carriers by enabling law enforcement to focus on the high risk carriers. Studies have suggested that a significant portion of these accidents are caused by carriers with poor safety and inspection records.

ELECTRONIC SCREENING SYSTEMS

Weigh in Motion (WIM) systems allow carriers to be inspected without having to stop at inspection stations. Carriers are equipped with automatic vehicle identification (AVI) devices which can communicate with inspection station equipment. There are obvious time savings for carriers, plus those with good safety and inspection records can expect fewer inspections. State agencies prefer these systems, as they reduce traffic at inspection stations and reduce the need for more stations to be built.

One goal of these systems would be to create a nationwide network so that carriers traveling across state lines would not have to stop at any inspection stations. Technical deployment presents few problems, as transponders used by carriers are accepted at all screening stations throughout the United States. However, operational and business issues present interoperability issues, as not all states use the same inspection standards nor use the same WIM system.

ELECTRONIC CREDENTIALING SYSTEMS

Credentialing involves a variety of state regulated activities:

> Motor carriers typically submit applications on a variety of paper forms relating to registering to operate as a motor carrier, demonstrating they have the required liability insurance, registering and titling vehicles, paying fuel taxes, applying for special oversize/overweight permits, applying for special hazardous materials hauling icenses and permits, paying federal heavy vehicle use tax, and complying with other state-specific regulations. (Orban 2001)

Providing this information via a Web site holds great promise for significant savings for carriers and state agencies. The challenge has been to adapt electronic credentialing with existing legacy systems.

COMMERCIAL VEHICLE INFORMATION SYSTEMS NETWORKS

To help states implement these three components, the USDOT has established the Commercial Vehicle Information Systems Networks (CVISN) Program. A state agency can qualify for Level One status by completing specific training workshops and establishing a plan to deploy each of the three components. In place since 1996, currently all states but Hawaii have completed a CVO business plan; forty-three states have completed the training workshops; and forty have completed Top Level One designs and programs (http://cvisn.fmcsa.dot.gov).

CVO and CVISN Benefits

The use of the SAFER data base allows states to identify those carriers that are likely to be in violation of state regulations, as well as having a poor safety record. More time and focus can be spent inspecting these vehicles, resulting in an initial higher violation rate and subsequent increased compliance rate (Brand et al. 2002). Fewer highway crashes result, producing benefits that include reduced highway delays to the public.

The increased use of WIM provides direct time saving benefits to carriers. Inventory costs are reduced. Air and noise pollution from trucks able to bypass inspection stations without slowing their speed is reduced.

Electronic credentialing also provides significant cost savings to states and private carriers. As illustrated by the experience in Washington State, "e-credentialing" allows carriers the ability to download and complete forms in their home offices and send them electronically to the state licensing agency. The wait time for approval of applications is reduced considerably. This information is then shared with all appropriate state agencies, providing additional safety and time benefits (ITS Joint Program Office 2004b).

ADVANCED PUBLIC TRANSPORTATION SYSTEMS

A key goal of all public transportation agencies is to reduce the use of the single occupancy vehicle. Lower traffic congestion and reduced air pollution are logical results. ISTEA provides funds to test and deploy innovative transit related technologies. In some cases, congestion mitigation funds are available for use as well (Harris et al. 2002).

The goals of a public transit or bus system are to provide quality service to the public by providing on-time service and routes that maximize ridership by responding to the travel needs of the greatest number of people in a given metropolitan areas. This service includes giving safety a high priority by being able to respond to accidents and breakdowns as quickly as possible.

Transit agencies will provide a variety of services, including buses, subways, light rail, ride matching programs, and vanpools. This discussion will focus primarily on bus travel.

Automatic Vehicle Location

The use of automatic vehicle location (AVL) transponders placed on buses assists schedulers and the public to know where buses are located in real-time. Knowing this information has several benefits. Dispatchers can alert bus drivers that they are ahead or behind schedule, or if they are off route (Weatherford 2000).

Delays due to unexpected traffic congestion may cause buses to run behind schedule. A lack of expected congestion may allow buses to arrive at a stop earlier than expected. Another factor that contributes to "early running" is that the driver may not stay at a stop for a specified time period if the number of passengers is less than expected. If the headway between buses is a half hour or more, this behavior may severely diminish public service, as patrons would have to wait longer times for the next bus (Bullock et al. 2005).

Likewise, as a bus nears an urban downtown destination, the delay time may be longer. As a result, schedule changes can be made if the delay is recurrent. Control of when buses leave the terminal may be changed (Hammerle 2005).

Also, the data collected by the use of AVL can allow schedulers and route planners to respond to service requirements much more efficiently and effectively. Accurately assessing demand along a specific route and responding to that demand with sufficient buses is a key task for schedulers and route planners. Knowledge of bus location, along with ridership counts can provide invaluable information that will increase service effectiveness. Operating costs and revenue per mile data can assess resulting system efficiency.

When crashes, incidents, or breakdowns do occur, dispatchers can also identify bus locations immediately and facilitate appropriate responses of emergency or maintenance personnel.

Without the AVL equipment, schedule information is collected periodically by "riders" that will be stationed at selected bus stops and time a sample of arrival and departure times for specified buses. This information, collected several times a year, provides a sample of schedule adherence information that is not real time nor can be collected for every bus at every stop (Weatherford 2000).

PRE-TRIP PLANNING

Even though AVL technology is used primarily to increase efficiency of bus operations, agencies soon realized that the same technology could be used to identify arrival times for bus patrons. Searching for ways to increase ridership, the communication of this information was also viewed as an effective marketing tool. The usage has been shown to have a significant and positive impact on customer satisfaction (Schweiger 2003).

One example of pre-trip planning using ITS applications is the Portland, Oregon, Transit Tracker System. GPS technology is used to determine how far each bus is from a bus stop. This information is then transferred to displays at the most heavily used transit stops and to a website. Arrival countdown information estimates when a bus will arrive and displays this information as well. A survey of users in the spring of 2003 found that the overwhelming majority used the system and felt that it has saved them time. Many were confident enough in the accuracy of the data to make other related decisions such as having sufficient time to "run errands" prior to arriving at the bus stop. Overall, patrons had a more positive impression of the transit agency (Pecheux and Vandergriff 2005).

TRAFFIC SIGNAL PRIORITY

Buses using traffic signal priority (TSP) can experience fewer delays when traveling along their routes. When a bus approaches an intersection, it transmits a signal to the traffic signal controller. Additional green time is allowed, preventing the bus from having to stop at the intersection (Casey 2000). Alternatively, if the light is red when a bus approaches an intersection, the system could truncate the red light time and progress the cycle to green more quickly.

TSP can lead to reduced operational costs, as buses make fewer stops and use less fuel. If delay along a route is significantly reduced, fewer buses may be required. (Casey 2000) In some cases, if delay is noticeable by patrons, then lowering delay will increase ridership (Chada and Newland 2002).

The effectiveness of TSP depends upon a variety of factors, including the type of system installed, the amount of traffic along a given bus corridor, and the amount of cross traffic at an intersection. The most effective systems are those using traffic signal adaptive systems such as SCOOT that allow real time signal changes. TSP works best when conditions of heavy traffic or light traffic do not exist.

Of continuing concern is the amount of traffic delay to nontransit vehicles. The amount of additional green time allotted to buses is one means of dealing with this issue. TSP systems in place allot between four and ten additional seconds, no matter how heavy the bus traffic. Experience in various metropolitan areas has provided a variety of positive results, with studies concluding that delay is reduced by up to 34 percent without adverse impact on non-transit traffic (Chaba and Newland 2002).

AUTOMATIC PASSENGER COUNTS

Automatic Passenger Count (APC) technology records the number of passengers to board at a given bus stop and the number who alight or leave the bus. It replaces manual ride counters and provides similar levels of accuracy at much lower cost (Kimpel, et al. 2002). APCs are often deployed in conjunction with AVL and other operations software and computer aided dispatching systems. As such they can provide a range of data that can be used for planning and scheduling purposes.

The number of boarding riders per hour can be identified, allowing planners to identify those stops that are underutilized. Similarly, they can identify stops that are heavily utilized and consider adding busses to a given route. Operations staff can identify headway data (the amount of time between each bus on a given route) and make adjustments where appropriate. Total passenger counts for bus stops can be analyzed and possible bus stops added along routes. If travel time information is provided to passengers, APC data can serve as the basis to predict arrival times (Strathman 2002).

SILENT ALARM

The silent alarm is a safety device activated by a bus driver when there is an incident that prevents him from using the intercom. Once triggered, a covert microphone is deployed that allows dispatch personnel to listen to activity on the vehicle. If drivers are faced with unruly passengers, or passengers with weapons, they may feel more safe by contacting dispatch for help without passengers knowing they have done so. Once the silent alarm is activated, the vehicle location is displayed in the dispatch center, along with the closest vehicles containing supervisory personnel. Dispatch can relay the vehicle location to law enforcement, fire, or emergency personnel as needed (Harris et al. 2002).

APTS Benefits

AVL deployment produces a better quality service. Transit agencies have reported up to a 40 percent reduction in emergency response times if buses are using AVL technology. Overall efficiency and adherence to schedules has improved more than 20 percent for some agencies (Goeddel 2000). A study of the transit system in Denver reports that dispatchers and supervisors felt they had more control over the operations of buses as they traveled on their routes (Weatherford 2000).

CONCLUSION: OVERALL ITS DEPLOYMENT EVALUATION AND ASSESSMENT

ITS deployment continues to face several challenges. Comparing data from the ITS Deployment Surveys provides one measure of to what extent ITS applications have been adopted nationwide. Collected from self-reported data from cities and states, the 2004 data set represents a larger number of large and medium sized cities (108 to 78), plus the 2004 data includes information provided by states as well (Table 6.2).

The data, although not exactly comparable, provides insights into ITS deployment. All comparable indicators reflect increases in adoption. However, thirteen years after ISTEA, many states and metropolitan areas have not accepted ITS applications as much as possible. The reasons for a lack of ITS adoption are several,

---

TABLE 6.2

Deployment Component	% Miles Covered 1999	% Miles Covered 2004
Freeway Management—Miles under electronic surveillance	22	32
Incident Management—Freeway miles covered by service patrols	35	43
Incident Management—Arterial miles covered by service patrols	3	10
ATIS—Freeway miles covered	22	31
ATMS—Signalized Intersections under centralized or closed loop control	46	50
ETC—Toll lanes with electronic toll collection	43	81
APTS—Fixed buses with AVL	30	47

Source: http://itsdeployment2.ed.ornl.gov/its2004/default.asp.

---

and they represent continuing challenges and opportunities for those who champion ITS deployment.

From the inception of ITS, it was recognized that institutional barriers had to be overcome:

> ITS planning and deployment required coordination among jurisdictions, data sharing, unique technical knowledge, andinvolvement of nontraditional players. (DeBlasio 2000, 152)

All of these changes require a different institutional structure and culture than that based upon an exclusive focus on capital improvements. The primary goal of state and local departments of transportation has been to build roadways, without much need to maintain them. Operations, or the management of a roadway system, has been a secondary emphasis of traditional public transportation organizations. ITS applications require the opposite: operations and maintenance must be the long term focus.

There remains a lack of technical understanding among transportation officials, especially concerning the adoption of appropriate ITS architecture. Departments of transportation have been traditionally staffed with civil engineers. Effective ITS requires systems engineering experience and background, which brings with it an understanding of the need for management and operations skills. The lack of appropriate skills may also lead to a lack of commitment and belief in the benefits of ITS applications (Lockwood 2000).

The role of public officials towards the private sector must change as well. Private organizations must be accepted as equals, as partners in the effort to deploy ITS applications (DeBlasio et al. 1999). Given the complexity of the ITS applications that must be deployed, traditional public-contractor relationships must be avoided. Public officials must also play roles that may be unfamiliar, such as placing an increased focus on marketing and assisting private partners in efforts to achieve greater traveler awareness of ATIS (Lawther 2004).

Lack of adequate funding for all surface transportation projects contributes to an incremental approach to adopting ITS. Often what has been deployed has been heavily dependent on "one-time" federal funding without sufficient thought given to the longer term operations and maintenance costs (DeBlasio 2000). The need to explore sources of funding other than fuel tax (Wachs 2003) coincides with efforts to gain resources from the private sector (USGAO 2004). In addition, adding ITS operations costs as a line-item in the on-going state and local transportation budgets is a welcome outcome of changes in organizational culture mentioned above (Lockwood 2000).

The incorporation of ITS support in the traditional transportation planning process is essential. At present, many metropolitan planning organizations use the planning process as a means to support projects that favor members of the planning boards (Ankner 2005). Mainstreaming ITS into the traditional planning process entails one or more of the following three conditions:

- Endorsement of ITS by elected officials and transportation managers
- Improved communication and coordination across geographic boundaries and between agencies
- Collection of data and use of information (Jackson et al. 2000)

Efforts to achieve anyone of these three conditions also help to achieve the other two. The use of collected data can highlight the benefits of ITS applications, and in turn lead to greater endorsement of additional ITS efforts. Improved regional coordination, in many cases made possible by ITS efforts such as Traffic Incident Management Programs, is likely to grow to the extent that previous efforts are successful. Over time, achieving these conditions should lead to greater support for more ITS projects within transportation planning.

Even with these challenges there are countless instances of ITS benefits in each of the specific areas mentioned above. Traveler satisfaction with 511 services remains extremely high. Incident management programs have reduced delays from 10 to 45 Percent. Freeway management systems have handled up to 22 percent more traffic at speeds up to 48 percent faster. Electronic toll collection increases capacity as much as 300 percent when compared to attended lanes. Continuing research should publicize these results, supporting marketing efforts to gain increased public support for ITS.

ISSUES AND TRENDS

ITS represents a sea change in surface transportation (Sussman 2000). Acceptance and change in ITS deployment started incrementally, and has gradually evolved to a more regional acceptance in many areas.

ITS success requires transportation officials to recognize and accept the trends that in many cases have been stimulated by ITS technologies. The shift in professional focus must be from capital planning to management and operations. Thinking in long-term frames, characteristic of capital projects, must be shifted to real-time control and communication of information. An emphasis only on public financing must be replaced by innovative financing arrangements that include greater use of public private partnerships. Public transportation organizations must shift from a more narrow urban and rural focus to a more regional focus, recognizing that more dynamic relationships across organizational boundaries will be more successful (Sussman 2005).

Perhaps most important is placing a high priority on meeting customer needs and increasing customer satisfaction. As stated by transportation officials attending a U.S. General Accounting Office sponsored conference on the future of surface transportation:

> By linking transportation policies and services to customers' needs and preferences, the primary mission of transportation agencies will change from building highways, bridges, and mass transit systems to moving people and goods...Developing new services based on customers' needs and input will be a substantial departure from the largely bureaucratic decision-making that characterizes transportation organizations today. (USGAO 1999, 4)

The recently passed Safe, Accountable, Flexible, and Efficient Transportation Equity Act: A Legacy for Users (SAFETY-L&U) recognizes the importance of public satisfaction and support. ITS deployment and acceptance will invariably increase as a result.

BIBLIOGRAPHY

Allred, C. 2004. "Coordinating Incident Response." *Public Roads, March-April*: 7–11.

Aultman-Hall, L., S. Bowling, and J. Clemons-Asher. 2000. *ARTIMIS Telephone Travel Information Service: Current Use Patterns and User Satisfaction.* Washington, D.C.: 79th annual meeting of the Transportation Research Board, January.

Brand, D., T. Parody, J. Orban, and V. Brown. 2002. "A Benefit/Cost Analysis of the Commercial Vehicle Information Systems and Networks (CVISN) Program." Paper presented at the annual meeting of the Transportation Research Board, Washington, D.C.

Bullock, D. and T. Urbanik. 2000. "Traffic Signal Systems: Addressing Diverse Technologies and Complex User Needs." Paper presented at the annual meeting of the Transportation Research Board, Washington, D.C.

Bullock, P., Q. Jiang, and P. Stopher. 2005. "Using GPS Technology to Measure On-Time Running of Scheduled Bus Services." *Journal of Public Transportation* 8 (1): 21–40.

Cambridge Systematics, Inc. 2001. Twin Cities Ramp Meter Evaluation: Final Report. Oakland, CA: Author.

Casey, R. 2000. "What Have We Learned About Advanced Public Transportation Systems?" in United States Department of Transportation. *What Have We Learned About ITS?* Washington, D.C.: Author: 87–106.

Chada, S. and R. Newland. 2002. *Effectiveness of Bus Signal Priority: Final Report.* Tampa: University of South Florida, Center for Transportation Research.

Chen, K. and J. Miles (eds.). 2000. *ITS Handbook 2000.* Norwood, MA: Artech House.

Colgan, C. S., & Quinlin, G. 1997. "The Catch-22 of Congestion Pricing." *Transportation Quarterly*, 51 (4): 117–133.

Conway, A. and C. M. Walton. 2005. "Potential Application of ITS Technologies to Improve Commercial Vehicle Operations, Enforcement and Monitoring." Paper presented at the annual meeting of the Transportation Research Board, Washington, D.C.

DeBlasio, A., D. Jackson, A. Tallon, G. Powers, and J. O'Donnell. 1999. *Successful Approaches to Deploying a Metropolitan Intelligent Transportation System.* Cambridge, MA: John A. Volpe National Transportation Systems Center.

DeBlasio, A. 2000. "What Have We Learned About Cross-Cutting Institutional Issues?" In United States Department of Transportation. *What Have We Learned About ITS?* Washington, D.C.: Author: 151–169.

511 Deployment Coalition. 2005. *511 National Progress Report.* Washington, D.C.: Author.

Farradyne, P. B.. 2000. *Traffic Incident Management Handbook.* Washington, D.C.: U.S. Department of Transportation, Federal Highway Administration.

Fenno, D. and M. Ogden. 1998. "Freeway Service Patrols: A State of the Practice." Paper presented at the annual meeting of the Transportation Research Board, Washington, D.C.

Goeddel, D. 2000. *Benefits Assessment of Advanced Public Transportation System Technologies, Update 2000.* Cambridge, MA: John A. Volpe National Transportation Systems Center.

Hadi, M. 2002. "Experience of Signal Control Agencies with Adaptive Control in North America." A paper presented at the annual meeting of the Intelligent Transportation Society of America, Long Island, California.

Hallenbeck, M. 1998. *Choosing the Route To Traveler Information Systems Deployment: Decision Factors for Creating Public/Private Business Plans.* Washington, D.C.: Intelligent Transportation Society of America.

Hammerle, M., M. Haynes, and S. McNeil. 2005. "Use of Automatic Vehicle Location and Passenger Count Data to Evaluate Bus Operations for the Chicago Transit Authority."

Paper presented at the annual meeting of the Transportation Research Board, Washington, D.C.

Harrington, W., A. Krupnick, and A. Alberini. 2001. "Overcoming Public Aversion to Congestion Pricing." *Transportation Research Part A* 35: 93–111.

Harris, M., M. Hardy, R. Casey, and J. Schwenk. 2002. *A Ride through SaFIRES—Lessons Learned from SaFIRES, an APTS Operational Test in Prince William County, Virginia.* Cambridge, MA: John A. Volpe National Transportation Systems Center.

Helman, D. 2004. "Traffic Incident Management." *Public Roads* 68(3).

Inman, V. and J. Peters. 1996. *Travtek Global Evaluation and Executive Summary.* McLean, VA: Federal Highway Administration, Office of Safety and Traffic Operations, R&D.

Institute of Traffic Engineers. 1995. *Improving Traffic Signal Operations: A Primer.* Washington, D.C.: United States Federal Highway Administration.

ITS Joint Program Office, US Department of Transportation. 1996. *Implementation of the National Intelligent Transportation Systems Program: 1996 Report to Congress.* Washington, DC: Author.

ITS Joint Program Office, US Department of Transportation. 1998. *Intelligent Transportation Systems in the Transportation Equity Act for the 21st Century.* Washington, D.C.: Author.

ITS Joint Program Office, US Department of Transportation. 2004a. *CVISN Safety Information Exchange for Commercial Vehicles in Connecticut: A Case Study.* Washington, D.C.: Author.

ITS Joint Program Office, US Department of Transportation. 2004b. *CVISN Electronic Credentialing for Commercial Vehicles in Washington State: A Case Study.* Washington, D.C.: Author.

Jackson, D., E. Deysher, and A. DeBlasio. 2000. *Mainstreaming ITS Within the Transportation Planning Process: A Summary of Strategies Within Ten Metropolitan Areas.* Cambridge, MA: John A. Volpe National Transportation Systems Center.

Jensen, M., C. Cluett, Karl W., A. DeBlasio, and R. Sanchez. 2000. *Metropolitan Model Deployment Initiative Seattle Evaluation Report Final Draft.* Washington, D.C.: United States Department of Transportation, FHWA-OP-00-020.

Kang, S. and D. Gillen. 1999. *Assessing the Benefits and Costs of Intelligent Transportation Systems: Ramp Meters.* Berkeley, CA: California PATH Research Report UCB-ITS-PRR-99-19.

Khattak, A., F. Targa, and Y. Yim. 2003. *Investigation of Traveler Information and Related Travel Behavior in the San Francisco Bay Area.* Berkeley, CA: California PATH Research Report UCB-ITS-PWP-2003-6.

Kimpel, T., J. Strathman, D. Griffin, S. Callas, and R. Gerhart. 2002. *Automatic Passenger Counter Evaluation: Implications for National Transit Database Reporting* Portland, OR: Portland State University, Center for Urban Studies.

Lappin, J. 2000. "What Have We Learned About Advanced Traveler Information Systems and Customer Satisfaction?" in United States Department of Transportation. *What Have We Learned About ITS?* Washington, D.C.: Author: 65–85.

Lawther, W. 2004. "Public Outreach for Advanced Traveler Information Systems Public Private Partnerships: The Changing Role of Public Officials in Transportation." *Public Works Management and Policy,* 9 (2): 120–131.

Lawther, W. and E. Berman. 2004. *Second Annual Evaluation of the SmartRoute Systems Advanced Traveler Information Services Contract For Miami-Dade, Broward and Palm Beach Counties.* Orlando, FL: Author.

Lee, C., B. Hellinga, and K. Ozbay. 2005. "Quantifying Effects of Ramp Metering on Freeway Safety." Paper presented at the annual meeting of the Transportation Research Board, Washington, D.C.

Little, C. and J. Wooster. 1994. *IVHS and Environmental Impacts: Implications of the Operational Tests*. Cambridge, MA: John A. Volpe National Transportation Systems Center.

Lockwood, S. 2000. "The Institutional Challenge: An Aggressive View," in D. Nelson (ed.) *Intelligent Transportation Primer*. Washington, D.C.: Institute of Transportation Engineers: 24–21.

Orban, J.C. 2000. "What Have We Learned About ITS for Commercial Vehicle Operations? Status, Challenges and Benefits About CVISN Level 1 Development," in United States Department of Transportation. *What Have We Learned About ITS?* Washington, D.C.: Author: 108–126.

Maas, G., M. Maggio, H. Shafie, and R. Stough. 2001. "Incident Management and Intelligent Transportation Systems Technology: Estimating Benefits for Northern Virginia," in R. Stough (ed.) *Intelligent Transport Systems: Cases and Policies*. Northampton, MA: Edward Elgar Publishing: 207–224.

Margiotta, R., K. Voorhies, and T. Lomax. 2004. *Measuring and Communicating the Effects of Traffic Incident Management Improvements*. Washington, D.C.: National Highway Cooperative Research Program, Research Results Digest, 289.

McQueen, B., R. Schuman, and K. Chen. 2002. *Advanced Traveler Information Systems*. Norwood, MA: Artech House.

Miller, M. 1998. *Testing a Proposed Decision Oriented Framework to Understand ITS Deployment Issues: A Case Study of the TravInfo ATIS Project*. Berkeley, CA: California Path Research Report: UCB-ITS-PRR-98-35.

Mylvaganam, C. and Borins, S. 2004. *"If you build it..."*: *Business, Government and Ontario's Electronic Toll Highway*. Ontario: University of Toronto Press.

Mobility 2000. 1990. Proceedings of a National Workshop in IVHS. Dallas, TX: Author.

National Transportation Operations Coalition. 2005. *National Traffic Signal Report Card: Technical Report*. Washington, D.C.: Author.

Pecheux, K. and P. Vandergriff. 2005. "Customer Use of and Satisfaction with Real-Time Bus Arrival Information in Portland, Oregon." Paper presented at the annual meeting of the Transportation Research Board, Washington, D.C.

Pederson, C. 1998. *The Intelligent Transportation Systems (ITS) Metropolitan Model Deployment Initiative (MDI): Lessons Learned from the Non-Selected Partnerships* (Executive Summary). Washington, D.C.: U.S. Department of Transportation.

Peirce, S. and J. Lappin. 2003. *Acquisition of Traveler Information and Its Effects on Travel Choices: Evidence from a Seattle-Area Travel Diary Survey*. Cambridge, MA: John A. Volpe National Transportation Systems Center.

Perez, W. and M. Carter. 2000. "Metropolitan Model Development Initiative: National Evaluation." Paper given at the annual meeting of Intelligent Transportation Society of America.

Piotrowicz, G. and J. Robinson. 1995. *Ramp Metering Status in North America: 1995 Update*. Washington, D.C.: U.S. Department of Transportation.

Schintler, L. 1999. *Partners in Motion and Customer Satisfaction in the Washington, D.C. Metropolitan Area*. Fairfax, VA: Institute of Public Policy, The George Mason University.

Schuman, R. and E. Sherer. 2001. ATIS U.S. Business Models Review. Washington, D.C.: U.S. Department of Transportation and ITS Joint Program Office, November 15.

Schweiger, C. 2003. Real-Time Bus Arrival Information Systems: A Synthesis of Transit Practice. Washington, D.C.: Transportation Research Board, Synthesis 48.

Shaver, K. 2002. "Smart Traffic System a Failure: Personal Notification Service Lacked Data, Customers and Profits," *Washington Post*, December 17:B01.

Skabardonis, A., K. Petty, Pravin V., and R. Bertini.1998. *Evaluation of the Freeway Service Patrol (FSP) in Los Angeles*. Berkeley, CA: University of California, California PATH Research Report UCB-ITS-PRR-98-31.

Skabardonis, A. 2001. "ITS Benefits: The Case of Traffic Signal Control Systems." Paper presented at the annual meeting of the Transportation Research Board, Washington, D.C.

Smith, B. 2000. "Transportation Management," in D. Nelson (ed.) *Intelligent Transportation Primer*. Washington, D.C.: Institute of Transportation Engineers: 3-1 to 3-8.

Smith, L. 2002. *Services and Technologies: Electronic Toll Collection*. Berkeley, CA: University of California, Institute of Transportation Studies.

Synder, W. and X. de Souza-Briggs. 2004. "Communities of Practice: A New Tool for Government Managers," in J. Kamensky and T. Burlin (eds.), *Collaboration: Using Networks and Partnerships*. Lanham, MA: Rowman and Littlefield: 171–272.

Strathman, J. 2002. *Tri-Met's Experience With Automatic Passenger Counter and Automatic Vehicle Location Systems*. Portland, OR: Portland State University, Center for Urban Studies.

Sullivan, E. 2000. *Continuation Study to Evaluate the Impacts of the SR 91 Value-Priced Express Lanes: Final Report*. San Luis Obispo, CA: Cal Poly State University.

Sussman, J. 1996. "ITS: A Short History and a Perspective on the Future." *Transportation Quarterly*, 50(4): 115–125.

Sussman, J. 2000. "What We Have Learned About ITS: Final Comments," in United States Department of Transportation. *What Have We Learned About ITS?* Washington, D.C.: Author: 171–176.

Sussman, J. 2005. *Perspectives on Intelligent Transportation Systems*. New York: Plenum Publishing Corporation.

United States Department of Transportation. 2001. *Regional Traffic Incident Management Program: An Implementation Guide*. Washington, D.C.: Federal Highway Administration.

United States Department of Transportation. 2005. *Summary of ITS Integration Projects*. (http://www.its.dot.gov/resources/IntegrationProject/index.htm). Last accessed September 11, 2005.

United States General Accounting Office. 1997. *Challenges to Widespread Deployment of Intelligent Transportation Systems*. Washington, D.C.: Author,GAO/RCED-97-74.

United States General Accounting Office. 1999. *Surface Transportation: Moving into the 21st Century*. Washington, D.C: Author, GAO/RCED-99-176.

United States General Accountability Office. 2004. *Highways and Transit: Private Sector Sponsorship of and Investment in Major Projects Has Been Limited*. Washington, D.C.: Author, GAO-04-419.

Wachs, M. 2003. *Improving Efficiency and Equity in Transportation Finance*. Washington, D.C.: The Brookings Institution, Transportation Reform Series.

Weatherford, M. 2000. *Assessment of the Denver Regional Transportation District's Automatic Vehicle Location System*. Washington, D.C.: Federal Transit Administration.

Whelan, R. 1995. *Smart Highways, Smart Cars*. Norwood, MA: Artech House.

Yermack, L., R. Fielding, and P. Leshinsky. 2000. "Electronic Toll and Traffic Management," in D. Nelson (ed.) *Intelligent Transportation Primer*. Washington, D.C.: Institute of Transportation Engineers: 8-1 to 8-14.

Zimmerman, C, J. Marks, J. Jenq, C. Cluett, A. DeBlasio, J. Lappin, H. Rahka, and K.Wunderlich. 2000. *Phoenix Metropolitan Model Deployment Initiative Evaluation Report (Draft)*. Washington, D.C.: U.S. Department of Transportation, FHWA-JPO-00-015.

7 Toll Roads

*Patrick Fisher, Johnathan Gerber, and
David C. Nice*

INTRODUCTION

A very old concept in transportation systems is charging users a fee for the use of a particular route or corridor. In some cases the proceeds have been used to help defray the costs of building and maintaining the system. In other cases, as occurred during the Middle Ages, local nobles demanded fees from travelers using natural transportation routes, such as rivers. This chapter will discuss the use of toll roads in the United States, with attention to the shifting degree of interest over the years and the varying use of toll roads from state to state.[1]

THE EARLY DAYS OF TOLL ROADS

The earliest toll roads in the United States began with the development of turnpike companies soon after the United States won its independence (Kulash 2001). In 1792 the Philadelphia and Lancaster Turnpike in Pennsylvania became the first turnpike chartered in the United States. A boom in turnpike construction began, resulting in the incorporation of more than 100 turnpike companies in the United States, primarily in Connecticut, New York, and Massachusetts (Federal Highway Administration 2005). By today's standards, the early turnpikes were fairly primitive roads, although they were the only improved roads in some areas.

Over time, however, state and local governments became increasingly involved in building roads and maintaining them, and they tended to prefer financing roads with tax revenues. Tax financing was needed because many citizens wanted and needed in roads in many different locations. Many of those routes would not generate enough traffic to finance a major road using tolls; state and local officials found that a more practical strategy was to raise funds via taxes and, when necessary, to redistribute funds from where they could be raised to areas where new roads were needed. Interest in toll roads gradually declined until the twentieth century (Young 2005).

A RENEWED INTEREST IN TOLL ROADS DURING THE EARLY AND MIDDLE PARTS OF THE TWENTIETH CENTURY

With the advent of the automobile and with growing public demand for better (and more expensive) highways, however, the federal government began to study the possibility of building toll roads across the country. In 1939 the U.S. Bureau of Public Roads rejected the toll option for financing interstate highway construction because agency officials believed that toll charges would drive away most motorists. As a result, the interstate corridors would not generate enough toll revenue to retire the bonds issued to finance them (http://www.fact-index.com/t/to/toll_road.html).

The financial success of the Pennsylvania Turnpike after it opened in 1940, however, increased the credibility of toll road financing (http://www.fact-index.com/t/to/toll_road.html). After World War II, many of the populous states in the eastern part of the country were struggling to balance their citizens' demands for better highways with the need for a politically acceptable method of covering the immense costs of expressways. To a large degree, therefore, toll roads in the mid-twentieth century were a product of short-on-funds states coming up with a way to finance major new construction before the federal subsidies of the Interstate Highway Act of 1956 began. For example, the state of Illinois in 1953 created the Illinois State Toll Highway Commission to build an expressway system in the Chicago suburbs because the state had already committed $1.1 billion to the construction of five expressways in the Chicago metropolitan area (Young 2005). By 1956, most limited access highways in the eastern United States were toll roads (http://www.fact-index.com/t/to/toll_road.html).

The prospects for an extensive network of toll roads throughout the country, however, declined with the passage of the Federal-Aid Highway Act of 1956. The act, which provided for a coast-to-coast expressway system connecting important cities and industrial centers to one another, was legislated as a tax-supported system, not a toll system. Since its creation, the Federal-Aid Highway program has operated under the assumption that tax-supported roads were preferable to toll roads (http://www.fact-index.com/t/to/toll_road.html). The measure funded non-toll roads with 90 percent federal dollars and a 10 percent state match, giving little incentive for most states to expand their toll road system.

During deliberations over the Interstate System, Congress struggled with how to handle existing turnpikes in Interstate corridors. One proposal was to build toll-free Interstate highways parallel to the turnpikes, but that would have jeopardized the rights of bondholders by diverting traffic away from the turnpikes. Another option was to repay the bondholders and remove the tolls, but this would have diverted hundreds of millions of dollars from the highway construction program. After extensive debate, Congress finally decided to incorporate toll facilities in the Interstate System to ensure connectivity without additional expense. With the implementation of the 1956 act, a number of toll roads that previously existed were designated at Interstate routes, but were able to continue to collect tolls under agreements which specified that when the toll road bonds were paid off the highways would become toll free. With the implementation of federal aid to the states to build the Interstate System, proposals for additional toll roads lost much of their appeal, and by 1963, when the last of the toll roads planned before 1956 was completed, no new toll roads were being seriously considered (http://www.fact-index.com/t/to/toll_road.html). The lack of interest did not persist, however.

TOLL ROADS IN THE LATTER PART IN THE TWENTIETH CENTURY AND BEYOND

The toll road concept began to reemerge by the late 1970s, amid rising concern that the United States was falling behind in building and maintaining highway infrastructure. Policy makers felt that raising additional tax revenues was politically risky, and often preferred to defer maintenance and reconstruction of all kinds. Many roads and highways across the country were approaching the end of their design life and/or showing signs of serious wear (Federal Highway Administration 2003; (http://www.fact-index. com/t/to/toll_road.html). A series of reports also revealed that thousands of road and highway bridges needed considerable renovation or replacement (Nice 1992; Bureau of Census 2003, 693).

In that environment, toll charges may be a politically appealing way to raise additional funding, in part because tolls may shift a considerable share of the cost of a highway to nonresidents, such as tourists. For example, officials of the Oklahoma Turnpike Authority estimate that approximately 40 percent of their toll revenues come from nonresidents (http://www.pikepass.com/why/%20turnpikes.htm). State and local governments across the country have become increasingly reliant on charges and fees of many types to finance many programs since the 1960s (*Significant Features of Fiscal Federalism* 1994, 58). Much of that trend is due to public and interest group resistance to tax increases in many parts of the country.

Traffic congestion has also helped stimulate interest in toll roads, in part due to the belief that the tolls will generate revenues that could not be obtained in any other way. Those added revenues can then be used to finance transportation improvements, including the addition of new routes or more lanes. In addition, however, charging higher tolls during periods of heavier traffic congestion or on heavily congested routes may cause people to alter their transportation plans (traveling at less busy times or on less busy routes or switching to public transportation). Some proposals would also permit motorists traveling alone to drive in carpool lanes for an additional fee (sometimes called HOT lanes) and, consequently, increase utilization of the carpool lanes, although some critics complain that policy injects a class bias into a facility originally built to encourage carpooling. Drivers unconcerned with the extra charge for the lane use would, presumably, be more likely to use the extra-price lanes than would poor people (see Federal Highway Administration 2005, 2–5; Sneath 2005, 7; Swope 2005, 26, 28–29). According to one study in California, people from a variety of income groups are willing to pay tolls to use the high-occupancy lanes (see Dornan and March 2005 9–10; March 2005, 11), although the problem remains that a given toll charge will consume a larger share of a low-income person's income than of a high-income person's income.

A recurring source of interest in toll roads is linked to economic development concerns. A growing economy often generates additional demand on the transportation system, and transportation improvements may help to spur further economic growth (Dye 1990, chapter 7; http://www.ohioturnpike.org/history.html, 1–2). Increasing competition among states and localities for jobs and investment in recent years (Saiz and Clarke 2004) has enhanced the appeal of all manner of policies that might attract new business activity to the state and help it to retain existing firms. Toll-financed transportation improvements could very well be one transportation improvement that would attract or help retain businesses.

The low interest rates of recent years have also enhanced the appeal of financing transportation improvements by borrowing funds, using them to pay for improvements, and charging tolls to pay off the bonds. This approach also has the benefit of placing the cost of the improvements on the shoulders of the people who benefit directly from the improvements (Sneath 2005, 14–15). However, a route that generates relatively low traffic volume may not produce enough toll revenue to pay off the bonds.

Interest in toll road programs has also increased in the past two decades because the federal government has given the states increased flexibility in highway funding, allowing for the development of new toll roads. The Intermodal Surface and Transportation Efficiency Act (ISTEA), passed by Congress in 1991, was designed to give state and local governments greater flexibility in spending their federal transportation money, including a limited opportunity to build more toll roads. Though the measure was originally seen as a means to give the states considerably more discretion in how they spent their allotment federal transportation funds, to a large degree the states did not utilize this increased discretion, and for the most part states did not move toward policies that encouraged the creation of toll roads (Fisher and Nice 2002).

The Transportation Act for the 21st Century (TEA-21), signed into law by President Clinton in 1998, also provided new provisions that influenced federal toll road policies. TEA-21 continued the transformation of the nation's 1950s-era highway building program into a more flexible transportation program that allowed the states to potentially create a limited number of toll roads. Among the provisions of TEA-21 was a pilot program under which a state may collect tolls on an Interstate highway for the purpose of reconstructing or rehabilitating the Interstate highway that could not be adequately maintained without the collection of tolls (http://www.fact-index.com/t/to/toll_road.html). The states' discretion over toll collection, however, can be manipulated for political purposes. A four-mile stretch of the New Jersey Turnpike, for example, came under the jurisdiction of the Turnpike Authority in 1992, as the New Jersey Department of Transportation "sold" the road in order to balance the state budget for the year.

A major source of increased interest in toll roads in recent years is improved technology. Electronic toll collection, which allows electronic equipment to identify vehicles and record large amounts of data, is transforming toll collection. The emergence of electronic vehicle identification allows states or other levels of governments to add new policies, including value pricing and weight-distance charges, which can make the collection of tolls considerably more efficient (Kulash 2001; Sneath 21; Swope 2005, 26). By not requiring vehicles to stop, electronic toll collection benefits the traveling public by reducing lines at tollbooths, reducing vehicle operating costs, and conserving fuel. The number of toll facilities with electronic technology has increased from 49 in 1995 to 161 by 2003 (http://www.fact-index.com/t/to/toll_road.html).

Investors in electronic toll collection in New Jersey spent more than $300 million to install an electronic toll system, which will be repaid primarily by identifying and charging toll violators. Thus, the toll roads in New Jersey count on catching booth runners to pay off loans for the project. Video cameras installed at the toll booths take photos of license plates. Once identified, the violators are fined and charged a $25 administration fee to cover the cost of installing the electronic system (*Civil Engineering* 1998). California authorities estimate that their cameras record approximately 99 percent of all license tags (California Department of Transportation 2004, 13).

The use of toll roads in the northeastern states has become more efficient due to the installation of the so-called E-ZPass. Conventional toll collection methods require drivers to deposit coins, tickets, or tokens at toll plazas. This challenges highway capacity because the number of vehicles that can be processed at toll plazas is limited. With E-ZPass electronic toll collection technology, however, account information on an electronic tag installed in a motor vehicle is read by a receiving antenna at the toll plaza. The toll is then electronically deducted from the driver's prepaid account. New Jersey, New York, Massachusetts, Pennsylvania, Delaware, Maryland, and West Virginia all currently utilize the E-ZPass (New Jersey Department of Transportation 2005).

With changes in technology and greater reliance on toll financing, some observers believe that the private sector can play an expanded role in many nations' highway systems (see Lockwood, Verma, and Schneider 2000). Private toll roads may be an additional way of financing and constructing highways in the near future. The private sector may be willing to invest in highway construction and assist with highway operations if there is a high probability of making profits through the collection of tolls. However, recent U. S. court rulings prohibiting the use of eminent domain powers to acquire private property for private developments have greatly reduced the feasibility of building purely private roads on any large scale in the United States.

Nevertheless, public-private partnerships, where government and the private sector work together to develop, finance, construct, operate, own, and maintain highway facilities remain an alternative to traditional tax-supported public roads, particularly if needed land is already publicly owned or if ownership of the road is public or will become public at some future date Those partnerships can take many forms, including hiring a private company to manage an existing toll road, floating bonds to the private sector with the requirement that tolls from the project will be used to retire the bonds, partial public guarantees of bond proceeds, and many other combinations. Two experiments currently underway in the United States are Virginia's Dulles Greenway and the adding lanes to a highway southern California. A number of other countries are also trying various public-private partnerships for managing or upgrading existing roads or building new ones (Lockwood, Verma, and Schneider 2000, 78–88; Federal Highway Administration 2005).

TURNPIKES ON THE EAST COAST

A striking feature regarding toll roads in the United States is the very pronounced regional patterns in toll road use. The most extensive toll road systems are found along the East Coast and in a belt extending from New Jersey and New York west to Chicago. The pattern is rooted in the historical development of America's highway system.

As noted earlier, Pennsylvania's experience with toll roads dates back to the 1790s. The modern Pennsylvania Turnpike—the first turnpike of the modern motor vehicle era—was created in 1937 during the Great Depression. The Pennsylvania Turnpike Commission was created with the support of President Franklin Roosevelt's WPA program, which sought to lower unemployment. Since bankers were hesitant to support the unproven nature of a toll superhighway, the project was financed mainly by a loan from the New Deal's Reconstruction Finance Corporation for almost $41 million at 3.75 percent. The WPA also provided an additional $29 million in grants (Pennsylvania Turnpike Commission 2005).

The Pennsylvania Turnpike had many innovations. The turnpike, when possible, was laid out on southern exposures to let the sun heat the ice and snow on the roads. Toll roads off of the turnpike were located on downhill grades to allow drivers time to react. Even today the Pennsylvania Turnpike has one of the lowest fatality rates in the country. The original 160-mile route of the Pennsylvania Turnpike has been expanded to 514 miles, carrying more than 150 million vehicles a year at a toll of just over 4 cents a mile (Pennsylvania Turnpike Commission 2005).

From colonial times, the corridor between New York and Philadelphia has been heavily traveled, first by stagecoach and later by motor vehicles. As a result, New Jersey has been a key link in the East Coast travel chain. Since the 1950s, New Jersey has two major toll roads: the New Jersey Turnpike and the Garden State Parkway.

The older of these toll roads—The New Jersey Turnpike—took astonishingly little time to be constructed. In 1948, the New Jersey state legislature passed the New Jersey Turnpike Authority Act, which created the New Jersey Turnpike Authority "to construct, maintain, repair, and operate Turnpike projects." Nationally recognized highway engineering firms from across the country were brought in to estimate traffic demands and determine the best route for the 118-mile-long Turnpike. The Turnpike was divided into seven simultaneous projects to expedite its construction (http://www.nycroads.com/roads/nj-turnpike 2005). As a result, the Turnpike was remarkably completed in only 25 months at a cost of $255 million. At the time it was built, the New Jersey Turnpike was considered the cutting edge of highway construction; when the interstate highway system was built it copied many of New Jersey's design guidelines.

The engineers who oversaw the construction of the Turnpike had to adhere to a uniform set of standards. First, it was determined that the Turnpike would be a controlled-access highway with relatively few entrances and exits—access to the turnpike would only be at interchanges that were spaced considerable distances apart. Also, the roadways were to have extra-wide traffic lanes, wide shoulders on both sides of the traffic lanes, and grades and curve radii kept to a minimum (http://www.nycroads.com/roads/nj-turnpike 2005).

The completion of the New Jersey Turnpike provided another piece of what would be called the "eastern turnpike complex." The first piece of the "complex" was completed in 1940 with the opening of the Pennsylvania Turnpike, followed in 1947 with the opening of the Maine Turnpike. Their turnpikes would be followed with the completion of controlled-access toll expressways in New Hampshire by 1950, Ohio in 1955, in New York and Indiana in 1956, in Massachusetts in 1957, in Connecticut and Illinois in 1958, and finally in Delaware and Maryland in 1963. By that year, motorists could travel from Maine south to Virginia, or west to Illinois, without stopping at a traffic light. Much of the "eastern turnpike complex" was eventually integrated into the Interstate Highway System (http://www.nycroads.com/roads/nj-turnpike 2005). The relatively continuous network from Illinois to Pennsylvania demonstrates that coordinated state action can sometimes results in major achievements, although the absence of similar networks in most parts of the country suggest that coordinated state action without federal assistance is not easy.

Since it opened in 1952, the New Jersey Turnpike has operated on a ticket system in which motorists, upon entering the turnpike, receive a magnetically encoded ticket which indicates the vehicle class and point of origin that is surrendered when the motorist exits. The toll now ranges from $4.60 for off-peak E-ZPass users to $5.50 for cash users to drive the entire length of the Turnpike (http://www.nycroads.com/roads/nj-turnpike).

The Garden State Parkway was constructed between 1946 and 1957. Its initial impetus was to connect suburban northern New Jersey with resort areas along the Atlantic coast as well as to alleviate traffic on traditional north-south highways in the state. With only eighteen miles of roadway completed by 1950, financing the Parkway had become difficult until officials devised a plan modeled on the successful New Jersey Turnpike. In 1952 the New Jersey state legislature passed legislation to create the New Jersey Highway Authority, which was to construct and maintain a self-sufficient toll parkway the length of the state from north to south http://en.wikipedia.org/wiki/Garden_State_Parkway 2005).

Following the successful model of the New Jersey Turnpike Authority, the New Jersey Highway Authority adopted the power to issue bonds to finance construction of the Garden State Parkway. The payment of interest and principal on the bonds would be covered largely by tolls and concessions. In 2003 the New Jersey Turnpike Authority and the Garden State Parkway were merged into one agency.

Gilmore Clarke, a protégée of Robert Moses, was the landscape architect and engineer in charge of the construction of the Parkway. Clarke's design prototypes for the Parkway combined the efficient attributes of the parallels in the German Autobahn routes of the 1930s with the Merritt Parkway (located in Connecticut) model that stressed a planted "green belt" for aesthetic purposes. And like the German Autobahn and Merritt Parkway, the Parkway was built with wide planted medians to prevent head-on collisions and mask the glare of on-coming headlights (http://en.wikipedia.org/wiki/Garden_State_Parkway 2005).

In northern New Jersey, the Parkway serves as a functional commuter highway and does not appear different from expressways built in the 1950s. In southern New Jersey, however, the Parkway takes on more of a bucolic nature, passing through pine barrens with forested medians as wide as six hundred feet (http://en.wikipedia.org/wiki/Garden_State_Parkway 2005).

Since its creation, additional bonds have helped finance expansion projects on the Garden State Parkway. In central New Jersey, the original four-lane parkway has been widened to as many as fourteen lanes. Like the New Jersey Turnpike, the Garden State Parkway makes use of the dual-dual arrangement in the twelve-lane and fourteen-lane sections.

Unlike the New Jersey Turnpike, which keeps interchanges at a minimum, the Garden State Parkway has a total of 305 entrances and exits. Also, unlike the Turnpike, which charges tolls only at interchanges, the Parkway has eleven 35-cent barrier tolls located throughout the state along with the nineteen entrance and exit tolls. The frequency of the toll plazas, now a much criticized feature of the Parkway, was originally justified by Parkway engineers as relieving the monotony of driving (http://en.wikipedia. org/wiki/Garden_State_Parkway 2005).

All of the cash toll plazas operate under a system in which motorists who do not have the exact change may submit an envelope with the coins and mail it later. This system, however, has proved to be quite ineffective: in a typical year only about 4 percent of all envelopes were returned, translating into a loss of more than $125,000 per year (http://en.wikipedia.org/wiki/Garden_State_Parkway 2005).

In 2005, Acting Governor Richard Codey proposed selling or leasing the rights to operate the New Jersey Turnpike and Garden State Parkway to private investors in order to fill the state's $4 billion budget deficit. No estimate was given for the sale of the Garden State Parkway, but it has been estimated that the New Jersey Turnpike alone could be sold for between $10 billion and $20 billion, a potential massive windfall for the state of New Jersey (http://en.wikipedia.org/wiki/Garden_State_Parkway 2005).

The New York Thruway was authorized by the New York Sate Legislature in 1950 and opened in sections in the mid-1950s. It is the longest toll road in the United States, stretching 426 miles from Buffalo in western New York to the Bronx in New York City. It is operated by the New York State Thruway Authority, an independent public corporation that built and manages the turnpike, which finances the turnpike through toll revenue bonds, and self-liquidating by receipt of tolls, rents, and concessions (http://en.wikipedia.org/wiki/New_York_State_Thruway 2005).

For the most part, the history of turnpikes on the East Coast generally supports the hypothesis that once a toll road is built it is extremely difficult to remove tolls at a later date. An exception to this, however, is the Connecticut Turnpike, which was authorized in 1954 and completed in 1958. The $464 million in construction costs were originally covered by tolls collected from eight barrier stations along the route. In 1983, however, an accident in which a tractor-trailer collided with three cars at a toll plaza, killing seven people and injuring many more, prompted state officials to consider removing the eight toll plazas on the turnpike; the tolls were removed in 1985. The removal of the barrier tolls was made possible by a hike in the state gasoline tax (http://www.nycroads.com/roads/ct-turnpike 2005).

In addition to being a safety hazard, the tolls on the Connecticut Turnpike were criticized for many years by New York officials for another reason: the tokens used by the automatic toll machines fit easily into the token machines used the New York City subway. As a result, some people purchased Connecticut Turnpike tokens for one-fourth the cost of New York City subway tokens and used them in subways.

Florida has an extensive system of toll roads, which have provided approximately two-thirds of the new lane miles and almost all of the limited access highways built in the state in the last fifteen years (Sneath 2005). Florida's dramatic population growth in recent decades has produced enormous demands on its transportation system. One toll route, the Everglades Parkway (or "Alligator Alley") extends across the southern portion of the state, from Fort Lauderdale to Naples. A second route extends from just south of Ocala to Homestead, which is southwest of Miami. A third route extends west from the Orlando-Kissimmee area to the west coast. A fourth route extends northward from the Tampa metropolitan area to Homosassa Springs. Taken together, the Florida system is one of the largest in the country and is an important component of several metropolitan area transportation systems, including Miami-Fort Lauderdale-Palm Beach, Tampa-St. Petersburg, and Orlando-Kissimmee. Toll roads are particularly attractive in Florida because of its large tourism industry; tolls shift a significant share of the costs of the roads to nonresidents.

TOLL ROADS IN OTHER PARTS OF THE COUNTRY

Generally speaking, as we move westward from the East Coast, the proportion of states with toll roads declines considerably, at least in part because the eastern states were more likely to have sufficient population density to produce traffic congestion and the traffic volume needed to make toll roads financially viable during the pre-Interstate era. However, toll roads are a significant component of the transportation systems of a number of states beyond the East Coast.

Kansas and Oklahoma have two of the most significant toll road systems west of the Mississippi River. Oklahoma has almost 600 miles of toll routes, including 261 miles that are included in the Interstate Highway system. All of the Kansas Turnpike's mileage (approximately 240 miles), by contrast, is included in the Interstate system. Kansas initially committed to toll highways before the federal government began providing funds for building Interstates, and each state has a board of directors for overseeing its system's operation (see the Web sites for each state's turnpike for details).

A striking difference between the two states' systems, however, is that Kansas has a single route, while Oklahoma has several. The Kansas Turnpike extends from Kansas City, Kansas, to Topeka, then to Wichita, and then south to the Oklahoma border. The longest route in Oklahoma makes up most of Interstate 44 within the state and extends from the northeastern corner of the state to just north of the Oklahoma-Texas border south of Lawton (different sections of the route carry different names). A second route extends from a point on Interstate 40 southeast of Muskogee to a point on Interstate 35 just north of Perry. A third route extends from Henryetta on Interstate 40 south to Hugo, just north of the Texas border. A fourth route, the Cherokee Turnpike, makes up part of U.S. Highway 412 from just east of U.S. 69 to near the Arkansas border. A fifth route, the Chickasaw Turnpike, extends from Fitzhugh, near Ada, to near Davis. Oklahoma's relatively complex and extensive system of toll roads reflects, in part, a concern for extending expressways into portions of the state not covered by the Interstate highways, particularly into areas with major recreational facilities, institutions of higher education, or high traffic volume.

In the Appalachian region, Kentucky and West Virginia have significant but limited toll roads. Kentucky's system is somewhat larger and includes two routes. West Virginia has a single route covering 87 miles. Kentucky and West Virginia have many things in common, including a history of economic difficulty, some rugged terrain, which increases the cost of road building, and a number of neighboring states with toll road systems. Policy researchers have known for years that state governments often borrow ideas from their neighbors (Walker 1971).

Both Colorado and California have toll roads, but the systems are fairly small in comparison to the sizes of the states, especially in California. Its system was created after the adoption of federal funding for Interstate Highways and is centered in Orange County. California's venture into toll roads grew out of the combination of growing traffic congestion and the difficulty of raising additional tax revenues. As if to underscore the premise that California's toll roads are primarily local facilities, the boards of directors of its two toll agencies are made up of representatives of significant local governments in the area. The two toll road agencies reported combined revenues of approximately $200 million in Fiscal Year 2004, and additional routes are currently being considered (http://www.thetollroads.com/home/about_history.html 2005; California Department of Transportation 2004).

Like California, Colorado's recent use of toll highways has a strong local emphasis. Colorado's toll route provides a bypass around the eastern and northern sides of Denver, a metropolitan area that has grown dramatically in the last thirty years, with a corresponding increase in traffic. Denver is also the junction of three major Interstate Highway routes, which generate a substantial amount of through traffic. Officials are currently considering modest expansions in the toll system; a considerable number of routes and projects have been assessed (Colorado Department of Transportation 2005).

SOME CONCLUDING THOUGHTS

Toll roads have fared somewhat unevenly as components of the American highway system. Interest in toll roads has shifted considerably over time and varies from states with no toll roads at all to states with several hundred miles of toll routes. America's toll roads are a very small proportion of our national highway network (less than 5,000 miles out of nearly 4,000,000 miles of public roads. Bureau of the Census 2003, 691; Federal Highway Administration 2003, 1). However, toll roads are vital components of the transportation systems of a number of states and localities. Whenever tax increases are politically difficult and highway systems need additional capacity, toll roads may be a practical option for making improvements.

Tolls may also be helpful for managing traffic congestion, with higher tolls on more congested routes or during times of heavy traffic volume to encourage people to use alternate routes or public transportation or to drive during low-volume times if possible. The use of toll roads have become considerably more attractive with the development of new technologies that enable motorists to pay tolls without stopping. In addition, tolls place much of the cost of a road on the people using it; by contrast, much of the local revenue used for roads comes from general revenues (March 2005, 2).

Toll financing presents a number of possible complications, however. Some citizens complain that toll charges and motor fuel taxes force them to pay for the same road twice, a sentiment often expressed by the trucking industry (March 2005, 11). This problem may be less serious if motorists see specific benefits associated with the tolls.

A related concern is that the expectation that the tolls will be spent to maintain and/or improve the toll route can contribute to a fragmentation of a state or nation's highway system. If officials try to use the toll revenue to free up motor fuel tax revenues, which can then be spent elsewhere (Dornan and March 2005, 7–9, 12), motorists may feel that the tolls they pay are not producing sufficient improvements in the toll roads. More generally, shifting to greater reliance on toll financing is much more practical in densely populated areas with high traffic volume. Rural highways are often unable to generate enough traffic to finance a route from tolls.

Efforts to increase the role of private firms in highway systems also present several complications. As noted earlier, the U. S. Supreme Court has ruled that governments cannot use eminent domain powers to seize land that is then turned over to a private owner. A number of states have state laws with similar provisions. Consequently, many routes cannot realistically be developed for private owners, although private firms can play numerous other roles.

Local residents may be concerned if a major highway is owned or managed by "outsiders" who have no commitment to their state or community (Dornan and March 2005, 7). In a related vein, transportation decisions that benefit a private operator may not benefit other parts of the transportation system (if, for example, a private operator excluded particularly heavy trucks from its route and shifted the wear and tear generated by that traffic, with its attendant costs, to other roads).

One other concern regarding private firms involves the sharing of risks and rewards (Lockwood, Verma, and Schneider 2000, 89). Private firms, seeking to maximize profits, may try to skim off as much of the toll revenue as they can and to cut costs, which may lead to skimping on maintenance. If a private firm finds itself in financial trouble, its owners may try to obtain a bailout from governmental rescuers. The dangers, then, are that the private firm may try to obtain all of the rewards while shifting the risks to government.

With either public or private management, some observers have expressed concern that the new tolling technologies may be a threat to privacy (March 2005, 11). Some of the electronic toll systems can be adapted to tracking individual motorists, whether on or off the toll road, and cameras at toll booths can place specific individuals at specific locations at particular times. While the overwhelming majority of that information would be completely innocuous, some people are uncomfortable with the possibilities, particularly in conjunction with other threats to privacy in recent years.

NOTE

1. Our discussion will be limited to toll roads and highways and will exclude toll bridges and tunnels, largely because the latter institutions are heavily a function of localized geographic features, such as major rivers.

REFERENCES

Colorado Tolling Enterprise Traffic and Revenue Feasibility Study. 2005. Colorado Department of Transportation webdocument.

"Connecticut Turnpike: Historic Overview." 2005. http://www.nycroads.com/roads/ct-turnpike. Accessed August 2.

Dornan, Daniel, and James March. "Direct User Charges." *Public Roads* 69, no. 1 (July–Aug., 2005): 1–14.

"E-ZPass." 2005. New Jersey Department of Transportation. http://ezpass.com/static/info/omdex. shtml. Accessed August 2.

Fisher, Patrick and David Nice. 2002. "Variations in the Use of Grant Discretion: The Case of ISTEA." *Publius* 32 (1): 131–142.

"Garden State Parkway." 2005. Wikipedia. http://en.wikipedia.org/wiki/Garden_State_Parkway. Accessed July 7.

"Garden State Parkway: Historic Overview." 2005. http://www.nycroads.com/roads/garden-State. Accessed July 7.

"The History of the Pennsylvania Turnpike." 2005. The Pennsylvania Turnpike Commission. http://www.paturnpike.com/geninfo/history/history.aspx. Accessed August 2.

"Innovative Uses of Tolling." 2005. Federal Highway Administration. http://www.fhwa.dot. gov/innovativefinance/ifp/inntoll.htm.

Kansas Turnpike Web site: http:www.ksturnpike.com/history/html.

Kentucky Transportation Cabinet, Division of Toll Facilities. 2005. http:/www./transportation. ky.gov/toll/.

Kulash, Damien. 2001. "Transportation User Fees in the United States." *Transportation Quarterly* 55 (3): 33–50.

Lockwood, Stephen, Ravidra Verma, and Michael Schneider. "Public-Private Partnerships in Toll Road Development: An Overview of Global Practices." *Transportation Quarterly* 54 (Spring 2000): 77–91.

March, James. "The Future of Highway Financing." *Public Roads* 69, no. 3 (Nov.–Dec., 2005): 1–12.

"New Jersey Toll Roads Seek Violators." 1998. *Civil Engineering* 68: 8.

"New Jersey Turnpike: Historic Overview." 2005. http://www.nycroads.com/roads/nj-turnpike Accessed July 7.

"New York State Thruway." 2005. Wikepedia. http://en.wikipedia.org/wiki/New_York_State_Thruway. Accessed August 2.

Ohio Turnpike: History. 2005. http://www.ohioturnpike.org/history.html.

Oklahoma Turnpike Web site: http://www.pikepass.com/why/%20turnpikes.htm.

"Pricing." 2005. Federal Highway Administration. http://www.fhwa.dot.gov/policy/2002cpr/ pdf/ch16pdf.

Sneath, Brady. 2005. Florida's Toll Agencies. Florida Department of Transportation webdocument.

Statistical Abstract. 2003. Washington, D.C.: Bureau of the Census.

Swope, Christopher. 2005. "The Fast Lane." *Governing* 18, no. 8 (May): 24–30.

Toll Facilities in the United States. 2003. Washington, D.C.: Federal Highway Administration report FHWA-PL-03-017.

"Toll Road." 2005. Wikipedia. http://www.fact-index.com/t/to/toll_road.html. Accessed July 7.

"Toll Roads: Background and History." 2005. California Department of Transportation. http:// www.thetollroads.com/home/about_history.html.

"Toll Roads in the United States: History and Current Policy." Federal Highway Administration. 2005. http://ww.fhwa.dot.gov/ohim/tollpage/cover.htm. Accessed July 7.

Transportation Corridor Agencies: 2004 Annual Report. 2004. California Department of Transportation webdocument.

"Why Does the Interstate System Include Toll Facilities." 2005. Federal Highway Administration.http:// fhwa.dot.gov/infrastructure/tollroad.htm.

Young, David M. 2005. "Toll Roads." Encyclopedia of Chicago. http://encyclopedia.chicagohistory.org/pages/1257.html. Accessed July 7.

Part II

Transportation and Federalism

8 State Departments of Transportation: From Highway Departments to Transportation Agencies

Andrew R. Goetz

State departments of transportation (state DOTs) are responsible for the development and maintenance of state transportation systems, including air, highway, maritime, rail, and public transit modes. Each of the fifty Unted States states has such a department, although the names and functions of some of these state agencies may be somewhat different.

The state DOTs play a critical role in the nation's transportation system for several reasons. First, because of the decentralized nature of the federal system that constitutes U.S. governmental structure, states have considerable rights and powers, and jurisdiction over state affairs. For much of early U.S. history, the provision of transportation was largely the domain of the private sector, but to the extent that government became involved in infrastructure provision, it was principally at the state and local government level. Second, when the federal government spearheaded national highway programs in the twentieth century, state highway agencies were called upon to conduct the planning, construction and maintenance as part of a federal-state partnership. And third, because of this state-level orientation, most of the funding for transportation infrastructure continues to be managed by the state DOTs. Thus, the broad visions for transportation policy tend to be cast at the national level, but the specific form and shape of these policies are forged at the state, as well as local, level.

This chapter will first consider the history of state DOTs by chronicling their evolution from highway departments to intermodal agencies. A brief discussion of contemporary administrative structures at state DOTs will then be followed by a consideration of major policy issues facing state DOTs today as they confront the challenges of the intermodal era.

HISTORY OF STATE DOTS[1]

THE EARLY YEARS

Every state DOT started as a Department of Highways, typically in the late 1800s/early 1900s. Prior to that time and throughout much of United States history, the private sector was largely responsible for transportation provision, while state and local governments became involved in subsidizing the right-of-way infrastructure. Private shipping lines, railroads, canal and riverboat operators, and electric streetcar companies met much of the nation's early transportation needs until the beginning of the twentieth century. Early roads and canals were oftentimes subsidized by local and state governments on a project-by-project basis. The national government was slow to become involved in transportation provision, but did so only on certain large-scale projects such as Zane's Trace, the National Road, or the land grants to railroads to encourage westward settlement (Dilger 2003). But there was no organized federal or state department of transportation until the twentieth century.

Federal and state government involvement in transportation was instigated by the need for more and better roads. The "good roads movement" began in the late 1800s, initially spurred by three major constituencies: bicyclists (who started the movement), railroads, and farmers (Sampson, Farris, and Shrock 1990; AASHTO 1991). Both railroads and farmers desired better rural roads to facilitate agricultural goods movement to railheads, while bicyclists wanted better roads for bicycling. It is somewhat ironic that railroads and bicyclists would champion better roads, given that automobiles and trucks would quickly come to dominate the new roads and ground transportation overall to the detriment of both the railroads and bicyclists. Yet, because of this early impetus, states began to develop road networks in the 1890s, including the establishment of state aid systems and state highway departments. New Jersey was the first to establish a state highway department (in 1892), and in 1893, the federal government established the Office of Public Road Inquiry (renamed the Bureau of Public Roads [BPR] in 1918) within the Department of Agriculture. Logan Waller Page, the first director of the Office of Public Roads, drafted a model bill for creating state highway departments that many state legislatures subsequently adopted. One of its features was the promotion of an administrative structure that emphasized scientific rationality and Progressive-era technical expertise, thus rebuking machine-style politics that had become rife with graft and corruption. Accordingly, Page felt that highway engineers, not politicians, should run the state highway departments (AASHTO 1991), a practice that has persisted throughout much of the twentieth century.

The newly emerging automobile and truck industry began to serve as the major catalyst for the good roads movement by the early 1900s, and the states and federal government responded to the growing need to develop better roads. In fact, by 1915, forty-five states (out of forty-eight states, at that time) had established state aid systems for highway development and 40 states had created state highway departments (Sampson, Farris, and Shrock 1990). The first Federal Highway Aid Act was promulgated in 1916, providing $75 million based on a 50 percent federal matching formula to plan, build, and maintain highways under the direction of the state highway departments.

In order to qualify to receive federal funds, states were required to create highway departments run by engineers approved by the federal BPR. By 1917, all forty-eight states had a state highway department (Dilger 2003). The American Association of State Highway Officials (AASHO) [later renamed the American Association of State Highway and Transportation Officials (AASHTO)] was started in 1914, and became an important conduit in facilitating information exchange between the fledgling state highway departments and the BPR (AASHTO 1991). In 1922, the Highway Research Board (HRB) [later to be renamed the Transportation Research Board (TRB)] of the National Research Council was also created to encourage highway engineering research and technical information exchange.

State highway departments expanded road-building throughout the 1920s, spurred by another federal highway act and by the adoption of state gasoline taxes to help fund state highway expansion programs. The Federal Highway Aid Act of 1921 focused federal funds on a designated system of primary highways not to exceed 7 percent (later changed to 8 percent) of all state highway mileage (Sampson, Farris, and Shrock 1990). In 1919, Oregon, Colorado, and New Mexico became the first states to impose a state gasoline tax for the purpose of highway building and maintenance (AASHTO 1991). Other states quickly followed, setting a pattern of highway funding that has proven to be highly successful in generating large revenues without engendering widespread public consternation. Despite some initial resistance from the oil companies, the state gasoline tax proved to be politically palatable as most constituencies supported its use in road building and improvement efforts. Because of the rapidly increasing use of automobiles and trucks, the tax raised such substantial revenues that some political leaders began to divert some of these funds to non-highway purposes. In response, state road engineers launched vigorous campaigns to enact laws and amend state constitutions restricting the use of gasoline taxes to highway-only purposes (AASHTO 1991), a legacy that continued until the recent era of more funding flexibility.

Extensive road-building expanded in the 1930s due largely to federal New Deal funding that targeted road construction as one of numerous public works projects to provide employment for workers during the Great Depression. Decisions to build highways were increasingly based on larger social and economic considerations, as opposed to being solely traffic-based. To some degree, the federal funding from New Deal agencies such as the Public Works Administration and the Works Progress Administration to build new highways bypassed the BPR and state highway departments, much to their chagrin. Some of the funds were transferred directly to cities and towns where employment needs were the greatest, thus circumventing the federal-state process that had been established in 1916. The Federal Highway Aid Act of that year actually prohibited federal expenditures in communities with populations exceeding 2,500 (Dilger 2003), but this urban exclusion no longer applied by the 1930s. Consequently, state highway departments reluctantly began to take more interest in urban highway projects, deviating from their previously rural orientation. In response to a request from President Roosevelt to report on the feasibility of transcontinental toll road proposals, the BPR, under the leadership of chief Thomas MacDonald, issued a study *Toll Roads and Free Roads* in 1939 that became the basis for the concept of the

Interstate Highway System, and emphasized a more prominent role for state highway departments (AASHTO 1991).

Attention to highway building had to be postponed for several years due to the onset of World War II, with its attendant gas rationing and travel restrictions. But the need for an upgraded national system of highways was underscored by the demands that the military placed on road transport to move personnel and equipment to coastal embarkation points. In 1944, some transportation specialists proposed that a new highway system could be built as part of a balanced transport network directed by a new national agency in which rail, water, air carriers, and truckers would be equally represented (AASHTO 1991). But powerful trucking and farming interests preferred traditional road-building arrangements, thus precluding attempts to create an intermodal transportation agency at that time.

The Interstate Era

After the war, as business demand increased and automobile use skyrocketed, there was widespread public support to upgrade the nation's highway system. Existing roads and highways were inadequate to meet the demands of an expanding and suburbanizing population that was becoming increasingly reliant on automobiles and trucks. In the Federal-Aid Highway Act of 1944, Congress approved the concept of an Interstate Highway System based on the 1939 BPR study, but it took another twelve years before a workable financing plan could be agreed upon. The Federal-Aid Highway Act of 1956 authorized $25 billion over twelve years to begin building a 41,000-mile National System of Interstate and Defense Highways in accord with high design standards—all roads had to be multi-lane, limited-access highways for high-speed travel. The Act raised federal taxes on gasoline to create the Highway Trust Fund, and increased the federal share of highway expenditures to 90 percent of allowable costs. It also reasserted the federal-state highway partnership, thus providing state highway departments with a new *raison d'etre*: building the Interstate Highway System.

For the foreseeable future, the central mission of state highway departments would be the planning, design, and construction of Interstate highways based on traffic needs and traditional highway engineering practices. The 1956 Act emphasized highway construction above all, and did not require consideration of "non-highway" issues, such as effects on land use, economic development, social regeneration, environmental impacts, or broader transportation objectives. State highway departments were deliberately insulated from these broader concerns by federal and state highway department leaders, as well as by the trucking and road-building industries (AASHTO 1991).

Admittedly, the construction of the Interstate Highway System was a massive undertaking, and has been described as "the most ambitious public works program since the Roman Empire" (AASHTO 1991). Although state highway departments had been building roads for decades, the scale and magnitude of the Interstate system dwarfed everything that had come before. Thus, it was incumbent upon state highway departments to mobilize quickly and focus their efforts on this enormous challenge. Many state highway departments in the East and Midwest were more developed and thus better prepared for the onset of the Interstate program, while some in the South and

West took longer to ramp up (AASHTO 1991). Yet all the state highway departments were very enthusiastic about the opportunity to build highways during the Interstate era, sharing the widespread public support for highways that existed at that time.

This enthusiasm began to wane during the 1960s, as a trickle of public opposition to highway building began to grow into a flood of outrage, triggering the "freeway revolt" era. Much of the early construction of the Interstate system occurred in rural areas, where land-use conflicts were confined to access issues for farmers or businesses. When construction began to intensify in urban areas, many residents were displaced, homes were demolished, neighborhoods were split, and public opposition to highways began to grow. The 1960s also marked the beginning of a major environmental movement that led to the promulgation of the National Environmental Policy Act of 1969 requiring Environmental Impact Statements for all federal projects, including highways. Environmentalists increasingly began to see automobiles and highways as major contributors to air, noise, and water pollution, as well as voracious consumers of petroleum. Highway building began to change our landscapes, contributing to urban sprawl, consumption of open space, and encroachment into wildlife habitats. Furthermore, the highways themselves, which were supposed to relieve traffic congestion, generated additional demand that resulted in even higher levels of congestion well in excess of what state highway engineers had predicted. Many urban highways, built to accommodate traffic for a twenty-year period, became congested soon after they were completed. Even as soon as the early 1960s, there was a growing realization that highways would not be able to solve all transportation problems.

The 1962 Highway Act was the first to acknowledge that changes in standard highway operating procedures were necessary. State highway departments were required to involve local officials in a broader-based planning process that should be "continuing, cooperative, and comprehensive" (the 3-C process). Federal mandates also required that urban transportation planning should involve metropolitan planning organizations (MPOs)—voluntary associations of local governments focused on regional concerns including land use, transportation, housing, and urban development. Recognizing that a more comprehensive approach to urban transportation was necessary, federal funding for transit began with the Urban Mass Transportation Act of 1964.

Also by 1964, AASHO began to recognize that state highway departments might need to expand beyond highways and to embrace other modes of transportation, as reflected in the following passage (AASHO 1964, p. 66):

> The Association can neither close its eyes to other forms of transportation nor say smugly that it is concerned only with highways, for in some limited areas, transportation needs will require other modes, in addition to highways, and they must be planned to complement each other.
>
> The distinct possibility exists that, in the foreseeable future, some state highway departments may have their authority expanded to include other modes of transportation, in addition to highways.

Indeed, these changes were already occurring at the federal level, as the Bureau of Public Roads was merged into a newly created Federal Highway Administration (FHWA), which in turn became part of a new cabinet-level Department of Transportation

(DOT) in 1966. This Department included the Federal Railroad Administration, Federal Aviation Administration, the Coast Guard, the St. Lawrence Seaway Development Corporation, the Urban Mass Transportation Administration (which joined DOT in 1968, and later was renamed the Federal Transit Administration), and several other modal offices. Most of these administrations had already existed in different departments, so the Department of Transportation Act of 1966 sought to bring these modal administrations together under a one-department umbrella.

After the federal government created the DOT, several states changed the names of their highway departments to transportation departments. New Jersey, the first state to create a highway department, also became the first state to change its name to a department of transportation, in 1967. New York followed shortly thereafter, and by 1973, 20 states had made the change. In 1973, AASHO decided to change its name to the American Association of State Highway and Transportation Officials (AASHTO) to reflect the changing role that many, but not all, of its member departments began to adopt. Many highway departments did not immediately change their names, and a few never did. The Colorado Department of Highways did not become a department of transportation until 1991. New Mexico became the State Highway and Transportation Department in 1987 thus keeping "highway" in its name; but in 2003, it changed its name again to become simply the New Mexico Department of Transportation.[2] As of 2006, only one state, Nebraska (Nebraska Department of Roads) retains the term "highway" or "roads" in its official name.

Just from this discussion of official names, it is obvious that the transition to becoming a department of transportation has been a slow process. Some state departments have been very active in expanding their involvement to include other modes of transportation. AASHTO expanded its focus by creating several standing modal committees in 1976, and by seeking broader involvement with other modal agencies and private sector organizations (AASHTO 1990). Yet, just because their names were changed did not mean these state departments necessarily embraced the wider implications of becoming a true department of transportation. It was difficult for many highway departments to change their emphasis, given that much of the organizational structure that had developed to meet the demands of roads and the Interstate Highway System was still in place.

In fact, Interstate highway construction continued to dominate state DOT activities through the 1970s and 1980s. By 1965, just nine years after its start, the Interstate Highway System was halfway completed, with over 21,000 miles constructed. The second half of the System's construction would prove to be slower-paced and much more difficult than the first, as environmental and social concerns began to erode public support that had existed previously. State departments still saw their primary mission as completion of the Interstate program, but they encountered a tremendous amount of public and local political resistance particularly on many segments of urban highways. To many highway engineers struggling to complete the Interstate system, the change from being a highway department to a department of transportation could have been perceived as a symbolic sign of capitulation. Yet throughout the late 1960s, 1970s, and 1980s, state highway departments/DOTs continued to work to finish the Interstate system, reaching over 42,000 miles completed by 1989. In addition, these departments were responsible for numerous state roads and highways outside of the Interstate system. As new construction was being completed by the end of this period, attention was turned toward rehabilitation and maintenance of existing roads and highways, and increasingly toward other modes and non-highway activities.

By 1990, state DOTs as a whole were starting to become more involved in aviation, public transportation, rail, water, and intermodal transportation (AASHTO 1990). After airline deregulation in 1978, state DOTs were increasingly drawn into helping local authorities provide more airport capacity and air service to smaller communities. State aviation funding doubled from approximately $300 million in the late 1970s to over $600 million by 1988. Likewise, state DOTs became more involved in public transportation planning, funding, technical assistance, and in a few states, even operation of mass transit systems. As federal funding for transit declined during the 1980s, state funding increased from $1.8 billion in 1981 to $4.2 billion by 1989. The Multi-State Technical Assistance Project (MTAP) was created by fifteen states and AASHTO in the late 1980s to fund technical assistance and networking among state transit managers. By 1989, twenty states had joined the project.

Many state DOTs created rail divisions during the 1970s and 1980s to coordinate state involvement in both freight and passenger rail transportation. As the freight rail industry restructured and consolidated during this time, many rail lines were abandoned. In order to provide continued rail access to many small communities, states created and funded rail service programs. Augmented by the federal Local Rail Service Assistance (LRSA) program, states acquired 9,600 miles of rail lines and rehabilitated 13,000 miles of track that would have been abandoned. With the demise of private sector passenger rail service and the difficulties that Amtrak has faced, states have become more involved in passenger rail. States began providing financial assistance to Amtrak to operate service in those states under the "403(b) program", while a few state DOTs (e.g., California, Maryland) actually began to operate rail services directly. Furthermore, interest in high-speed rail systems prompted several states to undertake feasibility studies, though no new high-speed lines were ever built.

Economic globalization, characterized by increasing trade and passenger volumes, has placed more pressure on transportation systems to keep goods and people moving. These trends have been most evident in the maritime industry, as shipping lines and ports have struggled to keep up with ever-increasing demand. States have begun to help local coastal communities expand and improve harbor facilities to accommodate the larger post-Panamax ships and technological innovations in port operations. Perhaps the most important of these innovations has been the containerization revolution and the rise of intermodal freight movement. Increasing emphasis is being placed on the seamless transfer of containers from ships to trains to trucks, relying on an unprecedented level of coordination and cooperation among previously separate and highly competitive transportation industries. By 1990, state DOTs were just beginning to realize the implications of this revolution in transportation, but it was becoming clear that the 1990s and beyond would be greatly influenced by the intermodal concept.

THE INTERMODAL ERA

The key event that signaled the beginning of a new era in transportation was the promulgation of the landmark *Intermodal Surface Transportation Efficiency Act (ISTEA) of 1991*. It was the first major piece of federal transportation legislation that used the term "intermodal" instead of "highway." Congress sought to change the direction of transportation policy and planning by expanding the scope beyond highways to include more attention to other modes and broader concerns such as economic progress, a cleaner environment, energy conservation, and social equity. ISTEA discouraged continued reliance on highways intended largely for single-occupancy vehicles, while encouraging the seamless movement of goods and people between modes of transportation. The legislation reflected a growing concern with sustainable development, i.e., development that meets the needs of the current generation without jeopardizing the ability of future generations to meet their needs. More emphasis was placed on developing transportation systems that would be economically and energy efficient, environmentally sound, and safe and secure.

In order to achieve these goals, Congress authorized $156 billion for the development of a comprehensive intermodal system involving highways, transit, railroads, and water transportation. It designated a 161,000-mile National Highway System (composed of Interstate and other important highways) serving major population centers, border crossings, military bases, ports, airports, and other major travel destinations as the primary network of federally-aided highways (Meyer and Miller 2001). It created the Surface Transportation Program (STP) to provide more flexibility to states and local governments in using highway funds for non-highway purposes, including public transit, bicycle and pedestrian facilities, carpool programs, and historic preservation. It explicitly tied the availability of transportation funding to environmental goals by requiring that proposed transportation projects be in conformity with air quality standards as set forth in the *Clean Air Act Amendments of 1990*. ISTEA also strengthened the influence of the larger Metropolitan Planning Organizations (MPOs) by expanding their funding and project selection authority for certain categories of federal funds.[3] Furthermore, these MPOs were given responsibility for developing long-range regional transportation plans and short-range regional transportation improvement programs in cooperation with state DOTs, regional transit agencies, and local governments.

For state DOTs, ISTEA required the planning process to focus on the development and implementation of the *intermodal* transportation system of the state, and attempted to mandate much greater cooperation with MPOs and other local planning organizations in the process of transportation planning. States were required to have a statewide transportation plan that was coordinated with the transportation plans of their metropolitan areas. Under ISTEA, the Federal Highway Administration and Federal Transit Administration issued statewide transportation planning rules that identified twenty-three factors that state plans had to consider, grouped into four major categories (Federal Highway Administration/Federal Transit Administration 1995, 1996):

I. System Performance and Preservation
1. Transportation needs (strategies and other results) identified through six management systems (pavement, bridges, safety, congestion, public transportation, and intermodal);
2. Transportation system management and investment strategies designed to make the most efficient use of existing transportation facilities (including consideration of all transportation modes);
3. Methods to reduce traffic congestion and to prevent traffic congestion from developing in areas where it does not yet occur, including methods which reduce motor vehicle travel, particularly single-occupant motor vehicle travel;
4. Preservation of rights-of-way for construction of future transportation projects;
5. Identification of corridors for which action is most needed to prevent destruction or loss (including strategies for preventing loss of rights-of-way);
6. Methods to enhance the efficient movement of commercial motor vehicles;
7. The use of life-cycle costs in the design and engineering of bridges, tunnels, or pavements;

II. Coordination and Collaboration Among Stakeholders
8. The coordination of transportation plans and programs developed for metropolitan planning areas of the state with the statewide transportation plans and programs and the reconciliation of such plans and programs as necessary to ensure connectivity within transportation systems;
9. Connectivity between metropolitan planning areas within the state and with metropolitan planning areas in other states;
10. The use of innovative mechanisms for financing projects, including value capture pricing, tolls, and congestion pricing;
11. The transportation needs of non-metropolitan areas (areas outside of MPO planning boundaries) through a process that includes consultation with elected officials with jurisdiction over transportation;
12. Investment strategies to improve adjoining state and local roads that support rural economic growth and tourism development, Federal agency renewable resources management, and multipurpose land management practices, including recreation development;
13. The concerns of Indian tribal governments having jurisdiction over lands within the boundaries of the state;

III. Mobility and Access for People and Goods
14. International border crossings and access to ports, airports, intermodal transportation facilities, major freight distribution routes, national parks, recreation and scenic areas, monuments and historic sites, and military installations;
15. Long-range needs of the state transportation system for movement of persons and goods;

16. Methods to expand and enhance appropriate transit services and to increase the use of such services (including commuter rail);

IV. Environment and Quality of Life

17. Federal, state, or local energy use goals, objectives, programs, or requirements;
18. Strategies for incorporating bicycle transportation facilities and pedestrian walkways in appropriate projects throughout the state;
19. Recreational travel and tourism;
20. State plans developed pursuant to the Federal Water Pollution Control Act and the Coastal Zone Management Act;
21. The overall, social, economic, energy, and environmental effects of transportation decisions (including housing and community development effects on the human, natural, and man-made environments);
22. The effect of transportation decisions on land use and land development, including the need for consistency between transportation decision-making and the provisions of all applicable short-range and long-range land use and development plans (analyses should include projections of economic, demographic, environmental protection, growth management, and land use activities consistent with development goals and transportation demand projections);
23. Strategies for identifying and implementing transportation enhancements where appropriate throughout the state;

The first factor required state DOTs to develop, establish, and implement six management systems for the purpose of providing planners with system-wide data and information to improve planning and decision making. This systematic approach contrasted with the project-by-project approach traditionally used within state DOTs (Lindquist 1998). One of the requirements was a management system for intermodal transportation facilities and systems. According to ISTEA, a state's intermodal management system "shall provide for improvement and integration of all of a state's transportation systems and shall include methods of achieving the optimum yield from such systems, methods for increasing productivity in the state, methods for increasing the use of advanced technologies, and methods to encourage the use of innovative marketing techniques, such as just-in-time deliveries" (Dempsey 2000). In response to slow adoption and confusion over the delineation of the management systems, Congress decided as part of the National Highway System Designation Act of 1995 to make the management systems optional, with the exception of the congestion management system for some metropolitan areas. But many elements of ISTEA permanently affected policy and planning at state DOTs.

In 1998, Congress promulgated the Transportation Equity Act for the 21st Century (TEA-21), which continued the intermodal philosophy of ISTEA. TEA-21 authorized $217 billion for the nation's intermodal surface transportation system, including significant increases in funding for the Congestion Mitigation and Air Quality (CMAQ) program (35% increase) and transit (50% increase) (Dempsey, Goetz, and Larson 2000). TEA-21 tried to simplify the planning process by replacing ISTEA's twenty-three planning factors with the following seven (Goetz et al. 2004):

1. Support economic vitality by enabling global competitiveness, productivity, and efficiency;
2. Increase the safety and security of the transportation system for motorized and nonmotorized users;
3. Increase the accessibility and mobility options available to people and freight;
4. Protect and enhance the environment, promote energy conservation, and improve air quality;
5. Enhance the integration and connectivity of the transportation system, across and between modes, for people and freight;
6. Promote efficient system management and operation; and
7. Emphasize the preservation of the existing transportation system.

As its name implies, equity also became a more important concern in TEA-21. To emphasize the equity dimension of this legislation, each state was guaranteed a minimum return of 90.5 percent of the funds that each had contributed to the federal highway trust fund by way of gasoline taxes and other user fees. States that contributed more to the trust fund than they received in return (donor states) had objected to the sizeable subsidies they had been providing to those states that received more than they contributed (donee states). The donor/donee state issue was explicitly recognized as an important element in TEA-21, so that some minimum level of geographic equity among the states would be maintained.

Another equity dimension of TEA-21 involved a concern for environmental justice, first expressed in connection to federal transportation agencies as part of a presidential Executive Order, Federal Actions to Address Environmental Justice in Minority Populations and Low-Income Populations, in 1994. Environmental justice grew out of a concern for historical patterns of disproportionately adverse health and environmental impacts on minority and low-income populations from decisions regarding the locations of toxic waste facilities, incinerators, and other noxious land uses. Transportation was implicated in terms of the negative externalities from highways and other transportation facilities located in minority and low-income areas, as well as the uneven distribution of benefits from transportation provision. States, as well as MPOs, were required to address environmental justice issues as part of their long-range transportation plans and short-range transportation improvement programs.

TEA-21 also continued the public involvement emphasis of ISTEA by requiring that transit operators and freight industry representatives have an explicit role in the transportation planning process, and that opportunities for involvement by the general public (especially minority and low-income populations) should be improved and expanded (Meyer and Miller 2001; Goetz et al. 2004).

It is still too early to tell whether the Safe, Accountable, Flexible, and Efficient Transportation Equity Act—A Legacy for Users (SAFETEA-LU) of 2005 will be a significant departure from ISTEA and TEA-21. After two years of failure between the Bush administration and Congress to reach an agreement on funding levels, SAFETEA-LU authorizes a total of $286 billion over four years for surface transportation projects. This figure is far less than what Congress had initially wanted for transportation, but the Bush administration, under fiscal stress from the large outlays for the Iraq War and the general war on terrorism, insisted that transportation spending be curbed. Nevertheless, SAFETEA-LU has been characterized by the media as containing an inordinate number of earmarked "pork-barrel" projects, symbolized by the $231 million "bridge to nowhere" in Alaska (Clarren 2005). The focus on projects such as this, however, trivializes the real concerns and thus undermines support for badly needed legitimate transportation infrastructure projects that continue to go unfunded.

ADMINISTRATIVE STRUCTURE AND POLICY ENVIRONMENT OF STATE DOTS

State DOTs, similar to the federal USDOT, are part of the executive branch of government. Accordingly, the governor of each state typically appoints the director, executive director, or secretary (and other top-level executives) of the state DOT, and thus transportation policy is directed from the governor's administration. (As an illustrative example, Figure 8.1 is the organizational chart for the Colorado Department of Transportation.)

The state general assembly, or legislature, also plays an important role in formulating state transportation policy, most directly through one or more transportation

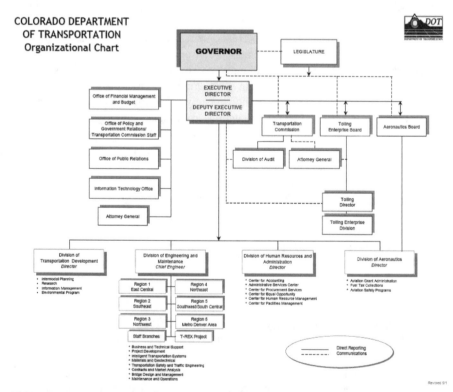

FIGURE 8.1   Organizational chart for the Colorado Department of Transportation.

committees within the legislature. The chairpersons of the transportation committees in the state senate and house can exert a large influence on policy, and the legislature overall typically is responsible for allocating funds for transportation.

In many states, the governor appoints members of a state transportation commission or board, composed of business and community leaders from different areas of the state, who serve an important role as advisors or even executors on policy and budget matters. In Colorado, for example, the powers and duties of the Transportation Commission include:

- Formulating general policy with respect to the management, construction, and maintenance of public highways and other transportation systems in the state;
- Advising and making recommendations to the Governor and the General Assembly relative to transportation policy; and
- Promulgating and adopting Transportation Department budgets and programs, including construction priorities and approval of extensions of abandonments of the state highway system. (The General Assembly appropriates the budget for the Division of Aeronautics and the administrative budget for the Department.) (Colorado Department of Transportation 2005)

The transportation commission or board may have a staff support office in the state DOT, perhaps in coordination with an office of policy and government relations.

The director, executive director, or secretary of the state DOT oversees all of the functions and divisions of the department, typically including such areas as planning, development, engineering, construction, operations, maintenance, finance, public affairs, human resources, and administration. State DOTs may also have different modal divisions, with highways, rail, ports, aeronautics, and public transit represented as separate entities or within an intermodal division.

CONTEMPORARY POLICY ISSUES AT STATE DOTS

Transportation policy for state DOTs has two components: (1) a common element that applies to all state DOTs as a group, and (2) individual state policies as an expression of executive and legislative initiatives in each state. State DOTs as a group are represented by the American Association of State Highway and Transportation Officials (AASHTO), which forges policies of common interest. But states also vary in their transportation policies, depending on historical, geographic, political, and other factors.

The general transportation policy of state DOTs, as expressed by AASHTO (1999, pp. I-1, I-2),

recognizes the connectivity, economic, social, environmental, energy, national security, and technological concerns of the nation and emphasizes intermodal transportation systems and program flexibility. . . . The national transportation system must provide adequate options, easy access, and transferability among all modes for the most timely and cost-effective movement of goods and people. . . . Programs should be structured to allow the maximum degree of flexibility in funding and program implementation possible to provide transportation services that will address connectivity, urban mobility, suburban congestion, rural access, movement of significant commodities, international trade, environmental protection, safety, and economic development and growth.

This general policy statement is in accord with the goals of the ISTEA and TEA-21 federal legislation. At this broad level, it is hard to detect policy differences between the federal and state governments. Upon closer inspection of the policy issues, differences begin to emerge in terms of how state DOT policies and practices as a group may differ from federal or local policies, and how individual state DOT policies and practices may differ from each other. There are many policy issues that currently confront state DOTs, including safety, funding, environmental impacts (air quality, noise, wetlands), land use, energy, technology, social and environmental justice, and economic development, among others. In keeping with the theme of this chapter, the following discussion will focus on contemporary policy issues in the development of the intermodal transportation system, with specific issues relevant to each of the major modes.

INTERMODALISM—PASSENGER AND FREIGHT

As early as the 1960s, state DOTs (then departments of highways) began to recognize the inevitability of an intermodal approach to policy and planning, when AASHTO (then named AASHO) declared that, "the Association can neither close its eyes to other forms of transportation nor say smugly that it is concerned only with highways" (AASHO 1964). Since that time, state DOTs have become increasingly intermodal and now have policy statements and administrative structures that explicitly recognize intermodalism.

Nevertheless, given the legacy of state DOTs as highway departments and responsible for the construction of the Interstate Highway System, there remains a strong highway orientation in state DOTs collectively and individually. State DOTs are responsible for the planning, construction, operations, and maintenance of state highway systems, which typically account for the largest share of their budgets and activities. This orientation is also not surprising considering that transportation modes that use highway and roadway systems continue to be overwhelmingly dominant in both passenger and freight transportation. Automobiles and light trucks account for nearly 90 percent of all passenger-miles traveled in both intercity and intracity trips (Bureau of Transportation Statistics 2005), while truck transportation encompasses roughly 70 percent of all freight tonnage and 80 percent of the value of U.S. shipments (Federal Highway Administration 2002). State DOTs are on the front lines in facilitating passenger and freight movement on highways and state roadways, and thus have a major task just keeping up with highway maintenance and bridge repair, let alone trying to confront capacity issues and increasing levels of congestion.

The degree to which state DOTs have become true intermodal agencies has varied depending on the geography, settlement history, politics, and leadership within each of the states. Most of the states that have been cited by previous research as examples of best practices in intermodal planning tend to have large and growing populations with relatively high population densities and a large number of metropolitan areas. The most frequently mentioned states contained in a catalog of intermodal planning case studies based on coverage in previous literature were Florida, Washington, Wisconsin, Oregon, California, and Maryland (Peyrebrune 2000). Many of these and other states with strong intermodal programs also have seaports or major freight activity. Florida, for example, has experienced very rapid population growth, has high population density, a large number of metropolitan areas, and several ports, which seem to be natural pre-conditions for a more intermodal orientation. On the other hand, geographically large, mostly rural, inland states with low population densities do not generally rate as high when it comes to intermodalism. These are natural conditions that tend to predispose some states over others in the context of a broad transportation perspective.

The geography and settlement history of many states in the West and South specifically reflect these points, although they are applicable to states in the East and Midwest as well. In a recent study assessing intermodal planning at state DOTs in seven southern and western states, Goetz et al. (2004) found geographic factors to be critical. Even though many of the southern and western states have experienced rapid population and economic growth in recent decades, with populations concentrated in the major metropolitan areas, they tend to be large states in geographic area, and thus have large rural areas whose inhabitants are often a powerful political force. Thus, inevitably, there is a fundamental tension between the major metropolitan centers that cry out for more intermodal solutions, and the rural areas throughout the state which demand improved transportation coverage. Hence a large component of funding is necessarily tied to roads and highways throughout the state. Such decisions regarding geographic resource allocations are central to the issue of the degree of progress in intermodal policy and planning at state DOTs across the nation.

Influenced by these geographic and historical realities, political factors play an obvious role in state transportation policy. Over time, there has developed a very strong highway lobby, including representatives from the motor vehicle, petroleum, rubber, and construction industries, that has steadfastly supported federal, state, and local government investment in highway and roadway systems. State DOTs, individually and as represented by AASHTO, have historically had a strong alliance with pro-highway lobbies given their longstanding highway orientation. More recently, other lobbying groups, such as the Surface Transportation Policy Project (STPP), have sought to create a more balanced transportation system, by encouraging more investment in transit and other alternative modes. As a group, state DOTs have probably been less receptive to the transit and alternative mode lobbies than either the federal or local levels, largely due to the historical, geographic, and administrative factors previously mentioned. But some state DOTs have been more receptive, and their policies and plans reflected it.

Intermodalism as an issue does not correspond directly to political affiliation, although certain tendencies are noticeable. Support for highways tends to be stronger among Republicans, while transit tends to have a stronger Democratic constituency. This is partly attributable to the rural/urban dichotomy, where more Republican rural areas rely almost exclusively on highways, while more Democratic urban areas are dependent on transit to a greater degree. Suburban areas tend to be more Republican and highway-oriented, although support for transit in suburban areas has been growing in recent years as evidenced by increasing ridership on and investment in suburban commuter rail systems. At the state level, individual transportation policy may reflect the divide between "red" Republican states and "blue" Democratic states. That said, there is a considerable degree of support for intermodalism across the political spectrum. Freight intermodalism is strongly supported by both parties, with perhaps even more support among Republicans. Intercity passenger rail has bipartisan support, with many key leaders coming from the Republican side. Support for aviation also is bipartisan.

Finally, leadership and cooperation with other transportation agencies play a large role in whether a state truly embraces an intermodal approach to policy and planning. The ISTEA legislation introduced several innovations into transportation policy and planning practices including: increasing flexibility for state and local governments to redirect highway funds to accommodate other modes and modal connections; enhancing the role of metropolitan planning organizations (MPOs) in regional transportation planning; and increasing the number and variety of stakeholders that should be involved in the transportation planning process (Goetz et al. 2004). Prior to ISTEA, state DOTs had a larger role in local and metropolitan transportation planning, as the MPOs had previously served in a more limited advisory role (Goetz, Dempsey, and Larson 2002). Since ISTEA, state DOTs had to become more collaborative organizations, especially in conjunction with MPOs and transit agencies, as well as other stakeholders. Some state DOTs have adjusted to this new reality better than others, and the success of their policy and planning programs is evidence of the effectiveness of their leadership.

The following discussion highlights specific issues in state DOT policies for each of the major modes.

Aviation

States have become more involved in aviation over the last several decades, though this mode is largely private in orientation, and typically involves the Federal Aviation Administration and local airport authorities on the government side. State aviation agencies, however, are playing a greater role in overseeing commercial passenger service, private general aviation, and air cargo activities within their states. Airline transportation is the largest commercial intercity passenger mode (based on passenger-miles), far outdistancing bus or rail. General aviation plays an important role in serving large corporations or other major businesses transporting company personnel in planes that firms either own or lease. Air cargo is important in transporting high-value, time-sensitive commodities as part of package delivery and other lighter industry movements (Goetz 2006).

After airline deregulation started in 1978 and many smaller communities and rural areas began losing major airline service, states have been concerned about service provision to these places. The intermodal landside connection between airports and the places they serve has become an increasingly important issue to states, as more people and goods are traveling farther over more congested roadways to reach commercial service airports. General aviation airports also come under state jurisdiction as a primary function of a state's smaller airports typically involves the retention and expansion of business enterprises within their service areas (Goetz 2007; Ohio Department of Transportation 1989).

Highways

Highways have been and will continue to be the "bread-and-butter" of state DOTs. The budgets of virtually every state DOT are still dominated by spending on traditional highway maintenance and construction, although some large-scale projects, such as Colorado's T-REX highway and light rail expansion, and the ambitious Trans-Texas Corridor plan, are decidedly intermodal in character (Goetz et al. 2004).

One of the major challenges facing state DOTs is how to generate enough funding to maintain and expand state highway systems. The demand for freight and passenger transportation as measured by vehicle miles of travel has been increasing faster than population growth, and projections indicate continued strong growth, especially in freight transportation. States provide over 50 percent of highway funding, while local governments and the federal government provide about a quarter of the funding each. But most states have been experiencing severe fiscal crises in recent years, and highway funding has been cut back significantly in many states. States have had to enact creative financing alternatives, including increased use of bonding backed by anticipated highway revenues, such as Grant Anticipation Revenue Vehicle (GARVEE) bonds. More states are also building new toll roads or converting existing high occupancy vehicle (HOV) lanes to high occupancy toll (HOT) lanes, in order to increase revenues to support highways. In 2002, twelve states were indexing their fuel taxes directly to the Consumer Price Index, thus helping to adjust for inflation (AASHTO 2002a). A few states have increased their gas tax, or have raised additional revenues through project-specific referenda. In virtually all states, however, highway infrastructure needs vastly outnumber available dollars.

Pipelines

An often overlooked mode, pipelines are becoming more important to state DOTs as they provide relatively inexpensive transportation of vital petroleum and natural gas resources throughout their networks. Heretofore strictly a private sector concern, states have had to consider pipeline transportation issues in terms of impacts on highway and rail modes especially in the case of pipeline disruptions, caused by natural disasters, terrorist activities, or other events. Pipeline capacity issues are a continuing concern for pipeline firms, and states may become more involved in helping to facilitate expanded pipeline infrastructure.

Public Transportation

The state role in facilitating and, in some cases, providing public transportation has grown considerably over the last two decades. In the first half of the twentieth century, mass transportation in the form of electric streetcars, subways, elevated rail lines, and bus systems, were owned and operated largely by private companies. As competition from automobiles and highways intensified after 1950, all of these operations were taken over by public sector agencies, first by city governments, and then later by regional transit departments. These agencies initially in the 1960s and 1970s relied heavily on federal funding for capital, and later, operating expenses. During the 1980s, federal funding for transit started to decline, and local, regional, and state sources of funding began to increase. By 1998, state support for transit reached $6.5 billion compared to $4.8 billion provided by the federal government (AASHTO 2000).

A particularly important multimodal policy issue is the role of state DOTs in public transportation provision, administration, and coordination. Most transit operations (bus, light rail, heavy rail, commuter rail, ferry systems, etc.) are conducted by regional or local transit agencies. Intercity bus service is provided mainly by the private sector, while intercity rail is largely the domain of Amtrak. But there are some states (e.g., Maryland, California) that now offer major statewide transit services themselves, thus their state DOTs have become transit operators and have taken on the role of transit planning directly. Other states are also considering similar large-scale expansions in the public transportation arena. Although much smaller in scope, many states currently administer rural public transportation programs. More states are providing increased funding for transit, thus necessitating a greater transit focus at the state level. Pennsylvania, for example, has a long-established program of fiscal assistance to local transit agencies (AASHTO 1990). Another role that state DOTs are increasingly being asked to play in regards to transit policy involves coordination with local/regional transit agencies and metropolitan planning organizations in the development of a transit component in the statewide transportation plan. As metropolitan and micropolitan areas continue to grow outward and coalesce with one another, the need for coordination of transit provision at the state level has become more important. Local and regional agencies' authority ends at jurisdictional boundaries, but the need for inter-regional transit coordination and perhaps new inter-regional transit service will increase and thus require the involvement of state DOTs.

Rail—Freight and Passenger

The private railroad industry dominated both freight and passenger transportation in the US from the 1850s to the 1930s. Facing competition from the trucking industry on the freight side, and automobiles and airlines on the passenger side, the rail industry declined in importance from the 1930s to the 1980s. As a result of the Rail Passenger Act of 1970, private railroads were relieved of their regulatory obligations to provide passenger service, as the federal government created the National Railroad Passenger Corporation (Amtrak) for that purpose. As a result of this and subsequent regulatory reform legislation, especially the Staggers Act of 1980, that allowed railroads more flexibility to merge and abandon unprofitable services, the freight railroad industry was able to stabilize and become more profitable over the last twenty years. Newer intermodal technologies such as containerization and double-stacking, and expanded markets in coal, grain, and intermodal freight, have also helped to generate the freight rail industry's renaissance. On the passenger side, intercity rail has languished as

Amtrak has struggled (outside of the Northeast and a few other corridors) to provide competitive service.

During the period of rail industry decline, state DOTs started to become more involved in rail issues. As private railroads abandoned passenger lines, and Amtrak rationalized its network, some state DOTs began to subsidize passenger services. As some freight rail lines were abandoned, state DOTs assisted in the acquisition and operation of local shortline and regional railroads (AASHTO 1990). State DOTs have also cooperated with the railroads and the federal government to begin eliminating many highway at-grade rail crossings, thus improving both highway and rail safety.

More recently, state DOTs have started to play a larger role in facilitating railroad infrastructure expansion as part of a number of public-private partnerships in conjunction with the railroads. In recognition that the utilization of rail transportation for both freight and passengers relieves pressure and congestion on the highway system, state DOTs have been more inclined to support rail infrastructure relocation and expansion projects. The Mid-Atlantic Rail Corridor Study brought five state DOTs (New Jersey, Pennsylvania, Maryland, Delaware, and Virginia), three railroads (Amtrak, CSX, and Norfolk Southern), and the I-95 Corridor Coalition together to identify $6.2 billion worth of improvements needed to ensure effective freight and passenger rail service over a 20 year time period (AASHTO 2002b). The Alameda Corridor Project was a major public-private partnership ($2.4 billion) involving Caltrans (California DOT), two railroads (BNSF and UPSP), the ports of Los Angeles and Long Beach, the LA Metropolitan Transportation Authority, and the federal government, to improve rail access between the ports and intermodal railyards in southern California. Other completed and planned rail improvements sponsored in part by the state DOTs can now be identified across a majority of states (AASHTO 2002b).

Furthermore, according to AASHTO (2002b), there is now an opportunity and need for states and the federal government to become even more involved in freight rail infrastructure expansion. Total domestic freight tonnage is expected to increase by 57 percent and import-export tonnage will increase by nearly 100 percent by 2020. Since the trucking industry now carries about 78 percent of domestic tonnage, it is expected that the highway system will have to carry an additional 6.6 billion tons of freight by 2020. Since the highways are already experiencing significant congestion, and the social, economic, and environmental costs of adding new highways are prohibitively high, state DOTs are wondering whether expanding the capacity of the rail system may be a more cost-effective way of increasing the capacity of the total transportation system. AASHTO (2002b) has found, "that relatively small public investments in the nation's freight railroads can be leveraged into relatively large public benefits for the nation's highway infrastructure, highway users, and freight shippers," and thus advocate increased public expenditures for this purpose. This represents a major policy departure from the highway-dominated approach of state DOTs in years past.

On the passenger side, AASHTO supports further development and investment in the intercity passenger rail system, in both higher-density corridors and longer-distance routes, to help relieve congestion on overcrowded highways and in the air transportation system, and to provide additional options in moving people. AASHTO (2002c) has made it clear that their focus here is "about intercity passenger rail, not Amtrak, although necessarily, Amtrak plays an important role in the story." Amtrak currently operates nearly all intercity passenger rail services throughout the nation, but thirteen states (California, Illinois, Maine, Michigan, Missouri, New York, North Carolina, Oklahoma, Oregon, Pennsylvania, Vermont, Washington, and Wisconsin) have contracted with Amtrak to operate additional state-supported intercity passenger rail services. Most of the state focus is on corridor services, which are typically under five hundred miles in length and are competitive with other modes on the basis of speed, frequency, and reliability. Some of the more successful corridor services include the Northeast Corridor (Boston-New York-Philadelphia-Washington) that features Amtrak's high-speed Acela trains, the California corridors (Sacramento-San Francisco-Los Angeles-San Diego), and the Pacific Northwest corridor (Eugene-Portland-Seattle-Vancouver). Furthermore, thirty-eight state DOTs are currently participating in intercity passenger rail corridor planning and development.

Water

Waterborne modes of transportation include ocean shipping and inland waterways. Ocean shipping has grown significantly in recent decades, especially in the trans-Pacific markets as import volume from China, Japan, Korea, Hong Kong, Singapore, Taiwan, and other states in East and Southeast Asia has skyrocketed. Capacity issues now face the major ports on the West Coast (Los Angeles, Long Beach, Oakland, Seattle, Tacoma, Portland) as well as intermodal linkages with inland highway and rail networks. Major East Coast ports (Boston, New York, Newark, Baltimore, Hampton Roads, Charleston) also face many of the same issues, especially concerns with intermodal transfer facilities.

Even though inland water transportation has a lower share of freight movement than either truck or rail, it still plays a significant role in moving bulk commodities efficiently at relatively low cost. The Mississippi and Ohio river systems, as well as the Great Lakes-St. Lawrence Seaway system, account for the majority of inland waterway transportation in the United States. As highway congestion and fuel costs increase, water transportation will continue to be an effective mode. One fully loaded barge carries the equivalent of fifty-eight trucks, while one tow (fifteen barges) carries the equivalent of 58 rail cars or 870 trucks (ODOT 2004). In terms of fuel use, one river barge can travel as far on a tablespoon of fuel as a train on a cup or a truck on a gallon (ODOT 2004).

State DOTs with ocean and/or inland port activities in their states have become much more involved in planning and developing infrastructure to facilitate waterborne movements, particularly on the landside. The Alameda Corridor project in California is a primary example, but several other states have engaged in major efforts to integrate port activity in their planning, such as the Washington State Freight Action Strategy (FAST) Corridor project.

CONCLUSION

State DOTs are undergoing a remarkable transformation from being solely highway departments to multimodal transportation agencies. Historically having primary responsibility for state and national highway networks, including the Interstate Highway System, state DOTs are now playing a much greater role in aviation, pipeline, public transit, rail, and water modes. The policy challenges that state DOTs face now and in the future are significant in light of growing demand for both freight and passenger transportation, and the squeeze on state budgets for infrastructure provision. It is likely that more intermodal public-private infrastructure projects, involving state DOTs, federal and local agencies, and private firms, such as the Alameda Corridor project, will be on the horizon. The importance of these projects will underscore the necessity of continuing an intermodal approach to transportation in state DOT policy.

NOTES

1. Much of this section is extracted from a National Center for Intermodal Transportation (NCIT) research project. Goetz et al. (2004) Assessing Intermodal Transportation Planning at State Departments of Transportation.
2. After New Mexico changed its name to a department of transportation, Transportation Secretary Rhonda Faught humorously began fining employees $1 every time they inadvertently said "Highway Department," in reference to the New Mexico Department of Transportation.
3. Large MPOs (representing metropolitan areas with populations greater than 200,000) were given authority to allocate Surface Transportation Program-Metro (STP-Metro) funds, and in some states, Congestion Mitigation and Air Quality (CMAQ) and Transportation Enhancement funds in "consultation" with the state DOT (Goetz, Dempsey, and Larson 2002).

BIBLIOGRAPHY

American Association of State Highway Officials (AASHO). 1964. *AASHO, The First Fifty Years, 1914–1964*. Washington, D.C.: American Association of State Highway Officials.

American Association of State Highway and Transportation Officials (AASHTO). 1990. *Moving America Into the Future: AASHTO 1914–1989*. Washington, D.C.: American Association of State Highway and Transportation Officials.

American Association of State Highway and Transportation Officials (AASHTO). 1991. *The States and the Interstates: Research on the Planning, Design and Construction of the Interstate and Defense Highway System*. Washington, D.C.: The American Association of State Highway and Transportation Officials.

American Association of State Highway and Transportation Officials (AASHTO). 1998. *The Changing State DOT*. Washington, D.C.: The American Association of State Highway and Transportation Officials.

American Association of State Highway and Transportation Officials (AASHTO). 2000. *Survey of State Involvement in Public Transportation, 1998*. A Report of the Standing Committee on Public Transportation. Washington, D.C.: The American Association of State Highway and Transportation Officials.

American Association of State Highway and Transportation Officials (AASHTO). 2002a. *Transportation: Invest in America, Bottom Line Report, 3rd Edition.* Washington, D.C.: The American Association of State Highway and Transportation Officials.

American Association of State Highway and Transportation Officials (AASHTO). 2002b. *Transportation: Invest in America, Freight-Rail Bottom Line Report.* Washington, D.C.: The American Association of State Highway and Transportation Officials.

American Association of State Highway and Transportation Officials (AASHTO). 2002c. *Intercity Passenger Rail Transportation.* Standing Committee on Rail Transportation. Washington, D.C.: The American Association of State Highway and Transportation Officials.

Arnold, Eugene D., Jr.; Patricia A. Weichmann; and Jeffrey A. Capizzano. 1999. *A Survey of Transportation Planning Practices in State Departments of Transportation.* Charlottesville, VA: Virginia Transportation Research Council.

Balloffet and Associates, Inc. 1995. *Examples of Statewide Transportation Planning Practices.* Prepared for Federal Highway Administration/Federal Transit Administration. Publication No. FHWA-PD-95-018. Conducted by Washington, D.C.: Federal Highway Administration.

Boske, Leigh B. 1998. Multimodal/Intermodal Transportation in the United States, Western Europe, and Latin America: Government Policies, Plans, and Programs. Lyndon B. Johnson School of Public Affairs, Policy Research Project Report 130. Austin, TX: University of Texas.

Boske, Leigh B. 1999. Case Studies of Multimodal/Intermodal Transportation Planning Methods, Funding Programs, and Projects. Lyndon B. Johnson School of Public Affairs, Policy Research Project Report 132. Austin, TX: University of Texas.

Clarren, Rebecca. 2005. A Bridge to Nowhere. Salon.com. August 9, 2005. (http://www.salon.com/news/feature/2005/08/09/bridges/print.html)

Colorado Department of Transportation. 2005. (http://www.dot.state.co.us).

Crain and Associates, Inc. with Pacific Consulting Group. 1996. Institutional Barriers to Intermodal Transportation Policies and Planning in Metropolitan Areas. Transit Cooperative Research Program Report 14. Transportation Research Board, National Research Council. Washington, D.C.: National Academy Press.

Dempsey, Paul Stephen. 2000. The Law of Intermodal Transportation: What It Was, What It Is, and What It Should Be. *Transportation Law Journal* Vol. 27, No. 3 (Summer): 367–417.

Dempsey, Paul Stephen; Andrew R. Goetz; and Carl Larson. 2000. *Metropolitan Planning Organizations: An Assessment of the Transportation Planning Process*, A Report to Congress, Volumes 1, 2, and 3. Denver, CO: University of Denver Intermodal Transportation Institute and National Center for Intermodal Transportation.

Dilger, Robert Jay. 2003. *American Transportation Policy.* Westport, CT: Praeger.

Federal Highway Administration. 2002. *The Freight Story: A National Perspective on Enhancing Freight Transportation.* Washington, D.C.: Federal Highway Administration, U.S. Department of Transportation.

Fontaine, Michael D. and Miller, John S. 2002. *Survey of Statewide Multimodal Transportation Planning Practices.* Charlottesville, VA: Virginia Transportation Research Council.

Goetz, Andrew R. 2007. "Transportation and Energy," in *The Geography of Ohio*, ed. A. Kieffer. Kent, OH: Kent State University Press.

Goetz, Andrew R.; Paul Stephen Dempsey; and Carl Larson. 2002. Metropolitan Planning Organizations: Findings and Recommendations for Improving Transportation Planning. *Publius: The Journal of Federalism* 32:1 (Winter): 87–105.

Goetz, Andrew R.; Joseph S. Szyliowicz; Timothy M. Vowles; and G. Stephen Taylor. 2004. *Assessing Intermodal Transportation Planning at State Departments of Transportation.* Denver: National Center for Intermodal Transportation.

ISTEA (Intermodal Surface Transportation Efficiency Act) of 1991, Conference Report, H.R. No. 102-404, 102nd Congress (Nov. 27, 1991).

Lindquist, Eric. 1998. Unintended Consequences of Policy Decisions: Whatever Happened with the Intermodal Surface Transportation Efficiency Act Management Systems? *Transportation Research Record 1617*, Paper No. 98-0470, pp. 112–117.

Lipsman, Michael A. and Walter, Clyde Kenneth. 1998. Response of State Transportation Planning Programs to the Intermodal Surface Transportation Efficiency Act of 1991. 1998 Transportation Conference Proceedings.

Martinez, Robert. 1993. "Perspective from the Office of Intermodalism," in *ISTEA and Intermodal Planning: Concept, Practice, Vision.* Special Report 240, pp. 47–54. Transportation Research Board. Washington, D.C.: National Academy Press.

Meyer, Michael D. 1999. "Statewide Multimodal Transportation Planning," pp. 339–368 in *Transportation Planning Handbook,* 2nd edition, John D. Edwards, Jr. (ed.). Washington, D.C.: Institute of Transportation Engineers.

Meyer, Michael D., and Eric J. Miller. 2001. *Urban Transportation Planning,* 2nd edition. Boston: McGraw Hill.

National Cooperative Highway Research Program (NCHRP). 2001. *Managing Change in State Departments of Transportation.* NCHRP Web Document 39 (Project SP20-24[14]). Washington, D.C.: Transportation Research Board, National Research Council.

Noerager, Kimberly and Lyons, William. 2002. *Evaluation of Statewide Long-Range Transportation Plans.* Prepared for: Office of Intermodal and Statewide Planning, Federal Highway Administration, U.S. Department of Transportation. Washington, D.C., April.

Ohio Department of Transportation [ODOT]. 1989. *Ohio Transportation Facts.* Columbus, OH: Department of Transportation, Bureau of Transportation Technical Services.

Ohio Department of Transportation [ODOT]. 2004. *ACCESS OHIO, 2004-2030 Statewide Transportation Plan.* Columbus, OH: Ohio Department of Transportation.

Peyrebrune, Henry L. 2000. Multimodal Aspects of Statewide Transportation Planning. National Cooperative Highway Research Program, Synthesis of Highway Practice 286. Transportation Research Board, National Research Council. Washington, D.C.: National Academy Press.

Sampson, Roy J.; Martin T. Farris; and David L. Shrock. 1990. *Domestic Transportation: Practice, Theory, and Policy, 6th Edition.* Boston: Houghton Mifflin Company.

Siwek, Sarah J. and Associates. 1996. *Statewide Transportation Planning Under ISTEA: A New Framework for Decisionmaking.* Prepared for Federal Highway Administration/Federal Transit Administration. Washington, D.C.: Federal Highway Administration.

Surface Transportation Policy Project. 1998. *TEA-21 User's Guide: Making the Most of the New Transportation Bill.* Washington, D.C.: Surface Transportation Policy Project.

TransManagement, Inc. 1998. *Innovative Practices for Multimodal Transportation Planning for Freight and Passengers.* National Cooperative Highway Research Program Report 404. Transportation Research Board, National Research Council. Washington, D.C.: National Academy Press.

Transportation Research Board. 1993. *ISTEA and Intermodal Planning: Concept, Practice, Vision.* Special Report 240. Washington, D.C.: National Academy Press.

Transportation Research Board. 1996. *National Conference on Intermodalism: Making the Case, Making It Happen,* New Orleans, Louisiana, December 7–9, 1994. Conference Proceedings 11. Washington, D.C.: National Academy Press.

Transportation Research Board. 1997. *Statewide Transportation Planning,* Transportation Research Circular Number 471, June. Washington, D.C.: National Academy Press.

Transportation Research Board. 2000. *Statewide Transportation Planning,* Transportation Research E-Circular Number E-C015, April. Washington, D.C.: Transportation Research Board, National Research Council.

Weiner, Edward. 1999. *Urban Transportation Planning in the United States: An Historical Overview.* Westport, CT: Praeger.

Zoller, Ted. D., and Jeffrey A. Capizzano. 1997. Evolution and Devolution: A National Perspective on the Changing Role of Metropolitan Planning Organizations in Areawide Intermodal Planning. Report No. VTRC 97-R19, Virginia Transportation Research Council.

9 State Programs to Support Passenger Rail Service

Patrick Fisher and David C. Nice

AMTRAK AND THE HISTORY OF PASSENGER RAIL IN THE UNITED STATES

Passenger rail service was the dominant mode of intercity transportation in the United States as late as the 1920s. Passenger rail travel in passenger miles, however, fell almost 80 percent between 1920 and 1970. At the end of World War II, there were over six thousand intercity passenger trains operating in the United States; by 1970 this number had dwindled to four hundred. In much of the country intercity passenger trains could not attract enough riders to remain economically viable (Dilger 2003). Prior to the creation of Amtrak, many private railroads allowed passenger service to deteriorate because the service lost money. On those routes, ridership usually declined sufficiently that the Interstate Commerce Commission would eventually grant the railroads permission to discontinue the operation (Oberstar 2001). As a result, Amtrak was created by the federal government in 1971 as a means of encouraging passenger rail travel once again while relieving private railroads of the financial losses generated by passenger service.

Amtrak began its operation facing many obstacles. First, its equipment was outdated, and much of it was in poor condition. Second, track conditions were poor, especially in the Northeast. Third, critics complained that Amtrak service was inappropriately distributed across the country, although the critics differed among themselves regarding which areas had too much service and which, too little. In addition, Amtrak initially had relatively limited influence over the employees providing passenger service; they were employed by the railroad that owned the tracks on which each train operated. Finally, Amtrak was forced to tackle the fundamental problem of reversing the long-term decline in passenger train ridership (Nice 1998).

Since Amtrak was created, it has succeeded in stopping the decline in rail passenger traffic and has produced increased passenger volume most years. Between 1972 and 1991, passenger miles more than doubled. Amtrak, therefore, has been able to siphon some of the growing travel demand in the United States (Nice 1998), but Amtrak's passenger volume still ranks far below auto and air travel. Following the terrorist attacks of September 11, 2001, Amtrak saw a short-term boost in ridership. Millions of Americans, concerned about air safety, took the train instead of flying after the attacks; as a result, Amtrak ridership for 2001 was the highest in its history. Amtrak was hailed by many for its performance during the crisis, and many suggested that train travel would once again gain in popularity. The record increase in ticket revenue after September 11, however, did not have a lasting effect on Amtrak's financial situation (Dilger 2003).

Since its creation, Amtrak has always had numerous critics inside and outside of government. Denunciation of Amtrak reached such a point that Congress created an eleven-member Amtrak Reform Council (ARC), which in 2000 issued a scathing assessment of Amtrak. The ARC criticized Amtrak for failure to anticipate delays in its new high-speed rail service in the northeast, poor labor productivity, inability to understand costs, refusal to produce a capital needs assessment, tardiness in analyzing the economics of its route system, and an unwillingness to follow a congressional directive to cooperate with the ARC (Wilner 2000). Three members of the council, however, declined to sign the report, and one of them filed a seven page dissent that critiqued many aspects of the report. Amtrak's leaders also criticized the report on a variety of grounds, including a failure to grasp some basic aspects of Amtrak's financing (Perl 2002, 207–211). Amtrak still has many supporters both inside and outside of government. And considering all the obstacles that Amtrak has faced, it can be argued that it has done a reasonably good, if not spectacular, job. As Robert Dilger (2003) states, "for nearly 30 years Amtrak's management was in a no-win situation. For most of its existence, Amtrak was evaluated by Congress and the White House as if it were a business, yet Amtrak's management was not provided the authority to act as a business."

However, America's transportation system overall faces a number of practical difficulties. The current system, with its heavy reliance on automobiles and airplanes, has an enormous appetite for oil, most of which is now imported. In addition, most of the proven oil reserves in the world are in the Middle East, a region that seems to be perennially wracked with conflict. Growing demand in world oil markets and recent hurricanes in the Gulf Coast region have helped foster dramatic increases in oil prices.

Another problem facing the U. S. transportation system is its safety record. Motor vehicle accidents, primarily involving cars, trucks, and motorcycles, kill tens of thousands of people every year and injure many more. Cars, trucks, and planes also generate considerable pollution and are increasingly subject to congestion problems in densely populated areas. Many Americans do not have access to a car, and many more cannot drive due to health problems. As the population ages, the latter group will certainly grow. Greater use of rail transportation could help to alleviate all of these problems (American Association of State Highway and Transportation Officials 2002, 7–8; Nice 1998, ch. 8; Perl 2002; Wilner 1994, 109–111), as the experience of a number of other countries clearly demonstrates (see Perl 2002, 20, 27–30).

Since Amtrak's creation, federal funding has been limited and, at times, uncertain. Amtrak's precarious political standing can be seen by the fact that despite an increase in national Amtrak ridership in recent years—twenty-five million passengers in 2004, up from twenty-one million passengers in 1998—funding has been cut—$1.22 billion in federal funding in 2004, down from $1.67 billion in 1998 (National Association of Railroad Passengers 2005a). States and local governments, however, may contribute directly or indirectly to improvements in their Amtrak service. More than one-third of all states have directly subsidized Amtrak service at some point since 1971, and several local governments have hired Amtrak to operate commuter trains. In addition, a number of states and localities have helped to finance improvements in track, train stations, railroad crossings, and other infrastructure.

REGIONAL HIGH-SPEED TRAINS

Currently the northeastern United States has the only American high-speed rail route, but the Transportation Equity Act of the 21st Century (TEA-21), passed by Congress in 1998, called for creation of more high-speed corridors. In regard to high-speed rail, American policy makers need to face two questions: Are high-speed trains desirable? And, if so, what is the means to implement the development of high-speed rail in the United States? If more high-speed trains are built in the United States, it increasingly appears that regional high-speed rail initiatives will determine the future face of high-speed rail in the United States. The success of most of those initiatives is tied to the willingness of states to work together. Unfortunately, that willingness is not consistently present in American federalism.

High-speed rail refers to a series of technologies involving trains traveling at top speeds of 90 to 300 mph (Federal Railroad Administration 2003). High-speed rail service is increasingly being considered as an alternative to automobiles and air as a mode for travel. In Europe and Japan, high-speed trains are already a common mode of transportation and have demonstrated that high-speed rail can be viable and practical. The American experience to date also demonstrates that service improvements, even of a more incremental nature, will attract more riders to passenger trains.

The lack of adequate, consistent federal funding for Amtrak has limited its ability to modernize, particularly outside the Northeast Corridor. Consequently, some proposals to improve passenger rail service envision the states taking a leading role in bringing high-speed rail service to various parts of the United States (see General Accounting Office 1999; American Association of State Highway and Transportation Officials 2002). Most of the proposed high-speed corridors cover more than one state; as a result, interstate cooperation is vital to the success of most of the corridors. The proposed routes are generally less than five hundred miles long and in heavily populated, traffic-congested areas in order to provide the most cost-effective services (see American Association of State Highway and Transportation Officials 2002, 4, 6–8, and ch. 2). The record so far presents a somewhat mixed picture, with some indications of cooperation and achievement but also with signs of practical difficulties.

Among the hopeful signs are the progress that state involvement has already made in a number of the corridors (American Association of State Highway and Transportation Officials 2002, 17–19 and ch. 6), although not all of those improvements are interstate in nature. The most substantial progress is found in California, which has spent roughly $1.6 billion in state funds to improve passenger rail service. The service improvements have helped to produce dramatic increases in ridership, with the number of riders on the San Joaquin Corridor increasing more than tenfold between 1974 and 2001. A significant portion of that increase is due to more frequent service and to coordinated bus service that links a number of the train stations with nearby communities.

California supports three different routes. One extends from San Diego to Los Angeles, with extensions to Santa Barbara and San Luis Obispo. A second operates primarily between San Jose and Sacramento via Oakland, and the third, the San Joaquin Corridor, links Oakland and Sacramento with Bakersfield. Overall, the state-supported corridors in California are the second, third, and fifth busiest passenger rail corridors in the United States (see the *Amtrak Fact Sheets* on Amtrak's Web site for updates).

The Pacific Northwest has another successful corridor improvement program, one which involves Oregon, Washington, and the Province of British Columbia. The program has helped finance track improvements, purchased new equipment, and subsidized train operations from Eugene, Oregon, to Portland, Seattle, and Vancouver, British Columbia. In addition, Oregon has helped develop a large network of bus service coordinated with the trains. The resulting upgrades in service helped increase passenger volume by more than 500 percent between 1992 and 2001 (see the *Amtrak Fact Sheets* 2005, on Amtrak's Web site).

The most dramatic corridor improvement program involves the Northeast Corridor, which extends from Boston to Washington, D.C., and includes the fastest passenger service in the country. This corridor, which serves a densely populated region, has received more than four billion dollars in federal funds since 1976 and $1.8 billion in state and other funds. Much of that money has been devoted to track improvements and extending electric power on the corridor to Boston. Amtrak also developed the Acela trains, which have helped increase speed along the corridor. There seems to be little doubt that many of the improvements would not have been made without a large federal contribution.

A number of northeastern states have contributed state funds for passenger service that connects with and in some cases uses the Northeast Corridor. The most recent addition extends Amtrak service from Boston to Portland, Maine, and is supported by the state of Maine. New York, which has provided financial support for a number of trains and for track improvements over the years, currently helps to finance the Adirondack, which links New York City and Montreal. Pennsylvania has funded track improvements and rail station renovations, as well as its Keystone trains between Philadelphia and Harrisburg. Several of those trains continue beyond Philadelphia to New York City. Vermont now supports two trains, one of which extends to New York City and the other, to Washington, D. C. (*Amtrak State Fact Sheets* 2005).

The most complex high-speed corridor development plan centers on Chicago, builds on some previous state improvements, and includes nine states and three thousand miles of routes. Current plans envision two levels of service, with high-speed trains on the lines with highest traffic potential and more conventional service on the other routes. The corridor may eventually be extended to reach New York, Pennsylvania, and Canada (see American Association of State Highway and Transportation Officials 2002; Wisconsin Department of Transportation 2000).

A number of improvements have already been made on several of the Midwest corridors, including Chicago-Detroit, Chicago-Milwaukee, and Chicago-St. Louis. Passenger volume on the Chicago-Milwaukee corridor, which has been assisted by the states of Illinois and Wisconsin, rose by more than 30 percent between 1996 and

2001. The state of Michigan helped to finance the development of a new, high-tech train control system that uses satellites to monitor the location of trains on the Chicago-Detroit corridor, help maintain a safe distance between trains and safe train speeds, and monitor grade crossing equipment to make certain that it is functioning properly. The new system allows passenger trains to operate safely at higher speeds (Michigan Department of Transportation 2002).

THE INTERSTATE CORRIDOR PROPOSALS

The implementation of high-speed rail in the United States has revolved around the concept of regional corridors. Early on it was realized that if high-speed rail was going to be successfully built in the United States, the states needed to play a prominent role. In 1992 the U.S. Department of Transportation designated five high-speed rail corridors across the country, later expanded to twelve corridors. The regional corridors are a creation of state and regional initiatives and represent the potential start of a network of high-speed rail lines. Given the importance of regional corridors as a means of advancing the creation of high-speed rail in the United States, we will explore some of the proposed regional corridors in detail, with an emphasis on how the states have worked together towards the goal of building high-speed rail.

As noted above, the most complex of the high-speed corridor proposals centers on Chicago, with high-speed connections to Detroit, Cleveland, Cincinnati, St. Louis, Milwaukee-Minneapolis, Quincy, and Carbondale. Somewhat lower speed service would reach Grand Rapids, Port Huron, Kansas City, Omaha, and Green Bay. The proposed improvements in infrastructure and rolling stock would require an investment of about four billion dollars over ten years, although improvements in stations and adjacent areas would increase the total cost.

If fully implemented, the Midwest Regional Rail Initiative (MWRI) would change the face of intercity passenger rail service in the Midwest. The MWRI is the combined effort of nine midwestern state departments of transportation, which have worked since 1996 to plan and implement a three thousand-mile high-speed rail system to connect the region. With a hub located in Chicago, the system planned by the initiative would dramatically increase available service and decrease overall trip times. Under the plan, approximately 90 percent of the Midwest's population will be within one hour of a MWRI station (Midwest Regional Rail Initiative 2004).

The states included in the corridor have cooperated in developing a fairly detailed plan of the needed improvements, including timetables for completing work on the various routes (see *Midwest Regional Rail System* 2000). However, the plan assumes that the federal government will cover 80 percent of the infrastructure costs and that the states will fund purchase of the rolling stock needed for the new trains. Given the many demands on state funds and the federal budget, those funds are likely to be difficult to find in the near future. However, gradual improvements have already taken place on some of the routes, and the surges in petroleum prices during 2005 may help to stimulate interest in rail service.

The Pacific Northwest Rail Corridor is much simpler than the Midwest Corridor. The Pacific Northwest Corridor extends from Eugene, Oregon, to Vancouver, British Columbia. In addition to the two states and one province involved, Amtrak, the two railroads owning the track, commuter rail organizations, and various communities are participants. Plans for this corridor include improving track and other facilities, acquisition of additional passenger train equipment that permits higher speeds on curving track and permits more frequent service, and improvements in stations and in connections with other transportation systems. The total cost of the system from 1998–2018 has been estimated at just over two billion dollars, with most of the funds needed for track and facility improvements. As of 2000, none of the participants was willing to make a long-term financial commitment to make the plan a reality (*Executive Summary: Amtrak Cascades Plan* 2000), although a number of improvements have already been made.

The most expensive corridor improvement plans, with investment needs of more than eight billion dollars, are in California (American Association of State Highway and Transportation Officials 2002, 56, 112–130). The plans include several corridors and four possible extensions. The first is the Capitol Corridor between Auburn and San Jose by way of Oakland. Improvements in the corridor between 1992 and 2001 helped increase ridership more than fourfold. Future plans call for increasing speeds and more frequent service; track improvements (including bridge and tunnel work) and additional rolling stock, with capital costs of just over one billion dollars. A possible extension of the corridor to Reno, Nevada, would generate additional costs.

A second California Corridor extends from San Diego to San Luis Obispo. This corridor has already benefited from substantial state, local, and private outlays for infrastructure improvement and additional rolling stock, as well as state subsidies of operations. Long-term plans call for more than $2.5 billion in infrastructure investments, including new tunnels and track realignments to permit higher speeds. Given the considerable traffic congestion in southern California, the expectation that the congestion will become worse in future years, and the dramatic increases in passenger volume in this corridor since 1973, planners expect the projected improvements will triple annual ridership by 2018.

The third California Corridor extends from Bakersfield in the south to Oakland and Sacramento. In spite of the fact that the southern terminal of the line is a comparatively small community (relative to Los Angeles or San Diego), ridership on this corridor has risen dramatically over the years, in part due to major state investment in infrastructure and in part due to the development of an extensive system of feeder buses that bring eighteen million people within the reach of the system. Additional infrastructure improvements, higher train speeds, and more frequent service are expected to increase ridership by nearly 300 percent by 2018. California officials are also discussing the possibility of extending that service to Los Angeles, but that would require construction of a new rail line from Bakersfield to Los Angeles, a project that would be fairly expensive.

The California Coast Corridor extends from San Francisco to Los Angeles; much of the route is used by Amtrak's Coast Starlight. State-supported improvements on this corridor have been very limited so far, except for the southern portion that is also part of the San Diego to San Luis Obispo Corridor. Substantial investment in infrastructure, primarily for track and signal improvements, and additional rolling stock to permit more frequent service are expected to produce significant increases in passenger volume. However, ridership on this corridor is expected to lag behind the others in California, in large measure due to competition from the airlines.

The Southeast Corridor demonstrates some of the most important interstate cooperation among states in the pursuit of high-speed rail. Virginia, North Carolina, South Carolina and Georgia have joined together to form a four-state coalition to plan, develop and implement the Southeast Corridor. In 2000, the governors from the four states committed themselves towards working together for the purpose of high-speed rail in the region when they endorsed a report entitled "Southeast High Speed Rail Corridor: A Time to Act" that was developed by the four state transportation departments. According to the report, the benefits of high-speed rail include: enhanced environmental quality, energy savings, economic development from improved travel and tourism, and the reduced need for additional highway and airport construction. The support for high-speed rail by the four states could be summed up in the words of North Carolina Governor Jim Hunt, who claimed that "a significant portion of the region's economic future is riding with high-speed rail. It is critical that we act now to begin developing high-speed rail in the South" (Southeast High Speed Corridor 2000).

North Carolina and Virginia in particular have taken the lead in working together to develop a detailed vision for the Southeast Corridor and have partnered to address the future needs of high-speed rail service. In 2001, the legislatures in both states approved the creation of a twelve-member commission to evaluate the feasibility of establishing high-speed rail service in the two states, with each state appointing six members. As North Carolina Transportation Secretary Lyndo Tippett stated, "the success of high-speed rail in North Carolina depends on the success of high-speed rail in Virginia and other neighboring states; no one state can build this new system alone—all states must work together as a region" (Southeast High Speed Rail Corridor 2001).

North Carolina and Virginia have cooperated with the development of an environmental impact statement for the Charlotte-Washington high-speed rail program and coordinated forty-four public meetings held in both states to solicit comments on the program in the production of a document that examined nine alternatives. The first phase of the study—referred to as the Tier I Environmental Impact Statement (EIS)—examined the potential impacts on both natural and man-made environments along the nine possible routes. Due to public and business demands and the strong potential ridership, the two state departments of transportation included a connection to Winston-Salem that was not part of the original plan. After outlining why the recommended alternative was selected in June 2002, North Carolina and Virginia began proceeding on the next phase, Tier II, which will provide a detailed analysis on the impacts of track location, station arrangement and final design (Southeast High Speed Rail Corridor 2002). North Carolina and Virginia are also working together develop a short- and long-term equipment strategy for trains operating on the Southeast Corridor, with the goal of initiating an equipment procurement for new corridor trains (Amtrak 2003). Due in a large part to the states' ability to work together, it is expected that North Carolina and Virginia can begin obtaining necessary permits need to begin construction of the Southeast Corridor in 2005. If such a timetable were met, this would allow the Southeast Corridor to become operation by 2010.

Besides working closely with one another, the state governments of both North Carolina and Virginia have also been supporting passenger rail service through significant funding as well. Both states are putting significant investments in existing rail corridors in order to provide improved passenger rail service. Currently in the works is a plan to include a $2 billion investment that would reduce travel time to two hours between Charlotte and Raleigh, one hour and forty-five minutes between Raleigh and Richmond, and one and a half hours between Richmond and Washington (Amtrak 2003). While infrastructure improvements are the primary cost—a good share of the work would involve a series of incremental changes such as straightening curves to push existing rail speeds up to 110 mph—new train sets are also necessary: at least eight high-speed train sets would be needed for the proposed service between Washington and Charlotte (Southeast High Speed Rail Corridor 2003a; *Amtrak Fact Sheets* 2005).

If one state government stands out in its support of high-speed rail in the Southeast, it is North Carolina. The North Carolina government has been the lead state in working with the other southeastern states to develop high-speed rail service. In addition, North Carolina has worked with the Northeast Corridor states to develop a future high-speed rail network from Florida to Maine (Southeast High Speed Rail Corridor 2003b). North Carolina already supports two passenger trains, both of which connect with the Northeast Corridor.

Georgia, on the other hand, has shown less of an inclination to work with other states in the development of interstate high-speed rail and instead has focused on commuter and intercity rail in the Atlanta metropolitan area. The state is also actively pursuing a new Atlanta-Macon commuter rail service and construction of a new multimodal passenger terminal in Atlanta (Amtrak 2003).

Interest in high-speed rail in the southeast is due in part to the fact that population, traffic and air pollution are growing in the southeast at rates far in excess of the rest of the nation. Business leaders in the region have also given encouraging signals—the chambers of commerce in Virginia, North Carolina, South Carolina, and Georgia are strong advocates of high-speed rail (Amtrak 2003). Another factor benefiting high-speed rail in the region is the fact that the Southeast Corridor has been identified as economically viable. The U.S. Department of Transportation (1997) reported the Southeast Corridor could generate more revenue than any other proposed high-speed rail route in the country. The DOT estimated that the Southeast Corridor could generate $2.54 in benefits for every dollar spent to develop and operate it—making it the only proposed route to cover its operating costs from passenger revenues.

Despite strong state support for the Southeast Corridor, however, establishing a federal/state funding partnership is needed to facilitate project development. The corridor will probably need large sums of federal dollars in order to be successfully implemented. There is only so much the states can do on their own without federal financial help, even with strong political support at the state level. Certainly major improvements have to be made before high-speed passenger rail service becomes a reality in the Southeast. Between Charlotte and Atlanta, for example, the 262-mile line was entirely double tracked at one time, but only 58 percent remain doubled tracked today. As a result, current top speeds on the route are only generally between 50 and 60 mph (Georgia Rail Consultants 2004).

Another proposed high-speed passenger rail corridor in the south is the Gulf Coast High-Speed Corridor, which covers 719 miles from Houston through New Orleans to Birmingham. By being designated a high-speed corridor, the states that are part of the Gulf Coast Corridor (Alabama, Louisiana, Mississippi, and Texas) are eligible to receive federal funds, which combined with state and local funds will finance the development of high-speed rail. In fiscal year 2004, for example, a total of $1.5 million was made available by the federal government to the states of the Gulf Coast Corridor. In return for federal funding, the Gulf Coast states along the route are expected to make a commitment to work with private railroad companies and the federal government to gradually upgrade existing railroad rights-of-way, so that speed of more than ninety miles per hour can be achieved (U.S. Department of Transportation 2005).

Louisiana, Mississippi, and Alabama have a history together to obtain funding for high-speed rail. Designation of the route as the Gulf Coast Corridor follows two decades of work by these three states, which created the Southern Rapid Rail Transit Commission (SRRTC) in 1982 to analyze options for enhancing rail passenger service along the Gulf Coast. In 2001, the Commission produced a high-speed rail corridor development plan, identifying the scope, cost and benefits of proposed rail upgrades on the corridor (Amtrak 2003). The plan detailed trip times and improvements required to improve speeds and reduce congestion on the line. In 2003, the SRRTC began a preliminary engineering analysis.

Despite the development of the SRRTC, of all the proposed high-speed rail corridors, the Gulf Coast Corridor may be the one with the least amount of political support at the state government level. Currently none of the states of the Gulf Coast Corridor are investing in upgrades to existing rail corridors in order to provide improved passenger rail service (U.S. Department of Transportation 1998). Though the Louisiana DOT claims that "Louisiana has actively encouraged development and application of a full spectrum of guided ground transport technologies, ranging from upgraded conventional rail services to magnetic levitation" (Federal Railroad Administration 2003), little has been done to promote high-speed rail. Similarly, though Mississippi is assessing the environmental consequences of a new rail alignment parallel to Interstate 10 that would permit faster service (Amtrak 2003), little else is being done by the state government to advance high-speed rail. As members of the SRRTC, Louisiana and Mississippi, at least have a formal mechanism to work with other states in regards to the development of high-speed rail. This is not the case, however, with Texas. Texas is not a member of the SRRTC and has shown little inclination to coordinate efforts with other states of the Gulf Coast Corridor.

Alabama's role in the development of regional high-speed rail corridors is important because the state sits strategically in between the Gulf Coast Corridor and Southeast Corridor. The Alabama government, however, has generally been only at best a lukewarm supporter of high-speed rail. Proposals for high-speed trains from Birmingham to Atlanta, for example, have been repeatedly criticized by the state DOT as cost-prohibitive or unworkable (Nicholson 2003).

Furthermore, Alabama faces an ominous hurdle in regards to securing funding for high-speed rail. According to federal law, states must provide matching money for federal high-speed rail dollars. This may seem straightforward enough, but Alabama law prohibits the state's allotment of federal gas tax money going to anything but highway maintenance and construction. Despite efforts to release some Alabama DOT funds for rail, the state legislature has been hostile to such endeavors. Two major obstacles to securing funds for high-speed rail in Alabama are the state DOT, which through the years has shown little enthusiasm for high-speed rail, and the Alabama Roadbuilders Association, a powerful lobbying group that works aggressively to keep highway dollars going to highways (Nicholson 2003). Despite these obstacles, however, Alabama's important position in the Gulf Coast Corridor high-speed designation has encouraged Alabama leaders to hope that a strong federal commitment will help relieve some of the political problems of implementing high-speed rail at the state level.

Due to the lack of political support by the state governments, plans for high-speed trains in the Gulf Coast Corridor are in acute need for large amounts of federal dollars. It is safe to say the amount of federal funding will probably make or break high-speed rail in the region. There is fear among supporters of the Gulf Coast Corridor that the plan could fall apart if Amtrak's role in its development were eliminated or greatly curtailed. "Without Amtrak, high-speed rail is dead for the foreseeable future," claims John Smith, the mayor of Meridian, MS (Nicholson 2003). While nearly all supporters of the Gulf Coast Corridor agree that significant federal funding is necessary, not all agree that Amtrak is necessarily a prerequisite for high-speed rail in the region. For example, the Southeastern Economic Alliance, a coalition of chambers of commerce in fourteen Southern cities explicitly argues that "high-speed rail corridors should be viewed separately from national passenger rail service (Nicholson 2003). Concern for rebuilding the Gulf Coast states after the 2005 hurricanes may help to foster support for a high-speed system to boost the economy.

State political support for passenger rail is unquestionably much stronger in the northeast. The Northeast Corridor rail line between Boston, New York, and Washington, is the most successful passenger rail line in the country: two hundred million travelers use Amtrak and seven commuter rail systems over a portion of the Northeast Corridor every year (Amtrak 2003). Due in a large part to its population density, political support for passenger rail has always been strongest in the Northeast. The Northeast Corridor has by far the most railroad passengers and it was a logical place to implement the nation's first high-speed rail service.

Though high-speed trains have been highly successful elsewhere, particularly in Europe and Japan (Strohl 1993), it has only been since 2000 that high-speed trains have been operational in the United States. Amtrak's new flagship high-speed rail serve, the Washington-New York-Boston Acela Express began on December 11, 2000 and was immediately operating at two-thirds capacity or better. Originally dubbed "American Flyer" when it was initiated in 1992, the name change to Acela is supposed to reflect "acceleration" and "excellence." With the opening of the Acela train service, Americans for the first time began experiencing high-speed rail travel similar to what Europeans and the Japanese have enjoyed for decades; Acela trains can operate between Washington and New York in two hours and thirty-five minutes and New York to Boston in three hours and twenty-five minutes. Amtrak has invested substantial funds in upgraded track, new train sets, and electrification of the Boston-New York corridor in order to get high-speed rail operational in the northeast. It is estimated that Amtrak will invest more than $4 billion to implement high-speed service for the Northeast Corridor (General Accounting Office 1995).

To a large degree, high-speed rail in the Northeast Corridor has been a success. For 2003, Acela revenues were projected to exceed costs by $180 million, enabling the Northeast Corridor to generate an operating profit, setting it apart from all other passenger train lines in the United States. According to Amtrak (2003), ridership on the Acela service is growing faster than projected and Amtrak's portion of the air/rail market has grown to over 50 percent between New York and Washington and to over 30 percent between New York and Boston.

Outdated infrastructure remains a problem facing the implementation of high-speed rail in the Northeast Corridor. The peak speed for Acela trains is 150 mph on a forty-mile stretch of track. Though 150 mph is more than twice as fast as most people travel on the highway, Acela trains are still considerably slower than the fastest trains in Europe and Japan (Karow 2000). Acela trains have the potential to go faster, but their operating speed is limited by the existing tracks. Shared rights-of-way with rail freight pose another difficult hurdle for high-speed rail in the Northeast Corridor. In Europe, most high-speed lines are dedicated solely to high-speed passenger trains; slower passenger service and all freight operations are relegated to other rail lines. On the Northeast Corridor, however, hundreds of 80 mph commuter trains and 30 mph freight trains operate on the same line (Amtrak 2003).

Besides the fact that it is the only current high-speed rail in operation in the United States, the Northeast Corridor in many respects is distinct from other rail service in the United States. Although Amtrak owns about 85 percent of the right-of-way along the Northeast Corridor between Boston and Washington, it is a relatively small user of the corridor. Seven commuter railroads operate about 91 percent of the passenger trains that use the corridor each year (General Accounting Office 1995). The Northeast Corridor also stands apart from other rail service in the nation in terms of the prominent role the federal government has played—the federal government has always played a significant role in the development of the Northeast Corridor.

The Northeast Corridor may be distinct, but as the first high-speed rail in the United States it is a model for other corridors, and its profitability may make it an attractive model to follow. Amtrak sees Acela as a forerunner of its aim to establish a new-style rail system, based upon increased partnership between the public and private sectors. Though federal government involvement and aid for high-speed rail have been greater for the Northeast Corridor than elsewhere, the states themselves have played significant roles. There has been sustained state involvement in financial investment, technological innovation, and economic development. In terms of financial investment, for example, New Jersey has invested $100 million in capital in the Northeast Corridor while Massachusetts has spent $85.5 million ("Transportation Corridors" 1995).

THE MATTER OF CONNECTIONS AND SPILLOVER EFFECTS

Some analysts recommend that governments coordinate and connect regional high-speed trains to other transportation venders in order to serve passengers more efficiently and effectively. In Europe it is common place for the second hop of a "flight" to be a train, not a plane. For example, when you buy a ticket on United Flight 1021 from Washington to Lyons, your second ticket is a "code share" with French National Railways and after arriving in Paris you pick up a train right at Charles DeGaulle Airport that takes you to Lyon. If you call Air France to buy a ticket from Paris to Brussels, you are in fact buying a train ticket, not a plane ticket (RePass 2001a).

As congested airports in Europe become busier, policies have shifted to high-speed trains for trips of 3 hours or shorter (Vranich 1997). There is potential for doing this in the United States. Amtrak already has a partnership with United Airlines to enable travelers to combine rail and air travel, and Amtrak also has a more limited agreement with Icelandair. SAS Airlines have been looking into marketing U.S. East Coast cities as part of one travel package, combining flights with passenger rail. Continental Airlines has been considering the option of selling a flight's second or third leg as a train ride, and has been working with Amtrak to make that happen (RePass 2001a).

Amtrak and state and local transportation officials also recognize the value of surface transportation that is coordinated with passenger rail service. Some communities are too small to produce enough passengers to justify direct rail service, and a considerable number of American communities are not located on a rail line that is in good enough condition to support passenger rail service. When buses serve train stations at times that are convenient to rail travelers, train ridership is likely to rise and bus ridership may as well. Amtrak also connects with a number of commuter rail systems and with Canada's VIA passenger rail system.

Track improvements needed for high-speed, intercity passenger service would also produce spillover benefits for the private freight railroads and commuter trains that operate on many routes. Particularly as the railroads come under increasing pressure to deliver goods by a particular deadline in order to compete with the trucking industry, many track improvements would make timely freight delivery a good deal easier.

THE HIGH-SPEED RAIL INVESTMENT ACT

The High-Speed Rail Investment Act is a legislative proposal that would authorize Amtrak to issue $12 billion in federally subsidized bonds for intercity rail purposes. The goal of the bill is to develop high-speed rail service throughout the United States. According to James Oberstar (2001), one of the cosponsors of the bill, "by preserving our Nation's rail passenger service network through difficult times, Amtrak has set the stage for developing a national network of high-speed trains that can play a major role in relieving air and highway traffic congestion" (300). Among the supporters of the bill are the National League of Cities, which argues that increased investment in passenger rail is critical to the reduction of the road congestion and suburban sprawl (Ward 2001).

First introduced in 2000, the bill enjoyed support from the Clinton administration and many in Congress, but was not brought to a vote during final negotiations. This was in a large part due to the opposition of Senator John McCain, who chairs the Senate Commerce, Science and Transportation Committee. Although McCain supports service in congested corridors, he does not believe that a national passenger rail network can be justified. Senator McCain's home state is headquarters to two major airlines, one of which has been a vociferous critic of Amtrak.

Opponents to the High-Speed Investment Act were numerous, and among others included the American Bus Association (ABA), which feared that it would negatively affect intercity bus service. Other critics argued that the act was flawed because it would permit Amtrak to spend billions on trains that travel as slow as 40 mph (Vranich and Hudgins 2001), a prospect that seems unlikely given the express purpose of the act. To a large degree, critics of government subsidizing high-speed rail tend to do so on limited government, ideological grounds. According to the conservative Cato Institute, "the federal government does not run a national airline. The justification for a national passenger railroad has evaporated" (Vranich and Hudgins 2001). Similarly, the Heritage Foundation sees federal high-speed rail investment as a boondoggle and argues that railroads in the United States should be completely privatized (Utt 2001). The nation's freight railroads, however, have been extremely cool to the idea of letting private companies operate passenger trains on their (the freight railroads') track. Conservatives tend to be less vocal in criticizing subsidies of air and highway travel.

HIGH-SPEED TRAINS: WORTH THE COST?

To supporters, high-speed rail can move commerce more efficiently and can improve competitiveness and the standard of living in the United States (Itzkoff 1991). High-speed rail can provide travelers with a alternative to automobiles and airlines that many would welcome. High-speed rail is also supported by some as a national defense priority. From a national security standpoint, high-speed trains could add capacity to the U.S. transportation system since a nationwide high-speed rail network could help move troops and relocate populations quickly (Duffy 2001), particularly if civilian aircraft were needed for military purposes.

High-speed rail is an extremely safe means of transportation. For example, in the first thirty years of the Shinkansen high-speed rail in Japan, with enormous traffic volume, there was not a single passenger death from a train accident (Strohl 1993).

From an energy perspective, high-speed trains can potentially be justified as a means of reducing America's dependence on oil, especially oil from other countries. This benefit would be most pronounced with electrified rail service, which is more expensive to build than diesel service but does not require oil fuels for propulsion.

High-speed trains would certainly improve train service quality and thus make traveling by train more desirable. Subsidies for high-speed trains would not be inconsistent with subsidies for other modes of transportation. In the wake of September 11, 2001, Congress quickly passed a $15 billion bailout for the airline industry, much of which is still in financial difficulty. Moreover, much of the technology used in modern aviation was financed by the national government. The nation's road and highway system also benefits from many public subsidies.

The goal for passenger rail is to provide an intercity railway passenger service that is attractive and sufficiently competitive with other modes of travel (Strohl 1993).

The business traveler and the private traveler will have different perceptions arising from their purposes of travel. While time is likely to be major determinant for the business traveler, financial costs are probably more of a determinant for private travelers. High-speed rail, if offered at a reasonable cost, thus would have the potential to appeal to business travelers and non-business travelers alike, as the Northeast Corridor's experience reveals.

A criticism of Amtrak and the current passenger railroad structure in the United States is that too much effort is spent on long-distance trains and that short-distance trains are much more practical in the United States, and much more cost-effective. Long-distance trains account for a majority of Amtrak's route-miles. The justification for this is that trains are important to people who live in or are trying to reach small communities where alternative public transportation does not exist or is unaffordable and to people who cannot drive, lack access to a reliable car, or cannot fly (Capon 2001). Moreover, long-distance trains may provide the equivalent of corridor service for people taking trips of moderate length and help connecting high-speed corridors generate additional traffic volume. Proposals for regional high-speed trains, however, are only for short- to medium-distance routes and thus probably have a greater chance of being economical.

High-speed rail also fares well compared to alternative means of high-speed ground transportation, such as Magnetic Levitation (Maglev) technology. Maglev developers claim that their system can achieve higher speeds, have lower energy consumption costs, and produce less noise and vibration the high-speed trains. A study by Vukan Vuchie and Jeffrey Casello (2002), however, found that even though there is a small travel time advantage to Maglev, the benefits of high-speed rail strongly outweigh this. The German government reached similar conclusions (Perl 2002, 32–41). A significant advantage of high-speed rail is that, unlike Maglev, it is compatible with existing rail networks, significantly reducing investment costs.

Many argue, however, that high-speed rail is simply not worth the financial costs. A common criticism of many high-speed train proposals is, in fact, that they do not go fast enough. And admittedly, in comparison to passenger trains in Europe, the usage of the term "high-speed" might be a bit of a misnomer. Yet, Jean-Pierre Ruiz, executive vice president of Talgo, a company that manufactures rail equipment, including much of the rolling stock used in the Pacific Northwest Corridor, argues that "in some cases it just doesn't make sense to go 150, 170, 200 mph. For example, in the Pacific Northwest, Washington state considered building trains that would do 180 mph. If you take a look at Seattle to Portland—which is the longest distance in the corridor at 182 miles—you could build a 180 mph corridor that would require a dedicated track with all the grade crossings closed for $20 billion, most of it spent on infrastructure and very little on equipment, signaling systems, etc. And you would go to Seattle to Portland, with seven stops in between, in about 85 minutes. Or you can build a system that can go 110 mph that gets you to Portland in two-and-a-half hours. It's still more convenient than air. Am I going to take passengers from the highways? Yes, and I only spent $2.8 billion. What you're trying to be is time competitive" (Ytuarte 2002).

On some routes, air travel simply makes more sense as a means of intercity travel than passenger rail, even at high speeds. The California Department of Transportation did a study to determine the full costs of intercity travel by high-speed rail, highway, and air for one California corridor. The financial costs as well as external, social costs (accidents, congestion, pollution, and noise) were analyzed and it was found that the full cost of air transportation is significantly less than the other two modes, at least as long as fuel prices remain reasonably low. High-speed rail, however, fared favorably compared to highways; high-speed rail and highway had approximately the same full cost, with highways having higher external costs and high-speed rail having higher internal costs (Levinson et al. 1999). The advantages of air travel, however, are limited in a number of major cities now by traffic congestion, and building new, large-capacity airports is extremely expensive.

POLITICAL AND ADMINISTRATIVE ISSUES

Current corridor improvements and the regional high-speed rail proposals are based on creative federalism, with its combination of national, state, and local government participation in the effort, along with a number of private actors (Leach 1970, 15–16: Nice and Fredericksen 1995, 8). The national government's involvement is mostly channeled through Amtrak and the Federal Railroad Administration, but the proposed future improvements also assume a major infusion of federal dollars on a continuing basis (American Association of State Highway and Transportation Officials 2002, 55).

State and local governments have also helped support passenger rail service, and the proposed corridors all involve substantial, continuing state and local participation for a wide variety of purposes, from financing capital and operating costs to coordinating local transit service with passenger rail schedules. Most of the states have been relatively cautious regarding the costs of the proposed corridors, however.

Private sector involvement takes many forms. A large majority of Amtrak's routes are on privately owned railroad lines, and any significant track improvements require cooperation from those railroads. Passenger train operations must also be coordinated with freight operations on those lines. Moreover, Amtrak's rolling stock has all been built by private companies, although Amtrak employees have rebuilt some of that equipment over the years. Many of Amtrak's supplies, such as food, are also from private firms. When more separate organizations are involved in an initiative, greater effort to coordinate those actors is likely to be needed.

A comparison of the states that are part of the proposed corridors and the states that have supported Amtrak service over the years reveals considerable overlap between the two groups. All of the states that have ever subsidized Amtrak service are included in one of the proposed corridors, although the corridors also include a number of other states as well. The link between Amtrak subsidies and corridor inclusion appears to be rooted in the prospects for relatively cost-effective service. Those prospects are, in turn, related to a number of state characteristics.

Two of the most fundamental of those characteristics are the population density of the state and the total population. Population density is strongly associated with which states are included in the corridor plans (see Table 9.1). Population is also related to whether states are in a corridor program (see Table 9.2). Table 9.1 and Table 9.2 show

TABLE 9.1

State Population Density and Inclusion in High-Speed Rail Corridor

In a Corridor?	Population Density		
	Highest Density	Moderate Density	Lowest Density
YES	100% (12)	85% (23)	9% (1)
NO	0% (0)	15% (4)	91% (10)

gamma = .98
significant at the .002 level

TABLE 9.2

State Population and Inclusion in High-Speed Rail Corridor

In a Corridor?	Population			
	Largest	Moderately Large	Moderately Small	Smallest
YES	100% (15)	88% (14)	43% (6)	20% (1)
NO	0% (0)	12% (2)	57% (8)	80% (4)

gamma = .90
significant at the .002 level

that corridor states tend to be states with large populations and dense populations, both of which are helpful in making rail service more economical because they improve the odds of having an economically viable number of passengers.

SOME MAJOR DIFFICULTIES

Other than the difficulties created by the federal framework of American govern-ment, there are a number of other hurdles facing high-speed rail in the United States. Obstacles to making high-speed trains an integral part of America's transportation infrastructure include: (1) American's love affair with the car and the comparatively low price of gas, at least until recently; (2) the population sprawl of many American metropolitan areas—sprawl that reduces the efficiency of rail service; (3) the long distances between many population centers; and (4) the land use priority problems along many of the paths that might be traversed by high-speed trains on specialized track systems (Strohl 1993).

The transportation culture of the United States has hampered the development of high-speed trains. Europeans take for granted passenger rail's role as a fundamental part of their transportation system. This, however, is unquestionably not the case in the United States. As Table 9.3 demonstrates, the United States' financial support for passenger rail service ranks among the lowest in the world, although federal funding is

TABLE 9.3
Capital and Operating Support from Governments to Major National Railways (U.S. Dollars)

Country	Per Capita Rail Funding
Belgium	834.39
Switzerland	162.65
Luxembourg	160.69
France	67.66
Slovenia	46.98
Italy	46.09
Netherlands	44.36
Ireland	43.75
Sweden	39.09
Croatia	37.40
Britain	36.98
Slovakia	26.27
Norway	24.92
Spain	22.76
Hungary	21.06
Czech Republic	20.08
Germany	18.60
Romania	15.75
Yugoslavia	13.83
Estonia	7.67
Finland	5.95
China	5.21
Canada	5.09
United States	3.28
Poland	3.13
South Korea	3.11
Turkey	1.55
Portugal	1.48
Saudi Arabia	0.82
Cameroon	0.23
Algeria	0.20
Senegal	0.17
Chile	0.17
Malaysia	0.16
Taiwan	0.15

Source: National Association of Railroad Passengers, http://www.naprail.org/pc.htm. Figures for 1999.

supported by a large majority of Americans. The European experience is often praised by those supporting government subsidies for passenger rail. The American transportation culture, however, is more supportive of automobiles than trains, and public policy in the United States is skewed against passenger rail. In 2003, for example, the federal government provided $32 billion to highways (doubled in twenty years, accounting for inflation), but only $1 billion for Amtrak (cut more than a third in twenty years) (National Association of Railroad Passengers 2005b). Improved passenger rail service, which could help the country alleviate traffic, energy, and environmental problems, is less readily accepted by leaders in the United States (Dilger 2003). Critics of this position point out that developments in passenger ridership across different transportation modes are not dramatically different in the United States from Japan and a number of European countries (Perl 2002, ch. 2), a finding that suggests the American situation is not as distinctive as we tend to think.

Those who advocate a more balanced transportation system usually argue that more government funding is needed to encourage innovative transportation concepts such as high-speed rail. Opponents of a more balanced transportation system argue that such an approach is "social engineering" and that the nation's traffic congestion does not suggest policy failure. Rather, traffic congestion results from policy success (Dilger 2003). According to this free market approach, fewer people are taking passenger trains because they would rather drive and any attempt to get people to drive less is inappropriate. Bear in mind, however, that governments provide a variety of direct and indirect subsidies for road and highway transportation and air transportation, and there is little likelihood that those subsidies will end in the foreseeable future.

A lack of consistent political support negatively impacts funding for high-speed rail. As a result, high-speed rail outside the Northeast Corridor is, to a significant degree, stalled at the planning and development stages. Amtrak President George Warrington told Congress that it would potentially cost several hundred billion dollars to build a national high-speed rail system (Luberoff 2001), depending on the extent of the system, speeds, and frequency of service. Even the regional high-speed corridors that have received the most attention need investments of approximately $60 billion dollars, and a number will need operating subsidies as well (American Association of State Highway and Transportation Officials 2002, 56). To cover these costs, state officials anticipate major infusions of federal funds (American Association of State Highway and Transportation Officials 2002; Mathews 2001), which does not appear to be forthcoming at present.

Road and air transportation programs in the United States are protected by a wide array of powerful interest groups. This unquestionably works against the development of high-speed rail. The relatively low standing of trains compared to highways can be seen with the congressional passage of the Transportation Equity Act for the 21st Century (TEA 21). Passed in 1998, TEA 21 provided $218 billion over six years for transportation projects in the United States. Relatively little of that, however, was allocated to rail. The act authorized only $40 million for high-speed corridor planning and $150 million to aid in the development of improved technology. Yet, the states are increasingly allocating money to rail projects. Since 1990, demand for more passenger train service has resulted in the appropriation of hundreds of millions of dollars for rail infrastructure in several states: $250 million in Illinois, $50 million in Wisconsin, and $10 billion in California, among others (RePass 2001b). Without doubt, the future of high-speed rail in the United States is going to be determined to a large degree by the willingness of the states, as well as the federal government, to contribute to the development of regional high-speed rail networks.

At the same time, the historical record indicates that placing too much reliance on state initiatives is perilous. In the early 1980s, a proposal to build a high-speed rail line from Los Angeles International Airport to downtown Los Angeles and San Diego included the premise that private financing would be enough for the system. The proposal encountered opposition from critics who complained that predicted ridership levels were too optimistic and who feared that the private financing would prove inadequate and leave California with the financial burdens that remained. Other critics complained of the adverse environmental effects of high-speed rail going through prosperous neighborhoods and communities. Potential investors felt the project was too risky, a reaction that left the system unable to raise sufficient funds. It was, consequently, abandoned, although the state of California did proceed to support more gradual improvements in passenger rail service (Perl 2002, 151–156).

A high-speed rail proposal in Ohio met a similar fate. Reformers there pressed for a high-speed system. The Ohio proposal, unlike California's, included a state sales tax increase to finance a system capable of speeds of 150 miles per hour. Some backers of the plan hoped that it would produce economic benefits for Ohio by giving it a leading role in high-speed rail technology. Other parts of the country would then purchase products and expertise from Ohio to build their own systems. However, the plan fell victim to the recession of the early 1980s; voters turned down the tax increase by a wide margin in 1982 (Perl 2002, 158). Some supporters of rail improvements have not given up hope, but they have clearly grown more cautious.

Texas provides another example of a state effort that failed. Texas officials created an independent authority, which was to select a private firm to build and operate a high-speed rail system connecting Dallas-Fort Worth, Houston, and San Antonio. State funding, however, was limited to planning activities. The costs of building and maintaining the system would presumably be borne by the private firm. However, Southwest Airlines, which provided considerable service among those cities, filed lawsuits against the state rail authority and also threatened to terminate all of its air service to San Antonio after the mayor proposed that the city assist the rail effort. Public hearings to assess environmental impacts generated considerable criticism of the proposed service, and private investors were reluctant to commit the funds needed for the project. The effort was abandoned (Perl 2002, 161–170).

CONCLUSION

To supporters, high-speed rail can move commerce more efficiently and can improve competitiveness and the standard of living in the United States (Itzkoff 1991). High-speed rail can provide travelers with a alternative to automobiles and airlines that many would welcome. High-speed rail is also supported by some as a national defense priority. From a national security standpoint, high-speed trains could reduce the vulnerability of the U.S. transportation system since a nationwide high-speed rail network could help move troops and relocate populations quickly (Duffy 2001). High-speed rail is also an extremely safe means of transportation (Strohl 1993).

While high-speed rail has considerable support, the price tag is high. Amtrak has estimated the nationwide cost over twenty years would be $70 billion. Due to the estimated costs of implementing high-speed rail, the states are counting on the federal government to cover a large share of the costs. Thus, even though much of the initiation and planning is being done by the states, the success of high-speed rail corridor programs will depend on the availability of federal funding to support the state planning and construction work. While federal funding sources support construction and maintenance of the national highway, air and transit systems, there is no similar funding to support state efforts to implement high-speed rail service. The lack of matching federal funds has severely hampered the development of high-speed rail systems.

In regard to the federal government's role in developing high-speed rail, an important question with proposed regional high-speed rails is the degree to which Amtrak should be involved in developing new high-speed rail corridors across the country. Mayors and governors want to have the federal government help pay for the projects, but also want the resulting systems to respond to state and local governments. Amtrak has generally been responsive to state and local concerns, but some officials may eventually want to try another operator.

Traditionally, nearly all states have been limited to planning and funding activities solely within their own boundaries. This has created major headaches as states have moved to promoting high-speed rail. In this regard, Amtrak can potentially play a valuable role. Since Amtrak operates a national passenger rail system, it can provide the cross-border regional coordination that is necessary to the successful creation of new high-speed rail systems. Amtrak is also the only U.S.–based organization with experience in providing high-speed service (http://amtrak.com/about/government).

Previous experience with multistate support of passenger rail service suggests potential problems with achieving concerted action. In May of 1971, several states (Illinois, Indiana, Ohio, Pennsylvania, and New York) worked together to support extending a New York City–Buffalo train to Chicago. The service ended in January of 1972, however, because the states failed to make the promised payments to help support the service (Zimmerman 1981). In January of 1985, the Gulf Coast Limited, a state funded train serving Louisiana, Mississippi, and Alabama, ceased to operate. Although Alabama and Louisiana had approved continuing to fund the service, Mississippi did not (*Passenger Train Journal* 1985). These examples illustrate the difficulty of achieving multistate action. Thus, most of the state-funded routes over the years have been entirely or primarily within a single state and supported by only one state.

It is safe to say that the efforts of states to work together on high-speed rail have been uneven, to say the least. Efforts to achieve multistate cooperation for passenger rail improvements have utilized a variety of institutional arrangements (American Association of State Highway and Transportation Officials 2002, 52–53). For example, a number of the tasks, including planning and coordination, involved in creating the Midwest corridors are the responsibility of the Midwest Interstate Passenger Rail Compact Commission, but implementation of the planned improvements is largely the responsibility of the individual states. In the Northeast, the Coalition of Northeastern Governors has a wide range of policy interests, one of which is passenger rail service. The Coalition has tried to encourage interstate cooperation in the Northeast and worked with the federal government and private railroads to improve service. The governors tend to support a continuing flow of federal funds to support rail improvements, as well as continued state involvement. In the Southeast, Virginia and North Carolina formed the Virginia-North Carolina Interstate High-Speed Rail Commission to study the feasibility of high-speed service as part of a broader system of transportation improvements in the two states. None of these organizations has yet played a major role in financing or operating high-speed service. Whether a multistate organization could play a major role in those arenas has yet to be seen. For the time being, significant progress seems to depend on: (1) substantial support from the federal government, as has been the case for the Northeast Corridor, or (2) gradual improvements that are largely carried out by individual states, possibly as part of a broader regional plan. The state-supported improvements so far have generally involved routes that are entirely or primarily in one state. Whether two or more states would work together on costly improvements to a shared route and on a continuing basis remains to be seen.

Federalism often makes it difficult for states to coordinate planning for entities such as rail that require states to work together. Given the nature of federalism in the United States, it can be argued that the degree of cooperation among the states in the development of high-speed rail has been impressive. The states want high-speed rail and have been able to work with one another to a significant degree in this endeavor. The problem, however, remains funding. And in this regard, the states need the help of the federal government. Without significant federal funding, the ability of the states to implement a high-speed rail network is severely limited. High-speed rail is unquestionably technologically feasible. The question is weather or not it is politically feasible. In order for the high-speed rail corridors to become a reality, the federal government is going to have to play a prominent funding role.

REFERENCES

Amtrak. 2003. "Amtrak's Vision for America's High-Speed Rail Program." http://amtrak.com/about/government. Accessed July 26.

Amtrak Fact Sheets. 2005. Washington, D.C.: Amtrak (web documents).

"Amtrak's Crisis Hinders Fast Trains." 2002. Accessed February 2.

Applegate, David M. 2001. "U.S. Needs High-Speed Trains." *The Crusader* 43 (November 16).

Capon, Ross B. 2001. "Should Congress Approve the High-Speed Rail Investment Act?: Pro." *Congressional Digest* 80 (12): 308–12.

Dao, James. 2005. "Acela, Built to Be Rail's Savior, Bedevils Amtrak at Every Turn." *New York Times* April 24, 1.

Dilger, Robert. 2003. *American Transportation Policy.* Westport, CT: Praeger.

Duffy, Jim. 2001. "A National Defense Priority: High-Speed Rail." *Mass Transit* 27 (4): 6.

Executive Summary: Amtrak Cascades Plan for Washington State, 1998–2018 Update. 2000. Olympia: Washington Department of Transportation.

Federal Railroad Administration. 2003. "High Speed Ground Transportation Corridors." Accessed July 26.

General Accounting Office. 1995. "Amtrak's Northeast Corridor: Information on the Status and Cost of Needed Improvements." Accessed April 13.

Georgia Rail Consultants. 2004. *Macon-Charlotte Southeast High Speed Rail Corridor Plan.* Atlanta: Georgia Rail Consultants.

"High-Speed Rail." 2003. Federal Railroad Administration. Accessed November 5.

Intercity Passenger Rail Transportation. 2002. Washington, D.C.: American Association of State Highway and Transportation Officials).

Itzkoff, Donald. 1991. "Bob Casey: High Speed Rail's True Believer and Catalyst." *Railway Age* (August): 14.

"The Journal." 1985. *Passenger Train Journal* 16 (1): 5–7.

Karow, Julia. 2000. "Almost on Time: High-Speed Trains in the U.S." *Scientific American* (December 4).

Leach, Richard. 1970. *American Federalism.* New York: Norton.

Levinson, David, Adib Kanafani, David Gillen. 1999. "Air, High-Speed Rail, or Highway: A Cost Comparison in the California Corridor." *Transportation Quarterly* 53 (1): 123–31.

Luberoff, David. 2001. "A Ticking Timetable." *Governing* (January): 64.

Mathews, Robert A. 2001. "The Future of Passenger Transportation." *Railway Age* (January): 16.

Midwest Regional Rail Initiative. 2004. Brochure published in December.

Midwest Regional Rail System: Executive Report. 2000. Madison, WI: Wisconsin Department of Transportation.

National Association of Railroad Passengers. 2005a. "Administration Plan Would Kill, Not Reform, Amtrak Service." Press Release March 24.

———. 2005b. "National Association of Railroad Passengers Homepage." Accessed May 22.

Nice, David. 1998. *Amtrak.* Boulder, CO: Lynne Rienner.

———, and Patricia Fredericksen. 1995. *The Politics of Intergovernmental Relations*, 2nd ed. Chicago: Nelson-Hall.

Nicholson, Gilbert. 2002. "Amtrak's Woes Could Derail Potential for High-Speed Rail." *Birmingham Journal* July 8.

Obserstar, James L. 2001. "Should Congress Approve the High-Speed Rail Investment Act?: Pro." *Congressional Digest* 80 (12): 298–300.

Perl, Anthony. 2002. *New Departures.* Lexington, KY: University Press of Kentucky.

Press Release. 2002. Lansing, MI: Michigan Department of Transportation.

RePass, James P. 2001a. "Planes to Trains: Coming to America?" *Railway Age* (January): 45–51.

———. 2001b. "First the Northeast, Next...?" *Railway Age* (May): 49–51.

Southeast High Speed Rail Corridor. 2000. "Four Governors Push for High Speed Trains Through Southeast." Accessed February 29.

———. 2001. "North Carolina and Virginia form Commission to Develop High-Speed Rail." Accessed August 24.

———. 2002. "Departments Get Approval to Proceed with Next Phase of Southeast High-Speed Rail Corridor." Accessed November 6.

———. 2003a. "Draft Implementation Plan for Southeast High-Speed Rail." Accessed July 25.

———. 2003b. "Tier II Environmental Studies Begin." Accessed July 25.

Strohl, Mitchell P. 1993. *Europe's High Speed Trains.* Westport, CT: Praeger.

Surface Infrastructure: High-Speed Rail Projects in the United States. 1999. Washington, D.C.: General Accounting Office, GAO/RCED-99-44.

"Transportation Corridors: The Health of States and Regions." 1995. *Transportation Matters* 1(2) July.

"Trop Peu, Trop Tard, Trop Amtrak." 2001. *The Economist* 360 (8234): 22–23.

U.S. Department of Transportation. 1997. "High Speed Ground Transportation for America.."

———. 2005. "Gulf Coast High-Speed Corridor."

Utt, Ronald D. 2001. "Should Congress Approve the High-Speed Rail Investment Act?: Con." *Congressional Digest* 80 (12): 307–13.

Vance, James E. 1995. *The North American Railroad*. Baltimore: John Hopkins University Press.

Vranich, Joseph. 1997. *Derailed: What Went Wrong and What to Do About America's Passenger Trains*. New York: St. Martins.

———. 2001. "Should Congress Approve the High-Speed Rail Investment Act?: Con." *Congressional Digest* 80 (12): 303–07.

Vuchie, Vukan. 2002. "An Evaluation of Maglev Technology and Its Comparison with High Speed Rail." *Transportation Quarterly* 56 (2): 33–49.

Ward, Janet. 2001. "Investment in Rail is an Idea on the Right Track." *City and County* (April): 4.

Wilner, Frank. 1994. *The Amtrak Story*. Omaha: Simmons-Boardman.

———. 2000. "Amtrak Slam." *Traffic World* (January 17): 13–14.

Ytuarte, Christopher. 2002. "Taking the Initiative." *Railway Age* (May): 49–52.

Zimmerman, Karl. 1981. *Amtrak at Milepost 10*. Park Forest, IL: PTJ Publishing.

10 Metropolitan Planning Organizations and Regional Transportation Planning

James Wolf, Thomas W. Sanchez, and Mary Beth Farquahr

INTRODUCTION

Metropolitan Planning Organizations (MPOs) were established as part of the Federal-Aid Highway Act of 1962 that gave these organizations a role in regional transportation planning for metropolitan areas with populations of fifty thousand people or more. The Intermodal Surface Transportation Efficiency Act of 1991 (ISTEA) and the ensuing Transportation Efficiency Act for the 21st Century (TEA-21) extended and enhanced the responsibilities of MPOs for regional transportation planning. The 2005 reauthorized federal transportation legislation (SAFETEA-LU), although controversial at times, offered no substantive changes in how MPOs perform transportation planning. From the beginning, MPOs have played a role in transportation planning and, through legislation, continue to have an impact on regional governance. This chapter will discuss the changing role of MPOs in transportation planning. It reviews the history of MPOs, the roles that MPOs play in metropolitan transportation planning as well as approaches used by MPOs as they work with local, state, federal and non-governmental partners. This chapter also reviews the research concerning the performance of MPOs since the 1991 ISTEA legislation to the present.

METROPOLITAN PLANNING ORGANIZATIONS: ORIGINS AND ROLES IN TRANSPORTATION PLANNING

ORIGINS AND HISTORY OF MPOS

The Federal-Aid Highway Act of 1962 gave MPOs a visible role in the transportation-planning process for metropolitan areas with a population of fifty thousand or more.

Segments of this chapter were published November, 2006 from *The International Journal of Public Administration*: "Assessing Progress: The State of Metropolitan Planning Organizations under ISTEA and TEA-21" by James F. Wolf and Marybeth Farquahr. Reproduced by permission of Taylor & Francis Group, LLC, http://www.taylorandfrancis.com.

State governors were required to designate an agency or an organization to ensure that transportation projects in these metropolitan areas were part of a comprehensive, cooperative and continuing planning process: the three "Cs" of the planning process. Entities such as a state agency, a regional council of governments, a planning district, or a free-standing transportation planning organization could be designated as the state MPO. Even with the support of legislation, the role of MPOs in transportation planning was severely reduced. When funding was lost, during the 1980s, their capacity was further reduced. Frequently, these organizations became not much more than compilers of transportation projects that were identified by state departments of transportation. Some turned to entrepreneurial strategies such as contracting for completing transportation analyses for local jurisdictions to maintain their financial viability.

But in the 1990s, federal transportation legislation sought to strengthen the role of MPOs through the provision of improved authority to coordinate transportation programs within a region. Specifically, the Intermodal Surface Transportation Efficiency Act of 1991 (ISTEA) and the ensuing Transportation Efficiency Act for the 21st Century (TEA-21) reenergized the efforts of MPOs to increase the capacity of metropolitan governance. ISTEA created a new world for regional transportation, and MPOs assumed a major role in transportation planning, becoming a critical focal point for the new emphases in federal transportation policy. Transportation planners now had to consider all modes of transportation rather than the traditional modes. The clear expectation was that highway-centered transportation plans would expand their focus to include not only mass-transit, but also air, freight, bicycle, and pedestrian travel (intermodal). This new perspective involved connectivity, efficiency of linkages, integration of transportation assets, and efficiency of point-to-point travel.

In 2005, the federal transportation bill was reauthorized amidst much debate and controversy. The reauthorization process, often characterized as very contentious, involved no less than ten extensions that can be attributed to the lack of agreement over total funding levels and the formula for distributing gas tax revenues to states. Although a lengthy process, the reauthorization legislation eventually passed, and overall, the bill offers minimal substantive changes that affect MPOs, or the funding they receive, the modal foci, or their planning roles and responsibilities.

THE ROLE OF MPOs IN TRANSPORTATION PLANNING

Building on their historical transportation-planning role, MPOs (under ISTEA) had responsibility for establishing, maintaining, and improving the planning processes. Most importantly, they assumed a leadership role in the development of two plans that involved significantly expanded planning criteria in addition to their annual plan of work. The Constrained Long Range Plan (CLRP) included projects over a twenty- or twenty-five-year time frame, while the Transportation Improvement Program (TIP) was a shorter derivative of the CLRP that detailed specific projects planned for immediate implementation. The TIP covers a minimum of three years and is updated every one or two years depending on state planning rules and the needs of the region.

The CLRP consists of the region's transportation systems improvement priorities and specific plans. It includes systems level plans that may be intermodal or multimodal. These plans, ideally, should link with plans for regional land-use, economic development, and housing plans. The CLRP includes new projects as well as plans for efficient use of existing transportation resources. According to law, both the long- and short-range plans must be fiscally constrained meaning that there had to be an identification of revenue sources for projects, quite unlike many previous MPO long-range plans that often had been little more than a wish list for state and local jurisdictions.

These short- and long-range plans—originally fifteen, but later, during the ISTEA period, consolidated to seven—must address a set of criteria. The ISTEA criteria included consideration for economic vitality, safety and security, accessibility and mobility, quality of life (including environment and energy conservation), integration and connectivity, system management and operation, and preservation of existing systems. The plans must provide explicit participation opportunities for stakeholders, as well as the general public. Larger MPOs were given a measure of control over allocation of a portion of the transportation funds, while those in nonattainment air quality areas had additional constraints and special funding.

MPO STRUCTURES AND PROCESSES

MPOs vary in organizational size, structures, funding levels, and program emphasis. Local traditions for metropolitan cooperation and size of population are particularly important in understanding the differences among MPOs. Nearly one-fifth of MPOs are free-standing organizations with their own governing bodies and professional staffs. The majority of MPOs, however, are housed in other local, regional or state agencies. Nearly one-third are part of regional councils of government (COGs) or planning commissions and, the remainder are located in either city, county, or state departments of transportation (DOTs). An Association of Metropolitan Planning Organizations (AMPO) survey of member's reports that the mean population served is 1 million but the median is only slightly more than 200,000. The staff size ranged from 1 to 129 with a median size of five employees (Association of Metropolitan Planning Organizations 2004).

Many MPOs have successfully created a cadre of political leaders who can provide direction and enthusiasm for metropolitan planning, which, according to Goetz, Dempsey and Larson, is important because strong leadership among the elected members of the governing board contribute to successful MPOs (Goetz, Dempsey, and Larson 2002). Strong political leadership also facilitates collaboration among different actors and organizations and as such, builds consensus for regional solutions to shared problems.

The typical MPO governing board consists of elected leaders from member jurisdictions. These voting members are mostly appointed and consequently do not represent all metropolitan interests equally (Frug 2002). Many MPO boards effectively over-represent newly expanding suburban interests at the expense of central cities and inner suburbs. On the other hand, one might expect a time lag between increased population outside central cities and the redesignation of the MPO policy board that would adjust for the population change. And because racial and ethnic representation is implicit to geographic representation, racial and ethnic minorities continue to struggle for acceptable representation on transportation boards and commissions (Bullard 2004).

This is significant because MPO boards wield powers to adopt and endorse regional transportation plans, approve budgets, approve agreements, adopt rules, and oversee operating procedures. MPO plans, budgets, contracts, and agreements all directly impact the location and extent of transportation investment.

A detailed examination of the voting boards of fifty large MPOs in the United States found that:

1. Less than one-third of board members from urban jurisdictions represent eligible votes. A "one-area, one-vote" voting structure significantly underrepresents urban areas of large MPOs.
2. When board votes are weighted in proportion to the metropolitan population that they represent, urban votes comprise two-thirds of all board votes. Non-representative members significantly influence the balance of votes.
3. Only sixteen of the selected fifty MPOs use some type of weighted voting structure. While some MPOs employ weighting schemes to correct for geographic or demographic imbalances, few use it on a regular basis.
4. MPO boards overrepresent white constituents. Because they under-represent urbanized areas, MPO boards also under-represent racial minorities (Sanchez 2005).

Evidence suggests that imbalanced representation can influence the patterns of transportation investments made by MPOs. A recent study with a sample of twenty large MPOs found that the ratio of urban to suburban votes was correlated with the allocation of transportation funds between highway and transit modes. They found that for each additional suburban voter on an MPO board, between 1 and 7 percent fewer funds were allocated to transit in MPO budgets (Nelson et al. 2005).

Technical committees and advisory committees along with competent staffs constitute the core organizing elements for most MPOs. The technical committees advise the policy committees and board on the technical elements of transportation and a substantial part of MPO work is done by these groups as they study issues and make proposals to the policy groups. The technical committees consist of representatives from local and state professional staffs and often specialists from universities and consultant organizations. These committees are most familiar with the details of the policies and operational problems of the region.

Advisory committees also contribute to the overall MPO planning processes. The most important standing committee is the citizen advisory committees that result from specific federal requirements for citizen participation in the MPO process. There may also be a variety of other standing committees or short term special committees that deal with issues such as a bicycle/pedestrian, freight, or land-use. Most of these advisory committees regularly review MPO planning issues and usually report directly to the MPO policy boards.

The professional staffs provide administrative and technical support that enables the often large number of policy, technical, and advisory committees to do their work. These staffs include transportation planners, researchers, and technicians who work with geographical information systems (GIS), modeling, and other technical operations as well as administrative workers who provide the day to day support of MPO committees. Most MPOs augment in-house staffs by using technical, consultant, and university groups that stand ready to meet their demands for technical expertise. First, the work of the technical and policy committees needs to be coordinated. Then MPO staffs must develop the capacity to support the logistics necessary for an extensive planning process that involves many jurisdictions and nongovernmental members. The number of reports, meeting minutes, and notices that MPOs produce is extensive and, effective MPOs have been found to be those that have developed efficient, streamlined administrative processes (Gayle 2004; Goetz, Dempsey, and Larson 2002). Increasingly, MPOs recognize that their staff's require the traditional committee support capabilities as well as consensus-building competencies thereby allowing MPOs to carry out complicated planning processes in very complex institutional settings.

MPOs have also developed technical skills that bring them credibility and influence (Gayle 2004; Wolf and Farquhar 2006). One of the most essential administrative and technical capacities is the ability to take advantage of information technology, especially modeling and communication technologies. The Internet sites of most large MPOs play a key role in supporting the administrative demands of the MPO processes. As the MPOs develop transportation models, complete air quality conformity analyses, provide support for using GIS, evaluate alternatives to projects, and generate other planning scenarios, their value to the local and regional planning processes increases. These technical capacities create opportunities for MPOs to enter into more discussions concerning regional issues. For example, MPOs' transportation models attract the interest of local jurisdictions and private companies because they use the models' output in their activities. The GIS outputs are seen as particularly popular, useful, and credible.

PLANNING REQUIREMENTS AND MPOs

ISTEA and TEA-21 created planning requirements that directly affected MPO planning activities. Key to these requirements is that MPOs are required to create short range and long range plans that are fiscally constrained, involve multi-modal elements, relate transportation plans to air quality, land-use, and equity concerns as well as provide opportunities for citizen participation. Systems management and operations received increased attention, particularly in the later years of the ISTEA and TEA-21 period. Each of these elements is reviewed in this section.

CONSTRAINED FISCAL PLANNING

Under ISTEA, MPOs assumed extensive analytical and consensus-building tasks that required review of proposed projects for these plans. These projects had to include information about the sources of financing, which for many MPOs represents one of the most difficult of their new tasks (Gage and McDowell 1995). While challenging, most MPOs have been able to complete the plans and many involved in the process believe that the constrained requirement infused the regional planning process with a new level of realism and credibility (Chang and Salvucci 1996). The fiscal constraint element has forced an awareness of actual limits into the process, stimulated more scrutiny of costs and phasing of projects, promoted identification of additional revenue sources, encouraged local agencies to seek a bigger funding shares, and concentrated federal money on big projects (Bishop, Wornum, and Weiss 1997).

However, difficulties persisted throughout the ISTEA and TEA-21 period. MPOs had trouble with the requirements for ensuring that the plans were fiscally constrained, developing and documenting project selection criteria, presenting the planning documents in a format that could be easily understood by lay people and policy board members, and creating planning documents that could track status of projects over time (Advisory Commission on Intergovernmental Relations 1997). A particularly vexing task has been the struggle to create and use methodologies and procedures for project cost estimation, especially for estimating the costs and revenue for out years (U.S. Government Accounting Office 1996; Bishop, Wornum, and Weiss 1997; Gage and McDowell 1995; Mierzejewski and Marshall 1998; Wade 1998). The frequency of updating the TIP and the long range plan continues to tax MPOs' capacities. The requirement to update the TIP every three years is expensive and requires continued staff and policy maker attention. In Rothblatt and Colman's study of MPOs, they subsequently recommend that the short-term plans be extended beyond the three-year requirement (Rothblatt and Colman 2001).

INTERMODAL TRANSPORTATION

Since the early years of ISTEA, intermodal plans have constituted a central feature of MPO operations. The move away from focusing on single modes—most often highway and transit was mandated by the ISTEA and TEA-21 legislation. The MPOs began to focus on enhancing the integration of highway, transit, freight, airports, ports, bicycle, and pedestrian modalities. During the ISTEA/TEA-21 period, most large and small MPOs began to incorporate intermodal criteria in their planning efforts (U.S. Advisory Commission on Intergovernmental 1995; Lewis and Howard 1999; Wade 1998). MPOs serving the largest metropolitan areas are more likely to include intermodal elements in their project planning (Wolf and Farquhar 2006).

Highways and Transit

The principle mode for transportation has been, and continues to be highways. These projects form the major element of practically all MPO plans. In addition, most MPOs, particularly in large urban areas, include mass-transit modes such as rail and bus, and frequently, van pooling and ridesharing programs. Some of these intermodal plans are simply a compilation of the separate highway and transit activities, while others explicitly reflect the intermodal approach, that is integrating highway and mass transit plans. Large MPOs that already rely heavily on mass-transit continue looking toward expanding existing rail and bus services.

Local transit agencies were instantly affected by the ISTEA and TEA-21 planning mandates and thus are now more directly involved in MPO processes. Some funding opportunities required transit involvement in MPO processes, which was new for both MPOs and transit agencies. In the past, transit agencies could work independently with federal funding agencies but now; MPOs are required to check transit cost data much more frequently than before. This results in more involvement of MPOs and transit agencies. Since ISTEA, transit agencies have been given a more formal role in MPO policy in the form of participation on their technical boards and committees (Denbow 2004). However, these relationships are often more "of the consult and coordinate type rather than full collaborative partnerships" (Goldman and Deakin 2000).

Freight, Aviation, and Ports

Few MPOs include representatives from freight, airports, and rail on their governing boards. However, these groups often participate in MPO technical advisory committees. Partnerships between MPOs and industry groups have begun to emerge (Goldman and Deakin 2000). Participation by freight, aviation, and port operations in MPO planning activities present problems, because these modes frequently involve private organizations that do not have to participate in MPO planning processes. While many do not want to participate for business reasons, others simply do not have the structural and planning processes that would allow them to articulate with public transportation planning processes (Arnold, Weichman, and Capizzano 1999). Many MPOs have been reluctant to seek a more active role for freight because they have little experience working with this industry. Furthermore, MPOs rarely take on freight issues as priority concerns because local political officials often view freight as a political negative due to the perceived impacts of increased freight traffic. In addition, freight projects present complex financing issues and local leaders are often hesitant to take on such projects because they may be viewed as favoring particular companies (Goldman and Deakin 2000).

As MPOs move toward creating intermodal management systems, efficient movement of freight receives increased attention. A 2003 AMPO survey reported that 80 percent of respondents include freight in their long range plans, but only a third include freight in the TIP projects plans and only 16 percent have a priority list of freight projects. A key limitation was the lack of adequate data to integrate freight into their planning process (Association of Metropolitan Planning Organizations 2003). Some large MPOs, including Boston, Chicago, San Diego, and San Francisco have integrated freight into their multimodal plans. San Francisco, for example, has created a standing freight advisory council (Rothblatt and Colman 2001). The Pittsburgh, Pennsylvania MPO participates in the Southwestern Pennsylvania Freight Forum that is a venue for representatives from rail, air, trucking, and waterways to work with the freight industry to promote regional growth. Specific issues include safety and security, linking with environmental issues, commercial vehicle size and weight policies, urban goods, and congestion mitigation (Johnson 2004).

Planning for aviation facilities are included in most MPO plans for larger metropolitan areas (Lewis and Howard 1999; Wolf and Farquhar 2006). The St. Louis MPO, for example, has specific plans and annual project recommendations for its airport capital improvements, is examining a potential heliport system, and participates in a Regional Aviation Technical Advisory Committee. Yet, Rothblatt and Colman conclude that airport authorities have minimal cooperative relationships with MPOs. MPO involvement in aviation is more likely to be in the form of administrative support to an advisory committee rather than leading planning activities for large projects. They suggest that this low level of cooperation may be due to the nature of airport authority operations. They are autonomous enterprise agencies that often support improvements through debt rather than relying on federal grants and second because airports often have shorter planning time horizons than the twenty-year focus for MPOs long-term plans. As illustrated here, there are few incentives for airports to participate in MPO activities (Rothblatt and Colman 2001).

Pedestrian and Bicycles

Both pedestrian and bicycle modalities are present in practically all MPO plans and projects. Three studies found that over 90 percent of the MPOs included bicycle and pedestrian plans, while over 80 percent listed specific pedestrian and bicycle projects (Lewis and Howard 1999; Association of Metropolitan Planning Organizations 2003; Wolf and Farquhar 2006). While these two modes claim a very small amount of ISTEA/TEA-21 monies, they are incorporated into most MPO plans. Projects include technical training for engineers to create bicycle/pedestrian accommodations, walkable community workshops, planning assistance to local governments, design guidelines, and data collection activities (Association of Metropolitan Planning Organizations 2003). An AMPO 2003 survey of 140 MPOs reports that 80 percent of MPOs have some form of planning processes that formally included bicycle or pedestrian issues. But while some of these committees were more concerned with safety issues, the AMPO found that most incorporated planning efforts to expand the capacity of bicycle and pedestrian modes of transportation (Association of Metropolitan Planning Organizations 2003). The San Francisco regions MPO takes an active role in bicycle programs. It leads a Regional Bicycle Working Group that oversees plans and activities that include data collection and analysis, projects to enhance bicycle/transit connections, marketing and outreach, bike-to-work week, bicycle maps and conducts best practices training programs for local agencies. In another example, Seattle illustrates ways that MPOs focus on bicycles and pedestrians. The Bicycle Pedestrian Advisory Committee coordinates with and advises MPO Regional Council staff, policy boards, and other advisory committees on bicycle and pedestrian-related planning issues.

Linking Transportation to Related Planning Processes

The ISTEA/TEA-21 period has brought much closer MPO involvement with other related regional planning and policy issues. At times, this results from required collaboration, such as with air quality, and at other times with more permissive requirements such as in the cases of land-use, economic development, and environmental justice. MPOs have become increasingly involved in each of these three spheres as well as increased their contact with federal, regional and local agencies also working in these areas.

Environmental Air Quality

Metropolitan regions are required to track a group of air pollutants that are caused by mobile sources produced mainly by transportation modalities. These include ozone, particulate matter, carbon monoxide, nitrogen dioxide, sulfur dioxide, and lead. MPOs assess the affects of mobile sources on metropolitan air quality and must demonstrate conformance with the federal National Ambient Air Quality Standards. Through a system of regional monitoring of air quality samples, metropolitan areas will be designated as to whether or not they meet air quality standards. They must also demonstrate that any new project will not exacerbate the air quality in the region. Those failing to meet standards are designated as non-attainment areas. Most large MPOs experience significant difficulty integrating the air quality requirements of the Clean Air Act into the ISTEA planning processes. While those with air quality problems receive more funding, they face serious constraints when new projects are introduced, because they can't "bust" the air quality emission budget. For many MPOs in this situation, a substantial amount of its planning effort goes to finding ways to conform to the region's air quality plan (Goldman and Deakin 2000; Howitt and Moore 1999; Mierzejewski and Marshall 1998; Rothblatt and Colman 2001; Wade 1998).

MPOs must work with the regional and state air quality agencies to ensure that the transportation plans are in conformity with the air quality improvement plans. The relationship between these state and regional air agencies with MPO planning processes is often reactive. In the first ten years of the ISTEA/TEA-21 era, air agencies possessed limited capability in transportation demand modeling, and seemed politically wary of challenging transportation agencies. At the same time, many MPOs in non-attainment areas believed they lacked a meaningful voice in the state air quality implementation plans developed by state air quality agencies (Goldman and Deakin 2000). The cooperation that does exist, manifests itself at the technical committee level. Goldman and Deakin's study concludes that conformity standards is mostly considered an afterthought by MPOs and therefore, success is largely limited to technical, not policy, issues (Goldman and Deakin 2000). At the same time however, Howett and Moore find that MPOs are becoming more active in regional air quality issues, which is a major change in both air quality and transportation planning. While far from smooth, the relationship between air quality regulatory processes and transportation planning "… have become more closely linked than ever before" (Howitt and Moore 1999).

Land-Use and Transportation Planning

Few MPOs have any direct role in land-use. Nevertheless, MPOs do have indirect influence in local land-use decisions through their ability to influence the location of new transportation facilities, but only a limited number of MPOs explicitly recognize their ability to influence land-use decisions (Rothblatt and Colman 2001). Reports on the degree of cooperation between MPOs and local planning and zoning agencies are mixed. One study concludes that most local land-use agencies were not interested in working with MPOs. While this reluctance is beginning to abate, this study reports that MPOs have not had an easy time becoming a significant actor in local land-use decisions (Goldman and Deakin 2000). MPOs with serious air quality problems were more likely to consider land-use issues in their transportation planning (U.S. General Accounting Office 2002). Two-thirds of MPOs serving large metropolitan areas incorporate some elements of transportation and land-use issues into their planning processes. Nearly one-third of the large MPOs report making widespread and comprehensive attempts to join transportation and land-use aspects and a similar number adopted substantial individual activities that link transportation and land-use even though these activities may not be part of a comprehensive approach. These larger MPOs are most likely to participate in land-use and transportation discussions, because of their problems in meeting air quality standards most likely due to traffic congestion issues (Wolf and Farquhar 2006).

One approach used by MPOs to join land-use planning to transportation involves combining different kinds of planning and visioning forums. The Olympia, Washington, area MPO, for example, sponsored a conference on land-use and transportation. The event brought together policy makers and professionals to explore specific ways to join the two issues in local and regional planning processes. The Los Angeles MPO sponsored a series of visioning activities in the Los Angeles area that included developing different scenarios of land-use and transportation, educational materials and visioning events throughout the region (Wilbur Smith Associates 2004). Other MPOs have taken a more direct approach to linking transportation projects to land-use. One MPO in the northeast combined land-use sensitive projects with a major bridge construction project. It planned a commuter rail component on the bridge and led a drive to change local zoning to allow for intensive development along the rail stations (Wolf and Farquhar 2006).

Economic Development

Economic development efforts represent another potential area for coordination with MPO transportation planning. To a limited extent MPOs did initiate projects to take advantage of the TEA-21 Livable Cities program. These projects, sometimes with federal support and at other times locally initiated, often provide technical assistance to local communities for project planning. The MPOs can use federal funds which may be programmed for transportation related enhancements that accompany an alternative development proposal. These programs may also offer specific financial or planning incentives. For example, if a locally proposed transportation project were within a specified or a preferred area, it would be more likely to receive higher priority in the funding allocation processes (Wolf and Farquhar 2006).

Environmental Justice

The issue of environmental justice and social equity within metropolitan transportation planning processes is primarily being addressed through the environmental justice component of MPO programs. Title VI of the Civil Rights Act of 1964 and President Clinton's Executive Order 12898 established environmental justice as a federal policy with Clinton's order stating that "each Federal agency shall make achieving environmental justice part of its mission by identifying and addressing, as appropriate, disproportionately high and adverse human health or environmental effects of its programs, policies, and activities on minority populations and low-income populations."

Both the U.S. Department of Transportation (USDOT) and the Federal Highway Administration (FHWA) issued Environmental Justice Orders (USDOT Order 5610.2 and FHWA Order 6640.23) in 1997 and 1998, respectively. These orders described how environmental justice elements can be incorporated into existing federal programs. The USDOT cited three core principles of environmental justice that can be used for analysis and decision-making including both procedural and substantive elements. They are:

1. To avoid, minimize, or mitigate disproportionately high and adverse human health and environmental effects, including social and economic effects, on minority populations and low-income populations;
2. To ensure the full and fair participation by all potentially affected communities in the transportation decision-making process;
3. To prevent the denial of, reduction in, or significant delay in the receipt of benefits by minority and low income populations (USDOT 2000, p. ii).

Three issues constitute the core of equity and environmental justice issues for MPOs. The first relates to the more formal political processes used by MPOs. Specifically, they concern the formal membership and voting processes. The second concerns the ISTEA/TEA-21 requirement for public participation in the MPO planning processes. Finally, the third equity issue concerns how the specific groups are served or underserved by the transportation programs.

MPOs are part of the environmental justice effort in two ways. First, they often undertake technical studies to review distribution of transportation services for different socioeconomic and ethnic groups. These studies are assigned to staff and special committees. Our MPO Web site analysis identified eighteen of the larger MPOs with these kinds of environmental justice activities. Second, MPOs are involved in funded programs seeking to improve the mobility of the economically disadvantaged. Many of these initiatives are part the Welfare Reform legislation that created job access programs, designed to aid low-income populations find and maintain gainful employment. Nearly half of the MPOs in our Web site analysis included reports of various forms of reverse commuting projects that help individuals in the Welfare Reform program find transportation to and from their place of employment. MPOs also have programs aimed at serving the elderly and disabled. Baltimore, for example, has an "Out and About" travel guide program for elderly and individuals with disabilities. Its specialized rideshare program serves the same population in place of more costly paratransit programs

CITIZEN PARTICIPATION AND TRANSPORTATION PLANNING

The 1997 Advisory Committee on Intergovernmental Relations study reports increased MPO efforts to gain timely and effective citizen involvement in the development of both the long and short range plans. Seventy-eight percent of MPOs established initiatives to encourage citizen participation. The report concludes that there were more opportunities for involvement available to citizens, more staff available to support these processes, new techniques to promote citizen involvement were developed, a sense that MPOs were listening, and a feeling that this involvement would make a difference in the planning processes (U.S. Advisory Commission on Intergovernmental Relations 1997). Goetz and his colleagues report that the four MPOs in their study felt most successful about their citizen involvement activities (Goetz et al. 2002). Each had extensive citizen involvement programs and felt that this was an advantage that contributed to their overall planning efforts. Involvement early in the process seemed particularly valuable because it uncovered potentially difficult conflicts, which provided time to avert litigation and delay (U.S. General Accounting Office 1996; Goldman and Deakin 2000; McDowell 1999).

At the same time, it is not entirely clear that public involvement represents a deeply or enthusiastically held MPO value. Gage and McDowell found that, at best, the MPO directors rated their efforts as slightly ineffective (Gage and McDowell 1995). The American Society of State Highway Transportation Officials and their member states have been critical of participation procedures because they seem to serve more as a "lightening rod" for controversial projects. Often, these activities are seen as bringing out those with strong opposition on a one-issue basis, though they do not create a consistently engaged public (Goldman and Deakin 2000).

SYSTEM MANAGEMENT AND OPERATIONS

As the clamor by citizens for relief from spending endless hours in traffic grows and the possibility of building major new highway systems declines, MPOs have taken on more responsibility for optimizing the existing highway transportation system. Over the past few years, with the encouragement of ISTEA and TEA-21 planning requirements, many MPOs shifted emphasis from focusing primarily on planning for new projects to management and operation of the existing metropolitan transportation systems. Rothblatt and Colman conclude that even though MPOs will continue to attend to their traditional role in planning for major new transportation projects, they will also have to become "proficient in monitoring the system and identifying performance measures and feedback, and adept at developing and implementing low-cost projects to improve overall performance of the transportation system" (Rothblatt and Colman 2001). Preservation of the existing transportation systems becomes increasingly important with this emphasis. An AMPO survey of members concerning system management and operations defined this program emphasis in the following way:

> An integrated program to optimize the performance of existing infrastructure through the implementation of multi- and intermodal, cross-jurisdictional systems, services, and projects designed to preserve capacity and improve security, safety, and reliability of the regional transportation system. Transportation systems management and operations includes regional operations

collaboration and coordination activities among transportation and public safety agencies, and improvements such as traffic detection and surveillance, arterial management, freeway management, demand management, work zone management, emergency management, electronic toll collection, automated enforcement, traffic incident management, roadway weather management, traveler information services, commercial vehicle operations, traffic control, freight management, and coordination of highway, rail, transit, bicycle, and pedestrian operations. (Association of Metropolitan Planning Organizations 2003)

Many MPOs are spending nearly 75 percent of their total budget on management and operations activities (Rothblatt and Colman 2001). Congestion management takes up a considerable amount of MPO efforts, particularly in the larger metropolitan areas. This involves relieving traffic congestion through transportation demand management (TDM) approaches (Rothblatt and Colman 2001). Intelligent Transportation Systems (ITS) and safety, particularly related to homeland security, have become important elements of this management and operations focus.

Focus on ITS was stimulated by federal ISTEA funding and ensuing federal requirements. ITS emphasizes the role of high technology and communication technologies for monitoring travel flows, relieving traffic congestion, improving traffic flow, improving air quality and safety. ISTEA required MPOs to develop strategic ITS plans and integrate them into the on MPO planning process. MPOs also provide technical planning and support to local jurisdictions and public and private transit operators. These efforts focus on creating real-time information for identifying and coordinating regional transportation facilities. ITS improvements seek to ensure that transportation facilities and technologies are compatible across transportation modes and jurisdictions so that common improvements can be made. ITS may work to create and enhance traffic monitoring systems. These systems sometime called one-stop information centers, provide for central data management, management, and emergency response to incidents and, verification and coordination of corrective action. Other ITS projects include coordination of traffic signalization, traffic operation centers, variable message signs providing information about congestion hotspots, pending delays or potential disasters, weather or construction, global positioning systems (GPS) on buses and a proposed 511 phone number to provide nationwide traffic information. ITS often uses closed circuit television to monitor flow at intersections, automatic vehicle location (AVL) for transit vehicles and signal pre-emption for emergency vehicles.

A more recent element of MPOs' system operations and management activities involves security. Historically, MPOs have been involved in coordinating transportation systems with other security related agencies. They have focused on a broad range of hazards, particularly, evacuation during natural disasters and coordinating efforts to get transportation systems functioning again after a disaster. Since September 11, 2001, security of the transportation systems has given many MPOs, particularly those in target rich areas, added responsibility for considering security threats from terrorism as part of its planning and operations role. MPOs often find themselves in the center of planning and coordination of evacuation plans, airport facilities, and E-911 services.

Some MPOs have established technical advisory committees to create emergency evacuation routes, enhance coordination among modalities, and to construct roles such as an emergency management director somewhere in the MPO organization.

Meyer argues that MPOs can play a crucial role in these activities including promoting coordinated planning, provide centralized location for information on transportation systems conditions. More specifically they can play such roles as helping regions create the capacity for prevention, surveillance/monitoring, information dissemination/ communications, incident response, and system recovery. He notes that MPOs can be particularly helpful in the institutional learning phase of a security/ disaster incident (Meyer 2005).

INTERGOVERNMENTAL PARTNERS FOR MPOS

Metropolitan Planning Organizations must work closely with other MPOs, local governments, state governments (particularly state departments of transportation), and federal agencies. To a large degree, MPOs' ability to influence the transportation planning process depends on the effectiveness of their relationships with their intergovernmental partners.

FEDERAL PARTNERS

Federal influence in MPOs' work comes from both the federal funding of MPO activities and federal rules that govern funding of federally supported projects in metropolitan areas. MPO planning increasingly reflect the rules of the federal legislation. For example, both ISTEA and TEA-21 require MPOs to work through government and non-governmental agencies. There is more consideration given to developing intermodal facilities and capabilities among highway, transit, bicycle, freight, and pedestrian modes than there was before ISTEA, and the requirements that MPOs use intermodal strategies do drive some MPO decisions.

While MPO plans do often consider land-use, economic development, and equity in their planning work, they are not as frequently included as those with more explicit and mandated federal planning requirements. For example, rules for intermodal planning and air quality conformity rules are directly tied to funding consequences. As a result, MPOs' attention to air quality grows as difficulty in meeting air quality standards are encountered (U.S. General Accounting Office 2002). Federal rules concerning land-use, and economic and community development are more permissive and do not normally have the same influence except when they are seen as a way to contribute to meeting air quality standards and thereby allow a new transportation project to proceed.

Certification is one way that the federal agencies try to hold MPOs accountable for meeting planning requirements. MPOs and SDOTs must conduct self-certification reviews annually that must examine major issues such as how they undertake planning regulations and how they consider the seven planning criteria (see Table 10.1). Even with problems created by nonstandard reporting criteria; McDowell's review of the

---

TABLE 10.1
ISTEA Planning Criteria

Economic vitality
Safety and security
Accessibility and mobility
Quality of life
Integration and connectivity
System management and operation
Preservation of existing systems

---

certification process found that overall the certification process provides an incentive for MPOs to follow planning criteria in order to avoid funding penalties and also allows MPOs share practices (McDowell 1999).

THE STATES

State highway agencies have traditionally been the major player in transportation planning. ISTEA/TEA-21 changed this to some degree by adding the regional overlay provided by MPOs, but older patterns remain strong (Katz, Puentes, and Bernstein 2003). States dominate MPO processes in most areas and this relationship has continued to be problematic (McDowell 1999; Rothblatt and Colman 2001). Several studies support the conclusion that the manner in which state DOTs relate to the MPO process largely determines MPOs success, and that developing more collaborative relationships between MPOs and state DOTs has been difficult (Gage and McDowell 1995; Katz, Puentes, and Bernstein 2003). At best, MPOs are seen by states as an additional partner; at worst, as is often the case, state DOTs see MPOs as an obstacle to accomplishing work.. A Brookings Institute assessment published in 2003 concludes that most states have not evolved sufficient powers and responsibilities in their metropolitan areas and that they maintain substantial control. This report concludes that:

> (The)…federal law has been largely subverted….(and)…many state DOTs still wield considerable formal and informal power, and retain authority over substantial state transportation funds….The governor and the state DOT still have veto authority over MPO-selected projects….state political leverage is far greater than the MPOs. (Katz, Puentes, and Bernstein 2003, p. 5)

Several MPOs include more than one state, and cooperation is severely tested when MPOs have to work with two or more states. At a minimum, MPOs have to develop relationships with several state agencies, and the states must then work more closely with each other when they focus on a particular region. Institutional histories and simple habits of working vary among states, thereby challenging regional planning processes and policies.

MPO planners themselves also often neglect to fully include state transportation plans in their work. Schweitzer and Taylor's interviews with statewide and regional planners find that only a small minority of regional planners report using or referring to their state's transportation plan. At the same time, these MPO planners do use the state data and expertise. While coordination between state DOTs and MPOs occur, these activities are not necessarily tied to the state plans. They do rely heavily on state environmental agencies for data and express interest in working toward greater cooperation with the state in freight planning (Schweitzer and Taylor 2002). Many agencies have moved closer to cooperation by including a state DOT representative on MPO governing boards (Rosenblatt 1994).

LOCAL GOVERNMENTS

Local governments should both cooperate with their planning partners, but at the same time, preserve local control in areas deemed essential for local interest. Political leaders and professional staffs from local governments play a critical role in MPO planning success. They cooperate during the CLRP process as well as in many of the works of technical committees not directly tied to the CLRP. Negotiating skills become essential as local governments work to get their specific interests and projects included in plans. The large MPOs facing air quality problems find the need for cooperation the most. At the same time, efforts to link land-use with transportation is one area where local prerogatives constrain governance at metropolitan levels (Gainsborough 2001). The Goldman and Deakin study finds that most local agencies were not interested in working with MPOs on land-use issues. While local resistance to working with MPOs around land-use has abated somewhat, MPOs have not had an easy time becoming a significant actor in regional debates or in local land-use decisions (Goldman and Deakin 2000).

SUMMARY AND CONCLUSION: THE PRESENT AND FUTURE OF MPOs AS REGIONAL INSTITUTIONS

Clearly, MPOs are, at some level, players in metropolitan transportation planning. This is particularly the case in larger metropolitan areas. Also, regions that face more serious problems meeting air quality standards create more critical roles for MPOs. The ISTEA and TEA-21 period has added substantial responsibilities. The requirement to develop the CLRP and shorter-term TIP put MPOs in a position to take a more central role in regional transportation planning and programming. They rely on organizing strategies that emphasizes the use of policy, technical, and advisory committees that are augmented by professional staffs and consultants. During this ISTEA and TEA-21 period, many MPOs, particularly in large metropolitan areas, have enhanced both their administrative and technical capacities as they work to meet federal planning requirements.

MPOs have also moved beyond simply compiling local and state highway plans and include both multi-modal elements as well as coordination with related policy and program areas. Now, highway and transit planning are increasingly integrated with other modes including freight, airports, bicycles, and pedestrian programs. The federal requirement to meet air quality standards as they develop the CLRP and TIP leads to difficult planning processes for those large MPOs classified as or at risk of being classified as a non-attainment area in terms of air quality. MPOs also work with other non-transportation areas land-use, economic development, and equity. Finally, as MPOs have moved from the early ISTEA period to the later years of TEA-21, MPOs have shifted some of their focus away from planning new projects to systems maintenance and operations. They have given increased attention to intelligent transportation system technologies, and, in certain metropolitan areas, homeland security.

However, the questions about the MPO role in regional transportation planning persist. The traditional intergovernmental partners in transportation planning at federal, state and local levels remain deeply involved in MPO processes, and the institutional histories of regional governance of these actors mitigate a powerful MPO role. While MPOs have gained some autonomy in limited areas, the state governments continue to be the key player in these planning processes. Local governments obviously participate heavily in MPO processes, but they guard their own institutional prerogatives and seek to advance their own interests. In most areas, the council of government model dominates MPO approaches to governance. One-third of MPOs are part of COGs and another third are tied to regional planning commissions, an even weaker form of regional cooperation. MPOs use the COG norms of inform and confer approaches more than to cooperate and collaborate (Goldman and Deakin 2000). As a result, MPOs traditionally do not take on controversial issues and many resist calling a vote on a matter when a consensus has not been reached. This creates timid MPO agendas (Goldman and Deakin 2000). Also, MPOs' ability to forge regional action is hampered by increased use of federal and state earmarking of transportation projects. Earmarked projects are automatically placed in the MPO plans, thus reducing the opportunity for meaningful consideration of how the projects fit into regional plans. The increasing use of earmarking also reduces the amount of dollars, and therefore projects, that will receive a hearing at the metropolitan level (Wolf 2004).

At the same time, MPOs have a different history than councils or governments in several important respects. This does offer them opportunities to play a more important role in regional governance. Most significantly, the federal mandates that require regional projects to go through an MPO planning process and the direct federal support of MPO activities provides MPOs with more leverage than most COGs enjoy. Federal rules require that plans and projects undergo a planning and review process at a regional level, a significant departure from many of the traditional COG processes. Requiring a review process that necessitates getting a project into the plan in order to receive federal funds creates a dynamic different from many controversial issues that COGs face: delay through committees, studies, and overt avoidance. Requiring regional reviews means that the process has to be joined and completed. MPO policy boards may not always represent regional perspectives and priorities, but the chance of this happening is greater than for many other COG processes.

MPOs separate source of federal funding also provides MPOs with a degree of autonomy not enjoyed by many other regional efforts. There is a 1 percent take-down from federal funds for planning purposes, and these funds go directly to the MPOs.

These operating funds provide some promise of long-run stability for these agencies. They can develop administrative capacities to operate a sophisticated planning and review process. Support for the policy boards and technical committees, for information distribution, and for developing planning, consensus, and technical capacity all contribute to a more competent and legitimate metropolitan organization. The technical and policy committees, professional staff, and consultants create administrative capability that support MPO planning processes, and build MPO capacity to be a viable regional governance institution.

In conclusion, the future of MPOs as an important actor in regional transportation remains uncertain. While MPOs have extended their sphere of activity and left their mark on regional transportation as well as on other policy issues, they have not developed substantial institutional autonomy. MPOs' degree of institutionalization remains fragile. Their future will depend to a large extent on existing local political, social, and economic historical contexts, as well as on shifts in intergovernmental policies.

REFERENCES

Advisory Commission on Intergovernmental Relations. 1995. *MPO Capacity: Improving the Capacity of Metropolitan Planning Organizations to Help Implement National Transportation Policies.* Washington, D.C.: Association of Metropolitan Planning Organizations.

Association of Metropolitan Planning Organizations. 2003. *AMPO Bike-Ped Survey Results.* Washington, D.C.: Association of Metropolitan Planning Organizations.

Association of Metropolitan Planning Organizations. 2003. *AMPO Survey Results.* Washington, D.C.: Association of Metropolitan Planning Organizations.

Association of Metropolitan Planning Organizations. 2003. *AMPO Survey: MPOs Need More Freight Resources.* Washington, D.C.: Association of Metropolitan Planning Organizations.

Association of Metropolitan Planning Organizations. 2004. *AMPO Survey Results: Institutional Survey.* Washington, D.C.: Association of Metropolitan Planning Organizations.

Arnold, Eugene D., Partricia Weichman, and Jeffery A. Capizzano. 1999. *A Survey of Transportation Practices in State Departments of Transportation.* Charlottesville, VA: Virginia Transportation Research Council/Virginia Department of Transportation and the University of Virginia.

Associates, Wilbur Smith. 2004. *Noteworthy MPO Practices in Transportation Land Use Planning Integreation—Final Report.* Washington, D.C.: Association of Metropolitan Planning Organizations.

Bishop, Elbert R., Christopher Wornum, and Martin Weiss. 1997. Experience of Metropolitan Planning Organizations with Intermodal Efficiency Act Financial Planning Requirements: Interviews and Analysis. *Transportation Research Record* (1606):1–9.

Bullard, Robert. 2004. *Highway Robbery, Transportation Racism and New Routes to Equity.* Cambridge, MA: South End Press.

Chang, D. Tilly, and Frederick P. Salvucci. 1996. *Analysis of Financial Planning Requirements in Transportation Planning.* Cambridge, MA: New England University Transportation Center/Massachusetts Institute of Technology.

Denbow, Rich. 2004. MPOs and Transit Agenies—Sitting Together at the Table? *Metros: A Quaterly Newsletter of the Association of Metropolitan Planning Organizations* 1.

Frug, Gerald. 2002. Beyond Regional Government. *Harvard Law Review* 115 (7):1766–1836.

Gage, Robert W., and Bruce D. McDowell. 1995. ISTEA and the Role of MPOs in the New Transportation Environment: A Midterm Assessment. *Publius* 25 (3):133–154.

Gainsborough, Juliet F. 2001. Slow Growth and Urban Sprawl: Support for a New Regional Agenda? *Urban Affairs Review* 37 (5):728–729.

Gayle, Stephen, Karin McGowan, and Rae Rupp. 2004. *The Nuts & Bolts of an MPO: 2004 AMPO Annual Conference: Powerpoint Presentation*. Washington, D.C.

Goetz, Andrew, Paul Stephen Dempsey, and Carl Larson. 2002. Metropolitan Planning Organizations: Findings and Recommendations for Improving Transportation Planning. *Publius* 32 (1):87.

Goldman, Todd, and Elizabeth Deakin. 2000. Regionalism Through Partnerships? Metropolitan Planning Since ISTEA. *Berkeley Planning Review* 14:46–75.

Howitt, Arnold M., and Eliazabeth M. Moore. 1999. Implementing the Transportation Conformity Regulations. *TR News* (202):15–23, 41.

Johnson, Scott. 2004. Freight Professional Development PowerPoint Presentation. Paper read at Association of Metropolitan Planning Organizations' Annual Meeting, October 12–14, 2004.

Katz, Bruce, Robert Puentes, and Scott Bernstein. 2003. *TEA-21 Reauthorization: Getting Transportation Right for Metropolitan America*. Washington, D.C.: Brookings Institution.

Lewis, Carol, and Ruben Howard. 1999. *An Examination of Policy Implications of Criteria That Determine Regional Transportation Priorities*. Houston, Texas: Center for Transportation Training and Research Texas Southern University.

McDowell, Bruce D. 1999. *Improving Regional Transportation Decisions: MPOs and Certification*. Washington, D.C.: Brookings Center on Urban and Metroplitan Policy.

Meyer, Michael D. 2002. The Role of the Metropolitan Planning Organization (MPO). In Preparing for Security Incidents and Transportation System Response. Atlanta. GA (Draft).

Mierzejewski, Edward A., and Margaret A. Marshall. 1998. Review of Long-Range Transportation Plans in Florida's Metropolitan Planning Organizatioans. *Transportation Research Record 1617* (Paper No. 98-1305):122–129.

Nelson, A.C., T.W. Sanchez, J.F. Wolf, and M.B. Farquahr. 2005. Metropolitan Planning Organization Voting Structure and Transit Investment Bias: Preliminary Analysis with Social Equity Implications. *Transportation Research Record* 1895:1–7.

U.S. General Accounting Office. 2002. *Environmental Protection: Federal Incentives Could Help Promote Land Use that Protects Air and Water Quality*. Washington, D.C.

Rosenblatt, Donald N. 1994. North American Metropolitan Planning: Canadian and U.S. Perspective. *Journal of the American Planning Association* 60 (4):501–520.

Rothblatt, Donald N., and Steven B. Colman. 2001. *Best Practices in Developing Regional Transportation Plans*. San Jose, CA: Mineta Transportation Institute College of Business-San Jose State University.

Sanchez, Thomas W. 2005. *Patterns of MPO Representation and Board Structure in Relations to Transportation Planning and Decision-Making*. Washington, D.C.: Brookings Institution.

Schweitzer, Lisa, and Brian Taylor. 2002. A Comparative Analysis of State-Regional Relations in Statewide Transportation Planning After ISTEA. Paper read at Transportation Research Board 2002 Annual Meeting CD-ROM.

U.S. Advisory Commission on Intergovernmental Relations.1997. *Planning Progress: Addressing ISTEA Requirements in Metropolitan Planning Areas*. Washington, D.C.: Association of Metropolitan Planning Organizations.

U.S. General Accounting Office. 1996. *Urban Transportation: Metropolitan Planning Organiza-tions' Efforts to Meet Federal Planning Requirements: Report to Congress.* Washington, D.C.: U.S. Government Printing Office.

U.S. General Accounting Office. 2002. *Environmental Protection: Federal Incentives Could Help Promote Land Use that Protects Air and Water Quality.* Report: GAO-02-12. Washington, D.C.: U.S. Government Printing Office.

Wade, Montie. 1998. *Synthesis of Highway Practice 252: Response of Small Urbanized Area MPOs to ISTEA.* Washington, D.C.: Transportation Research Board.

Wolf, James F. 2004. New Governance in Metropolitan Regions: The Role of Metropolitan Planning Organizations. Paper read at American Society for Public Administration, April, 2004, at Portland, Oregon.

Wolf, James F., and Marybeth Farquhar. November, 2006. Assessing Progress: The State of Metropolitan Planning Organizations Under ISTEA and TEA-21. *International Review of Public Administration* 28:1057–1079.

11 Transportation Management Associations: Toward a New View of Public Policy and Administration

Göktuğ Morçöl and Ulf Zimmermann

Transportation management associations (TMAs), sometimes known as transportation management organizations, are nonprofit organizations formed by business owners to solve local transportation problems. Although they function in small geographic areas and number fewer than two hundred, TMAs have exercised an increasingly significant role in the formation of transportation policies and the delivery of transportation services in many of our metropolitan areas in the last two decades.

Because of the proliferation of such nongovernmental actors in policy making and implementation, TMAs have become a "public administration problem" (Salamon 2002). While in some cases TMAs were created voluntarily by local businesses and nonprofit organizations, and independently of local governments, in others governments encouraged, facilitated, or even mandated their creation. It appears that government is either abandoning certain public powers, such as regulating and planning transportation, to self-interested nonprofits or is itself devolving public responsibilities to private agents. These developments and the increasing complexity of metropolitan governance thus require a new view of the scope and nature of public policy making and administration.

TMAs play significant roles in transportation policy and this poses problems to public administration. The significance of TMAs is obscured not only by their low visibility in the federal system but also by their limited numbers—no more than two hundred, as noted, but this is four times the number that existed in the early 1980s. First prevalent in California, they have since spread across the United States from suburban "edge cities" to central business districts, transportation corridors, and other high activity hubs in cities and counties. Similarly, in the 1980s TMAs were simply one of the tools of transportation demand management (TDM), but since then their functions have broadened to include public education, promoting local economic development, running local transportation systems, and transportation policy advocacy in the 1990s (Loveless & Welch 1999; Ferguson 2000, 181; *TMA Handbook* 2001, 6–61).

The significance of TMAs lies not only in their growing numbers and their geographic, spatial, and functional diversification but also in their growing influence in policy making and implementation. Their impact on public policy is enhanced through formal and informal relations with other business organizations (i.e., local business associations and chambers of commerce) that participate in the public policy process. In some states and communities, TMAs are associated with, or even directly funded by, business improvement districts (BIDs)—special districts formed by property owners that have the powers to tax the business constituents of their districts to fund these improvements. TMAs and BIDs not only influence public policies and deliver public services, but some also leverage large amounts of public money to be used in projects in their areas, thus often extending their financial powers far beyond their small operating budgets. Because of their influence in public policy, these private business organizations have been variously termed "private governments" (Pack 1992; Lavery 1995), "parallel states" (Mallett 1993), and "quasi-governmental entities" (Ross & Levine 2001, 244).

ROLES OF TMAs IN TRANSPORTATION POLICY: PRIVATIZATION, TOOLS, PARTNERSHIPS, AND NETWORKS

Some see the increasing role of private business organizations in public policy as the result of the privatization trend of recent decades. Ferguson, Ross, and Meyer (1992), for example, argue that TMAs should be seen as a form of privatization of public transportation services (16). TMAs are mainly organizations of private businesses. In legal terms they are nonprofits. The 1998 TMA survey found that a majority of them were incorporated as tax-exempt nonprofit organizations: over one-third (37%) of them as 501 (c) (3) organizations, 17 percent as social welfare—501 (c) (4)—organizations, and 17 percent as business league—501 (c) (6)—organizations (*TMA Handbook* 2001, 6–62). This survey also showed that a large majority of their members (75%) were representatives of businesses, whereas only 14 percent were representatives of government agencies and 9 percent of nonprofit organizations (*TMA Handbook* 2001, 6–59). About 90 percent of TMA members are representatives of for-profit firms (Ferguson 2000, 182). In the 1980s, particularly in California and a few Northeastern states, where governments were pushing for the creation of TMAs, government representatives played more active parts in them; but over time the percentages of the representatives of public agencies decreased and those of corporate members increased (Ferguson & Davidson 1995, 49).

The governance of TMAs is also predominantly private. A survey of 110 TMAs in the early 1990s showed that large majorities of board members (68% on average) represented businesses, with only 21 percent and 14 percent representaing nonprofit organizations and public agencies, respectively (Ferguson, Ross, & Meyer 1992, 64). In the late 1990s the percentage of business people among board members increased to 84 percent (Ferguson 2000, p. 182). Although public agencies often have representatives on TMA boards, only about half of them were voting members (Dunphy & Lin 1990, 48–50).

As Farazmand (2001) points out, the big wave of privatization came in the 1980s, during the Thatcher and Reagan administrations in Britain and the United States, respectively. Fueled by public choice theorists, this wave of privatization successfully contended that some of the functions of the welfare state, and public sector ownership in general, were unnecessary. This resonated with policy makers of the time as it did with populist, anti-government political forces. While Farazmand and others are critical of privatization and favor reorganization of public agencies instead, the public choice school contends that the competitive pressures privatization puts on public agencies leads to service improvements in government (Chandler & Plano 1988, 100, 105–106).

Salamon (2002) offers a different perspective: Nonprofits such as TMAs can be seen not as forms of privatization, but as policy implementation "tools" of local governments. Indeed, in the 1980s, local government officials in California, Maryland, and New Jersey actually wanted to use TMAs as tools to change commuting behaviors in certain areas. Their notion was that local TMAs would be more effective than remote governments because of their intimacy with local conditions, as a New Jersey DOT representative explained:

> TMAs serve as an extension of the Department's Bureau of Mobility Management . . . the TMAs provide the same type of services to their constituents that the Department staff would provide and in a much more personal and immediate fashion . . . in the regions where the problems are occurring on a day-to-day basis. (Dunphy & Lin 1990, 58)

A similar view of TMAs is that they are "the vanguard of a new form of governance—a new grassroots approach to dealing with local problems that is neither fully public nor fully private but represents a melding of the public and private interests in the form of collaborative partnership" (Orski 1982, 314).

Each of these views (privatization, tools, and partnership) offers some insights, but none is sufficient to explain the complex roles of TMAs and other business organizations in public policy making and service delivery. The network governance perspective is more helpful in explaining the increasing importance of TMAs and other such business organizations in the public policy process. In this perspective, public authority is inevitably shared with an array of nonprofit and for-profit organizations in the increasingly complex governance networks. Network governance theorists (e.g., Teisman & Klijn 2002) suggest that the classic separation between hierarchies and markets is disappearing and the public and private sectors are becoming interdependent. According to Teisman and Klijn, the rise of the "network society" has made the private sector more prone to inter-organizational alliances and partnerships, and public organizations are following suit. They also contend that network governance is complex because of the interdependencies and negotiation processes among different actors. Before elaborating on network governance later, a short history of TMAs will help highlight their significance.

HISTORY

Urban scholars, such as Judd and Swanstrom (2004, 337–340), point out that the strains on city government finances, partly due to the loss of federal aid in the 1980s, helped shape the environment in which "special entities" like TMAs and BIDs were created.[1] Mallett (1993) stresses that even more important than these financial difficulties were the spatial and structural changes that had been taking place since the 1950s in urban areas in the United States. These financial difficulties were largely the consequence of these spatial and structural changes and produced the conditions for the emergence of TMAs and BIDs. Two complementary developments after World War II were particularly important. On the one hand, suburbs evolved from bedroom communities into job centers, which introduced suburban traffic congestion. TMAs were created to deal with these suburban problems. On the other, this suburban job growth came at the expense of central city downtowns and BIDs were created to combat this decline. As seen below, these two trends seem to have converged, at least in some states such as Georgia where TMAs and BIDs have become intertwined as forms of business involvement in transportation policy.[2]

PREDECESSORS OF TMAS AND DEVELOPMENTS IN THE 1970S

TMAs are successors to commuter assistance programs, launched by employers as early as the 1920s. Then, during World War II, the federal government encouraged ridesharing programs in communities to reduce fuel consumption (Dunphy & Lin 1990, 4). But today's TMAs emerged out of the developments in the 1970s when, in addition to employer involvement in commuter assistance and trip reduction programs and oil shortages, federal legislation mandated or encouraged reduction in air pollution and federal transportation system management programs.

The 1970 Clean Air Act (CAA) had strong repercussions for transportation policies, and the oil crises of 1973–1974 and 1979–1980 gave new impetuses to energy conservation efforts. The national ambient air quality standards set by the 1970 act and its definition of nonattainment areas created a framework for transportation policies. Subsequent acts in the 1970s further defined this framework. The 1977 and 1980 CAA amendments mandated reductions in air pollution from auto emissions and encouraged using alternative modes of transportation. Earlier, the 1974 Emergency Highway Energy Conservation Act had already authorized funding ridesharing demonstration programs and the 1974 Federal Energy Act had offered tax breaks for energy conserving investments (Dunphy & Lin 1990, 11).

In response to the oil crises some corporations also took measures to facilitate employee transportation. Connecticut General and 3M, for example, offered commuter assistance programs that included ridesharing, vanpooling, bus services, staggered work hours, and subsidizing public transit fares for their employees. Even oil companies like Conoco started ridesharing programs to counteract negative publicity (Dunphy & Lin 1990, 5–6).

The 1980s—The Emergence of TMAs

The first TMAs were established in the 1980s (Dunphy & Lin 1990, 44). This was an era in which urban transportation policies were transformed, as Plant observes (1988), and in these years private sector funding for transportation programs was increased. He points out that the imbalances between highway and other modes, the inability of the government to respond effectively to public needs, the passivity of the transportation system in responding to demands, the public's dissatisfaction with them, and the Reagan administration's desire to make changes in transportation all contributed to this transformation.

Under these conditions, federal transportation policies shifted toward "transportation (or "travel") demand management" (TDM) policies, which encouraged better use of existing transportation resources and facilities instead of the traditional approach of increasing the supply of these (Dunphy & Lin 1990, 15–16). TDM policies involved actions to reduce traffic by alternative means of transportation—ridesharing, vanpooling, bus service, bicycling, transit subsidies, and alternative work scheduling (flex-time) (Ferguson 2000).

To implement TDM policies, jurisdictions instituted "traffic mitigation" or "trip reduction" ordinances (Ferguson 2000). In the 1980s, several local jurisdictions in California issued such ordinances and required employers to make plans for coming into conformity with the local TDM plans. In some jurisdictions the ordinances required employers and developers to establish TMAs; in others TMAs were created through negotiated agreements between employers or developers and local governments (Ferguson, Ross, & Meyer 1992, 30–32).

The 1990s—The Growth of TMAs

In the 1990s the creation of TMAs accelerated substantially. The Clean Air Act (CAA) Amendments of 1990 and the Intermodal Surface Transportation Efficiency Act (ISTEA) of 1991 were the twin propellers of this accelerated growth, especially because they were uniquely coordinated, as Howitt and Altshuler (1999) put it. The 1990 CAA amendments commanded a new priority for environmental goals in urban transportation and ISTEA defined the financial and institutional mechanisms of accomplishing these goals. Together they created a legal framework that enabled and encouraged the spread of TMAs to states beyond California and the Northeast.

The 1990 amendments called for a strict control of vehicular emissions, particularly in severe and extreme ozone nonattainment areas (Ferguson, Ross, & Meyer 1992, 36). They also mandated the creation of employer trip reduction (ETR) programs in the ten most severely polluted nonattainment areas. These ETRs gave a major impetus to the creation of new TMAs. That Congress made the programs voluntary in 1995, in the face of resistance from businesses in places like Baltimore, Chicago, and Philadelphia (Howitt & Altshuler 1999, 242), did not, however, prove to be a disincentive to the creation of new TMAs.

One reason was that ISTEA provided the financial resources to implement the programs created by the 1990 CAA amendments and expanded the roles of local and regional governmental agencies, particularly metropolitan planning organizations (MPOs), in transportation policy. Urbanized areas with populations of two hundred thousand or more were designated as transportation management areas and required to make long-range plans. ISTEA required that in transportation management areas the planning process had to include a congestion management system, which typically involved using TDM strategies (Weiner 1999, 180–181). Some MPOs, such as the Atlanta Regional Commission, have actively encouraged the creation of TMAs in their regions. Two programs created by ISTEA have been particularly important for the funding of TMAs: the Congestion Mitigation and Air Quality Management Program (CMAQ) and the Transportation Enhancement Program (Horan, Dittmar, & Jordan 2001, 226).

The Transportation Equity Act for the 21st Century (TEA-21) of 1998 continued and enhanced the ISTEA programs, establishing the Transportation and Community and System Preservation Pilot Program, which gave grants to local communities to encourage demonstration programs of integrated transportation. Despite some opposition during its implementation, TEA-21 also increased CMAQ funding (Horan, Dittmar, & Jordan 2001, 238).

SIGNIFICANCE

Numbers and Geographic and Spatial Distributions of TMAs

Although there appears to be no definitive count of TMAs, it is clear from the information that is available that their numbers have increased rapidly since the 1980s. Surveys conducted in the late 1980s and in the 1990s reported somewhat varied counts; Table 11.1 shows the results from four different sources.

The *TMA Handbook* (2001) notes that in the 1990s, a few TMAs ceased operation, but others emerged. The figures in Table 11.1 show that, despite these losses, their

TABLE 11.1
Numbers of TMAs in the 1980s and 1990s

Year	TMA Directory (1995)	Ferguson & Davidson (1995)	Ferguson (1997)	TMA Handbook (2001)
1989		72	52	
1990	50		72	
1991			110	
1992			134	
1993		136		
1995	100		170	
1998				135

overall numbers doubled, or even tripled, in that time. What is more interesting is that the TMAs that ceased to exist were in environments in which they had previously been mandated, as in the several California jurisdictions we mentioned that required the creation of TMAs in the 1980s as part of their TDM strategies. As the mandates were lifted in the 1990s, some developers and other businesses decided to discontinue their TMAs. All the new ones that emerged in the 1990s were in states that did not mandate their establishment. The *TMA Handbook* reports that in 1993 most TMAs were located in California, Florida, and New Jersey. According to Ferguson's (1997) meta-analysis of surveys, between 1989 and 1995 almost half the TMAs were located in California, and almost one-fourth of them were in the Northeast, the nation's most traffic-challenged regions. In the late 1990s, TMA formation shifted to other states, particularly those that had experienced significant growth in population and traffic congestion, such as Colorado and Georgia. Neither of these states had any TMAs in the early 1990s, but in 1998 Colorado had seven and Georgia five (*TMA Handbook* 2001, 6–63). The first TMA in Georgia (Commuter Club) was established in 1996 (see Table 11.2).

Parallel to their increasing geographic spread, TMAs also became more spatially diversified in metropolitan areas in the 1990s. In the 1980s TMAs were a suburban phenomenon. Of the seventy-two found in 1989, only two were in downtowns (Dunphy

TABLE 11.2
Transportation Management Associations in Georgia

TMA Name	Year TMA Established	Location	Affiliated CID (BID)	Year CID (BID) Established	CID (BID) Annual Assessment
Commuter Club	1996	Suburban activity center	Cumberland CID	1987	$ 4 million (1999)
Buckhead Area TMA	1997	Intown	Buckhead CID	1999	$2.2 million (1999)
Perimeter Transportation Coalition	1998	Suburban activity center	DeKalb and Fulton Perimeter CIDs	1999 (DeKalb), 2001 (Fulton)	$1.2 million (2002; DeKalb only)
Clifton Corridor TMA	1998	Intown	No affiliated CID	N/A	N/A
Cobb Rides	1999	Suburban activity center	Town Center Area CID	1997	$1.5 million (2001)
Hartsfield Area TMA	1999	Airport	No affiliated CID	N/A	N/A
Downtown TMA	2000	Intown	Atlanta Downtown Improvement District	1995	$1.65 million (1999)
Midtown Transportation Solutions	2001	Intown	Midtown Improvement District	2000	N/A

and Lin 1990). This pattern changed significantly in the 1990s. The *TMA Handbook* (2001 6–60) reports that in the late 1990s only 14 percent of TMAs could be classi- fied as exclusively suburban; among the remaining TMAs, 30 percent were regional in scope, 13 percent were citywide, 20 percent of them served central business districts, 10 percent transportation corridors, 6 percent activity centers, and 8 percent noncon- tiguous service areas. The figures in Table 11.2 show that the TMAs in Georgia also are spatially diversified: four of them are intown, three are in suburbs, and one covers the area around Atlanta's Hartsfield-Jackson airport.

TMA FUNCTIONS AND SERVICES

The functions performed by TMAs have also become more diversified in the 1990s. In addition to implementing TDM policies (ridesharing, vanpooling, bus service, bicycling, transit subsidies, and alternative work scheduling), they have begun to provide a wide variety of services, from public education and transportation policy advocacy to working with local economic development organizations and running local transportation sys- tems (Loveless & Welch 1999; Ferguson 2000, 181; *TMA Handbook* 2001, 6–61).

The diversification of their functions illustrates the increased importance of TMAs in transportation policy. This expanded activity and reach also poses challenges to, public policy making and administration. Particularly their influence in strategic land-use planning is an area that has the potential for interfering with the powers and responsibilities of local governments, as discussed below.

TMA REVENUES AND BUDGETS

Measured by the size of their operating budgets and the numbers of their employees, TMAs are small organizations. According to Dunphy and Lin (1990) TMA budgets ranged between $70,000 and $400,000 in the late 1980s. Roughly a decade later, the *TMA Handbook* (2001) reports that their budgets ranged between $50,000 and $300,000. While there are obviously some discrepancies in the figures cited by Dunphy and Lin and the *TMA Handbook*, the important point here is that their average budget is in fact barely sufficient to employ an executive director and perhaps a few other staff, considering that the executive director salaries range between $20,000 and $100,000 (*TMA Handbook* 2001, 6–61). But these numbers do not tell the whole story. TMAs' economic and political powers are enhanced by two important factors: For one, their formal and informal affiliations with BIDs and other business associations magnify their reach exponentially and, for another, this compounded influence enables them to leverage large sums of public dollars which in turn enable them to dictate (or at least strongly influence) local and state governments' transportation investments.

The *TMA Handbook* (2001, 5–4 and 5–5) documents that the funding sources of TMAs vary substantially; in-kind and other private contributions, public seed funding for start-up programs, and membership dues are the most important ones. In-kind and other private contributions are important, because in many cases TMA are established, funded, and/or directly operated by other business associations or chambers of commerce. Although there are no figures available, in Georgia business associations, such as Central Atlanta Progress and the Midtown Alliance, created and currently house and staff their respective TMAs (see Downtown TMA and Midtown Transportation Solutions in Table 11.2).[3]

Such affiliation of TMAs with BIDs is particularly significant. TMAs like the Tysons Corner TMA in Northern Virginia and the West Houston Association in Texas use funds generated by special assessment districts (BIDs) in their areas (Dunphy & Lin 1990, 40). Because BIDs are not funded by dues from voluntary members, but by taxes levied on businesses in their jurisdictions, their financial resources are much greater than those of TMAs. The figures of annual assessments of CIDs (community improvement districts, as BIDs are known in Georgia) in Table 11.2 provide a basis for comparing the budgets of BIDs and TMAs. Budgets figures are not available for all the TMAs in Georgia, but the Buckhead Area TMA (BATMA) collected $112,000 in membership fees in 1997 and 1998 (*BATMA Workplan FY 1998–99*; www.batma.org/about/workplan.pdf; accessed March 10, 2003). But the assessments for BATMA's affiliated CID were $2.2 million in 1999. If we use the nationwide TMA budget figures cited by the *TMA Handbook* (2001)—between $50,000 and $300,000—as a basis for comparison, the CID annual assessments in Table 11.2 show that BIDs (CIDs) are far richer organizations.

What is the connection between the two types of organizations? There are no nationwide studies on this issue. The affiliations of TMAs with CIDs in Georgia may be a geographically limited but potentially significant example. Although there are stand-alone TMAs (see the Clifton Corridor and Hartsfield Area TMAs in Table 11.2) in Georgia, most of them are affiliated with CIDs.

In Georgia, the legal basis of TMAs was established with a 1984 amendment to the state constitution. Article IX, Section VII, Paragraph II lists "public transportation" among the services of CIDs. The enabling laws passed by the state legislature expanded this function of CIDs empowering them to create and operate TMAs. Although providing transportation and traffic-related services is only one of the seven functions that are listed for CIDs in the Georgia constitution, it is significant that transportation services are the main activity of almost all CIDs; some focus also on land-use planning and two (the downtown and midtown districts) spend a significant amount of money for security services in their jurisdictions (Reese 2001; www.midtownalliance.org/improvement_district/mid.htm; accessed May 7, 2003). It is not surprising that six out of eight TMAs listed in Table 11.2 are affiliated with CIDs. Four of those six CIDs were established before their TMAs. It is also noteworthy that two TMAs (Buckhead and Perimeter) were established first and their respective CIDs were created later chiefly to fund transportation-related projects.

The financial resources of TMAs are enhanced not only through their affiliations with BIDs, but also through the public monies BIDs can leverage for TMA-related projects, as noted. Ferguson, Ross, and Meyer (1992, 58) indicate that corporate membership dues and government contributions were the two main sources of income for the 110 TMAs they surveyed in the early 1990s and that government contributions were about 25–35 percent of total TMA revenues. The *TMA Handbook* (2001, 6–63) reports that about 50 percent of the total revenues of TMAs were obtained from membership dues in the early 1990s; in the late 1990s, this decreased to one-third and they began relying more on funding from state and local agencies. In Georgia, the CIDs not only have substantial budgets of their own, owing to their self-taxation, but attract public dollars at rates of 1/6 to 1/10 (Reese 2001). The Cumberland CID, for example, boasts that it leveraged $400 million in public dollars between 1988 and 1993 (www.com-muterclub.communityimprovedist.htm; accessed December 18, 2002), whereas their 1999 budget was a mere $4 million (see Table 11.2).[4]

TRANSPORTATION MANAGEMENT ASSOCIATIONS AS A PUBLIC ADMINISTRATION PROBLEM

Business organizations such as TMAs and BIDs are praised as innovative problem solvers and efficient service providers (Ross & Levine 2001, 245), but they are also criticized for their lack of accountability, violating the rights of residents in their respective areas, and creating social and economic segregation in metropolitan areas (Ross & Levine 2001, 245; Briffault 1999; Lavery 1995).

ACCOUNTABILITY, RESIDENTS' RIGHTS, AND SPATIAL SEGREGATION

The accountability of TMAs and other business organizations in public policy making and service delivery is indeed an important issue, but in the context of the emerging network governance, the notion of accountability needs to be redefined. What do we mean by accountability in this context? Should and can business organizations be held accountable for their actions like public agencies? Part of the issue is with legal definitions. There are different legal frameworks governing BIDs and TMAs in differ-ent states. BIDs are incorporated as nonprofits in some states (Houstoun 1997, 2000), while CIDs in Georgia are governmental entities, special districts with limited func-tions and jurisdiction. Most TMAs are incorporated as nonprofits. The *TMA Handbook* (2001)—the official publication of the Association for Commuter Transportation, the national umbrella organization of TMAs and other transportation-related organiza-tions—restricts the definition of TMAs to those with nonprofit status but acknowl-edges that there are other forms, such as informal unincorporated groups working for transportation solutions. Regardless of their legal statuses, TMAs and BIDs do have significant influence on and play roles in transportation policy and service delivery. Therefore, accountability is a relevant issue.

Smith (1999, 189) identifies two types of accountability: administrative/proce-dural, which is concerned with whether the legal and bureaucratic rules are met, and programmatic, which pertains to the substantive contents of a program. Thurmaier and Wood (2002) refer to accountability *to* someone and accountability *for* something. Although based on somewhat different conceptualizations, both typologies have some administrative/procedural accountability *to* someone and programmatic accountability *for* something.

In the case of BIDs and TMAs both are applicable, but the latter is more so. Ad-ministrative/procedural accountability is more pertinent to hierarchical/bureaucratic relations within and between organizations. BIDs and TMAs can be held accountable administratively and procedurally to grant-giving governmental agencies for the public money they receive. However, this would be very limited in scope and effectiveness since it would at best measure the outputs of their programs, but not their community and societal outcomes (impacts). The community and societal impacts of the TMA and/or BID programs that the grant money is used for are far more important. As private nonprofit organizations, many of these entities use their own monies for projects that have impacts in their areas and larger communities. Transportation programs implemented in a pivotally situated suburban shopping mall or a transportation corridor, for example, can have repercussions for an entire metropolitan region. The impacts of these projects are not measurable only by referring to the legal bureaucratic procedures they employ. The programmatic accountability of TMAs and/or BIDs for these projects is therefore far more important.

But it is not easy to establish programmatic accountability, because in the network governance environment in which these organizations operate there may not be clear lines of authority or responsibility in the implementation of a program. In programs that are conducted collaboratively with local or other governments or other nonprofit or for-profit organizations, the lines of authority and responsibility are considerably blurred. In Georgia, there are examples of CIDs conducting feasibility studies for projects, planning for land-use and transportation improvements, and then pushing their projects and ideas up on the agendas of local and state government agencies. Who should be held programmatically accountable for the projects that are planned by CIDs and implemented by governmental agencies? One of the issues in program evaluation that is growing in importance is to determine the "goals" of a program—or "benchmarks" for success—when there are multiple stakeholders and implementers, so that the effectiveness of the program could be established vis-à-vis that goal or benchmark. In the network governance environment of TMAs and BIDs the task of determining commonly accepted goals, benchmarks, and lines of authority and responsibility is therefore becoming even more challenging.

Nevertheless, there are studies that highlight the issues of accountability as they relate to BIDs and TMAs. The legal studies by Barr (1997), Briffault (1999), Garodnick (2000), and Lavery (1995) discuss the accountability of these organizations to local governments, to their members or taxpayers, and to the residents in their areas/jurisdictions. These studies emphasize the violation of the "one person one vote principle" (BIDs have differentiated voting schemes that grant property owners votes in proportion to the size of their properties) and the violation of the rights of residents and the homeless in their jurisdictions. The violation of the "one-person one-vote" principle is particularly cited because BIDs have the governmental authority to collect taxes from all commercial property owners in their jurisdictions. Because most TMAs are voluntary organizations, this is less of an issue for them.[5]

TMAs have their own problems, however. As mentioned earlier, local governments in California mandated the creation of TMAs in the 1980s. These governments required developers to establish TMAs by tying the granting of building occupancy permits and the approval of rezoning requests to the creation of TMAs in their developments. Some developers, understandably, in turn required membership in TMAs as part of their lease agreements or covenants and conditions in deeds (Dunphy & Lin 1990). Ferguson, Ross, and Meyer (1992) report that, as of 1992, these mandatory membership practices were on the wane.

But another kind of membership problem continues. TMAs typically restrict membership rights of residential property owners and tenants in their areas who are directly impacted by their activities. The Buckhead Area TMA (BATMA) in Atlanta, for example, designates two classes of membership, voting and nonvoting. Large commercial property owners have voting membership, residents and small commercial property owners have only nonvoting membership (BATMA Bylaws at www.batma. org/about/bylaws.pdf; accessed March 12, 2003). This differential membership scheme may not be a legal problem at the moment, but it shows that TMAs like BATMA can avoid procedural accountability to certain designated categories of residents and business owners in their areas. To prevent resistance to these policies, some TMAs and their affiliated CIDs in Georgia informally include residents in their strategic land-use planning practices.[6]

In terms of the societal outcomes or programmatic impacts, there have been some studies of TMAs modifying travel behavior, but they are spotty. Ferguson, Ross, and Meyer (1992, 102) report that over half (54%) of the TMAs they surveyed had never undertaken any evaluation studies. Ferguson and Davidson (1995, 45) report that Florida conducted an evaluation of its TMAs in the early 1990s.

Ferguson (1997, 360–361) identifies three modes of evaluation for TMAs: (1) level of participation in their programs (request for information, signing up for activities, and actual participation in carpools, vanpools, and bus programs); (2) transportation system effects (number of trips, vehicle miles traveled, and hours of travel); and (3) broader policy effects (higher level of service, reduced traffic congestion, and reduced pollution). Among these, the first mode, participation levels, is the easiest one to study, and there are a few studies conducted in this mode. Evaluations in the other two modes are rare. Ferguson cites two studies in Los Angeles and San Francisco that found only modest reductions in the rates of driving alone, corroborating the results of earlier studies reported by Dunphy and Lin (1990). Dunphy and Lin also report that these studies found that the presence of very large employers in a TMA's area affects drive-alone rates most significantly because it is easier to find rideshare matches with a large employer. According to these studies, TMAs are most successful in organizing flextime and staggered shifts, thus effectively reducing peak-hour traffic. But overall traffic in TMA areas is not affected much.

PUBLIC EDUCATION, POLICY ADVOCACY, AND PLANNING

Public education and policy advocacy became increasingly important TMA functions in the 1990s. Most TMAs use their Web sites and other means of communication to persuade their members and others in their areas to drive their cars less and take advantage of their programs like ridesharing and reduced rates for public transit passes. They and their affiliated BIDs also act as lobbying groups to attract public investments to their areas and push the transportation projects they favor up on the agendas of state and local governments. There appear to be no systematic studies on the influence of these entities on state and local government policy making, but in a few but significant legal cases, like the lawsuits against New York's Grand Central Partnership, it is argued that these entities have extraordinary leverage in influencing public policies because of the economic and political power of the businesses among their members (Garodnick 2000).

The political influences of TMAs and BIDs may be seen as yet another example of interest groups using their powers to influence public policy. However, when they engage directly in strategic land-use planning, it becomes a more serious issue of using governmental powers. Except that states may impose guidelines or restrictions, land-use planning is the prerogative of local governments. In Georgia CIDs such as Cumberland, Midtown, and Buckhead have developed plans for their areas on their own (with participation open to the public), which propose changes and developments in transportation infrastructure (streets and sidewalks), street-level retailing, and green space, and thus are tantamount to land-use planning. As noted in the documents of these CIDs, their plans also include "changes in development and zoning regulations, adoption of urban design standards" (www.commuterclub.com/blueprint.htm; accessed December 18, 2002).

CIDs in Georgia have not usurped governmental powers, however. In fact, they have been granted the right to make plans by local governments, and they exercise this right in collaboration with governmental entities. In the 2000 amendments to the cooperation agreements between the CIDs in Cobb County (Cumberland and Town Center) and the county government, "planning, development, and improvement consistent with Cobb County's coordinated and comprehensive planning" is designated as a "service" of CIDs. Similarly, Atlanta's Downtown, Buckhead, and Midtown CIDs have the power of "construction and maintenance of local, collector and arterial streets."

The planning authorities and political influences of TMAs and BIDs also have larger, societal ramifications. They are criticized by some for creating social segregation in cities through differential provision of services (see Briffault 1999; Lavery 1995; Mallet 1993; Ross & Levine 2001, 245 for these criticisms). As such, BIDs and TMAs may be contributing to the service-delivery gap between the rich and the poor. (It's not that poorer areas cannot form TMAs or BIDs—there are some, such as in South Fulton County, just south of Atlanta, but they do not have the business resources to attract the huge public investments the rich ones have.)

Arguably, they also are engaged in activities that are essentially public in nature. BIDs and TMAs may relieve local governments from their obligations to deliver services (as we mentioned before, many local governments willingly turned over some authority and money to these entities), but, the critics argue, in the process they can circumvent the public policy process and become part of the coercive powers of the state.

CONCLUSIONS: TMAs, NETWORK GOVERNANCE, AND PUBLIC POLICY MAKING AND ADMINISTRATION

TMAs and other private business organizations that exercise public authority pose challenges to conventional public policy making and administration theory and practice. These are not conventional public bureaucracies that can be held accountable to the public through elected representatives or hierarchically structured bureaucracies. These private business organizations participate directly in public policy making and service delivery with little or no public oversight. Phenomena such as TMAs and other private business organizations acting in such a fashion can be better understood via the evolving theories of networks.

Kickert, Klijn, and Koppenjan (1997), O'Toole (1997), and Frederickson (1999) all agree that the functions of government have been transformed in recent decades as governance has become dominated by networks in which government is only one actor. According to Kickert and his colleagues, the failures of governmental policies in the 1960s and 1970s; the increasingly interdependent, complex, and global nature of the world economy; and the increasing ethnic and economic diversification of societies led to the emergence of policy networks as the main mechanisms of policy making and implementation in Western democracies. They point out that in such network governance the role of "sovereign authorities" has diminished and the "rational central rule approach" does not work any more (1997, 1–9).

Frederickson (1999) observes that contemporary public administration takes place in the context of a declining relationship between jurisdiction and public management, the erosion of the importance of geography due to globalization of economies, and the disarticulation of the state and its capacity to deal with complex social problems. Under these circumstances, the meaning of "public" has broadened, and the distinctions between public and private organizations have become fuzzier. Consequently, he observes, public policies are made and implemented more and more in networks or network constellations, as illustrated particularly well in metropolitan areas.

TMAs and other business organizations participating in transportation policy making and service delivery exemplify the emergence of network governance. They are examples of the broadening of the meaning of "public" and the erosion of the distinctions between public and private. Although their membership is composed largely of the representatives of private, for-profit organizations, they have some powers usually reserved for governments (e.g., planning). Although they are bound by the legal norms set by public authorities, they are, for the most part, not subject to the bureaucratic control of governments. Although there are occasional evaluations of TMAs by state governments (e.g., in Florida), in general they are not regularly audited, monitored, or controlled by governments. More important, their creation is actively encouraged—in some cases even mandated—by government agencies, and they use their economic and political power to influence transportation and land-use policies. These private organizations are becoming increasingly significant actors in network governance.

Bresser and O'Toole (1998) emphasize that government agencies are not "authorities" but "actors," albeit still very significant actors in network governance. Despite the fact that the boundary between public and private has been blurred, there are still organizations, such as local and state agencies, that are "more public" and have more authority. They can set the legal ground rules for other actors' performance and steer network actors toward broad policy goals. In transportation policy, as we discussed earlier, federal, state, and local governments played very major roles in the creation of the environment that enabled and encouraged the establishment of TMAs. While this did not give them hierarchically superior roles in transportation policy networks, they remained major and powerful actors that can set the stage for others.

These network conditions pose new challenges to public administrators. As O'Toole (1997) points out, public administrators must learn the new network realities and develop skills to deal with them. Frederickson (1999) concurs and emphasizes that the primary skills required in networks are negotiation and diplomacy. Beyond O'Toole's and Frederickson's observations, the expanding scope of public administration in governance networks means basically two things: First, our concept of public administration will have to be broadened to include such organizations as TMAs. TMA managers and their boards will have to be considered new actors in the administration of public policies. TMA managers are partners with the traditional public administrators, because in the new network governance TMAs work interdependently with governments. And second, as such, TMA managers have the obligation to collaborate with traditional public administrators in improving the conditions not only of their own nuclear areas, but also those of the community at large.

NOTES

1. Judd and Swanstrom (2004) contend that such special entities were created because they could circumvent official fiscal constraints. Such entities were typically private but promoted by the mayors of the time who encouraged public/private partnerships either to help with local problems as TMAs do or help with funding public projects as BIDs do.

2. BIDs are included here because in some states, such as Georgia, transportation management is the primary reason for the creation of BIDs and most TMAs are affiliated with BIDs.

3. Interviews in Georgia indicate that business associations create TMAs as legal entities for mainly two reasons. First, TMAs provide the organizational structure through which public monies (e.g., grants and state transportation investments) can be "leveraged." Second, TMAs are legal entities that allow organizations and individuals who are not business owners, such as public agencies and residents, to participate in the discussion and solution of local transportation problems. It should also be noted that in Georgia the state constitution sanctions TMAs as programs of BIDs, as discussed below, and the Atlanta Regional Commission (the largest and most important MPO in the state) encourages local businesses to create TMAs.

4. CIDs use their own monies to fund transportation improvement studies. Also when state and local DOTs get their budgetary allocations (or when federal grants become available), the CIDs are the only organized interest groups ready with a concrete plan for spending transportation funds. Since CIDs typically represent the metropolitan area's most heavily trafficked nodes, counties (and the state) are willing to accept their requests. The feasibility studies that CIDs conduct with their own money prior to proposing their projects make their requests particularly attractive to the local and state governments.

5. Only where there are significant overlaps between the members of BIDs and TMAs and where the two types of organizations are legally affiliated, as is the case in Georgia, then the one person one vote principle becomes a problem for TMAs as well.

6. Interviews in Georgia indicate that the Cumberland, Midtown, and Buckhead CIDs actively recruited residents in their areas for their strategic planning processes.

REFERENCES

Barr, H. (1997). More like Disneyland: State action 42 U.S.C. § 1983, and business improvement districts in New York. *Columbia Human Rights Law Review, 28*(2), 393–430.

Bresser, H. T. A., & O'Toole, L. J. (1998). The selection of policy instruments: A network-based perspective. *Journal of Public Policy, 18*(3), 213–239.

Briffault, R. (1999). A government for our time? Business improvement districts and urban governance. *Columbia Law Review, 99*(2), 365–477.

Chandler, R. C., & Plano, J. (1988). *The public administration dictionary.* Santa Barbara, CA: ABC-CLIO.

Dunphy, R. T., & Lin, B. C. (1990). *Transportation management through partnerships.* Washington, DC: Urban Land Institute.

Farazmand, A. (2001). Privatization of public enterprise reform? Implications for public management. In A. Farazmand (Ed.), *Privatization or public enterprise reform? International case studies with implications for public management.* Westport, CT: Greenwood Press.

Ferguson, E. (1997). Privatization as choice probability, policy process and program outcome: The case of transportation management associations. *Journal of Transportation Research, Part A: Policy and Practice, 31*(5), 353–364.

Ferguson, E. (2000). *Travel demand management and public policy.* Aldershot, UK: Ashgate.

Ferguson, E., & Davidson, D. (1995). Transportation management associations: An update. *Transportation Quarterly, 49*(1), 45–60.

Ferguson, E., Ross, C., & Meyer, M. (1992 May). *Transportation management associations in the United States: Final report.* Washington, D.C.: U.S. Department of Transportation, Technology Sharing Program (DOT-T-92-22).

Frederickson, H. G. (1999, December). The repositioning of American public administration. *PS,* 701–711.

Garodnick, D. R. (2000). What's the BID deal? Can the Grand Central Business Improvement District serve a special limited purpose? *University of Pennsylvania Law Review, 148*(5), 1733–1771.

Horan, T. A., Dittmar, H., & Jordan, D. R. (2001). ISTEA and the new era in transportation policy: Sustainable communities from federal initiative. In D. Mazmanian & M. E. Kraft (Eds.), *Toward sustainable communities: Transition and transformations in environmental policy* (217–245). Cambridge, MA: The MIT Press.

Houstoun, L. O. Jr. (1997). *Business improvement districts.* Washington, D.C.: Urban Land Institute.

Howitt, A. M., & Altshuler, A. (1999). The politics of controlling auto air pollution. In J. A. Gómez-Ibánez, W. B. Tye, & C. Winston (Eds.), *Essays in transportation economics and policy* (223–256). Washington, D.C.: Brookings Institution Press.

Judd, D. R., & Swanstrom, T. (2004). *City politics: Private power and public policy* (4th ed.). New York: Pearson Longman.

Kickert, W. J. M., Klijn, E. H., & Koppenjan, J. F. (1997). *Managing complex networks: Strategies for the public sector.* Thousand Oaks, CA: Sage.

Lavery, K. (1995). Privatization by the back door: The rise of private government in the USA. *Public Money and Management, 15*(4), 49–53.

Loveless, S. M., & Welch, J. S. (1999). Growing to meet the challenges: Emerging roles for transportation management associations. *Transportation Research Record, 1659,* 121–128.

Mallett, W. J. (1993). Private government formation in the D.C. metropolitan area. *Growth and Change, 24*(3), 385–416.

Orski, C. K. (1982). The changing environment of urban transportation. *Journal of the American Planning Association, 48*(3), 304–316.

O'Toole, L. J., Jr. (1997). Treating networks seriously: Practical and research-based agendas in public administration. *Public Administration Review, 57*(1), 45–52.

Pack, J. R. (1992). BIDs, DIDs, SIDs, SADs: Private governments in urban America. *Brookings Review, 10*(4), 18–22.

Plant, J. F. (1988). Beyond the beltway: Urban transportation policy in the 1980s. *Journal of Urban Affairs, 10*(1), 29–40.

Reese, K. (2001, November 1). Dollars-and-sense solution. *Georgia Trend, 17*(1), 55–59.

Ross, B. H., & Levine, M. A. (2001). *Urban politics: Power in metropolitan America* (6th ed.). Itasca, IL: F. E. Peacock Publishers, Inc.

Salamon, L. M. (2002). The new governance and the tools of public action: An introduction. In L. M. Salamon, & O. V. Elliott (Eds.), *The tools of government: A guide to the new governance* (1–47). New York: Oxford University Press.

Smith, R. (1999). Government financing of nonprofit activity. In E. T. Boris & C. E. Steuerle (eds.), *Nonprofits and government: Collaboration and conflict* (177–210). Washington, D.C.: The Urban Institute Press.

Teisman, G. R., & Klijn, E. (2002). Partnership arrangements: Governmental rhetoric or governance scheme? *Public Administration Review, 62*(2), 197–205.

Thurmaier, K., & Wood, C. (2002). Interlocal agreements as overlapping social networks: Picket-fence regionalism in metropolitan Kansas City. *Public Administration Review, 62*(5), 585–598.

TMA Directory (1995). Washington, DC: Association for Commuter Transportation.

TMA Handbook: A guide to successful transportation management associations. (2001). Washington, D.C.: Association for Commuter Transportation.

Weiner, E. (1999). *Urban transportation planning in the United States: An historical overview* (2nd ed.). Westport, CT: Praeger.

12 Urban Transportation Policy: The Baltimore Experience

Z. Andrew Farkas

INTRODUCTION

Throughout the history of the United States transportation has been an important factor in the *concentration* of population and employment. Transportation is a factor in the formation of settlements and change of urban form. During the colonial era, small ports on the East Coast served as gateways to the unsettled interior. Later, some of them became large urban centers. Baltimore expanded in this way from its port, and St. Louis later developed around its *break bulk* and gateway location on the Mississippi River. Atlanta flourished at the crossing of railroads. Transportation then became instrumental in the *deconcentration* of cities. Streetcar suburbs sprang up at the termini of streetcar lines laid at the end of the nineteenth century. The recently formed power and light companies owned streetcar companies and land on the urban fringe. They expanded the streetcar lines outward, developing the land as they went. Suburban development in turn created greater demand for electricity.

Prior to World War II, as households moved to the suburbs in greater numbers and the Depression caused serious job loss, transit ridership declined. The deconcentration of cities gathered new momentum during the post-war period. The rapidly expanding economy created unprecedented demand for automobiles. Energy prices remained under control, and automobile user fees were low. The Federal Aid Highway Act of 1956 imposed taxes on motor vehicle fuels and established an abundant source of funding for the Interstate and Defense Highways and other federal and state roads.

Metropolitan areas of the United States have continued to undergo deconcentrations of population and employment (Hughes 1992; Pisarski 1996). The Interstate and other highways have reduced travel costs for travelers and freight haulers, improved safety, and increased regional connectivity. The *malling* of America has created the opportunity to work in suburban villages and industrial campuses with abundant free parking. Real fuel prices have declined steadily from their peaks in the 1970s. Suburb-to-suburb commuting to employment has become a large and rapidly growing component of metropolitan trip-making. According to Pisarski (1996), driving to work alone was the mode of choice for all workers in the 1980s and walking, carpooling, and taking public transit to work declined. This trend continued but moderated during the 1990s (see Table 12.1).

The declining share of workers commuting by transit has been further evidence of the automobile's dominance, but the number of passenger trips has fluctuated, influenced by federal transit policies and economic conditions. The lowest number of passenger trips, 6.5 billion, occurred in 1972, but then trip-making gradually increased, as many transit systems were placed into public ownership (APTA 2005). By 1990 passenger trips reached 8.8 billion trips, but dropped to 7.7 billion in 1995 during the economic downturn of the early 1990s. The number jumped to 9.7 billion by 2001 during the economic expansion of the late 1990s, but in 2002 the number fell a bit to 9.6 billion, as another economic downturn began to take effect.

The single occupant vehicle (SOV) has brought about an unprecedented level of mobility and economic opportunity for most Americans in metropolitan areas. On the other hand, that dominance by the SOV has contributed to urban maladies of congestion and delay, poor air quality, and inaccessibility to employment opportunities for the urban poor.

Most metropolitan areas of the United States experience vehicular congestion during peak hours, wasting many hours of travel time for commuters, business clients, and freight haulers. Congestion has been an acceptable and common occurrence throughout

TABLE 12.1

Means of Transportation to Work Metropolitan Areas, 1980, 1990, 2000

	Percent of Total Workers								
	Drove Alone			**Car Pool**			**Public Transit**		
Metropolitan Area	1980	1990	2000	1980	1990	2000	1980	1990	2000
Atlanta	68.7	78.0	77.0	19.6	12.7	13.6	7.6	4.7	3.7
Baltimore	59.8	70.9	75.4	22.3	14.2	11.5	10.3	7.7	6.3
Boston	56.0	65.8	73.9	17.0	9.8	8.8	15.6	14.2	8.9
Cleveland	67.9	77.7	82.3	16.0	10.5	8.7	10.6	6.2	3.5
Dallas	71.2	77.6	78.8	20.6	14.0	14.0	3.4	3.2	1.8
Minneapolis	63.1	76.0	78.3	19.9	11.2	10.0	8.7	5.3	4.5
Philadelphia	60.0	67.8	73.3	18.0	11.9	10.3	13.0	11.6	8.7
Pittsburgh	60.7	70.7	77.4	19.4	12.9	9.7	11.5	8.5	6.2
San Diego	63.8	70.9	73.9	17.4	13.8	13.0	3.3	3.3	3.4
San Francisco/ Oakland	57.9	15.7	12.7	12.9	16.4	13.9	9.3	63.1	68.1
Tampa	72.0	78.8	79.7	18.4	13.3	12.4	1.8	1.5	1.3
Washington, D.C.	53.7	62.9	70.4	22.9	15.8	12.8	15.5	13.7	9.4

Source: U.S. Bureau of the Census, 1980, 1990, 2000 Census of Population.

TABLE 12.2
Most Congested Urban Areas 2002

Urban Area	Travel Time Index*	Rank
Los Angeles, CA	1.77	1
San Francisco-Oakland, CA	1.55	2
Chicago, IL-Northwestern, IN	1.54	3
Washington, D.C.-MD-VA	1.50	4
Boston, MA	1.45	5
Atlanta, GA	1.42	6
New York, NY	1.40	7 (tie)
Miami-Hialeah, FL	1.40	8 (tie)
Denver, CO	1.40	9 (tie)
San Diego, CA	1.39	10

*Index represents ratio of peak period travel time to free flow travel time. A value greater than one indicates congested road conditions.
Source: David Shrank and Tim Lomax, The 2004 Urban Mobility Report, Texas Transportation Institute: College Station, TX, 2004.

automotive history, but in many areas it is now truly onerous (see Table 12.2). The Texas Transportation Institute estimates that average delay per peak period traveler has grown from sixteen hours in 1982 to forty-six hours in 2002, costing in excess of $63 billion (Shrank and Lomax, 2004). Congestion also wasted more than 5.6 billion gallons of fuel in 2002. Most large metropolitan areas have serious or severe air quality standard non-attainment designations. The sources of pollution are many and varied, but mobile sources, that is, motor vehicles, contribute greatly.

Many urban expressways were built during a time of lax environmental regulation. Urban expressways, coupled with urban renewal projects, were often located in low-income residential areas, removing residents and employment opportunities and then isolating the remaining residents from each other with physical barriers and open space. Continued deconcentration of employment has left urban pockets of poor and minority residents, especially African Americans, in locations that are less accessible to employment opportunities, resulting in a "spatial mismatch" between housing and jobs (Kain 1993). There has been much debate over whether *race* (prejudice) or *space* best explains inaccessibility to employment, but both play a role.

The Baltimore Metropolitan Area mirrors the national trends. The Baltimore area has experienced growth in population and employment, but a decentralization of growth. Between 1980 and 2000, the area's population increased from 2.17 million to 2.5 million (BRTB, March 2004). Between 1980 and 1990, the number of workers in the metropolitan area commuting from suburb-to-suburb increased by 41.7 percent, and between 1990 and 2000 it increased another 24.1 percent (Steiss and Tabugbo 1993; 2000). The number commuting from suburb-to-city declined by 9.5 percent and 5.6

percent, respectively. Because of the increase in workers but slight decrease in jobs in Baltimore City, city-to-suburb commuting experienced the largest relative increase of 48.0 percent. The "reverse commute" has become a significant component of the commuting pattern.

The percentage of workers in the metropolitan area driving alone grew from 59.8 percent to 75.4 percent between 1980 and 2000, while the percentage of commuters in car/vanpools decreased from 22.3 percent to only 11.5 percent (Table 12.1). Users of transit declined from 10.3 percent to 6.3 percent of all commuters.

Modal shares varied greatly within the metropolitan area, depending on the level of urbanization and location. The percent of workers in Baltimore City using SOVs in 2000 was 54.7 percent of the total, while transit use was 19.0 percent. In Howard County, a suburban county located between Baltimore and Washington, DC, SOV use was 81.9 percent and transit use was only 2.5 percent (CTPP 2000).

The major roads in the Baltimore Area are frequently congested during peak hours. These roads serve as routes for intercity passenger and freight transportation along the East Coast and for commuting and freight distribution throughout a huge market area. Although not among the most congested, Baltimore has a travel time index value of 1.36 and ranks fifteenth among eighty-five metropolitan areas (Shrank and Lomax 2004). Baltimore residents experience some of the longest commutes in the nation (Brewington 2005).

Baltimore has been designated a severe ozone non-attainment area for years, having the fifth worst air pollution in the nation (Besa et al. 1995). Ground level ozone is a meteorologically caused pollutant, enhanced by hot, humid days with little air flow and much automobile commuting. On such days, a plume of ozone typically flows north along and to the east of I-95 from Washington, DC, through Baltimore City and suburban counties.

Low-income residents of Baltimore City suffer the added difficulty of inaccessibility to employment. Many of the jobs in the Baltimore suburbs are beyond the reach of city residents (Abell Foundation 1999). One-third of households in Baltimore City do not own an automobile (Haines 2004). The dispersed nature of job growth makes public transportation from inner-city neighborhoods inconvenient (Farkas 1992). Mass transit travel times for reverse commutes have been significantly longer than for central business district-oriented commutes, and transit's accessibility to suburban activity centers from several areas of the city has been low. The availability of other reverse commute service options have been few, consisting of unreliable van services or expensive taxicabs (Abell Foundation 2001).

It is evident that there are direct linkages among road network expansion, economic development, increased automotive travel, environmental degradation, and inaccessibility to suburban employment for the urban poor. An unresolved question concerns whether some of these links can be broken. Can society provide better mobility for all and improve air quality and accessibility to employment in a cost-effective manner? The answer is a cautious—yes. It is possible to develop strategies for *sustainable mobility*, but it will require local institutional vision, effective education of the public, and the political will to bring about major changes in transportation policy.

POLICY OPTIONS FOR TRANSPORTATION FINANCE

Finance drives much of transportation policy making. The federal government collects motor fuel taxes on gasoline and diesel and other user fees. States collect motor fuel taxes on gasoline and diesel, retail sales taxes on fuel, vehicle weight fees, registration fees, drivers license fees, vehicle license fees, facilities tolls, and emission certification fees. Motorists pay a large portion of the capital costs of facilities. The general public pays for some of the capital and operating costs of roads, particularly local roads, in the form of income, property, and sales taxes.

The establishment of fuel taxes and a trust fund by the Federal Aid Highway Act of 1956, essentially the *earmarking* of motor vehicle taxes exclusively for road construction, meant instant emphasis on road building. The Interstate and Defense Highway funding formula was clearly biased toward building of limited-access highways rather than local roads or transit (Dunn 1981). The share of funding was set at 90 percent federal and 10 percent state and local funds for Interstates, while for other federal-aid highways the share was 50 percent federal and 50 percent state and local.

In the 1970s, the federal highway trust fund was tapped to support ailing transit systems. Federal capital grants, covering virtually all of the construction and equipment purchasing costs, may have contributed to overbuilding or *gilding* of local transit systems. Transit operating subsidies were then required to maintain adequate service levels. Even so, large transit systems throughout the nation have had to raise fares, cut services, and seek new funding, because they are experiencing financial difficulty (Colias 2005).

In the early 1970s, Maryland established its multi-modal trust fund, where state fuel taxes, licensing, and vehicle registration fees go into a fund for all modes of transportation. State officials have often touted the wisdom behind this fund, emphasizing that it supports highways, seaports, BWI Airport, and mass transit, as needed, but it is a policy clearly in opposition to *pay as you go* or *pay as you benefit*. State officials have more recently pointed out that there is insufficient revenue in the trust fund for transit (or for roads, if more money is dedicated to transit). Controversy continues as various transportation interests decry the lack of convenient transit, adequate roads or insufficient development and marketing of the seaports or airport. Thus, state officials have been grappling politically with whether the fuel tax should be raised during a time of constrained state budgets. The last two Maryland governors have decided not to submit requests to the legislature for fuel tax increases, but the issue of funding will surely arise in the future.

The raising of fuel taxes is an issue with its own unique aspects. It is one of those taxes that does not usually cause a visceral reaction by the public against it, because they see the results of those taxes—road and transit facilities—and usually perceive improvement of those facilities as beneficial. On the other hand, the current system of fuel taxes and registration fees is clearly regressive, taking a larger percentage of household income of those in low-income categories. There are criticisms against alternative forms of paying for roads as well. Tolls are often described as paying for roads twice, that is, the toll is in addition to the fuel tax. There are also concerns with and how to charge the increasing numbers of motorists that use alternative fuel or hybrid vehicles. Distance-based user fees, using transponders and GPS, are being proposed to address that concern (Sorensen and Taylor 2005).

POLICY OPTIONS FOR MOBILITY AND AIR QUALITY

It is widely acknowledged that states and metropolitan areas cannot afford to *build their way* out of congestion through more road construction. Urban activists, editorial writers, and some transportation planners describe new roads as merely *inducing* greater demand for roads, quickly filling the expanded road capacity. This situation is actually a simple example of micro-economic theory; the increase in supply (of road capacity) reduces the price (monetary and time costs of automotive travel) and increases the quantity consumed (of road capacity). A shift of the demand curve outward from population and income growth causes the quantity consumed to increase further. Actually, judicious road construction can reduce congestion and facilitate greater mobility for significant periods of time; it depends on the situation.

It is evident that the demand and supply relationship for roads does not hold for public mass transit. Even so, the same activists and editorial writers state that more emphasis must be placed on mass transit to enhance mobility for low-income commuters, reduce congestion, and improve air quality. As the data have already illustrated, merely providing transit service has been insufficient inducement to use it in large numbers. According to Pucher and Renne (2003), public transportation accounted for less than two percent of urban travel in 2001. Even the lowest income households made only 5 percent of trips by public transit. All minority groups make the vast majority of trips by automobile. Research by Hill (1994) showed that while African-Americans at all income levels used transit for a higher proportion of work trips, 11 percent in 1990, than other ethnic groups, a large majority of them, 74 percent, used the private vehicle for commuting to work.

Because relatively few commuters use transit, transit's beneficial impact on air quality has been small. Air quality has nonetheless improved in metropolitan areas because of automobile emission standards imposed on automakers in the 1970s (Koontz 1998). The Baltimore Metropolitan Area has exhibited similar results, according to Maryland Department of the Environment data (Energy and Environmental Analysis 1995). While vehicle-miles of travel have increased since 1970, the air quality in Baltimore has improved with reductions in vehicle emissions. However, Baltimore's air quality still does not meet federal standards for ground level ozone.

Hope for additional emissions reduction rests in part on the use of low-emission and zero-emission vehicles (LEVs and ZEVs). LEVs tend to be hybrid internal combustion and electrically powered or alternative fuel powered vehicles; they are becoming popular with consumers. The only ZEV technology currently available is electric vehicles, but their appeal is very small, because they can only travel short distances before requiring recharge.

While LEVs and ZEVs may well continue auto emissions reduction and fulfill the public policy goal of cleaner air in the nation's cities, there will still be the difficulty of maintaining mobility and accessibility to employment for metropolitan residents. Grid-lock with LEVs and ZEVs during peak hours would not allow metropolitan residents or freight haulers to travel faster, even if the air they breathe while stuck in traffic is dramatically improved. Some modification of travel behaviors will be needed to reduce the cost of time spent on the commute to work.

POLICY OPTIONS FOR MANAGING TRANSPORTATION DEMAND

Economists have for many years argued that public policy should first *internalize the externalities* of the automobile, i.e., place the full costs of automobile use, including congestion and pollution, on the user (Vickrey 1963; Zettel and Carll 1964). The user would be faced with an overt monetary price for travel and would presumably make more rational choices, thereby lessening the externalities or negative effects of auto-mobile travel. Without pricing, the queue (and the amount of time spent in the queue) rations road space, during peak and off-peak times.

Congestion pricing of roads consists of variable tolls that vary by time of day and level of congestion. Change in the travel behavior of commuters resulting from congestion pricing may lead to shifts in traffic from peak to off- peak periods, changes in routes, increases in ride sharing, and transit, and decreases in trip making. These effects of pricing are believed to increase the efficiency with which the road system is used and reduce the demand for additional capacity. In addition to lessening the need for new capital investment, pricing could increase transit ridership, assuming transit is a convenient option. Pricing could reduce energy consumption by reducing trips and improving traffic flow, and it may also bring some decline in the level of environmental pollution.

In years past, the technology was not readily available to charge motorists through-out a network for peak period travel. The suggested means of applying congestion pricing was to vary tolls on tunnels and bridges. Several such applications have been underway. New York's Triborough Bridge and Tunnel Authority has been studying op-tions for pricing of its bridges and tunnels. The New York State Thruway has variable tolls for trucks on the Tappan Zee Bridge north of New York City. The New Jersey Turnpike utilizes discounts from the normal toll on trucks during peak hours to take trucks off local roads. Lee County, Florida, has variable tolls on two bridges. In this case, travelers during times prior to and after peak periods receive a 50 percent discount off the regular toll (Samuel 1998).

The technology does now exist for pricing of congested networks. *Intelligent transportation systems* can count vehicles, identify them, and display user fees on variable message signs on roadways. Much of the interest in applying congestion pric-ing lies in the realm of pricing of High Occupancy Vehicle (HOV) lanes. HOV lanes, an example of which is the Shirley Highway HOV lanes in Northern Virginia, allow vehicles with two or more adults to travel in exclusive lanes during peak hours. The pricing of HOV lanes or HOT lanes (High Occupancy free/Toll others) is frequently described as *value pricing*, whereby a single commuter can pay a toll to travel in the HOV lane and avoid congestion. Poole and Orski (2003) estimate that most HOV lanes nationwide are underutilized, thus providing many opportunities for HOT lanes that allow SOVs to use them for a fee.

HOT lane projects in operation are located in Orange County and San Diego, California; Minneapolis; and Houston (Egan 2005; Burris and Stockton 2004; Havinoviski 2004). The most widely known HOT lane demonstration project in the country is the Interstate 15 Value Pricing Project near San Diego. FHWA awarded the San Diego Association of Governments almost $8 million to operate the project in cooperation with the California Department of Transportation, the Federal Transit Administration, and other agencies. I-15's unrestricted lanes frequently exhibited severe (Level F) congestion during morning and evening peak hours, while the HOV lanes were underutilized (Lawrence 1998).

The electronic toll collection system for the I-15 project, called FasTrak, requires a transponder on each participating automobile. The system then identifies the vehicle and deducts a toll from a customer's prepaid account. The toll varies based on actual traffic speed on I-15's unrestricted lanes. Electronic signs located at the entrance to the HOV lanes indicate the current toll. Tolls may vary from $0.50 to $4.00 for a one-way trip on the eight mile facility to maintain free flow. Prior to the introduction of FasTrak, I-15 HOV lanes carried an average of 9,200 vehicles per day (Lawrence 1998). Three months after introduction in June 1998, an average of 12,400 vehicles per day were using the HOV lanes. FasTrak revenue is required by state law to be spent on transit, carpool services, and the HOV facilities.

The implementation of a congestion pricing program does impose other costs on society. Congestion pricing incurs capital costs required to install the system and operating costs for administrating the program. There are also some potential side effects that may result. They include queuing in response to price changes, accidents, enforcement costs, spill over of traffic to other roads, and the relocation of businesses.

Equity concerns associated with congestion pricing involve income, gender, race, age, employment, and residential location. Value of time is positively correlated to income. The higher the income, the higher is the value of time. Since the major objective of congestion pricing is to reduce travel time, the people to benefit most from pricing are those of middle to high income (Small et al. 1989). Low-income drivers will be adversely affected financially by road pricing (Egan 2005). Because the proportion of out-of-pocket costs is inversely related to income, congestion pricing is most likely to force low-income people to change their travel behavior.

Revenues from congestion pricing could be used to compensate low-income drivers through reduction of other regressive road user fees or direct rebates (Small et al. 1989). Goodwin (1989) has suggested using the revenue to increase spending on road infrastructure and public mass transit. He believes that this approach would more likely satisfy freight haulers, public transportation users, environmentalists, and motorists. This writer suggests that transponders and *smart cards* now allow differential pricing of congestion. Low-income commuters, identified through some means test, could be charged a lower toll in proportion to income, while high-income commuters would be charged a higher toll. Both groups' behavior would be affected by a price, but one appropriate to the income level.

Giuliano (1994) concluded that there is inequity between men and women drivers.

Males tend to have more flexible work schedules than females, who typically have more family-related duties and may not be able to avoid peak-periods. She has argued that redistributing toll revenue based on income would not address the negative impacts on females. However, Johnston-Anumonwo (1992) found that women, more so than men, have suburban jobs. Thus, women may be able to avoid a congestion price facing those that commute to a central business district.

A concern of the business community is the possible competitive disadvantage to those businesses in a congestion priced area vis-à-vis those businesses in an area without congestion pricing. Higgens (1994) suggested that businesses whose customers and suppliers are affected by congestion pricing might receive property tax or other business tax rebates. If congestion pricing reduces congestion, then certainly businesses would benefit from that condition.

Because of various costs and concerns many planners and local officials are fearful of the potential political resistance to congestion or value pricing. The fear appears to be unfounded, given the popularity of value priced lanes with commuters in California (Argetsinger and Ginsberg 2005). San Diego's I-15 value pricing project has gained extensive public acceptance (Havinoviski 2004; Supernak et al. 1999). A majority of the users of I-15's unrestricted lanes and HOV lanes thought the program was fair. Evaluations of congestion pricing projects, including I-15 FasTrak, Lee County's Bridge Tolls, and Tappan Zee Bridge Tolls, show that travel behavior is modified by congestion pricing; yet, there is public acceptance of it (Adler et al. 1999; Berg et al. 1999).

While state and local governments generally have been reluctant to price automobile trips, they have relied to some extent on other measures of transportation demand management (TDM). The objective of TDM is to increase the efficiency of roads by reducing SOV trips, particularly during peak travel times, by administrative or economic measures. Studies have indicated that with sufficiently strong financial incentives/disincentives, travel behavior regarding mode choice can be changed (Wachs 1990). Short of pricing the automobile trip, which is organizationally and technologically complex, reducing the subsidy for urban parking would be a simpler, but effective TDM strategy.

Parking fee strategies, e.g., parking surcharges and subsidized parking for ride-sharers, are widely acknowledged to be among the most effective at promoting ride-sharing or transit (Delaware Valley Regional Planning Commission 1994; Wilson and Shoup 1990; Feeney 1989). Yet, these strategies have not been popular among local governments either, for some of the same reasons that other pricing schemes have not been widely accepted. The more popular incentives are typically transit support or supply strategies, such as ride-share matching, transit promotion and marketing, but they are among the least effective strategies at changing mode choice (COMSIS, Inc. 1994; Giuliano et al. 1993).

When parking costs are low and the convenience of parking is high, then commuting by automobile is more often the preferred method of travel by individuals at all income levels. Pickrell (1991) observed that free parking can be worth more than free gasoline. According to the 1990 Nationwide Personal Transportation Survey, 90 percent of commuters who drove to work had free parking (Transportation Research Board 1997). Employers have traditionally subsidized the cost of parking as a way to provide an important employee perk at taxpayers' expense. Employer-paid parking has received favorable treatment in the tax code, first as a tax-deductible business expense and as a tax-exempt fringe benefit for employees. Employees who paid for parking could not deduct those costs as a work-related expense.

To redress the imbalance in modal subsidy Shoup (1997) proposed a program for cashing out parking subsidies. Employees would receive a taxable cash allowance to use for parking, transit, or other modes. Shoup estimated that cashing out parking subsidies in Los Angeles would result in reducing the number of vehicle-trips to downtown by 9,000/day or the SOV share from 69 percent to 55 percent. Recent federal legislation has allowed cashing out of parking subsidies.

Shoup (1999) has also argued for cities to limit parking rather than have minimum numbers of spaces required at new developments. Developers would not be compelled to provide an abundant number of parking spaces, but could provide fewer spaces toward a more pedestrian or transit oriented development. Greenberg (2005) has calculated that minimum parking requirements increase cost per urban dwelling unit by an average $85,000 for each parking space required by zoning regulations.

POLICY OPTIONS FOR LAND USE AND GROWTH MANAGEMENT

It has been suggested that land use policies and plans that favor increasing residential and employment area densities would improve employee access, reduce automobile commute trips and increase transit ridership. Pushkarev and Zupan (1977) illustrated that as high densities make the automobile a less convenient transportation choice, as in the case of high-density European and Canadian cities and New York City, transit use reaches respectable levels. Cervero (1994) showed that with increased density through developments that cluster work places and residences near rail stations shares of commute trips by rail transit increase. These kinds of developments are described in the literature as *transit oriented development*.

High-density suburban developments generate much automobile traffic, but they may also provide the conditions for mass transit to achieve cost-effectiveness. Mixed-use developments that combine commercial/industrial activities with low to moderate-income housing could increase job accessibility and reduce trip-making. However, it should be noted that as household incomes rise, optimal travel declines; that is, people do not necessarily travel to the nearest opportunity for employment, shopping, or school. Thus, residents of mixed-use developments do not necessarily work at the same development.

Giuliano (1995) has argued that the patterns of land use after many decades of development are in place and essentially fixed and because of the current pricing of transportation, land use is of little importance to location decisions and to travel behavior. She states, "...efforts to shift travel to other modes, either by promoting higher-density land use patterns or building of massive rail systems are doomed to fail if current automobile pricing policies are maintained."

There may appear to be a divergence of opinion regarding the ability of land use planning and growth management to influence commuting behavior, but there is instead a difference in scale. Certainly, high-density commercial developments connected by transit to high-density residential developments could bring about an incremental increase in transit use (Barnes 2005). Yet, with the overall pattern of the built environment in place, along with rising incomes and current automobile pricing, travel behavior in total will reflect the existing pattern and favor the automobile.

It has also been suggested that transportation infrastructure, rail transit in particular, despite its centrifugal effects in the past, can cause redevelopment in urban areas. According to Bourne (1991), urban redevelopment (population turnaround and land use succession) is associated with urban areas having "... growing and diversified service-based economies; historic and amenity-rich central cores; relatively strong public transit systems; interventionist public administrations (that channel growth, revenues, and infrastructure into inner-city areas); active municipal housing construction programs and a relatively long history of inner city living." Nelson's (1999) extensive research on the Atlanta rapid rail system's development impacts around rail stations indicated that transit in concert with other development tools can be an agent of redevelopment in the city. Portland, Oregon, is known for its light rail system and land use controls that seem to channel high-density residential and commercial development along rail lines.

Whether Baltimore meets Bourne's criteria or has similar development strategies as Atlanta or Portland is debatable; yet, light rail and other transit initiatives have been sold to the public in part for their redevelopment potential. There is little evidence that light rail has spurred redevelopment in Baltimore. One merely has to travel along Howard Street to confirm this view. It should be clear to policy makers that while transportation is a necessary condition for development, it is insufficient by itself to spur growth. If insufficient transportation capacity inhibits growth, then certainly increased capacity may spur it. Otherwise, additional factors must be present for economic growth to occur. It has been stated well and succinctly that "...a transit system cannot by its mere presence catalyze miracles in the inner city" (Loukaiton-Sidiris and Banerjee 1996).

POLICY OPTIONS ON ACCESS TO JOBS

Much research was conducted on reverse commuting policy in the early 1970s, because job growth was occurring in the suburbs, while unemployment among urban residents remained high. Under Republican administrations in the 1980s, entrepreneurial reverse commute services were heavily touted as a solution to inaccessibility to employment. Reverse commuting programs fell into disfavor in the early years of the Clinton administration, when urban redevelopment became the focus of urban policy. Later, the reality of the costs of redevelopment made policy makers acknowledge the role that reverse commuting must play.

Welfare-to-work initiatives have anchored reverse commute projects within the welfare reform movement. Various public officials have described reverse commuting as the *to* in welfare-to-work. The Transportation Equity Act for the 21st Century (TEA-21) provided funding opportunities for metropolitan areas through job access and reverse commute provisions.

New markets for private sector commuter services, including reverse commute services, have opened up. Such services have become established because of public and private sector financial support and because they can increase access to jobs and other activities at lower cost than that of mass transit. Yet, a comprehensive review of reverse commute services over many years by Rosenbloom (1992) concluded that the majority of such services were financially unsuccessful. Rosenbloom acknowledged that there were some exceptions. Hughes (1992) suggested that reverse commute services with a comprehensive approach of providing workers and transportation service and having links to the suburban business community could be successful. This writer reached similar conclusions based on three case studies of reverse commute providers with relatively comprehensive approaches in Chicago, Philadelphia, and Orlando (Farkas 1993).

In 1998, TEA-21 established the Access to Jobs and Reverse Commute Program in support of welfare to work legislation. USDOT's initial competitive service grants gave way to congressional earmarks in subsequent years, because the selection process and program effectiveness were called into question (Peterson and Sandoval 2004). It became unclear whether the program effectively moved individuals, literally and figureatively, into the workforce. One government assessment found that most services supported by the program were not financially viable over the long run. Peterson and Sandoval concluded that the program has had too little evaluation of its efficacy and that its goals were noble but vague.

One program that has gained popularity and is an excellent example of the clash between the goals of reducing congestion/improving air quality and increasing mobility of low-wage labor is that of supplying cars for free or low cost to former welfare recipients. A welfare-to-work transportation grant supported such a program in Fairfax County, Virginia (Reid 1999). The Fairfax program has provided social service clients with money to pay for half of the cost of a used car. The program also has provided counseling on finance of automobile expenses, such as insurance. Anne Arundel County's welfare-to-work efforts include a *free car* program whereby used government fleet cars are donated to charities, which then give the cars to former welfare recipients that have found jobs (Reid 1999). While it appears that encouraging additional car ownership among low-income employees may add to congestion, not to do so could raise serious equity issues and would complicate the achieving of other public policy objectives.

BALTIMORE'S TRANSPORTATION PLAN

Transportation policy in the Baltimore Metropolitan Area, as in other areas, is formulated by transportation agencies and elected officials on federal, state, and local levels. On the one hand, transportation policy is formulated by a centralized system on the federal and state levels, because most of the funding of transportation projects comes from federal and state governments. On the other hand, it is a decentralized system, because much of the decision making regarding the mix, timing, and location of transportation infrastructure occurs on the metropolitan, city, and county levels. These systems of transportation policy development are melded through the long-range transportation planning process. Each urbanized area with a base population of 50,000 must have a transportation planning process and transportation plan in order to receive federal capital and operating funds.

The Baltimore Area's transportation system consists first and foremost of express-ways, toll bridges and tunnels, and primary and secondary roads and streets. These facilities are planned, designed, constructed and maintained by the State Highway Ad-ministration and Maryland Transportation Authority in cooperation with the Baltimore Regional Transportation Board and various jurisdictions' departments of public works. The road network is in the historic radial pattern emanating from and traversing the Baltimore Central Business District. The radial pattern of roads and streets, following historic routes of ingress and egress from a compact city, does not serve well current dispersed travel. The Baltimore Beltway, I-695, was built, as was the case in many metropolitan areas, to allow interstate travelers to bypass the city entirely. The beltway, again as in many metropolitan areas, has become a *main street* for local commuting, frequently becoming subject to recurring and incidental congestion.The Maryland Transit Administration (MTA), a modal administration of the Maryland Department of Transportation, is a state agency operating a local transit service. MTA operates regularly scheduled bus service in all jurisdictions of the metropolitan area, except Carroll County. MTA operates the Suburban Transit Program to provide peak-period bus service to suburban areas and park-and-ride lots. The MTA also is the source of state and federal funding for the Washington Metropolitan Area Transit Authority and for city and county transit services throughout the state.

MTA also operates rail services, but the network is rather piecemeal, with one rapid-rail line in the northwest, one light rail line running north to south, and a com-muter rail corridor running from the northeast of Baltimore south to Washington, DC. There has been a noticeable lack of interconnection of these systems. For example, the light rail station at BWI airport is not near the commuter rail line at the BWI sta-tion (although shuttle service between the two exists). The MTA, to its credit, has now made a high priority of creating interconnections, such as the Camden Station Transit Terminal, where the commuter rail and light rail lines intersect.

All fixed route transit service providers in the Baltimore Area provide para-transit services that comply with the Americans with Disabilities Act. Since the late 1970s, MTA has provided mobility service, lift-equipped bus service and taxicabs to transport persons who are unable to use standard transit buses because of disabilities. Many for-profit, non-profit, and social service agencies also provide demand responsive services to their clients throughout the metropolitan area.

The latest Baltimore Area transportation plan represents the area's transportation objectives and actions in fulfillment of the requirements of the Intermodal Surface Transportation Efficiency Act of 1991, the Clean Air Act Amendments of 1990, and TEA-21. In addition Maryland's Neighborhood Conservation and Smart Growth Act requires counties to meet certain criteria with regard to investing in transportation facilities. Because the Baltimore Area is a Severe Ozone Non-attainment Area, the transportation plan must be updated every three years and approved by the U.S. Envi-ronmental Protection Agency.

The transportation plan is a compendium of strategies and actions for planned changes through the year 2030 (Baltimore Regional Transportation Board 2004). The plan covers the transportation systems of the jurisdictions comprising the Baltimore Area as well as the state transportation system within the area. The plan is multi-modal in orientation, addressing highways, transit, bicycle/pedestrian, rail, and ground access to aviation and maritime facilities.

The Baltimore Regional Transportation Board (BRTB) is the designated Metropolitan Planning Organization for the Baltimore Area. The BRTB consists of representatives from the cities of Annapolis and Baltimore; the counties of Anne Arundel, Baltimore, Carroll, Harford, and Howard; and the Maryland Department of Transportation, the Maryland Department of the Environment, and the Maryland Office of Planning. The Baltimore Metropolitan Council staff conducts the analyses and modeling to determine the expected results of various assumptions and scenarios.

The BRTB conducts public outreach efforts, which are designed to make the public aware of the transportation planning process and to solicit public opinion on transportation issues and planning results. The plan incorporates the land use plans of the member jurisdictions and addresses issues of land use, environmental concerns, and economic development. The BRTB identified five goals for the region with input from citizens and other advisory groups: a Regional Process Goal, encouraging interjurisdictional cooperation; Physical Form/Land Use Goal, fostering community character and transportation efficiency; Accessibility and Safety Goal, enhancing regional connectivity; Economic Development Goal, promoting a balanced transportation system; and an Environmental Quality Goal, promoting a sustainable transportation system that protects natural resources.

The transportation plan assumes that there will be an increase in population from 2.5 million in 2000 to 2.9 million in 2030, but that congestion will be much more pronounced in 2030 than it is now (BRTB 2004). The radial design of the existing road network will be even more unsuitable for the increase in suburb-to-suburb travel in the future. The BMC's travel demand modeling indicates that the baseline condition, consisting of the existing transportation network plus committed improvements to 2008, exhibits an increase in severely congested daily vehicle-miles traveled increasing by 190 percent. Vehicle hours of delay will increase by more than 400 percent.

The transportation planning process developed a Preferred Alternative of project investments, consisting of expansions of highway and transit capacity and some TDM initiatives.Modeling the impact of the Preferred Alternative compared with the baseline condition yields about the same level of daily vehicle-miles traveled, while reducing the severely congested vehicle-miles traveled by 11 percent for the morning peak hours. Transit ridership increases by about 10 percent. Nitrogen oxide and volatile organic compound emissions grow slightly because of increased average vehicle speeds (BRTB 2004).

The net result of the Preferred Alternative is that there will be some miniscule improvement over the horrendous conditions that would exist in 2030 with the baseline network. One should note that there are always difficulties with modeling transportation scenarios: the time period is, however necessary, exceptionally long; the models are notoriously inaccurate with regard to transit share, emissions, and TDM impact; and the perceived costs facing the traveler and their influences on travel behavior are not well understood.

In addition to unfavorable travel conditions, the motorist of the future may have to pay substantially more for transportation facilities. The Preferred Alternative's projected capital cost is approximately $6.7 billion, but conditions could change very easily. Thus, the plan calls for new public/private partnerships, increased privatization, and improved coordination to decrease operating costs and suggests that increased user fees and fuel and other taxes may be necessary.

The Preferred Alternative's TDM strategies consist of park and ride facilities, regional commuter assistance programs in each jurisdiction, transit improvements, bicycle and pedestrian facilities, intelligent transportation systems, alternative fuels/clean technology vehicles, and land use/growth management (BRTB 2004). TDM strategies that were rejected were: congestion pricing of existing toll facilities, congestion pricing of radial freeways, parking pricing (essentially a parking surcharge), and a transit fare discount program. The latter strategy was rejected because it duplicates parts of an existing transit fare discount program. The congestion and parking pricing strategies were rejected because they are alleged to have limited trip and emissions reduction potential, increased traffic diversion impacts on local roadways, adverse economic development impacts in the city, and adverse economic impacts on low-income groups.

The Baltimore Area's long-range plan, as did the ones before it, dismisses out-of-hand many TDM strategies because of their supposed limited impact on travel behavior. Limited trip and emissions reduction potential certainly does apply to park and ride facilities and commuter assistance programs, but not to congestion and parking pricing strategies. The plan also does not address the trip-making obstacles facing the urban poor. This writer contends that there is insufficient focus on TDM strategies that would manage demand rather than build park-and-ride lots. Area transportation officials may not want to influence travel behavior greatly because of political consequences. The reasons for the rejection of the pricing TDMs, while important, are not insurmountable, as the literature has shown.

SUMMARY AND CONCLUSIONS

In the United States, suburbanization has caused tremendous growth in suburb-to-suburb and city-to-suburb (reverse) commuting. The fastest growing commuting mode in metropolitan areas has been SOVs. One reason is that when incomes go up, automobile ownership goes up. The second reason is the abundance of free parking in the suburbs with a significant amount of free parking in downtown areas. The third reason is that public policy has supported expanding road infrastructure, while the full costs of automobile use are not incurred by the automobile user. The dominance of automobiles in metropolitan trip-making has provided unprecedented mobility (not for everyone), but also concerns over congestion and poor air quality. LEVs and ZEVs can address the air quality problem but not congestion and the costs of delay. Automobile-oriented suburbanization has left large concentrations of the inner-city poor and minorities in locations that are less accessible to employment opportunities, reinforcing the *spatial mismatch* between housing and jobs.

Some argue that more roads are needed to solve the problems of congestion, inaccessibility, and air pollution. Some judicious building of roads in high growth areas is needed to open up bottle-necks that have developed, but as has been concluded by most mainstream observers, we can no longer simply build our way out of such problems.

Many argue that transit is still the answer; if there were other choices, if rail systems were more extensive and interconnected, then riders would choose transit. First, because of transit's current small share of work trips in metropolitan areas, there would have to be a *massive* shift in mode choice to do away with congestion and poor air quality. Second, the offering of choices does not guarantee selection. In fact, more choices for commuting allow commuters not to choose transit. One merely has to compare the growth in transit supply over the last twenty-five years with the reduction in transit's mode share to conclude that more choice alone is not the answer. Third, new rail transit systems are very expensive to build and require high levels of ridership to be cost-effective. Land use planning and growth management may not affect travel behavior significantly because of current transportation pricing and regional development patterns. Public policy must address the road pricing issue.

Federal transportation policy has been promoting congestion or value pricing for congestion management and as a new source of revenue. With the development of intelligent transportation systems and the use of transponders, scanning devices, and other systems to count and identify vehicles, it is possible to levy tolls on automobile users based on the level of congestion. Road pricing would increase revenues as well as ration road space, but it would place a financial burden on low-income commuters. Such commuters would have to pay a burdensome toll, travel at other times, or use other modes or congested routes. To avoid some of the financial impacts of pricing, part of the revenue could be rebated to low-income commuters, used to lower the more regressive fuel taxes and registration fees and to subsidize alternative transportation modes. Prime candidates for subsidy are reverse commute services operated by small entrepreneurs, automobile ownership assistance programs for low-income employees, and high volume mass transit services where appropriate.

The Baltimore Metropolitan Area can no longer dismiss congestion or value pricing of roads or other measures, such as parking surcharges. Its public officials should muster the political courage to propose local demonstration of road and parking pricing, rather than continue to fear political retribution. There are HOV lanes being planned in the Baltimore Area and they would be excellent candidates for pricing. In order to gain acceptance of such measures, public officials must educate and lead the public concerning the problems of congestion, poor air quality, and inaccessibility and the potential role of pricing in solving these problems. The public seems unaware of the cause and effect relationships in metropolitan transportation; a major public education initiative should accompany the long-range transportation planning process.

REFERENCES

Abell Foundation. Reverse Commuter Programs: Are Workers and Employers Getting Good Mileage from Them? *The Abell Report*, 14, August 2001, 1–6.

Abell Foundation. *Baltimore Area Jobs and Low-Skill Job Seekers: Assessing the Gap*. Abell Foundation: Baltimore, 1999.

Adler, T., Ristau, W., and Falzarano, S. Traveler Reactions to Congestion Pricing Concept for New York's Tappan Zee Bridge. *Transportation Research Record*, 1999, 1659, 87–96.

American Public Transportation Association. *Public Transportation Ridership Statistics*, 2005, http://www.apta.com/research/stats/ridership/.

Argetsinger, A., and Ginsberg, S. Lessons of California's Toll Lanes. *Washington Post*, June 20, 2005, 197, A1, A4.

Baltimore Region Travel Trends 1980–2000. *BRTB Notes*, March 2004, 5, 1.

Baltimore Regional Transportation Board. *Transportation 2030: The Baltimore Regional Transportation Plan*, Baltimore Metropolitan Council: Baltimore, 2004.

Barnes, G. The Importance of Trip Destination in Determining Transit Share. *Journal of Public Transportation*, 2005, 8, 1–15.

Berg, J. T., Kwanda, K., Burris, M., Swenson, C., Smith, L., and Sullivan, E. Value Pricing Pilot Program. *TR News*, 1999, 204, 3–10.

Besa, G., Bascom, R., and Wilson, D. D. The Ozone Pollution Map: A Technology-Based Approach to Improved Public Awareness of the Nature of Ground-Level Ozone Pollution and to a Greater Acceptance of Effective Control Measures. *Proceedings of the Baltimore Symposium on Urban Environmental Justice Research and Education*, Baltimore: International City/County Management Association, 1995, 14–15.

Bourne, L. S. The Roepke Lecture in Economic Geography, Recycling Urban Systems and Metropolitan Areas: A Geographical Agenda for the 1990s and Beyond. *Economic Geography*, July 1991, 196.

Brewington, K. Marylanders' Commutes Among Longest in Nation. *Baltimoresun.com*, March 31, 2005, http://www.baltimoresun.com/news/traffic/bal-md.commute31,1,921328,print.story?coll=bal-home-headlines.

Burris, M., Stockton, B. HOT Lanes in Houston—Six Years of Experience. *Public Transportation*, 2004, 7, 1–21.

Cervero, R. California Rail-Oriented Office Development: How Successful? *Transportation Quarterly*, 1994, 48 (1), 33–44.

Colias, M. Budget Gap Threatens Chicago Transit. *Baltimoresun.com*, April 14, 2005, http://www.baltimoresun.com/news/nationworld/nation/wire/sns-ap-chicago-transit-woes,1,7733673.story.

Census Transportation Planning Package (CTPP 2000), Table 1, Profile of Selected 1990 and 2000 Characteristics; U.S. Census Bureau: Washington, DC, 2000.

COMSIS, Inc. *Effectiveness of Employer Management Program*, presented at Air Quality and Mobility Workshop, Baltimore, MD, May 24, 1994.

Delaware Valley Regional Planning Commission. *Transportation Control Measures: An Analysis of Potential Transportation Control Measures for Implementation in the Pennsylvania Portion of the DVRPC Region*. Delaware Valley Regional Planning Commission: Philadelphia, 1994.

Dunn, J. *Miles to Go: European and American Transportation Policies*, MIT Press: Cambridge, MA, 1981.

Egan, T. Paying on the Highway to Get Out of First Gear. *New York Times*, April 28, 2005, A1.

Energy and Environmental Analysis. *An Overview of Baltimore Area Air Quality Trends*, Energy and Environmental Analysis: Arlington, VA, 1995.

Farkas, Z. A. Factors of Successful Private Sector Reverse Commute Services. *Transportation Research Record*, 1993, 1402, 3–8.

Farkas, Z. A. Reverse Commuting: Prospects for Job Accessibility and Energy Conservation. *Transportation Research Record*, 1992, 13–49, 85–92.

Feeney, B. A Review of the Impact of Parking Policy Measures on Travel Demand. *Transportation Planning and Technology*, 1989, 13, 229–244.

Giuliano, G. The Weakening Transportation-Land Use Connection. *Access*, 1995, 6, 3–11.

Giuliano, G. Equity and Fairness Considerations of Congestion Pricing. *Curbing Gridlock: Peak-Period Fees to Relieve Traffic Congestion*, 2 (242), National Academy Press: Washington, DC, 1994.

Giuliano, G. The Weakening Transportaion Land Use Connection. *Access*, 1995, 6, 9.

Giuliano, G., Hwang, K., and Wachs, M. Employee Trip Reduction in Southern California: First Year Results. *Transportation Research-A*, 1993, 27A (2), 125–137.

Goodwin, P. The "rule of three": A Possible Solution to the Political Problem of Competing Objectives for Road Pricing. *Traffic Engineering and Control*, 1989, 495–497.

Greenberg, A. How New Parking Spaces May Effectively Increase Typical U.S. Urban Housing Total Unit Costs from $52,000 to $117,000. In *Compendium of Papers* (CD-ROM), presented at the Transportation Research Board, 84th Annual Meeting, Washington, DC, January 9–13, 2005.

Haines, M. (Ed.) 2001 National Household Travel Survey. *BRTB Notes,* October 2004, 53, 3.

Havinoviski, G. Warming Up to HOT Lanes. *Traffic Technology International,* August/September 2004, 39–40.

Higgens, T. J. Congestion Pricing: Implementation Considerations. *Transportation Quarterly*, 1994, 48 (3), 287–298.

Hill, E. *Assessing Travel Behavior by Blacks in the United States: A New Perspective*, Research and Special Programs Administration: Washington, DC, 1994.

Hughes, M. *The New Metropolitan Reality: Where the Rubber Meets the Road in Antipoverty Policy,* The Urban Institute: Washington, DC, 1992

Johnston-Anumonwo, I. The Influence of Household Type on Gender Differences in Work Trip Distance. *Professional Geographer*, 1992, 44 (2), 161–169.

Kain, J. The Spatial Mismatch Hypothesis: Three Decades Later. *Housing Policy Debate*, 1993, 3, 371–460.

Koontz, M. Clean Air and Transportation: The Facts May Surprise You. *Public Roads*, 1998, 61 (1), 42–46.

Lawrence, S. Congestion Pricing. *ITS International*, September/October 1998, 66.

Loukaiton-Sidiris, A., and Banerjee, T. There's No There There. *Access*, 1996, 9.

Nelson, A. C. Transit Stations and Commercial Property Values: A Case Study with Policy and Land-Use Implications. *Journal of Public Transportation*, 1999 2 (3), 77–95.

Peterson, E., and Sandoval, J. Analyzing Job Access and Reverse Commute Programs in the Chicago and San Francisco Metropolitan Regions, *2004 Annual Meeting CD-ROM*, Transportation Research Board, Washington, DC, 2004.

Pickrell, D. The Role of Parking Charges in Highway Congestion Pricing. *Testimony Presented to the U.S. Senate Subcommittee on Water Resources, Transportation, and Infrastructure*, United States Senate: Washington, DC, 1991.

Pisarski, A. *Commuting in America II: The Second National Report on Commuting Patterns and Trends,* Eno Transportation Foundation, Inc.: Landsdowne, VA, 1996.

Poole, R., and Orski, C. *HOT Networks: A New Plan for Congestion Relief and Better Transit,* Reason Foundation: Los Angeles, 2003.

Pucher, J., and Renne, J. Socioeconomics of Urban Travelers: Evidence from the 2001 NHTS. *Transportation Quarterly*, 2003, 57 (3), 49–77.

Pushkarev, B., and Zupan, J. *Public Transportation and Land Use Policy*, Indiana University Press: Bloomington, 1979.

Reid, A. On the Road from Welfare to Work. *Washington Post*, February 2, 1999, A1, A8.

Rosenbloom, S. *Reverse Commute Transportation: Emerging Provider Roles*, Federal Transit Administration: Washington, DC, 1992.

Samuel, P. Variety Shows Promise. *ITS International*, July/August 1998, 47–48.

Shoup, D. The Trouble with Minimum Parking Requirements. *Transportation Research Part A: Policy and Practice,* 1999, 33A, (7/8), 549–574.

Shoup, D. Evaluating the Effects of Cashing Out Employer-Paid Parking: Eight Case Studies. *Transport Policy*, 1997, 4 (4), 201–216.

Shrank, D., and Lomax, T. *The 2004 Urban Mobility Report*, Texas Transportation Institute: College Station, TX, 2004. Small, K. A., Winston, C., and Evans, C. A. *Road Work: A New Highway Pricing and Investment Policy*, The Brookings Institution: Washington, DC, 1989.

Sorensen, P., and Taylor, B. Paying for Roads: New Technology for an Old Dilemma. *Access,* 2005, 26, 2–9.

Steiss, T., and Tabugbo, L. *Commuting Trends in the Baltimore Region: A Comparison of 1970, 1980, and 1990 Census Data*, Staff Paper 9302, Baltimore Metropolitan Council: Baltimore, 1993.

Supernak, J., Golob, M., Kawanda, K., and Golob, F. San Diego's I-15 Congestion Pricing Project-Preliminary Findings. Paper prepared for the *78th Annual Meeting of the Transportation Research Board*, Washington, DC, 1999.

Transportation Research Board. Coordinated Intermodal Transportation Pricing and Funding Strategies. *Research Results Digest*, 1997, 14.

Vickrey, W. Pricing in Urban and Suburban Transport. *American Economic Review Papers and Proceedings*, 1963, 53 (2), 452–473.

Wachs, M. Transportation and Demand Management: Policy Implications of Recent Behavioral Research. *Journal of Planning Literature*, 1990, 5 (4), 333–341.

Wilson, R., and Shoup, D. Parking Subsidies and Travel Choices: Assessing the Evidence. *Transportation*, 1990, 17 (2), 141–158.

Zettal, R., and Carll, R. The Basic Theory of Efficiency Tolls. *Highway Research Record,* 1964, 47, 49–50.

13 Environmental Impact on Transportation Policy: The Case for California's Zero Emissions Vehicles (ZEV) Mandate

Sarmistha Rina Majumdar

INTRODUCTION

The automobile is a prime example of a practical and a useful invention. It is inextricably linked to our daily lives. Used for a variety of purposes ranging from transportation to entertainment, it has been taken for granted in this country. Uniquely enabling individuals to independently traverse immense distances, it has rendered society auto-centric. As a result, any changes in the policy governing the technology of this individualized mode of transport are of great importance not only in transportation, but also in land use planning and in the urban political economy.

The ubiquitous use of the automobile in our society poses a serious threat to the environment. Though technological advancements like catalytic converters and fuel-efficient engines have helped to achieve significant environmental gains via a reduction in pollution per vehicle, such environmental gains seem to be lost through the more intensive and extensive use of automobiles (Nilsson and Kuller 2000). For example, the average car, yielding approximately 27.5 miles per gallon, emits 35 tons of carbon monoxide over its lifetime. It also emits significant quantities of other harmful gases such as hydrocarbons and oxides of nitrogen. As a major source of air pollution, especially in urban areas, automobile emissions cause concern at the state, federal, and international levels. Continual efforts are being made to reduce pollution through technical (engineering) fixes as well as through policy incentives.

The technical issues involve fuel switching and use of alternative fuel technologies, emission controls and reduction of fuel consumption per unit distance traveled. Non-technical issues involve reduced vehicle use per capita through development of transit systems, ride sharing, fuel taxes, car excise taxes, road and congestion pricing, and telecommuting. No matter which approach is adopted to address those problems, each approach requires policy solutions. This is mainly because vehicle emissions problems are unique among pollution problems such as those associated with industrial emissions and effluents. According to Plaut (1998), the most crucial difference that sets vehicle emissions apart from other pollution problems is the inability to apply Pigouvian[1] and similar or related "direct" pricing techniques to resolving vehicle emissions externality problems. It is difficult to impose direct taxes on automobile emissions because of two unique problems. First, it is impracticable to precisely monitor direct emissions from automobiles and impose commensurate charges. Second, it is difficult to gauge the level of social harm or disutility from vehicle emissions, as the rate of emissions varies widely depending on when and where the automobile is operated. The second problem makes the development of any efficient vehicle emissions pricing scheme hard to formulate, even theoretically.

To address the serious problem of emissions from motor vehicles, the state of California passed a mandate on zero emissions vehicles (ZEV) in 1990. This mandate aimed at the gradual introduction of battery powered electric vehicles to help improve its air quality, especially in the south coast basin, which covers the counties of Los Angeles, San Bernardino, Riverside, and Orange. In the following section, the air quality in the state prior to the passage of the mandate and other factors that led to the adoption of this mandate, will be discussed in greater details.

THE CASE FOR THE ZERO EMISSIONS VEHICLES IN CALIFORNIA

THE ENVIRONMENTAL ISSUE

The state of California has tried to control the problem of air pollution from automobile emissions through an early focus on air quality management. It has developed its own legislative framework—the California Clean Air Act of 1988 (amended in 1989), which operates within the guidelines set by the federal Clean Air Act.[2] This has enabled it to adopt strict air quality standards far more stringent than the federal standards. For example, the federal pollution standard index (PSI) is 100, while the California clean air standard is 75PSI.

The strict air quality standards have helped to reduce the number of worst smog episodes in the state in the 1990s to less than half their number in the 1950s. Also, stage one smog episodes[3] have been cut by more than half since the 1970s and stage two smog episodes were absent during the 1988–1991 period. In fact, during the same period the south coast basin enjoyed the cleanest air quality in a forty-year history of air quality monitoring[4] (Grant 1994). Despite stringent air quality standards, the south coast basin's experience of occasional failure to meet state and federal standards was a portent of serious trouble ahead. An increase in human population and in the number of registered vehicles, posed a serious threat to the attainment of air quality targets upon which federal funds depend (Los Angeles Times 2000). Also, gasoline leaks from cars not subjected to smog checks coupled with emissions from heavy-duty trucks that were misreported by diesel engine manufacturers, made the problem of smog forming gases more serious than was previously estimated (Cone 1999).

As seen in Tables 13.1–13.6, the state of California's emission figures for criteria[5] pollutants like carbon monoxide, oxides of nitrogen, sulfur dioxide, and volatile

TABLE 13.1
Total Pollutant Emissions in Tons per Year for Carbon
Monoxide from Highway and Off-Highway Vehicles

State	1985	1987	1989
California	8,572,848	7,964,008	8,131,817
Florida	5,077,256	4,687,772	4,672,123
Illinois	4,104,638	3,808,067	3,410,297
Massachusetts	2,113,735	1,936,414	1,842,647
Ohio	4,020,037	3,749,055	3,562,413
Pennsylvania	3,962,597	3,637,075	3,297,434
New Jersey	2,525,828	2,447,456	2,268,591
New York	4,597,534	4,416,455	4,149,152
Texas	7,433,493	6,856,586	6,145,815
Washington	472,042	1,686,864	1,707,314
Total	42,880,008	41,189,752	39,187,603

Source: EPA Office of Air and Radiation, Air Data—Net Tier Report 1985–1989.

organic compounds from highway and off highway vehicles, surpassed that of other states in the nation. For example, in the case of carbon monoxide, the state of California requires that the carbon monoxide content of air not to exceed or equal 20 ppm (parts per million) for a one-hour average or 9 ppm for an eight-hour average. The federal standard is 35 ppm for a one-hour average and 9.4 ppm for an eight-hour average. The state has violated both standards in emissions.

In the case of oxides of nitrogen, the state standards require that it should not exceed .25 ppm for a one-hour average while the federal standard is .52 ppm for one-hour average. The state has violated both the standards. As shown in Table 13.2, California's annual emission of oxides of nitrogen from both highway and off-highway vehicles exceeded that of other densely populated states in the nation.

The emission of sulfur dioxide from automobiles (mainly those with diesel engines), is linked to increases in lung diseases and breathing problems for asthmatics. The state's emission figures surpassed that of other densely populated states (see Table 13.3).

It is evident from Table 13.4 that volatile organic compounds, the precursors of bad ozone, were at a much higher level in the state of California in comparison with other states in the nation.

Also, ground level ozone, the key ingredient in the formation of smog, caused a serious concern in the state. Usually, the presence of bad ozone near ground level above .15 ppm (parts per million) leads to the issuance of health advisories. Smog alerts are issued when ozone concentration reaches a level higher than .15. The state of California, noted for its stringent air quality standards, requires all its counties not to equal or exceed an ozone level of 0.09 ppm. The federal requirement is 0.12 ppm.

It is true that in the 1980s the number of high-ozone alert days were only a half of

TABLE 13.2
Total Pollutant Emissions in Tons per Year for Oxides of
Nitrogen (NOx) from Highway and Off-Highway Vehicles

State	1985	1987	1989
California	1,131,184	1,120,852	1,173,167
Florida	515,909	506,969	541,180
Illinois	496,226	490,280	502,225
Massachusetts	234,658	229,776	233,092
Ohio	478,310	455,651	457,305
Pennsylvania	439,891	418,201	413,636
New Jersey	293,460	291,586	293,614
New York	497,951	488,322	490,454
Texas	964,771	942,650	953,358
Washington	172,942	259,153	271,395
Total	5,225,302	5,203,440	5,329,426

Source: EPA Office of Air and Radiation, Air Data—Net Tier Report 1985–1989.

what they were in the 1950s, but still the problem of smog persisted. It was so severe in the south coast basin that this "Super Bowl of Smog," even with the toughest standard in the world, failed to attain state and federal standards on several days of the year from 1976–1989 (Air Quality Management District 2002). See Table 13.5.

TABLE 13.3
Total Pollutant Emissions in Tons per Year for Sulfur Dioxide
(SO$_2$) from Highway and Off-Highway Vehicles

State	1985	1987	1989
California	142,370	156,617	175,610
Florida	52,439	56,016	62,489
Illinois	42,984	45,775	48,941
Massachusetts	19,956	21,131	22,801
Ohio	44,433	46,725	49,774
Pennsylvania	37,553	39,049	41,402
New Jersey	32,385	35,362	38,573
New York	42,444	45,122	48,288
Texas	100,263	105,989	114,487
Washington	27,336	30,095	33,630
Total	542,163	581,881	635,995

Source: EPA Office of Air and Radiation, Air Data—Net Tier Report 1985–1989.

TABLE 13.4
Total Pollutant Emissions in Tons per Year for Volatile Organic Compounds (VOC) from Highway and Off-Highway Vehicles

State	1985	1987	1989
California	1,093,077	991,669	971,118
Florida	721,903	629,099	594,472
Illinois	489,843	449,950	374,760
Massachusetts	247,986	219,563	198,272
Ohio	474,025	446,039	378,860
Pennsylvania	462,090	419,812	348,836
New Jersey	319,448	299,309	248,167
New York	559,415	518,564	445,809
Texas	966,119	863,425	718,792
Washington	208,136	204,610	194,236
Total	5,542,042	5,042,040	4,473,322

Source: EPA Office of Air and Radiation, Air Data—Net Tier Report 1985–1989.

Another criteria air pollutant of concern is fine particulates (PM10). Fine particulates originate from the incomplete combustion of fuel in gasoline-powered cars. It also poses a serious threat to public health. A review of the annual emission figures for fine particulate matter in the state of California, indicates that its level was significantly higher in the 1980s in comparison with other states in the nation during the same time period. See Table 13.6.

The poor air quality had a deleterious effect on public health. It led to increased incidences of respiratory related health problems among people of all age groups. The

TABLE 13.5
Ozone Air Quality of the South Coast Basin of California: The Number of Days Exceeding State and Federal Standards

Year	State Standard (0.09ppm)	Federal Standard (0.12ppm)	Health Advisory (0.15ppm)	Stage 1 Alert (0.20ppm)	Stage 2 Alert (0.35ppm)	Basin Maximum
1976	237	194	166	102	7	0.38
1979	226	191	169	120	17	0.45
1982	191	149	121	63	2	0.40
1985	206	158	136	83	7	0.39
1987	196	160	130	66	0	0.33
1989	211	157	120	54	0	0.34

Source: Historic Ozone Air Quality Trends, Air Quality Management District.

TABLE 13.6
Pollutant Emissions in Tons per Year for Particulate Matter (PM10) from Highway and Off-Highway Vehicles

State	1985	1987	1989
California	76,280	79,886	83,953
Arizona	12,260	14,525	14,998
Florida	40,658	42,277	44,701
Illinois	29,774	31,071	31,784
Massachusetts	14,459	14,985	15,334
Ohio	31,250	32,227	32,845
Pennsylvania	25,541	25,797	25,932
New Jersey	17,012	17,675	18,119
New York	29,939	30,991	31,656
Texas	63,741	65,288	66,444
Washington	17,447	18,449	18,993
Total	358,361	373,171	384,759

Source: EPA Office of Air and Radiation, Air Data—Net Tier Report 1985–1989.

smog prevented people from the daily activities supposedly promoting health: jogging, biking, and exercising (California/EPA's Office of Environmental Health Hazard Assessment and The American Lung Association of California Fact Sheet 2002). Various health studies conducted in the state indicated the existence of a significant relationship between daily mortality and increasing pollution at all temperatures (Shumway, Azari, and Pawitan 1988). In addition, agricultural production of important state crops suffered as a result of increase in ambient zone. Even the trees in the forests of southern California and Sierra Nevada mountains were not spared (Research Notes of CARB 1989). Further, the state's failure to comply with federal standards in air quality also meant huge cutbacks in federal funding for transportation and other related programs. The multitude of problems attracted media attention. Their nationwide focus on the state's air quality and the quality of life soon helped the city of Los Angeles to earn the unenviable reputation of being the 'worst polluted city' in the nation.

POLITICAL ISSUES

The problem of air pollution from automobiles in the state of California could have been resolved through the selection of various cost-effective transportation control measures like ride sharing or trip reductions plans, expansion of public transportation networks along with changes in land use patterns or retirement of older and polluting cars. A review of some of these options has revealed that they were implemented in various parts of the state. But their scales of operations were insufficient to bring about significant changes in air quality, as they were not uniformly adopted throughout the state. For instance, restrictions on solo driving had great potential in reducing the number of cars on roads and highways. But any reduction in automobile usage calls for greater use of public transit facilities[6] and ride-sharing programs.

According to the 1990 U.S. Census Report, only 5.1 percent of California's working population used public transit in their daily commute to work. Its poor usage could be attributed not only to its lack of development but also to the presence of a strong car culture in the state of California. Also, the fact that ownership of automobiles confer certain psycho-social benefits—protection, autonomy, prestige, and other socially desirable attributes like skill, competence, and masculinity—only helped to reinforce people's attachment to their cars (Hiscock et al. 2002) and reject other transportation options.

The implementation of the ride sharing policy option in southern California aroused strong public opposition to the program. Initially, participation in the program was made mandatory for employers with one hundred or more employees at the workplace. Public resentment especially from middle class voters and organized business groups, resulted in pressure on the state government for change. Strong and effective opposition from the interest groups finally succeeded in bringing about the changes in the legislation. It was made mandatory only for those employers with 250 or more employees, and optional for those with fewer employees. The program was effectively hamstrung; there was relatively little change in solo driving rates[7] (Baldassare et al. 1998).

Further, in a 1991 survey of solo drivers in Orange County, respondents' opinions were sought on proposals to discourage solo driving. Of them, 27 percent favored congestion fees, 31 percent favored parking charges at work, and 41 percent favored smog fees to discourage solo driving. The majority of the respondents were predisposed towards opposing any kind of ridesharing policies (Baldassare et al. 1998). The findings of the aforementioned study by Baldassare and colleagues supported previous research findings by Teal (1987) and Hwang and colleagues (1990) that economic incentives (fees and cash bonuses) are capable of reducing solo driving among young and lower socioeconomic status commuters who carpool and take public transit, but not among the higher-status commuters. To induce changes in the latter groups' travel behavior, further development of mass transit is necessary. If a policy aims to reduce solo driving per se, cash incentives would prove to be most effective. But to achieve overall reduction among all commuter groups, this strategy would not be very effective. The main reason is the time and money lost by lower-status commuters in making the required changes in their travel behavior. That would militate against the political acceptability of such a policy option (Baldassare 1998).

Another policy option that had the potential to address the air pollution problem from automobiles was congestion pricing.[8] In urban areas, it could have reduced congestion, ownership of cars, fuel usage, and emissions of carbon monoxide and volatile organic compounds proportionately more than any other gases[9] (Acutt et al. 1997). But its political acceptability was, and is, questionable.[10] The existence of strong opposition from the public towards any charging schemes for the usage of highways and roads, has made it politically unacceptable. The public may tolerate the rationing of road use with

HOV lanes but highly resents the idea of paying coercive congestion tolls (Harrington et al. 2001). The fees collected are usually considered as an "additional tax."

Further, the lack of public awareness of congestion reduction and other benefits stemming from those fees made it seem unattractive. Also, when there exist few (or if any) viable commuting alternatives, and motorists are more or less forced into a rigid pattern of single-occupancy vehicle use, resentment is expected to mount (Harrington et al. 2001).

THE ZERO EMISSIONS VEHICLE MANDATE

The state of California, finding itself in a state of loss both environmentally and politically, considered the electric vehicle[11] as the major enabler of its clean air goals (Koenenn 1991). Also, it is the only state in the nation that can establish its own vehicle emission standards (Grant 1994). This helped the South Coast's Air Quality Management District (AQMD)[12] to outline the need for the introduction of zero emission vehicles (commonly known as electric cars), to bring air quality to federal standards by 2007 (Stammer 1989). The California Air Resources Board, responding to the 1990 Clean Air Act amendments and instructions from California's assembly (Turrentine 1994, 107), tried to implement Air Quality Management District's (AQMD)[13] plan by adopting the zero emissions vehicle mandate in 1990.

The electric vehicle (EV) technology has been in existence since the early 1900s. Prior to 1990, it played no role in the state government of California's plans to battle smog. Then in 1990, engineers at Aero Vironment[14] improved the technology significantly. This led to the design and successful development of the modern electric car. Conceived in a secret mission project named Santa Ana[15] and financed by General Motors, the improved EV broke all previous electric vehicle records in speed and battery efficiency. Later, hailed as GM's innovative electric car, the "Impact," it drew the attention of Air Resources Board. Eight months later, the state's Air Resources Board decided in an 8–0 vote to adopt the electric car technology which led to the passage of the mandate in late 1990 (Cone 1996).

The mandate required that 2 percent of new vehicles sold in the state (or about 40,000 cars) should be zero emission vehicles during the period of 1998–2000. Otherwise, automobile manufacturers would face stiff penalties (Cone 1992). The number increased to 5 percent for the years 2001–2002 and 10 percent for 2003 and subsequent model years. The strict requirements of the mandate met with stiff opposition from auto manufacturers. The chairman and chief executive officer of Chrysler Corporation, Robert Eaton (1994), pointed out that there are few people who actually want to buy these electric cars and they are not willing to pay more than the cost of a conventional car. He also made it clear that in order to offset the cost of manufacturing electric vehicles, the price of the conventional gasoline powered vehicle has to be raised by $2,100. Under such pressure from the automobile industry, California Air Resources Board (CARB) made several revisions in the mandate.

In the reviews of 1996 and 1998, the board removed the deadlines for 1998 and 2001. It also relaxed the original figure for 2003 from 10 percent to 4 percent and automakers were allowed to substitute so-called near-zero emission vehicles for the remaining 6 percent (Pollack 2000). As a result of the ZEV mandate, more than 1,000 conventional automobiles were converted to electric vehicles in the state (Koenenn 1991). Also, in the four year-period ending September 2000, about 2,300 new ZEVs had been sold in the state (Ball 2000).

Auto manufacturers continued their attempts to modify the mandate. Steve Douglas, a Sacramento based representative of the Alliance of Automobile Manufacturers, argued that the ZEV mandate requires people to pay (as much as) $20,000 more for a vehicle which has only one-third the range of a conventional car or truck, requires a three-to-five hour recharging time and a limited public infrastructure for recharging (O'Dell 2000). Under such pressure from the auto industry, many others outside the auto industry, speculated on the withdrawal of the mandate, given the current absence of a market for a fledgling technology. Undeterred, CARB in its September 7, 2000, biennial review, decided to leave the mandate unchanged (Pollack 2000). From 1998 to 2003, four thousand electric vehicles have been sold in the state and there are many more buyers were waiting for them.

The ZEV mandate continues to exist in the state, albeit mutedly. Amendments to it have been made to align its requirements with the status of the fledgling EV technology. Given the mandate's potential to bring about the required changes in air quality and in the transportation scenario of southern California, it would be a political suicide for CARB to eliminate the mandate it originally passed in 1990 (O'Dell 2000). Supporters of the mandate hail CARB's decision. They countercharge that the auto industry is ignoring its long-term benefits and assert that relaxing the mandate would crush the fragile electric vehicle market and affect adversely other emerging "clean" technologies (*Los Angeles Times* 2000). Interest groups like the Sierra Club, The American Lung Association, and Southern California Edison also heavily supports the mandate and help to keep it alive. Actually, many consider the mandate for ZEVs, as the best hope for continued development of truly clean private transportation (O'Dell 2000).

STATE INITIATIVES TO IMPLEMENT THE MANDATE

To make electric vehicles attractive to potential buyers, AQMD initially offered a $5,000 per vehicle subsidy for 1,200 vehicles. The state and federal governments also offered significant tax incentives (Lents 1997). Utility companies offered incentives in the form of deductions for recharging at night, when the electric power load is reduced. Also, to make Los Angeles an electric-vehicle-ready city, the City Council approved plans for the massive installation of battery-charging outlets at public and private parking facilities throughout the city (Koenenn 1991).

Statewide public outreach programs were launched to convey the messages on the environmental merits of ZEVs to the public, environmentally challenged communities, car dealers, air districts, city governments, businesses with fleets, media, and to public agencies. It included educational workshops for auto dealers, fleet operators, and local government organizations and visits to high schools and colleges to spread the message about ZEVs. Also, to showcase the latest ZEV technologies available in the state, the first ZEVent was held on August 2000, in Sacramento, California. It provided information on the latest technology along with the offer of competitive lease rates on EVs in the region.

CONCLUSION

The importance of the ZEV mandate has gradually waned over the years. This can be attributed to the limitations of the expensive battery technology and the strong opposition from the automobile industry. Nevertheless, this technology forcing regulation has made the state of California the nationwide pioneer in mandating ZEVs. The ambitious nature of the mandate has helped to focus attention on ZEVs not only in the state but also in the nation. States like New York, Massachusetts, Maryland, Vermont, among others, have displayed varying levels of interest in electric vehicles. It is an idea whose time has come around again. The events of September 11, 2001, render it, perhaps, more appropriate than ever. The technology holds the promise of reducing the nation's dependence on imported crude oil from countries on the verge of or in political crises.

In the absence of a mandate like this or something similar, the nation would not have seen much progress on the research and development of electric vehicles. It may not have even reached the stage where it is currently now. The auto industry may rebuff that assertion. But it has a long history of not taking any serious initiatives unless compelled to by public pressure or law or regulation: witness the case of seat belts and the recent Firestone debacle. Also, the mandate has had an indirect impact on the production of superclean internal combustion engine cars in the nation. It has led to the production of the new generation of clean cars, which partially meets the requirements of the ZEV mandate. Undoubtedly, the limitations of the electric vehicle technology may have affected its commercial viability, but have helped to shift the focus to hybrids and other zero emission vehicles that are fueled by fuel cells.

NOTES

1. Pigouvian or direct taxes are charges that are assessed upon the polluter and upon the quantity of emissions (Plaut 1998, 193).
2. The first Federal Clean Air Act was passed in 1963. First amended in 1963 and later in 1970, it required reductions in auto emissions by states, under federal guidelines. The latest amendment of 1990, allows other states to adopt California's rigid standards, including the ZEV mandate (Turrentine 1994, 105).
3. A 200 PSI is considered to be a *stage one* smog episode. At this stage, usually health warnings are issued and people are advised to avoid vigorous outdoor activities. A 275 PSI is considered to be a *stage two* smog episode and people are advised to stop all physical activities. A 400 PSI is considered to be a *stage three* smog episode and at this stage, everyone is advised to stay indoors.
4. For example, in 1991, the ozone level reached its peak on 131 days of the year compared with an average of about 195 days in the mid 1970s. The stringent state standards were exceeded only on 184 days, with peak levels reaching three times the standard level (Grant 1994).

5. The term refers to those air pollutants that are regulated by the state and federal Clean Air Acts (California/EPA's Office of Environmental Health and Hazard Assessment and The American Lung Association of California 2002).

6. Increased subsidy to public transport can help to lower its cost and improve the quality of service and thereby reduce the demand of travel by cars (Acutt 1997, 27).

7. According to Baldassare et al. (1998, 112), "Southern California's experience to date underscores the importance of finding ridesharing programs that are both politically acceptable and can change travel behavior to a large enough degree that they will significantly improve air quality and traffic conditions."

8. It increases the cost of travel by imposing a congestion fee, often regarded as a tax increase (Harrington et al. 2001).

9. This is because driving becomes smoother with reduced congestion (Abbot et al. 1995).

10. Economic efficiency does not serve as the sole decisive factor in public decisions (Acutt 1997).

11. The basic principles of the electric vehicle were demonstrated by the Scottish inventor, Robert Davidson nearly 160 years ago. In 1892 the first electric vehicle, powered by battery, could run for 13 hours on a 10-hour charge. In 1900, EV sales accounted for 38 percent of new vehicle sales. But the EV lost its market with the appearance of cars with electric starters, mainly the Cadillacs in 1912. Those were not only easy to start but were available at a fraction of the cost of the electric cars. Further interest in the EV waned with the availability of abundant and cheap gasoline (Lents 1997).

12. It is a regional agency, responsible for regulating emissions in the Los Angeles region.

13. AQMD has a 20 years blueprint for clean air in Los Angeles. According to this plan, 35 percent of medium and heavy duty vehicles, 22 percent passenger cars, 15 percent light-duty trucks, 100 percent urban buses and 50 percent off road engines should be zero emissions by 2010 (Lents 1997).

14. A firm noted for their innovative ultra-light aircraft and solar powered racecars (Cone 1996).

15. Santa Ana is the name of the wind that drives smog out of Los Angeles (Cone 1996).

BIBLIOGRAPHY

Abbot, P.G. The environmental assessment of traffic management schemes: a literature review. *Transport Research Laboratory Report, no. 174*, 1995.

Acutt, M.Z. and Dodgson, J.S. Controlling the environmental impacts of transport: matching instruments to objectives. *Transportation Research (D)*, 1997, vol. 2(1), 17–33.

Air Quality Management District. Briefing paper: L.A. Smog, 2002, available at http://www.aqmd.gov/news/lasmog.html.

Baldassare, Mark, Ryan, Sherry, and Katz, Cheryl. Suburban attitudes toward policies aimed at reducing solo driving. *Transportation*, 1998, vol. 25, 99–117.

California/EPA's Office of Environmental Health Hazard Assessment and The American Lung Association of California, Air Pollution and Children's Health, A fact sheet. 2002, available at http://www.oehha.ca.gov/public info.html.

Clifford, Frank. Air board targets utility vehicles, minivans, pickups. *Los Angeles Times*, December 10, 1997, A-1.

Cone, Marla. Vehicles blamed for greater share of smog. *Los Angeles Times*, October 30, 1999, 1.

Cone, Marla. 1990 vote was the spark that drove electric cars. *Los Angeles Times*, December 8, 1996, A-3.

Cone, Marla. GM and the Juicemobile: To satisfy California's tough anti-smog laws, General Motors jumped on the electric car bandwagon. But can the wounded giant follow through with a car we'll want to buy? *Los Angeles Times*, June 12, 1992, 8.

Eaton, Robert J. An essential balance: Society, the consumer and technology, executive. Speech delivered at the Commonwealth Club of California, in San Francisco on December 9, 1994.

Grant, Wyn. Transport and air pollution in California. *Environmental Management and Health*, 1994, volume 5(1), 31–34.

Harrington, W., Krupnick, Alan J., and Alberini, Anna. Overcoming public aversion to congestion pricing. *Transportation Research (A)*, 1999, vol. 35, 93–111.

Hiscock, Rosemary, Macintyre, Sally, Kearns, Ade and Ellaway, Anne. Means of transport and ontological security: Do cars provide psycho-social benefits to their users? *Transportation Research (D)*, 2002, vol. 7, 119–135.

Hwang K. and Giuliano G.. *The determinants of ridesharing: literature review*. Working paper no. 38, 1990, University of California, Berkeley: University of California Transportation Center.

Koenenn, Connie. Ready! Set!…Charge? *Los Angeles Times*, August 7, 1991, E-1.

Lents, James M. Electric vehicles are critical to healthful air. *Business Forum*, 1997, vol. 22(1), 41–46.

Los Angeles Times. Keep spark in electric car market. Editorial, print media edition: Record edition, Los Angeles, California, August 21, 2000, 8.

Nilsson, Maria and Kuller, Rikard. Travel behavior and environmental concern. *Transportation Research (D)*, 2000, 211–234.

O'Dell, John. California: Auto industry zero emissions claim rejected. *Los Angeles Times*, August 9, 2000, C2.

Plaut, Pnina O. The comparison and ranking of policies for abating mobile-source emissions. *Transportation Research (D)*, 1998, vol. 3, no. 4, 193–205.

Pollack, Andrew. California upholds rule for pollutionless car by '03. *New York Times*, September 9, 2000, 7.

Research Notes of CARB, no. 89-5. Ozone risks to California forests based on research report titled, Risks to California forests due to regional ozone pollution by Donald C. Peterson, Jr.

Shumway, R.H., Azari, A.S., and Pawitan, Y. Modeling mortality fluctuations in Los Angeles as functions of pollution and weather effects. *Environmental Research*, 1988, vol. 45, 224–241.

Stammer, Larry B. Air officials see scant easing of California smog. *Los Angeles Times*, June 13, 1989, part 1, col. 6, 1.

St. Pierre, Nicole. No dream: California skies are bluer. *Business Week*, February 26, 2001, 10.

Teal, R.F. Carpooling: who, how and why. *Transportation Research (A)*, 1987, vol. 13, 143–158.

Turrentine, Thomas S. Lifestyle and life politics: Towards a green car market. Doctoral dissertation, 1994, University of California, Davis.

14 You Can't Get There from Here: Issues in Rural Passenger Transportation

John J. Gruidl, Christopher D. Merrett, and David Connelly

Jeremy is in his early forties living in an isolated town of nearly two thousand residents located in the mountainous western United States and is caring for his elderly parents. Because his town is facing bad times as reflected by a declining population and dearth of economic opportunities, Jeremy has been without a job for several months. He wants to work and get off the welfare rolls, he has the skills and the ambition, and there are jobs in a nearby university town only twenty-five miles away. But he was forced to sell his automobile to pay for some unexpected medical expenses and there is no bus service. The neighboring town does have public transit vans available on a request basis. However, service is erratic as the van cannot handle the numerous requests. Jeremy decides that the time and hassle is not worth the entry-level wage that he would earn and elects to continue to receive welfare benefits.

Nancy is a professional business consultant living in a midwestern town with twenty thousand people. She appreciates the recreational opportunities and community connections of small town life. However, a business meeting with a client in Boston generally becomes a three-day trip because travel each way consumes a day. She must first drive to a small city that is two hours away. From the small city, she catches a flight to Chicago and then takes another flight from Chicago to Boston. She is well-respected within her field and would be able to attract more clients on the east coast, but she does not bid on the projects because of the travel demands.

As the cases of Jeremy and Nancy illustrate, rural communities face a different set of challenges than urban centers in passenger transportation. The long distances between communities and the scattered, sparse populations create difficulties and inefficiencies in providing services. Furthermore, the past thirty years have brought tremendous changes in the economic and social fabric of rural communities and in transportation policy. The goal of this chapter is to provide an overview of the changes and issues faced by the rural passenger transportation system. We also provide two case studies of innovative responses by local and state transportation providers to address the challenges posed by the unique characteristics of today's rural America.

Section 1 begins by describing early twentieth century rural America as a fabric of homogeneous localities that consisted of small, independent farmers and the communities that served them. This section continues by describing the rural America of today that is more like a quilt with diverse localities distinguished by different socio-economic characteristics. This view implies the complex and variable mobility needs and commuting patterns for most rural residents. With such community diversity, a "one size fits all" development approach will lead to inadequate and disappointing results. Instead, each locality must be assessed individually and the transportation strategies devised must be tailored to the locality's unique needs.

Section 2 examines the federal policy backdrop. The past fifteen years have brought increased federal funding for rural transportation and devolved responsibility for planning to the state level. Another point in the policy discussion is the deregulation of air, rail, trucking, and intercity bus that has produced mixed results for rural communities.

Section 3 overviews each of the primary modes of passenger travel in rural America: roads and bridges, public transportation, passenger train, intercity bus, and air. Section 4 provides two examples of innovative responses at the state and local level, one dealing with public transit provision and the other with effective regional planning for road and bridge investment. Section 5 summarizes and concludes.

SECTION 1. THE CHANGING FABRIC OF RURAL AMERICA

In the early twentieth century, America was faithful to the Jeffersonian ideal of a society of small, independent farmers. Rural communities and farms were the center of American life. Most of the country's population lived in rural areas, and most people living in rural areas were farmers producing sustenance for the country. A typical rural community in 1900 consisted of a small town or village with numerous small farms within a few miles. People lived out their entire lives within their community, having most needs, economic and otherwise, fulfilled close to home. They had little contact with areas beyond the community.

The invention of the automobile caused a major shift in rural life. Farmers and other rural residents were quick to replace horses with cars.

> The allure was powerful—a machine that required much less immediate care, that could travel long distances quickly and without rest, and that could carry heavy loads without complaining. Automobiles were not only practical, but modern and sophisticated, the mark of success and a "cutting-edge" sensibility. They also helped relieve the loneliness and isolation of farm families living outside of towns. (Schauer 2003a, 3)

Farmers soon discovered that cars and trucks got jolted and stuck in muddy fields and ruts. They became interested in building better roads that connected farms to town and to markets. The paved roads were gradually improved and yielded to state highways and sometimes to four-lane divided highways. Later, rural residents wanted to be connected by the latest concept in roads, interstate highways. With each of these improvements, farmers and rural residents became better connected to one another and to urban places. However, the other result was nearly a complete dependence on the automobile as a mode for passenger travel (Schauer 2003b).

Technological change in the twentieth century, however, was not confined to the automobile. More efficient machines in planting and harvesting crops revolutionized farming. Yields increased dramatically and much less labor was required to produce crops. Over time, fewer and fewer farmers were needed to produce the nation's expanding agricultural output. Many farmers, as well as other rural citizens, left the countryside for factory and managerial positions in the booming industrial sector. The loss of farmers also had a profound impact on rural communities that had developed largely to serve the neighboring farms and farm families. The shrinking number of farms and farm families meant that many communities lost population and had to consider other economic options in order to remain viable.

The rural America of the early twenty-first century bears little resemblance to the Jeffersonian ideal. Rural America is no longer self-sufficient and homogeneous, but instead is globally connected and diverse in its demographic, economic, and social characteristics. Improvements in communication and transportation have reduced rural isolation and removed many of the cultural differences between rural and urban areas. Television, phone service, and transportation systems have helped bring rural and urban dwellers much closer together in terms of culture, information, and lifestyles.

Although the decline in farm employment has been long-term, recent years have brought especially dramatic socio-economic changes to rural areas. The percentage of people living in rural areas has declined, so that now approximately 17 percent of American residents live in rural areas[1] (United States Department of Agriculture, Economic Research Service). During the 1990s, many rural communities lost population, while others gained due to in-migration from other areas (Figure 14.1). Population losses were concentrated in the Great Plains, a region that remains heavily dependent on farming for its economic base. Many young people left the Great Plains for economic opportunities elsewhere leaving behind a disproportionate share of elderly people. Meanwhile, as Figure 14.1 makes apparent, many other rural areas gained population, including those areas in the intermountain West, areas bordering major metropolitan areas in the Northeast, and other areas where climate, recreation, and employment opportunities are favorable (Rosenbloom 2006).

People moving into rural places are attracted by low-cost housing, friendliness, and the human scale of the smaller communities while recognizing the disadvantages, such as fewer economic resources and fewer cultural attractions, than the cities. Certain rural areas have attracted many retirees and recreation-minded younger people. In fact, the Economic Research Service classifies more than three hundred rural counties as recreation counties, many being in the west. These counties grew almost three times as fast as the other rural counties during the 1990s (United States Department of Agriculture, Economic Research Service 2005a).

Even among the recreation counties, there are economic and social differences. The ski resort counties, primarily in the west, have wealthy, well educated, and healthy residents, although they also have relatively high rates of reported crime. In contrast,

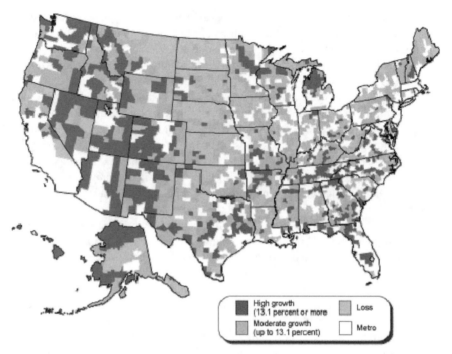

High growth
(13.1 percent or more

Moderate growth
(up to 13.1 percent)

Loss

Metro

FIGURE 14.1   Nonmetro population change, 1990–2000. Note: Metro/nonmetro status based on 2003 definition. The U.S. population growth rate for this period was 13.1 percent. Source: U.S. Census Bureau, map prepared by Economic Research Service.

south Appalachian resort counties have among the poorest, least educated residents among all recreation county types, with relatively poor health indicators, yet relatively low crime rates (United States Department of Agriculture, Economic Research Service 2005a).

In the West, rural population growth rates in the 1990s outpaced growth rates in the cities (Rosenbloom 2003). Many were affluent newcomers who capitalize on technology and transportation and, in many cases, are able to work from their house. Technology clearly is helping some rural communities. Those communities that have adopted new technologies and information systems are at an advantage in attracting new residents and businesses.

As some rural communities have experienced a sudden growth in population, the subsequent expansion of new housing has led to land-use patterns sometimes referred to as "rural sprawl." What happens is this: for reasons of cost and convenience, housing developments are built on land previously used as farmland that surround rural towns and villages. Then services and shopping facilities, often in the form of strip malls with large parking lots, spring up nearby. Because consumers look for the convenience of free and abundant parking and the draw of a new store, the central business district loses significant patronage. Downtown businesses are left with few options—close or relocate outside the central business district closer to the new development where they hope to capture back some of their customers. Meanwhile, residents see an increase in distances that they must travel to conduct daily business and shopping, and the automobile becomes the essential mode of transportation.

At the same time, some rural areas, especially in Texas, Florida, and the Southwest, are having an influx of poorer immigrants, particularly Hispanics. These immigrants are making rural places more diverse ethnically. Although some new residents may work on farms, many more work in food processing plants and other manufacturing companies. The rural communities are sometimes strained in providing the necessary services to the immigrants, such as schools, housing, and job training.

Underlying the population shifts are changes in the economic bases of rural communities. Rural America has shifted from a dependence on farming to a striking diversity of economic activities. Rural communities are now likely to depend economically on service businesses, including both consumer and business services, such as insurance, banking, and education. The shift to a service economy follows the national trend in which traditional industries like manufacturing and farming contribute a lower share of total employment. Yet, manufacturing remains critical to the economic welfare of many rural communities in spite of the "out-sourcing" of many manufacturing jobs overseas.

Another important social change in rural communities is the dramatic shift of farm and other rural women into the labor force over the past three decades. In 1977, 40 percent of farm women worked off the farm; by 1998 nearly 80 percent did so (Rosman and Van Hook 1998). In spite of this, poverty persists in many rural communities as women work in low-wage jobs.

The changing fabric of rural America has implications for passenger transportation. First, the diversity of rural areas suggests that a "one size fits all" approach to transportation is unlikely to be successful. With each locality having different mobility needs and commuting patterns, it is important that each locality craft its own transportation strategies. Recent federal legislation has required that state and local government be more responsible for the planning and implementation of transportation. This approach seems appropriate given the diversity of rural America. It will be increasingly important for rural places to follow effective, comprehensive planning approaches that engage a wide variety of stakeholders.

Second, it is clear that rural Americans have a complex set of rural mobility needs (Rosenbloom 2003). Older persons, ethnic minorities, poor families, women in the labor force—each have distinct transportation needs. It is a tremendous challenge to meet the needs of these various groups at the same time as resources in rural communities are generally declining.

Finally, changing economies in rural localities have brought about a greater variety of home-to-work commutes. While many rural residents have a "home office," many also commute frequently to suburbs or rural communities in different counties. The passenger transportation system must serve these commuters in a way that preserves the rural ambiance that so many find attractive. Finally, the shift to a service economy and multiple job-holders in a family mean that there is more variability in the timing and scheduling of work (Rosenbloom 2003). Residents are unlikely to follow a typical daytime work schedule. This presents a challenge for rural transit providers to meet their variable and complex transportation needs.

SECTION 2. THE FEDERAL POLICY ENVIRONMENT

Not only have rural communities changed, so too has the transportation policy context in which the rural passenger transportation system must operate. Several significant changes in federal policy occurred over the past thirty years including devolution of highway planning from the federal government to the states, the deregulation of transportation industries, notably trucking, air, and rail, and increased federal outlays for surface transportation, including highways, highway safety, and public transportation.

In 1991, the Intermodal Surface Transportation Efficiency Act (ISTEA) largely devolved federal highway planning to the states, which, along with local areas, own the vast majority (97% in 2002) of roads (United States Department of Agriculture, Economic Research Service 2005b). ISTEA initiated a comprehensive planning process that enlisted local, state, tribal, and public/private interest groups, and emphasized the connection of transportation improvements to clean air and water quality.

The 1998 Transportation Equity Act for the 21st Century (TEA-21), ISTEA's successor legislation, reinforced state and local transportation roles. The program gave states and localities more flexibility in allocating highway and bridge funding, a portion of which were required to be spent in rural America. Bridge funds, in particular, were required to be spent on lower/local road classifications, many of which are in rural areas. Under ISTEA and TEA-21, each state was required to set up a statewide transportation planning process (incorporating environmental concerns and intermodal connectivity), a transportation plan, and a transportation improvement program. States also were required to include local governments as well as other public and private organizations in the transportation planning process (Stommes and Brown 2002).

Federal funding of surface transportation has increased significantly since the passage of ISTEA in 1991. TEA-21 authorized $217.9 billion for all federal surface transportation programs (highways, highway safety, and public transportation) between 1998 and 2003, a 40.3 percent increase over ISTEA's funding. The latest piece of federal legislation called SAFETEA (Safe, Accountable, Flexible, Efficient Transportation Equity Act) was signed into law in August 2005. SAFETEA again significantly increases federal spending on surface transportation, this time to $286.4 billion over six years (Congressional Research Service 2005).

Increased federal funding and greater state/local control over those funds has improved rural roads and expanded public transportation in rural America. The quality of roads in rural America generally increased during the 1990s, with interstate highways improving the most. The share of rural interstates (as measured in miles) rated by the U.S. Department of Transportation as poor or mediocre declined from 35 percent in 1993 to 12.3 percent in 2002 (United States Department of Agriculture 2005b).

In spite of the federal largess, it is important to recognize that roads are primarily funded by state and local monies. In fact, in 1994, 68.7 percent of total transportation expenditures were from state and local government, compared to 31.3 percent from the federal government (Stommes and Brown 2002). Furthermore, although the federal government is requiring more local participation in funding decisions, the actual extent of representation by small, rural governments and organizations varies widely among the states. In some states, it remains difficult for rural constituents to gain the political support and funding to improve their roadways and other transportation modes.

Another significant change in policy began in 1978 with the Airline Deregulation Act, the first legislative act of many that accounts for the current deregulation of all transportation modes under federal statutes. Rail, intercity bus, and motor carrier deregulation followed the airlines, with most federal regulations sharply reduced or eliminated by the mid-1990s. Although deregulation has lowered prices for passengers nationwide, its effect on rural America has been mixed, as the following discussion illustrates.

When the airline industry was deregulated by the Airline Deregulation Act of 1978, the Civil Aeronautics Board was eliminated and air carriers were allowed to set fare structures and enter and exit markets without federal interference. To ensure continued service to smaller and more isolated communities, the legislation established the Essential Air Service program, which provides subsidies directly to airlines to maintain service to those small communities that were served at the time of deregulation. This program, with an annual funding level of $50 million, supports scheduled air service to more than one hundred rural communities, mainly in the Midwest, the Rocky Mountain states, and Alaska (Stommes and Brown 2002).

Deregulation significantly reduced the cost of air travel making it an option for many more people so that now customer demand drives the airline industry. This has lead to a sharp increase in overall domestic airline traffic, with air carriers concentrating their operations around hub airports. As a result, some rural communities have experienced significant declines in their air service, while others have benefited from increased service, and still others have experienced relatively stable service since 1978.

Following deregulation of the airline industry, the Bus Regulatory Reform Act of 1982 was enacted, which relaxed entry requirements for intercity bus companies. Certainly, intercity bus transportation is important in providing mobility to rural residents and deregulation has generally resulted in better long-haul service, more complete fare information, and a greater diversity of services, including enhanced charter and tour service. Yet many rural residents have not benefited from bus deregulation. Data from the Department of Transportation indicate that more than eleven thousand locations received intercity bus service in 1982, but only five thousand communities were served in 2000. Many of those service reductions took place in rural areas, as bus companies were no longer required to cross-subsidize low-revenue routes with profits from high-revenue routes (Stommes and Brown 2002).

Although freight transportation is not the focus of this chapter, deregulation of rail and trucking industries has greatly impacted freight transportation. Since rail infrastructure had been overbuilt at the time of deregulation, there has been consolidation and mergers among existing railroads. The national rail network has been steadily shrinking. Meanwhile, deregulation in the trucking industry led to explosive growth in small trucking companies. Trucking firms have become increasingly competitive since deregulation, offering more frequent service, smaller loads, and faster service times (Stommes and Brown 2002).

SECTION 3. OVERVIEW OF THE RURAL PASSENGER TRANSPORTATION SYSTEM

The rural transportation system is not a unified, centralized system of travel options. Instead, it is dispersed and decentralized, involving many travel modes, such as roads and bridges, public transportation, intercity bus, passenger rail, and air.

Furthermore, no single entity controls the system. Instead, it is a mix of federal and state government, state and local government, public and private sector, and profit and non-profit entities. For example, although most construction funding for roads and bridges comes from federal and state government, city and county government are responsible for the maintenance of most roadways. In a similar way, federal and state governments provide most capital funding for rural public transit, yet actual operations are usually a local responsibility. Rail rights-of-way are usually privately owned and maintained. On the other hand, airports are usually owned by public or quasi-public agencies.

However, the components of the transportation system—roads, rail, bus, air—are linked with one another. As with any system, a change in one component will affect the other components, sometimes in unanticipated ways. For example, the deregulation of railroads has caused recent mergers of railroad companies. Rail companies have abandoned many rural branch lines that are no longer economically viable. This has meant a loss of rail freight service to these rural communities. In turn, this has contributed to increased trucking on rural roads which increases road maintenance needs. The initial decision to deregulate railroads has had the unintended and unanticipated effect of reducing the fiscal capacity of local and state governments to properly maintain roads.

Ultimately, the system is judged by its effectiveness in forming vital economic and social connections. This is particularly important for rural areas because of the long distances and sparse, scattered population. We now review each of the major travel modes that comprise the rural system.

RURAL ROADS AND BRIDGES

The road system in rural America is generally well developed with an established network of local roads, county and state highways, and interstate highways. As discussed previously, the quality of rural roads and bridges has generally improved since 1991 due in part to increased federal spending. In fact, overall, rural roads are in better condition than those in urban areas. While less than 14 percent of rural roads as measured in miles were in poor or mediocre condition in 2002, more than 29 percent of urban roads were so classified (United States Department of Agriculture, Economic Research Service 2005b).

In spite of the overall improvement in the quality of the road system, there are indications that some rural roads are at, or near, carrying capacity. For example, rural traffic (as measured by vehicle miles traveled) grew by 29.8 percent from 1990 to 2003. Over that same time frame, the national road network increased in length by only 2.6 percent. This suggests that road travel demand is growing more rapidly than the supply of highways, especially in rural areas on the urban fringe (United States Department of Agriculture, Economic Research Service 2005b).

Rural bridges also improved in quality during the past fifteen years. The percentage of rural roadway bridges rated as deficient by the U.S. Department of Transportation declined from 32.8 percent in 1993 to 26 percent in 2003. States with the highest percentage of deficient bridges are clustered around the Mississippi and Missouri rivers and along the East Coast (United States Department of Agriculture, Economic Research Service 2005b).

There are several important issues for rural roads and bridges (Dye Management Group 2001):

- In spite of recent improvements, a significant percentage of county and local roads remain deficient. There is a backlog of maintenance and preservation needs.
- Occurrences of motor vehicle accidents on rural roads present problems. The fatality rate for rural roads (per 100 million vehicle miles of travel) is more than twice that of urban areas. This is due to several factors: speed, alcohol use, and slower response times to accidents along with delayed "times of arrival" to a hospital equipped to handle the type of injuries that have occurred, both of which are related to the long distances in rural areas between the accident location and the sources of help.
- Funding is limited for expansion improvements to local roads and bridges that are outside the federal-aid system.
- Planning for road improvements in rural areas could be improved by obtaining more public input, coordinating with other plans and with the land use and development process, and by planning strategically with a regional and system-wide perspective.
- A large percentage of rural counties have a high rate of "carlessness," households without access to cars. These counties tend to be characterized by persistent poverty and high concentrations of African American, Hispanic, or Native American residents. Residents without access to cars are particularly dependent on public transportation (United States Department of Agriculture, Economic Research Service 2005b).

RURAL PUBLIC TRANSPORTATION

Rural public transportation, the rural analogue to bus service in metro areas, is available in approximately 60 percent of rural counties nationwide, for a total of about twelve hundred systems. These "Section 5311" transit systems, identified by the federal statute that establishes them, are county- or city-based and tend to be found in the more populated rural areas. Few are found in the most rural, isolated areas. These systems range in size from one to over fifty vehicles.

Specialized transportation services for the elderly and persons with disabilities are available under the Section 5311 program. Federal funding is provided to private nonprofit groups and certain public organizations for capital expenses, including purchase-of-service agreements whereby an agency pays a transportation provider for services. There are approximately 3,700 of these systems throughout the country and they serve both urban and rural clients (Stommes and Brown 2002).

Recognizing the particular need for public transportation in poor places, the Job Access and Reverse Commute (JARC) grant program was implemented in 1998 to encourage development of new transit services and expand existing routes for low-income individuals seeking access to jobs. From 1998 to 2003, $750 million was authorized for JARC, with $150 million allocated for rural areas.

In recent years, local governments and nonprofit agencies have developed strategies to address the limited mobility options for low-income individuals in rural areas. One popular approach has been the "Wheels to Work" program, which offers low-income individuals the opportunity to purchase cars through attractive auto loan financing options.

In 2000, 62 percent of rural public transportation users were female, 31 percent were elderly, and 23 percent were disabled (United States Department of Agriculture, Economic Research Service 2005b).

Important issues in rural public transportation include:

- Approximately 40 percent of counties do not have a public transportation service.
- Furthermore, service, when provided, is primarily local and generally does not extend across political boundaries, such as county lines.

INTERCITY BUS AND RAIL PASSENGER SERVICE

In the past, most rural communities had bus service. However, this has changed due to deregulation in 1982, reduction of air fares, and declining populations in many rural communities, particularly on the Great Plains. Intercity bus service is no longer subsidized and companies are not required to operate lines if they are not profitable.

Currently, the intercity bus industry serves about 4,300 locations down from more than 15,000 in 1980, with many service discontinuations occurring in rural areas (United States Department of Agriculture, Economic Research Service 2005b). The rural area with the least access to bus service is the Great Plains where the population is particularly sparse. According to ridership surveys, intercity bus passengers tend to be lower income, female, minority, less educated, and older than air and rail passengers (Dye Management Group 2001).

When discussing rail passenger service in rural areas, Amtrak, a federally subsidized, for-profit corporation established in October 1970, is the only service provider. However, when Amtrak passenger service began in May 1971, only about half of all passenger rail routes were taken over by Amtrak. Many rural towns lost passenger rail service at that time. Although Amtrak offers a national network, it mainly links major metropolitan areas, with fewer than two hundred rural communities on its routes and minimal passenger rail connections with county transit systems. With disappointing performance leading to the recent dismissal of Amtrak's chief executive, it seems unlikely that Amtrak can operate without public subsidies. Furthermore, it appears that Amtrak's strategy is to focus on high-speed service which means fewer trains serving small, rural intermediate points (United States Department of Agriculture, Economic Research Service 2005b).

Clearly, both intercity bus service and passenger rail have reduced their service to rural areas. Those most impacted by these reductions are the less affluent rural residents who cannot afford air travel and those residents traveling to other rural areas, rather than to major cities served by airlines.

COMMERCIAL AIR SERVICE

With the decline of intercity bus and passenger rail service, rural communities increasingly depend on scheduled air service for business and pleasure trips. In general, rural residents have benefited from lower air fares following deregulation of the passenger air industry. Some rural communities have been able to add flights to their regional airports, while at the same time others have had to close commercial air service.

Following September 11, 2001, commercial air service suffered a downturn with smaller communities especially hard hit. The number of flights to regional airports dropped 19 percent between 2000 and 2003 with the Northeast and Midwest affected most (United States Department of Agriculture, Economic Research Service 2005b). Nevertheless, many rural communities believe that access to air service is an essential factor in attracting and retaining businesses and residents. Currently, the Essential Air Service subsidy program (established by the Airline Deregulation Act of 1978) serves more than 100 rural destinations, mostly in the West and Alaska, to ensure that these communities have passenger air service. However, the high cost of subsidizing such service limits its availability.

SECTION 4. INNOVATIVE EXAMPLES OF RURAL TRANSPORTATION

Given the many challenges in rural transportation, it is worthwhile to discuss examples of innovative responses by state and local government. Two such examples are presented here. The first is an effort in Illinois to better coordinate public transit provision. The second discusses a regional planning initiative in Iowa for effective prioritization of road and bridge investments.

EXAMPLE #1 PUBLIC TRANSIT IN ILLINOIS

The Illinois Department of Transportation and others have been frustrated by a lack of coordination in public transit in some regions. In these regions, there are multiple public transit providers that were working independently and not coordinating their service delivery. For example, one county that receives relatively high federal and state subsidies for public transit has four transit providers. The providers were not communicating, were concerned about "turf," and were not willing to work together to coordinate their services. The result was service duplication within the largest town, no service beyond the city limits, and many poorly served people, including disabled individuals (ICCT 2006). When there are multiple transit providers with different goals that do not collaborate, the result can be "ineffective and inefficient service, and problems such as duplication of service, underutilization of resources, inconsistent service, gaps in service, inconsistent safety standards and customer inconvenience" (ICCT 19).

In response to this situation, the Illinois General Assembly passed legislation forming the Interagency Coordinating Committee on Transportation (ICCT) with the goal of better integrating public transit provision in regions. The ICCT provides technical assistance to transit providers. It wants regions to upgrade and coordinate their services, similar to the RIDES program described below.

Rides Mass Transit District (RIDES) is the public transportation provider for 11 southern Illinois counties. RIDES was originally designed to be a demand-responsive system (i.e., to respond only to specific requests from individuals), but has evolved established deviated routes because of the regularity of riders and the need for human services transportation. RIDES coordinates the transportation of aging adults, individuals with disabilities, and the general public. To eliminate unnecessary miles and empty vehicles, RIDES reserves the right to mix clients or general public riders on any route. Under the RIDES system, reduced administrative costs and efficient use of vehicles throughout the service day create high-quality responsive service. RIDES illustrates the advantages of the coordinated use of a single regional system. (ICCT 2006)

Example #2 Regional Planning for Roads in Iowa

The second example also involves taking a more regional approach to rural transportation. The Region 16 transportation planning district is a five-county area in southeastern Iowa coordinated by the Southeast Iowa Regional Planning Commission. In Region 16, funds for roads and bridges were previously allocated to the four largest counties as a percentage of the total funds available. Counties focused on improvements on residential street and county roads, without considering the regional impact of the improvements. Furthermore, if a community received a relatively small amount for improvements, say $100,000 in one year, the money was not spent efficiently because it took too long to save for larger, more beneficial projects.

Region 16 created a subcommittee that studied the allocation process, listed ways to improve it, and provided recommendations to the board of directors. They developed an application process by which communities that have road improvement needs must apply to the subcommittee for funding. The subcommittee then collaborates with the board of directors to prioritize the projects according to level of benefit perceived for the entire region. The change in allocation policy has resulted in a competitive application process that identifies regional priority projects. The new process of prioritizing all projects on a regional level, as opposed to a county level, has improved the local road and highway infrastructure without increases in state and federal funds (Norris 2006).

This process in Region 16 in southeastern Iowa is in keeping with the shifts in federal policy that encourage more stakeholder involvement in decision-making regarding investments in roads and bridges. The result in Region 16 is a system that uses the federal and state highway funds to best meet the region's needs, rather than a system that disperses the funds throughout the communities for use at their discretion. In both of the above examples, we can see that a regional approach to service provision and transportation planning can be effective in improving the transportation system.

SECTION 5. SUMMARY AND CONCLUSIONS

This chapter has provided a broad survey of rural passenger transportation. This is a time of major transition for the system. In part, this is precipitated by changes in rural America itself. Rural America is becoming more diverse in its socioeconomic make-up. In the past two decades, some rural communities have thrived, while others have been left behind as globalization and technology have altered the economic landscape. Furthermore, the policy environment has also shifted. The major factors include increased federal funding, devolution of many responsibilities to state governments, and deregulation of air, rail, trucking, and inter-bus.

The rural transportation system is not a unified, centralized system. Instead it has a mix of funding agencies and modes of travel. In recent years, the quality of roads and bridges in rural America has generally improved. However, many less-affluent individuals without access to cars find their alternatives, such as inter-city bus and public transit, unavailable or inconsistent in service. Meeting the mobility needs of an increasingly diverse and scattered population is a great challenge.

The innovative examples presented in Section 4 suggest that the regional approach is essential in planning rural road and bridge improvements and in providing effective public transit. It will be increasingly necessary for state and local agencies to take a strategic, system-wide, and regional approach to address the rural transportation needs of the twenty-first century.

NOTE

1.   There are many definitions of "rural." In this chapter, we use the county-based definitions of metro and nonmetro from the Office of Management and Budget. In 2003, OMB defined metro areas as (1) central counties with one or more urbanized areas, and (2) outlying counties that are economically tied to the core counties as measured by work commuting. Nonmetro counties are outside the boundaries of metro areas. For more information, see http://www.ers.usda.gov/Briefing/Rurality/WhatisRural. In this chapter, the terms "rural" and "nonmetro" are used interchangeably.

REFERENCES

Congressional Research Service. 2005. The Library of Congress CRS Report for Congress Received through the CRS Web, Order Code RL33119 Safe, Accountable, Flexible, Efficient Transportation Equity Act — A Legacy for Users (SAFETEA-LU or SAFETEA): Selected Major Provisions. October 18, 2005. Available at http://www.ruraltransportation.org/library/crstealu.pdf.

Dye Management Group Inc. 2001. Planning for Transportation in Rural Areas. Prepared for the Federal Highway Administration in Cooperation with the Federal Transit Administration, July 2001, 1–96.

Interagency Coordinating Committee on Transportation. 2006. Report to the Governor and General Assembly of Illinois. January 24, 2006. Springfield, IL.

Norris, Michael. 2006. Interview with Michael Norris, Transportation Planner at the Southeastern Iowa Regional Planning Commission, February 10, 2006

Rosenbloom, Sandi. 2006. Facing Societal Changes: The Need for New Paradigms in Rural Transit Service. Community Transportation, 11: 16–27. Available at http://www.ctaa.org/images/rosenbloom.pdf.

Rosenbloom, Sandi. 2003. "The Changing Demographics of Rural America: What Are the Implications for Transportation Providers," TR News, Number 225, Transportation Research Board of the National Academies, March-April 2003, 12–17. Available at http://trb.org/news/blurb_detail.asp?id=1426.

Rosman, Michael and Mary P. Van Hook. 1998. "Changes in Rural Communities in the Past Twenty-Five Years: Policy Implications for Rural Mental Health." Downloaded from http://www.narmh.org/pages/refone.html on November 22, 2005.

Schauer, Peter. 2003a. "Rural Passenger Transportation: Finding a Way to Get Where They Need to Go," TR News, Number 225, Transportation Research Board of the National Academies, March-April 2003, 3. Available at http://trb.org/news/blurb_detail.asp?id=1426.

Schauer, Peter. 2003b. "The Trip To Town: Rural Transportation Patterns and Developments Since 1900," TR News, Number 225, Transportation Research Board of the National Academies, March-April 2003, 4, 11. Available at http://www.narmh.org/pages/refone.html http://trb.org/news/blurb_detail.asp?id=1426.

Stommes, Eileen S., and Dennis M. Brown. 2002. "Transportation in Rural America: Issues for the 21st Century," Rural America, Vol. 16, No. 4, Winter: 2–10. Available at http://www.ers.usda.gov/publications/ruralamerica/ra164/ra164b.pdf.

United States Department of Agriculture, Economic Research Service. 2005a. Rural America at a Glance. Economic Information Bulletin Number 4, Washington, D.C., September 2005. Available at http://www.ers.usda.gov/publications/EIB4/EIB4.pdf.

United States Department of Agriculture, Economic Research Service. 2005b. Rural Transportation at a Glance. Agriculture Information Bulletin Number 795, Washington, D.C., January. Available at http://www.ers.usda.gov/publications/aib795/aib795_lowres.pdf.

United States Department of Agriculture, Economic Research Service. Map of population change. Washington, D.C., 2003. Available at http://www.ers.usda.gov/Emphases/Rural/Gallery/popc9000.htm.

United States Department of Agriculture, Economic Research Service. Measuring rurality: What is rural? Washington, D.C., November 30, 2005. Available at http://www.ers.usda.gov/Briefing/Rurality/WhatisRural.

Part III

Transportation Policy

15 Spatial Modeling in Transportation

Simon P. Anderson and Wesley W. Wilson

INTRODUCTION

Alternative transportation infrastructure improvements necessitate the evaluation of equilibrium outcomes both with and without the improvements across the alternatives. Transportation, however, is a derived demand. That is, it is directly linked to the products transported and, hence, depends on the spatial differences in the origin and terminal locations. The products travel from origin to destination over transportation networks and geographic space. The transportation may be provided by different modes that may compete with each other or may be essential to completing a service, and, therefore, have both substitution and complementarities across modes. There are few models that have the capacity to integrate some or all of these factors into an equilibrium framework.

In this chapter, we describe the Samuelson (1952) and Takayama-Judge (1964) model (S-TJ Model) and then add a transportation market to the model. We then develop a "full spatial" equilibrium model in which mode choices drive modal demand functions. The chapter concludes with an application. Specifically, the Army Corps of Engineers use a model that is comparable in many respects to the S-TJ Model. We first describe this model and then point to differences in welfare measurement between this model and the full spatial model. The general finding of this research is that there are substantial differences in the two models. These differences arise from the S-TJ Model's assumption that geographic dimensions of the regions are fixed. In the full spatial model, the regions are endogenous and depend on the costs of transportation.

Samuelson (1952) and Takayama and Judge (1964) develop a model of trade over space. In this model, there are multiple regions with both demands and supplies of a product. If transportation costs are too high or if transportation is not possible, equilibrium is established by standard local supply and demand conditions. In such a case, there are price differences in the commodity across the regions. Transportation allows these price differences to be arbitraged. In equilibrium, either prices differ in the two markets by a transportation cost or else no trade occurs. Commonly, these models treat transportation as given. However, the model is can be fully endogenized through the addition of transportation supply. In the model developed in the next section, we solve the model for two regions with no trade, with trade at a given transportation rate, and

255

then complete the model with the addition of transportation supply. In transportation planning, the key policy variables underpin the transportation supply function. Specifically, improvements to the transportation infrastructure reduce the cost of providing transportation. The reductions in cost reflect a shift down in the supply function, reducing the transportation rate, and facilitating trade between regions.

In the S-TJ framework, the regions themselves are exogenously fixed in the sense that the size of the regions are unaffected by the transportation rate. In some cases, such an assumption is perfectly suited to modeling trade and transportation policy. For example, this applies to trade between countries and isolated regions wherein suppliers (transportation demanders) have no other options. However, in many transportation settings, regions are adjacent to one another. The total supply of a product is an aggregation of suppliers distributed throughout the regions. Transportation policy may impact the decisions of the individual suppliers on the routes or modes they choose. Since, for any given region, suppliers are spatially distributed, transportation policy affects the size of the region over which suppliers are aggregated to form the region's supply function. Thus, the size of the region and, therefore, the level of supply are determined endogenously in the equilibrium. The welfare consequences of an improvement to the transportation infrastructure in the S-TJ setting does not include the shifts in the regional borders and may therefore overestimate the welfare impact of improvements to the transportation infrastructure.

A full spatial model is developed as an alternative description that explicitly addresses this point. In this model, suppliers of a product are taken to be spatially distributed over a region. The individual suppliers are taken as the demanders of transportation. They choose a mode and routing option to get the product to market. The modal splits and the routing options transcend into regional supplies of a product and, hence, into transportation demands. As in our development of the S-TJ Model, transportation equilibrium obtains through the summation of modal supplies and completes the model. Also, in parallel with our development of S-TJ, improvements to the transportation infrastructure reduce the costs of transportation services. This reduction in costs facilitates trade between regions.

The chapter concludes with an illustration. While a number of differing infrastructure improvements can be made with modest modifications to the model, the particular improvement analyzed is a lock improvement. Locks are an essential component of the inland waterway system and are necessary for navigation. The locks and dams in the inland waterway system are managed by the U.S. Army Corps of Engineers (USACE). In determining whether improvements are made and the type of improvements, USACE evaluates the costs and benefits of alternatives. Their methodology to determine the costs and benefits of lock improvements has come under tremendous recent scrutiny, and a core criticism centers on the lack of an appropriate spatial equilibrium model. Their model uses a fixed region akin to S-TJ and demand structures that are perfectly inelastic to a threshold rate. In our application, we describe the model used by USACE along with comparisons to S-TJ. We then use the full spatial model to compare the welfare consequences of lock improvements against USACE's methodology. This comparison identifies differences that could seriously impact the calculations of net benefits accruing to transportation infrastructure improvements.

THE SAMUELSON AND TAKAYAMA-JUDGE APPROACH

In this section, we briefly review the classic spatial model of Samuelson (1952) and Takayama and Judge (1964).[1] In the S-T-J Model, there is a set of regions trading a good. Each region is endowed with a set of demand and supply functions. If markets are completely separated (i.e., no trade is allowed or is cost prohibitive), markets are cleared in the usual way. That is, demand and supply functions are equated for each region to give equilibrium prices and quantities.

Transportation, however, if not too costly, allows trade to occur between regions and causes price differences between regions to be arbitraged. To illustrate this point, suppose that there were no transportation costs. The prices in the regions then must be the equal in equilibrium. No difference can be sustained because goods would flow from any low price region to a higher price one if transportation were costless. With costly transportation, differential prices will reflect transportation costs: transportation will arbitrage excessive price differences between the regions.

AN ILLUSTRATIVE EXAMPLE—PROHIBITIVE TRANSPORTATION COSTS

Consider a simple example of two regions with linear demand and supply functions given by:

$$D_1 = \alpha_1 - p_1$$
$$D_2 = \alpha_2 - p_2$$
$$S_1 = p_1$$
$$S_2 = p_2$$

where the subscripts represent two different regions, 1 and 2. Suppose that $\alpha_2 > \alpha_1$: since supply parameters are the same, trade flows from Region 1 to Region 2. Accordingly, we can think of 1 as the supply region and 2 as the demand region. In this case, if there is trade, then it will flow from the low demand region (1) to the high demand region (2).

However, if trade costs are too high, then autarky will prevail and each market clears independently of the other. It is straightforward to find the equilibrium without trade as

$$p_1^* = \tfrac{1}{2}\alpha_1, \, p_2^* = \tfrac{1}{2}\alpha_2, \, D_1^* = S_1^* = \tfrac{1}{2}\alpha_1, \, D_2^* = S_2^* = \tfrac{1}{2}\alpha_2$$

In this simple model, the prices and quantities (both produced and sold) in the high demand region (2) are greater.

TRANSPORTATION COSTS AND THE DEMAND FOR TRANSPORTATION

Transportation allows price difference to be arbitraged across regions. The point is most simply illustrated with zero transportation costs. The equilibrium can be found by equating excess demand to excess supply. The excess demand equations are simply the residual demands for each region. Obviously, if the equilibrium price under trade is greater than α_1 demand in region 1 is zero. This will hold as long as α_2 is large enough relative to α_2. Equilibrium then is determined in market 2, which is supplied by both Region 1 and Region 2 suppliers. Excess demand in Region 2 is simply $ED = \alpha_2 - 2p_2$, which is then set equal to the excess supply from Region 1 suppliers, which is equal to p_2 as long as the price is high enough that domestic demand in Region 1 is crowded out. That is, given the assumption that α_2 is sufficiently high relative to α_1 so that demand is zero in Region 1, excess supply is simply Region 1's supply function. Since transportation costs are zero, $p_1 = p_2$ and so $ES = p_1 = p_2$. The equilibrium prices and quantities under trade are then:

$$S_1^* = S_2^* = p_1^* = p_2^* = \tfrac{1}{3}\,\alpha_2, \quad D_1^* = 0, \quad D_2^* = \tfrac{2}{3}\alpha_2,$$

and, this outcome holds as long as

$$\alpha_2 \geq 3\alpha_1$$

However, if α_2 is lower than $3\alpha_1$, but, still exceeds α_1, then Region 1 consumers will consume some of the good, and the rest will be exported. We can find the outcome for this case using the same technique as above, equating excess demand and excess supply. Region 2's excess demand function is the same as above, i.e. $ED = \alpha_2 - 2p_2$, and costless transportation again implies perfect price arbitrage, so that $p_1 = p_2$. What changes is Region 1's excess supply function, which now needs to account for domestic consumption eating into domestic production. Thus, $ES = 2p_1 - \alpha_1$, which is simply domestic supply minus domestic demand. Pulling these equations together yields the equilibrium prices and quantities under trade as:

$$S_1^* = S_2^* = p_1^* = p_2^* = \frac{\alpha_1 + \alpha_2}{4}, \quad D_1^* = \frac{3\alpha_1 - \alpha_2}{4}, \quad D_2^* = \frac{3\alpha_2 - \alpha_1}{4},$$

that holds as long as

$$\alpha_2 \in [\alpha_1, 3\alpha_1],$$

Transportation, however, is costly. Let t represent the cost per unit of the good transported. For now, consider the case of one mode providing transportation from Region 1 to Region 2. The excess demand and excess supply equations above still apply to the case of costly transportation, but transportation can no longer arbitrage prices to be the same. Instead, arbitrage implies that price differences cannot exceed the transport cost. That is, the price differences are bounded by the constraint $p_2 \leq p_1 + t$. If there is trade in equilibrium, this holds with equality (so $p_2 = p_1 + t$) and differential prices simply reflect the cost of transporting the good to the demand region. On the other hand, if prices are closer together than t ($p_2 < p_1 + t$), there can be no trade since arbitrage cannot be profitable. The equilibrium types then are like the ones we have already described: if transport costs are too large, the autarkic equilibrium prevails. For lower costs, there is trade, and the supply region will export its total production only if its domestic demand is weak relative to that in the demand region.

The autarky regime is the simplest to describe. As demonstrated above, autarky prices are $p_1^* = \tfrac{1}{2}\,\alpha_1$ and $p_2^* = \tfrac{1}{2}\,\alpha_2$, so that autarky remains as long as the price difference is less than the transportation cost. Equivalently, $\alpha_2 - \alpha_1 \leq 2t$ means there will be no trade.

In the case of lower transport cost but weak demand in the supply region, then demand in the low demand Region, 1, is zero. To characterize this case, we equate excess demand and excess supply so $\alpha_2 - 2p_2 = p_1$ and use the price difference equation given by $p_2 = p_1 + t$. Solving, the result is $p_1^* = \frac{\alpha_2 - 2t}{3}$ and $p_2^* = \frac{\alpha_2 + t}{3}$. Each region's domestic production equals its domestic supply, and quantity consumed in Region 1 is zero, while in Region 2 it is given by the demand curve as $D_2^* = \frac{2\alpha_2 - t}{3}$. For this regime to be pertinent, it must be the case that $p_1^* \geq \alpha_1$, otherwise there would be positive consumption in the supply region. This condition is $\alpha_2 - 2t \geq 3\alpha_1$. Notice that the quantity transported from 1 to 2 is the full quantity produced in 1, namely, $p_1^* = \frac{\alpha_2 - 2t}{3}$. This equation also forms the demand for transportation, and is a decreasing function of t.

For low transport cost and relatively strong Region 1 demand, not all Region 1's production will be exported. Equating excess demand and excess supply, in this case, implies $\alpha_2 - 2p_2 = 2p_1 - \alpha_1$, and, again, the price difference equation $p_2 = p_1 + t$ holds. Solving these equations gives $p_1^* = \frac{\alpha_1 - \alpha_2 + 2t}{4}$ and $p_2^* = \frac{\alpha_1 + \alpha_2 + 2t}{4}$. Once again, these are also the respective expressions for the domestic supplies, S_1^* and S_2^* respectively. The quantities consumed are $D_1^* = \frac{3\alpha_1 - \alpha_2 + 2t}{4}$ and $D_2^* = \frac{-\alpha_1 + \alpha_2 - 2t}{4}$ respectively.[2] From the first of these, it is clear that we need the condition $3\alpha_1 - 2t > \alpha_2$ to hold in order for D_1^* to indeed be positive. The quantity transported in this case is given by $T = \frac{(\alpha_2 - \alpha_1)}{2} - t$, and constitutes the demand function for transportation.

The results of both cases are similar. Specifically, as demand in the excess demand region grows, quantities transported increase, and, as the transportation rate increases, quantities transported fall. In the latter case, as demand in the excess supply region grows (i.e., α_1 increases), less is transported.

The model, to this point, has the cost of providing transportation as exogenous. It merely indicates the interrelationship of demand and supply conditions in each region without and with transportation charges. We address this issue in the remainder of this section.

TRANSPORTATION MARKET EQUILIBRIUM

There is considerable interest in modeling equilibrium in the transportation market as an end in itself. The models in the previous sub-sections illustrate the construction of demand for transportation. In this sub-section, we add in the supply of transportation. In the literature, transportation firms are typically taken as price-takers. The supply of transportation then emanates from cost functions. In the simplest case, suppose that costs are a constant (c) per-unit of output shipped. The equilibrium transport rate t is simply this cost (i.e., $t = c$ per unit shipped). Any improvement in cost conditions (a reduction in c) then reduces transportation costs and facilitates trade between the regions.

In a slightly more complicated case, suppose that the marginal cost of a transportation firm is linearly increasing in output shipped, i.e., $MC = cq$. If there are N such providers, then transportation supply function is given by $T^S = N\frac{t}{c}$. In the context of the demand models established above, transportation demand and supply are set equal to find equilibrium. An improvement in cost conditions of transportation suppliers increases transportation supply and reduces the transportation rate. This, in turn (and as above) facilitates trade between the two regions.

FULL SPATIAL MODEL OF RAIL AND BARGE COMPETITION

Development of the full spatial model requires some detail on the locations of shippers, the geography of the transportation network, and the options available to shippers. To this end, we follow our previous work (Anderson and Wilson 2004, 2005). In what follows, we take shippers to be the suppliers of the product that is shipped. These shippers are located over a space. Shippers ship to a single terminal market and can ship by rail, barge, or a combination of truck and barge. We assume that commodities flow to a single terminal market.[3] Further, the present case is confined to rail and truck-barge alternatives. That is, shippers cannot use truck only as an alternative.[4]

The river-canal system runs from North to South and terminates at the terminal market, which may reflect a final transshipment port (e.g., New Orleans). Let the East-West distance from the river be in the x direction, and let the North-South direction up and down the river be denoted by $y \geq 0$. The river is divided up into "pools." A pool is a body of water between fixed points. For our purposes, and, as discussed in greater detail below, USACE planning purposes, pools are bodies of water between two locks.

For the first part of the analysis below, the river there is a single river terminal in each pool. The cost of barge shipping from the pool is w_i per shipment. We also start out with a single rail terminal per pool. Let the cost of rail transportation be R_i. However, shipments still have to reach the terminals, and they travel by truck to do so. Shipping by truck is perfectly competitive. The shipping rate by truck is constant per unit per unit distance shipped, at rate t. Truck transport is assumed to follow the Manhattan metric, meaning that distances must be traversed East-West and North-South only. Hence, the cost of shipping by truck to a river terminal location $(\bar{y}, \bar{x})$ from coordinate (y, x) is $t|x - \bar{x}|$. Thus, the cost of shipping to the terminal market is given by the summation of truck and barge costs which is $t|x - \bar{x}| + w|y - \bar{y}|$.

Below, we also allow for rail transport to be made from many points, and likewise for barge. Both are assumed to follow the block metric (actually, for river, this is straightforward since the river flows due South). The corresponding rates per unit per mile are b for barge and r for rail, and we assume that $t > r > b$, so that, if transport modes are priced at cost, the combination of truck and barge is the cheaper option for locations close to the river since the high per mile cost of trucking is offset by the low per unit cost of barge (see Anderson and Wilson 2004).

In what follows, we first assume that each shipment point (i.e., coordinate (y, x)) is associated to a shipment of unit size up to a reservation value that is high enough that it plays no role in what immediately follows. Later, we introduce a downward sloping demand at each point in space.

SINGLE RIVER TERMINAL PER POOL, SINGLE RAIL TERMINAL

A focal point of this chapter is to develop a full spatial model from which welfare changes from a transportation infrastructure improvement can be evaluated and compared with USACE modeling efforts. To illustrate the restrictive assumptions implicit in the USACE and S-TJ Models, we first give a set of conditions that when applied to the full spatial model generates the fixed region assumption within a spatial context. To fix regions and satisfy the properties of the S-TJ and USACE approaches, there are a number of assumptions that can be imposed on the model. These are:

1. There is a single river terminal for each pool
2. There is a single rail terminal for each pool, and it is coincident with the river terminal;
3. The quantity of agricultural production from each point in space is fixed;
4. All land within a given distance from the river is viable for farming for the range of transport cost variations considered (fixed extensive margin); and
5. Farmers within the latitudes that define the pool must ship from the pool terminal by either river or by rail).

Each of these assumptions is described below. The objective here is to build a model that has origin-destination demands (for a given commodity) at the pool level. We have assumed that there is but one destination pool so that each demand can be simply identified by its originating point. To generate this feature from a spatially extended economy, we, therefore, suppose that each farmer within the latitudes that define the pool must ship to the river terminal that is in this pool. That is, there is a single river terminal and all farmers situated between the locks must ship to that terminal. The river terminal also doubles as a rail terminal so that farmers have a choice of whether to ship by river or by rail. Further suppose that each farmer has a fixed amount of produce to ship on the river and that the number of farmers is fixed. For example, suppose that there is a fertile valley that is cultivated, and that outside of this valley, the land is too barren to farm. Then suppose too that all these farmers will find it worthwhile to ship by rail from the terminal on the river, and that there is no other rail terminal around. This means that the price for the agricultural produce is more than sufficient to cover the rail transport costs, plus the truck transportation cost needed to get the produce to the terminal (and also covers any harvesting costs, plus, in the long run, the cost of planting and other farming costs—as well as still leaving the farming crop the most profitable land use). This basic pattern is illustrated in Figure 15.1.

The farmers now only have to choose which mode to use for shipping the produce to the final market (downstream to New Orleans, say). Clearly they will choose the one that is less expensive. Suppose that rail shipping from terminal i in pool $_i$ costs R_i per ton shipped. As long as the barge price per ton, w_i, is below R_i, then all produced will be shipped by barge. The resulting barge demand curve is given in the Figure 15.2.

Note that the rail price here, which is assumed exogenously given, is a Zap price in the sense that if the barge price rises higher than R_i, all shipments will go by rail instead of by barge. In this model, the barge price w_i is determined as an equilibrium price given that it endogenously includes all delay costs at locks downstream. A brief description of how this works is as follows. For any set of barge prices (w_i's), there corresponds a set of shipments (nothing from pool i if w_i exceeds R_i, and the full demand from pool i otherwise). These shipments then determine a set of lock congestion times, and hence induce a new set of barge prices. The equilibrium is an internally consistent set of barge prices (a fixed point in technical terms) such that the barge prices induce exactly the set of shipments that give rise to the barge prices.

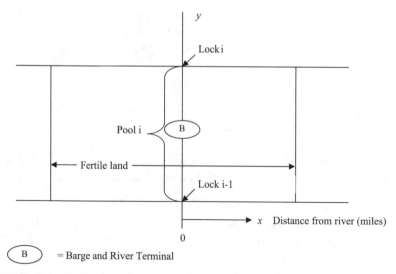

FIGURE 15.1   Stylized network and transportation infrastructure.

Now return to the demand schedule, and suppose that all land within the pool latitudes is equally fertile, and stretches out in both directions. Then the costs of shipping will draw a natural bound on the width of land farmed. Call the furthest away points the extensive margin of cultivation, so that all land within the extensive margin is farmed, and all land outside is not farmed. The extensive margin is illustrated in Figure 15.3. It has a lozenge shape and is furthest from the river at the latitude of the river terminal. This is because the costs of truck shipping determine the extensive margin for any given barge rate, and these costs are lowest for any given horizontal (East-West) distance the lower is the North-South distance.

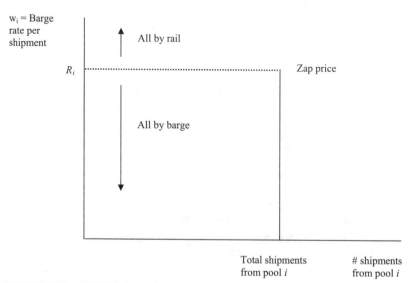

FIGURE 15.2   ORNIM demands.

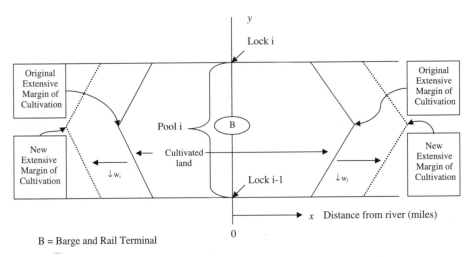

FIGURE 15.3   Extensive margin of cultivation and lower barge rates.

In the model, allowing the extensive margin to change effectively allows the Samuelson-Takayama-Judge region to change endogenously and generates a demand function with a non-zero slope. In our geography, the gathering area (the region from which shipments occur) expands in the East-West directions. Below, we also develop a case for which there are expansions in the North-South directions as well.

Consider now a drop in the barge rate. By making shipping less expensive, this moves the extensive margin of cultivation outward to the dashed lines in Figure 15.3. This feature generates some degree of elasticity in the demand curve for barge transportation, i.e., as the price of barge traffic falls, the extensive margin shifts out and more land is cultivated for shipment.

A further reason for demand elasticity is at the level of the individual farmer within the catchment area (i.e., inside the extensive margin). As the price of barge shipping falls, the profit per unit from shipping a ton of produce rises. This effect induces farmers to produce more, and the longer the time-frame, the more response is expected. In the short-term, a lower barge rate at harvest time causes farmers to exert more effort into reducing waste and ensuring the whole crop planted is harvested. They will also be more inclined to ship rather than use the produce for other local purposes (such as feeding to hogs or converting to ethanol in the case of corn). In the longer run, more land will be cultivated with the crop in question, and more intensive farming techniques (applying more workers and machinery as well as using higher yield seed types) will be used. For all these reasons the individual demands will be sensitive to the barge price. The implications for demand are sketched in Figure 15.4.

There are other important factors in demand even in this simple sketch (i.e., even before we introduce more elaborate infrastructures). Perhaps the most important of these is that the farmers farthest down-river in the pool might find it more profitable to ship from the next terminal downstream rather than from the upstream terminal to which they were assigned in the above argument.

Suppose now that farmers are to choose the pool from which to ship. We revert

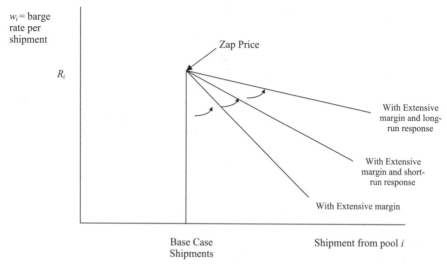

FIGURE 15.4   Demand effects: Base case, extensive margin, short and long runs.

for simplicity to the basic geography of Figure 15.1 where the extensive margin of cultivation is fixed by nature and assume too that there is no supply flexibility (no barge price responsiveness) within the extensive margin. Consider a farmer towards the southern end of the pool, facing the decision of whether to truck north to ship from the pool i or whether to truck south, and ship from the terminal in the next pool down, pool $i - 1$. We naturally expect the barge rate to be lower further south ($w_{i-1} < w_i$) because a smaller distance is traversed on the river and one less lock is crossed. The farmer must, therefore, weigh the costs of trucking to the two alternative terminals. The indifferent farmer defines the market boundary for the catchment areas of the two pools. Those farmers further north of the boundary will ship to the pool terminal, and conversely, those further south of it will ship to the pool $i - 1$ terminal.[5]

The situation is illustrated in Figure 15.5, and again, points to another source of substitution from shippers located over geographic space. The Figure 15.5 also shows the effects of an increase in the barge rate in pool i. This means that shipments from pool i shrink as its barge price rises. They shrink on two margins here. First, shippers in the South switch to the pool below. Second, shippers in the North switch to the pool above. What is important in this simple sketch is that the number of shipments on the river does not change, but their allocation to the pools on the river does. The demand immediately upstream and immediately downstream changes with the local price as farmers substitute away from the more expensive option. However, they do not switch into rail; instead, they switch into a different pool demand. We next consider more elaborate infrastructure patterns.

Alternative Rail Shipping Location

Suppose that there is an alternative rail shipping location to the one at the river terminal. For expediency, let the rail terminal be located at the same latitude as the river terminal,

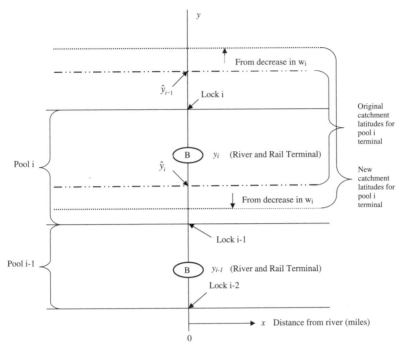

FIGURE 15.5 Endogenous pool markets and barge rates.

and moreover impose the restriction that all farmers between the latitudes of the locks defining the pool ship from either the river or the rail terminal. The demand for the pool is then dictated by the location of the farmer indifferent between the rail and the river terminal. Given the assumption that transportation follows the block metric, the locus of indifference is at the longitude where the difference in the distance to the river terminal and the distance to the rail terminal just offsets the rail-barge transportation cost difference.[6] Figure 15.6 illustrates this infrastructure and economic behavior.

As the barge rate falls, the indifference longitude moves east linearly. Note that the demand for barge transportation falls continuously to zero, and reaches zero at a price above R_i because barge has an advantage for farmers near the river terminal by since its proximity enabling them to pay lower trucking costs to ship to the river rather than the rail terminal. Also note that the barge mode zaps the rail mode at a critical price where it is just cheap enough to attract farmers at the railroad terminaland, therefore, all the farmers in the hinterland of the rail terminal.

Having established the pattern under the constraint that farmers must ship from their own pools, we next relax this constraint to allow for "lock-jumping." This is an important feature of the spatial setting. In Figure 15.7, we take a snap-shot of two adjacent pools and delineate the demand addressed to river shipments in each pool as well as shipments from the rail terminals in the pool area. Figure 15.7 is constructed by finding the indifference longitudes between each rail and river terminal in each pool, and the indifference latitudes between the two rail terminals and the two river terminals. We then complete the graph by determining the locus of indifference between the barge terminal of each pool and the rail terminal of the other pool.

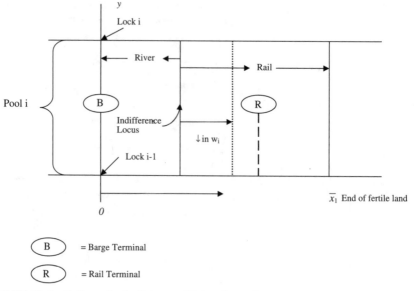

FIGURE 15.6   Rail terminal off-river and linear demands.

As we noted before, the effects of a barge price decrease for a pool increase the number of shipments from that pool. This increase is drawn in part from decreasing the demand for the adjacent pools. However, there is now an additional effect that some of the increase is drawn from the nearby rail point AND the rail terminals in adjacent pools too.

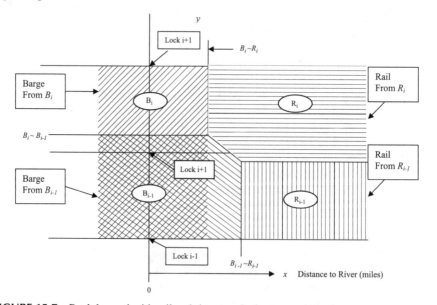

FIGURE 15.7   Pool demand with rail and river terminals at same latitude.

MANY RAIL TERMINALS

Next assume that there are many points in a pool area from which rail shipments may be made. In other words, the rail network is reasonably dense, and there are multiple branch lines. The specific geography can be modeled at a micro level by specifying all the actual possible rail pick-up points and then following the lines of the analysis of the preceding section. Note that this introduces the issue of multiple rail prices (one from each possible shipment point), and also specifying how these prices are determined. We, therefore, approximate a dense rail network by assuming that rail transport is available all over the geographic space. The advantage of this approximation is to give a clearer picture of the overall system equilibrium shipment pattern.

We retain for now the assumption that there is a single river terminal per pool. Once again, to emphasize the demands at each pool are independent of demands in the adjacent to pools in both the S-TJ and, as discussed below, the USACE models, we first solve the model with the assumption that all shipments originating between the two latitudes defining the pool must ship from that pool's river terminal if shipping is done by the river (i.e., truck-barge is used). We then relax this assumption and let prices dictate the pool from which farmers initiate barge movements.

As above, let t denote the cost per unit shipped per unit distance using truck. Further, let w_i be the cost of shipping from the river terminal in pool i. We now also must specify how much rail shipping costs differ from different points. To accomplish this, we shall use a block metric system just as we did above for the trucking sector. What this means is that transportation can be viewed as following a grid network, and distances are traversed only North-South and East-West. We suppose that the cost of rail shipping is linear in the (block) distance shipped, at rate r per unit shipped per unit distance. Thus, we can specify shipping costs from any point in space. We know that rail shipping is cheaper the closer to the river is the origin, as is also true for truck-barge (since the rail traffic effectively must traverse the same East-West mileage as the truck traffic). Rail is also cheaper the closer the origin to the destination. For barge though, this is not true if the origin point is South of the pool river terminal. In that case, the further South, the greater the shipping cost because a greater distance must be traveled North by truck to reach the terminal. However, of the points north of the terminal, further South is better because it is synonymous with closer to the river terminal.

To find the catchment area for barge within the pool latitudes for this case, it suffices to find the indifferent farmer location such that the farmer pays just as much shipping by truck to the terminal and then by barge thereafter as he does shipping by rail throughout. Figure 15.8 illustrates the resulting spatial catchment area. Notice that it reaches furthest East at the latitude of the river terminal: this is because the relative advantage of barge is highest there because transportation by truck needs no North-South component.

Figure 15.8 also illustrates the effects on the barge catchment area of decreasing the water rate, w_i.[7] Notice that the decrease in the barge rate causes the catchment area to expand in a parallel fashion. This means that if the density of farmers is uniform over space, then the demand function for the pool is a linear function of the barge rate, w_i.[8]

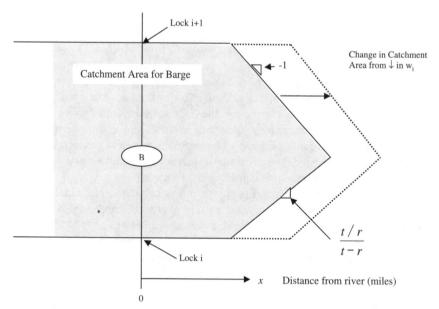

FIGURE 15.8   Pool demands and lock-jumping.

We now allow the farmers to ship to whichever river or rail terminal they wish. This means that the terminal in the pool below may well attract traffic from farmers from the South of a pool above. This is the situation illustrated in Figure 15.9.

The picture looks quite like that of Figure 15.8, with the catchment areas having the same shape, except that they are shifted upwards (above the pool latitudes) because of the possibility of trucking down to the river terminal in the next pool down. Note that this lock-jumping feature also entails there being continuity in the longitudinal boundary (as illustrated) as we pass from one pool catchment area to the next one down. The latitudinal boundary between two pools' catchment areas is horizontal, as given in Figure 15.9, because of the assumption of block distance in trucking: trucks must also travel in North-South and East-West patterns only. While a crow-flies distance would give a more intricate pattern, it would not fundamentally alter the qualitative result of the figure.[9]

MANY RAIL TERMINALS AND MANY RIVER TERMINALS (DENSE INFRASTRUCTURE)

The models above have assumed that there is a single river terminal per pool. In practice, there are often several locations within a pool at which barges can be loaded. Having just analyzed the case of many rail terminals over space, we now develop the model for the case of many river terminals. Again, for clarity, we suppose that any point on the river is a candidate barge-loading location. There is a difference between the case of many rail terminals and many river terminals: in the former case, anywhere in the two-dimensional geographic space is a potential loading point, while in the latter case

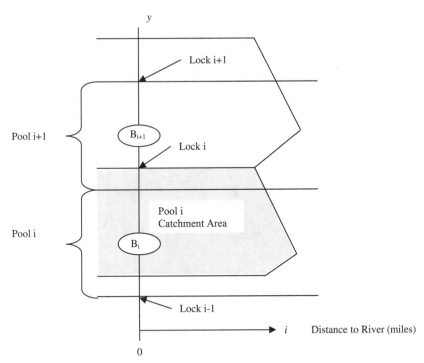

FIGURE 15.9 Endogenous markets.

the loading points are constrained to points along the river. This means that trucks must be used to reach the river to use barge, while rail goes directly from the point of production.

We now need to also specify the rate per unit distance traveled by barge. Call this rate b. Barge must be used in conjunction with truck (which operates at rate t), and so truck-barge combines the most expensive mode (truck) with the least expensive mode (barge). Letting the rail rate per unit per unit distance be r, we assume that $t > r > b$. This pattern of costs ensures that both modes (rail and the joint truck-barge one) are viable in equilibrium. Moreover, truck-barge dominates in the neighborhood of the river. We also suppose that barge shipping entails an extra cost whenever locks are crossed: denote the cost associated with Lock i as c_i.

Since the terminal market is at location $y = 0$, $x = 0$, the cost of making a shipment from a location with coordinates (y,x) is therefore $r|x| + ry$ using rail. Using the truck-barge mode, the cost is $t|x| + by + \sum_{\{i|y_i < y\}} c_i$ where the summation encompasses the total cost of traversing all locks between origin (y) and destination (0). For comparison with what has come before, we start out by maintaining the hypothesis that each shipper must ship from his own latitude (x) if shipping by barge. This gives rise to the following pattern of barge shipment areas.

Figure 15.10 embodies the idea that crossing a lock adds to the cost of barge shipping.[10] The existence of this cost, though, means that farmers may prefer to ship down (by truck) below the costly lock.[11] Indeed, Figure 15.10 clearly indicates that such an

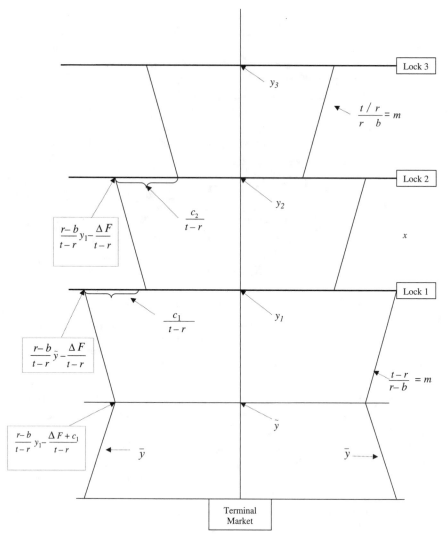

FIGURE 15.10   Catchment area of barge, case of many river terminals per pool, many rail terminals, "lock-jumping" not allowed.

arbitrage opportunity exists. Figure 15.11 shows the spatial pattern of the truck-barge catchment area once we allow for such lock-jumping.

Notice the similarity between Figure 15.11 and Figure 15.9 that shows the catchment area for barge in the case of a single river terminal per pool and many rail terminals, when lock-jumping is allowed. In both cases, arbitrage behavior by shippers (in terms of lock-jumping in response to price differentials) renders the catchment area boundaries continuous (cf. the discontinuities apparent in the counterpart Figures 15.8 and 15.10 without the ability for shippers to ship from terminals other than in a shipper's own

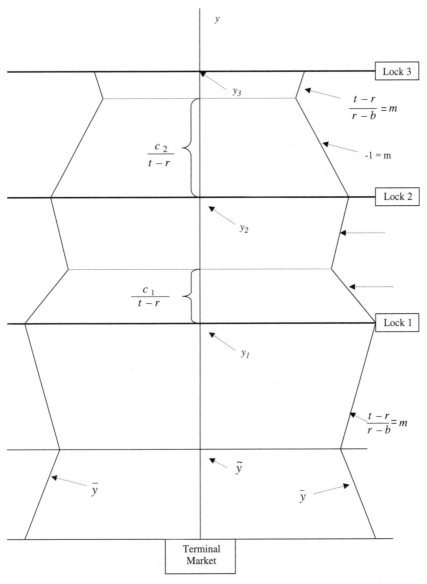

FIGURE 15.11 Catchment area for barge, case of many river terminals, may rail terminals, "lock-jumping" allowed.

pool area). The difference between the two figures is that the barge catchment area bulges out at the latitude of the terminal when there is a single river terminal. When terminals are all along the river, the catchment area follows a similar pattern, except that the bulges correspond to the latitudes of the locks since locations just above the locks must incur costly truck transportation in order to "jump" the locks.

WELFARE AND PLANNING MODELS

We next turn to the comparison of welfare across the different models, and the relation between the welfare derived from the spatial model developed here and the world of Samuelson-Takayama-Judge and ORNIM.

The US Army Corps of Engineers uses estimates of future user benefits in planning infrastructure developments. In the case of evaluating the economic case for lock improvements, the USACE uses a particular suite of models called ORNIM (Ohio River Navigation Investment Model). The ORNIM Model (implicitly) imposes a particular spatial structure. It uses as input data demands at the level of river pools, which are bodies of water between two points (e.g., adjacent locks). Demands are defined as the annual volume of traffic for a particular commodity between an origin and a terminating pool. These demands are assumed to be not substitutable between originating or terminating pools.

This assumption follows the tradition of Samuelson (1952) and Takayama and Judge (1964) (S-TJ). The S-TJ set-up does allow for spatial differences between locations. These differences are arbitraged through a competitive transportation sector. However, the set-up treats all supply or demand nodes as spaceless points, and does not consider the underlying geographic dispersal of supplies or demands that are funneled together to form the point demands. Allowing for a richer spatial structure, where producers choose whence to ship, suggests that the net demands at neighboring shipment points ought not be treated as independent, but instead the allocation of shipments from a particular location depends also on prices for shipping from neighboring shipment points. That is, the market area generating a given pool demand depends not only on its own price, but also on the prices at neighboring pools. As such, the regions of Samuelson-Takayama-Judge and ORNIM are, in a sense, themselves endogenous.

THE OHIO RIVER NAVIGATION INVESTMENT MODEL (ORNIM)

The basic idea in ORNIM is that a fixed set of shipments must be made. These are categorized as Origin-Destination-Commodity triples. The origins and destinations are pools. In what follows, we index a particular Origin-Destination-Commodity triple by i. The shipments that are made for any commodity between any pair of pools are derived from a forecast model. The forecast levels are based on past levels of shipments of the commodity between the specified origin and destination.

Shipments are assumed to either go by one of two shipping modes, rail or barge. If a shipment goes by rail, it goes overland at rail rate R_i per ton which is exogenous to the model. If it goes by barge, the rate is w_i, which is endogenous to the model. The barge rates, w_i, are determined by historical data using a base year level plus a correction for changing congestion from traffic on the river through various locks.

The algorithm works as follows. Start with a given set of waterway rates, w_i, and a set of rail rates, R_i. First, all shipments go by the cheaper mode, and so choose the waterway if and only if w_i is less than R_i. This step yields a set of quantities to be shipped by river. For each i, either all the shipment is shipped by river (if $w_i < R_i$) or else none is (if $w_i > R_i$), leaving rate equality ($w_i = R_i$) as the only possible reason for observing a mixed shipment.[12]

Having determined the set of shipments made by river for a given w_i (these are the full prices faced by shippers, including time costs, etc.), the next step is to update the w_i from the induced shipments. This procedure is the task of the module WAM (Waterway Analysis Model) in the ORNIM suite.[13]

WAM takes the total shipments and considers the geography of the waterway to derive congestion costs that depend on shipping levels through the locks. This process generates a new set of barge prices which are then fed back to the first module of determining induced shipments. An equilibrium is, therefore, a fixed point of this algorithm whereby a set of barge prices induce a set of shipments that, in turn, induce the original barge prices.

Given the above algorithm, the benefit-cost analysis of a structural change (e.g., lock refurbishing) is readily performed. This surplus analysis uses the rail rate (which acts as the default option) as the benchmark. Since a shipment either goes by rail or waterway, the shipment sent by barge returns a surplus equal to shipment size times the net saving over the rail option.

The model is commendable for carefully separating out the perfect competition assumption of price-taking shippers from the computation of the equilibrium barge rate. This warrants the two-stage procedure used in the model, and is moreover appropriate because of the presence of congestion externalities (which are determined in the waterway cost calculation in WAM).

The above description of the Zap-price demand formulation applies to the basic ORNIM and TOW-COST Models (TCM) used by the USACE. Recognizing the abrupt behavioral assumption that the entire shipment must go by one mode or the other, a second model, the ESSENCE Model, introduces some elasticity into this process. In particular, ESSENCE stipulates that the demand for barge shipments depends on the barge price in a continuous manner, with higher shipments demanded at lower price, in line with standard economic analysis. The demand curve is parameterized by a value N which indicates the elasticity of demand (with respect to the rail-barge differential, $R_i - w_i$).[14] The case $N = 1$ is easiest to explain. This gives rise to a linear demand function.[15] Reviews of the basic ORNIM model point to several concerns. The demand forecast model has been quite roundly criticized by Berry et al. (2000).[16] Moreover, the demands are assumed fixed at the pool Origin-Destination-Commodity level. This is the issue we concentrate upon in the current paper. Even with data limitations, it may be possible to generate the observed demands at the pool levels from an underlying spatial economy and let the data constrain parameters.

WELFARE ANALYSIS

There are several potentially important sources of welfare gains and losses that are not captured by the ORNIM approach, which are discussed in this section. The first is illustrated most simply by using the model closest to ORNIM, namely our first model above (Section 3) in its stark form whereby there is a fixed amount of arable land, and no scope in terms of production at either intensive or extensive margins. Hence the total amount shipped is completely invariant to the barge rate or rates. In this model, the only important issue (and the one we highlight here), concerns substitution between pools by shippers: other points are made later in more elaborate versions of the model. This issue is at the heart of our criticism of using the framework of Samuelson-Takayama-Judge to model transportation demands that emanate from locally dispersed production: no such substitution is allowed.

To see the issue, refer back to Figure 15.5, which illustrates the effects on the market for pool i shipments resulting from a decrease in the barge rate, w_i. To make things even simpler, suppose too that the uppermost pool is pool i and let the location denoted Lock i in Figure 15.5 represent the furthest North extent of the arable land (call this $\bar{y}$). Now, as we noted in Section 3, the critical latitude that divides the catchment area for pool i from that for pool $i - 1$ is linearly increasing in w_i. This property implies that the demand for shipments from pool i is also linear. However, the ORNIM Model sets it as a constant amount. This divergence in assumptions can potentially lead to a substantial difference in the welfare evaluation of a change (the empirical importance is discussed further below). This is illustrated in Figure 15.12.

Figure 15.12 represents the demand addressed to the river terminal in pool i as a function of the barge rate for shipments from pool i, w_i. The demand, as derived from the spatial model, is linear in w_i. This linearity reflects the important feature of the traffic diversion effect. Namely, as the barge rate falls (due to an improvement in transit times at lock $i - 1$ following lock rehabilitation there, say), and keeping the barge rate from the downstream locks (such as Lock $i - 2$) constant, shippers in the northern reaches of pool $i - 1$'s catchment area switch to using the pool i terminal. In Figure 15.12, the

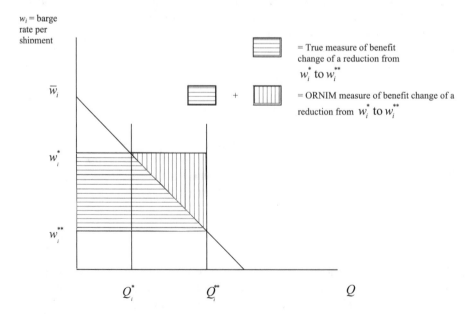

FIGURE 15.12   Welfare benefits of a reduction in the barge rate in pool i.

original (pre-improvement) barge rate is represented as w_i^*. After improvement, it falls to w_i^{**}. The ORNIM approach takes the demand at pool i as constant—a quantity of shipments Q_i^{**} in the figure, which we assume for illustration to be the level to which the quantity shipped rises after the reduction in the barge rate.[17] The measured welfare improvement under ORNIM simply then corresponds to the reduction of costs (w_i^* $- w_i^{**}$) on the assumed volume of traffic (Q_i^{**}). The total improvement is measured as the product, $(w_i^* - w_i^{**})Q_i^{**}$, as given as the full shaded rectangle in the figure. However, this neglects the induced lower volume of shipments at the initial high rate (the traffic diversion effect) whereby the high rate renders pool i pricier for more shippers than pool $i-1$. The total benefit is then properly measured as the area left of the true demand curve (the linear one in the figure) between the two prices (the horizontally shaded area in the figure). This constitutes only part of the rectangle measured by ORNIM (the cost saving as if there were a high volume of shipments), but this neglects the fact that diverted shipments escape cost rises.

The size of the difference depends on the size of the cost reduction, the elasticity of the true demand, and where the demand forecast lies. Note that the ESSENCE Model also shares with ORNIM the problem that the demands are based on the S-TJ formulation: no traffic diversion effect is included. In our development of the first model, the case of the single river terminal and single coincident rail terminal in Section 3, we next allowed for an increase in the extensive margin of cultivation in addition to the traffic diversion effect. This effect serves to render the demand more elastic (see also Figure 15.4). If a lower barge price also encourages more production due to substitution into crop production, demand is larger still, and more so the longer the time period under consideration (again, see Figure 15.4). The ESSENCE Model may pick up the latter effects, but it does not pick up the demand diversion one since it is based on S-TJ.

Before proceeding, a further caveat is in order. This concerns the nature of the ORNIM quantity forecast. ORNIM must forecast demands years into the future, and a crucial point concerns for what prices the forecast is valid. Of course, for the original ORNIM/TOW-COST specification, since demand is assumed totally inelastic up to the Zap price, this issue does not matter because it does not arise. However, it matters crucially if the demand has some elasticity.[18]

The second and third models presented above introduce a further source of possible welfare gains that are not accounted for in the ORNIM approach. In these models, the rail sector earns rent at locations that it serves. The rail price is determined by the constraint that rail shipping has to meet and beat the competition from the truck-barge alternative shipping mode. This process is described in detail in Anderson and Wilson (2005). In our model, railroads beat the competition by practicing spatial price discrimination.[19] A reduction in the barge rate now causes an expansion of the catchment area, as before, and the benefits from this are measured as the area under the barge demand curve, as above. However, there is also an effect on the rail rate from locations still served by rail. The rail rate must fall to beat the new tougher competition. If there is no demand expansion from this price reduction, this is simply a transfer of surplus from railroads to farmers. There is no efficiency effect, but simply redistribution of benefits. However, there is an additional efficiency effect if farmers respond by raising production when faced with lower shipping rates.[20] This means that there is an additional surplus benefit that is not captured simply by looking at the demand for barge transport, and this is due to the competitive effect in the rail sector. A full treatment of the extra economic surplus emanating from the lock rehabilitation should include this spill-over effect into the other transportation sector. It is overlooked in ORNIM because the ORNIM Model takes the rail rate as given.

SUMMARY AND CONCLUSIONS

This chapter describes, develops, and compares alternative models of equilibrium in the transportation market and the corresponding measures of welfare benefits accruing from transportation infrastructure improvements. The most famous model considered here is the S-TJ Model that we described and solved in the context of a simple framework. In this framework, regional demands and supplies are connected through a transportation network which allows price differences across regions to be arbitraged. The model is completed through the addition of the transportation sectors. The NRC has recommended that this model be considered for use in evaluating transportation improvements to the waterway. However, in this network, suppliers of a product in a region have important alternatives that render the region over which demand and supply endogenous, i.e., determined within the equilibrium. As a matter of theory, the S-TJ model could make the regions arbitrarily small (as long as all choices are fully specified), in which case, it collapses to a full spatial model comparable to that presented in Section 3.

The model presented in Section 3 is a full spatial model developed in the context of transportation decision making by disaggregated suppliers of a product who also make the mode/routing choices of transportation. The model is first developed with a set of assumptions that fix the regions of supply. In this case, the suppliers choose only the mode to use, and are taken to use the cheapest mode. The result yields a perfectly inelastic demand function up to the point with the rail rate is reached and zero thereafter. The model is then extended to allow for an extensive margin of cultivation with the result that as modal rates fall, the extensive margin of production increases and more products are transported. The model also accommodates changes in the intensive margin of production (e.g., farmers cultivate more intensively as mode rates fall). The model is then amended to allow suppliers in one region to ship from another (e.g., farmers haul out of region to another pool). Again, this points to another added source of substitution. The remainder of the cases describes alternative rail shipping locations and river terminals to illustrate how the market areas and substitution effects differ with alternative transportation infrastructure.

To illustrate the calculation of welfare effects, in Section 4, we describe models used by the USACE to evaluate the benefits of lock improvements on the waterway. The basic USACE planning models assume that the pool level demand is perfectly inelastic up to a threshold point (where the alternative mode dominates). We develop a full spatial model and then consider the assumptions under which this framework can be consistent with the USACE ones. We also indicate possible sources of over-estimation and under-estimation of benefits within the USACE Model when compared to the full spatial model.[21] One major potential source of divergence between the full spatial model and the one used by the USACE is attributable to their taking the pool level demands to be independent of barge rates at neighboring pools. In a full spatial model, it is readily apparent that marginal shippers will switch river terminals in response to barge rate changes (or lock rehabilitation that reduces waiting times at some locks). Accounting for this traffic diversion effect can yield welfare changes from improvements that are not picked up in the USACE approach, which assumes no substitutability across pools is possible. Such substitutability is a natural economic phenomenon akin to arbitrage activity: shippers will switch whenever they find a better deal. Accounting for this behavior can generate welfare changes even when there is no induced extra economic activity (crop production, say) due to the barge rate decrease. Both the standard ORNIM/TOW-COST Model and the ESSENCE variant are subject to these critiques since they are based on the Samuelson-Takayama-Judge spatial equilibrium model. Somewhat ironically, the National Research Council (2004) review of the latest round of the Upper Mississippi-Illinois waterway cost/benefit analysis, proposed that the USACE consider the use of spatial competition models of the Samuelson-Takayama-Judge type. As we have seen, such a proposal may encounter theoretical flaws which are shared by both the ORNIM and ESSENCE Models. Additional benefits will accrue following a barge rate reduction if shippers can adjust, and these are not captured in the standard ORNIM/TOW-COST Model. Arguably, the ESSENCE Model can pick up such effects, though its crucial elasticity parameter (N) would need to be calibrated. However, rather than calibrating that model, it would seem preferable to work directly with the spatial model that is to generate it, as indeed was suggested by Berry et al. (2000). Using the spatial model directly would obviate functional form concerns that the constant elasticity version in ESSENCE brings up. Another form of potential benefits is more subtly hidden in the market. It is not captured (or addressed) in the USACE Models, but it is evidenced in the explicitly spatial view of the underlying market. In particular, the USACE Models take the rail rate as exogenous. The spatial approach indicates that there is not one, but many rail rates at the pool level. Furthermore, rail has to beat the competition from truck-barge in order to get shipping contracts, so these rail rates are endogenously determined. If barge rates fall, competition will get tougher and even shippers who remain with rail will gain the rent because the railroads must lower price to meet tougher competition.[22] If each shipping point generates a downward sloping demand, then waterway improvements may generate additional welfare gains as shippers experience lower prices and expand output.[23] Thus, the full effects on benefits from infrastructure improvements may spill over (and be measured from) other markets as well as the truck-barge market itself.

ACKNOWLEDGMENTS

Much of this research was conducted under support from the Navigation Economic Technologies (NETS) program of the Institute for Water Resources of the Army Corps of Engineers. We gratefully acknowledge their support and comments. We especially appreciate the comments of Keith Hofseth and Kevin Hendrickson who read early versions of this chapter and provided a number of useful comments.

NOTES

1. Samuelson in turn drew on Enke (1951). Enke proposed the problem of determining spatial transportation patterns (under a linear demand system). His solution was inspired by the analogue to the problem in an electric system, and he could measure equilibrium prices and quantities with voltmeters and ammeters. Samuelson (1952) then set up and solved the problem as a linear programming problem. Takayama and Judge (1964) converted the Samuelson-Enke problem into a quadratic programming problem and found the solution algorithm (still for linear demands).

2. It is readily checked that total production equals total consumption, i.e., $S_1^* + S_2^* = D_1^* + D_2^* = \frac{a_1 + a_2}{2}$.

3. As demonstrated in previous work, the model can be adapted to allow for multiple terminal markets (Anderson and Wilson 2005).

4. This development is made for convenience and exposition, but, in Anderson and Wilson (2004), the assumption is relaxed and analyzed.

5. The indifference boundary is determined as follows. Let the terminals be located on the river ($x = 0$) at y_i and y_{i-1}, with $y_i > y_{i-1}$, and let $w_i > w_{i-1}$. The indifferent farmer is at a latitude $\hat{y}$ such that total transport costs are equalized. This means that $t[y_i - \hat{y}] + w_i = t[\hat{y} - y_{i-1}] + w_{i-1}$. Simplifying, $\hat{y}_i = \frac{y_i + y_{i-1}}{2} + \frac{w_i + w_{i-1}}{2t}$.
    Note that this is simply the midpoint if both barge prices are equal. Otherwise, the higher is the price in pool i, the further north the indifferent latitude.

6. Specifically, the distance satisfies $tx + w_i = t(x_R - x) + R_i$ where the location of the rail terminal is x_R. Rearranging, $x = \frac{x_R}{2} + \frac{R_i + w_i}{2t}$. This indifference location moves east linearly with decreases in the barge rate, w_i, and therefore generates a linear demand for the pool.

7. The water rate here, w_i, is the rate from the river terminal down to the destination. It constitutes the full price for the trip, and does not need to be broken down into a rate per mile.

8. The same property (linearity) is true in the current formulation if the density of farm production is the same at any latitude. Even if it differs across latitudes, it still has the linearity property.

9. Using the actual road net would likely yield an intermediate pattern.

10. This figure, and the subsequent one, also allow for shipping by truck directly to the final (terminal) market. This explains the lowest catchment area on the figures (i.e., below $\hat{y}$): this constitutes truck-only traffic. In Figure 15.10, there is also a term ΔF that influences the position of the extensive margin for truck-barge: this represents the fixed cost advantage to rail traffic (and includes lock-crossing costs at locks further downstream). See Anderson and Wilson (2004) for further details.

11. Analysis of this issue was one of the prime purposes of Anderson and Wilson (2004).

12. Since the w_i are calibrated from congestion data, this should almost never happen in practice with the algorithm.

13. The presentation of Oladosu et al. (2004) invokes a procedure whereby shipments are allocated to where $R_i - w_i$ is highest. This is equivalent to the description in the text.

14. The formula for the volume of shipments demanded is $[\frac{R_i - w_i}{R_i - w_0}]^N$ where w_0 is a base period price for the waterway. This is a constant elasticity of demand form with respect to the price differential $R_i - w_i$. The elasticity with respect to w_i is $\frac{-Nw_i}{R_i - w_i}$.

15. One way to think of it is to imagine a uniform density of types of shipper between the old price (w_0) and the rail price (R_i). The differences in preferences across shipper types could arise from differential evaluations of the time or reliability of barge relative to rail.

16. Berry et al. (2000) offer a tough critique of the approach used to justify expanding lock

capacity. Their review was based on a one-day conference presentation, and the main findings are presented in an Executive Summary, although they do not go into much detail. The main points include: Forecasts of future demands lack credibility; Demand elasticity is arbitrary, and ought to be estimated; Missing factors (other terminal points, regional economies); Congestion pricing should be investigated, along with alternative infrastructure investment. They concluded that the project ought to be delayed until the justification is properly documented. For the present purpose, the following quote is revealing: the specific form of the N equation does not match the form of the appropriate spatial demand models ... there is no value of N that would reproduce the various shapes of demand functions that are easily generated from spatial demand models (Berry et al. 2000, 14).

17. Clearly, the estimated benefits depend crucially on the starting position, i.e., the demand forecast.

18. There is considerable recent empirical evidence that demand functions are continuously downward sloping. The research by Boyer and Wilson (2005), Henrickson and Wilson (2004), and Train and Wilson (2004) use very different methodology and data, and, in most cases, find strong evidence that demand functions are not perfectly inelastic to a Zap price. Further, unlike both the ORNIM and ESSENCE Models, demands do not necessarily fall to zero at the price of the next best alternative.

19. In addition, the exogeneity of rail rates in ORNIM also implies that enough railroad capacity is available to meet whatever traffic goes by rail. If there is a capacity constraint on the rail sector, the railroad's pricing rule is correspondingly adjusted to incorporate this. Further details are given in Anderson and Wilson (2005).

20. Recall that we are using farmers as the illustrative example. Various elasticity effects may be larger or smaller for other commodities that use the river system.

21. In Anderson and Wilson (2004), we developed an equilibrium model of the barge market with shippers located over geographic space and deciding how to ship to market. This model explicitly allows for flow constraints on the waterway due to locks, so that the cost of using the waterway increases with the level of traffic. The model yields a unique equilibrium with barge rates, quantities, and congestion determined endogenously for given rail and truck rates. The model allows for shippers to by-pass locks and points to a stacking property of pool level demands that requires evaluation of lock improvements to be made at a system level. In Anderson and Wilson (2005), we extended the framework to endogenize railroad prices and show the railroad sets prices so as to beat the competition. The effects of waterway improvements on rail customers are purely distributional only if quantity shipped is insensitive to prices.

22. The same principle applies with rail capacity constraints. Then the railroad prefers to serve the shippers from which it can receive the highest markups. Such locations are the captive shippers to railroads, i.e., the shippers located furthest from the waterway. Lower barge rates reduce the rail rates that can be charged to these shippers as well.

23. These basic insights also apply when shippers may choose the final shipping point from a menu of possible options.

REFERENCES

Anderson, Simon P., and Wesley W. Wilson (2004). Spatial Modeling in Transportation: Congestion and Modal Choice. Mimeo, University of Oregon. Available at http://www.corpsnets.us.

Anderson, Simon P., and Wesley W. Wilson (2005). Spatial Modeling in Transportation II: Railroad competition. Mimeo, University of Oregon. Available at http://www.corpsnets. us.

Berry, Steven, Geoffrey Hewings, and Charles Leven (2000). Adequacy of research on upper Mississippi-Illinois river navigation project. Northwest-Midwest Institute.

Boyer, Kenneth, and Wesley W. Wilson (2005). Estimation of demands at the pool level. Mimeo, University of Oregon. Available at http://www.corpsnets.us.

Curlee, T. Randall (2004). The Restructured Upper Mississippi River-Illinois Waterway Navigation Feasibility Study: Overview of Key Economic Modeling Considerations,Oak Ridge National Laboratory report, prepared for the Mississippi Valley Division, U. S. Army Corps of Engineers.

Curlee, Randall T., Ingrid K., Busch, Michael R. Hilliard, F. Southworth, andDavid P. Vogt, (2004). Economic foundations of Ohio River Investment Navigation Model. Transportation Research Record No. 1871.

Enke, Stephen. (1951). Equilibrium among spatially separated markets: solution by electric analogue. *Econometrica*, 19, 40–47.

Henrickson, Kevin E., and Wesley W. Wilson (2005) A model of spatial market areas and transportation demand. Forthcoming, Transportation Research Record. Available at http://www.corpsnets.us/inlandnav.cfm.

National Research Council (2004). Review of the U.S. Army Corps of Engineers Restructured Upper Mississippi River-Illinois Waterway Feasibility Study. Committee to Review the Corps of Engineers Restructured Upper Mississippi River-Illinois Waterway Feasibility Study, available at http://www.nap.edu/catalog/10873.html.

Oladosu, Gbadebo A., Randall T. Curlee, David P. Vogt, Michael Hilliard, and Russell Lee (2004). Elasticity of demand for water transportation: effects of assumptions on navigation investment assessment results. Mimeo, Oak Ridge National Laboratory.

Samuelson, Paul A. (1952). Spatial Price Equilibrium and Linear Programming. *American Economic Review*, 42, 283–303.

Takayama, T., and G. G. Judge (1964) Equilibrium among spatially separated markets: a reformulation. *Econometrica*, 32, 510 524.

Train, Kenneth and Wesley W. Wilson (2005). Shippers' Responses to Changes in Transportation Rates and Times: The Mid-American Grain Study. Mimeo, University of Oregon. Available at http://www.corpsnets.us/inlandnav.cfm.

16 Decentralization and the Transport Sector: Some Observations

François Vaillancourt with Philippe Wingender

INTRODUCTION

The purpose of this chapter is to present some aspects of decentralization in the transport sector. This is of interest since decentralization in various sectors is a policy option for government activities including transportation. The chapter is divided into three sections. The first section presents definitions of decentralization, plausible assignment of responsibilities by level of government and statistical evidence on the extent of decentralization in eight countries. The second presents the salient points of the literature on decentralization of responsibility for providing transport with regard to four modes, namely road, rail, ports and airports. The third discusses revenue issues for the transportation sector in a decentralized setting.

DECENTRALIZATION: TYPES, POLICY RECOMMENDATIONS, AND IMPORTANCE IN THE TRANSPORTATION FIELD

This section first presents what is meant by decentralization. It then examines what is the proposed division of power between levels of government in the area of transportation by economists and ends by presenting some evidence on the extent of decentralization in a small number of countries.

WHAT IS DECENTRALIZATION[1]

The term "decentralization" generally covers three types of institutional arrangement. Note that the perspective used herein presenting them is a top down one where all powers are initially at the central level and can be allocated to other levels. One could also examine what powers should be given by lower levels of governments to the central one from a bottom up perspective.

Deconcentration

Deconcentration occurs when the territorial distribution of central functions allows decentralized bodies with decision-making authority to resolve the problems that the administration must deal with, primarily because being closer to the ground they have a better understanding of local conditions. According to Delcamp, territorial decentralization, as he terms it, means "a transfer of decision-making power or responsibility for implementation to an administrative entity within the same legal person."[2]

Central government thus retains its powers and responsibilities for a given function, but has that function performed/implemented outside the capital, say by administrative agencies or offices located in the regions. What is important is that officials and managers working in the regions are able to take decisions without having to refer back to the capital for advice and thus are no longer merely links in a chain.

Delegation

Delegation is the retaining by central government of authority and responsibilities but delegating service delivery and administration to sub-national (provincial, cantonal, etc.) or local governments (referred to throughout this paper as sn/l governments). It is worth noting in this respect that authority is delegated to a government; the politicians accountable to citizens for managing the delivery of the services that have been delegated are therefore not the same than those managing central government. Therefore, *if the requisite funding is available* at the sub-national/local level, or, in other words, if no account need be taken of the problem of unfunded mandates, services will be adequately administered, which will confer a certain degree of autonomy on sn/l governments with regard to the delivery of delegated services. Functional duplication must be avoided.

Devolution

Devolution is the transfer of responsibilities and authority from central government to sn/l governments. This transfer means that central government loses all rights of oversight over the quantity and quality of services provided as well as modes of delivery. Examples include the responsibilities of American states, Canadian provinces, and Swiss cantons. Devolution may also be accompanied by continued funding by central government funding or national standards, which will ensure a certain level of service in terms of quantity and quality. The outcome in such cases is a mix of delegation and devolution whose precise balance varies from country to country.

Table 16.1 presents each type of decentralization from three standpoints: political authority, implementing authority, and funding authority. This table also illustrates the similarities and differences between the three types of decentralization and on examination reveals that delegation is the most complex form of decentralization.

TABLE 16.1
Three Aspects of the Three Types of Decentralization

Type	Political authority	Implementing authority	Funding authority
Deconcentration	National elected representatives	Central government officials	National budget
Delegation	National and sn/l elected representatives	Sn/l government officials supervised by central government officials	Sn/l budget, with or without contractual payments by central government, taken from the national budget
Devolution	Sn/l elected representatives	Sn/l government officials (including groups of central government officials)	Sn/l budget, taxes or central government transfers from the national budget

Source: Gauthier and Vaillancourt (2002).

THE DIVISION OF RESPONSIBILITIES IN THE TRANSPORTATION FIELD

Economists have examined what is the proper division of powers for various types of government activity. We summarize the recommendations of three studies for the transportation activities in Table 16.2.

TABLE 16.2
The Division of Responsibilities in the Transportation Field: Summary of Three Studies

Activity/Author	Fox and Wallich (1999)	Prud'homme (1992)	Shah (1994) Policies/ regulations	Shah (1994) Implementation/ administration
Airports	F	SN/L	F	F
Ports	–	L	–	–
Railroads	–	F/SN	F	F
Roads				
• National/intercity	F/SN	F	F	SN/L
• Regional/rural	–	SN	SN	SN/L
• Urban/local	L	L	L	L
Public transport-urban	L	–	–	–
Public transport-Intercity	F	–	–	–

Note: F: federal (central); SN: sub-national (region, state, province,…); L: local.

Examining Table 16.2, we find that:

- All three authors examine road transport in detail and concur in assigning authority by area served. Urban/local roads are more decentralized than national roads/motorways.
- Airports are assigned at the federal level by two of the authors. In contrast, Prud'homme believes that this sector lends itself to decentralization.
- Rail transport is assigned by Shah and by Prud'homme to the federal level.
- Only Prud'homme deals with ports, which he considers to be highly amenable to decentralization.

DECENTRALIZATION IN THE TRANSPORTATION FIELD; SOME EVIDENCE

We end this first section with a brief overview of decentralization and the importance of transport in government expenditure for eight developed countries for 1990, 1995, and 2000. The countries and years were selected because of the availability of the data and their similarities in terms of economic development and institutions. Five of the countries selected are federations, Spain is de facto a federal state and two are unitary countries. The countries differ geographically, ranging from very large countries, like Canada, the United States, and Australia to small ones like mountainous Switzerland and flat Denmark. Data were taken from the IMF's Government Finance Statistics 2005. In Table 16.3, we present some information on political organization and geographical size and four indicators of the importance of government spending in the economy, centralization and transport expenditure. Government share of GDP is given by the share of public consumption on GDP that is it excludes debt service and government transfers to individuals.

Most indicators are fairly stable throughout the period selected, but important declines in the share of central government expenditure in transport can be seen in the Australian and Canadian cases. In both cases, we can trace this decline to the privatization of national airlines and railways. In the 1990s, Canada privatized Air Canada and the Canadian National Railway. Australia privatized Australian Airlines and the Australian National Railroad. This explains the drop in the share of the central government. What can explain differences between countries? The following factors seem to matter:

- The role of the private sector in transportation. Private sector involvement in the provision of transportation services will often occur in sectors where the central government is otherwise present; put differently, air and train transportation are more likely to be privatized than local roads and public transit.
- The institutional framework of the country. Everything else equal, one expects federal countries to be more decentralized and countries more decentralized overall to be more decentralized in the transportation area. Using 1995 (mid-point) data, the five federal countries have an overall share of central government expenditures in total government expenditures of 53 percent and a central share in transport

TABLE 16.3
Eight Countries, 1990–1995–2000, Size, Public Spending and Centralization Indicators Total Transport

Country	Type of government	Size (km²)	Year	Government share of GDP (consumption)	Central share of total government expenditure	Transport share of total government expenditure	Central government share of transport expenditure
Australia	Federation	7,683,000	1990	17.2	57.1	6.9	21.5
			1995	18.9	58.3	5.8	20.2
			2000	18.1	59.3	5.9	10.6
Canada	Federation	9,970,610	1990	20.2	43.9	5.1	21.0
			1995	19.9	42.9	4.8	23.3
			2000	18.2	40.8	3.7	8.7
Denmark	Unitary	43,094	1990	25.3	55.6	2.8	52.2
			1995	25.7	56.4	2.8	50.5
			2000	25.8	51.9	2.8	45.2
Germany	Federation	357,025	1990	18.3	59.0	4.5	50.5
			1995	19.0	59.2	4.4	53.2
			2000	19.0	n.a.	n.a.	n.a.
Spain	Quasi-federation	504,750	1990	15.5	n.a.	n.a.	n.a.
			1995	16.7	69.8	4.2	45.8
			2000	17.5	69.1	4.1	39.5
Switzerland	Federation	41,288	1990	13.7	49.7	8.4	40.8
			1995	15.1	51.8	7.5	43.0
			2000	14.7	52.0	7.3	43.0
United Kingdom	Unitary	229,988	1990	20.5	74.9	2.8	40.9
			1995	19.7	77.6	2.4	48.4
			2000	18.7	n.a.	n.a.	n.a.
United States	Federation	9,809,418	1990	18.9	55.9	4.7	28.9
			1995	18.6	52.9	4.7	27.7
			2000	17.5	50.4	4.8	26.6

Source: IMF Government Finance Statistics and International Financial Statistics, various years.

expenditures of 33.5 percent while the other three have shares of respectively 67.9 percent and 48.4 percent. Correlation between ranks for both indicators is 0.53.

- The size of the country. Everything else equal, one expects larger countries to be more decentralized. In this respect, the rank correlation between the two indicators is 0.62. The three largest countries Canada, the United States, and Australia are the three most decentralized in terms of transport expenditure and the smaller countries like the United Kingdom and Denmark are among the most centralized.
- The use of various transportation modes. The greater the share of trucks and cars in overall transportation output, the greater decentralization as measured by expenses should be as roads are more often a sn/l responsibility.

DECENTRALIZATION OF TRANSPORTATION RESPONSIBILITIES

Here we present the main observations made in the literature with regard to the four sectors. We first discuss the road and rail sectors, which both have large-scale networks, followed by the port and airport sectors in which major hubs play an important role. Ports (airports) differ from road and rail networks in that they play a role as a point where infrastructure is concentrated to allow transhipment between a slow mode of transport that is cheap per ton (or, in the case of airports, a fast mode of transport that is expensive per ton) and a contact point with road and often rail networks. They often also play a role in several cases as an international gateway to a country for goods (or passengers) and therefore have a role in ensuring security (goods, people, disease, etc.) and collection of customs duties.

ROAD SECTOR

On average, the road network is used for between 60 percent and 80 percent of passenger and freight movements[3] in any given country. It consists of a variety of elements such as residential streets, rural roads, major urban boulevards, and motorways that have a component that is at once local, regional, and, in some cases, national. Roads are a network and are mutually interdependent. They only have utility as components of a network that must meet the needs of a variety of users. Some roads are only used by a few vehicles a day, whereas other parts of the network such as motorways are used by tens of thousands a vehicles a day. One road may be used primarily by cars, whereas others may be used by heavy load vehicles inflicting highly variable degrees of wear and tear. However, the most important issue here is that there are several types of user which can be divided into two main categories, namely local users and non-local (transit) users. The presence of these two types of user has implications with regard to the management of a given road because the preferences of local users in terms of trip, fluidity, and safety differ from those of transit users (regardless of whether trips are at the national or even international level), as do the levels of government that are likely to meet their demand for public services in the road sector.

Administering a road network is more complex than other types of public infrastructure (such as sports complexes, fire stations, etc.) for two reasons: the existence of junction points and the fact that roads often run through several jurisdictions. It is therefore important to establish which authority will be responsible for coordination, construction and maintenance. The large externalities which are generated by certain decisions taken by sn/l authorities, and which justify the application of standards relating to quality, safety and development, make decentralization a complicated process. Furthermore, individual sections of a given road can vary in terms of age, condition, construction materials and standards. Landscape, environment and climate impose constraints on the type of road that can be built, which varies from one region to another, and also influence the degree of wear and tear, all of which must be taken into account in the construction and maintenance of a road network. Any decentralization project must therefore give due consideration to the skills and know-how of different levels of government.

A variety of relationships can be forged between different levels of government, depending upon the type of model and degree of decentralization sought, as argued in the first section. A distinction must be drawn between so-called functional decentralization and financial decentralization. The former refers to the process that consists in decentralizing operations relating to functions such as planning, policy making, implementing work, etc; the latter refers to the funding of those operations. Note that these two forms of decentralization are relatively independent of one another and that this has major implications for the viability of the reforms undertaken in different countries.[4]

There are two approaches[5] that provide an analytical framework for a decentralization process. An initial approach is to look at tasks and responsibilities relating to roads administration. These are divided into three major categories: administration, construction and renovation, and maintenance.

Administration can be further subdivided into planning, coordination of junction points, implementation of policies, regulations, and standards of quality and safety. This dimension affords significant economies of scale[6] and it is therefore advisable in many cases to entrust it to the central authority. Central government is thus able to impose standards and procedures with the aim of standardizing certain social, environmental and technical attributes of the network; it can also encourage local or regional governments to take account of national interests in their planning and decision making. Lastly, central government can assist the administrative function through policy research and assessment, the provision of facilities that might sometimes be beyond the means of smaller or less wealthy regions, as well as through other measures.[7]

The second category, construction and renovation, includes engineering work, cost analysis, work scheduling, submission of contracts, and calls for tender. These responsibilities call for a good level of expertise and technical know-how. Furthermore, road construction requires the use of heavy equipment and in many cases substantial financial investment. This seems to favor a large role of central governments but the presence of private enterprises in this sector of activity allows sn/l governments to assume these responsibilities more efficiently, so it would seem, than central governments.[8] This is from a World Bank study of forty-two developing countries that shows that in countries where road maintenance had been decentralized, delays were less frequent and road conditions better. In aggregate, the share of paved roads in poor repair fell from 22 percent to 12 percent with decentralization and that of unpaved roads in poor repair from 33 percent to 15 percent.[9] Another study compared the performance of the road sector for 1985 in a sample of seventy-six developing countries and found that decentralization helped to improve the condition of unpaved roads, but that the condition of paved roads and the share of paved roads in the network as a whole remained unchanged.[10]

The third category of expenditure, network maintenance is usually less demanding in terms of funding and technical resources, although more intensive in terms of labor and frequency. This responsibility is one that sn/l governments would seem to be better able to manage by virtue of their ability to maintain networks at lower cost[11] Under this approach it would therefore seem appropriate to consider the nature of the tasks and responsibilities to be fulfilled when allocating responsibilities by level of government. Indeed, a study by Humplick and Moini-Araghi in 1996 considered the optimum structure for road supply (construction of new roads and maintenance of the existing network). The authors analyzed data from thirty-five industrialized and developing countries over a ten-year period, as well as South Korea over the period 1968 to 1992 and another panel of eight German Länder over the period 1980–1992. Through a double-cost approach, that is to say by incorporating road production and usage costs into their analysis, they found that decentralization allowed maintenance costs to be minimized, thereby making it possible to provide better quality roads at lower cost. It seems that the best results are obtained when central government shared in planning, coordination, policy making and development of quality and safety standards. The authors found no link between the level of decentralization and the minimizing of construction costs. Other factors such as competition between private suppliers and the quality of contractual procedures appeared to be more important.[12]

The second approach consists of establishing the nature and characteristics of roads in order to determine which level of government should be given responsibility for each. While the appropriate classification of roads obviously depends on the specific situation of each country, there are four major categories that are generally used, national, regional, rural, and urban networks. The difference between them lies in the function they perform and the type of user they accommodate. The national network is composed of roads that are of national interest, that is to say more than simply the interest of neighboring communities. Regional networks consist of roads linking major urban communities and also rural access roads that are of benefit to a large part of a region, state, or province. Rural networks are roads providing access to peripheral communities and urban networks which allow traffic to flow inside towns and villages.

The level of government responsible for a particular network should be the one responsible to road users. If a road is used by local users, local government will be more alert to their preferences and thus better able to meet local demand. In contrast, the maintenance of a road used by a large number of transit users, but under the control of local government, would probably not reflect the preferences of such users. They would have no effective means of persuading the level of government responsible to take account of their preferences, since they have no right to vote in the jurisdiction concerned. Likewise, the management of a road of national interest under the responsibility of a sn/l government will not necessarily be geared towards meeting the objectives favored by the central government as appropriate for society as whole.

TABLE 16.4
Decentralization in the Road Sector

	Administration	Construction/renovation	Maintenance
National network	Central	Central or regional	Central or regional
Regional network	Regional/central	Regional	Regional
Rural network	Regional/central	Local	Local
Urban network	Local/metropolitan	Local	Local

Source: Adapted from Gutman (1999) and Darbéra (1993).

There can be no doubt that attempting such a classification of roads is a hazardous exercise in that road use cannot be readily identified and the technical, financial, and political considerations to be taken into account often complicate matters. Nonetheless, this approach provides us with an interesting starting point from which to assign different responsibilities within the transport sector.

It is also possible to combine the two approaches outlined above. Table 16.4 provides a general framework for dividing responsibilities between different levels of government. It is similar to the one summarized in Table 16.2, but leans more slightly towards the centre in the distribution of powers.

RAILWAYS

Railway networks differ from road networks by requiring greater technical expertise to operate and maintain and by their restricted accessibility. They also differ in that privatization of some rail activities is more common than of road activities. Hence, rail freight is private in Australia, Canada, and the United States; [13] the public sector plays a greater role in Europe, but the United Kingdom has privatized its railway network.

A distinction must be drawn in the rail sector between different types of users and infrastructure. Rail transport primarily concerns the movement of goods, or freight, and passengers. While the private freight sector is highly efficient in the United States, where 550 firms share a network of over 270,000 km, Germany and France offer examples where freight is concentrated in the hands of a few firms. In the passenger sector, a distinction can be drawn between long-distance trips, in many cases by high-speed train (TGV), and regional/urban area trips. While long-distance movements are managed at the central level in most Western European countries,[14] decentralization in both Europe and North America may be found at the regional level. The regions, (Länder, Cantons, Autonomous Communities or Provinces) or urban authorities are, therefore, to varying degrees, responsible for the organization and funding of regional/urban passenger rail transport.[15] There are several models of decentralization in which relations between the national and regional levels depend on various factors such as territorial scale, population density, regional heterogeneity, political traditions, degree of regional autonomy, and the financial situation of networks. Coordination, planning, and funding issues, which in many cases warrant central government intervention, therefore pose different problems in individual countries and regions. Some countries, such as Switzerland and the Netherlands, exhibit very high levels of coordination with regard to transfers, tariffs, and investment steering, for example. There are also cases such as Germany, Italy, and Spain—much larger countries with marked differences and lower levels of coordination between regions. Thus, the role of central government varies significantly from one country to another.[16]

Decentralization in the regional rail transport sector assumes a variety of forms in Europe, but the areas where the greatest differences lie are those relating to infrastructure management and network operation. Some countries have separated infrastructure from operations, as in the case of Sweden which in 1988 set up the Banverket, the administration responsible for the single national network, and of France which in 1997 set up Réseau Ferré de France. These central bodies are responsible for planning, investment, and infrastructure maintenance. Other countries such as Switzerland, Germany, Spain, Italy, and Denmark have many public and private regional networks operating alongside the national network. While the national network competes with these regional networks in Switzerland and Germany in the passenger sector, regional transport in Spain and Italy is restricted exclusively to regional networks.

On the operations side, France has awarded network operation to a national monopoly, the Société Nationale des Chemins de Fer (SNCF), and following the reform of 2002 the regions now have to reach agreement with the national operator regarding the supply of services. Sweden, on the other hand, has granted access to its network to private operators since 1996. The regions, which are responsible for organizing timetables and tariffs, are therefore free to choose between the national company SJ and one of the fifteen private companies for the supply of transport services[17] This type of decentralization is also to be found in the Netherlands, Switzerland, Germany, and Denmark. Italy and Spain have public or semi-public enterprises responsible for the management of transport supply and regional network infrastructure; there is therefore a single operator for each regional network. Table 16.5 lists the decentralization models adopted by a number of European countries.

Some countries have a long tradition of decentralization in the rail sector. Regional passenger transport in Switzerland, for example, has always been the responsibility of the cantons; this highly coordinated system is one of the most efficient in the world. Moreover, the Swiss rank second in terms of rail mobility with average per capital travel of 2,200 km a year. Exceptionally dense network coverage, frequent services on all lines,

---

TABLE 16.5
Decentralization in the Regional Rail Sector in a Few Countries, 2004

	Single operator	Multiple operators	
Single network (national)	France	Sweden	
Multiple networks (national and regional)	Spain Italy	Germany Denmark	Switzerland Netherlands

and inter-modal coordination make the Swiss network highly efficient.[18] There are other examples such as Italy and Spain where the decentralization of regional networks has produced excellent results. The Lombardy network, Ferrovie Nord Milano Esercizio, is the most efficient in Europe with 327 km of track, 500 trains a day and 50 million passengers a year Ferrocariles de la Generalitat de Catalunya, the Spanish regional network, has only 195 km of track yet carries 60 million passengers a year.[19] These examples of the regional management of passenger transport, among the most efficient in Europe, succinctly illustrate the benefits of decentralization in the rail sector.

Evidence from traditionally more centralized countries such as Germany and France that have only recently decentralized their regional transport service, in 1997 and 2002 respectively, show some impact of the reforms. The Länders, which are now responsible for funding and organizing regional rail services, can choose as their operator either the national network DB-AG or one of 150 private providers. The outcome has been an acceleration in the growth of regional traffic, while the Länders' budget allocation for regional passenger transport has risen from DM 8.7 billion in 1996 to over DM 15 billion four years later.[20] What remains to be established, however, is whether the increase in expenditure is due to higher costs or to the emergence of a demand previously masked by centralization. The sector needs to be studied in greater depth. In France, following the promising results of an initial trial period involving seven regions in 1997, full responsibility for regional rail transport was transferred to the regions in 2002. It is therefore up to the regions to determine the scale and frequency of supply and to sign a contract with SNCF for the delivery of services. It is still too soon to draw any firm conclusions at this stage, although there would appear to be problems with the transfer of the financial resources.[21] The results achieved by the regions involved in the trial over the period 1996–1999 are nonetheless highly encouraging: supply growth measured in terms of train/coach kilometers of over 17 percent, compared with merely 1.4 percent in the other regions (apart from Ile-de-France and Corsica); introduction of quality standards into agreements with the SNCF with a system of bonuses and penalties, resulting in improvements in punctuality, the quality of stations and trains, access for persons of reduced mobility, passenger reception services and facilities in stations, user information services, and so forth. The funding assigned to regional rail services in the regions involved in the trial between 1997 and 2000 amounted to FRF 4.7 billion, more than twice the total amount for all other regions combined.[22] Incentives offered to the regions helped to increase productivity not only by improvements to the use of rolling stock, that is to say faster trains, shorter intervals between trains and shorter changes for passengers, but also by revamping regional train services that had become less attractive due to lack of investment.[23]

PORTS

The decentralization process with regard to port management has reached an advanced stage in Europe, where almost all countries have one form or another of regional port management.[24] The local attributes of infrastructure and the labor force, and the commercial nature of activities such as handling and forwarding, explain in part the degree to which port administration has been decentralized. Nonetheless, the existence of major externalities such as reduced transport and distribution costs and time together with the need to coordinate freight transport planning and development, can justify State involvement in port management and administration.[25]

Ports differ from other transport infrastructure in that they are sited at specific locations serving an area of economic influence or hinterland.[26] Some trading ports can serve several regions or even countries, whereas others are simply fishing ports or harbors for local recreational activities. Classifications vary according to country, as in the case of countries such as France which, *inter alia*, has seventeen ports of national significance under central government control or Japan which has four ports referred to as "specifically designated major ports."[27] Market liberalization, new technology, developments in maritime transport and the integration of transport modes are all factors that have fuelled competition between ports. This context, which requires a decentralized form of management, allows ports to pursue commercial activities efficiently and flexibly. This is how North American ports, for example, have been able to adapt to demand from cargo forwarders in a state of complete organizational transition in response to developments in the container industry, communications technology and cargo handling.[28] And yet a port cannot function simply as a commercial enterprise, and port management must undoubtedly remain a concern for governments.

Management at an exclusively local level would not permit pursuit of a national development strategy and the economic logic of a private firms would easily not tolerate pursuit of a goal relating to the common good such as, for example, access to areas poorly served by the road network or the maintenance of services for certain types of economically unprofitable freight traffic. Ports can act as an economic engine for growth within a given region, open up a region to the international economy and, in some countries, allow the collection of foreign currency revenue. Ports are also part of the national border and port regulations on police and customs procedures must be dealt with at central level.[29] Besides efficient management, ports must also be able to enjoy coordinated investment by central and sub-central governments. Ports must be integrated into industrial networks within a country by an inland transport network, either road or rail. It is therefore important to ensure the consistency of port development plans with those for inland transport infrastructure. Central government can also involve itself at other levels such as dredging, ice-breaking and the provision of navigational aids.[30] Investment in major infrastructure such as channels, dikes, docks, and locks to allow ports to be used by high-capacity vessels is also considered to be a matter for central government.

Decentralized port management can take a variety of forms but will usually provide for two basic entities, namely the port authority and the port enterprise. Four spheres of activity are divided between these two entities: regulation, planning and coordination; the management of port operations (security, police, and maintenance); investment; and commercial activities relating to the port.[31]

The port authority may be a public body, either centralized or decentralized, or it may be semi-public or private. Centralized public management means that planning, development, and investment decisions, as well as commercial strategy and sometimes even pricing policy, will all be the responsibility of a central authority. This means that central government takes charge of regulation, the cohesion of the port marketplace, and port operations. It can therefore decide whether or not to delegate trade activities to private port enterprises, depending upon whether the port is a landlord port or an operating port. This type of management leaves local port authorities little room for maneuver and seems incompatible with the current competitive climate in which ports operator. Decentralized public management allows greater participation by local authorities, although central government must remain responsible for drawing up a national ports policy which sets out the rules of management, funding, assignment criteria, public investments, the obligations of ports with regard to public service obligations and regional interests, that is to say the area of coordination and regulation. Participation by sub-central governments can assume a variety of forms ranging from infrastructure funding, support for investment projects and acquisition of a share in the capital of the landlord port.[32] Private management means that the port is the property of individual investors, holding companies or conglomerates, and that the latter are responsible for the port authority.

The port enterprise can similarly take a variety of forms such as a private company, public or semi-public enterprise, cooperative, partnership, and so forth.

Decentralization has enabled European and North American ports to develop an adaptability and ability to innovate in response to the new realities of maritime transport. Fierce competition between ports, advances in communications and cargo-handling technologies, and the upgrading of facilities for modern container vessels are all factors that have led to the emergence of a decentralized framework for management and planning.[33] And yet experience with decentralization in the port sector has not been universally positive. The decentralization of ports in Japan, for example, has not been as successful as hoped.

The financial position of Japanese ports is currently precarious. The nature of the funding and sharing of responsibilities between different levels of government is such that after 40 years of decentralization the Japanese port sector is currently facing problems with overcapacity and a budget deficit.[34] While there are several accounting and political factors involved, problems relating to financial transfers between different governments have created a situation in which revenue is no longer linked to expenditure. Under the Act on Ports and Havens, regional governments are responsible for the funding of ports, but planning and investment decisions are made at the local level. This situation has resulted in a port development policy that is no longer aimed at reducing distribution times and costs but at job creation and transfers in the form of investment. Because of the way funding provided for in the act is structured, local authorities only have to pay for part of the investment decisions they take. Despite the regional and national review committees, in particular those of the Ministry of Transport, assigned the task of auditing development plans, local development plans are seldom turned down. Japan illustrates the case of a decentralization process in which the financial incentives encourage the local authorities to act in a suboptimal manner from the national standpoint.

Moreover, the same criticisms made of the decentralization of Japanese ports have also been applied to North American ports where some commentators have criticized the overcapacity of port facilities, port development plans that fail to take sufficient account of the economic potential of coastal sectors, as well as the environmental impact of large-scale construction work such as dikes, canals, locks, etc. In addition, the decentralization of North American ports has created a situation in which the very large number of actors makes it fairly difficult to coordinate policies, planning, and operations.[35]

AIRPORTS

Airports have similar attributes to ports. They too have local infrastructure, employ local labor, and are used for commercial activities. Airports are also major tools for economic development and, like ports, are points of entry to a country, which therefore involves areas such as customs, immigration and security. Government intervention is therefore warranted by these issues of public interest. However, while ports are primarily used for movements of goods, airports play an important role in the movement of passengers.

While public policy towards airports began to change in the 1970s, privatization accelerated during the 1980s with the privatization of the British Airport Authority (BAA 1987). In several cases, airports were sold off either wholly or partially to the private sector. There are three types of ownership:[36]

- Corporatization: a separate autonomous administrative entity is set up to manage the airport. This is a type of administrative decentralization that encourages a "business" approach, allows a distinction to be made between regulatory agency and operator and also enables greater retention of the revenue arising from operations.
- Private participation: this can be accomplished through management contracts or the leasing of the airport for a given period of time.
- Full or partial privatization: some or all of the ownership rights to the airport are sold off.

In practice, various forms of management can not only coexist but may also replace each other over time. In Denmark, for example, until 1990 airports were operated by a public company owned by the Danish government. This company was subsequently transformed into a publicly listed company which was fully public-owned. In 1994, a 25 percent share was sold off to the private sector and in 2000 a majority shareholding was in the hands of the private sector. In 2004, one-third of the share capital is held by the Danish government and the remainder by various private investors. In Canada, as part of the National Airports Policy, the federal government created airport authorities to which is entrusted the management of twenty-six airports identified as part of the National Airports System. The criteria for selecting airports were that they had to handle more than two hundred thousand passengers a year or be located in a provincial capital. The central government has remained the owner of the airports but has leased them for sixty years to the local authorities. The creation of these airport authorities was designed to make airport operators more efficient and flexible compared with the previous situation. To allow investment and ensure that airports are profitable, the federal government has delegated responsibility for setting user charges to the airport authorities without legislating at the national level.[37]

The decentralization of airports, which in several countries led to the creation of an autonomous entity, allowed gains to be made in terms of efficiency. The overall financial situation and the decentralization airport management system have tended to improve.[38] This was particularly evident in Canada where, according to a review by Transport Canada in 2001, the transfer of airports was a success not only in financial terms, in that the airport authorities of the four largest airports managed to generate budget surpluses, but also with regard to customer services, security and operations. In addition, decentralization was a spur to investment in Canadian airports in that in 2001 over \$5 billion were invested by the private sector alone.[39] One explanation for this is the introduction of airport improvement fees paid for by passengers. One should also note that until a reform in 2005, some aspects of airport leases created disincentives to good management.[40]

REVENUES

Different levels of government all need revenue to finance their activities, including transport. The two possible sources are own revenues, mainly from user fees and taxes and transfers from other levels of government. We first discuss own revenues then turn to transfers. We discuss these two sources of revenues in the context of government provision of transport services. Obviously, when private firms are providing the services, these issues do not matter except when a subsidy is provided to the private firms by a government either on a short-term basis such as subsidies to American airlines following September 11, 2001[41] or a long-term one, such as implicit subsidies through payment to transport mail.

Hence, airlines, shipping firms, trucking, and some railroads appear to not be concerned by this discussion, except if they make use of services not fully paid for such as roads or ports/airports. The issue probably has greater salience for urban public transit, however provided (train, bus, etc.), passenger services of railroads, and users of roads. In the case of passenger railroads and public transit, the costs are usually not covered by user fees; this can be justified by the reduction in both pollution and congestion that railroad/transit users generate for others. Hence one will need to fund in part these costs through tax revenues levied either by the jurisdiction directly responsible for the transport entity or by a higher jurisdiction that will give transfers to this entity. In the case of road, it is sometimes argued that as a class road users contribute to the costs of non toll roads through taxation of fuels and thus that there is no need for general tax revenues to subsidize roads.

OWN REVENUES

Let us first discuss taxation by the jurisdiction responsible for the service thus subsidized. The main criterion for assigning a tax base to one level of government or another is the mobility of the tax base, that is to say its ability to move from one tax jurisdiction to another in order to escape all or part of its fiscal obligations. The greater the mobility of the tax base, the more it should be taxed at a higher level of government in order to avoid tax evasion and the shifting of burdens between local governments. The property tax base is immobile and therefore a good source of funding for local services such as waste collection or fire fighting when users' costs cannot be employed. Taxes on labor (income tax and payroll tax) and consumption (VAT, excise duties) apply to the activities or individuals and households, agents that are more mobile than land but less mobile than capital. Corporations have a number of instruments at their disposal (transfer pricing, financial structure, etc.) with which to shift their tax burden.

Having stated the general principle, let us turn to taxes associated more specifically with transport such as fuel taxes, administrative fees (logbook, registration plates, driving license) and user charges (tolls, annual road tax). Whether roads should be funded by means of special tax levies, tolls, or general revenues (income taxes) is one key aspect of transportation policy. Some parts of a road network can be viewed as an "open system,"[42] that is to say one in which it is not possible to control the number of network users, as for example in a city or on country roads where tolls would be too expensive and cumbersome to manage. Other components such as national motorways can be seen as a closed system to which access is easily controlled; they thus can be more easily funded through tolls.

Table 16.6 summarizes the tax allocation put forward by Shah (1994). His study notes that the correct assignment of taxes and user fees depends in part on how responsibilities for roads are assigned. It is worth adding that:

- Fuel taxes can be used not only to finance roads, but also to reduce pollution and road congestion by reducing the use of private vehicles, particularly for commuting. In such cases part of this revenue must be assigned without taking account of responsibilities for roads.[43] This also raises the issue of what percentage of these taxes should be allocated to road funds, where such funds exist. Note that the relevance of such funds has been challenged (Gwilliam and Shalizi 1999).
- The choice of levying mechanism is not straightforward either. The report on *Reforming Transport Taxes and Charges*,[44] prepared by the European Conference of Ministers of Transport clearly illustrates this in its discussion of current mechanisms when it states that "Fuel taxes ... though efficient in relation to CO_2 emissions, [they] cannot be differentiated to provide effective incentives for reducing congestion, pollution, noise and accident costs" (p. 7). It is therefore proposed that use be made of km charges varying according to time and place, while recognizing that cordon tolls and differentiated road tolls might also be effective. The allocation of this revenue to different levels of governments is not discussed. Note that work on the United States has shown that political factors such as the share of nonresidents among users and the behavior of neighboring states partly governs choices in this area (Levinson 2001).

TABLE 16.6
Assignment of Tax-Raising Powers

Type	Determination		Collection and administration	Comments
	Base	Rate		
Taxes on thermal units	F/SN/L	F/SN/L	F/SN/L	According to impact of pollution
Fuel	F/SN/L	F/SN/L	F/SN/L	According to responsibility for roads
Taxes on emissions	F/SN/L	F/SN/L	F/SN/L	According to impact of pollution
Toll posts, road tax	F/SN/L	F/SN/L	F/SN/L	According to responsibility for roads
Parking fees	L	L	L	Control of local congestion
Registration/annual fees, transfer taxes	SN	SN	SN	Responsibility of state/province/SN
Driving licence and fees	SN	SN	SN	Responsibility of state/province/SN

Source: Shah (1994).

TRANSFERS

Let us now turn to the case of transfers. There are three issues: (1) how should they be funded, (2) how big should they be overall, and (3) how should the funds be distributed between recipients.

How Should They Be Funded?

There are several possibilities, two are discussed here. First, the amount is financed out of the general resources of the paying unit(s) and established in their annual budget. This is a very flexible solution, adaptable from one year to another. But it has two main defects: (1) recipient governments are not sure that they will receive a comparable amount (in real value) from one year to another, which renders very difficult any medium term planning and pluri-annual policies; and (2) annual budgetary debates are subject to ad hoc political arrangements, with unstable contours by definition. This issue or a variant of it surfaced in France in 2005 with the debate on the funding of the STIF (Syndicat des transports d'Ile-de-France), the greater Paris transportation body responsible for public transit. Until July 1st 2005, this was a national body funded out of the central government revenues. As of that date, it becomes an autonomous regional body funded by a specific subsidy. The issue is thus the size of the subsidy with the central government offering an amount deemed too small by the regional authorities; they have refused to name members of the board, replacing those the central government relinquished as of July 1st 2005, as a protest. It is interesting to note that this occurs within a constitutional framework that states that any transfer of responsibilities from the central government to a sn/l must be accompanied by a transfer of resources equivalent to those used previously in providing the service.[45] One of the key issues, according to the regional authorities, is the presence of deferred maintenance expenditures that should be compensated for by a lump-sum payment; this raises the incentives issues associated with planned transfers of responsibilities

Second, the exact calculation of the amount is explicitly stated in the constitution or in a law in the form of revenue sharing from at least one but preferably several or all specific tax sources used at the central level. Using only one tax source for sharing purposes may result in the central government not collecting it as vigorously as if it was only a central source of revenues since its collection efforts reward in part subnational governments. The advantages of this solution are that: (1) with a specific legal foundation, the political debate on how much transfers take place when the constitution is amended or the law is passed, and not on a annual basis when the budget is decided; (2) it avoids important variations in the amounts available if the tax sources are sufficiently diversified and chosen in such a way that macroeconomic cycles are partly alleviated.

How Big Should the Transfers Be?

The answer depends in part on the institutional framework of the country as shown in part in Table 16.3. There is no general answer as to the appropriate percentage that transfers should represent in total transportation spending by sn/l but one general principle is that the level of government receiving funds should have at the margin some responsibility for raising funds, i.e., should not be solely funded by transfers but also by taxes whose rates it sets. One interesting issue is that when an existing program has reached its objectives, it remains in place. According to some observers, this is the case of the United States. The federal highway program was created in 1956 and subject to renewal every six years, the current law expired in September 2003, but Congress and the president have been unable to agree either on the contents of the new law or on how much to spend on roads and transit over the next six years. As a consequence, the current law was extended for a series of short intervals. On July 29th, Congress adopted the Safe, Accountable, Flexible, and Efficient Transportation Equity Act, which authorizes $286.4 billion in spending for federal highway projects over six years, and renews all federal highway, public transit, safety, and research programs until fiscal 2009.[46]

According to Utt (2005),

> for the first several decades of the federal highway program's existence, virtually all of its energy and resources were devoted to the task it was created to fulfill: to build a 42,000 mile high-speed, limited-access interstate highway system from coast to coast and border to border, connecting all of the cities in between. That task was largely completed by the early 1980s, and with no similarly compelling and clear objective to guide it, successive Congresses began the process of diverting the trust fund's resources to other purposes. While the diversions initially focused on non-road, transportation-

related investments such as transit, over time nontransportation projects such as nature trails, museums, flower plantings, and historic renovation became eligible for trust fund spending.

Of particular concern is the use of earmarked or pork barrel projects.

> The propensity to earmark has become an increasingly severe problem in federal budgeting, and virtually all discretionary spending programs have experienced an escalation in the number of earmarks included. The 1987 highway bill contained 152 earmarks, 538 were added to the 1991 bill, and 1,850 were included in 1998's TEA–21. Trends underway in current deliberations suggest that the final 2005 version will have as many as 5,000 to 6,000. (Utt 2005)

Utt suggests that one answer to this problem is to do away with the federal program by putting states in charge. This would reduce the percentages of transfers used for transportation financing in the United States.

How Should the Funds Be Distributed?

Transfer schemes require that the amount each jurisdiction will receive be determined by an appropriate formula. This will vary according to the purpose of the grant. If grants are made to stimulate the production by all or some sn/l of specific public services that generate positive externalities, then the central government may want to use a formula with a component linked to the benefits outside populations receive, such as their size. If grants are made to alleviate vertical fiscal disequilibrium, then need as measured by such indicators as population, specific populations, topography, or urban density may be appropriate. Finally, in the case of grants aimed at alleviating horizontal disequilibrium (equalization grants), revenue capacity, and needs may both be taken into account. Jurisdictions with higher than average capacity should receive less (pay more); jurisdictions with lower than average capacity should receive more (pay less). Extra funding for governments facing additional charges caused by socio-demographic challenges, their geographic location, or both would necessitate some form of cost equalization.

Given the above, it is interesting to examine the distribution of grants to American states. According to Utt (2005),[47]

> Under current law, federal trust fund spending on highways and transit is distributed among the states according to a complicated mathematical formula that attempts to relate resources to need. The formula has changed little since it was developed decades ago and today contains pervasive inequities that consistently reward some states with more money than they pay in ("donee" states) while shortchanging others ("donors"). The donee states are clustered mostly in New England and the Middle Atlantic, while the donor states are mostly in the South and the Great Lakes region.... Lower-income states ship

money off to the richer ones. Mississippi, ranked 50th by income, is a donor state, shipping money off to Connecticut, a donee state ranked number one in the nation by personal income.

One does observe that this formula does not respect the principles set out for an equalization formula since some better off states receive large transfers and some poorer states receive small transfers. Is this inappropriate? Yes, if equalization is the only goal of the formula; no, if it has other goals such as alleviating congestion in large urban areas. Examining the program, one sees that there are goals in addition to equalization such as air quality and congestion as well as political considerations (bonuses to donee states, hold harmless provisions) that determine transfers to a specific state. Whether the transfers are the correct ones, given these various goals, is a question that would need deeper analysis than this chapter can offer. But we would argue that the statement (Utt 2005) below is incorrect since it does not account for interstate externalities:

> One way to do this is to change the flawed formulas that govern the program, but an even better way would be to begin the process of "turning back" federal highway funding to the states and allowing each state to retain the federal fuel tax receipts collected within its borders. Moreover, while the existing system of subsidies for those mountain and plains states with low population densities should be maintained, there is no reason why motorists in Texas, Georgia, and other donor states should be subsidizing the wealthier citizens of Connecticut, New York, and Pennsylvania.

CONCLUSION

Decentralization is a complex phenomenon that has given rise to much discussion as well as reforms throughout the world. In this chapter we have attempted to identify the lessons learned from decentralization in a specific domain, namely how decentralization has encouraged efficiency in the transport sector through intergovernmental competition and emulation. While there is a consensus on the theory, the empirical findings with regard to decentralization do not always allow any clear and definitive conclusions to be drawn. The analysis is often complicated by structural, historical and, political factors that have a nonnegligible impact on the results of reforms and decentralization programs. The topic therefore deserves more research in view of both the substantial gains in terms of efficiency that decentralization has allowed to be made in many cases of reform and the predictions of theory.

ACKNOWLEDGMENT

This chapter is reproduced here with permission from the OECD material found in *Decentralisation, Intergovernmental Competition/Emulation and Efficiency: Lessons from and for the Transport Sector* (7–40) by François Vaillancourt and Philippe Wingender Round Table 131 on Transport and Decentralisation, OECD, Paris, September 2006, 133 pages.

NOTES

1. This sub-section of the chapter draws on Gauthier and Vaillancourt (2002).
2. Delcamp (1995), p. 733.
3. Gutman (1999), p. 87.
4. Humplick and Moini-Arighi (1996a), p. 33.
5. See, for example, Humplick and Moini-Araghi (1996a) and Gutman (1999).
6. Humplick and Moini-Araghi (1996a), p. 38.
7. Darbéra (1993), p. 206.
8. Humplick and Moini-Araghi (1996b), p. 30.
9. World Development Report 1994, p. 75.
10. Humplick and Estache (1995), p. 95.
11. Humplick and Moini-Araghi (1996a), p. 38.
12. Humplick and Moini-Araghi (1996a), p. 38.
13. Batisse (2003a), p. 58.
14. Faivre d'Arcier (2002), p. 390.
15. Batisse (1999), p. 49.
16. Batisse (2003a), p. 53.
17. Batisse (1999), p. 49.
18. Batisse (1999), p. 48, and Batisse (2003a), p. 54.
19. Batisse (2003a), p. 56.
20. Batisse (2003a), p. 55.
21. Batisse (2003b), p. 5.
22. Faivre D'Arcier (2002), p. 393.
23. Crozet and Heroin (1999), p. 193
24. Terrassier (2002), p. 1.
25. Terada (2002), p. 10.
26. Chapon (2002), p. 304.
27. Terada (2002), p. 4.
28. Newman and Walder (2003), p. 160.
29. Chapon (2002), p. 305.
30. Terrassier (1999b), p. 4.
31. Terrassier (1999a), p. 1.
32. Terrassier (2002), p. 4.
33. Newman and Walder (2003), p. 160, and Terrassier (2002), p. 4.
34. Terada (2002), p. 12–14.
35. Newman and Walder (2003), p. 163.
36. Cortes (2002), p. 7.
37. Ibid, p. 3.
38. ICAO (2001), p. 3.
39. Valo (2001), p. 4–5.
40. With in some cases, an implicit tax back rate of 100% of improved revenues. See Aéroports de Montréal Presentation to the Standing Committee on Transportation. http://www.cacairports.ca/english/policy/ADMComitedestransportsvisitedu21marsang.ppt.
41. Through the Air Transportation Safety and System Stabilization Act ("ATSSA"); see http://www.fed-soc.org/Publications/Terrorism/airlinebailout.htm for more details.
42. Robinson and Stiedl (2001), p. 55.
43. Turgeon and Vaillancourt (2002), p. 178.
44. *Reforming Transport Taxes and Charges.* European Conference of Ministers of Transport, Council of Ministers CEMT/CM(2003)3/FINAL, May.

45.   See article 72-2 Tout transfert de compétences entre l'Etat et les collectivités territoriales s'accompagne de l'attribution de ressources équivalentes à celles qui étaient consacrées à leur exercice http://www.legifrance.gouv.fr/html/constitution/constitution.htm.
46.   Available at http://www.chicagotribune.com/news/nationworld/chi-0507300140jul30,1, 5197988.story?coll=chi-newsnationworld-hed.
47.   For more details see Federal Highway Funding Formulas and the Reauthorization of ISTEA; What's at Stake for Texas at http://www.senate.state.tx.us/SRC/pdf/trans.pdf.

BIBLIOGRAPHY

Batisse, F. "La régionalisation des transports ferroviaires est un phénomène mondial." *Revue Générale des Chemins de Fer*, Septembre 1999, pp. 44–52.
————. "La décentralisation dans les chemins de fer, un fait mondial qui n'est pas nouveau," *Revue Générale des Chemins de Fer*, February 2003, pp. 45–58.
————. "La décentralisation des transports ferroviaires a-t-elle atteint ses limites?" *Rail International*, June 2003, pp. 2–5.
Chapon, J. "La décentralisation en matière de transports: Une bonne chose à manipuler avec précautions." *Transports*, 415, September–October 2002, pp. 301–306.
Cortes, Z. "Airport's Privatisation and the Quality of the Services." Paper given at the Seminar on Airport Management: Security and Quality, Balanced Commitments, La Antigua, October 14–18, 2002.
Crozet, Y. and Heroin, E. "Le transport régional de voyageurs: Régionalisation et nouvelles incitations à la performance ferroviaire." *Politiques et Management Public, 17*(3), September 1999, pp. 171–191.
Darbéra, R. "An analytical framework for decentralizing roads with illustrations from France and Venezuela," in PTRC 21st Summer Annual Meeting, 13–17 September 1993, University of Manchester Institute of Science and Technology, Proceedings of Seminar B Highways, PTRC Education and Research Services, London, pp. 195–207.
Delcamp, A. "Les problèmes de la déconcentration dans les pays européens." *Revue Française d'Administration, 11*(4), 1995, pp. 730–740.
European Conference of Ministers of Transport, Council of Ministers, *Reforming Transport Taxes and Charges*, CEMT/CM(2003)3/FINAL, May 2003.
Faivre D'Arcier, B., "Les premiers pas de la régionalisation ferroviaire." *Transports*, 416, November–December 2002, pp. 389–398.
Fox, W.F. and Wallich, C. *"Fiscal federalism in Bosnia and Herzegovina: The Dayton challenge."* In *Fiscal federalism in developing countries*, R. Bird and F. Vaillancourt (eds.). Cambridge: Cambridge University Press, 1998, pp. 271–300.
Gauthier, I. and Vaillancourt, F., Déconcentration, délégation et dévolution: nature, choix et mise en place. Mimeo. World Bank Institute, 2002.
Gutman, J. "Decentralizing roads: Matching accountability, resource, and technical Expertise." In Beyond the center: Decentralizing the state, S.J. Burki, G.E. Perry, and W. Dillinger (eds.), pp. 87–98. Washington, DC: World Bank, 1999,
Gwiliam, K. and Shalizi, Z. "Road funds, user charges and taxes." *The World Bank Research Observer, 14*(2), 1999, pp. 159–185.
Humplick, F. and Estache, A. "Does decentralization improve infrastructure performance." In Decentralizing infrastructure: Advantages and limitations, A. Estache (ed.). World Bank Discussion Paper 290, Washington, DC, 1995.
Humplick, F. and Moini-Araghi, A., *"Is there an optimal structure for decentralized provision*

of roads?" World Bank Policy Research Working Paper 1658. Washington, DC: World Bank, 1996a.

Humplick, F. and Moini-Araghi, A. *"Decentralized structures for providing roads: A cross-country comparison."* World Bank Policy Research Working Paper 1657. World Bank: Washington, DC: World Bank, 1996b.

ICAO. *ICAO's policies on charges for airports and air navigation services* (6th ed.), 2001. Doc 908216 at www.icao.int/icaonet/dcs/9082_6ed.pdf.

Levinson, D. "Why states toll: An empirical model of finance choice." *Journal of Transport Economics and Policy, 35*(2), 2001, pp. 223–238.

Newman, D. and Walder, J.H. "Federal ports policy." *Maritime Policy & Management, 30*, 2003, pp. 151–163.

Prud'homme, R. On the dangers of decentralization. The World Bank, Infrastructure and Urban Development. Mimeo, December 1992.

Robinson, R. and Stiedl, D. "Decentralization of road administration: Case studies in Africa and Asia." *Public Administration and Development, 21*, 2001, pp. 53–64.

Rosenbaum, A. "Gouvernance et décentralisation: Leçons de l'expérience." *Revue Française d'Administration Ppublique, 88*, 1998, pp. 507–516.

Shah, A. "The reform of intergovernmental fiscal relations in developing and emerging countries." *Policy and Research Series, No. 23.* World Bank, Washington DC, 1994.

Terada, H. "An analysis of the overcapacity problem under the decentralized management system of container ports in Japan." *Maritime Policy & Management, 29*, 2002, pp. 3–15.

Terrassier, N., Évolution de la gestion et de l'organisation des ports, *Isemar, synthèse, 13*, January 1999.

———. La réforme portuaire au Canada: Une nouvelle politique de transports. *Isemar, synthèse, 16*, April 1999;

———. Ports et régionalisation. *Isemar, synthèse, 47*, September 2002.

Turgeon, M. and Vaillancourt, F. "The provision of highways in Canada and the federal government." *Publius, 32*(1), 2002, pp. 161–181.

Utt, R. Congress Gets Another Chance to Improve America's Transportation: Should It Be Its Last? 2005. Available at Heritage Foundation. http://www.heritage.org/Research/SmartGrowth/highway-reauth2005.cfm?renderforprint=1.

Valo, S. "The continuing evolution in Canadian airport privatization." Airports Council International—North America. December 21, 2001. Available at http://www.aci-na.org.

World Bank. *World development report 1994."* New York: Oxford University Press, 1994.

17 Context-Sensitive Design for Highways and Streets

Eric T. Donnell and John M. Mason, Jr.

INTRODUCTION

Prior to the advent of the automobile, highways in the United States consisted mainly of unpaved paths connecting only a few cities. At the turn of the twentieth century, the automobile was introduced and the principal goal of the transportation system was "getting the farmer out of the mud." Transportation funding focused on new construction projects in rural areas. Geometric design standards or guidelines were not available to those designing or constructing roads.

In the early 1940s, road construction focused on meeting the needs of the military. At the conclusion of World War II, roads were in disrepair and traffic congestion was developing in many urban areas. During this same period, the American Association of State Highway Officials (AASHO), now known as the American Association of State Highway and Transportation Officials (AASHTO), published the first set of criteria for geometric design of highways and streets. These criteria were eventually modified and formed the basis for construction of the Interstate Highway System. In 1956, the Federal-Aid Highway Act authorized funding to construct a forty thousand-plus mile system of access-controlled highways based on uniform geometric design criteria. A large proportion of the newly constructed highways passed through rural areas and connected urban areas. Initially, environmental impacts and public involvement were not fully realized; mobility and safety were considered top transportation facility priorities.

Interstate highway construction continued through the 1980s and early 1990s. The Intermodal Surface Transportation Efficiency Act of 1991, often cited as landmark legislation, required that transportation projects consider both environmental impacts and quality of life. Road design and construction had to focus on the preservation of the natural environment, social and environmental impacts, and preservation of historic property and scenic sites. Furthermore, engineering designs had to carefully balance these social, environmental, and cultural issues with the traditional commitment to safety and mobility. This initiative later became known as *context-sensitive design.*

The purpose of this chapter is to describe historical transportation policies that eventually lead to the concept of context-sensitive highway and street design. The chapter is divided into the following subsequent sections: transportation policy and geometric design; context-sensitive design of highways and streets; and, future transportation infrastructure investment needs. The section on transportation policy and geometric design describes the myriad legislation that helped shape the nation's current transportation planning and highway geometric design criteria. The next section contains information regarding the characteristics of context-sensitive design, available resources to achieve context-sensitive design, and describes several published case studies of successful context-sensitive highway and street design. The final section discusses the current state of the transportation system in the United States, the notion of integrating safety and mobility into all stages of transportation project development, and future infrastructure investments needs.

FEDERAL TRANSPORTATION POLICY AND HIGHWAY DESIGN

PRE-AUTOMOBILE ERA

Prior to the twentieth century, travelers used primarily rail and waterborne transportation modes. Roads were simply dirt paths that connected farms to cities. When wet, travel on roads was time-consuming and nearly impossible. Credit for the early road-building movement in the United States is given to bicyclists—their interest in paved roads in the late 1800s provided additional momentum to create the Office of Road Inquiry (ORI) within the Department of Agriculture. The agency was formed to improve rural road development by creating a state-aid plan and by offering technical assistance to local governments regarding methods to improve road quality. Roadway geometric design guidelines did not exist; however, development of the Model T Ford in 1908 increased the need for improved roads. A federal-aid plan was being debated that could offer funding support to states and local government agencies to improve road quality. The American Association of State Highway Officials (AASHO) was formed in 1914 and gave state agencies a unified voice for road betterment.

TRANSPORTATION IN THE WORLD WAR ERAS

In 1916, the Federal Aid Road Act was passed giving $75 million to states for rural road improvements. Opponents of the bill argued that federal-aid spending should be focused on interstate travel; however, this piece of legislation was primarily focused on "getting farmer's out of the mud." Funds were apportioned to states based on total area, population, and mileage of existing rural roads—the federal share of any project could not exceed 50 percent. State agencies were tasked with creating highway departments to select and administer rural road improvement projects. Engineers within each state highway department were required to prepare surveys, plans, specifications, and estimates for all projects. Final project approval was granted by the United States Secretary of Agriculture (Office of Public Roads was part of agency).

Because the United States would enter into World War I in 1917, the first federal-aid program was not overly successful. Rural road improvements were spread widely within and among states and thus no formally connected system of long-distance roadways existed. The Federal Highway Act of 1921 changed this. This legislation focused on improving farm-to-market roads and also on creating a formal system of interstate quality roads. Up to 60 percent of federal-aid funding could be used on these interstate roads—nearly 43 percent (3/7th) of federal-aid highways had to be constructed for the purpose of long-distance trip-making. Up to 7 percent of all roads in a state could be designated as federal-aid highways. No formally-adopted geometric design criteria existed, but road surface conditions and network connectivity were improving.

Highway construction continued to flourish throughout the 1920s until the beginning of the Great Depression in late 1929. Funding for the federal-aid transportation program was diverted in favor of non-highway purposes. During the 1930s, the Bureau of Public Roads (designated as such in 1919) received pressure to construct a rural highway network and a network of freeways to serve urban centers. The Federal-aid Highway Act of 1934 for the first time allowed states to use federal-aid funds for plans, surveys, and engineering investigations (America's Highways 1976). The Agricultural Appropriations Act, passed in 1936, expanded the allowable use of federal-aid highway funds to cover economic evaluations. Together, this legislation provided the impetus for states to create a planning function within their agency to identify and prioritize highway improvements and future development.

In 1939, the Bureau of Public Roads issued a report titled "Toll Roads and Free Roads." The report suggested that a system of toll highways was not economically feasible; however, it did recommend an interregional network of connected super-highways without tolls. The Federal Highway Act of 1940 permitted states to use federal-aid funds to design and construct highways, without matching, for the purpose of national defense. America's involvement in World War II began late in 1941, thus highway construction funding declined. At the conclusion of the war, roads were in disrepair and traffic congestion was developing in many urban areas. Some of the post-war problems were addressed in the Federal Aid Highway Act of 1944. Among other provisions, the legislation outlined a National System of Interstate Highways (up to forty thousand miles long) and recognized the need for urban extensions of rural federal-aid highways. A secondary federal-aid system of highways was also specifically noted—it was unlimited in size (America's Highways 1976).

Throughout the decades of the 1930s and 1940s, research studies were commissioned and uniform geometric design policies were established for highway construction. Examples included policies for sight distance, marking and signing passing zones on two- and three-lane highways, highway types (geometric), intersections at grade, rotary intersections, and transition curves. During this time period, roadside development was also considered. Although formal roadside design criteria did not exist there was recognition that construction left areas adjacent to the traveled way less than aesthetically pleasing. As such, most roadside development focused on beautification with some recognition that areas adjacent to through lanes be adequately safe.

TRANSPORTATION IN THE INTERSTATE HIGHWAY CONSTRUCTION ERA

The Federal Aid Highway Act of 1948 required the Bureau of Public Roads to study the needs for a national defense system of Interstate highways. The report found that more than $10 billion would be required to improve existing roadways designated as Interstate highways. To meet the needs of national defense, however, the report recommended a need for significantly more funding. Annual funding for federal-aid highway projects increased slowly through 1955. Adequate funding for the Interstate system, however, was not provided in subsequent legislation. In 1956, a landmark piece of legislation was passed that authorized $25 billion, to be allocated between fiscal years 1957 and 1969, to construct a "National System of Interstate and Defense Highways." The proposed network consisted of forty thousand miles of limited-access, multi-lane highways. All highways were to be constructed using uniform design standards; no highway-rail grade crossings were permitted; vehicle size and weight restrictions were imposed; and, traffic volumes forecast for 1975 had to be accommodated. Implicit in the policy was the notion that mobility and safety would be enhanced if all states were working to achieve the design objectives set forth in the policy. The federal funding share for each project would be 90 percent. After 1960, state funding for the Interstate system was appropriated based on the required cost to complete the system. Prior to that, it was appropriated based on state population, total area, and mileage.

Another important piece of highway legislation—the Highway Revenue Act—was passed in 1956. This act authorized funding for the entire Interstate system. It also created the Highway Trust Fund to be supplied by taxes on motor-vehicle users. Gasoline was the main user tax—it was increased to 3 cents per gallon in 1956 and is currently 18.3 cents per gallon. Taxes on tires and other motor fuels were also directed into the Highway Trust Fund.

Other highway project requirements were also implemented as a result of the Federal Aid Highway Act of 1956. As in the previous legislation, states were given the responsibility of initiating projects while the federal government reviewed and approved them. All federal-aid projects must be accompanied by a public hearing in an effort to integrate local community goals into the design. At first, a public hearing was held only during the route location stage of project development. A second public hearing, however, was often administered during the design phase. Major urban highway projects were underway during the decade of the 1960s. By 1965, all federal-aid projects within urban areas of fifty thousand or more were to contain a continuous, comprehensive, and cooperative transportation planning process.

The Department of Transportation was created in 1966 and began considering those affected by highway construction projects. Historic properties, parks, wildlife or waterfowl refuge areas, and other public lands were now being protected during project development— none could be impacted by highway development unless another reasonable and prudent alternative could not be provided. Section 4(f) of the Department of Transportation Act of 1966 provided the mandate to protect properties—the National Environmental Policy Act (NEPA) of 1969 set environmental goals and policies to complement Section 4(f). All federal government agencies, in cooperation with state and local agencies were now required to coordinate plans and programs that affect the environment. Reports and recommendations must contain a statement on the environmental impact on a proposed action. Together these policies led to creation of the following three classes of action to monitor environmental goals:

- Environmental impact statement (EIS),
- Environmental assessment (EA),
- Categorical exclusion (CE).

Actions requiring an EIS include new access-controlled highways or new construction of a new fixed rail transit system. When individual or cumulative impacts are not significant, a CE may be prepared to document environmental impacts. An EA is required when the significance of environmental impacts are not well known, thus providing details about which document to prepare. An overview of the NEPA process is shown in Figure 17.1.

When known environmental impacts will occur as a result of a highway project, state agencies are required to prepare an EIS. Formal preparation of an EIS involves the following steps:

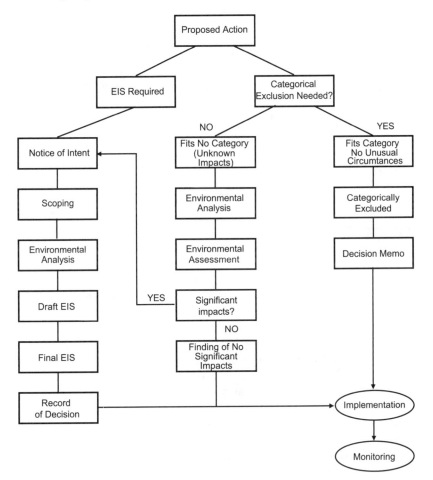

FIGURE 17.1 National Environmental Policy Act process (adapted from www.section4f.com).

- Define project purpose and need;
- Prepare and evaluate alternatives;
- Document affected environment;
- Quantify environmental impacts of alternatives and prepare mitigation measures;
- Document findings from scoping process and other project meetings;
- Prepare draft EIS and solicit comment;
- Prepare final EIS;
- Develop record of decision to identify selected alternative, present basis for the decision, and provide information on environmental mitigation measures.

The 1970s saw increased attention to environmental impacts and public involvement. Highway engineers routinely began to consider more than simply mobility and safety when deciding on route location and applying geometric criteria.

TRANSPORTATION IN AN INTERMODAL ERA

Construction of the Interstate system continued through the 1980s. When the Surface Transportation and Uniform Relocation Assistance Act of 1987 passed, funds were made available to states to complete Interstate system construction. As such, Interstate highway construction continued through the 1980s and early 1990s. The Intermodal Surface Transportation Efficiency Act (ISTEA) of 1991, often cited as landmark legislation, focused on improving transportation system efficiency. Funds of approximately $155 billion over six years were appropriated in the bill. Some highlights of the ISTEA bill included:

- Creation of a National Highway System (NHS), consisting of the Interstate system, roads important to national defense, and roads that provide intermodal connectivity.
- A flexible state and local transportation program to address congestion, air quality, accessibility, and intermodalism. Metropolitan planning organizations (MPOs) were responsible for cooperating with states to develop both long-range and short-term transportation plans and programs.
- Creation of an Intelligent Vehicle-Highway Systems (IVHS) program to promote the use of advanced technologies in transportation. This initiative is now known as Intelligent Transportation Systems (ITS).
- States were to develop and implement six management systems—highway pavement, bridge, highway safety, traffic congestion, public transportation facilities and equipment, and intermodal transportation facilities and systems—to support transportation planning requirements.
- A Congestion Mitigation and Air Quality Improvement Program to help states achieve national ambient air quality standards.
- Creation of a Surface Transportation Program (STP) where states can use funds for any federal-aid road (excludes local and rural minor collectors), bridges on

public roads, and for transit capital programs. Ten percent of each states funds must be used for transportation enhancements which include environmental-related activities.

Authorization of ISTEA in 1991 brought about heightened environmental awareness in the transportation project development process. With the passage of the National Highway System Designation Act of 1995, the National Highway System (NHS) was designated. It included nearly 161,000 miles of roadways to serve national interests and was a subset of roads eligible for federal aid. Section 304 of the act included design criteria of the NHS—excerpts from this section are as follows:

- Design standards for NHS projects must take into account planned traffic demand, safety, durability, and economy of maintenance; and,
- Design standards for NHS projects, except those also on the Interstate System, may also take into account: (a) the constructed and natural environment of the area; (b) the environmental, scenic, aesthetic, historic, community, and preservation impacts of the activity; and, (c) access for other modes of transportation. The secretary, in cooperation with state highway departments, may develop criteria to implement these provisions.

Road design and construction had to focus on the preservation of the natural environment, social and environmental impacts, and preservation of historic property and scenic sites. Furthermore, engineering designs had to carefully balance these social, environmental, and cultural issues with the traditional commitments to safety and mobility. The FHWA sought less-rigid design practices and later published *Flexibility in Highway Design* (FHWA 1997) a document that provides guidance on incorporating community values in the highway design process. This initiative later became known as *context-sensitive design*.

In June 1998, the Transportation Equity Act for the 21st Century (TEA-21) was signed into law. It essentially continued the initiatives begun in ISTEA. Authorization of funds for various surface transportation programs would thus continue for six years at a minimum of $198 billion. The main objectives of the legislation included: (a) improve traffic safety, (b) improve congestion, (c) protect and enhance communities and the natural environment, and (d) advance America's competitiveness and economic growth both domestically and internationally. The Highway Trust Fund would continue to provide funds for surface transportation programs, including transit. Each state transportation agency received a specific share of surface transportation funding based various programs designated in the TEA-21 legislation. However, each state agency was guaranteed a minimum share (90.5 percent) based on their contribution to the Highway Trust Fund.

A few key programs from the TEA-21 legislation are:

- Continuation of the NHS program funds. Publicly owned bus terminals, infrastructure-based ITS capital improvements, and natural habitat mitigation programs were all eligible for funding in addition to those outlined in ISTEA.

- Continued funding for Interstate system (including maintenance) projects.
- Continuation of STP funding for projects on federal-aid highways. Eligibility for STP funds now included environmental provisions such as natural habitat mitigation, stormwater retrofit, and anti-icing and de-icing). Ten percent of STP funds had to be set aside for transportation enhancements which included environmental projects.
- The transit program included a grant program for clean fuel buses and clean fuel bus facilities.
- Continuation of the Congestion Mitigation and Air Quality (CMAQ) Improvement program to meet the requirements of the Clean Air Act.
- Creation of the Transportation and Community and System Preservation Pilot program. This program permitted the study of relationships between transportation and community and system preservation and private-sector based initiatives. Part of the strategy associated with this program was to study alternatives to reduce environmental impacts of transportation projects.
- Continuation of planning requirement within Metropolitan Planning Organizations and statewide planning agencies.

In both ISTEA and TEA-21 legislation, intermodal transportation issues were given great attention and both local and state government agencies were given greater flexibility and input into transportation project development. As a result of the ISTEA legislation, there were fifteen metropolitan and twenty-three statewide planning factors that had to be considered in the metropolitan and statewide planning processes, respectively. These factors are listed in Table 17.1. As shown, many factors overlap among the groups. The main theme of the statewide factors is coordination among local agencies and continuous consideration of transportation system performance measures (i.e., mobility, safety, access, preservation, and environmental stewardship).

In the TEA-21 legislation, the planning factors created under ISTEA were collapsed in the following seven broad areas:

- Support the economic vitality of the state and its metropolitan areas, by facilitating global competitiveness, productivity, and efficiency;
- Increase the safety and security of the transportation system for all users;
- Increase the accessibility and mobility options for all users;
- Protect and enhance the environment, promote energy conservation, and improve quality of life;
- Enhance the integration and connectivity of an intermodal transportation system for all users;
- Promote system management and operation;
- Promote preservation of the existing transportation system.

As part of the ISTEA legislation, state transportation agencies and metropolitan planning organizations were required to prepare and continuously update long-range transportation plans and short-term transportation programs. Long-range transportation planning involved identifying transportation system improvement needs twenty years into the future. Impacts are considered, alternative improvements studied, and capital investment requirements are estimated. The process is fiscally constrained. Short-term

TABLE 17.1
Metropolitan and Statewide Planning Factors Established in ISTEA

Agency	Planning Factor
Metropolitan Planning Organization	Effects of all transportation projects
	International border crossings and promotion of access to critical areas and activities
	Road connectivity into and out of metropolitan areas
	Enhanced freight movement efficiency
	Enhancement and expansion of transit systems service and use
	Congestion relief and prevention methods
	Preservation and efficient use of existing transportation system
	Identify transportation needs using management systems
	Right-of-way preservation
	Use of life-cycle costs in bridge, tunnel, and pavement design
	Social, economic, environmental, and energy effects of transportation decisions
	Consistency of energy conservation and planning measures
	Relationship between transportation and short- and long-term land-use planning
	Expense programming of transportation enhancement activities
	Increase transit system security using capital investment
Statewide Planning	Identify transportation needs using management systems
	Any federal, state, or local energy goals and objectives
	Strategies to incorporate bicycle and pedestrian facilities into transportation projects
	International border crossings and access to ports, airports, and other intermodal facilities
	Transportation needs of non-metropolitan areas
	Any metropolitan area transportation plan
	Connection of metropolitan planning areas within state and with other similar agencies in other states
	Recreational travel and tourism
	Any State plan developed pursuant to the Federal Water Pollution Control Act
	Transportation system management and investment strategies designed to make efficient use of transportation facilities
	Social, economic, environmental, and energy effects of transportation decisions
	Congestion relief and prevention methods
	Enhancement and expansion of transit systems service and use
	Relationship between transportation and short- and long-term land-use planning
	Strategies to identify and implement transportation enhancements throughout state
	Use of innovative mechanisms for project financing (i.e., value pricing, tolls, etc.)
	Right-of-way preservation
	Long-range needs of state transportation system
	Methods to enhance commercial vehicle operations
	Use of life-cycle costs in bridge, tunnel, and pavement design
	Coordinate metropolitan planning organization transportation plans
	Investment strategies to improve state roads to support economic growth
	Concern of Indian tribal government having cross-jurisdictional boundaries

Source: Humphrey (1995).

programming involves the allocation of financial resources to a specific transportation project. Short-term programs typically include projects that will either be designed or constructed in less than three or four years. A typical planning, programming, design, and construction process is shown in Figure 17.2. At the planning level, transportation system goals and objectives are considered. This phase of the project development process is not project-specific. At the programming level, specific projects are typically identified and funding is allocated based on a general scope. Next, the alternatives

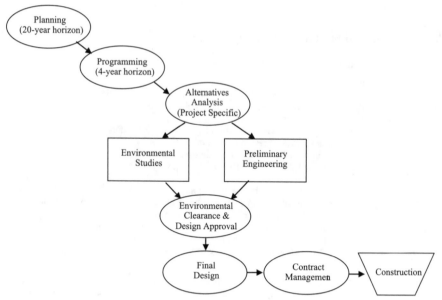

FIGURE 17.2   Typical transportation project development process (adapted from AASHTO, 2004).

analysis phase provides simultaneous consideration of environmental and preliminary engineering studies. Public involvement is typically at its highest level in this phase. After environmental clearance and design approval, final design ensues. After design, construction is begun. Context-sensitive design traditionally occurs during preliminary engineering, after the programming stage but prior to final design and construction.

The Safe, Accountable, Flexible, and Efficient Transportation Equity Act: A Legacy for Users (SAFETEA-LU) was passed on July 29, 2005. It provides for $286.5 billion in guaranteed funding for fiscal years 2004 through 2009. Several noteworthy provisions to the transportation project development process are as follows:

- SAFETEA-LU encourages federal transportation agencies to perform project delivery and environmental reviews concurrently as opposed to sequentially. Five states will be given the opportunity to pilot test the new review process.
- State transportation agencies are permitted to take over federal agency reviews of less-complicated transportation projects, specifically those designated as categorical exclusions.
- Requires transportation planning process to consider natural resources.

SUMMARY OF TRANSPORTATION LEGISLATIVE HISTORY

Prior to the turn of the twentieth century, there were no geometric design guidelines for the highway system in the United States. After the advent of the automobile, both federal and state transportation agencies formed and began to cooperatively establish transportation policy. Geometric design policies began to emerge in the 1940s and construction of the Interstate highway system began in the 1950s. During the early years of construction, roadway design and construction focused mainly on safety, mobility, and access. In the 1970s, public involvement and consideration of the environment were given consideration in the project development process. Beginning with the passage of the ISTEA legislation in 1991, explicit consideration of environmental, cultural, historic, and social impacts were provided for in long-range planning and short-term programming. Additionally, a formal public involvement process was typically initiated for large-scale transportation projects. As result of the ISTEA legislation, the concept of context-sensitive highway and street design began.

CONTEXT-SENSITIVE DESIGN OF HIGHWAYS AND STREETS

Context-sensitive design seeks to balance the considerations of roadway safety, mobility, enhancement of the natural environment, and preservation of community values. Context-sensitive design has often been referred to as "thinking beyond the pavement" where emphasis is placed on aesthetics and preservation of land—two considerations that were not principal design criteria during the Interstate highway construction era. Context-sensitive design strives to overcome the rigid segmentation of responsibility often encountered during the project development phase by allowing for community input. This concept also allows for a more in-depth evaluation of design alternatives that blend engineering considerations and the social and physical environment. Ideally, context-sensitive design eliminates communication barriers between transportation project stakeholders and a public agency. The following sections describe the characteristics of context-sensitive design, available context-sensitive design resources, and several case studies from the United States.

CHARACTERISTICS OF CONTEXT-SENSITIVE DESIGN

The 1990s became a decade of flexibility in highway design. Design teams are facing realities unlike those in previous eras because of the increased number of vehicles on the nation's highways, increased importance of public involvement, neighborhood and historic preservation requirements, community and economic development, environmental sensitivity, and concern for bicyclists and pedestrians (Peaks and Hayes, 1999). To achieve roadway design excellence, all of these factors must be considered and merged with the transportation project development process. A national workshop entitled Thinking Beyond the Pavement (1998) sought ideas for integrating highway development with communities and the environment. Several qualities for excellence in transportation design were outlined at the workshop:

- Early stakeholder consensus on the project purpose and need;
- Ensure a safe facility for the transportation user and the community;
- Preserve environmental, scenic, aesthetic, historic, and natural resources while striving for a project in harmony with community values;
- Achieve project excellence in the minds of the community and the design team;

- Efficient and effective use of resources by all highway development parties;
- Minimize disruption to the community; and,
- Provide added, lasting value to the community.

To achieve excellence in transportation design, the first challenge is harmonizing the project development process and community values. It is important to recognize, however, that balancing the two is not easily achievable as the general population, elected officials, community planners, and transportation professionals often do not maintain similar project viewpoints (Heanue 1998). For instance, land use decisions are taking place at all levels of government on a continuous basis. Because land use decisions are never made at one time or at one level of government, harmonizing transportation and community values becomes very complex. To provide a balance between transportation and community values, a workshop entitled *Thinking Beyond the Pavement* identified key characteristics that would yield highway design excellence (Thinking Beyond Pavement Conference Notes 1998):

- Honest, early, and continuous communication between all stakeholders;
- Develop project alternatives that are tailored to the circumstances;
- Establish a multi-disciplinary project team that includes the public;
- Understand the valued resources of the community before beginning the design process;
- Garner consensus on the project scope before pursuing engineering design;
- Use creative and innovative public involvement process; and,
- Secure process commitment from top political and elected officials.

BARRIERS TO CONTEXT-SENSITIVE DESIGN

While striving to achieve transportation harmonization by incorporating community values into the highway development process is a noble goal, barriers still must be overcome to achieve project success. First, the traditional highway development process involves rigid segmentation of responsibility among project parties. Second, traditionalists have maintained that any design deviating from the uniform standards was somehow substandard (AASHTO Quarterly 1998). Failure to recognize the flexibility in highway design alternatives may in fact result in a strenuous protest from the community. Finally, the lack of communication between the stakeholders and a transportation agency may be the toughest barrier to overcome during the highway development process. Design solutions not only must consider engineering and technological solutions, but they must improve the lives of the surrounding citizens and their environment (AASHTO Quarterly 1998).

CONTEXT-SENSITIVE DESIGN ISSUES

The Thinking Beyond the Pavement workshop (1998) identified certain issues that should be integrated into the context-sensitive design process. Liability, environmental compatibility, and design guidelines are shown in Table 17.2.

TABLE 17.2
Context-Sensitive Design Issues

Liability	Environmental Compatibility	Design Guidelines
• Tort liability should not be an impediment to flexible design. • Document reasons for deviating from design standards. • Communication between designers and legal counsel is required for flexible highway design.	• Link transportation and land-use planning. • Reducing capacity does not increase congestion. • Provide access for people *and* vehicles. • Public needs to be engaged in decision-making. • Solve problems, do not promote solutions.	• Provide public involvement on both small and large projects. • Seek consensus on project decisions by engaging all special interest groups. • Communication and visualization is important. • Research and document relationship between safety and flexible highway design.

A major issue concerning context-sensitive design arises out of community involvement. Often agencies or special interest groups desire a transportation solution that does not conform to transportation agency-adopted geometric design criteria. Conformance to existing design criteria may be extraordinarily expensive or may impose severe community impacts. When a design team is required to deviate from the design policy, a fear of liability arises. To combat this fear, it is important to recognize that documentation of decisions and proper communication with legal counsel will alleviate concerns. A "design exception" is the process by which deviations from design criteria are documents. Jones (1997) and Martin (1994) contend that tort liability concerns can be adequately addressed by providing a clear rationale justifying the exception. Awareness of the potential liability associated with design exceptions requires that documentation be persuasive and demonstrate the exercise of reasonable care. Design exception documentation should reflect not only that the exception was justified after considering engineering aspects, but also that the resulting design is safe.

In a recent survey by Mason and Mahoney (2003), only 11 percent of responding state transportation agencies (five of forty-six) have experience with design exception documentation being used in a tort case. Less than 20 percent (nine of forty-six) of responding agencies indicated that design exceptions have increased, or are expected to increase, as a result of implementing Context Sensitive Design.

Available Resources

This section describes various documents that are available as guidance documents for those interested in context-sensitive design implementation. A short narrative summary of the contents contained in each document are included in the discussion.

Flexibility in Highway Design (1997)

This document was published by the Federal Highway Administration (FHWA) in cooperation with the American Association of State Highway and Transportation Officials

(AASHTO), Bicycle Federation of America, National Trust for Historic Preservation, and Scenic America. The purpose of the report is to highlight the flexibility that exists in geometric design criteria and project regulations to understand the opportunities that exist to sustain community interests without compromising safety. The impetus for creating the document stemmed from both the ISTEA legislation in 1991 and the NHS Designation Act of 1995. An overview of the "flexible" transportation development process is presented as is an overview of geometric design guidelines. This process highlights the use of multi-disciplinary design teams early in the project development process (i.e., preliminary engineering and environmental studies). Finally, case studies of design flexibility are presented.

A Guide to Best Practices for Achieving Context-Sensitive Solutions (2002)

Published as National Cooperative Highway Research Program (NCHRP) report 480, this document describes methods for achieving context-sensitive solutions. It highlights barriers to context-sensitive design, and methods to overcome these barriers. Five pilot states (Connecticut, Kentucky, Maryland, Minnesota, and Utah) were tasked in the ISTEA and NHS Designation Act legislation to implement context-sensitive solutions. These pilot states, along with several other state transportation agencies, provided input to development of this publication. Issues discussed include effective decision-making, community values, achieving environmental sensitivity, ensuring safe and feasible solutions, and organizational needs. The report provides numerous suggestions for achieving context-sensitive solutions using various methods. The main methods include: (1) developing and implementing a public involvement plan, (2) identifying environmental and community constraints, (3) establishing appropriate project design criteria, and (4) developing and implementing a context-sensitive design process that can be tailored to meet specific project goals.

Context-Sensitive Design Around the Country: Some Examples (2004)

This document, published as Transportation Research Circular E-C067 by the Transportation Research Board, contains ten case studies of context-sensitive design. The document can be found at: http://trb.org/publications/circulars/ec067.pdf.

Performance Measures for Context-Sensitive Solutions: A Guidebook for State DOTs (2004)

The guidebook presents a framework that state transportation agencies can use to develop performance measures for context-sensitive design solutions. No evaluation measures are cited; rather, agencies are prompted to consider their own projects, each having a specific purpose and need. An outline of the framework is as follows:

- Guiding Concepts for Context-Sensitive Solutions Performance Measurement Programs
  - Context-Sensitive Solutions Measurement Program Framework
    - Balance between project (micro) and organization (Marco) measures

· Balance between process and outcome-based measures
o Creating and Implementing a Context-Sensitive Solution Measurement Program
  · Creating measures—requires leadership and consistent strategic planning
  · Implementing measures—develop a project-specific, collaborative, self-assessment approach (include all team members and stakeholders)
  · Timing of measures—regular assessment of performance measures, including project milestone assessment
- Project-Level Measure Focus Areas
  o Process-Related Focus Areas
    · Use of multi-disciplinary teams—develop project team based on project-specific needs
    · Public involvement—consider developing a plan; identify an external project champion; assess adequacy of project resources
    · Identify project problems, opportunities, and needs
    · Develop project goals or vision—be consistent with local plans; establish consensus among team stakeholders
    · Alternatives analysis—consider range of alternatives; match design criteria with project goals; evaluate alternatives against criteria
    · Construction and maintenance—involve construction and maintenance personnel in project development process
  o Outcome-Related Focus Areas
    · Achievement of project goals—did project support community values; were environmental resources preserved
    · Stakeholder satisfaction—consider elected officials; minimize construction impacts
    · Quality Assurance Review—use charts, peer reviews, and project reviews
  o Implement Project-level Measures
- Organization-Wide Measure Focus Areas
  o Process-Related Focus Areas
    · Training—quality, focus, quantity
    · Manual—consider manual changes as result of context-sensitive solutions
    · Policies—consider policy changes as result of context-sensitive solutions
    · Staff motivation strategies—consider awards program
  o Outcome-Related Focus Areas
    · Timeframe and budget
    · Stakeholder satisfaction—use survey of stakeholders; consider construction impacts
  o Implement Organization-Wide Measures

This document can be found at http://trb.org/publications/nchrp/nchrp_w69.pdf.

A Guide for Achieving Flexibility in Highway Design (2004)

Published by the American Association of State Highway and Transportation Officials (AASHTO), this text provides a summary of the project development process; a guide for achieving context-sensitive solutions through public involvement; review of highway geometric design criteria; and, tort liability issues. The suggested method to achieve context-sensitive transportation solutions is as follows:

- Identify stakeholders and solicit early, open, timely input
- Establish project purpose and need
- Conduct project scoping
- Build an effective public involvement campaign
- Plan and conduct public meetings
- Develop creative yet "engineered" design alternatives
- Document design decisions

A key component of context-sensitive solutions is public involvement. Aside from holding meetings to inform the public of various project milestones and design decisions, other creative public involvement methods exist. These include: creation of up-to-date project Web sites and visualization techniques to display project design alternatives.

CONTEXT-SENSITIVE DESIGN CASE STUDIES

The following section describes two examples of projects where context-sensitive design principles have been successfully applied in the United States. The first project is along U.S. Route 93 near Missoula, Montana; and, the second is the Danville-Riverside Bridge and Bridge Approach on state route 54 in Danville, Pennsylvania.

U.S. Route 93

U.S. Route 93 serves as a link between Interstate 90 in western Montana and two recreational sites: Flathead Lake and Glacier National Park. This fifty-six-mile section of two-lane rural highway experienced 42 fatalities and 727 injuries as a result of traffic crashes between 1995 and 1999. Passing and turning lanes did not exist and the roadway shoulders were not considered adequate for a roadway with average daily traffic volumes between six thousand and twelve thousand vehicles per day.

In the early 1980s, the Montana Department of Transportation (MDT) and Federal Highway Administration (FHWA) recognized the need for safety improvements on U.S. Route 93. As such, they collectively proposed to design and construct a four-lane highway to link the existing four-lane sections at both ends of the project limits. The project would traverse the Flathead Indian Reservation. This project was opposed by the Confederated Salish and Koonenai Tribes of the Flathead Nation (CSKT) as they felt that the environmental assessment of the proposed highway did not adequately address the environmental and cultural impacts.

Approximately fifteen years after the initial proposal to design and construct a four-lane highway across the Flathead Indian Reservation, the CSKT, MDT, and FHWA began working collaboratively to improve the safety and mobility issues on U.S. Route 93. A Memorandum of Agreement (MOA) was signed by all parties in December 2000.

This MOA served as guiding principles to the entire project team during the alternatives analysis and final design stages of project development. A few highlights from the MOA include (Public Roads 2002):

- The CSKT, MDT, and FHWA collectively prepared a final environmental impact statement and section 4(f) evaluation in June 1996 to highlight proposed project, design alternatives, and the social, environmental, and economic impacts.
- The CSKT, MDT, and FHWA deferred lane configuration, corridor preservation, mitigation measures, and other design decisions in the final environmental impact statement (modified in February 1998). The designated parties would continue to meet to decide lane configurations, design decisions, and mitigation measures throughout project development process.
- The CSKT, MDT, and FHWA developed preferred conceptual lane configurations, design features, and mitigation measures for the 30.8-mile section of U.S. Route 93 between Evaro and the Red Horn Road and Dublin Gulch Road intersections. This section would remain a two-lane highway with some passing, turning, and climbing lanes.
- A preferred conceptual plan for the 10.6-mile section of U.S. Route 93 between the Spring Creek Road and Baptiste Road intersection and MT Route 35 intersection was developed. This section would become a four-lane divided highway.
- The CSKT, MDT, and FHWA will prepare a supplemental environmental impact statement to evaluate alternative roadway alignment and new circumstances on an 11.2-mile section between U.S. Route 93 at the Red Horn Road and Dublin Road intersection and U.S. Route 93 at the Spring Creek and Baptiste Road intersection.
- A series of wildlife crossings would be constructed to allow for safe passage of deer, bear, elk, and other wildlife across the highway.
- A visitor's center would be constructed to display the reservation's tradition, culture, and landscape.
- A Project Oversight Group (POG) would be established and consist of representatives from CSKT, MDT, and FHWA that would establish and maintain design and environmental policies throughout project development process. Decisions will be made by consensus.
- A Technical Design Committee (TDC) would be established and consist of representatives from the CSKT, MDT, and FHWA who would provide oversight of design and construction plans. Project consultants would provide assistance to the TDC. Temporary representatives from local government agencies, the Montana Department of Fish, Wildlife, and Parks, and the U.S. Fish and Wildlife Service would also be included on the TDC, as appropriate.
- A liaison with other agencies impacted by the U.S. Route 93 construction would be created. Such agencies include local governments, U.S. Department of the Interior (Bureau of Indian Affairs), U.S. Army Corps of Engineers, and U.S. Fish and Wildlife Services.
- The cultural landscape would be restored along the entire length of the project.

The MOA was reached principally because of stakeholder involvement by the project team in the late 1990s. Local committees were established to discuss project needs and more than 600 property owners along the corridor were visited.

In all, forty-two wildlife crossings (eight bridges, oie overpass, and thirty-three culverts) were included in the project design. The design concepts were estimated to reduce fatal crashes by seventy by the year 2024 when compared to the existing conditions. Similarly, injury crashes were estimated to be reduced by 520. A traffic operational analysis indicated that mobility would improve under the proposed design scenarios when compared to the existing conditions.

Construction of the proposed U.S. Route 93 improvements is currently underway.

Danville-Riverside Bridge on Pennsylvania State Route 54

Built in 1904, the Danville-Riverside Bridge was a two-lane Parker Through truss bridge that spanned the Susquehanna River in Danville, Pennsylvania. Figure 17.3 is a photograph of the existing steel truss bridge.

FIGURE 17.3 Existing Danville-Riverside Bridge on Pennsylvania State Route 54. Photo courtesy of McCormick Taylor, used with permission.

The project history is extensive. In 1982, the Pennsylvania Department of Transportation (PENNDOT) identified structural deficiencies (e.g., narrow lanes and no shoulders, low vertical clearance, and poor sight distance) in the bridge and began the process of preparing and documenting design alternatives for a new bridge in an Environmental Assessment. Further, there were traffic congestion problems in Danville. Two of the three alternatives involved impacting historic sections in Danville while the other involved design and construction of a bypass around Danville with a new upstream river crossing. Because of controversy associated with impacting the Danville Historic District, the FHWA redesignated the project as an Environmental Impact Statement in 1989 and the project team started the project development process over again.

A Citizens Advisory Committee (CAC) was formed to facilitate interaction between the technical project team and the general public. The CAC was instrumental in forming a Community Design Task Force to assist in addressing design concepts, aesthetics, and community impacts. The draft Environmental Impact Statement submission considered only two alternatives, both requiring impacts to historic areas in Danville. A Record of Decision for the preferred alternative was issued by the FHWA in 1997.

Central to achieving a context-sensitive solution was an open public involvement process and continuous collaboration among various agencies. The Pennsylvania Historical and Museum Commission (PHMC) worked with the PENNDOT to determine which impacted properties in the historic district were contributing and non-contributing elements. A noncontributing property was demolished and a contributing property was eventually demolished because of its structural deficiencies that posed risk to the occupant. The PHMC was also concerned about the negative impact of the new bridge and bridge approach on local businesses. A Memorandum of Agreement between all relevant project parties stated that FHWA and PENNDOT would collaboratively prepare an Urban Design Plan that would integrate the project into the historic area. Essentially, a gateway would be created into the Borough of Danville as part of the project—pedestrians, bicyclists, parkland preservation, traffic noise, and parking would all be considered. The goal of the project was not only to create an aesthetically-pleasing, structurally-sound new bridge, the economic vitality of downtown Danville was to be maintained or enhanced.

A few design highlights from the project include:

- Historic appearance of bridge with decorative pedestrian railings;
- Historic street lamps on bridge and bridge approach;
- Creation of a bridge approach underpass with many historic features, including ornamental lighting and fencing, brick paver overpass crossings, and landscaping.

Figure 17.4 is a collage of photographs of the bridge and bridge approach after completing construction.

Paris Pike on U.S. Route 27/68 in Lexington, Kentucky

The Paris Pike, prior to 1997, was a two-lane highway that connected Lexington to Paris, Kentucky. This functioned as a principal arterial that served commuter as well as

FIGURE 17.4 Newly constructed Danville-Riverside Bridge approach. Photo courtesy of McCormick Taylor, used with permission.

tourist traffic because of its scenic route designation. In 1966, the Kentucky Transportation Cabinet initiated a study to identify both mobility and safety deficiencies along the existing Paris Pike. Findings from this effort indicated that enhancements were needed to Paris Pike to better serve the region's transportation system. Specifically, project travel demands may exceed capacity, geometric design features were inadequate based on existing criteria, and traffic safety was a concern (www.contextsensitivesolutions. org). An Environmental Impact Statement (EIS) was approved by both the Federal Highway Administration and Kentucky Transportation Cabinet in 1973 for design and construction of a four-lane highway. Design studies were subsequently initiated and right-of-way acquisition began in 1977. In 1978, an injunction was issued by the Federal District Court and the project was cancelled in 1980.

In 1986, a public hearing to discuss the project was held in Paris, Kentucky. A traffic safety memorandum was approved in 1987 and a supplemental EIS was submitted in 1988. The final, supplemental EIS was approved in 1991, and, in 1993, the court injunction was lifted. A Paris–Lexington Road Project Advisory Task Force, consisting of many local and statewide stakeholders, helped guide project development and were key contributors to the injunction being lifted. "Hayride tours" were used to involve local landowners. Such tours permitted the project team to understand the impacts of the proposed project.

Final design of the project consisted of two independent roadways through "zones of opportunity." These two independent roadways consisted of two lanes each—one roadway carried northbound traffic while the other carried southbound traffic. The roadway did not necessarily follow the existing two-lane highway alignment, rather often times was outside the existing right-of-way. The context-sensitive factors identified and maintained throughout design and construction of the Paris Pike included (www.contextsensitivesolutions.org):

- Soil from the project area was restored after construction because of its importance to the Kentucky horse farm industry.
- The roadway was designed and constructed to minimize impacts to historic properties and structures, including horse farm entrances and mortar-less stone walls. When impacted, new walls or farm entrances were built to match the historic ones.
- Timber guiderail was used to prevent vehicles from running off the road. This was used in place of more traditional, steel guiderail to retain the aesthetic character along the road corridor.
- Stone façade was applied to newly constructed structures to match rock outcroppings along the road corridor.
- Extensive landscaping, using native plants and trees, was done along the new roadway.
- Grass shoulders were used instead of paved shoulders.
- A quality-based prequalification process was used to guarantee that a contractor was obtained that could perform the context-sensitive construction of the proposed roadway.

Figures 17.5 and 17.6 are "before" and "after" photographs of a section of the Paris Pike. The "before" condition (Figure 17.5) shows the existing two-lane highway.

FIGURE 17.5 Existing condition on Paris Pike. Photo courtesy of Charlie Scott, Jones & Jones, Architects and Landscape Architects, Ltd., used with permission.

FIGURE 17.6   Newly constructed Paris Pike. Photo courtesy of Charlie Scott, Jones & Jones, Architects and Landscape Architects, Ltd., used with permission.

The "after" (Figure 17.6) shows the newly constructed four-lane section from a similar vantage point.

In Figure 17.5, note the stone wall and the narrow shoulders. In Figure 17.6, the stone wall remains, but an aesthetic guardrail is between it and the roadway. The paved shoulders have been widened in the "after" period. Also, it is important to note that only a single direction of travel is shown in Figure 17.6 while the same section is shown in Figure 17.5 with a single lane in each direction.

Figure 17.7 shows an aerial view of a completed section of the Paris Pike. As evidenced from Figure 17.7, the alignment closely followed the natural topography and significant landscaping was provided to improve aesthetics.

Conceptual Framework to Objectively Consider Context-Sensitive Solutions

In its current state, context-sensitive design is focused on developing collaborative transportation project solutions based on significant public involvement and application of appropriate engineering design criteria while preserving the community and natural environment. Public involvement typically begins after a project is programmed, but before undertaking alternatives analysis. Earlier public involvement (i.e., in long-range

FIGURE 17.7   Aerial photo of Paris Pike. Photo courtesy of Charlie Scott, Jones & Jones, Architects and Landscape Architects, Ltd., used with permission.

transportation planning process) may prove to be an even more effective context-sensitive design approach. This would provide citizens with an opportunity to decide which transportation projects should be included in long-term investments by state and local government agencies. Such early involvement on behalf of the community may increase support for projects before being programmed. Once the project is programmed and alternatives analysis is underway, increased public involvement in the long-range transportation planning process may reduce the level of opposition when preparing environmental assessments or environmental impact statements.

Prior to advancing to the alternatives analysis phase, a project purpose and need must be established when identifying conceptual solutions. Often, the purpose and needs reflect either safety or mobility issues, or both. Such concerns are generally left to the engineer to evaluate and mitigate. Input from project stakeholders will involve other issues such as community cohesion, impacts to aquatic resources and terrestrial habitat, impacts to historic property, among others. Developing alternatives must strike a balance between these issues. Once a preferred alternative is approved, preliminary engineering begins. Application of engineering design criteria and agency standards occurs during this stage. Cases have emerged where the desire of stakeholders and conformance to design criteria are not in agreement. The engineering community is then pressed out of its comfort zone into technical areas where little quantitative guidance exists.

When asked to consider transportation project solutions that violate established geometric design criteria, a quantitative evaluation is needed. The FHWA recently released the first version of the Interactive Highway Safety Design Model (IHSDM) for two-lane rural highways (Krammes 2002). Future enhancements consist of expanding the capability of the software to include multi-lane rural highways. In its present form, the software consists of six evaluation modules, including:

- Crash Prediction,
- Design Consistency,
- Policy Review,
- Traffic Analysis,
- Driver/Vehicle,
- Intersection Review.

The crash prediction module can be used to evaluate the safety performance (i.e., crash frequency and severity) of transportation designs. Inputs to the evaluation module include: horizontal and vertical alignment design elements, cross-section elements, sight distance, access density, roadside hazard rating, and traffic characteristics. The output is the expected crash frequency of each design feature in the project being evaluated. Such quantitative information could be used to evaluate design-decisions, compare the safety performance of design alternatives, or evaluate improvement projects on existing roadways.

The policy review module can be used to check project design-decisions against agency standards and policies. Violations of policy are highlighted and a message to the analyst indicates the location and nature of the policy violation. The design consistency module is similar to the crash prediction module except that it estimates and evaluates 85th-percentile, free-flow, passenger vehicle operating speeds at each point on a roadway alignment. The output of the module can identify potential speed inconsistencies of proposed or existing roadways.

The driver/vehicle module can be used to evaluate how a driver would operate a vehicle in a given roadway context. It provides output to identify locations where vehicle loss of control (i.e., skidding or rollover) might occur. The traffic analysis module can be used to evaluate traffic quality of service on proposed or existing roadways. The intersection review module can be used to perform a diagnostic review of an intersection and highlight safety concerns.

Agencies have traditionally been very reluctant to deviate from design criteria and only do so with caution. The design exception process is the current means used to document deviations from design criteria. The process is both deliberative and documentation-intensive. The frequency and reasons for design exceptions are expected to increase as more agencies adopt the context-sensitive design principles. State transportation agencies indicate in their formal design exception documentation that the safety implications of substandard geometric features should be assessed; however, few agencies provide specific guidance on how to do it (Mason and Mahoney 2003). The proposed Highway Safety Manual, being developed by the Transportation Research Board, will provide much needed knowledge and evaluation approaches to assist engineers in making design decisions.

SUMMARY

Context-sensitive design originated in the early 1990s as a result of the Intermodal Surface Transportation Efficiency Act and the National Highway System Designation Act. An underlying purpose of the legislation was to promote equal consideration of transportation project impacts and engineering design in the project development process. In its current state, context-sensitive design involves considerable public involvement after projects have been programmed for funding. A consequence of diverse stakeholder involvement is the concern over the application of minimum or limiting geometric design criteria to the preferred alternative. There is a need to integrate quantitative tools into the context-sensitive design process where engineers can compare safety and mobility measures for various alternatives. Increased public involvement, and quantitative decision-making methods, in the long-range transportation planning process would also alleviate concerns that may arise from design criteria deviation in later stages of project development.

When design criteria are not met, design exception documentation is required. There is a need to improve guidance associated with design exception preparation. Again, quantitative information that shows the safety, mobility, and cost impacts of deviating from existing criteria is necessary.

REFERENCES

A Guide for Achieving Flexibility in Highway Design. American Association of State Highway and Transportation Officials: Washington, DC, May 2004.

America's Highways 1776–1976: A History of the Federal-Aid Program. United States Department of Transportation, Federal Highway Administration: Washington, DC, 1977.

Context-Sensitive Design Around the Country: Some Examples. *Transportation Research Circular E-C067*. Transportation Research Board, National Research Council: Washington, DC, July 2004. http://trb.org/publications/circulars/ec067.pdf (accessed July 2005).

Context Sensitive Solution Web site. Federal Highway Administration. http:www.contextsensitivesolutions.org (accessed July 2005).

Flexibility in Highway Design. U.S. Department of Transportation, Federal Highway Administration: Washington, DC, 1997.

Heanue, K. E. Harmonizing Transportation and Community Values. *ITE Journal*, 1998, 68 (11), 32–35.

Humphrey, T. F. Consideration of the 15 Factors in the Metropolitan Planning Process. *NCHRP Synthesis of Highway Practice Report 217*, Transportation Research Board, National Research Council: Washington, DC, 1995.

Jones, R.O. Risk Management for Transportation Programs Employing Written Guidelines as Design and Performance Standards. *NCHRP Legal Research Digest Number 38*, Transportation Research Board, National Research Council: Washington, DC, August 1997.

Krammes, R. A. IHSDM: Evaluating the Safety of Highway Geometric Designs. *Civil Engineering News*, 2002, 13 (12), 48–51.

Martin, S. F. J. Design Exceptions: Legal Aspects. *Transportation Research Record 1445*, Transportation Research Board, National Research Council: Washington, DC, 1994, 156–159.

Mason, J. M.; Mahoney, K. M. *NCHRP Synthesis 306: Design Exception Practices*. Transportation Research Board, National Research Council: Washington, DC, 2003.

Moler, S. A Hallmark of Context-Sensitive Design. *Public Roads*, 2002, 65 (6), 6–13.

Neuman, T. R.; Schwartz, M.; Clark, L; Bednar, J.; Forbes, D.; Vomacka, D.; Taggart, C.; Glynn, M.; Slack, K.; Abere, D. *NCHRP Report 480: A Guide to Best Practices for Achieving Context Sensitive Solutions*. Transportation Research Board, National Research Council: Washington, DC, 2002.

Peaks, H. E.; Hayes, S. Building Roads In Sync with Community Values. *Public Roads*, 1999, 62 (5), 7–14.

Performance Measures for Context-Sensitive Solutions: A Guidebook for State DOTs. *NCHRP Web Document 69*, Transportation Research Board, National Research Council, Washington, DC, October 2004. http://trb.org/publications/nchrp/nchrp_w69.pdf (accessed July 2005).

Thinking Beyond the Pavement. *AASHTO Quarterly Magazine*, 1998, 77 (3), 27–34.

Thinking Beyond the Pavement: A National Workshop on Integrating Highway Development with Communities and the Environment. Maryland Department of Transportation, University of Maryland, May 3–5, 1998.

18 The Evolution of Policy and Regulation in the First Century of American Aviation

Bassel El-Kasaby, Patrick D. O'Neil, and Scott E. Tarry

AVIATION POLICY AND REGULATION

The evolution of aviation policy and regulation is characterized by a continuous ebb and flow of federal control punctuated by more significant and dramatic changes due to various crises and disasters. The following chapter traces this evolution from the industry's earliest days when, in an effort to foster its own development, industry pioneers reached out to the federal government for support and regulatory guidance. In a cycle of fits and starts that would last for decades, the federal government moved from a reluctant supporter and tentative regulator to create in 1938 the most pervasive regulatory environment in transportation. Federal regulations governed virtually all facets of the industry, including the provision of transportation services. Despite the industry's impressive growth and development under government control, some notable deficiencies eventually attracted the attention of political leaders who turned the calls of free-market economists into watershed regulatory reform in 1978. The debate continues today whether the industry owes its impressive growth in spite of or because of deregulation. More important, observers wonder if a return to a more extensive regulatory regime, harkening back to the three decades following WWII would help the industry handle its cyclical nature where periods of exceptional profits and growth are usually followed by difficult downturns.

This chapter is a broad survey of policy changes that illustrate the evolution of the relationship between the federal government and the air transport industry. The substantive coverage of any specific act or policy is necessarily brief, but the reader should gain an appreciation for the changing role of government in the industry and the difficulty of striking the right balance of market and government in a number of areas. The government has always struggled with what has been characterized as its "dual mandate" for aviation. The sometimes complementary and sometimes conflicting goal of simultaneously promoting and regulating the industry has a long history. That history shows the industry's awkward relationship with government and the government's own vacillation over its appropriate role.

The broad historical perspective taken here is important. Too often, sweeping generalizations about the industry are made in the context of especially good or devastatingly poor conditions. A broad view allows for a more complete understanding of how government and industry have struggled in their effort to craft a relationship that serves the interests of the industry as well as the general public. In the end, through all of its trials and tribulations, the industry has prospered, notwithstanding the current financial difficulties of the so-called legacy carriers, who continue to lose money even as passenger volumes grow. And while considerable political attention has been focused on the issue of airline security in recent years, government and industry continue to grapple with the general balance within their complex relationship. It is the continually shifting balance within that relationship that is explored here.

THE ERA OF PROTECTIONISM

Pre-World War II

Before the mid-1920s there was little interest in enacting federal legislation to control safety or spur the economic development of aviation. Access to the air was unrestrained. There was no licensing for pilots, for those who instructed pilots, or for those who worked on the aircraft. There were no standards in place governing the design or construction of aircraft to ensure minimal airworthiness, nor were there air traffic rules or guidelines for the conduct of flight once airborne (Komons 1989). Aviation was legally considered an "ultra hazardous activity," on par with pyrotechnics, explosives, and chemical manufacturing (Eichenberger 1997). Aviation technology was unreliable, and flying was considered a venture for wealthy thrill seekers, not a viable form of transportation or a potential tool of commerce. Historical accounts show that public distrust of aviation was substantial and investors believed that aviation was too dangerous and unreliable. During the 1920s, it became clear that a more structured regulatory environment was needed to set the stage for the commercialization of aviation as a mode of transportation (Smith 1991, p. 342).

Today, aviation is a highly regulated industry. Aviators and aviation professionals are constrained by an intricate web of controls aiming to foster the orderly development of the industry, while maintaining sufficient safety standards to engender public confidence. It is worth noting that current regulations exempt homebuilt and ultra-light aircraft and their pilots from many of the otherwise onerous licensing and certification requirements, perhaps as a suggestion of homage to the legacy of early free-spirited experimenters (14 C.F.R. §103 et seq.).

The importance of an adequate regulatory environment for the early development of the aviation market cannot be understated. For example, on the technical level, new technologies were often challenged because of patent problems (Witnah 1966).

Commercial flying was also hindered by public distrust of aviation in terms of safety (Davies 1972). In 1915, to address these and other issues, President Wilson created the National Advisory Committee for Aeronautics (NACA) attaching it to that year's Naval Appropriations Act. As a separate and independent body apart from the Navy, NACA was charged with the study of aviation and the provision of scientific solutions to problems associated with flight. NACA recommended, *inter alia*, the establishment of Airmail, facilitating the licensing of aviation patents, as well as measures aimed at fostering technology development (Witnah, 8).

NACA strongly recommended to Congress for the establishment of an airmail service to demonstrate that aviation could be a safe and reliable mode of transportation (Kane 2001). Airmail service was thus launched in May 1918. Following an initial rough start, a number of interagency operational and maintenance programs were instituted that corrected safety and reliability problems. By 1923, the airmail service possessed the best safety record of any aviation activity in the country. The improved reliability of airmail operations led to additional appropriations for construction of a system of lighted airways and airfields that, by mid-1924, formed a transcontinental system that enabled coast-to-coast airmail service in approximately twenty-nine hours eastbound, and thirty-four hours westbound (Heppenheimer 1995, p. 11).

In 1925, Representative Clyde Kelly of Pennsylvania introduced a bill that opened Airmail service to competitive bidding. The Kelly Act reflected the political belief of the time that private enterprise, not government, should provide transport and delivery of post and cargo. However, by the end of the decade it had become clear that Airmail could not be sustained without substantial subsidies from the government (Kane 1999).

In terms of safety, President Wilson and NACA called for a regime where the Department of Commerce would assume primary responsibility for licensing, inspection, and operations. In 1922, legal representatives from various aviation stakeholder groups met in Washington D.C. At this meeting, a committee of representatives from the American Bar Association, Commissioners on Uniform State Laws, aviation manufacturers and government passed a resolution seeking federal legislation and regulation for the promotion of aviation. The lack of significant federal leadership in aviation regulation led the states to explore other options. Representatives from thirty-two states met and produced the Uniform Aeronautics Act in which participating states agreed to standardized guidelines for sovereignty, ownership and liability, and adjudication of torts and crimes for aviation (Davies 1972). Although uniform standards were never achieved via the state action, a clear signal was sent to the federal government that it needed to assume a more prominent role in guiding the development of the industry.

Despite the efforts of many aviation associations and those with interests in aviation, there was a lack of support for federal legislation and regulation of aviation from the general public and legislatures, who had difficulty seeing aviation's potential. Support for federal regulation of aviation finally found a champion in the Secretary of Commerce, Herbert Hoover, who believed that the federal government should sponsor and regulate the American aviation industry. Noting that the aviation industry was one of the few American businesses that sought regulation by the government, Hoover mobilized the various aviation associations into an increasingly effective lobby for increased government involvement in the industry.

In 1925, Hoover responded to both the lobbyists for federal regulation and growing public and media criticism of aviation safety by forming the *Joint Committee of Civil Aviation of the U.S. Commerce Department and the American Engineering Council*. In 1925, calls for a more comprehensive regulatory framework were finally heeded (Davies 1972). In 1926, Congress passed the Air Commerce Act. The passage of the act firmly preempted state and local regulatory efforts, and heralded the beginning of the current federal regulatory regime. By mid-1926, the federal government was providing economic aid to growing airlines through postal subsidies and through regulations aiming to improve aviation technology and operational safety. In addition, the McNary-Watres Act of 1930 provided the Postmaster General, Walter Folger Brown, with broad regulatory powers over the commercial aviation industry. Subsidies were used to encourage mergers and penalize small players. These tactics drew strong criticism from industry and within the legislature (Komons 1979; Lewis 2001). Many legislators vigorously opposed any an airmail system that required federal subsidy. Other legislators were also extremely critical of the increased centralized authority and power of the federal government over the aviation enterprise, an enterprise that they believed should be guided by free market forces, not government regulation.

Thus began a running debate regarding the appropriate role of government in aviation. In the earliest stages of its development, when few people had experienced flight and even fewer understood its potential, the industry found it difficult to attract the attention and support of the federal government. In short, questions about its viability and relevance fostered reluctance among policy makers. Ironically, when the industry began to grow sufficiently to be taken seriously, opponents of government support argued that the industry didn't really need government to ensure its success and that the market should determine the industry's fate as well as the fortunes of those who decided to involve themselves in the business of air transport.

The conflict in Congress intensified when small commercial carriers, originally viewed the passage McNary-Watres as an opportunity to gain a viable source of revenue by gaining lucrative airmail contracts, were excluded because of their size and lack of aircraft passenger capacity. Free market proponents were further alienated when Brown proceeded to strengthen the air industry's financial situation by eliminating what he considered reckless competition among participants. Brown held a conference with airline executives in 1930 that established a handpicked collection of large, reasonably well-financed aviation companies that would prosper in the context of regulated competition. Numerous carriers deemed too small, poorly funded, or operationally inadequate were excluded from receiving airmail contracts. Other small companies were directed to merge to create large companies. Routes were divided between these large companies. Competition on these routes was prohibited, thus protecting company revenues. Companies, not benefiting under Brown's scheme, complained to the federal government that Brown had exceeded his legal authority and was not complying with the intent of the act. The Comptroller General, John R. McCarl, who had originally opposed McNary-Watres citing the potential for fraud, favoritism, and waste in creation of such a powerful and centralized system, challenged Brown. McCarl was especially critical of the government's award of lucrative transcontinental routes to airlines companies formed under Brown's direction (Komons 1978).

By 1933, political opposition and congressional investigations into Brown and his authoritative aviation regulation enabled President Roosevelt to order sweeping regulatory reforms of the industry (Komons 1979). On February 9, 1934 a congressional committee headed by Hugo Black, a southern Democratic populist, issued an order that immediately and effectively cancelled all domestic airmail contracts citing collusion, fraud, and favoritism on the part of Brown. All domestic airmail contracts were cancelled. Army pilots and aircraft were ordered to temporarily transport the mail. The Army's role in airmail transport was short lived, as it immediately became apparent that the Army was neither prepared nor equipped to replace experienced private air carriers. Three days prior to the Army's assumption of airmail operations, three pilots were killed in crashes en route to their initial assignments. By the end of the first week of airmail operations, five more Army pilots had been lost, six more seriously injured, eight aircraft had been destroyed and more than $300,000 of property damage had been accumulated (Heppenheimer 1995, p. 59). Continued Army mishaps and poor service in the provision of airmail produced significant public and political outrage that lead to formal restoration of commercial contracts with the passage of the Air Mail Act of 1934.

The act was intended to correct the previous over centralization of governmental power regulating airmail expanded the number of government agencies tasked with regulating aviation to three. The Interstate Commerce Commission (ICC) was charged with setting rates for each route, the U.S. Post Office controlled routes and operations, and the Department of Commerce was responsible for safety (Komons 1979; Preston 1998).

Brown's spoils conference and the subsequent political fallout offer a glimpse of a recurring theme in aviation policy. The government, in its effort to guide the industry, made choices that necessarily create winners and losers within the industry and to some extent within society. Brown's efforts to strengthen the industry make sense at a certain level, but they were not politically sustainable since his actions alienated those who were excluded from the process. This is a recurring theme in the evolution of government's role in aviation. Because government policy rather than market forces often determine success in the industry, those disaffected by the outcomes of such policies use the political process to seek redress.

Another recurring theme in aviation is that once a policy's opponents are able to muster their forces for change, they often strike quickly and change policies in ways that reflect their contempt for current policies rather than a clear understanding of the implications of the changes they propose. The hasty decision to use military pilots to carry the mail reflected policy makers' disgust for Brown's actions rather than a carefully considered plan to fix what was actually wrong with the industry at the time. While this behavior is certainly not unique to aviation, the industry has a rich tradition of policies driven by visceral reactions to crises.

By the mid-1930s, attempts to regulate the industry by three overlapping federal agencies had produced inefficient and often conflicting regulatory programs. This led to calls from the industry for more regulatory reforms to better manage competition (Richmond 1961). Roosevelt responded by proposing to consolidate the regulatory prerogative into a single agency (Baloug, Grinsger & Zelikow 2002). On June 23,

1938 the Civil Aeronautics Act of 1938 (McCarran-Lea) was signed into law. The act consolidated federal authority to regulate all economic and operational aspects of the aviation industry under one government agency. It also established complete federal control over airways and over state aviation activities. The Civil Aeronautics Act of 1938 is viewed as having legally preempted the regulatory field of aviation (Frederick 1946).

The act created the Civil Aeronautics Authority (CAA), as well as an independent Air Safety Board possessing accident investigation powers (Preston 1998, pp. 19–20). The CAA was charged with directing the expansion and maintenance of the civil airway system, operation of airway navigation facilities and the safety and regulation of air traffic. The organization was mandated to coordinate the development and maintenance of the nation's airports and to conduct a comprehensive survey of airports, providing Congress with recommendations supporting aviation infrastructure expansion. While purchase of these facilities by the government was prohibited and airports were to remain under "local ownership," they were now eligible to receive federal funding as long as they met federal policy guidelines (Bednarek 2001).

Unfortunately, the newly formed CAA suffered from many problems at its inception. The act did not establish clear lines of separation between the organization's executive, quasi-legislative and quasi-judicial roles. The CAA was additionally plagued by rumors of continuing conflict and disagreement between the chairman of the five-member board, Edward J. Noble, and the CAA Administrator, Clinton M. Hestor, in addition to charges by the press that neither were qualified for their respective positions.[1] Congress had intended to construct unambiguous lines of separation and authority between the organization's executive, quasi-legislative, and quasi-judicial roles. However, it had unintentionally placed provisions within the act that negatively impacted the CAA's internal balance of powers. Budgetary power and other executive functions had been placed under the control of the five-member authority. Because of these "unintentional" powers, the five-member board was able to assign certain tasks, some involving safety actions that clearly violated congressional intent, to the administrator.

The administrator was placed in the position of answering to legislative agents as well as to the executive in the performance of his duties. The CAA's board also had persistent conflicts with the Air Safety Board severely limiting the agency's effectiveness (Wilson 1979). By intention, the Air Safety board provided recommendations as a result of their accident investigations. But, corrective actions to prevent future accidents, stemming from ASB recommendations were under the purview of the five-member board. Members of the Air Safety Board felt that the Authority would take

---

1. Edward Noble was a liberal Republican and inventor of the Life Saver mint. Though possessing an interest in aviation and proven business ability, he lacked experience in public affairs and was prone to unwittingly offend and be offended by others. *American Aviation* criticized him for his lack of innovative ideas for development of American Aviation. Clinton M. Hestor also a Republican was a lawyer, with substantial legislative legal experience, but little technical aviation expertise. When Hestor told his wife of his appointment to the position of CAA Administrator she responded by stating "You are not qualified" to which he responded "I realize that myself" (Wilson 1979, pp. 12–15).

credit for recommendations following mishaps that rightly fully belonged to them (Wilson 1979).

In 1940, Roosevelt terminated the Civil Aviation Authority as an independent agency and divided federal regulatory power between two new organizations. The Civil Aviation Authority was renamed the Civil Aviation Administration and the five-member board was recast as the Civil Aeronautics Board (CAB) and placed in the Department of Commerce. The Air Safety Board was also abolished and safety responsibilities were placed under the direction of the CAB (Preston 1998). This last change produced a relatively stable CAA that would function within the Department of Commerce until the passage of the Federal Aviation Act of 1958. Following the passage of this act, the CAB would become an independent agency along with the newly formed Federal Aviation Agency.

World War II is a watershed in the development of aviation both in terms of its impact on the industry and the role of the federal government. While the war temporarily stifled the development of the civilian aviation sector, the efforts of the federal government to develop the nation's military aviation sector resulted in a phenomenal increase in the number of airports, the capabilities of aircraft, the number of pilots, as well as significant improvements in key technologies that would catapult the industry forward after the end of hostilities. In particular, war preparations included the first real federal funding of airports, signaling a fundamental shift in philosophy for the development of aviation infrastructure.

In the late 1930s, the threat of war prompted that passage of the Civilian Pilot Training Act of 1939. The CAA created the civilian pilot training program (CPTP) that, by the beginning of the war, had trained over sixty thousand pilots. In May of 1940, President Roosevelt called for the expansion of domestic aviation industry production to fifty thousand aircraft per year (Wilson 1979). In October of 1940, Congress directly appropriated to the CAA funding to develop public airports identified as critical to national defense under the Development of Landing Areas for National Defense (DLAND) initiative. DLAND helped create an airport infrastructure system that would be vital to the war and to the rapid growth of commercial aviation afterwards. By 1941, the war build up was driving large appropriations for pilot training, aircraft development and expanded aviation infrastructure that would enable the expansion of commercial aviation in post-war America. Funding for aviation grew from $14 million in 1939 to over $224 million in 1942 (Preston 1998, p. 292).

In addition to DLAND, the Army and Navy devoted substantial resources to the improvement of municipal airports throughout the country. Prior to this investment most of the nation's airports suffered from limited local investment and benign neglect on the part of the federal government (Gordon 2004). The military undertook operations and improvement of airports both through lease arrangements and outright purchase. In some cases municipal airports were appropriated into military service with the promise of returning ownership to original authorities within six months after the war. In the majority of cases, municipalities and private owners benefited from vastly improved aerodromes at the end of the war (Bednarek 2001, p. 158). These improved airports became centers of transportation commerce and contributed to the postwar growth of commercial aviation.

In November of 1944, the CAA proposed to Congress a National Airport Plan that would meet the nation's forecasted civil aviation needs following the end of the war. The plan recommended a system of federal and state aid to stimulate growth of airports. In May of 1946, President Truman signed the Federal Airport Act, which authorized the Federal-Aid Airport Program (FAAP). For the first time, federal funds were appropriated for the development of civil airports. In January of 1947, FAAP funding was released for construction or improvement of 800 airports. Modifications to the Federal-Aid Airport Program in August of 1955 by President Eisenhower extended the program timeframe, removed previous airport size and type restrictions that had limited eligibility, and increased funding (Rochester 1976).

Post-World War II

The war brought significant advances in aviation technology, promising to make transcontinental and transoceanic flight easier and more prevalent once hostilities ceased. In anticipation of rapid growth following WWII, the federal government undertook a variety of programs to provide financial incentives to own and operate aircraft, develop new technology, and support the expansion of America's domestic and international aviation markets.

A few noteworthy amendments to The Civil Aeronautics Act were enacted between 1946 and 1951. The amendments sought to encourage the financing of aircraft used for commercial purposes. The first amendment limited liability for owners who were not involved in direct operations of the purchased aircraft. The second amendment created a system for recording liens for aircraft parts. To ensure the continued operation of commercial aviation, even under emergency conditions, Title XIII was added to the Civil Aeronautics Act in 1951 authorizing provision of war-risk insurance to commercial air carriers when insurance could not be obtained.

The government's efforts to enhance aviation were not focused solely on the domestic industry. In a move analogous to its driving role in the development of the United Nations, the United States sought to foster the development of a global aviation regime. In 1944, the country hosted the International Civil Aviation Conference in Chicago. The fifty-three attending nations rejected the premise that the skies would be open to all air traffic and reaffirmed the principle of national sovereignty in ownership of airspace. The convention provided the foundation for the creation of the Provisional International Civil Aviation Organization (PICAO) and placed in motion the machinery that would produce uniform international flight safety and operational standards. The Bermuda Agreement followed this in February of 1946 in which the United States and Britain forged an air agreement for commercial services that would serve as a model for future bilateral agreements with the United States as well as those between numerous other nations (Groenewege 2003; Hanlon 1999).

International commercial aviation was enhanced with the ratification of the Convention on International Civil Aviation on August 9, 1946. Signed by twenty-six countries, including the United States, the agreement put into effect the conventions originally drafted by the Chicago Convention and created the International Civil Aviation Organization (ICAO) as a replacement for PICAO. U.S. development of international commercial markets was further advanced with the passage of the International Facilities Act of 1948. Under this act, the CAA administrator received the authority to improve foreign air facilities and train foreign nationals to operate and maintain these facilities, if the effort was viewed as benefiting U.S. commercial air carriers. As such the United States emerged at the end of World War II as a global leader in both the development and regulation of aviation.

While the transition from military to civil aviation following the war had its share of difficulties, the nation's air transport system soon took full advantage of the infrastructure, aircraft, and pilots produced as part of the war effort. The economic expansion that followed the end of the war unleashed a pent up demand for air travel. Airline companies grew rapidly and air traffic threatened to overwhelm the system. The federal government soon discovered that its role would need to evolve further if the American air transport industry was to develop safely and efficiently.

In August of 1957 President Eisenhower signed the Airways Modernization Act (Public Law 85-133) creating the Airways Modernization Board (AMB) to support domestic expansion. Congress formed the AMB as an interim committee, viewing it as a transitional step leading to the creation of an independent federal agency with authority to oversee a rapidly expanding American aviation industry.

By mid-1958, the twentieth anniversary of the Civil Aeronautics Authority, the industry had made tremendous progress. The number of aircraft in commercial service also steadily grew. Between 1950 and 1953, aircraft utilized in commercial service had grown by 17 percent, with the total available lift capacity increasing 42 percent, producing an annual increase of billion-ton miles (Preston 1998, p. 50). By 1958, international commercial travel had increased to the point where more transoceanic passengers traveled by air than by ship. In October of 1958, the Boeing 707, the nation's first turbo-jet commercial aircraft began service (Preston 1998). Although safety was still a concern, by 1957 aviation passenger fatality rates had been substantially reduced from 1938 levels. Air travel in 1957 was judged to be thirteen times safer than travel by automobile (Rochester 1976).

As aviation grew in size and importance, so did criticism of the federal government's ability to properly oversee the industry. Whether because they thought the government was inadequately prepared to handle the rapidly expanding industry or because they believed it was time for the government to give up its control and allow market forces to shape the industry's future, aviation stakeholders pressed the government for change. The CAA's subordinate role within the Department of Commerce was viewed as a substantial issue. The CAA's actions were considered fragmented because the time spent coordinating with the CAB, the Department of Defense, and with various coordinating committees and private groups, reducing time available for directing critical programs (Rochester 1976).

Legislative and industry pressure mounted until on August 23, 1958, when President Eisenhower signed the Federal Aviation Act into law. This act repealed the Air Commerce Act of 1926, The Civil Aeronautics Act of 1938, the Airways Modernization Act of 1957 and reorganization stipulations stemming from various presidential civil aviation directives. All aviation functions performed at the federal level were removed from the Department of Commerce and placed within two independent agencies, the Federal Aviation Agency (FAA) and the Civil Aeronautics Board.

The FAA as an independent agency was empowered with the regulatory authority to both promote economic growth and ensure the safety of air commerce, as well as control of the U.S. airspace. The FAA controlled research for all air navigation facilities, their installation, and operation. The FAA was also given what proved to be a critical responsibility to develop and operate a common system of air traffic management for military and civil aircraft. The CAB retained economic regulatory authority for air carriers and for accident investigation, but transferred safety rulemaking to the FAA.

The FAA continued as a separate agency pursuing the sponsorship and regulation of aviation until 1966 with the passage and signing of the Department of Transportation Act (Public Law 89–670). The act brought all governmental transportation, including the FAA, under the control of a single Cabinet-level Department. The new department was charged with guiding the expansion and coordination of national transportation systems. The Department of Transportation Act also created the National Transportation Safety Board (NTSB). The NTSB was charged with the determination and the reporting of the cause or probable cause of transportation accidents. The NTSB was additionally assigned the responsibility for appeal review of suspension, amendment or denial of transportation certificates and licenses.

By the end of the 1960s, the United States had further solidified its role in global aviation. Boeing, McDonnell Douglas, and Lockheed dominated the commercial aircraft market. The FAA and CAB jointly supervised the largest domestic air transport market in the world and wielded substantial influence in the development of international aviation as well. Once again, the industry seemed to outstrip the government's ability to keep pace. This was no more apparent than in the area of funding the enhancement of airports and airways that were increasingly unable to meet the demands of the industry. By now, however, the industry was no longer a sideshow in America's transportation system. While the industry's concerns were previously dealt with almost exclusively within the aviation community, by the early 1970s aviation's concerns became part of the nation's much broader political and economic context.

As the aviation industry grew, so did its demands on the general fund of the federal government. Unfortunately, its demands were increasingly going unmet as aviation found itself competing for resources with the expanded social programs of President Johnson's Great Society and the military's Cold War initiatives including the war in Vietnam. In a move that would have substantial long-term implications for the funding of aviation in America, President Nixon created the Airport and Airway Trust Fund by signing into law in 1970 the Airport and Airway Development Act, and Airport and Airway Revenue Act. No longer would aviation have to battle with other interests for money from the general fund; it would rely instead on user fees and taxes collected by aviation for aviation.

Levies were imposed on domestic passenger fares. International passengers were subject to a surcharge. Aviation fuel and airfreight waybills were taxed, aircraft registration was subject to additional annual fees and aircraft were now taxed according to takeoff weight. It was intended that this trust fund support long-term infrastructure improvement with tax generated funds protected from diversion to nonaviation uses. In November of 1971, Congress amended the act specifying that trust fund money usage was limited and could be used only to establish or improve air navigation and administrative program costs. Importantly, the Airport and Airway Development Act and the Airway Revenue Act marked an important shift how local airports and facilities were to be funded. In lieu of seeking support for taxation of local taxpayers, municipalities and airport authorities could seek financial support from the Federal Aviation Trust Fund (Preston 1998).

The decision to rely on a trust fund to provide resources for the development and support of aviation turned out to be a double-edged sword for an industry that has always been cyclical in nature. A trust fund is a great way to fund relatively stable sectors of the economy. It is less attractive for an industry that is prone to substantial swings between phenomenal success and devastating failure. At the trust fund's inception commercial aviation was still operating under the CAB's conservative approach to managed competition. By the end of the 1970s, however, the CAB was no longer in charge of guiding the industry and the nation's air carriers who were poised to embark on three decades of market driven competition that carried the industry to dizzying new heights and equally devastating lows.

Legislative actions in the mid 1970s also targeted improvement of aviation safety. The Independent Safety Board Act of 1974 specified that all air carrier accidents falling under 49 CFR parts 121 and 135 involving public and government aircraft would now be investigated by the NTSB. The act additionally specified that the NTSB would investigate any foreign mishap involving a U.S. carrier or U.S.-produced aircraft or major U.S.-manufactured aircraft component. The NTSB was also tasked with the investigation of incidents involving ATC, training, mid-air collisions, newly certified aircraft components, in-flight fires or breakup as well as general aviation accidents. Annex 13 of the Convention of International Aviation provided the NTSB with the ability to participate in investigations of commercial accidents worldwide (Wells and Rodrigues 2003).

In January 1975, President Ford signed the Transportation Safety Act of 1974 that gave the Secretary of Transportation the authority to set new regulatory and enforcement rules over shipment of hazardous materials. Title III of this act, effective in April of 1975, removed NTSB from the DOT establishing it as an independent authority to better produce unbiased mishap reports and recommendations. Objective and external safety investigation and reporting was further expanded with the creation of the offices of the Inspector General in the Department of Transportation in October of 1978. The newly formed office was given the authority to investigate, evaluate and provide recommendations for improvement throughout the DOT.

Rather than reducing its role, the federal government was in many instances reaffirming its authority over the industry. It is important to see airline deregulation which begins in 1978 in this context. In fact, one might argue that in many ways other aspects of the relationship between the federal government and industry were bolstered as a result of the decision to free the airlines of commercial regulations that had made the decisions of political appointments more relevant than the decisions of consumers in shaping the industry in the postwar era.

THE ERA OF DEREGULATION

PRE-SEPTEMBER 11

The industry became a focal point of academic and political debate in 1970s as a result of its successes as much as its failures. Its success as manifested in the growth of air travel and the maturation of the airline business model suggested to reform minded economists that the time had come to remove the restrictions imposed by government regulators so the industry could reap the efficiencies associated with unfettered competition. Populist political leaders also took note of how the CAB's managed competition had done little to bring air travel to the masses. High fares kept a significant number of Americans from enjoying the benefits of aviation (Peterson and Glab 1994).

The Airline Deregulation Act of 1978 (ADA) deregulated routes, flights, and fares. The ADA also eliminated the Civil Aeronautics Board (CAB) by phasing it out over a six-year timeframe. The FAA then assumed the remainder of the CAA's regulatory duties and the Department of Transportation (DOT) later assumed the remainder of the CAB's duties. Although deregulation as such was not extended to airports or air traffic control, major air transport markets benefited to a great extent from the airlines' freedom to set prices and routes. The airline industry grew significantly as air travel increased and travel costs dropped on major routes (GAO 1996). However, the benefits of deregulation were not distributed evenly. Not surprisingly, costs decreased more on higher traffic and long-distance routes than on thinner and shorter routes. Even though smaller airline markets did not fare as well in terms of travel cost savings or even service availability, on average consumers gained from lower fares and increased service.

Of course, "on average" benefits mean little to citizens who don't realize direct benefits. In fact, much of the academic debate about the success or failure of airline deregulation revolves around the issue of disparate impact throughout the system (Morrison and Winston 1995; Dempsey and Goetz 1992). Proponents of deregulation point to well-documented overall welfare gains and the growth of the industry, while critics note the numerous specific cases of service reductions and high fares experienced by smaller cities around the nation as well as the industry's financial difficulties at various times since deregulation.

Proponents of deregulation are quick to note that despite the claims of market critics that competition would lead to dangerous cost-cutting, travel safety has actually improved slightly since deregulation. However, these admittedly modest safety improvements must be considered in view of the fact that air travel had already become one of the safest modes of transportation. For example, by 2000, there were only 96 airline fatalities, compared to 770 rail fatalities, and 41,800 fatalities on U.S. highways (NTSB 2000). While enhanced safety could not be directly attributed to deregulation, it is important to note that deregulation was not an obstacle to such improvements. If anything, deregulation probably contributed indirectly to safety by creating an environment where advances in aircraft design, air traffic control, and maintenance standards were possible. The industry has also seen significant advances in navigation aids and related technologies driven at least in part by an expanded government role in the development and enforcement of regulations related to operational safety.

After deregulation, airlines adopted hub-and-spoke networks as a model for developing their routes (Bill 2002). As its name suggests, this distribution model consists of a number of spokes extended out from a central hub. The flight paths that lead from origin and destination cities are considered spokes, connected through a central hub. A hub is always a major airport that serves as a transfer point to get passengers from their originating airports to their ultimate destinations. This system allowed airlines to use their aircraft, equipment, and overall operations more efficiently, offering more routes and more frequent service. One disadvantage of this model compared to the point-to-point transit pattern that prevailed before deregulation is that it requires most flights to be routed through a hub. Hence, passengers not residing in hub cities or traveling to hub cities have to make at least one additional stop and change planes before reaching their final destination. Notwithstanding this inflexibility and a variety of other problems such as congestion and delays at busy hubs, the hub-and-spoke system has become the standard model for most major airlines (Hanlon 1999; Dempsey and Goetz 1992).

Deregulation created a number of regulatory or policy challenges that are still unfolding even after nearly three decades of experience with the market driven industry. In particular, government has been charged with: (1) preserving competition without managing it; (2) preserving service to rural and small communities that the market would otherwise ignore; (3) preserving efficient access at airports without actually mandating specific rules or behavior for the airlines or the airports; and (4) enhancing international air transport by liberalizing the market without actually opening the market.

This awkward role for government is a function of its ambivalence towards the market forces that are supposed to guide the industry in the deregulated environment. On one hand, policy makers are reluctant to return to a regulated environment for fear of giving up the lower fares most consumers have come to enjoy. On the other hand, the government's reluctance to unleash market forces has resulted in questionable policies throughout aviation. For example, the government managed competition by approving mergers and acquisitions that are arguably detrimental to market fairness. Moreover, the subsidies provided to small community air service have stifled innovation and competition while congested airports are prohibited from adopting market based pricing strategies. Finally, stringent restrictions on the flow of capital within the industry limit foreign ownership even as the government trumpets its efforts towards liberalization.

Pressure from competition strained airlines financially and several bankruptcies and takeovers took place within the industry following deregulation. The government is well equipped politically and administratively to deal with the issue of bankruptcies and mergers so that impact of those situations on competition is mitigated. The sophisticated U.S. antitrust regime operates to limit market practices that are detrimental to competition (Sherman Act 1890; Clayton Act 1914). Historically, the U.S. Department of Justice (DOJ) has served as the government's enforcement authority in this area. During the 1980s, however, the DOT retained the sole authority over airline mergers that had previously belonged to the Civil Aeronautics Board. While the DOJ lacked enforcement authority, it still made recommendations and objections to the DOT with regard to proposed mergers.

In 1989, after the merger frenzy that gripped and reshaped the industry in the wake of the passage of the deregulation act, the authority to evaluate and block airline mergers was relegated to the DOJ, which enforces section 7 of the Clayton Act and sections 1 and 2 of the Sherman Act. Section 7 prohibits mergers and acquisitions that threaten to hamper competition. Courts have interpreted the act to prohibit mergers that make it easier for an airline to successfully raise its price without that price being met by its rivals. Sections 1 and 2 of the Sherman Act prohibit price fixing and other monopolistic practices (Sherman Act 1890). This decision was arguably too late to have a meaningful effect on the consolidation of the industry, since most mergers and acquisitions that effectively eliminated many smaller potential competitors within the industry had been completed by that time.

Rural and small communities at risk of losing service after deregulation were guaranteed subsidized service under the Essential Air Service program (EAS). The program was initially authorized for ten years. It was hoped that by that time these communities would generate sufficient demand to sustain unsubsidized service. Communities that were served by certificated carriers were only able to maintain a minimal level of scheduled air service under the program. The program continues to be available to some communities today in a more limited form. The program is administered by the Department of Transportation (DOT), which provides subsidized service to about 140 rural and small communities across the country.

The EAS program typifies the government's unwillingness to treat aviation like other industries and allow the market to genuinely determine levels of service. Ironically, instead of allowing small communities to develop their air service markets in ways that might sustain commercial service without subsidy, the program actually creates clear disincentives for innovation and change that might meet the transportation needs of small and rural communities. While the airline industry has seen substantial innovation and change, EAS communities have been locked into a level of service that shows no appreciable improvement over what they initially received as part of the original subsidy program nearly thirty years ago.

Another irony of the deregulated airline market is that while the airlines are free to charge fares determined by the basic principles of supply and demand, airports are prohibited from charging differential rates based on the relationship between supply of and demand for runway capacity. Airlines routinely charge passengers more for flights that depart at preferred times and provide discounts to fill flights operating on less congested schedules. Yet, airports are not allowed to do the same with their runways, even as over-scheduling of flights during peak hours lead to congestion and delays and increased costs that are ultimately passed to the consumer. Instead, the government attempts to both pressure and persuade the airlines into limiting their operations during peak times at congested airports.

The pros and cons of congestion pricing and other mechanisms for managing access more efficiently are too complex to discuss in detail here. It is worth noting, however, that even though this issue has receded into the background as a result of the industry's struggles, the problem did not completely disappear. It is also worth noting that the current system is simply a relic of an era in which the rules of federal funding for airports as well as the demands placed on those facilities made sense. The funding streams at large commercial service airports and the demands for access to those airports are such that the old system should be evaluated carefully and not held a sacrosanct.

As noted earlier, the United States signed and ratified the Chicago Convention in 1944 thus paving the way for an air transport regime dominated by bilateral agreements between states that agree to open their air transport markets in a limited, but reciprocal fashion. This regime created a framework for liberalization primarily within a bilateral framework. In this context, states are able to negotiate more liberal agreements on routes, frequencies, fares, and designation of airports and carriers that are mutually beneficial. In fact, significant progress has been made by the United States and other nations to liberalize their various bilateral agreements. These so-called open skies agreements are undoubtedly less restrictive than the Bermuda-style bilateral agreements, but there are important caveats that must be noted. Many of the renegotiated bilateral agreements legitimize agreements between carriers that may have adverse effects on competition if the markets were ever actually opened. Thus the impact of renegotiated bilateral agreements must be evaluated in the context of strategic alliances and the "code sharing" agreements that facilitate close coordination between potential competitors.

On the international level, the DOJ has the prerogative to review airline alliances. These usually involve code sharing arrangements wherein a carrier uses its partner's two-letter airline designator code for listing its own flights in computerized reservation systems. This typically occurs in tandem with agreements to coordinate check-in procedures, baggage handling, and gate arrangements. Occasionally, such an alliance would also involve stock investments between partner airlines. Even though antitrust review authority was transferred to the DOJ, the DOT still has the sole discretion to confer antitrust immunity to international code-share partners.

Ironically, numerous code sharing alliance agreements have been granted antitrust immunity in the name of liberalization. However, the need for such immunity is questionable if these arrangements are genuine steps towards liberalization. More perplexing perhaps is the fact that open skies agreements have garnered support in the United States inasmuch as they limit further liberalization. For example, U.S. law continues to prohibit foreign carriers from engaging in cabotage and limits foreign ownership of domestic carriers. U.S. cabotage rules forbid all but domestic carriers from carrying passengers between any two points within the country. By the same token, U.S. law prohibits foreign ownership of more than 25 percent of the voting stock in a domestic airline or more than 49 percent of the overall equity therein. Furthermore, the right of establishment of a U.S. airline is reserved exclusively for U.S. citizens and corporations (Hanlon 1999). This is again an artifact of a political and commercial environment that no longer exists. Restricting foreign capital and foreign operators from competing in the U.S. domestic market suggests that the nation is still reluctant to trust the market and reflects disbelief in the concept of open skies.

One of the oft-cited concerns about liberalizing the aviation market and relying on competition to marshal the industry is that if allowed to self-regulate, airlines would engage in "dangerous competition." The term is used and interpreted in a number of ways, but two of the interpretations are worth noting here. The first is that competition will necessarily lead to cost cutting and cost cutting will necessarily lead to problems with safety. The second interpretation, which has surfaced at various times since 1978, is that the airlines will engage in fare wars by which they will slowly, but surely destroy themselves or as Robert Crandall, the former head of American Airlines said, suffer death from a thousand cuts (Peterson and Glab 1994).

Even before the recent financial difficulties of the major carriers, concerns were raised about the safety of their low cost competitors. Despite a virtually flawless safety record by Southwest Airlines, a successful low-cost carrier, incumbent carriers began warning of impending disaster as early as the late 1980s, when low-cost carriers began to claim market share with their no-frills, point-to-point services. The celebrated case in point is the ValuJet crash in 1996. The fatal crash of the low-cost carrier's DC-9 into the Florida Everglades became fodder for the ensuing media frenzy over the safety of low-cost carriers and a *cause célèbre* for the traditional major airlines and critics of the FAA. Ironically, the crash was not the result of lax maintenance or unsafe operations by the airline. Rather the crash was determined to be the result of illegal activity by a maintenance contractor who decided to ship oxygen generators in the aircraft's cargo hold without properly securing and protecting the highly flammable devices.

In the end though, the ensuing investigation into ValuJet's corporate practices brought to light a basic conflict in the FAA's mission: its dual mandate to promote the industry and foster safe travel. Despite numerous and serious safety violations, ValuJet airline was allowed to continue operating until the fatal crash. The agency was accused of carelessly emphasizing its role as promoter over its role as regulator. In the aftermath, the FAA's mandate was officially changed and safety was declared to be its first priority.

In a similar case, the crash of TWA 800 in 1996 aroused a vigorous national debate about the risk of terrorism. One would reasonably expect such a crash to focus public and policy makers' attention on the financially ailing airlines, their maintenance practices, and their aging fleets. Even though the TWA crash was ultimately ruled to be accidental and related to design defects in the fuel delivery system of the aircraft and the fueling practices of the airline, it spurred the creation of the White House Commission on Aviation Safety and Security (Gore Commission), which emphasized the risk of terrorism to aviation. The commission was specifically charged with examining the state of aviation security and drawing measures to combat terrorism (White House Commission 1997).

Among other things, the commission called for increased funding to develop screening technologies. This led to the creation of computerized passenger screening programs, increased use of bag matching, and the implementation of other technologically advanced detection and imaging systems. The commission acknowledged that the implementation of such measures must be balanced against constitutionally protected individual rights. Even though the commission's recommendations were deemed valid and necessary, when it came to implementation, most of these recommendations were not followed. This is not surprising given that the industry was faced with the prospect of shouldering virtually all the costs associated with these recommendations. In addition, by the time the commission produced its rather costly and intrusive remedies, it had been established that the crash that provided the impetus for the commission's creation was not the result of terrorism. Of course, virtually all of the commission's recommendations were revisited more seriously in 2001 and many were rapidly implemented.

POST-SEPTEMBER 11

On September 10, 2001, terrorism and airline security were low priority issues for the industry and government alike. In addition, few industry observers were expressing concerns about the fact that the industry was facing a significant market correction after enjoying record profits in the later 1990s. Instead, the topics of the day were modernization of the Air Traffic Control (ATC) system, increasing airport capacity to reduce congestion and delays at the nation's busiest airports, and extending the regulatory standards imposed on the largest commercial service airports to airports with more limited scheduled service. Each of these issues represented significant, controversial, and costly regulatory and administrative changes with the FAA and the aviation industry.

It is an undeniable measure of the impact of the terrorist attacks of September 11 that these issues were not only put on hold, they were in many ways reshaped by policy decisions stemming from the attacks. In fact, for at least the first few years after the attacks, each and every policy initiative in aviation was discussed and debated against the backdrop of the nation's response to the terrorist attacks. The reaction to the attacks is interesting as it harkens back to other crises and critical junctures in the industry's development. With speed and energy that reflect the emotions of the time, the government moved quickly to protect the industry from financial distress and to implement broad ranging and far reaching security policies and regulations.

In response to the financial difficulties created by September 11, the Air Transportation Safety and System Stabilization Act was passed into law on September 22, 2001. The act authorized up to $10 billion in Federal loan guarantees for airlines and $5 billion in direct aid for losses sustained as a result of the attacks. The act also allocated $120 million to ensure that service to small communities was not interrupted. Interestingly, this policy made no effort to distinguish between successful and failing carriers. In fact, support was based on the airline industry's standard measure of capacity, available seat miles, so airlines were actually rewarded for having the most aircraft or seats flying prior to the attacks, even if those seats were empty.

The act further provided compensation to air carriers for insurance premium increases, expanded the government's ability to provide insurance and reinsurance directly and indirectly to airlines, and set a liability cap for terrorist acts (Air Transportation Safety and System Stabilization Act 2001). In order to provide restitution to the victims and their relatives, the ATSA further created the September 11th Victim Compensation Fund. This unprecedented measure gave victims the option of recovery from the government according to a predetermined formula. In exchange, the victims and their families waived all rights to further litigation, with the exception perhaps of the right to sue the terrorists themselves and terrorist organizations responsible for the attacks. By doing so, the government sought to protect the airlines from the staggering cost of litigation, while providing the large number of victims with prompt compensation. (Air Transportation Safety and Systems Stabilization Act 2001). These measures highlighted the need for new mechanisms to protect against such risks. The creation of the Victim Compensation Fund can be described as a *post facto* federal tort reform measure to sidestep the state-based common law liability regime

In the same vein, the Terrorism Risk Insurance Act of 2002 (TRIA) provided immediate insurance protection to businesses impacted by terrorist attacks. The act provides federal assistance to insurance companies for claims related to acts of terrorism. The TRIA was originally intended to make terrorism risk coverage available in the short term, and will expire in December, 2007 unless renewed. By sharing losses with the insurance industry, the government hoped to reduce the financial burden of terrorism coverage. The government aimed only to allow the market to adjust, eliminating the need for further intervention. Critics have argued, however, that the act served to create a dependency in this market, and has created unrealistic market expectations in the long run (Terrorism Risk Insurance Act 2002).

Another major reform initiative was the passage of the Aviation and Transportation Security Act in November of 2001. The act established the Transportation Security Administration (TSA). The TSA was originally organized within the U.S. Department of Transportation but was subsequently moved to the Department of Homeland Security (DHS) in 2003. The organization was charged with developing safety procedures and policies to ensure the safety of air traffic and other modes of transportation from the risk of terrorism. With the establishment of the TSA, the FAA was stripped of most of its regulatory powers relating to aviation security. The act was a small part of a larger overhaul under the pennant of homeland security. Once created, the DHS eventually became the parent organization of the Border Patrol, Coast Guard, Immigration Service, as well as the newly created Transportation Security Administration (Aviation & Transportation Security Act 2001).

The TSA's first responsibility was the federalization of airport baggage screeners. This function had been previously delegated to the FAA, which carried it out by contracting with private firms. Even though baggage screening currently accounts for most TSA activities, the agency's mandate is much broader, involving all sectors of transportation. While the TSA provides screening at most airports, the act contains an opt-out provision, allowing airports to revert to private screeners under certain conditions, beginning in November 2004. Currently, only five airports are using private screeners under the TSA's Screening Partnership Program. Studies comparing these airports to federalized facilities found no statistically significant differences in performance (Federal Human Resource 2004). The TSA currently employs over 40,000 people and provides security at over 500 airports across the United States.

Arguably the most controversial TSA activities is the use computerized profiling systems. Collectively, these systems use passengers' personal information, some of which is routinely collected by the airlines, such as name and address. This information is used to check against various lists, such as the TSA's no-fly list and the FBI most wanted list. Passengers are then assigned a terrorism risk score. High-risk travelers are subjected to additional screening, or even turned over to the authorities. The criteria used in assigning risk scores, as well as many other aspects of these programs are not publicly available (Sweet 2004). The program, originally known as CAPPS I, was further developed after September 11 as CAPPS II. CAPPS II raised serious civil rights concerns, due to both the potential for illegal profiling and discrimination and the inevitable impact of the system on passengers' privacy rights. Following public criticism and congressional concerns, CAPPS II was terminated, and the agency is currently developing a new version of the program known as Secure Flight. Under this new program, the TSA is attempting to achieve its security purpose without compromising passengers' rights (GAO 2004).

As passenger levels approach pre-September 11 levels, the TSA is contending with a new dilemma: ensuring safety without causing undue inconvenience, delay, and civil rights violations. This new dual mandate is reminiscent of the FAA's dilemma arising from the conflict inherent in promoting the industry and fostering safety. How the TSA will resolve the conflicts inherent in its mission remains to be seen. As the TSA is struggling to develop and grow, the organization has already come under attack from critics who argue that federalized screening should be abolished in favor of a market-driven model. The TSA has also come under attack after a series of widely publicized incidents, as well as pressure from civil rights advocates who question the prerogative of the organization and certain aspects of its operation such as passenger profiling and the use of no-fly lists.

Recovery from the impact of September 11 has been a slow and painful process for the airline industry. With the exception of a few low-cost carriers and some enterprising regional airlines, the industry has struggled to find firm financial footing. Arguably the initial impact of the terrorist attacks has dissipated as passengers have returned to the skies, but the traditional carriers have continued to struggle with high fuel costs and labor agreements that make competing with their low-cost counterparts difficult at best.

What then is the relationship between the government and the aviation industry? Interestingly, with the exception of the initial stabilization plan, the government has been careful not to be seen as propping up the industry or engaging in the re-regulation of commercial aspects of the airline business. Of course, we have not seen the wholesale disappearance of major carriers that has been predicted by some and may still be in the offing. Major carriers have moved into bankruptcy and in many ways are being treated by the government like firms in other industries. In the meantime, little has been done to remove the financial or regulatory burden placed on the industry in the wake of September 11. There are signs that some of the TSA's policies and procedures are being evaluated and may be changed in the future, but there seems to be little imperative to do anything in the name of financial expediency for the ailing carriers.

In the end, the rather awkward relationship between the federal government and the industry persists and the somewhat ambiguous commitment to market forces by policy is still in place. We may see things change dramatically if major carriers move from reorganization to liquidation, but it would not be a surprise to see the government move cautiously if the industry goes through another round of consolidation. Perhaps more important for the industry's future, the FAA has returned its full attention to the issues that occupied its agenda prior to September 11. The financial circumstances in the industry and overarching concerns about security will undoubtedly shape its strategies and resource commitment to ATC modernization and improving and increasing airport capacity, but progress will be made.

APPENDIX: SELECTED LEGISLATIVE ENACTMENTS

Act or Law with Implications or Provisions

Naval Appropriations Act (1915)
- The act established *the National Advisory Committee for Aeronautics* (NACA).
- NACA's stated purpose was to direct and conduct a scientific study of problems associated with flight, seeking practical solutions.
- NACA played an important role in the development of military aeronautics during the war as well as actively advocating federal control of civil aviation.
- Following WWI, NACA pushed for legislative action that would enable the Post Office to reestablish the airmail service, hoping to prove that aircraft were capable of safe and reliable commercial operations.

Contract Air Mail Act (Kelly Act) (1925)
- The act authorized a scheme of competitive bidding enabling private companies to acquire contracts for feeder and transcontinental airmail routes.
- The act signaled the beginning of a major federal legislative period occurring in the mid-1920s where the government assumed a much greater role in the sponsorship, funding, and regulation of commercial aviation.
- The act reflected the political belief of the time that private enterprise should provide postal delivery, not the government.
- The Kelly Act contained few provisions pertaining to safety and standardization of pilots, aircraft, and maintenance.

Air Commerce Act (1926)
- Under the Air Commerce Act, Congress charged the federal government with the following responsibilities:
  - Operation and maintenance of the airway system.
  - Construction and maintenance of air navigation aids.
  - Institution of a regulatory system to promote and ensure air commerce safety.
- The act specifically charged the federal government with the growth and development of aviation and advocated the creation of organizations to meet these goals.

McNary-Watres Act (1930)
- The act was enacted to stimulate the growth of commercial aviation by encouraging private industry to manufacture and operate of aircraft large enough to carry passengers.
- The act signaled a marked increase in the centralization of authority and power over commercial aviation within the federal government.
- The Postmaster General was given broad powers which some considered as dictatorial over the commercial aviation industry. Under the act, the Postmaster General possessed the authority to grant airmail contracts without competitive bidding, the ability to expand or consolidate airmail routes as deemed necessary, and the power to direct smaller airline's to merge as a stipulation for being able participate in airmail transport.
- The driving force behind this legislation was Postmaster General Walter Folger Brown, who proceeded to eliminate competitive bidding and use increased government subsidized airmail rate structures to reward only those companies deemed capable supporting the expansion of commercial aviation.

Air Mail Act of 1934 (1934)
- The passage of the act placed the airline industry under the control of three separate federal agencies. The post office controlled routes and operations, the ICC established rates and the Department of Commerce regulated aircraft configurations and safety. For the aviation industry this meant that in order to conduct business they would have to listen to and comply with three separate voices, often with overlapping authority and often contradicting each others directions.

- The act brought the Interstate Commerce Commission (ICC) into the administration of air law. Under the act the ICC determined compensation rates for each route.
- The ICC was given authority to terminate any contract extended beyond the initial period within 60 days of notification.
- The Postmaster General and the ICC were given oversight and regulatory authority over individual accounting practices of contracted airline companies.
- The Secretary of Commerce was given the authority to specify speed, load capacity, and safety equipment for use on airmail routes. In addition, the secretary had authority to fix and regulate work hours and compensation for private airline company's pilots and mechanics.
- A previous decision by the National Labor Board (Decision 83), limiting airline pilots to flying a maximum of 85 hours per month was imposed on airmail carriers.

The Civil Aeronautics Act of 1938 (McCarran- Lea Act) (1938)
- The act amended or repealed all existing and previous aviation legislation.
- The act's passage was in response to three factors:
    - It was the unique demand by private industry for federal intervention to control the "chaotic" economic conditions of American aviation, where destructive competition ravaging the aviation industry.
    - The act was in partial response to requests by the airline industry seeking relief from what the industry considered inefficient regulation and oversight by three overlapping federal agencies; the Bureau of Aviation, the Interstate Commerce Commission and the Post Office.
    - It was in response to the President Roosevelt's Committee on Administration Management Report, also known as the *Brownlow Report* seeking broader federal organizational reform and consolidation.
- The passage of the McCarran-Lea Act gave the federal government full economic and operation regulatory authority over the airline industry.
- The CAA was created as a as an independent and powerful, centralized federal agency, with complete legal authority to make rules and regulations that completely controlled all economic and operational aspects of aviation for air carriers.
- Under the Civil Aeronautics Act, the CAA's Administrator was specifically tasked with:
    - The encouragement of the civil aviation industry through the development of air commerce.
    - The expansion of the civil airway system and navigation facilities and the safety and regulation of air traffic operating in this system.
    - Airport development and maintenance with the intention of constructing a national system, although the Administrator was prohibited purchasing any airport facilities.
    - Conducting a survey of the nation's existing airports to present recommendations about future airport developments for the nation.

Civilian Pilot Training Act (CPTP) (1939)
- The act authorized the Civil Aeronautics Authority to construct a Civilian Pilot Training Program (CPTP) conducted by educational institutions for the training of students to obtain their instruction as private pilots.
- The act was enacted by the growing realization that the United States would eventually be drawn into the Europe conflict and aviation would inevitably play a vital role in the conflict.

Federal Airport Act (1946)
- The act established the *Federal-Aid Airport Program (FAAP)*, the first peacetime program of financial aid aimed exclusively at promoting development of the nation's civil airports.

International Aviation Facilities Act (1948)
- It authorized the CAA Administrator to improve air navigation facilities abroad and to train foreign nationals to operate such facilities whenever it benefited U.S. air carriers.
- The act gave the administrator responsibility for maintaining a record of deficiencies in aviation facilities used by U.S.-flag carriers and to plan appropriate programs for their correction. Public Law 463 (1948) The legislation authorized the Secretary of the Interior to acquire, construct, operate, and maintain public airports near national parks and monuments in cooperation with local

government agencies and with the assistance of CAA in accordance with the Federal Airport Act. Title XIII of the Civil Aeronautics Act (1951) The act authorized the Secretary of Commerce to provide war risk insurance to U.S. air carriers when such insurance could not be obtained commercially on reasonable terms and conditions.

- The program also included non-premium war risk insurance for aircraft under contract to the Departments of Defense and State, or committed to Defense for emergency use. Public Law 211 (1955) The law made major changes in the Federal-aid airport program and removing 1958 as the time limit prescribed by the original act, as amended in 1950.
- The changes established a four-year program which placed the total funding for fiscal 1956 at $62.5 million and provided $63 million for each of the fiscal years 1957–59.
- The law also made all types and sizes of airports eligible for aid, included development of airport buildings as eligible items, and provided that funds apportioned yearly to States under an area population formula would remain available for two years.

Airways Modernization Act (P.L. 85-133) (1957)

- The act established the Airways Modernization Board charged with the development and modernization of the national system of navigation and traffic control facilities to serve present and future needs of civil and military aviation.

Federal Aviation Act of 1958 (P.L. 85-726) (1958)

- The new statute repealed the Air Commerce Act of 1926, the Civil Aeronautics Act of 1938, the Airways Modernization Act of 1957, and those portions of the various Presidential reorganization plans dealing with civil aviation.
- The act assigned the functions exercised under these repealed laws, which had been dispersed within the Federal structure, to two independent agencies: the Federal Aviation Agency (FAA), which was created by the act, and the Civil Aeronautics Board (CAB), which was freed of its administrative ties with the Department of Commerce.
- The FAA came into existence with the signing of the Act, but assumed its functions in stages. It also took over the responsibilities and personnel of the Airways Modernization Board, which were transferred to it by Executive Order 10786.
- The FAA inherited as a nucleus the organization and functions of CAA on Dec 31, 1958. Later the Executive Order 10883 terminated the Air Coordinating Committee, transferring its functions to FAA.

Department of Transportation Act (P.L. 89-670) (1966)

- The act brought 31 previously scattered Federal elements, including the FAA, under the wing of one Cabinet Department.
- The purpose of the new department was to:
  - Assure the coordinated, effective administration of the transportation programs of the federal government.
  - Facilitate the development and improvement of coordinated transportation service, to be provided by private enterprise to the maximum extent feasible.
  - Encourage cooperation of federal, state, and local governments, carriers, labor, and other interested parties toward the achievement of national transportation objectives.
  - Stimulate technological advances in transportation.
  - Provide general leadership in the identification and solution of transportation problems.
  - Develop and recommend to the president and the Congress national transportation policies and programs to accomplish these objectives with full consideration of the needs of the public, users, carriers, industry, labor, and the national defense.
- The legislation provided for five initial major operating elements within the department. An administrator headed four of these organizations:
  - The Federal Aviation Administration (previously the independent Federal Aviation Agency).
  - The Federal Highway Administration.
  - The Federal Railroad Administration.
  - The Saint Lawrence Seaway Development Corporation.

- The new department also contained the U.S. Coast Guard, which was headed by a commandant and had previously been part of the Treasury Department.
- The DOT Act also created within the new department a five-member *National Transportation Safety Board (NTSB),* charged with:
  - Determining the cause or probable cause of transportation accidents and reporting the facts, conditions, and circumstances relating to such accidents.
  - Reviewing on appeal the suspension, amendment, modification, revocation, or denial of any certificate or license issued by the Secretary, or by an Administrator.
- In the exercise of its functions, powers, and duties, the board was made independent of the secretary and the other offices and officers of the department.
- Two important differences between President Johnson's proposal and the final DOT Act were:
  - The Maritime Administration was left out.
  - The actions of the FAA Administrator relating to safety, and the decisions of the NTSB, were designated "administratively final" with appeals only to the courts.

Veteran's Pension and Readjustment Act of 1967 (P.L. 90-77) (1967)
- The act authorized the Veterans Administration to reimburse eligible veterans for 90 percent of the cost of flight training necessary for a recognized vocational objective.
- The legislation specified that:
  - The eligible veteran must have a private pilot certificate (or have completed the required flight-training hours), with at least a second class medical certificate, and;
  - The flight school courses meet FAA standards and must be approved both by FAA and the appropriate State agency.

Federal Aviation Act of 1958 Amendment—Noise Abatement Regulation (P.L. 90-411) (1968)
- The act vested in the FAA Administrator the power, after consultation with the Secretary of Transportation, to:
  - Prescribe, and amend standards for the measurement of aircraft-engine noise and sonic boom.
  - Prescribe noise standards as criteria for aircraft certification.
  - Require the retrofit of existing aircraft with quieter engines or noise-abating devices.
  - Enforce operating procedures that reduce noise.
  - Ban overland supersonic flights of civil aircraft.

Airport and Airway Development Act (P.L. 91-258) (1970)
- Title I was the *Airport and Airway Development Act of 1970* and Title II was the *Airport and Airway Revenue Act of 1970.*
- The legislation responded to problems posed by civil aviation's extraordinary growth during the 1960s on which the number of aircraft handled by FAA's air route traffic control centers had increased by 110.6 percent, while aircraft operations at FAA's airport towers had increased by 112 percent. Airport and airway development programs, inadequately funded, had failed to keep pace with this growth in aviation activity, resulting in a severe strain on the air traffic control system.
- The new legislation assured a fund of about $11 billion over the next decade for airport and airway modernization by establishing *an Airport and Airway Trust Fund* modeled on the *Highway Trust Fund*; it freed airport and airway development from having to compete for General Treasury funds. Into the trust fund would go new revenues from aviation user taxes levied by the Airport and Airway Revenue Act, and other funds that Congress might choose to appropriate to meet authorized expenditures.
- Revenues would be raised by the following levies on aviation users in the following way:
  - An 8 percent tax on domestic passenger fares.
  - A $3 surcharge on passenger tickets for international flights originating in the United States.
  - A tax of 7¢ a gallon on both gasoline and jet fuel used by aircraft in noncommercial aviation.
  - A 5 percent tax on airfreight waybills.
  - An annual registration fee of $25 on all civil aircraft, plus:
    1. in the case of piston-powered aircraft weighing more than 2,500 pounds, 2¢ a pound for each pound of maximum certificated takeoff weight, or

    2. in the case of turbine powered aircraft, 3.5¢ a pound for each pound of maximum certificated takeoff weight.

- The principal advantages of the user-charge/trust-fund approach to revenue raising and funding were that it provided a predictable and increasing source of income, more commensurate with need; permitted more effective and longer range planning; and assured that the tax revenues generated by aviation would not be diverted to non-aviation uses.
- The major weaknesses of the Federal Airport Act, which was repealed by the new legislation, were the inadequate funding and the nature of the formula for distributing those resources.
- Under the new Airport Development Aid Program, by contrast, airport aid received a greatly increased annual authorization of $280 million for each of the next five fiscal years; also provided an improved distribution formula. Of the annual $280 million, $250 million in matching funds would be distributed in the following manner among airports serving air carriers certificated by CAB and airports serving general aviation primarily to relieve congestion at airports serving other segments of aviation:

  One-third as follows:
  1. 97 percent of this third among the several states, one-half in the ratio of each state's population to the total U.S. population, and one-half in the ratio of each state's area to the total area of all the states;
  2. 3 percent of this third among Hawaii, Puerto Rico, Guam, and the Virgin Islands, the first two places receiving 35 percent shares each, and the last two, 15 percent shares each.
  - One-third among airports serving CAB-certificated air carriers in the ratio of each such airport's passenger enplanements to the total number of passengers enplaned at all such airports.
  - One-third at the discretion of the Secretary of Transportation.
  - The remaining $30 million of the annual $280 million would be apportioned by the secretary as follows for developing in the several states and in Puerto Rico, Guam, and the Virgin Islands airports serving segments of aviation other than CAB-certificated air carriers:
    1. 73.5 percent among the several states, one-half of this in the ratio of each state's population to the total population of all the states, and one-half in the ratio of each state's area to the total area of all the states;
    2. 1.5 percent for Hawaii, Puerto Rico, Guam, and the Virgin Islands in shares of 35 percent, 35 percent, 15 percent, and 15 percent, respectively; and 25 percent at the discretion of the Secretary.
- In its provisions concerning planning, the new legislation reflected both lessons of experience and the emergence of certain new planning factors. Experience under the Federal Airport Act with the National Airport Plan (NAP), which covered a period of five years and was revised annually, led to the requirement in the new law for a National Airport System Plan (NASP) covering at least ten years and revised only as necessary.
- A significant feature of the new legislation was its provision for planning grants. The law authorized a total of $75 million for grants to planning agencies for airport system planning, and to public agencies for airport master planning; however, planning grants could not exceed $15 million in any one fiscal year; nor could any such grant exceed two-thirds of an airport project's cost.
- Another important provision of the bill gave FAA the responsibility for the safety certification of airports served by air carriers.

Independent Safety Board Act of 1974 (1974)

- The act tasked the NTSB with the investigation of:
  - All accidents involving 49 CFR parts 121 and 135 air carriers.
  - Accidents involving public (government aircraft).
  - Foreign aircraft accidents involving U.S. airlines and U.S. manufactured transport aircraft or major components.
  - Accidents involving air traffic control, training, mid-air collisions, newly certified aircraft/engines and in-flight fire or breakup.
  - General aviation accidents, some of which are delegated to the FAA for fact finding (probable-cause determinations are not delegated).

Transportation Safety Act of 1974(1975)
- Title I of this law gave the Secretary of Transportation new regulatory and enforcement authority to combat the risks of transporting hazardous materials in scheduled commerce services, specifically limited radioactive materials that could be shipped on commercial passenger aircraft to those intended for research or medical use.
- FAA prohibited air carriage of hazardous material unless its container had been inspected to determine that, in all outward respects, it complied with packaging and marking requirements. In the case of radioactive materials, FAA also required scanning with a radiation-monitoring instrument. The rule was based on a proposal published shortly after an incident on Apr 5–6, 1974, in which improperly shielded radioactive material had exposed airline passengers to unnecessary radiation.

Public Law 94-452 (1978)
- Established the *Offices of Inspector General* in the Department of Transportation (DOT) and several other departments and agencies. The independent offices were to conduct objective audits and investigations of programs and operations.

Airline Deregulation Act of 1978 (1978)
- Allowed immediate fare reductions of up to 70 percent without CAB approval.
- Allowed the automatic entry of new airlines into routes not protected by other air carriers.
- CAB's authority over fares, routes, and mergers was to be phased out entirely before 1983, and, unless Congress acted, CAB itself would shut down by Jan. 1, 1985.
- The prospective abolition of CAB brought to a culmination the work of Chairman Alfred E. Kahn at that agency. Moreover, by Oct 1978, the major emphasis of deregulation had changed from an ideological campaign against government regulation to a key element in the president's effort to curb inflation. This was highlighted by the president's appointment of Kahn as head of his anti-inflation program, which was announced on this date.
- Smaller communities, from which the airlines might wish to shift their operations, were guaranteed essential air services for ten years under the act, with a government subsidy if necessary. Along with the subsidies for smaller-city service, the act provided for the inclusion of commuter airlines in the FAA equipment loan guarantee program and in uniform methods for establishing joint fares between air carriers. It also authorized the use of larger aircraft by commuter airlines. These special provisions for commuter airlines boosted their already-booming growth rates, and led to important new FAA regulations later in 1978.
- The Airline Deregulation Act also revived the aircraft loan guaranty program, raising the total amount that could be guaranteed for any eligible participant from $30 million to $100 million, expanding the eligible participants to include charter air carriers, commuter air carriers, intrastate air carriers, and extending the term of eligible loans to 15 years. Congress withdrew authority for the program in 1983, however, FAA ceased issuing new loan guarantees after June 30 of that year. Over its life, the program had guaranteed 106 loans totaling $900 million. Twelve airlines had defaulted on 23 of the loans for a loss of $182 million, but FAA had been able to recover $132 million.

International Air Transportation Competition Act of 1979 (1980)
- Reduced the Civil Aeronautics Board's power to regulate U.S. international airlines, while authorizing the Board to retaliate against the airlines of nations that discriminated against U.S. carriers.
- Revised the rules governing Federal use of foreign air carriers.
- Defined circumstances under which foreign-registered aircraft might operate on U.S. domestic routes.

Tax Equity and Fiscal Responsibility Act (P.L. 97-248) (1982)
- The act increased the aviation user taxes in the following way:
  - Raising the airline passenger ticket tax from 5 to 8 percent.
  - Increasing the general aviation gasoline tax from 4 to 12 cents per gallon.
  - Levying a jet fuel tax of 14 cents per gallon.

- Re-imposing the 5 percent for air cargo tax and $3 as international departure fee.
- These taxes were earmarked as renewed funding for the *Airport and Airway Trust Fund*, which had received no tax revenues since Sept. 30, 1980.

Airport and Airway Improvement Act (1982)

- The act stipulated formulas for apportioning airport development funds between primary, commuter, reliever, and general aviation airports, including a guarantee that reliever airports receive at least 10 percent of available funds.
- Also authorized FAA to use a total of 6.327 billion from the *Airport and Airway Trust Fund* for airway facilities and equipment over the six years beginning with fiscal 1982; this funding helped to finance the planned modernization of the *National Airspace System* (NAS).

Airport and Airway Safety and Capacity Expansion Act (1987)

- The act extended the authority for the *Airport Improvement Program* (AIP) for an additional five years. The legislation authorized $1.7 billion each fiscal year through 1990 and $1.8 billion each year for fiscal years 1991 and 1992.
- Other provisions of the act included:
  - Authorization for a *State Block Grant Pilot Program.*
  - A requirement that ten percent of the funds available under AIP be expended with *the Disadvantaged Business Enterprise Program.*
  - A redefinition of primary airports to include all airports emplaning more than 10,000 passengers annually.
  - Expenditures for soundproofing public schools and hospitals without a noise compatibility study.
  - Establishment of a discretionary fund set-aside for projects to enhance system wide capacity, safety, security, and noise compatibility.

Omnibus Budget Reconciliation Act of 1990 (1990)

- Authorized funding for FAA and other Federal entities for FY91-92. Title IX of that legislation included as subparts three acts pertaining to aviation:
- The *Aviation Safety and Capacity Expansion Act* included permission for FAA to draw on the Trust Fund for up to 75 percent of its operations and maintenance costs and authorized $5.5 billion for modernization of air traffic Facilities & Equipment over the two years. It also empowered the Department of Transportation to authorize airports to levy Passenger Facility Charges of up to $3 per enplaning passenger. Other features of the law provided: encouragement of capacity development at former and current military airports, continuation of the Essential Air Service program, and development of a system of Auxiliary Flight Service Stations, and more flexibility for FAA in procurement contracts.
- The *Federal Aviation Administration Research, Engineering and Development Authorization Act* further defined FAA's research functions. It included a mandate for the establishment of a Catastrophic Failure Prevention Program to develop technologies to combat the failure of parts and equipment that could result in aircraft accidents.
- The *Airport Noise and Capacity Act* required airlines by mid-1999 to phase out Stage 2 noise-level jets, although those carriers that met this deadline for 85 percent of their fleet might apply to operate their remaining Stage 2 aircraft until the end of 2003. The law also directed the Secretary of Transportation to prepare a national noise policy by mid-1991, and placed limitations were upon airports' authority to impose noise restrictions.

Aging Aircraft Safety Act (1991)

- Required FAA to undertake rulemaking requiring certain airworthiness reviews and inspections for airliners in service more than 15 years.
- The act also directed FAA to established programs to insure that U.S. air carriers properly maintained their older aircraft and to encourage foreign airlines to do the same.
- Although the legislation did not specifically address commuter aircraft, FAA extended its aging aircraft program to that sector.

Intermodal Surface Transportation Efficiency Act (1991)
- Designed to help develop Intermodal travel through a range of actions, one of which was improving access to the country's airports.
- On May 11, 1992, the Department of Transportation (DOT) invited the 50 states to submit proposals for development of Intermodal transportation plans, including aviation as well as surface modes.

Airport Improvement Program Temporary Extension Act of 1994 (P.L. 103-260) (1994)
- The act renewed FAA's authority to award *Airport Improvement Program* grants through June 30, 1994.
- The law provided for the gradual phasing out of compensation that certain FAA employees had received under the *Pay Demonstration Project* after that project's termination on June 17, 1994.

General Aviation Revitalization Act of 1994 (1994)
- Under this law, manufacturers could not be liable for accidents happening more than 18 years after the production of general aviation aircraft, engines, or parts.
- The legislation was followed by an upturn for this sector of the industry.

Wendell H. Ford Aviation Investment and Reform Act (P.L. 106-181) (2000)
- The act, known as *AIR-21*, provided a significant increase for the agency's (FAA) two capital accounts, *Facilities and Equipment* and the *Airport Improvement Program*.
- Both accounts were covered by stipulations aimed at guaranteeing spending levels, provisions that did not apply to FAA's Operations account.

Air Transportation and System Stabilization Act (P.L. 107-42) (2001)
- Restricted liability limits and awards against air carriers as a result of Sept. 11 terrorist attacks.
- Provided immediate fiscal and tax relief for airlines as well as limiting potential civil liability resulting form the use of their aircraft in the attacks.

Aviation and Transportation Security Act (P.L. 107-71) (2001)
- Established the *Transportation Security Administration* (TSA) tasked with the responsibility for security in all modes of transportation for the U.S.
- The TSA was given the authority to hire, as federal employees, thousands of workers to replace private airport passenger and baggage screeners.

Terrorism Insurance Act (2002)
- The act provided insurance protection to businesses impacted by terrorist attacks.

REFERENCES

Aviation and Transportation Security Act, 49 U.S.C. (2001).

Baloug, B., Grisinger, J., & Zelikow, P. (2002) *Making democracy work: A brief history of twentieth century federal Executive reorganization.* Charlottesville, VA: Mill Center of Public Affairs. Retrieved from http://milercenter.virginia.edu.

Bednarek, J. (2001). *America's airports: Airfield development, 1918–1947.* College Station, TX: Texas A&M University Press.

Bill, G. (2002). *Aviation: The first 100 years.* Hauppauge, NY: Barron's Educational Series.

Clayton Act, 15 U.S.C. §§ 12 et seq. (1914).

Davies, R.E.G. (1972). *Airlines of the United States since 1914.* London: Putnam.

Dempsey, P., & Goetz, A. (1992). *Airline deregulation and laissez-faire mythology.* New York: Quorum Books.

Eichenberger, J. A. (1997). *General aviation law.* New York: McGraw-Hill.

Federal Human Resources Week (2004). No differences found in performance of federal and private screeners. *Federal Human Resources Week* vol. 11, no. 5.

Frederick, J. H. (1946). *Commercial air transportation,* rev. ed. Homewood, IL: Richard. D. Irwin.

Gordon, A. (2004) *Naked airport: A cultural history of the world's most revolutionary structure.* New York: Metropolitan Books, Henry Holt.

Groenewege, A. D. (2003). *The compendium of international civil aviation,* 3rd ed. Canada: International Aviation Development Corporation (IADC).

Hanlon, P. (1999). *Global airlines: Competition in a transnational industry,* 2nd ed. Oxford, UK: Butterworth Heinemann.

Heppenheimer, T. A. (1995). *Turbulent skies: The history of commercial aviation.* New York: John Wiley.

Kane, R. M. (1999). *Air transportation,* 13th ed. Dubuque, IA: Kendall/Hunt Publishing.

Komons, N. A. (1989). *Bonfires to beacons: Federal civil aviation policy, under the Air Commerce Act, 1926–1938.* Washington, D.C.: Smithsonian Institution Press.

Lewis, D. (2000). *Airline executives and federal regulation: Case studies in American enterprise from the airmail era to the dawn of the jet age.* Columbus: Ohio State University Press.

Morrison, S.A. & Winston, C. (1995). *The evolution of the airline industry.* Washington D.C.: The Brookings Institution.

NTSB—United States Air Carrier Operations (2000). *Annual review of aircraft accident data.* NTSB/ARC-04/01 PB2004-106609, Notation 7502A. National Transportation Safety Board, Washington, D.C.

Peterson, B. S. & Glab, J. (1994). *Rapid descent: Deregulation and the shakeout in the airlines.* New York: Simon & Schuster.

Preston, E. (1998). *FAA Historical chronology: Civil aviation and the federal government 1926–1996.* Washington, D.C.: U.S. Department of Transportation.

Richmond, S. B. (1961). *Regulation and competition in air transportation.* New York: Columbia University Press.

Rochester, S. (1976). *Takeoff at mid-century: Federal civil aviation policy in the Eisenhower years 1953–1961.* Washington, D.C.: U.S. Department of Transportation, Federal Aviation Administration.

Sherman Act, 15 U.S.C. §§ 1 et seq. (1890).

19 Transportation and Energy: Policy Dilemmas for the Twenty-First Century

Mary M. Timney

Transportation policy is energy policy although the two are developed separately. Twenty seven percent of all energy used in the United States annually is consumed by the transportation sector. The mix of highways vs. rail and private transport vs. mass transit has a direct impact on energy consumption and policy. Transportation is also a major source of air pollution; policies to reduce smog and other pollutants also have an impact on transportation policy and energy policy.

Energy policy deals largely with supply and demand of fuels, including incentives to energy industries to increase production as well as to energy consumers to reduce demand through efficiency or conservation. Transportation policy deals principally with developing transportation infrastructure—highways, mass transit systems, rail, and water. Air transport is not generally included with ground transportation policy although airport siting also drives demand for highway access.

The transportation sector uses the following energy sources: petroleum, renewable energy (ethanol), natural gas, and electricity. Petroleum is the major energy source used in transportation, for automobiles, freight trucks, freight rail, air transportation, and buses. Transportation uses sixty-six percent of petroleum end products, the equivalent of 13.62 million barrels per day in 2004 (Annual Energy Review 2004, p. 132). More than 60 percent of the U.S. crude oil supply is imported (Annual Energy Outlook 2005, p. 157); consequently, transportation and energy are also linked to foreign policy. Non-OPEC countries supply about 60 percent of the U.S. market, the largest amounts coming from Canada (2.1 million barrels per day) and Mexico (1.6 million barrels per day) (Annual Energy Review 2004, p. 132). Of OPEC countries, Venezuela and Saudi Arabia each provide about 1.5 million barrels per day (ibid.). Domestic production of petroleum was about 5.7 million barrels per day in 2003 (Annual Energy Outlook 2005, p. 157). Figure 19.1 shows the amounts of crude oil imported into the United States per day in 2004 by country.

The future availability of petroleum to fuel the U.S. transportation system will be constrained by exploding demand in the emerging economies in China, India, South Korea, and other Asian nations. The U.S. Department of Energy forecasts that U.S. transportation energy demand will "grow from 26.9 quadrillion Btu in 2002 to 34.2 quadrillion Btu in 2015 and 39.4 quadrillion Btu in 2025" (International Energy Outlook 2005, p. 22). In the emerging economies, "transportation sector energy consumption

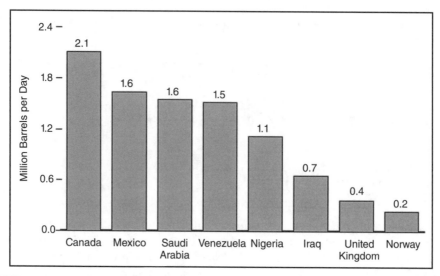

FIGURE 19.1   Selected countries, 2004. Source: Energy Information Administration/Annual Energy Review 2004, p. 132.

is projected to grow by 3.6 percent per year, from 26.2 quadrillion Btu in 2002 to 46.1 quadrillion Btu in 2015 and 58.9 quadrillion Btu in 2025" (ibid, p. 23). China alone is expected to see growth of an average of 6.0 percent per year (ibid). Thus, by 2025, the new economies will require 48 percent more energy for transportation than will the United States.

The interconnection of these policy areas requires a complex approach to energy policy, transportation planning, and development. Complicating it further is the importance of the automobile industry to the U.S. economy and the growing demand, since the early 1990s, for large SUVs that have relatively low fuel efficiencies. The continuing growth in demand for petroleum in the United States that these vehicles represent coupled with the increasing demand in emerging economies will put pressure on supplies and force prices up worldwide. U.S. transportation has traditionally been based on the assumption of low energy costs. Rising costs and diminishing supplies will require a rethinking of both energy policy and transportation policy in the United States.

This chapter examines the policy issues related to transportation in the United States. It provides an overview of transportation and energy policy in the twentieth century and their relationship with other policy areas, especially air pollution, regional development, and foreign policy. Current policy issues will then be identified and analyzed in a comprehensive way to develop a set of factors that public managers can use to address transportation needs for the future. Transportation provisions of the 2005 Energy Policy Act and other legislation sponsored by the Bush administration will be examined. Future concerns and proposals for innovations in transportation are offered in the conclusion of the chapter.

U.S. ENERGY POLICY, 1900–1980

Until the mid-1970s, the federal government did not have an official energy policy. In the early years of the twentieth century, oil was seen as a limited resource and efforts were made in World War I to husband then-existing supplies to ensure that ships, military vehicles and planes would have sufficient fuel reserves for the duration of the war. The Texas fields were the principal domestic source of oil at the time. The automobile industry was in its infancy and commercial air traffic had not yet developed. After the war, domestic supplies of oil began to decline, but imports from the Middle East soon became available. Later discoveries in Venezuela and Oklahoma ensured that U.S. oil consumption could grow, encouraging the development of the modern automobile industry, cross-country trucking, and commercial air transportation.

The large oil fields in the Middle East grew in importance as the U.S. appetite for petroleum expanded. U.S. oil companies formed a partnership with the Saudi Arabian government and established Aramco, the Arab-American Company, to develop those fields for export. A policy to encourage the companies, and indirectly to subsidize the Saudis, was developed between the State Department and the Treasury Department in the early 1950s. Known as the "Golden Gimmick," U.S. companies were allowed to credit taxes on profits earned from oil pumped in Saudi Arabia and pay them instead to the Saudi government, enriching the Saudi economy and developing an important ally in the region (Timney 2004, p. 18).

Imported Middle Eastern oil was cheaper than domestically produced oil in Oklahoma and Texas. To protect this powerful industry, price floors were established to make imported oil more expensive; domestic oil producers also received generous oil depletion allowances through the tax system. The U.S. government, in effect, subsidized the oil industry through tax policy (Ibid.). Domestic oil production began to diminish in the 1960s and imported oil began to comprise a larger share of U.S. crude supply. By 1975, imported oil provided 42 percent of U.S. crude oil stocks, 59.5 percent of which came from OPEC countries (Energy Information Administration, Annual Energy Review 2004, p. 133).

Post-World War II development in the United States—both economic and suburban—was directly tied to the availability of cheap energy, principally oil and natural gas. The expansion of urban areas to distant suburbs was made possible by the development of the Interstate Highway System. The resulting sprawl was too widespread for cost-effective mass transportation systems so automobile use increased and the two-car suburban family became the norm. Massive traffic jams became common in large cities which led transportation planners to design more and bigger highways. In the early 1950s, photochemical smog became a serious health problem, especially in Los Angeles. By the 1960s, research established that smog was formed by the interaction of sunlight with automobile exhaust.

In 1973, the Organization of Petroleum Exporting Countries (OPEC), dramatically raised oil prices on the world market. The cartel had been formed in the 1960s and included Nigeria and Venezuela as well as Middle Eastern producers, the countries with the largest known oil reserves in the world. The Iranian government also placed an embargo on exports to the United States and overnight the price of gasoline in the nation doubled—from 35 cents to 70 cents a gallon. Prices of all other energy sources increased dramatically, including heating fuel and electricity. This energy crisis provided the impetus for U.S. policy makers to develop the first national energy policy.

The impact of price increases fell heavily on the transportation industry, raising the costs of driving an automobile and everything shipped by truck or rail across the country. The U.S. economy had developed with a dependency on cheap energy prices so the inflationary impact of major price increases was felt across all sectors. Inflation rose to double digits in the mid-1970s, much of it the result of higher energy prices.

Another policy that had an impact on gasoline consumption at the time was the Clean Air Act. Enacted in 1970, the CAA required reductions of automobile emissions to curb smog and other pollutants in the nation's major cities. Most of the automobiles produced in the U.S. at the time had fuel consumption of less than 15 miles per gallon. Pollution controls added to cars after 1970 further reduced fuel efficiencies. The catalytic converter was approved in 1975 by the U.S. EPA for installation on all new vehicles not only because it reduced emissions but also because it had a lower fuel efficiency penalty than other technologies.

The Nixon and Ford administrations reacted to the 1973 energy crisis by establishing the Federal Energy Administration and developing energy conservation programs. The policy emphasis then and throughout the Carter administration was on conservation and improving efficiency. It was generally agreed across political affiliations that the amount of energy wasted in the United States should be recovered as a first policy step. A second goal was to break away from dependence on foreign sources of oil, especially in the Persian Gulf. President Gerald Ford appointed a task force chaired by Vice President Nelson Rockefeller to develop a plan for energy independence. The plan, which was never implemented because Ford did not win election in 1976, emphasized utilizing coal as a primary energy source and advocated research and development of coal gasification and liquefaction as a partial replacement for petroleum products. The United States has huge coal deposits that are the equivalent of oil reserves in the Middle East.

Energy experts at the time also focused on the low fuel economies of American automobiles. The U.S. automobile industry, which had the lion's share of the market at the time, steadfastly refused to build energy efficient products. The Carter administration developed a comprehensive energy policy as one of its earliest achievements and proposed Corporate Average Fleet Economy (CAFE) standards to improve average miles per gallon of passenger vehicles driven. These standards did not apply to light trucks which, at the time, were generally used by blue-collar workers and farmers. U.S. automakers had to scramble to design, produce, and market enough vehicles to achieve the necessary mix required to meet the average.

Foreign automakers—German, Swedish, and especially Japanese—took advantage of the weakness of Detroit's product lines and expanded exports of fuel efficient, well-made automobiles to the U.S. market. American consumers, seeking to reduce their out-of-pocket costs for gasoline, increasingly bought imported cars, especially after the second oil crisis in 1978 doubled gasoline prices once more. The market shares of Toyota, Honda, Nissan, and Volkswagen rose while those of General Motors, Ford, and Chrysler fell sharply.

American automakers did not regain some of that market share until the early 1990s when they brought out sport utility vehicles (SUVs). Because SUVs are built on a light-truck base, they are not subject to CAFE standards and, generally, have low average fuel economies, some below twenty miles per gallon. The popularity of these vehicles grew to the point that they accounted for about 50 percent of new vehicle sales in the early 2000s. In the fall of 2005, with gasoline prices hovering around $3 per gallon, sales of SUVs fell off and gasoline-electric hybrid vehicles, including SUVs, began to gain market share. Most of these vehicles are built by Japanese companies. Once again Detroit clung to a business model dependent upon the availability of relatively cheap energy, despite the growing evidence that those days are over.

By the end of the 1970s, a comprehensive energy policy was in place that provided tax benefits for conservation and solar energy products, funded research for coal conversion, and established efficiency standards for buildings, appliances, and automobiles. Oil and natural gas deregulation were being phased in to allow prices to be determined by the market. There was a national consensus among the states and the federal government that conservation and energy efficiency should be the base on which energy policy should be developed.

ENERGY POLICY SINCE 1980

When Ronald Reagan was elected this consensus was overturned. Declaring that the market should be trusted to provide affordable energy and energy alternatives, Reagan eliminated the energy programs and conservation tax incentives that had been put in place during the Carter administration. The bottom fell out of oil prices on the world market, partly as a result of the conservation efforts of the 1970s and the decline of OPEC's market power. Oil prices on the world market fell to below the 1978 crisis levels and Americans could once again fuel up for 75 cents a gallon. In 1991, the Persian Gulf War threatened a return of higher prices, but by the early 2000s, U.S. gasoline prices were still below $1.50 a gallon, about what they had been in 1982. Adjusted for inflation, gasoline prices were at or below the 1973 level of 35 cents per gallon.

The return of cheap energy, relative to income, also brought resurgence in housing construction and suburban development, necessitating more highway construction. Throughout the 1980s, there was no action on energy policy or air pollution policy at the national level because of political gridlock in Congress and between Congress and the White House. The Department of Energy, which Reagan had promised to dismantle during the 1980 campaign, was instead refocused on nuclear weapons as part of the administration's military buildup. States, however, continued to develop energy policies to protect the interests of their residents and to manage their own energy costs. Midwestern states began to lobby for the use of ethanol as automobile fuel, initially to reduce smog components.

In 1990, Congress and President G. H. W. Bush agreed on amendments to the Clean Air Act that required the use of ethanol or other additives and, for the first time, integrated transportation planning with achievement of ambient air standards. Regions defined as non-attainment areas—that is areas where the national ambient air quality standards had not been met—were required to "act within a set time frame to reduce emissions...(or face) sanctions, including the loss of federal-aid highway funds" (Weingroff, p. 12).

A major transportation policy was enacted in the Bush administration, the Intermodal Surface Transportation Act of 1991, better known as ISTEA (pronounced Ice Tea). This legislation developed out of several attempts by Senator Daniel Moynihan and the Senate Public Works Committee to establish an objective for "federal support for transportation (that) promotes clear national mandates for environmental quality, a strong economy, energy and resource conservation, and enhances the quality of life in neighborhoods and communities" (Weingroff, p. 17). Among ISTEA's many provisions were the following:

- Completion of the Interstate Highway System with the Central Artery/Tunnel project in Boston (the so-called Big Dig).
- Authorization of federal dollars for the Interstate Maintenance Program. Projects could be funded only if they did not add capacity, except for High Occupancy Vehicle lanes.
- Surface Transportation Program that provided flexible funds that could be used for a range of highway or transit projects
- Funding for transit programs
- Congestion pricing: a pilot program to test methods to increase the cost of driving as a way of convincing motorists to carpool or use mass transit.
- Funding for development of Intelligent Vehicle/Highway Systems (Weingroff, p. 47–48).

This act served as the transportation energy policy of the 1990s. The only transportation related energy policy that the Clinton administration sponsored was a 4.5 cents per gallon increase in the federal gasoline tax, with the monies dedicated to deficit reduction. This was not a large enough amount to encourage conservation, especially since the world market price of oil fell at about the same time that the tax was implemented. Oil consumption rose from about 15 million barrels per day in 1995 to over 18 million barrels per day in 2004, 70 percent of which is imported (see Table19.1).

Energy policy became a political issue again in 2001 when the state of California was faced with skyrocketing prices for electricity after implementing deregulation. President George W. Bush appointed a task force, headed by Vice President Dick Cheney, to develop a comprehensive energy policy for the nation. Both the president and vice president had worked in the oil industry and had many supporters from oil and other energy interests. The task force report was released in May 2001 and generated considerable controversy, both for its recommendations and for the way it was developed. The vice president refused to release the names of nongovernmental sources consulted during the task force proceedings. The General Accounting Office (GAO)[1] brought suit to force the release of the names. The Supreme Court ruled in 2004 in

---

1. GAO has since been renamed the Government Accountability Office.

TABLE 19.1
Petroleum Overview, Selected Years, 1950–2004

Year	48 States	Alaska	Total	Imports	Total	%Imports	%Total Growth	%Imports Growth
1950	5,407	0	5,407	850	6,857	13.6	—	—
1955	6,807	0	6,807	1,248	8,055	15.5	28.7	46.7
1960	7,034	2	7,036	1,815	8,851	20.5	9.9	45.4
1965	7,774	30	7,804	2,468	10,272	24.1	16.1	35.9
1970	9,408	229	9,637	3,419	13,056	26.2	27.1	38.5
1975	8,185	191	8,374	6,056	14,430	41.9	10.5	77.1
1980	6,980	1617	8,597	6,909	15,506	44.6	7.5	14.0
1985	7,146	1825	8,971	5,067	14,038	36.1	–10.5	–36.4
1990	5,582	1773	7,355	8,018	15,373	52.2	9.5	58.2
1995	5,076	1484	6,560	8,835	15,395	57.4	>1	10.2
2000	4,851	970	5,822	11,459	17,280	66.3	12.2	29.7
2004	4,522	908	5,430	12,899	18,329	70.4	6.1	12.6

(Thousand barrels per day)
Source: Energy Information Administration/Annual Energy Review 2004, p. 127.

favor of the administration, which had argued that executive confidentiality applied to the task force's business.

The group's recommendations emphasized the importance of increasing energy supplies, especially electricity generating capacity. The few recommendations for transportation included a modest proposal for increasing CAFE standards to "increase efficiency without negatively impacting the U.S. automotive industry" and instructed the Secretary of Transportation to "Look at other market-based approaches for increasing the national average fuel economy of new motor vehicles"(National Energy Policy 2001, Appendix One). Other recommendations included promoting congestion mitigation technologies and strategies, establishing a tax credit for fuel-efficient vehicles, and continuing to develop technologies for Intelligent Transportation Systems, fuel-cell-powered buses, and the Clean Buses program to get new bus technologies into general use across the nation. The report was controversial also because it recommended opening the Arctic National Wildlife Refuge (ANWR) for oil drilling.

Four years later, the Energy Policy Act of 2005 was signed into law on August 8. The act included only a few transportation-related provisions: tax credits up to $3,400 for purchase of hybrid vehicles; a requirement to triple the amount of biofuel (primarily ethanol) as a component of motor fuel by 2012; and authorization for research on hydrogen vehicles and the Freedom Car initiative, which would use fuel cells. Not included in the bill were the following: improved CAFE standards to cover SUVs, limited liability for MTBE producers,[2] and support for research on non-greenhouse gas-emitting energy sources that would meet Kyoto Protocol goals.

The 2005 energy policy reflects the administration's ties to the energy industries, as both the president and vice-president previously worked in oil companies. The legislation is premised on the assumption that growing energy demand is good for the country and that government policy should provide incentives to promote development of energy resources. Thus, the legislation included subsidies to the oil industry to develop new oil sources, but only modest support for reducing demand. During the summer of 2005, however, the price of oil on the world market reached record highs causing the price of gasoline in the United States to rise steadily above $2 per gallon. By September and October, after two major hurricanes devastated drilling platforms and refineries in the Gulf of Mexico, gasoline prices rose above $3 per gallon across the country. Sales of SUVs declined in September, potentially causing great dislocation in the American auto industry since these companies had not produced hybrid vehicles for the market.

The Bush administration belatedly developed a conservation promotion program to help cushion price shocks that Americans were already feeling from higher gasoline prices. The worst impact was forecast to be significant increases in the price of heating fuel and natural gas; Americans were once again encouraged to weather-strip their homes.

FUTURE CONCERNS FOR ENERGY POLICY AND TRANSPORTATION

The future of energy policy and transportation rests on a rediscovery by policy makers of the complicated policy arena of energy, transportation planning, and air quality control. Policy in each of these areas tends still to be developed in isolation of the others. Except for ISTEA, transportation policy has not recognized the importance of air pollution and energy policy. There has been no true national consensus on energy policy since the late 1970s.

Future energy policy will eventually have to focus on reducing demand, simply because of the high cost of oil linked to growing demand from the developing economies in Asia. Prices will inevitably rise as more and more people demand a share of shrinking resources. While the market will adapt and provide more fuel-efficient vehicles, it is limited in its ability to respond comprehensively. Only government can design comprehensive policies with both incentives and restrictions to achieve considered policy goals.

The link to global warming will also be a prime factor in future policy considerations. Transportation burns fossil fuels and their emissions contribute greenhouse gases to the atmosphere. The evidence of climate warming is growing steadily, as can

---

2. MTBE was added to gasoline in the 1990s as a provision of the Clean Air Act. It reduced pollution-causing emissions but was subsequently found to contaminate ground water. Its use was prohibited in 2000.

be seen, for example, in the expansion of open water near the Arctic Circle each summer, caused by melting of the polar ice cap.

Major advances in the complex of policy—energy, air pollution, and sustainability—are likely to come at the state and local level first. States now have the expertise to design energy policies that meet the specific needs of their own localities. With the completion of the Interstate Highway System, transportation policy can best be developed at the state and local level.

Public managers will need to design transportation policy that incorporates three elements: energy efficiency, clean air and water, and convenience. Many local and state governments are developing projects that capitalize on these elements. Communities in northern California along the Bay Area Rapid Transit system (BART) are developing transit villages that include housing, shops, and restaurants within walking distance of the stations to reduce the necessity for automobile use. Differential tolls on highways, bridges, and tunnels during rush hours provide an incentive for commuters to use mass transit instead of their cars, thereby reducing congestion and air pollution.

Regional plans can focus on promoting sustainable transportation. The Canadian Institute of Transportation Engineers defines the concept as promoting "a balance of the economic and social benefits of transportation with the need to protect the environment" (Chartier and Hollingworth 2004). It proposes site designs that promote walking, cycling, and transit through pedestrian friendly development that reduce dependence on the automobile. In Britain, major businesses are developing "green travel plans" to reduce congestion and transportation-related carbon emissions. Such plans include public transportation information, shuttle buses to railway stations, commuter centers, cycle parking with showers and changing rooms (Morris 2004).

One of the most ambitious and potentially far-reaching projects is the Cooperative Vehicle-Highway Automation Systems (CVHAS), an 11-state consortium that with Honda R & D is developing case studies for automated freight and public transport systems (Bishop 2001). The current membership includes the states of Arizona, California, Florida, Georgia, Illinois, Maryland, Minnesota, Missouri, New York, Utah, and Washington; the Federal Highway Administration; and Honda (www.cvhas.org). It is funded through pooled federal funds and has funded projects to improve safety and traffic flow through automation. CVHAS was funded through FY 2003, but three projects were still active in Fall 2006. Some funding is being used to develop a common encroachment permit for Vehicle Infrastructure Integration (VII) that can be used at any level of government to install VII equipment on their right-of-way (Siddiqui 2006).

The key to managing energy and transportation policy in the twenty-first century will be a coordinated effort to provide Americans with alternatives to the typical automobile-dependent lifestyle. Automated systems and so-called smart highways hold the greatest promise for accommodating individual vehicle use at lower energy consumption and highway congestion with greater safety. Such systems, models of which are in use in Europe and Japan, can electronically link trucks, buses and cars to move them efficiently while freeing drivers from the stress of stop-and-go traffic during rush hours. These systems can also improve the performance of public transit systems and provide real alternatives for commuters to lessen dependence on individual vehicles.

THE FUTURE OF ENERGY POLICY AND TRANSPORTATION

Although the Bush administration and current Congress are committed to continuing the growth of energy use in transportation, one can question the long-term feasibility of this policy. The economic costs of increased international competition for limited petroleum resources must ultimately raise the price of gasoline and other transportation fuels to a level that will foster demand for alternative modes. As the century ages, the effects of global warming will become more measurable and will challenge international efforts to develop comprehensive and fair agreements to slow or mitigate these effects. Since burning fossil fuels is a major contributor to greenhouse gases, limits on automotive use are inevitable at some point in the next hundred years.

There are many potential solutions that have already been initiated in Europe, Japan, and United States. Continued development of intelligent transportation systems along with rising fuel prices and global warming will eventually stimulate the U.S. government to support policies, both at home and internationally, that promote efficient energy use in transportation with significant reductions in air pollution.

REFERENCES

Bishop, R. Whatever Happened to Automated Highway Systems (AHS)? *Traffic Technology International*, August–September 2001. Downloaded October 13, 2005 from http://faculty.washington.edu/jbs/itrans/bishopahs.htm.

Chartier, G., Hollingworth, B. Promoting Sustainable Transportation Through Site Design: An ITE Proposed Recommended Practice. Institute of Transportation Engineers. *ITE Journal*, 2004, 74 (8), 44–45.

Energy Information Administration, *Annual Energy Outlook 2005 with Projections to 2025*. U.S. Department of Energy. February 2005. Available at http://www.eia.doe.gov/oiaf/aeo/.

Energy Information Administration. *International Energy Outlook 2005*. U.S. Department of Energy. July 2005. Available at http://www.eia.doe.gov/oiaf/ieo/index.html.

Morris, H. Green Travel Gains Support. Planning. London. July 23, 2004, 15.

National Energy Policy, Report of the National Energy Policy Development Group, May 2001. Available at: http://www.whitehouse.gov/energy/National-Energy-Policy.pdf. (Accessed September 2005).

Siddiqui, Asfand, October 13, 2006. Email communication. California Department of Transportation, Division of Research and Innovation.

Timney, M. M. *Power for the People: Protecting States' Energy Policy Interests in an Era of Deregulation*. M.E. Sharpe: Armonk, NY, 2004.

Weingroff, R. Creating a Landmark: The Intermodal Surface Transportation Act of 1991. U.S. Department of Transportation, Federal Highway Administration. Available at http://www.fhwa.dot.gov/infrastructure/rw01.htm. (Accessed July 2003).

20 Privatization of Transportation Systems

Wendell C. Lawther

INTRODUCTION

State and local public transportation officials have been privatizing many of their functions for years, as private construction firms are typically hired to build roads and bridges. Recent U.S. legislation, however, has encouraged additional forms of privatization. ISTEA and TEA-21, for example, gave states and metropolitan areas the flexibility to try new solutions to the major transportation challenges facing U.S. policy makers. In response, a range of programs and projects have resulted, many of which involve private sector involvement in the financing and construction of large infrastructure projects such as roads and bridges. The various forms of privatization include public private partnerships, design-build operate agreements, and most recently concessionaire arrangements that are similar to experiences more common in other countries.

As indicated by a recent USGAO (2004) report, however, the examples of private sector involvement in the United States have been relatively limited. Various barriers exist at the state level, as only twenty-three states permit privatization. Yet the most recent experience with the lease of the Chicago Skyway and planning for the Trans Texas Corridor roadways among others suggests that public private partnerships (PPPs) will become much more accepted as public agencies seek additional revenue support to meet growing demand for transportation services.

The continuing issue is the success or effectiveness of PPPs, as many such roadway projects are not considered financially healthy (George et al. 2004; Regimbal 2002). Other projects, such as the express lanes for SR91 in California, reflect increased public acceptance and growing usage. The much greater complexity of PPPs compared with traditional outsourcing approaches provides increased challenges to public agencies as increased private involvement occurs.

PRIVATIZATION: TYPES OF INSTITUTIONAL ARRANGEMENTS RELEVANT TO TRANSPORTATION SYSTEMS

In the international experience, there is a wide range of institutional arrangements that involve both public and private sectors. Figure 20.1 provides an overview of these arrangements. The list represents a spectrum of alternatives ranging from complete

Public Provision and Operation
Outsourcing
Operation and Management Contracts
Leasing
Build-Transfer-Operate (BTO)
Build-Operate-Transfer (BOT)
Design-Build-Finance-Operate (DBFO
Concessions
Build-Own-Operate
Divestiture by License
Divestiture by Sale
Private Provision and Operation

FIGURE 20.1   Types of private participation in infrastructure. Adapted from Guasch (2004).

public provision and operation to the same for the private sector. Moving from the top of the list downward, the extent and nature of the private sector involvement increases. There is a corresponding lessening of public control and decision making as it impacts the final product and every day operations.

With regard to transportation infrastructure arrangements in the United States, traditionally most involve outsourcing: public agencies have hired private construction firms to build roads and bridges.[1] In other cases, public agencies have built a traffic management center, for example, and have engaged private sector firms to manage daily operations.

Public Private Partnerships are represented by the next five types.[2] As will be discussed below, these types involve much different types of public and private roles and responsibilities.

Transportation agencies have been contracting out road and bridge construction projects for many years (NCHRP 2003). It has long been recognized that this approach leads to cost savings and is likely to produce a higher quality product:

- Employee workload: there may not be enough roadway projects to provide full-time employment for public employees over a long term;
- Public employees may receive higher levels of salaries than are usual for the private marketplace;
- Private firms are likely to offer lower pension and health care benefits;
- Greater expertise: private firms may have employees with greater expertise than is present among public agencies;
- Economies of scale: large firms can buy material in bulk.

In addition, a lower public payroll will likely provide political benefits for those in charge of the agency. The payroll cost of a private firm constructing a roadway will undergo much less scrutiny than the payroll of a public agency (Florida DOT 1999).

In dealing with privatizing a transportation system, however, the level of familiarity by DOT officials is much less. In this chapter, the term "transportation system" will be defined as the creation or adaptation of a roadway system—along with possible tolling—that includes build operate transfer (BOT) arrangements (and similar arrangements) among public and private agencies.

After defining PPPs and discussing key characteristics, the reasons for creating PPPs are analyzed. Representative types of PPPs are discussed in more detail. The major challenges facing public agencies as they enter into these agreements are then discussed, focusing more on the key issue of risk assessment and transfer. Finally, four case studies from the United States are presented, identifying success and failure to the degree possible.

PUBLIC PRIVATE PARTNERSHIPS: DEFINITION AND KEY CHARACTERISTICS

A public private partnership can be defined as:

> An arrangement of roles and relationships in which two or more public and private entities coordinate/combine complementary resources to achieve their separate objectives through joint pursuit of one or more common objectives. (National Highway Institute 1999)

Here the emphasis is placed on the importance of achieving separate objectives while pursuing the common partnership objective. Although the definition does not provide a full understanding of the "separate objectives" and the "common objective," it implies that an effective partnership must be judged in part on the achievement of both separate and more common objectives.

Linder (2000) provides additional insights into these objectives by suggesting effective PPPs require each partner to adopt the values and management approaches of the other. Public partners should act more like entrepreneurs, while private partners should "embrace public interest considerations and expect greater public accountability" (p. 21). Although fully understanding opposing partners viewpoints and organizational culture (Shenkar 2003) may help to increase the success of the partnership, this analysis does not provide as in-depth a picture of the key characteristics and roles needed to ensure success.

The risk of not fully participating in the efforts of partners to achieve the partnership goals is that partnership goal efforts may suffer. Only when all partners are committed to helping their counterparts achieve both individual objectives and partnership goals will the PPP succeed.

CHARACTERISTICS OF PPPs

Before identifying key characteristics of PPPs, there must be a discussion of what PPPs are not. Many authors (Guasch 2004) have suggested that all relationships between public and private organizations are partnerships. This chapter disagrees with this viewpoint, suggesting that traditional contracting relationships, in which a private sector organization works for a public agency is not a PPP. To the extent that participants in a PPP act in ways that reflect contracting out relationships, the PPP is at risk of failure.

PPPs have the following characteristics:

1. Resourcing (Grimsey and Lewis 2004). All partners contribute resources such as money, time, and expertise. The PPP seeks to maximize the value of all resources to best achieve partnership goals. These resources must be transferred to the partnership.
2. Sharing and allocation of risk. The public sector assumes some of the risk, and does not necessarily transfer all risk as it does under traditional contracting out relationships. Risk needs to be identified, calculated, assessed and managed (Atinkoye et al. 2003). In the United States, many public agencies are not familiar with risk calculations.
3. Relational. Instead of the vertical relationships between public agencies and their private contractors, PPPs require horizontal relationships, in which:
   • all partners are considered equals in the effort to achieve PPP goals;
   • the relationship is likely to be long term, as many PPP contracts are established for thirty years or more;
   • there is the expectation that relationships will evolve, as the contract can not anticipate all contingencies and future challenges that will occur (World Bank 2003; Guasch 2004).
4. Governance. To ensure continuity throughout the life of the project or partnership, a set of ground rules or a framework to the contract must be established. As individuals involved in the partnership change, these rules are needed so that the PPP doesn't have to "start from scratch" every time there are changes (Grimsey and Lewis 2004). Also, governance issues include the assignment of responsibilities for each partner engaging in collective efforts toward partnership goal achievement.

WHY PPPs: POTENTIAL BENEFITS

PPPs are seen as a means of closing the gap between projected public revenues and resources and what is needed to build, maintain and improve roadways and transportation infrastructure (Guasch 2004). Projects that are given lower priority for public support can be built much sooner (USGAO 2004). Private funds are one potential source that can be leveraged to help meet these needs, at little or no initial cost to the taxpayer (Levy 1996). In this manner these projects become not only financially feasible, but also politically feasible (Corry 2004; Stainbeck 2000). Private capital investments can design, build and operate the roadway. Revenue from tolls is used to provide a return on the investment.

Additional advantages include building projects at a much quicker rate than would occur otherwise. If the PPP contract is structured correctly, the public agency purchases the service that is reflected by the roadway's existence. The private consortium, also known as a special purpose vehicle (SPV) can be provided an incentive to maintain the roadway in as high a quality as possible, since it will not receive payments until the roadway is completed, with continuing revenue occurring if usage is maintained (Grimsey and Lewis 2004).

Private sector expertise may be greater than that of public sector, especially regarding the use of technological innovations to collect tolls (Levy 1996; Mylvaganam and Borins 2004). As a result, the roadway can be build at a lower cost than if the public agency built the roadway, especially since a private partner uses a more comprehensive, life cycle or whole-life approach (World Bank 2003; Perez 2004). Greater efficiency is achieved by the private sector because of less political influence on both technical and rate setting decisions (Amos 2004).

Overall, there is the perception that public agencies that outsource construction of roadway and bridge projects may not perform well. For example, in 2000 the State of Virginia's Joint Legislative Audit and Review Commission reviewed the six-year plan of the Virginia Department of Transportation. It found that costs had been underestimated by more than one third, as the $9 billion plan may cost another $3.5 billion. The cost difference was due to both not anticipating changes and major design flaws that were not recognized. Other problems cited in a USGAO study were a lack of data management for the Colorado DOT; a substantial increase in change orders in the Connecticut DOT, and a lack of sufficient staffing in the Texas DOT (USGAO 2002).

A system of incentives and sanctions can be deployed in a PPP, whereas there are limits on doing so with alternative delivery systems. Any cost savings that accrue from more efficient operations and maintenance can be gained by the private partner, thereby providing an incentive for greater efficiency (Guasch 2004; World Bank 2003).

TYPES OF PPPs

When privatizing transportation systems, PPPs can take a variety of forms, including:

- Build Operate Transfer (BOT): This is the most common form: the private company, usually an organization that represents a consortium of larger private interests, also known as a specific purpose vehicle (SPV) created for a specific project or roadway system, will first take employ design/build techniques to build a roadway (e.g., Ernzen, et al. 2000), taking advantage of their innovative and much faster completion time aspects. Then the SPV will operate and maintain the roadway (e.g., a toll road) for a specified period, often thirty years. At the end of this time, the operation of the toll road will transfer back to the public sector. The public partners may contribute to some costs, such as obtaining rights of way or supporting environmental impact studies (USGAO 2004).
- Build Transfer Operate (BTO): This arrangement is similar to the BOT, with two major advantages. First, the government owns the roadway immediately upon completion and the SPV leases and operates it. There may be financing advantages to this arrangement. Second, government ownership usually offers liability

protection not held by the private company, protecting it from uninsurable risk during the toll operations period. The building of express lanes for SR91 is an example.

- Design Build Finance Operate (DBFO): More common in Great Britain, under this form the private company is responsible for all functions indicated, but never owns the land or the completed roadway. It is given access to the roadway, and a license to operate it for a specified period. The private company does not collect tolls in this arrangement, as it is paid by the government using a shadow toll method.

  In some cases, there are separate contracts for design, construction and maintenance. In this fashion a considerable amount of risk is transferred to the private sector. In addition, any dependency on subsequent public budget cycles is avoided. Private partners find this arrangement attractive, as demand risk is limited. As the traveling public does not pay a toll, usage forecasts are much more accurate (Perez 2004).

- Concessions: This arrangement provides much greater responsibility and role to the private consortium, combining elements of the BOT arrangement with a longer term lease than is commonly found with BOT agreements. There is higher risk for the SPV, as all revenue is from collected tolls. There is also the expectation that additional investment in new or upgrading legacy infrastructure will need to occur over the life of the agreement. One approach is to incorporate new BOT projects as part of the Concession agreement, allowing the SPV a substantial equity in the new project (Guarsch 2004). This provides the SPV with greater flexibility to identify the nature and timing of these additional investments.

There are also many more incentives build into the PPP with a concession, to ensure higher levels of usage as well as to deploy additional infrastructure in a timely fashion. In theory, if there are no government guarantees regarding revenue, and usage of a toll road is the only revenue coming to a PPP, then there is maximum incentive for the service quality to be maintained (Grimsey and Lewis 2004).

PPPs: CHALLENGES AND DISADVANTAGES

INCOMPLETE CONTRACTS

Partners must recognize that the contractual foundation of the PPP is by its nature incomplete (i.e., it cannot be written to include every contingency or risk that may occur). Furthermore, negotiators are not rational: they make mistakes (World Bank 2003). As a result, there must be a commitment to deal with unexpected events and conditions that does not require extensive change orders or renegotiation of the basic contract.

NEED FOR APPROPRIATE LEGAL AND ENVIRONMENTAL FRAMEWORK

In the United States, individual states must enact or employ legislation that allows PPPs to be created: allowing franchises to be awarded to private companies to build a transportation project and operate it for a specified amount of time (e.g., thirty to fifty years). Twenty-three states have passed such legislation.[3] Since Design Build is a traditional element of BOT or Concessionaire approaches, state laws must allow for this arrangement. At present only thirty-two states allow the DesignBuild approach, with only twenty-eight states permitting its use for highways (USGAO 2004)

CREATION AND DEPLOYMENT OF APPROPRIATE INCENTIVES/SANCTIONS

In a general sense, public agencies must create sufficient financial incentives for private investors to enter into PPPs for transportation projects. These incentives, rate of return from toll revenue, for example, must be higher than those for other investments. Yet at the same time, there must be a public responsibility to identify what rate is in the best public interest, one that is not considered excessive (Pisarski and Tischer 2001).

In the examples discussed below, different methods have been implemented to deal with the reasonable rate of return issue. In the Chicago Skyway PPP, a limit on rates is specified. In the latter years of the lease agreement, however, there is an attempt to link toll rate increases with the rate of inflation. For the SR 91 express lanes, the rate of return was specified, but toll rates were left to the discretion of the SPV. Virginia's more regulatory approach allows the SPV to set toll rates, with the proviso that the regulatory body has the right to lower them if it feels they are unreasonable.

POTENTIAL FOR PRIVATE CONSORTIA TO BECOME INSOLVENT

In Europe, there have been many instances of private consortia experiencing financial difficulty. In part, the reasons may have included a lack of management expertise to operate highway facilities and operations. In these cases, the government has had to assume control and ownership of the highway project, assuming a great deal of debt in the process (Perez 2004).

RISK IDENTIFICATION, TRANSFER, AND MANAGEMENT

The vast range of risk types, the ability and means of transferring risk from the public to the private sector, and the management of risks by all partners present significant challenges to the effectiveness of a PPP. After characterizing risk, and presenting the goals of risk transfer, a few of the most relevant risk types will be discussed. Risk management, the process of limiting the existence of the risk and its impact, will be discussed in the PPP success factors section.

Risk occurs when either the outcome or the consequence of any decision is judged to be uncertain to any degree (Boothyard and Emmett 1996). All decisions, or groups of decisions, leading to achievement of a desired goal or outcome, have varying degrees of uncertainty and resulting risks. As such, risk is a concept that can be measured along a continuum from low to high.

Risk is another term for identifying the extent to which a problem in service or product delivery will occur. Risk also entails the responsibility with solving the problem, usually by using resources that otherwise would be profit for a private partner, or tax revenue for the public partner that could be spent elsewhere.

There is also a reward aspect of risk. If the private firm sets aside funds anticipating that risk is high and problems are likely, and the problems do not occur, then these funds are added to profit. Construction risks, for example, usually deal with the roadway not being completed by the date identified in the contract. If these risks occur, then payments are not received on time, and debt payments may be higher for the private firm. If the risks don't occur, and payments are received on time, then overall profit is higher.

For many routine services, risk is low, as the output is clearly identified and the process of achieving that output is highly standardized. The garbage put on the curb by a homeowner is either collected or not, and the process—emptying cans into a truck—varies little from one city to another. If someone's garbage is not picked up on a given day on a scheduled route, the private firm assumes all responsibility for collecting the garbage at an unscheduled time.

For PPPs, there are many risks that are high. One major goal of a PPP is that some high risks are shared, as responsibility is assigned (ideally) to the partner most able to prevent or lessen the risk.

TRANSFER OR SHARING OF RISK

In traditional contracting out relationships, the public sector attempts to transfer all risk to the private sector. This occurs by identifying the service or project output, and allowing the private firm to identify how to achieve the output. In the garbage collection example above, the contract between the city and the private firm may not mention the collection process, but will simply state that garbage is to be collected twice a week from all homeowners. The city is not at fault if any garbage is not collected, and shares no responsibility for correcting any problems that occur.

For an effective PPP, the goal is to transfer risk from a partner who has difficulty in handling it to one who can handle it much better (Nova Scotia 1997). In other words, there is a sharing of the risk. An added benefit is that in negotiating who should be responsible for what risk, roles and responsibilities of the partners are clarified. Furthermore, incentives can be provided in the context of risk sharing.

For example, in a BOT-type of PPP, the design aspects of a project may be assigned to the private partner. By specifying that a roadway will be operational by a certain date, and not mentioning how the roadway will be built, the risk that problems may arise because of poor design is transferred completely to the private partner.

With concessionaire PPPs, all construction risk can be transferred if the partnership contract states that the private partner will receive no revenue until the tollroad is operational and travelers begin paying tolls. This risk transfer also acts as an incentive, as innovation and efficiency may be maximized by the concessionaire in order to receive revenue as quickly as possible (Grimsey and Lewis 2004).

All risks should be negotiated among all partners as part of the formation of the

PPP. One crucial consideration made by public partners is the cost of risk transfer. The private consortia may provide all of the financing for a project, transferring all financing risk to the private sector. The overall cost of the project, however, may be higher than if the public partners decided to contribute to the needed financing (World Bank 2003).[4]

DEMAND OR TRAFFIC RISK

Demand or usage of the highway must be forecast in order to identify a basis on which revenues can be estimated, leading to private financing decisions. The actual demand, however, is dependent on many factors, and often is less than originally forecast. These factors include economic, unforeseen events (e.g., oil shortage, lack of public acceptance) and the existence of viable alternative roadways.

> Even with extensive investigation of traffic trends, scientific forecasts of future growth potential, and survey's of people's willingness to pay tolls, the traffic levels projects will actually attract are never truly known until they become operational. (Perez 2004, 24)

If demand is less than anticipated, the private consortia is likely to pressure public sector partners to raise toll rates to increase revenue. This may require a renegotiation of the original contract. Alternatively, the public sector could provide other means of funding, including

> direct funding subsidies or indirect funding incentives in the way of tax relief, development rights to properties located in proximity to the highway project, and other means. (Wooldridge et al. 2002)

Without this financial support, the SPV may go bankrupt, forcing the government to take over the operation of the roadway (Guasch 2004).

CONSTRUCTION RISK

Uncertainty in construction costs can be greatly removed with detailed engineering studies that are completed before the PPP contract. However, there are several risks that can increase costs, such as:

- Obtaining needed permits,
- Right of way agreements,[5]
- Design features that many conflict with each other (Chinyio and Fergusson 2003),
- Technology obsolescence (National Research Council 2002).

SERVICE INTERRUPTION/DELAY RISK

This risk occurs primarily during the operations and maintenance phase of a roadway project. It refers to the possibility that travelers may not be able to use the roadway in a timely manner once it has been operational. Causes of service interruption risks may include technology that is functioning improperly; construction delays; and accidents that block the roadway. Although it may be determined that this risk is low, when and if it does occur it may have a high impact. Under a BOT or Concessionaire contract, this risk is assumed by the private sector.

FINANCIAL RISK

The initial creation of the PPP depends upon accurately identifying financial risk so that private investors will believe they can achieve a reasonable return on their investment. When this estimate is correct, the project is deemed successful; failure occurs when demand is lower than anticipated.

The primary financial risk is closely linked to the accuracy of demand estimation. In recent years, demand for many toll roads build under a PPP arrangement have been overly optimistic (Regimbal 2004). Part of the problem can be attributed to faulty demand forecast models. Such models suffer from:

- The use of population growth assumptions used by MPOs for planning purposes;
- A steady state assumption that does not reflect the impact of economic cycles on demand;
- Not assuming demand differences due to weekend travel or truck usage;
- Lack of assessment of the likelihood that competing freeways would be build or expanded;
- Underestimating the value of time savings by motorists who may choose to travel the tollway; and
- Not fully understanding the "ramp up" period: the length of time it takes for the traveling public to accept the value of the tollway and increase usage (George et al. 2003).

The last two aspects are highly related and difficult to assess. Travel demand models have tried to assess how much time a given roadway will save a traveler compared to alternative freeways. What is clear is that the greater the value of time savings for the traveler, the lower the ramp up period. Beyond understanding that the more congested alternative roads are, the greater the time saving value for the traveler, present models do not accurately assess how and to what degree time savings is calculated by the traveler (George et al. 2003). One reason for the success of the SR91 express lanes may be that travelers have continually overestimated time savings (Sullivan 2000).

The key overall challenge for financial risk is the degree to which the public sector accurately understands the financial risk for the private sector and structures the resulting PPP as a result. As the number of PPPs increases world wide, and the experience or lessons learned grow, it is increasingly recognized that the public sector may have to contribute to the overall financial cost of a roadway project for it to succeed. Three options are possible:

- Cash support: either in the form of shadow tolls or periodic payments;
- Indirect support by increasing revenues through not building or improving competing freeways or through development rights;
- Indirect support by reducing costs through tax subsidies or tax exempt financing, right of way acquisition, and paying for surveying and environmental studies.

Determining when or under what conditions the public sector should choose which option is challenging and ultimately unanswerable (Miller 2003; USGAO 2004).

PUBLIC SECTOR MANAGERIAL CAPACITY AND POWER ASYMMETRIES

Much of the PPP literature assumes that all partners will act in harmony, with no partner acting unfairly toward the other. In some instances, however, this may not be accurate. To the extent that competition is limited, the public agency may find itself in a situation of supplier dominance. If the statement of work is unclear, or is expected to evolve, initial technical proposals may undergo significant changes (Guasch 2004). A given private SPV, realizing that it is in a position of dominance, may extract significant concessions from the private partners (Lonsdale 2005).

A similar situation may occur when and if the private partner may wish to renegotiate the initial contract (Guasch 2004). Although few United States projects have experienced this situation, if a private partner is suffering from diminished bond ratings, lower than expected usage, and overall financial difficulties, it may ask the public partners for a "bailout." A variety of proposals may be considered, including a change in toll rates and/or additional public support. Depending upon their "institutional strength" and managerial capacity (Boarnet et al. 2002), the public agencies may find themselves at a disadvantage in these negotiations.

PPP SUCCESS FACTORS

There are at least four categories of success factors that can be identified. First, the partnership should maintain adherence to the public interest. The roadway project must be viewed as legitimate by the public. There are at least three issues:

- The public must believe the toll rates are fair.
- If there are government financial contributions to the success of the project, these must be accepted as meeting a social objective such as decreasing traffic congestion.
- The financial arrangement that supports the PPP must be viewed as acceptable by all stakeholders as well as the traveling public (Grimsey and Lewis 2004).

A PPP roadway project must be viewed as necessary, significantly relieving a traffic congestion problem. The use of the PPP mechanism, as opposed to alternative funding approaches, must be accepted as appropriate.[6] The public must believe that the toll rate is not rising too quickly, nor is contributing to an excessive profit margin for the private consortia that constructs/operates the roadway. The existence of alternative, toll free roadways helps to limit the impression that toll roads are only for the wealthy.

A second category deals with the nature of the PPP contract, as well as the process leading to the initial choice of private partners:

- The procurement process must be competitive.
- The amount of risk transferred must be fair and clearly identified.
- Project based specifications should be output based as much as possible.
- Private partner management skills must be assured.

Third, the SPV must be successful in terms of making a reasonable return on the financial investment made in a roadway project. This means the public partners must play several roles throughout the life of the project including:

- They must assess what percentage constitutes a reasonable rate of return. Regulators in the SR91 express lane project set the rate at 17 percent.
- If the SPV is in danger of bankruptcy, the public partners must either "buy out" the SPV and become owners of a toll road, or renegotiate the contract to allow for higher rates or other solutions that generate more revenue. Neither of these latter two options indicates success.

Finally, the nature of the PPP evolution must be examined. The extent to which all partners have clearly identified their roles and responsibilities and have fulfilled their assigned and expected tasks must be evaluated. More importantly, as events and conditions change, roles and responsibilities change. The success of a PPP depends upon all partners recognizing the need for change and agreeing to adopt sometimes new and different tasks.

These roles may be challenging. If sanctions must be applied because the private partner has not met a milestone or in some other way violated a contractual agreement, the public partners must not shirk this duty. A viable risk management program, unfamiliar to many in the public sector, must be in place to monitor risk occurrence and resolution as the project progresses.

PPP CASE STUDIES

THE DULLES GREENWAY

In August 1986, the Commission on Transportation for the 21st Century, appointed by Virginia Governor Gerald Baliles, issued a report that identified transportation needs for the Commonwealth of Virginia. It estimated that $7 billion would be required to meet these needs. The commission indicated that the money would have to come from increased sales and gasoline taxes and bond issues (Levy 1996).

As part of the resulting legislative compromise regarding how much revenue enhancement could be enacted, and with the persuasive arguments from key consultants, the Virginia legislature passed the Highway Corporation Act of 1988. A key part of the legislation reads:

> ...it is in the public interest to encourage construction of additional, safe, convenient, and economic highways by private parties, provided that adequate safeguards are provided against default in the construction and operation obligations of the operators of the roadways.

The act further defined that the public interest should include factors such as the "relative speed" and the cost efficiency of the construction. It also permitted public funds to support such projects.

The legislation used a regulatory approach (Ybarra 2004), as the Commission of Transportation was given the authority to approve and regulate any private firms that would build a toll road. It has the authority to set toll rates, adjusting them in a manner not to discourage usage. The legislation also established a Certificate of Authority mechanism to approve projects. Guidelines for the application for this certificate include stating information about:

- The geographical area,
- Affected property owners,
- How rights of way would be obtained,
- Financing plan,
- Operations plan,
- Permits needed,
- Public utilities affected,
- Government plans affected,
- Certification from the Virginia Department of Transportation,
- Performance bonds.

No public funds were required, as the revenue from the tolls would provide a return on the private investment. In addition, state regulators decided that a reasonable rate of return for investors in the Dulles Greenway was 30 percent until debt service was met, reducing to 15 percent once toll revenues exceeded debt service (Levy 1996).

After public hearings were held in the spring of 1988, legislation was passed and the commission approved the application of the Toll Road Corporation of Virginia (TRCV). Initial tolls were set at $1.75 for the fourteen-mile limited access Dulles Greenway. Since it would connect with the already in place Dulles Toll Road, the total cost to commuters traveling the thirty-five miles from downtown Washington D.C. to Leesburg was $2.60.

TRCV partners included Lochnau Limited, a family owned investment firm headed by Magelen O. Bryant; Brown and Root construction firm; and Autostrade

Internationale, the firm that would operate the toll road facility. To obtain additional private financing, the TRCV changed from a corporation to a limited partnership entitled Toll Road Investors Partnership II (TRIP II). The projected project cost of $326 Million was financed as follows: 57.04 percent from Lochau Limited; 19.16 percent from Autostrade; and the remainder of the long-term financing from a consortium of ten lending institutions headed by John Hancock Insurance.

After early setbacks due to difficulties in obtaining rights of way as well as in obtaining the financing identified above, the construction finally began in September 1993. The roadway opened to travelers on September 30, 1995 (Levy 1996).

The initial results were disappointing, as only 8,000 travelers per day used the roadway, much less than the initially projected thirty-four thousand. In March 1996 the toll rate was cut to $.90, increasing daily usage to fifteen thousand (Perez 2004). In July 1997, tolls were raised to $1.15.

The lower than expected usage meant lower revenue and less funds available to pay investors and reduce debt. The first year had projected revenue of $27 million, with $7 million for operating costs and the remainder applied toward paying annual interest charges of $30 million. Investors granted approval for TRIP II to forego quarterly payments of $7 million, preventing bankruptcy (CBO 1998). Although the 1988 legislation prohibited a bailout of TRIP II, the Virginia State legislature considered but ultimately rejected it. They did approve an increase in the maximum speed to sixty-five miles per hour for the Greenway, hoping to increase ridership (USDOT 2004).

In the spring of 1999, the Virginia State Corporation Commission approved a restructuring of the project's debt. Insured zero coupon bonds, worth $360 million would replace $250 million of the original bank and insurance debt. These bonds would mature on January 1, 2036, the end of the contract for the PPP. Debt service for the first ten years would be minimized to match revised revenue projections, with principal and interest payments, increasing to $1.43 billion, with two thirds of this amount paid in the final twenty years of the project (Wooldridge 2002).

Tolls have gradually risen. Tolls were $1.75 as of Sept 1999, raised to $1.90 in September 2002. As of May 2005, the toll cost was $2.90 during rush hour; $2.50 at off peak, with discounts for smart tag holders (www.dullesgreenway.com). Usage has also risen with usage at over fifty-five thousand per day (Autostrade 2002). However, partnership losses continue at about $30 million per year (Vining et al. 2004).

EXPRESS LANES FOR SR-91

The legal framework for PPPs in California is Assembly Bill 680, passed in 1989. It permitted the creation of PPPs for construction of roadways in California, allowing private developers to build and the California Department of Transportation (Caltrans) to perform environmental and developmental tasks for a project. Caltrans would be reimbursed for their effort from the revenue stream when the roadway project was operational. Federal funds were allowed as seed money, with thirty-five-year leases allowed for private operations. Caltrans also proposed a BTO approach, reasoning that tort liability costs could be transferred to the public sector, thereby decreasing the project costs. The legislation allowed four demonstration projects to be chosen.

Unlike the regulatory approach adopted in Virginia, Caltrans established a two stage procurement process. A Request for Qualifications (RFQ) was issued in November 1989. There was a two stage approval process. First, the qualifications of each respondent to the RFQ were evaluated. Evaluation criteria included:

- Experience of principal organizations and consortia members,
- Record of financial strength,
- Ability to work cooperatively with a broad range of government agencies,
- Individual qualifications of key management (Levy 1996).

Next, the proposed projects would be evaluated on criteria including:

- Degree of local support,
- Degree proposal encourages economic development,
- Ease of project implementation,
- Expertise,
- Technical innovation.

By September 14, 1990, the four demonstration projects were chosen.[7] The California Private Transportation Corporation (CPTC) proposed converting the ten mile median strip within the Riverside Freeway (SR 91) to an electronic tolled four lane (two lanes in each direction) expressway for car pools (the roadway is through mountainous terrain and has only entrance and exits at either end). These lanes would be equipped with Automatic Vehicle Identification (AVI) systems, requiring each vehicle that entered these lanes to have a transponder and funds in an account to pay for the toll. The cost of the toll would vary by time of day, with higher costs during rush hour and lowest costs after midnight. CPTC estimated the cost at $80 million for construction of the lanes and $65 million for the AVI system.

The actual cost of the highway was $126 million, with $19 million funded equity and the rest (85%) debt (McDonald et al., 1999). The lease gave CPTC thirty-five years to pay off the loan and make a return to the investors. California did not regulate toll rates, but the CPTC was allowed no more than a rate of return of 17 percent for the project (CBO 1998).

The partners in the CPTC included Peter Kiewit, a more than one hundred-year-old construction company that also contributed knowledge concerning fiber optic technology and the AVI system; Cofiroute, the world's largest toll road developer, headquartered in France, and Granite construction, well known in California. Peter Kiewit and Cofiroute contributed 19 percent of the project costs; Granite, 25 percent; another $35 million in institutional debt; the Orange County Transportation Authority had $7 million in subordinated debt that would be repaid from toll revenue; and three banks loaned $65 million on a variable rate basis to be repaid over fourteen years.

The project was open to travel on December 27, 1995, and immediately was judged successful. By 1997, over eighty thousand vehicles were equipped with transponders. The toll road collected enough revenue ($10 million) by August 1998 to cover operation expenses and debt service. Travelers made an average of weekday thirty-two thousand trips (Boarnet et al. 2002). It is the world's first fully automated toll roadway, and the first congestion pricing arrangement in the United States (Shaheen et al. 2005).

When the roadway first opened, tolls ranged from $.25 to $2.50. In September 1997, the peak toll was increased to $2.95 (McDonald et al. 1999). Currently, tolls range from $1 to $6.25 for the ten mile trip, depending on the time of day. Peak tolls occur during 4–6 p.m. on Thursdays and Fridays. The goal of the variable pricing is to maintain free flow traffic.

During the first two years of operation, HOV vehicles were allowed to use the express lanes for free, resulting in a 40 percent jump in the use of these lanes. When HOV vehicles were charged a fee that was 50 percent of that for SOVs, HOV usage did not decrease throughout the roadway, but fewer HOVs used the express lanes. Fears that increasing tolls would cause less ridesharing have not materialized (Sullivan 2000).

Peak period congestion has been substantially reduced for all travelers on SR-91 as a result of express lane usage. However, travelers using the express lanes save approximately 30 minutes more than those using the freeway during peak periods (De Corla-Souza 2005). Increasing numbers of commuters are willing to pay the express lane charges to reduce travel time and increase safety of their trips. The favorable attitude to variable pricing, however, has declined but still is held by a majority of travelers (Sullivan 2000).

As part of the PPP agreement, Caltrans agreed to a non-compete provision, meaning that no efforts would be made to expand existing capacity on competing freeways. When Caltrans announced plans to expand SR-91 in 1999, CPTC sued. Caltrans rescinded its plans in 2002. The California Legislature approved the purchase of the SR-91 express lanes for $209.1 million in 2002 by the Orange County Transportation Authority. As part of the sale, completed as of January 2003, the non-compete provision was removed. (Shaheen et al. 2005). Secured by pledges of future toll revenue, this amount was financed with bonds that sold quickly to investors in November 2003 with a triple A rating (Ambac 2003). Annual revenues in 2004 totaled $26 million (Bailey-Campbell 2005).

CHICAGO SKYWAY

The Skyway is a 7.8 mile toll bridge which links I-90 from the Indiana-Illinois state line to the Dan Ryan expressway (I-94). Built in 1959, it is a closed access tollway that is also linked to the Ohio and Pennsylvania turnpikes, thereby serving as a main route from those eastern states to areas north of Chicago. In early 2004, the City of Chicago issued a Request for Qualifications (RFQ) offering long-term concession and lease to prospective bidders (Chicago 2004).

Ten bids were initially received by April 21, 2004. Preliminary assessment focused on two criteria: ability to manage tollways and ability to raise the necessary funds. By September, final bids were accepted from five consortia. No negotiation of the amounts bid were expected (Shields 2004).

On October 18, 2004, it was announced that the winning bidder was Skyway Concessions, Inc., a consortia composed of CINTRA Concesiones de Infraestructuras de Transporte S.A, a Spanish firm, and Macquarte Investment Holdings, Inc, an Australian investment bank. The two firms, who manage several toll roads in Canada, Europe and South America, bid $1.82 billion for a ninety-nine-year lease.

Key aspects of the deal included:
- Concessionaire has the right to collect all toll revenue, subject to toll limits
- Toll rate increases are limited to no more than:
    - $2.50 until 2008;
    - $3.00 until 2011;
    - $3.50 until 2013;
    - $4.00 until 2015;
    - $4.50 until 2017;
    - $5.00 after 2017, with 2 percent or inflation rate increases (whichever is greater) annually (Campomar 2004).
- The ninety-nine-year lease allows for Skyway Concessions, Inc. to depreciate all assets, in accordance with U.S. federal tax code;
- Skyway has the right to implement electronic tolling (note: a necessity) with city cooperation;
- City agrees to complete on going capital improvement program, with Skyway agreeing to deploy capital improvements costing $70 million within four years;
- Compliance with existing operating standards must occur, although flexibility is possible;
- Roadway must be maintained, and returned to the city in the same or better condition at the end of the lease period;
- Existing labor contracts were not assigned to Skyway, although all present employees must be granted an employment interview if they apply to Skyway;
- City has the right to inspect facilities and monitor operations, with Skyway paying these costs; Skyway must submit various reports, including financial and traffic (Seliga 2005).

In 2004, the Skyway's operating revenue was $43.2 million, generating over $33 million in surplus or profit after operating expenses were deducted. The concessionaire was attracted to this proposal because it estimated a 10 percent return on investment, due to the cost savings from depreciation, deployment of electronic tolling which should decrease operations costs, and expected steady growth in usage even as tolls increase. This last assumption is based on alternative routes that are heavily congested (Bunker 2004).

Trans-Texas Corridor Projects

In June 2002, the Texas Transportation Commission adopted the Trans-Texas Corridor Plan. This ambitious fifty-year plan envisioned a network of four thousand miles of highway crisscrossing the state, with each corridor encompassing five lanes for vehicles—three for cars and two for trucks—and six lanes for rail. There would also be easements for utilities to be placed along the routes. Total costs were estimated at $183.5 billion. With the passage of Proposition 15 by Texas voters in November 2001, a constitutional amendment allowed financing flexibility through a variety of means that included public private partnerships (TxDot 2002).

Supporters such as Governor Rick Perry viewed the plan as a necessary response to population growth—from 21 million to 50 million in the next few decades—as well as to negative environmental impacts from increasing NAFTA related truck traffic, air pollution, increased need for rural economic development, and other issues. Private funds would be needed to build the roadways to implement the plan. Corridors, 1,000 to 1,200 feet wide, would be built along side existing freeways (Lyne 2002).

One of the highest priority roadways is TTC-35, a corridor that would run parallel to the existing I-35 running from Dallas to San Antonio. In response to an unsolicited proposal made by Fluor Enterprises Inc. in November 2002, TxDot issued a Request for Competing Proposals and Qualifications in July 2003. By September 2003, three private firms had submitted responses: Cintra-Zachery, Fluor, and Trans-Texas Express. Within a month, all three were deemed qualified.

The next year was spent meeting with the three firms, working on gaining more detailed proposals. Final proposals were submitted by August 2004, with a selection of Cintra-Zachery in December 2004 as the preferred partner (Project Milestones). On March 11, 2005, the Texas Department of Transportation (Txdot) and Cintra-Zachery formalized a PPP to begin work on the first project that will be part of the Trans-Texas Corridor. Cintra has agreed to a $7.2 billion project: $6 billion will be spent building and operating a toll road from Dallas to San Antonio with a fifty-year lease, with an additional $1.2 billion returned to TxDot as concessionaire fees. The TTC-35 roadway is projected to be completed by 2010. Cintra will also help devise a master plan will identify specific projects, along with an implementation schedule, estimated project costs and toll revenue.

The established relationship between TxDot and Cintra is characterized as follows:

> a highly cooperative, mutual collaboration will be pursued, under the terms of the Contract Documents, to engage the Developer's innovation, private sector resources, entrepreneurial skills, risk sharing and management capabilities, and technical and financial expertise, and to engage TxDOT's governmental authority, planning capabilities, risk sharing and management capabilities, and technical and financial expertise, to bring the Project and Facilities to fruition. As such, this Agreement contemplates significant roles and responsibilities for the Developer that go beyond the typical work and services provided by engineering and construction firms under contracts routinely let by TxDOT. (TxDot 2005b: 6–7)

The first phase, an environmental study, will be completed by spring 2006 by TxDot and FHWA. It is anticipated that future more specific environmental hearings will be needed as the route is identified. Public hearings are being/will be held across the relevant corridor area to elicit comments regarding the final corridor route (TxDot 2005a).

Public comment on the resulting PPP has not been uniformly favorable. Some feel that large contributions to legislative and statehouse campaigns have lead to the PPP with Cintra (http://www.cleanuptexaspolitics.com/tollcorridormoney). Others decry the apparent lack of public disclosure of documents related the PPP (www.corridorwatch. org), as well as the lack of public input prior to the PPP agreement in March 2005. Opponents also decry the potential negative impact on the environment, the taking of private property for economic development, and the higher cost associated with tolls (Moreno 2005).

CONCLUSION AND ANALYSIS

Accountability to the public, leading to legitimacy and acceptance, can be gained in a variety of ways. Deliberate efforts must be made by all partners to elicit public input and involvement while the roadway is undergoing planning and throughout the construction period. Marketing and public relations are a necessary focus, especially for a new roadway project. Benefits of the project, in terms of time saved, increased reliability, and the option of using alternative, freeway routes helped acceptance for the SR91 express lanes. These benefits were clearly understood and experienced by travelers after the lanes were opened (Sullivan 2003). The efforts made by Autostrade and Virginia DOT to gain public acceptance no doubt contributed to greater acceptance (Levy 1996). The workshops held by TxDot to involve the public in choosing routes for Trans Corridor projects will invariably help this process.

Yet there are limitations on to what extent accountability can be achieved in the short term. When project financing is backloaded, as with the Chicago Skyway, the public may not fully consider the impact that toll rates will have twelve years from now and beyond, when tolls will be allowed to rise annually at the rate of inflation.

The choice of toll rates has an impact on public acceptance, as well as influencing the public agency roles after the roadway has been completed. The Dulles Greenway experience illustrates the potential for a "vicious cycle":

> tolls are set high in an attempt to cover financing and operating costs, demand is overestimated at the prospective toll (it is assumed that demand will be not much lower than it would be at zero price), the tolls discourage usage and thus total revenues are not high enough to cover financing and operating costs. Tolls are lowered, as a result demand increases, but total revenues do not increase substantially and still do not cover financing and operating costs; the builder/operator requests some form of bailout by government and if it does not get it, the firm slides into technical default. (Vining et al. 2004)

Much depends on the efforts public agencies will make in meeting public transportation goals that influence a given PPP roadway project. The controversy caused by the non-compete clause in the SR91 express lane partnership lead to public opinion turning against private management and operations and favoring a return to public control (Price 2001). Public transportation agencies will have to choose projects carefully if expanding or renewing competing alternative routes are among the options available using traditional pay as you go public financing approaches. If the public perceives that public agencies are deliberately not expanding alternative routes to influence higher usage of toll roads, legitimacy of the PPP will lessen.

The choice of the private SPV must be as transparent as possible. Using public procurement techniques to rate and evaluate bidders responses to a Request for a PPP Proposal seems preferable to the regulatory approach used in the case of the Dulles Greenway, as greater competition is assured. In the United States, with assistance from consultants, the ability of public agencies to adequately assess management skills and ability to obtain financing seems appropriate. The apparent reluctance by TxDot to release financial documents regarding its PPP with Cintra-Zachary, however, does not bode well for public acceptance nor does it increase confidence that the choice was made without political influence.

Identifying and adequately transferring and/or sharing risk remains a challenge for many American public agencies. If private SPVs are willing to assume all of the financial risk, and in doing so assume demand risk as well, then the public agency role is limited and relatively easy. If demand risk is high due to overly optimistic projections, as has been the case in many instances (George et al. 2003), then grappling with the issue of appropriate public sector financial support is much more unfamiliar and difficult for public agencies. The acceptance of tax-exempt financing as well as paying for some of the costs related to constructing a roadway is one approach that has been suggested (Miller 2003; Lockwood 2000; Boarnet et al. 2002; USGAO 2004). Value pricing approaches as exhibited by the SR91 express lanes also are more acceptable (Sullivan 2003). Some compensation for lower usage due to improving competing freeways, as in the case of SR 125 in California, may become more common (Poole 2005).

Ultimately there should be a balancing of the different goals of the public interest and the profit motives of private partners. This balancing goal will be a "moving target," as PPP relationships, roles and responsibilities evolve. The monitoring role of public agencies in the Chicago Skyway, ensuring maintenance of service quality, has yet to be fully developed. The degree to which a given partnership affects other efforts to reach public goals, such as ridesharing programs and other means of lessening congestion, will have to be assessed. Recognizing that all PPP contracts are incomplete, the success of a PPP will be measured in the degree to which evolving roles are identified, accepted, and fulfilled. In many instances this evolution is tied with incentives and sanctions and is judged by public opinion.

NOTES

1. For the most common arrangements from a financing perspective, see USDOT 2004.
2. A more extensive listing of PPP types is found in Grimsey and Lewis 2004.
3. These are Alabama, Arizona, Arkansas, Colorado, Delaware, Florida, Georgia, Louisiana, Maryland, Minnesota, Missouri, Nevada, North Carolina, Oregon, South Carolina, Texas, Utah, Virginia, Washington, and Wisconsin. Massachusetts also has enabling legislation, but it only applies to one project (USGAO 2004).

4. The Canadian government decided to finance construction of the 417 roadway for this reason. See Mylvaganam and Borins 2004.
5. See Dulles Greenway example in Levy 1996.
6. Public Finance Initiative contracts in Great Britain, for example, involve making value for money calculations. See, for example, Grimsey and Lewis 2004.
7. For additional information on the other three projects, see Levy 1996.

REFERENCES

Ambac. 2003. "New Ownership of Established Toll Road Solidified with Refinancing Bond Issue." Available at http://www.ambac.com.

Amos, P. 2004. *Public and Private Sector Roles in the Supply of Transport Infrastructure and Services.* Washington, D.C.: The World Bank Group, Transport Papers, TP-1, May.

Akintoye, A., M. Beck, and C. Hardcastle. 2003. *Public Private Partnerships: Managing Risks and Opportunities.* Malden, MA: Blackwell Science.

Autostrade International of Virginia O&M Inc. 2002. *Annual Report.* Sterling, VA: Author.

Bailey-Campbell, Pamela. 2005. "Managed Lanes are HOT in the US." Paper presented at the IBTTA Technology Workshop, Edinburgh, June 11–14.

Boarnet, M., J.F. DiMento, and G.P. Macey. 2002. *Toll Highway Finance in California: Lessons from Orange County.* Berkeley: University of California Policy Research Program.

Bunker, T. 2005. "Leasing the Mass Pike to Private Operators" *Policy Directions*, no. 14: 1–7.

Campomar, A. 2004. "Skyway's the Limit?" *Project Finance*, November: 29–31.

Chicago, City of. 2004. *Chicago Toll Bridge System: Request for Skyway Concessionaire Qualifications.* Chicago, IL: Author.

Chinyio, E. and A. Fergusson. 2003. "A Construction Perspective on Risk Management in Public Private Partnerships" in Akintoye, A., M. Beck and C. Hardcastle. 2003. *Public Private Partnerships: Managing Risks and Opportunities.* Malden, MA: Blackwell Science, 95–126.

Coory, D. 2004. "New Labour and PPP's" in A. Ghobadian, D. Gallear, N. O'Regan and H. Viney, *Public Private Partnerships: Policy and Experience.* New York: Palgrave, 24–35.

Congressional Budget Office. 1998. *Innovative Financing of Highways: An Analysis of Proposals.* Washington, D.C.: Author.

DeCorla-Souza, P. 2005. *Financing Infrastructure Solutions: Pricing Strategies.* Presentation made at the Freight Solutions Dialogue, June 7.

———. n.d. "Value Pricing as a Demand Management Strategy." Available at http://www.virginiaDOT.org/infoservice/resources/transconfdecorelasousa/.

Ernzen, J., G. Murdoch, and D. Drecksel. 2000. "Partnering on a Design-Build Project: Making the Three-Way Love Affair Work." *Transportation Record Board*, 1712: 202–211.

Florida Department of Transportation. 1999. *Operations, Management and Maintenance Issues Paper.* Tallahassee, FL: Author.

George, C., W. Streeter, and S. Trommer.2003. "Bliss, Heartburn, and Toll Road Forecasts," Fitch Ratings, Public Finance Special Report. Available at http://www.fitchratings.com.

Grimsey, D. and M.K. Lewis. 2004. *Public Private Partnerships: The Worldwide Revolution in Infrastructure Provision and Project Finance.* Northampton, MA: Edward Elgar Publishing.

Guasch, J. Luis.2004. *Granting and Renegotiating Infrastructure Concessions: Doing It Right.* Washington, D.C.: The International Bank for Reconstruction and Development/The World Bank.

Levy, Sidney. 1996. *Build Operate Transfer: Paving the Way for Tomorrow's Infrastructure.*
New York: Wiley.

Lockwood, S.C., R. Verman, and M. Schneider. 2000. "Public Private partnerships in Toll Road
Development: and Overview of Global Practices," *Transportation Quarterly* 54(2),
77–91.

Lonsdale, C. 2005. "Risk Transfer and the UK Private Finance Initiative: A Theoretical Analysis."
Policy and Politics 33 (2): 231–49.

Linder, S. 2000. "Coming to Terms with the Public-Private Partnership: A Grammar of Multiple
Meanings" in Pauline Vaillancourt Rosenau (ed.), *Public-Private Policy Partnerships.*
Cambridge, MA: MIT Press, 19–36.

Lyne, Jack. 2002. "Texas Governor Lays Out Plan for 4,000-Mile Road, Rail, Utility Network."
Available at http://www.onlineinsider.com (accessed February 18, 2005).

McDonald, J.F., E.L. d'Ouville, and L. N. Liu. 1999. *Economics of Urban Highway Congestion
and Pricing.* Norwell, MA: Kluwer Academic.

Miller, J.B. 2003. "Trends in North American Concession Arrangements: The Continuing
Courtship Between Government and the Private Sector." Power Point Presentation,
Massachusetts Institute of Technology, January 23.

Moreno, Sylvia. 2005. "Texans Are Divided Over Plan for Miles of Wide Toll Roads Funding,
Property Issues Debated." *Washington Post,* February 8, AO3.

Mylvaganam, C. and Borins, S. 2004. *"If you build it…": Business, Government and Ontario's
Electronic Toll Highway.* Ontario: University of Toronto Press.

National Research Council. 2002. *Privatization of Water Services in the United States*: An Assessment of Issues and Experience. Washington, D.C.: National Academy Press.

National Cooperative Highway Research Program. 2003. *Outsourcing of State DOT Capital
Improvement Delivery Functions.* Washington, D.C.: Transportation Research Board,
Project 20–24, November.

National Highway Institute. 1999. *Intelligent Transportation Systems Public-Private Partnerships—Participant Workbook.* Washington, D.C.: United States Department of Transportation, Federal Highway Administration, NHI Course No. 13603.

Nova Scotia, Province of. 1997. *Transferring Risk in Public Private Partnerships.* Nova Scotia,
Canada: Department of Finance.

Perez, B. 2004. *Achieving Public Private Partnerships in the Transport Sector.* New York:
iUniverse, Inc., the Diebold Institute for Public Policy Studies.

Pisarski, A. and M. Tischer.2001. "Transportation Policy—Interaction with a Changing World."
Washington, D.C.: Policy Analysis, Planning and Systems Analysis Working Group,
National Research and Technology Partnership Forum.

Poole, R. W. 2005. Orange County's 91 *Express Lanes: A Transportation and Financial Success,
Despite Political Problems.* Sepulveda, CA: The Reason Foundation, Policy Brief 39.

Price. W. 2001. "An Odyssey of Privatizing Highways: the Evolving Case of SR 91." *Public
Works Management and Policy* 5(4): 259–268.

Regimbal, J.J. 2004. *An Analysis of the Evolution of the Public-Private Transportation Act of
1995.* Charlottesville, VA: The Southern Environmental Legal Defense Fund.

Seliga, J. 2005. "Chicago Skyway Concession and Lease Agreement: Key Element." Presented
at The Chicago Skyway Transaction Seminar, Chicago, March 23.

Shaheen, S., C. McCormick, and R. Finson. 2005. *California's Innovative Corridors Initiative:
A New Model for Public-Private Partnerships in Transportation.* Berkeley: University
of California PATH Program.

Shenkar, O. 2003. *Public-Private Strategic Partnerships: The US Postal Service-Federal Express
Alliance.* Arlington, VA: IBM Endowment for the Business of Government.

Shields, Yvette. 2004. "Windy City Windfall: Officials Bask in Chicago Skyway Deal." *The Bond Buyer*, November 17.

Stainback, John. 2000. *Public/Private Finance and Development: Methodology, Deal Structuring, Developer Solicitation*. New York: John Wiley and Sons.

Sullivan, E. 2000. *Continuation Study to Evaluate the Impacts of the SR 91 Value-Priced Express Lanes: Final Report*. San Luis Obispo: Cal Poly State University.

———. 2003. "Implementing Value Pricing for US Roadways." *European Journal of Transport and Infrastructure Research* 3(4): 401–413.

Texas Department of Transportation, 2002. *Crossroads of the Americas: Trans Texas Corridor Plan*. Austin, TX: Author.

Texas Department of Transportation. 2005a. "Texas Moving Forward to Provide Congestion Relief to I-35: Public-Private Partnership Formed for Trans-Texas Corridor." News Release, March 11.

———. 2005b. *Comprehensive Development Agreement: TTC-35 High Priority Corridor*. Austin, TX: Author.

The World Bank. 2003. *Toolkit for Public Private Partnership in Highways*. Washington, D.C.: The International Bank for Reconstruction and Development.

U.S. Department of Transportation. 2004. *Report to Congress on Public Private Partnerships*. Washington, D.C.: Author.

U.S. General Accountability Office. 2002. *Transportation Infrastructure: Cost and Oversight Issues on Major Highway and Bridge Projects*. Washington, D.C.: Author, GAO-02-702T, May 1.

U.S. General Accountability Office. 2004. *Highways and Transit: Private Sector Sponsorship of and Investment in Major Projects Has Been Limited*. Washington, D.C.: Author, GAO-04-419, March.

Vining, Aidan R., Anthony E. Boardman, and Finn Poschman. 2004. "Public-Private Partnerships in the U.S. and Canada: Case Studies and Lessons" in Thai, Khi V., Armando Araujo, Roslyn Y. Carter, Guy Callendar, David Drabkin, Rick Grimm, Kirsten Jensen, Robert E. Lloyd, Cliff McCue, and Jan Tengen (eds.), *Changes in Public Procurement: An International Perspective (Volume Three)*. Fort Lauderdale, FL: Pracademics Press, 31–60.

Wooldridge, Stephen C., Michael J. Garvin, Cheah Yeun Jen, and John B. Miller. 2002. "Valuing Flexibility in Private Toll Road Development: Analysis of the Dulles Greenway." *Journal of Structured and Project Finance* 7 (4): 25–36.

Ybarra, Shirley. 2004. *Private Sector Participation in Transportation*. Testimony before House Committee on Government Reform Subcommittee on Energy Policy, Natural Resources And Regulatory Affairs, September 30.

21 Evaluating Intelligent Transportation Systems for Public Transit: A Cost–Benefit Approach

Margaret Morrow

INTRODUCTION

Cost–benefit analysis, a technique for systematically estimating the efficiency impacts of policies, has been applied with variable success, across a broad spectrum of policies. Weimer and colleagues (1999) identified the steps of cost–benefit analysis (CBA) as: (1) categorizing relevant impacts, (2) monetizing impacts, (3) discounting for time and risk, and (4) choosing among policies.

A review of the literature indicates that the majority of previous CBA studies of Intelligent Transportation Systems (ITS) technologies for the Bus Transit Management Systems (BTMS) component have not followed the approach above. Most have completed step one, categorizing the costs and benefits, and used it as a starting point for more accommodating analytical approaches such as impact assessments and survey research. But most have not included several important categories of costs and benefits.

In a 1997 study, GAO identified three barriers to performing CBA for ITS projects: (1) lack of knowledge about ITS at the state and local level; (2) lack of data on the costs and benefits; and (3) lack of funding for ITS, in the light of other transportation investment priorities (GAO 1997, p. 8). GAO's first and second barriers explain why approaches other than CBA have been used in previous studies.

The goals of this study were to address the second and third barriers by estimating the costs and benefits of ITS technologies for a BTMS component. With the second barrier removed, a net social benefit was derived for a BTMS. With the second and third barriers removed, deployment rates for ITS technologies will hopefully increase.

The study was developed using actual agency data. A CBA was conducted for the installation of a Traffic Signal Priority System (TSP) for the Tri-County Metropolitan Transportation District (Tri-Met). Tri-Met provides bus, para transit, and light rail service for the City of Portland Oregon. TSP was installed on eight routes (routes 4, 104, 9, 109, 12, 112, 14, and 72) over a one-year period beginning in June 2001 at an expected cost of $4.5 million.[1] TSP installation was staggered, with one route at a time being installed. The CBA examined three years of data, beginning one year prior to TSP installation and ending one year after TSP installation.

Tri-Met's preliminary justification for the system was based on its expected net benefits. Although a formal study was not conducted, Tri-Met's analysis indicated that benefits would include: removal of a bus from service on each route (approximately $200,000 * 8), and elimination of the need for the city to operate a trolley (approximately $850,000 annually), for a total net benefit of $2.45 million in the first year. The routes were selected based upon a number of criteria including: corridor ridership, on-time performance, the number of signals in the corridor, and the opportunity to save enough running time to remove a bus from service on that corridor (Crout 2001).

To perform the CBA study of Tri-Met's TSP, a literature review identified the categories of costs and benefits that are commonly included in a BTMS study. Then, the estimation and valuation methods used for each category were reviewed. Next, a methodology to perform the study was developed based upon the categories, estimation and valuation methods that were most appropriate. Finally, the CBA study was performed and fine-tuned using data from Tri-Met (Morrow 2005). The following sections of the cost–benefit study are included:

- The CBA methodologies that were tested,
- A discussion of the data analysis,
- A discussion of policy implications and conclusions.

METHODOLOGY

The CBA incorporates the categories containing significant quantifiable benefits as indicated by the literature review (Morrow 2005) including vehicle performance, passenger travel time, emissions, and equipment costs. Categories that were important, but could not be measured, are discussed in the omitted cost and benefits section of Morrow 2005. Categories with insignificant or undefined benefits, such as revenue increases, scheduling efficiencies, throughput, and labor relations costs, were not included in the study. Following is a description of the study design, and the cost–benefit categories accompanied by their associated estimation and valuation methods.

DESIGN

A pooled cross-section time-series design was used for all benefit categories. This design was selected because the project spanned more than a year and a control group would have been difficult to construct. Agency budget data was used to estimate cost categories. Overall, the general steps in the process consisted of estimating models for 36 months worth of data including the following variables for each month: vehicle miles, operator hours, vehicle hours, wait time, travel time, and emissions. Table 21.1 lists the effect parameters that were part of each model.

TABLE 21.1
Effect Parameters

Benefit Category	Variable	Unit of Effect	Cost Parameter
Vehicle Performance	Vehicle Miles	# miles traveled per day	$/mile = $.50
	Operator	# seconds operated per day	$/hr = $19.68
	Hours	# seconds driven per day	Present Value = $298,964
	Vehicle Hours		Annualized Value = $16,672
			Per hr factor = 3,268
			Interest rate = 2.5%
Passenger Travel Time	Wait Time	# seconds wait time per day	$/hr = $22.14
	Travel Time	# seconds travel time per day	$/hr = $11.07
Emissions	Emissions	# miles traveled per day	$/gal = $2.94
	Savings		m/gal = 4.5

Categories

For each category, the most appropriate estimation and valuation methods were selected and a justification for its use was identified. First, the benefit categories are presented, followed by the cost categories. Categories measured using the pooled cross-section time-series design includes: vehicle performance, and passenger travel time. Categories measured using agency budget data include equipment costs. The emissions category was measured using the results from the vehicle performance analysis. Additionally, the value of both benefit and cost categories that were left out of the study were contemplated.

Data for categories using the pooled cross-section time-series design was aggregated into a number of categories in the following order[2]:

- Either Route ID or Stop ID or link ID (leg of route—each piece between two stops was assigned an ID) depending upon characteristics of the variable;
- Schedule Type (weekday morning rush hour, weekday non-rush hour, weekday evening rush hour, non-weekday);
- Day of study.

Benefits for each schedule type were calculated separately, given that both traffic and route patterns differs significantly on different days of the week. For example, Saturday traffic differs significantly from weekday traffic, and a route may start/end in different places and have different stops on Saturday than on a weekday.

Following is a description of each category that was included in the study, the data elements that were measured, the estimation method that was used along with the reason for its selection, and the valuation method that was used along with the reason for its selection.

Vehicle Performance

Three variables were estimated in this category: (1) vehicle mile savings, (2) operator hour savings, and (3) vehicle hours savings. The three variables were selected because they capture the most significant portion of the vehicle performance related benefits. Additionally, the data to estimate them is readily available.

The valuation methods that were used for each variable are:

- Vehicle miles savings per year = cost-per-mile[3] *Δ miles traveled per year
- Operator hours savings per year = average wage rate[4] *Δ operator hours per year
- Vehicle hours savings per year = annual annuity cost of new bus[5] *(Δ vehicle hours per year/vehicle per hour factor[6])

The above valuation methods were selected for two reasons: first, they were the most commonly used in prior studies; in addition, all of the major transit agencies report miles, hours, and peak vehicle requirements to the Bureau of Transportation Statistics annually. Consequently, the information is readily available and is being used by both agencies and the federal DOT in the decision making process.

Vehicle Miles

In order to arrive at estimates for Δmiles traveled, the following estimation procedure was used. For each route, schedule type and day, the miles traveled on that route was calculated using data from the AVL system. The data was used to determine Y^s_{rt}, the bus miles traveled on route r and schedule type s on day t, where:

s = Schedule Type (weekday morning rush hour = 1, weekday non-rush hour = 2, weekday evening rush hour = 3, non-weekday > 3)
t = time period (day 1, day 2,...day 1095)
r = route (route 4 = 0, route 104 = 1, route 9 = 2, route 109 = 3, route 12 = 4, route 112 = 5, route 14 = 6, route 72 = 7)

For each schedule type, the following fixed effects[7] regression model was estimated:

$$Y^s_{rt} = b^s_o + Q^s_r + (m=1..35)\Sigma\ b^s_m P_{mt} + c^s_0 Z_{0t} + (k=1..7)\ \Sigma\ c^s_k\ Z_{rt} R_{kr} + e_{rt}$$
where:
R = 1 if k = r, 0 otherwise
Z_{rt} = 1 if TSP is in place on route r during time period t, 0 otherwise
P_{mt} = 1 if day t is within month m, 0 otherwise
P_{1t}, P_{2t}, ...P_{36t} are a series of dummy variables corresponding to month (1 = July 2000, 2 = August 2000...35 = May 2003)
m = monthly period ranging from 1 = July 2000 to 35 = May 2003
Q^s_r = the fixed effect for route r and schedule type s
c^s_0 = effect route 4 had on miles traveled
c^s_k = the partial effect route k had on miles traveled[8]

The estimated coefficients were then used to derive the daily effect of TSP on miles traveled on route r and schedule type s, ΔM_{rs} as follows:

$\Delta M_{rs} = (c^s_0 + c^s_k)$ for routes 104, 9, 109, 12, 112, 14, 72
$= c^s_0$ for route 4

Standard errors for ΔM_{rs} and t statistics were calculated as follows:

SE $(\Delta M_{rs}) = SE(c^s_0)$ for route 4
    = square root of (variance c^s_0 + variance c^s_k + (2*covariance(c^s_k, c^s_0))
        for routes 104, 9, 109, 12, 112, 14, 72
$t = \Delta M_{rs} / SE (\Delta M_{rs})$ for all routes

Summing ΔM_{rs} over all routes and schedule types results in the total annual effect of TSP on vehicle miles in the system as a whole, i.e.,

$\Delta AVM = (s = 1..4) (f_s \Sigma(r = 0..7) \Sigma \Delta M_{rs})$
where: f_s = number of times schedule type s in effect during a year (e.g. $f_{am\ rush}$ = 255)

Finally, ΔAVM was multiplied by the cost-per-mile factor to calculate vehicle miles savings.

Other variables might have been included in the model but were left out because they were either unavailable or did not vary. These include an indication for whether or not detours or construction was present on a route, an indication that a vehicle was purposefully turned back before it reached the end of the route, an indication that the structure of the route had changed, or an indication that a special event was occurring such as the annual Rose Parade.

Operator Hours and Vehicle Hours

The following estimation procedure was used for change in operator hours and change in vehicle hours. For each route, schedule type and day, the hours traveled on that route, Y^s_{rt} were calculated using data from the AVL system. A set of regression models similar to those discussed regarding travel miles saved was estimated for hours traveled, except the dependent variable in this model was hours traveled for route r and schedule type s during time period t. The daily effect of TSP on hours traveled on route r and schedule type s, $\Delta H_{rs,}$ was then obtained from:

$\Delta H_{rs} = (c^s_0 + c^s_r)$ for routes 104, 9, 109, 12, 112, 14, 72 = c^s_0 for route 4
    Standard errors for ΔH_{rs} and t statistics were calculated as follows:
SE $(\Delta H_{rs}) = SE(c^s_0)$ for route 4
    = square root of (variance c^s_0 + variance c^s_k + (2*covariance(c^s_k, c^s_0))
        for routes 104, 9, 109, 12, 112, 14, 72
$t = \Delta H_{rs} / SE (\Delta H_{rs})$ for all routes

Summing ΔH_{rs} over all routes and schedule types results in the total annual effect of TSP on operator hours required in the system as a whole, i.e.,

$\Delta AOH = (s=1..4) \ (f_s \ \Sigma(r=0..8) \ \Sigma\Delta H_{rs})$

Finally, ΔAOH was multiplied by the average wage rate factor to calculate operator hours savings.

In calculating change in vehicle hours, only peak-period schedules (rush hour) are pertinent since reducing hours in off-peak times does not reduce the number of vehicles needed to meet the peak load. Since the vehicle operates the same amount of hours as a driver operates, vehicle hours savings in the system as a whole was calculated as:

$\Delta AVH = \Sigma(r=0..8) \ \Sigma\Delta H_{r1}$[9] (or $= \Sigma(r=0..8) \ \Sigma\Delta H_{r3}$[10], whichever is greater). Then, ΔAVH was divided by the vehicle per hour factor, and then multiplied by the annualized cost of a new bus to calculate vehicle hours savings.

Emissions

One variable was estimated in this category—emissions savings. The variable was selected because transit agencies are most likely to have the resources available to calculate it.

The valuation method that was used is:

Emissions savings = EPA per-gallon cost of emissions damage[11] * (Δmiles traveled /average MPG[12])

The above valuation method was selected for two reasons: all of the major transit agencies report miles to the Bureau of Transportation Statistics annually. Consequently, the information is readily available and is being used by both agencies and the federal DOT in the decision making process; and the EPA makes the per-gallon damage estimates available for all major metropolitan areas. The estimates of Δmiles traveled that were used here were the same estimates used for the vehicle performance category.

Travel Time

Two variables were estimated in this category, passenger wait time savings and passenger travel time savings. Although the common practice in transit studies is to estimate the passenger time category based upon the wait time variable alone, the AVL system and passenger count equipment provide the data to determine exactly how many passengers were both waiting at a stop and how many passengers were on a vehicle between two points on a route. Consequently, both passenger wait time and passenger travel time were estimated.

The valuation methods used are:

- Passenger waiting times savings = Δ wait time * $22.14[13]
- Passenger travel times savings = Δ travel time * $11.07[14]

The Metro planning study (Metro 2002) revealed preferences method was selected for both of the above valuations because the information is readily available and is being used by other studies in the metropolitan area. Additionally, the bias introduced with stated preference models may be more significant than bias introduced by using the revealed preferences model. Economists are generally much more comfortable observing individuals' valuations of goods and services through their behavior in markets than eliciting their valuations through survey questionnaires (Boardman et al. 1997). Finally, although the average wage rate was used by all the previous studies, it most likely is not representative of people riding the bus.

Two different methods were used to estimate the effects for both passenger travel time and passenger wait time for several reasons including the fact that a random effects method was not an appropriate fit. The first generated more variables than the statistical package could manage with the full dataset, so the second was used as a check on the first one. Tests for appropriate specification and fit of the models would fill an additional study.

The first method involved selecting a random sample of two hundred stops/links from the full dataset, then estimating travel time variables. The advantage of this method is that a separate effect could be estimated for each stop. The stops were randomly selected, so statistical theory implies that they should be representative of the entire population of bus stops; and results can therefore be calculated and compared on a route-by-route basis. The disadvantage of this method is that the sample selected may not be representative of the entire population. However, because of the nature of the data, and the high number of dummy variables (one for each stop) it was impossible to work with the entire dataset.

The second method utilized the entire dataset, aggregating the stops or links by fare zone, and then estimating travel time variables. The advantage of this method was that it was possible to work with the entire sample because the number of variables was low. Thus effects of TSP on fare zones were uncovered. This view would not have been possible if the data had only been viewed by stop, link, route, and schedule type. Finally, the high number of observations in the sample increased the likelihood that the true estimates were found. The disadvantage of this method was that results for each route could not be determined. Results were generalized to an entire fare zone rather than individual stops within the zone.

Passenger Wait Time

The following estimation procedures were used to estimate the change in wait time. For each bus stop on a given route and day, the headway for a bus arriving at a stop was calculated as one-half the time between its arrival and the previous buses departure (or zero for the first bus in the morning). Data in the sample was aggregated as described previously (by stop ID, day type, and day of study). Additionally, each stop was categorized by its fare zone.

Method One—Passenger Wait Time by Bus Stop
The average daily wait time at stop b while schedule type s was in effect, Y^s_{bt}, was estimated. For each schedule type, the following fixed effects regression model was estimated:

$$Y^s_{bt} = b^s_o + Q^s_{kd} + (m=1..35)\Sigma\, b^s_m P_{mt} + c^s_0 Z_{dt} + (k=1..199)\, \Sigma\, c^s_d\, Z_{dt} B_{kd} + e_{dt}$$

where:

    d = bus stop ID (each route has between 100 and 240 stops, 200 random bus stops were sampled[15])

    Z_{dt} = 1 if TSP is in place on the route of which stop b is a part at the time corresponding to the tth wait time, 0 otherwise[16]

    Q_{kd} = the fixed effect for stop d and route k

    c^s_0 = the estimate for stop 40 on route 1, direction 0

    c^s_d = the partial estimate for all other stops

    The estimated coefficients were then used to derive the effect of TSP on waiting time for passengers boarding at stop b on route R while schedule type s is in effect for one year, ΔWR_{bs}, as follows:

$\Delta WR_{bs} = P_{bs} * (c^s_0 + c^s_b)$ for 199 stops

    $= P_{bs} * c^s_0$ for first stop in sample (stop 40)

    Where P_{bs} = number of passengers per year who board at stop b while schedule type s is in effect.

Standard errors for ΔWR_{bs} and t statistics were calculated as follows:

SE (ΔWR_{bs}) = SE(c^s_0) for stop 40

    = square root of (variance c^s_0 + variance c^s_k + (2*covariance(c^s_k, c^s_0))

        for all other stops

    t = ΔWR_{bs} / SE (ΔWR_{bs}) for all routes

The effect was averaged for all the stops on the route in the sample, and then multiplied by the total number of stops on the route:

$\Delta MWR_{bs} = ((\Sigma(b=1..C)\ \Delta WR_{bs})/C) * N)$

where C = # of stops on the route in the sample

    N = total # of stops on the route

    Summing ΔMWR_{bs} over all routes and schedule types results in the total annual effect of TSP on annual passenger waiting time in the system as a whole, i.e., $\Delta AWRT$ = (s=1..4) $(f_s \Sigma(r=1..8) \Sigma \Delta MWR_{bs})$. Finally, $\Delta AWRT$ was multiplied by \$22.14 to calculate passenger waiting times savings.

Method Two Passenger Wait Time by Fare Zone

In the second method, stops were categorized by their fare zone:

    f = fare zone (1 = inner city, 2 = zone 2 outbound, 3 = zone 2 inbound, 4 = zone 3 outbound, 5 = zone 3 inbound). The second method incorporated the wait time values for the entire sample of 1,321 bus stops. The following regression model was estimated for each schedule type:

$Y^s_{ft} = b^s_0 + Q^s_k + (k=1..4)\ \Sigma b^s_k B_{kf} + (m=1..35) \Sigma\ b^s_m P_{mt} + c^s_0 Z_{ft} + (k=1..4)\ \Sigma\ c^s_k\ Z_{ft} F_{kf}$

    $+ e_{ft}$

where:

Z_{ft} = 1 if TSP in place in fare zone f during time period t, 0 otherwise

Q^s_k = the fixed effect for zone k

$P_{mt=}$ 1 if day t is within month m, 0 otherwise

m = monthly period ranging from 1 = June 2000 to 36 = May 2003

F_{kf} = 1 if fare zone f is equal to k, 0 otherwise

c^s_0 = the effect of zone 1

c^s_k = the partial effect of zone K

The estimated coefficients were then used to derive the daily effect of TSP on waiting time on fare zone f and schedule type s in one day, ΔW_{fs}, as follows:

$$\Delta W_{fs} = P^* (c^s_0 + c^s_f) \text{ for fare zones central outbound, central inbound, outer outbound,}$$
outer inbound

$$= P^* c^s_0 \text{ for fare zone inner city}$$

where P = average daily passengers for the fare zone

Standard errors and t values were calculated using the same method as the previous models.

Summing ΔW_{bs} over all fare zones and schedule types results in the total annual effect of TSP on annual passenger waiting time in the system as a whole, i.e.,

$$\Delta AWT = (s=1..4) (f_s \Sigma(f=0..4) \Delta W_{fs}).$$

where F_s = number times schedule type s in effect during a year (e.g., f_{amrush} = 255). Finally, ΔAWT was multiplied by \$22.14 to calculate passenger waiting times savings.

Other variables that might have been included in both wait time models, but were left out because they were either unavailable or did not vary. They include: an indication for whether or not detours or construction was present on a route; an indication that the structure of the route had changed; an indication that a special event was occurring such as the annual Rose Parade; the congestion level; the activation parameters for TSP; an indication that the number of trips down the route had been reduced; and an indication of why the person was taking the trip so that their cost could be assigned by trip purpose.

Passenger Travel Time

The following estimation procedures were used to estimate Δtravel time. For each link (two adjoining stops) on a given route and day, the travel time between the two stops was calculated as the arrival time at the second stop minus the departure time from the first stop. Data in the sample was aggregated as described previously (by link ID, day type, and day of study). Additionally, each link was categorized by its fare zone.

Method One Travel Time by Link ID

The following estimation procedure was used to estimate the change in annual passenger travel time, ΔTT. For each link on a given route and day, the tth average travel time on link b (i.e., between stops b and b+1), Y^s_{bt}, was determined. A set of regression models similar to those discussed regarding passenger waiting time were estimated for travel time. The estimated coefficients were then used to derive the annual effect of TSP on passenger travel time for passengers who are on board during link b (i.e., boarded at or before stop b and did not exit prior to stop b+1) while schedule type s is in effect, ΔTR_{bs}, as follows:

$\Delta TR_{bs} = P_{bs}*(c^s_0 + c^s_b)$ all other 199 links
$= P* c^s_0$ for first link in sample (link 4241)
where P_{bs} = total number of passengers per year who traverse link b while schedule type s is in effect.

   The effect was averaged for all the links on the route in the sample, then multiplied by the total number of links on the route:
$\Delta MTR_{bs} = ((\Sigma(b=1..C) \Delta TR_{bs})/C) * N)$
where C = # of links on the route in the sample
   N = total # of links on the route

   Summing ΔMTR_{bs} over all routes and schedule types results in the total annual effect of TSP on annual passenger travel time in the system as a whole, i.e., $\Delta ATT=$ (s=1..4) (fs Σ(r=1..8) ΔMTR_bs). Finally, ΔMTP was multiplied by \$11.07 to calculate passenger travel times savings.

Method Two Travel Time by Fare Zone
Travel time was also estimated by fare zone, using a similar method as described for passenger wait time, with the exception that links rather than stops were categorized by fare zone, and travel time was estimated for each fare zone. Additionally, the other variables that might have been included but were not for various reasons are the same for travel time as for wait time.

Equipment Costs

Two variables were measured in this category: capital costs and operational costs. The actual budget figures from agency budgets were obtained so that figures are based upon actual costs not budgeted or projected costs.

DATA ANALYSIS

This section reports the results from the models discussed in section II. An analysis of the statistics for all of the models can be found in Morrow, 2005.

VEHICLE MILES

Table 21.2 lists the effect estimates, t value, annual benefits by schedule type, and annual benefits total for each route.

TABLE 21.2
Vehicle Miles Benefit

Route	Weekday AM Rush			Weekday PM Rush			Weekday Non-Rush			Non-Weekday			Total
	Effect miles per day	T	Annual Net Benefits	Effect miles per day	T	Annual Net Benefits	Effect miles per day	T	Annual Net Benefits	Effect miles per day	T	Annual Net Benefits	
4	-.74 (5.23)	-0.52	$350	39.85*** (8.53)	4.67	-$5,082	-457.76*** (36.27)	-12.62	$58,365	-750.63*** (58.37)	-12.62	$41,285	$94,918
104	-40.81*** (5.23)	-7.80	$5,203	41.88*** (8.53)	4.91	-$5,340	-459.71*** (66.57)	-6.91	$58,614	-629.76*** (97.54)	-6.46	$34,637	$93,114
9	-74.96*** (5.18)	-14.45	$9,559	28.82*** (8.46)	3.41	-$3,675	-444.07*** (66.41)	-6.69	$56,619	-777.62*** (96.96)	-8.02	$42,769	$105,272
109	16.42** (6.93)	2.37	-$2,094	32.66*** (11.30)	2.89	-$4,165	-223.19** (80.79)	-2.76	$28,458	-470.16*** (129.20)	-3.64	$25,859	$48,058
12	-22.68*** (6.40)	-3.55	$2,892	-270.24*** (9.10)	-29.67	$34,456	-227.96*** (70.34)	-3.24	$29,065	647.43*** (104.19)	6.21	-$35,609	$30,804
112	99.44*** (7.01)	14.19	-$12,680	131.24*** (11.42)	11.49	-$16,734	758.30*** (81.40)	9.32	-$96,684	959.62*** (129.91)	7.39	-$52,779	-$178,877
14	-33.45*** (6.15)	-5.44	$4,265	18.45 (10.05)	1.84	-$2,353	-283.21*** (74.57)	-3.80	$36,110	-337.77*** (114.94)	-2.94	$18,578	$56,601
72	-67.17*** (6.93)	-9.69	$8,565	-8.99 (11.30)	-0.80	$1,147	-619.97*** (80.79)	-7.67	$79,047	-675.38*** (129.20)	-5.23	$37,146	$125,906
			$16,061			-$1,746			$249,596			$111,886	$375,796

* p < .05, ** p < .01, *** p < .001; AM rush n = 5,935; PM rush n = 5,935; Weekday non-rush n = 5,951; non-weekday n = 2,569.

Overall, vehicle miles cost decreased $375,796 per year as a result of TSP. Savings occurred in all schedule types, except for the PM rush hour, and on all routes except for 112. For routes where a benefit occurred, the average annual savings was $125,847. All but three of the effect estimates were statistically significant at the .001 level.

The reduction in mean miles traveled after TSP was introduced occurred most probably because Tri-Met scheduled fewer trips, especially in the weekday non-rush hour schedule type. Other non-TSP factors that may have caused this change include: changes to the structure of the route, detours around construction zones, and dispatchers turning trips back before they reached the end of the route.

The cost increase in the PM rush was not a substantial amount; however, costs were incurred during that time on all routes except for routes 12 and 72. Unique non-TSP attributes of route 72 that may explain the difference in the PM rush hour include: it is the only route that does not go to downtown Portland and its PM trips do not travel the full route length. Both of these attributes increase the probability that a bus may encounter a lower number of route detours, and save a higher number of miles.

Two unique non-TSP attributes of route 12 may explain the difference in the PM rush hour. First, it is the only route traveling southwest of downtown. Second, it has more outbound trips during the evening rush hour. In terms of TSP, route 12's TSP is only installed on the portions of the route in fare zone 1 and 2, while TSP is installed almost the full length of all the other routes (except for 112).

Route 112 negative benefits across all schedule types. Probable explanations include: TSP is also only installed in fare zones 1, 2, and a small portion of 3; on the length of the route where TSP is installed, only 50 percent of the intersections were activated at the time of the study; and the route travels more northeast from downtown than the other routes. A probable non-TSP explanation is that beginning on September 11, 2001 a couple of miles distance was added to the end of the route.

Operator Hours

Table 21.3 lists the effect estimates, t value, annual benefits by schedule type, and annual benefits total for each route.

Overall a total savings in operator wages of $172,255 per year accrued as a result of TSP, which correlates with the vehicle miles savings (if less miles are traveled, it stands to reason that operators are also driving less). Savings occurred in all schedule types, and on all routes except for 12 and 112. The non-rush hour schedule types contained much higher benefits than the rush hour schedule types. One possible explanation for this is rush-hour gridlock, which hampers traffic and consequently TSP. The estimates indicate the gridlock effect is more severe in the evening. Tri-Met confirms that the PM rush hour typically has higher traffic volumes and ridership (Crout 2005). Estimated effects were significant for between five and seven of the routes (depending on schedule type).

The PM rush had the least amount of savings in operator hours, and then only on route 12. The reasons that route 12 experienced operator hours savings are the same as why route 12 had the most vehicle miles savings during the PM rush.

TABLE 21.3
Operator Hours Benefit

Route	Weekday AM Rush			Weekday PM Rush			Weekday Non-Rush			Non-Weekday			Total
	Effect 1000 seconds per day	T	Annual Net Benefits	Effect 1000 seconds per day	T	Annual Net Benefits	Effect 1000 seconds per day	T	Annual Net Benefits	Effect 1000 seconds per day	T	Annual Net Benefits	
4	2.42 (8.42)	-0.52	-$3,377	4.61 (8.42)	-0.52	-$6,439	-16.72 (8.42)	-0.52	$23,321	-42.00 (8.42)	-0.52	$25,260	$38,765
104	-2.29*** (0.37)	-6.22	$3,203	3.13*** (0.60)	5.19	-$4,375	-21.09*** (2.24)	-9.42	$29,407	-33.00*** (7.13)	7.12	$19,847	$48,082
9	-3.67*** (0.37)	-10.04	$5,127	4.10*** (0.59)	6.85	-$5,720	-13.47*** (2.23)	-6.05	$18,782	-46.97*** (7.08)	7.08	$28,245	$46,434
109	-0.50 (0.49)	-1.02	$697	3.55*** (0.80)	4.44	-$4,955	-13.02*** (2.97)	-4.38	$18,155	-31.53*** (9.44)	9.44	$18,961	$32,859
12	3.09*** (0.39)	7.86	-$4,321	-21.38*** (0.65)	-33.14	$29,804	24.21*** (2.39)	10.13	-$33,758	63.79*** (7.61)	7.61	-$38,364	-$46,640
112	-0.83 (0.49)	-1.70	$1,170	1.69* (0.81)	2.09	-$2,363	3.14*** (3.01)	1.05	-$4,381	36.98*** (9.49)	9.49	-$22,242	-$27,815
14	-2.60*** (0.43)	-5.99	$3,628	1.66* (0.71)	2.34	-$2,322	-11.58*** (2.63)	-4.40	$16,152	-16.29*** (8.40)	8.39	$9,796	$27,254
72	-3.67*** (0.44)	-8.41	$5,118	1.34 (0.80)	1.67	-$1,864	-23.70*** (3.46)	-6.84	$33,048	-28.29*** (11.00)	10.99	$17,014	$53,316
Total			$11,244			$1,767			$100,726			$58,518	$172,255

*p < .05, **p < .01, ***p < .001, n = 5,937 AM rush, n = 5,935, PM rush, n = 5,951 non-rush, n = 2,569 non-weekday.

However, route 12 negative benefits overall, despite positive vehicle miles benefits overall. A probable explanation for this occurrence is that dwell time (time a bus idles at the same spot) was included. Although, dwell time was included in the operator hour analysis, it was not included in the travel time analysis for route 12 or any of the other routes. This occurred because the links selected for route 12 did not include time when a bus dwelled at the same stop (the link ID would be the same stop combined). If increased congestion caused increased dwell time, then the travel time estimate is biased and the operator hours estimate is inaccurate.

Possible explanations for the negative benefits on both routes 12 and 112 include: both routes only have TSP installed in fare zones 1 and 2; and both have about the same number of TSP equipped signals (only 21 of route 112's 37 signals are equipped, while all of route 12 and 13's signals are equipped). Increasing the length of the route covered by TSP on these routes may help to increase their benefit levels to the levels of the other routes, as less operator time will be required. A non-TSP explanation for route 112 only is the additional distance added to the route on September 11, 2001.

Both routes 4 and 104 had overall benefits in the operator hour category, because their savings in the non-rush hour compensated for their rush hour costs. The throughput category, which was not included in the study, would have better captured this external cost, since gridlock may have been a contributing factor.

For future ITS evaluation studies, the throughput category will be required. The Transportation Equity Act for the 21st Century (TEA-21) prescribes that the U.S. Secretary of Transportation shall issue guidelines and requirements for the evaluation of operational tests and deployment projects for Intelligent Transportation Systems (ITS). The document fulfilling this mandate is titled "TEA-21 ITS Evaluation Guidelines Effect" (http://www.its.dot.gov/EVAL/evalguidelines_tea21evalguidelines.htm). The guidelines require that throughput costs be captured as a part of cost–benefit evaluations.

Vehicle Hours

The statistics and effect estimates for vehicle hours are identical to operator hours. However, the benefit calculation for vehicle hours differs from operator hours. Table 21.4 lists the individual route effects of TSP on vehicle hours. Only the PM rush hour schedule type was included for vehicle hours, since the primary costs captured in this category are new bus acquisition costs. Transit agencies typically require a fleet size large enough to accommodate their largest rush hour service, and according to the National Transit Database, for Tri-Met that is the PM rush hour.

Overall, vehicle hour costs savings were $458 per year as a result of TSP, which is a small portion of the annualized cost of purchasing a new bus, which is approximately $16,000. Only route 12 experienced savings, which amounted to roughly one-half of the annualized cost of purchasing a new bus. Estimates for five to six of the routes were statistically significant.

TABLE 21.4
Vehicle Hours Benefit

| Route | Weekday PM Rush | | |
	Effect 1,000 seconds per day	T	Annual net benefits
4	4.61 (8.42)	-0.52	-$1,669
104	3.13** (0.60)	5.19	-$1,134
9	4.10** (0.59)	6.85	-$1,483
109	3.55* (0.80)	4.44	-$1,284
12	-21.38** (0.65)	-33.14	$7,726
112	1.69** (0.81)	2.09	-$612
14	1.67** (0.71)	2.34	-$601
72	1.34** (0.80)	1.67	-$483
Total			$458

*p < .05, **p < .001.

EMISSIONS

The statistics and effect estimates for emissions are identical to vehicle hours. However, the benefit calculations differ. Table 21.5 lists the individual route effects of TSP on emissions.

Overall, emissions costs decreased $491,041 per year as a result of TSP. Since vehicles were traveling less miles because Tri-Met reduced the number of trips after TSP was introduced, fewer emissions were emitted. Savings occurred in all schedule types except for the PM rush hour, and on all routes except for 112. For routes where a benefit occurred, the average annual savings was $164,440. Route 112 negative benefits across all schedule types. The PM rush was the only schedule type with negative total benefits.

Reasons for the differences in the PM rush hour schedule type and route 112 are the same as the reasons listed in the vehicle miles analysis. All effect estimates except three were statistically significant.

PASSENGER TRAVEL TIME

The passenger travel time category contained two variables: wait time and travel time. The unit of analysis for wait time is a bus stop, and the unit of analysis for travel time

TABLE 21.5
Emissions Benefit

Route	Weekday AM Rush			Weekday PM Rush			Weekday Non-Rush			Non-Weekday			Total
	Effect miles per day	T	Annual Net Benefits	Effect miles per day	T	Annual Net Benefits	Effect miles per day	T	Annual Net Benefits	Effect miles per day	T	Annual Net Benefits	
4	-2.74 (5.23)	-0.52	$457	39.85*** (8.53)	4.67	-$6,640	-457.76*** (36.27)	-12.62	$76,264	-750.63*** (58.37)	-12.62	$53,946	$124,026
104	-40.81*** (5.23)	-7.80	$6,799	41.88*** (8.53)	4.91	-$6,978	-459.71*** (66.57)	-6.91	$76,589	-629.76*** (97.54)	-6.46	$45,259	$121,669
9	-74.96*** (5.19)	-14.45	$12,490	28.82*** (8.45)	3.41	-$4,802	-444.07*** (66.41)	-6.69	73982.7	-777.62*** (96.60)	-8.02	$33,789	$137,556
109	16.42** (6.93)	2.37	-$2,736	32.66*** (11.30)	2.89	-$5,442	-223.19** (80.79)	-2.76	$73,983	-470.16*** (129.20)	-3.64	33788.96	$62,796
12	-22.68*** (6.39)	-3.55	$3,779	-270.24*** (9.11)	-29.67	$45,022	-227.96*** (70.34)	-3.24	$37,979	647.43*** (104.19)	6.21	-$46,529	$40,250
112	99.44*** (7.01)	14.19	-$16,568	131.24*** (11.42)	11.49	-$21,866	758.30*** (81.40)	9.32	-$126,333	959.62*** (129.91)	7.39	-$68,965	-$233,732
14	-33.45*** (6.15)	-5.44	$5,573	18.45 (10.05)	1.84	-$3,074	-283.21*** (74.56)	-3.80	$47,184	-337.77*** (114.94)	-2.94	$24,275	$73,958
72	-67.17*** (6.93)	-9.69	$11,192	-8.99 (11.30)	-0.80	$1,499	-619.97*** (80.78)	-7.67	$103,289	-675.38*** (129.20)	-5.23	$48,538	$164,517
			$20,986			-$2,281			$326,138			$146,198	$491,041

$* p < .05, ** p < .01, *** p < .001$; AM rush n = 5,935; PM rush n = 5,935; weekday non-rush n = 5,951; non-weekday n = 2,569.

is a link, which is the coupling of two adjoining stops along a route. Two methods were employed to estimate both variables: (1) estimating the effect for two hundred randomly selected stops/links along the routes, then finding the average effect for all the stops/links for each route, and finally multiplying the average effect by the number of stops/links on the route, and (2) estimating the effect by fare zone.

For each variable and method, the effect estimates are presented and interpreted. The results of each method are compared.

Wait Time by Route

Table 21.6 highlights the differing stop and TSP configurations for the 8 routes and the stops included in the sample. The first column indicates the route number. The second column indicates the number of stops for that route that were included in the sample. The third column lists the percentage of signals on the route that were equipped with TSP. The fourth column indicates the total stops for the route. The fifth column indicates the length of the route where TSP was installed. The last column indicates the average daily ridership for the route.

Table 21.7 lists the effects of TSP on wait time using method one (averaging the bus stop benefits by route). First, the average effects for all the stops were calculated, and then it was multiplied by the number of stops on the route to derive the total annual benefit.

According to the estimate, overall, TSP resulted in a total wait time cost increase of $331,972 per year. Cost increases occurred in the am rush hour and the weekday non-rush hour schedule types, with the largest cost increases occurring during the non-weekday schedule type. A TSP explanation for this is a lower frequency of service during that schedule type. In other words, the number of buses traveling down the routes was reduced after TSP was introduced, so that the time a passenger had to wait for the next bus was increased. Tri-Met justified the purchase of TSP by conceptualizing that they would be able to eliminate service, consequently, the service reductions are counted as a result of TSP for the purpose of the study.

TABLE 21.6
Routes in Sample

Route #	# Stops in Sample	Percent Signals TSP Equipped	Stops on Route	Length Route TSP Installed	Avg. Daily Ridership
4	18	71%	154	80%	565
104	29	81%	178	80%	1119
9	15	94%	102	85%	271
109	26	47%	199	75%	1603
12	28	100%	162	40%	741
112	25	59%	184	55%	532
14	11	96%	118	80%	1054
72	34	94%	238	85%	2419

TABLE 21.7
Wait Time Benefit by Stop ID/Route

Route	# Stops	AM Rush		PM Rush		Non-Rush		Non-Weekday		Total Annual Benefit
		Avg. Annual Benefit Per Stop	Total Annual Benefit	Avg. Annual Benefit Per Stop	Total Annual Benefit	Avg. Annual Benefit Per Stop	Total Annual Benefit	Avg. Annual Benefit Per Stop	Total Annual Benefit	
4	154	-$77	-$11,852	$72	$11,062	-$55	-$8,513	$364	$56,080	$46,777
104	178	-$84	-$14,895	$41	$7,236	-$93	-$16,623	$43	$7,607	-$16,675
9	102	-$38	-$3,923	$3	$275	-$363	-$37,014	-$10	-$1,032	-$41,695
109	199	-$24	-$4,849	$110	$21,865	-$292	-$58,180	-$37	-$7,424	-$48,588
12	162	$36	$5,850	-$254	-$41,158	$117	$18,889	$177	$28,638	-$45,057
112	184	-$16	-$2,925	$33	$6,067	-$109	-$20,079	$58	$10,696	-$6,242
14	118	-$14	-$1,643	$81	$9,537	-$1,275	-$150,409	-$5	-$615	-$143,130
72	238	-$127	-$30,129	$219	$52,115	-$395	-$93,995	-$22	-$5,352	-$77,361
Total			-$64,367		$66,998		-$365,925		$31,322	-$331,972

All routes experienced wait time cost increases with the exception of route 4. Route 4's TSP configuration is similar to the routes that had cost increases. However, route 4 experienced the largest cost savings during the non-weekday schedule, an indication that service frequency, the number of trips down the route, has changed.

Routes 14 and 72 had the largest cost increases, with the majority of the increase occurring during the weekday non-rush. Both of these routes carry a high volume of passengers; however more research is needed to uncover why their costs were so much higher. Sample questions to research include: did construction occur along these routes; were there significantly more accidents; and have overall traffic flows increased.

Wait Time by Fare Zone

Five fare zones were included in the study: inner city, zone 2 inbound, zone 2 outbound, zone 3 inbound, and zone 3 outbound. The route maps included in section IV indicate where each zone begins and ends for each route. Table 21.8 lists the effects by individual fare zone.

According to the estimate, overall, wait time costs increased a total of $386,358 per year as a result of TSP. Comparatively small savings occurred in the rush hour schedule types, and large costs increases occurred in the non-rush hour schedule types. The reasons for the increases are the same as when analyzed by method one.

Wait time costs increased in the inner city and inbound fare zones, with the largest increases occurring in zone 2 during the non-rush hour. The outbound zones experienced cost savings, which indicates that TSP is more effective for travelers leaving the city than those going to it. Since TSP was almost always present in zones 1 and 2, those zones were most likely to show an impact from the system. All of the results were statistically significant.

Wait Time Benefits Calculations Differences

Table 21.9 displays the annual wait time benefits as calculated by both methods. Table 21.9 indicates that the two methods result in similar estimates of wait time costs and benefits. Overall, both methods indicate a wait time cost increase, or that passengers are spending more time waiting for buses. However, the route method indicates an approximately $50 thousand lower cost increase. Passenger counts for both models were almost identical, so the difference in estimates is because of differing coefficient values. The route method indicated savings in the non-weekday schedule type, while the zone method indicated a significant cost increase; and the route method indicated a cost increase for the AM rush hour, while the zone method indicated a savings. Both methods determined that a large cost increase occurred during the weekday non-rush hour.

The differing schedule type benefit values for the two methods indicate that further investigation is needed to determine if the best possible equation was employed to estimate wait time. Because of the scope of this effort, it is left for future work. The sign of overall net benefits does not differ, based upon which method is employed.

TABLE 21.8
Wait Time Benefit by Fare Zone

Fare Zone	Weekday AM Rush			Weekday PM Rush			Weekday Non-Rush			Non-Weekday			Total
	Effect seconds per day	T	Annual Net Benefits	Effect seconds per day	T	Annual Net Benefits	Effect seconds per day	T	Annual Net Benefits	Effect seconds per day	T	Annual Net Benefits	
Inner city	-6.48*** (.42)	-15.31	$24,659	-11.19*** (.35)	-31.89	$72,438	8.48*** (.44)	19.32	-$167,196	18.40*** (1.1)	52.96	-$108,111	-$178,210
Zone 2 - Outbound	-10.80*** (.41)	-26.03	$18,696	-14.17*** (.34)	-41.22	$40,969	-1.20** (.44)	-2.71054	$14,865	16.49*** (1.13)	45.47	-$73,163	$1,368
Zone 2 - Inbound	-4.78*** (.42)	-11.45	$19,117	-9.29*** (.35)	-26.85	$36,716	6.49*** (.45)	14.56661	-$131,621	15.70*** (1.13)	46.53	-$108,032	-$183,821
Zone 3 - Outbound	-58.24*** (.51)	-113.79	$27,503	-8.42*** (.42)	-19.84	$8,867	5.27*** (.55)	9.64209	-$22,114	5.61*** (1.38)	26.35	-$9,250	$5,006
Zone 3 - Inbound	-18.78*** (.52)	-35.80	$16,846	-2.60*** (.43)	-5.99	$2,676	7.41*** (.56)	13.23011	-$41,948	4.21** (1.42)	18.33	-$8,275	-$30,701
Total			$106,820			$161,667			-$348,014.45			-$306,831	-$386,358

* p < .05, ** p < .01, *** p < .001; AM rush n = 922,435; PM rush n = 922,259; weekday non-rush n = 938,555; non-weekday n = 404,240.

TABLE 21.9
Annual Wait Time Benefit Calculations Differences

	By Stop ID then Route	By Fare Zone
Weekday AM rush	−$64,367	$106,820
Weekday PM rush	$66,998	$161,667
Weekday Non-rush	−$365,925	−$348,014
Non-weekday	$31,322	−$306,831
Annual Net Benefits	−$331,972	−$386,358

TRAVEL TIME BY ROUTE

Table 21.10 highlights the differing TSP and link configurations for the eight routes. The first column lists the route, the second column indicates the number of links in the sample, the third column indicates the total number of links on the route, the fourth column lists the percent of the signals that are TSP equipped on the route, the fifth column lists the percent of the route that TSP is installed on, and the sixth column lists the average daily ridership for the route.

Table 21.11 lists the effects of TSP on travel time by averaging the link ID benefits by route. First, the average effect for all the links was calculated, and then it was multiplied by the number of links on the route to derive the total annual benefit.

Overall, when benefits are estimated using the average cost per link, a net savings of $534,131 per year results. Savings occurred for all schedule types, and all routes except for route 14. The PM rush hour schedule types experienced much greater savings than the other schedule types. An explanation not measured by the study that would explain the savings is that travelers leaving the city can select more dispersed

TABLE 21.10
Links in Sample

Route #	# Links in Sample	Links on Route	Length Route TSP Installed	Percent Signals TSP Equipped	Avg. Daily Ridership
4	32	153	80%	71%	565
104	16	177	80%	81%	1119
9	13	101	85%	94%	271
109	27	198	75%	47%	1603
12	26	161	40%	100%	741
112	28	183	55%	59%	532
14	18	117	80%	96%	1054
72	34	237	85%	94%	2419

TABLE 21.11
Travel Time Benefits By Link ID/Route

Route	# Links Per Route	AM Rush		PM Rush		Weekday Non-Rush		Non-Weekday		Total Annual Benefit
		Avg. Annual Benefit Per Link	Total Annual Benefit	Avg. Annual Benefit Per Link	Total Annual Benefit	Avg. Annual Benefit Per Link	Total Annual Benefit	Avg. Annual Benefit Per Link	Total Annual Benefit	
4	153	$49	$7,542	$39	$5,943	$154	$23,546	-$134	-$20,531	$16,500
104	177	$94	$16,645	$525	$92,875	$14	$2,511	-$119	-$21,132	$90,899
9	101	$42	$4,226	$247	$24,965	$605	$61,063	-$32	-$3,260	$86,994
109	198	$102	$20,262	$410	$81,220	$40	$7,831	$95	$18,874	$128,187
12	161	$61	$9,816	$264	$42,491	-$120	-$19,262	$377	$60,637	$93,682
112	183	$59	$10,742	$102	$18,740	$38	$6,970	$18	$3,244	$39,695
14	117	$14	$1,667	$366	$42,779	-$1,090	-$127,578	-$211	-$24,659	-$107,793
72	137	$163	$22,313	$545	$74,684	$351	$48,138	$298	$40,831	$185,966
			$93,213		$383,696		$3,218		$54,003	$534,131

routes, than those funneling into the crowded downtown areas. However, this would have been the case both before and after TSP. So, it is not apparent from the study that TSP altered the travel patterns in the city. The congestion category would have helped to understand TSP's impact on travel patterns. Otherwise, one can assume that TSP did speed up the process of leaving town for many passengers.

Route 14 experienced the majority of its cost increases during the weekday non-rush hour schedule type. Route 14's TSP configuration and number of links does not differ significantly from the other routes, so the probable explanation for the difference is not TSP related. Other possible non-TSP explanations include: it is the only route traveling southeast of town, construction has occurred during the non-rush hour schedule type and has slowed traffic; and a non-representative sample was drawn for the study. Further research is needed to reveal the cause.

TRAVEL TIME BY FARE ZONE

Table 21.12 lists the effects of TSP on travel time by fare zone. The route maps included in section IV indicate where each zone begins and end for each route. The analysis looked independently at inbound and outbound data for zones 2 and 3.

According to the estimates, overall, travel time costs decreased $79,895 per year. Savings occurred in all schedule type, and in the inner city and outbound fare zones. Inbound fare zones experienced cost increases across all schedule types. A possible explanation for this is that inbound traffic creates more grid-lock, which hampers the effectiveness of TSP.

The non-rush hour schedule types had the largest savings. Two probable explanations for the non-rush hour savings are: (1) the lack of rush-hour gridlock, which enhances TSP performance, and (2) the higher number of passengers traveling during the non-rush hour. Referring to the formula to calculate travel time benefits, the time savings is multiplied by the number of passengers, so the estimate is very sensitive to passenger count information.

According to the daily counts, Tri-Met carries approximately 685,000 passengers during the non-rush hour, 117,000 during the am rush, 152,000 during the PM rush, and 555,000 on the average non-weekday. Consequently, the effect estimate is higher for the weekday non-rush schedule type than the other schedule types because of the higher number of passengers. Effect estimates were significant for all but a few of the estimates.

TRAVEL TIME BENEFITS CALCULATIONS DIFFERENCES

Table 21.13 displays the annual net benefits calculated by each method. Table 21.13 indicates that the two methods result in different benefit calculations. The fare zone method resulted in significantly lower benefits; however, estimates were in the same direction. The passenger counts for the two methods were close, so cannot account for the difference. Consequently, the differing benefit values for the two methods

TABLE 21.12
Travel Time Benefit by Fare Zone

Fare Zone	Weekday AM Rush			Weekday PM Rush			Weekday Non-Rush			Non-Weekday			Total
	Effect seconds per day	T	Annual Net Benefits	Effect seconds per day	T	Annual Net Benefits	Effect seconds per day	T	Annual Net Benefits	Effect seconds per day	T	Annual Net Benefits	
Inner city	-7.59*** (.4)	-18.96	$14,434	-6.68*** (.46)	-14.50	$21,614	-4.64*** (.39)	-11.95	$45,726	-3.30*** (.64)	-5.14	$9,683	$91,457
Zone 2 Oubound	-1.57*** (.39)	-4.06	$1,594	-0.63 (.45)	-1.42	$910	-0.64 (.72)	-0.90	$3,974	-0.67 (.65)	-1.04	$1,494	$7,974
Zone 2 Inbound	1.03*** (.39)	-4.06	-$2,404	1.33*** (.21)	6.49	-$2,637	0.72 (.72)	1.00	-$7,320	1.30* (.65)	2.00	-$4,488	-$16,850
Zone 3 Oubound	-4.63*** (.48)	-9.69	$1,282	-4.46*** (.2)	-21.80	$2,349	-3.97*** (.82)	-4.85	$8,332	-4.45*** (.79)	-5.60	$3,672	$15,635
Zone 3 Inbound	3.27*** (.49)	6.60	-$1,718	8.24*** (.21)	39.94	-$4,232	2.29** (.84)	2.73	-$6,490	5.98*** (.82)	7.26	-$5,881	-$18,320
			$13,188			$18,005			$44,222			$4,480	$79,895

$* p < .05$, $** p < .01$, $*** p < .001$; AM rush n = 949,618; PM rush n = 966,290; weekday non-rush n = 1,150,630; non-weekday n = 494,499,

TABLE 21.13
Travel Time Benefits Calculations Differences

	By Link ID then Route	By Fare Zone
Weekday AM rush	$93,213	$13,188
Weekday PM rush	$383,696	$18,005
Weekday non-rush	$3,218	$44,222
Non-weekday	$54,003	$4,480
Annual Net Benefits	$534,131	$79,895

indicate that further investigation is needed to determine if the best possible equation was employed to estimate travel time. Because of the scope of this effort, it is left for future work. The sign of overall net benefits does not differ, based upon which method is employed.

CAPITAL AND OPERATIONAL COSTS

Table 21.14 lists the capital costs for the project as provided by Tri-Met. All are one time costs, with the exception of the annual operational costs which includes both personnel costs and hardware replacement costs (Lutterman 2002; Tri-Met 2001).

DATA ANALYSIS SUMMARY

Tables 21.15, 21.16, and 21.17 summarize the benefits of TSP by category, schedule type, and route. The three different charts include: benefits by category and schedule type calculated with the stop/link method, benefits by category and schedule type calculated with the fare zone method, and benefits by route. Both the present value of annual benefits and the present value of annual costs were calculated based upon the following assumptions:

TABLE 21.14
Capital and Operational Costs

Description	Notes	Cost
TSP Emitter Hardware	$1000/bus * 700 buses (+5% spares)	$735,000
Firmware	Software updates on the vehicle	$150,000
Other	Personnel, Software Updates in the Command Center	$615,000
City of Portland	Upgrading Intersections	$3,000,000
Annual Operational Costs	Mainly replacing failed emitters (Lutterman, 2002)	$2,000
	TOTAL	$4,502,000

TABLE 21.15
Net Benefits by Schedule Type using Stop ID/Link ID Estimates

Schedule Types	Annual Benefits Due to Effect on						Total
	Operator Hours	Vehicle Hours	Miles Traveled	Emissions	Travel Time	Wait Time	
Weekday AM rush	$11,244		$16,061	$20,988	$93,213	−$64,367	$77,137
Weekday PM rush	$1,787	$23,099	−$1,746	−$2,281	$383,696	$66,998	$471,533
Weekday non-rush	$100,728		$249,598	$326,138	$3,218	−$365,925	$313,753
Non-weekday	$58,518		$111,886	$146,198	$54,003	$31,322	$401,927
Net annual benefits	$172,255	$23,099	$375,796	$491,041	$534,131	−$331,972	$1,264,350
Present value of benefits							$11,065,672
Less present value of costs							$4,517,552
Present value of net benefits							$6,548,119

- A life expectancy value of ten years, which comes from the ITS Benefits and Costs Database sponsored by DOT (http://www.benefitcost.its.dot.gov/its/benecost.nsf/ SubsystemCosts?OpenForm&Subsystem=Transit+Vehicle+On-Board+(TV));
- A discount rate of 2.5 percent (OMB, 2003); and
- A terminal value of zero (terminal values are not provided by the ITS database).

The three views of the total benefits enhance analysis of the overall benefits.

Table 21.15 indicates that over its ten-year life span, TSP will result in a significant benefit of $6,548,119. The majority of the savings will occur in the travel time and emissions categories. Although transit agencies have traditionally focused on their own internal costs and benefits, the passenger/consumer costs and benefits ignored are tremendous. In this case, the large travel time, emissions, and wait time amounts significantly impact the bottom line.

The smallest amount of benefits occurred during the morning-rush hour schedule type. TSP appears to be hampered when travel patterns funnel people into the inner-city, creating higher congestion levels. This is puzzling because Tri-Met reports that when compared to the evening rush hour, the morning rush hour has lower traffic volumes and ridership (Crout 2005). Other possible reasons include: more morning construction detours and less trips scheduled. Overall, passenger wait time is the only category that experienced increased costs. So although reducing trips saved Tri-Met money, passengers had a higher price to pay.

Table 21.16 summarizes the benefits of TSP by category and schedule type. The benefits for travel time and wait time were derived by categorizing stops and links by their fare zone.

TABLE 21.16
Net Benefits by Category and Schedule Type

Schedule Type	Annual Benefits Due to Effect on						Total
	Operator Hours	Vehicle Hours	Meters Traveled	Emissions	Travel Time	Wait Time	
Weekday AM rush	$11,244		$16,061	$20,986	$13,188	$106,820	$168,298
Weekday PM rush	$1,767	$23,099	–$1,746	–$2,281	$18,005	$161,667	$200,511
Weekday non-rush	$100,726		$249,596	$326,138	$44,222	–$348,014	$372,667
Non-weekday	$58,518		$111,886	$146,198	$4,480	–$306,831	$14,251
Net Annual Benefits	$172,255	$23,099	$375,796	$491,041	$79,895	–$386,358	$755,728
Present Value of Benefits							$6,614,180
Less Present Value of Capital and Operational Costs							4,517,553
Present Value of Net Benefits							2,096,627

TABLE 21.17
Net Benefits By Route Using Stop ID/Link ID Estimates

Route	Annual Benefits Due to Effect on						Total
	Operator Hours	Vehicle Hours	Meters Traveled	Emissions	Travel Time	Wait Time	
Route 4	$38,765	–$1,669	$94,918	$124,026	$16,500	$46,777	**$319,316**
Route 104	$48,082	–$1,134	$93,114	$121,669	$90,899	–$16,675	**$335,955**
Route 9	$46,434	$722	$105,272	$137,556	$86,994	–$41,695	**$335,283**
Route 109	$32,859	$571	$48,058	$62,796	$128,187	–$48,588	**$223,884**
Route 12	–$46,640	$9,780	$30,804	$40,250	$93,682	–$45,057	**$82,820**
Route 112	–$27,815	$10,452	–$178,877	–$233,732	$39,695	–$6,242	**–$396,519**
Route 14	$27,254	$2,124	$56,601	$73,958	–$107,793	–$143,130	**–$90,986**
Route 72	$53,316	$2,253	$125,906	$164,517	$185,966	–$77,361	**$454,598**
Net Annual Benefits	$172,255	$23,099	$375,796	$491,041	$534,131	–$331,972	**$1,264,350**
Present Value of Benefits							**$11,065,672**
Less present value of capital and operational costs							**$4,517,553**
Present Value of Net Benefits							**$6,548,119**

Table 21.16 indicates that over its ten-year life span, TSP will result in a significant benefit of $2,096,627. Table 21.16 indicates that a lower non-weekday savings and a higher am rush hour savings in comparison to Table 21.15. The difference in travel time benefits accounts for much of the discrepancy. As in the previous summary, overall all schedule types experienced savings, and the only the wait time category experienced increased costs. Table 21.17 summarizes the benefits of TSP by route.

Table 21.17 indicates that all routes except for routes 112 and 14 experienced overall savings as a result of TSP. Route 112 experienced costs in the most categories (except for travel time and vehicle hours). Probable explanations include: TSP is only installed on 59 percent of the signals where it is planned to be installed, and TSP is only installed on approximately 50 percent of the route. Route 112 travels through a corridor that is crowded with small businesses with short city blocks. Tri-Met decided not to install TSP in the "downtown Portland" portions of the routes, because the blocks were so short that TSP would not have been effective. Route 112 has a large portion of terrain with short blocks also, so TSP may not be effective on this route.

Route 14 had the largest wait time and travel time increases. Further investigation should uncover whether other activity prompted the increases such as construction, specific route characteristics, or scheduling.

POLICY IMPLICATIONS AND CONCLUSIONS

Cost–benefit analysis provides critical information for establishing transportation policy at all levels of decision making. Table 21.18 identifies the three policy levels and areas

TABLE 21.18
Policy Levels and Areas Facilitated by CBA

Policy Level	Policy Area(s)
Transit Agency Personnel	Scheduling, Wait time accommodations, TSP System Management, Budgeting, Transportation Investments, CBA Requirements, Data Needs
City of Portland Personnel	TSP System Management, Congestion Management
Metropolitan, state, and federal	Transportation Investments, CBA Requirements, Data Needs

facilitated by the results of this CBA. Following the table is a discussion of the policy levels and the specific areas impacted.

For transit agency personnel, several policy areas are enhanced by the results of this study as indicated in Table 21.18, including: scheduling decision enhancements such as the spacing between headways on a route, the number of operators and vehicles needed to service a route, and service frequency. Prior to the wide-spread use of ITS, consumer benefits such as travel time savings required high-cost resources to capture. With the assistance of passenger counters and on-board computers, these benefits can be captured, and agencies can look at a more complete picture of costs and benefits.

Traditionally, scheduling policies are set according to agency benefits (producer benefits), as agencies operate as government service providers, and consequently can not easily raise fares (consumer costs) to cover their own costs. However, the CBA considered all social costs, the external/consumer benefits as well as internal benefits.

In the future, travel time benefits that were greater than all other costs and benefits combined, and wait time costs that were significantly higher than all the savings in the vehicle performance category, can be part of the scheduling policy decisions. If Tri-Met were to schedule headways, operators, vehicles, and service frequency with a focus on maintaining travel time savings and reducing wait time savings, benefits could climb higher.

If no changes are made to wait time, policies for wait time accommodations such as placement of bus shelters and bus arrival signs should be examined. Some of the stops in the study had significant wait time increases. Tri-Met initially conceptualized a reduction in wait time, resulting in increased safety. Although safety was omitted from the study, Tri-Met should consider the costs of safety risks associated with the extended wait time.

Tri-Met's TSP system management policies are another way to reduce wait time costs. Tri-Met policy determines system activation, equipment placement, route placement, and schedule type activation. The wait time cost increases indicate that changes need to be made to the TSP activation time along the route, prior to the stop.

Given that TSP was not successful on all routes, Tri-Met might consider not installing TSP on all routes, and consequently on all buses servicing those routes. Routes that did not have TSP installed on a majority of their length performed worse than other routes. Route 112, which travels northeast of town did not perform as well as other routes. Policy makers could use this information to decide whether or not to continue TSP on route 112 or install TSP on routes with similar characteristics to route 112.

Additionally, Tri-Met may also consider turning-off TSP during the weekday non-rush hour schedule, since wait time costs were negative at that time when estimated by either method. This change would be most effective for inbound traffic, which incurred higher wait time costs than outbound. This implies that AM rush-hour traffic gridlock may make TSP ineffective, and the lack of congestion at other times may complement its performance. Policy makers could use this information to determine how to expand TSP, and whether or not its use should be increased in various schedule types. Furthermore, information about traffic flow/congestion/throughput should be included in future analysis.

A few final policy areas Tri-Met should consider when setting TSP policies for routes include: the location and number of stops on routes, and the passenger volume. TSP performed well on route 72, which had the highest number of both stops and passengers. TSP benefits are exponentially incremented when passenger volumes are high. Additionally, Tri-Met indicated that stops which are located just before traffic signals hinder the performance of TSP (Crout 2005). Although stop orientation was not a part of the study, it should also be considered.

The City of Portland can also use the CBA results to set TSP system management policies. City personnel determine which intersections to equip with TSP equipment, the length of the green light, and the range algorithm. Route 112 had increased costs, and only 59 percent of the signals on route 112 were TSP equipped. Installing TSP on 100 percent of the signals could increase benefits. Additionally, installing TSP on a larger portion of the length of routes could enhance TSP's effectiveness.

Tri-Met's budgeting policies such as equipment and operator requirements needed to meet the schedule will be driven by scheduling policies previously discussed. For example, when planners determine that additional operators are needed to reduce off-peak wait time, then the cost of the operators must be budgeted for. With the wait time cost information in hand, budget analysts can weigh the wait time costs against the operator and vehicle hours costs.

CBA also enhances other budget policy decisions such as the amount to invest in new projects, and which projects to fund. Currently, Tri-Met's investment priorities are set by a five-year investment plan which established their investment priorities for a number of projects. Tri-Met's driving force is land use policies set by Portland's metropolitan planning organization, METRO. According to the plan, money should be focused on specific transit corridors and geographic areas (http://www.trimet.org/improving/tip/pdf/tip_exec_summary.pdf, 2003).

Tri-Met's investment policies could be enhanced by reviewing the net social benefits of planned projects and comparing them to TSP or other projects. Table 21.18 lists other studies that have identified a net social benefit value for an ITS investment (all the projects support transportation, some support transit). Tri-Met could use some of this information when deciding where to invest.

Comparing this study to other ITS investments indicates that TSP had higher net benefits than one of the other transit investments, fleet management systems. Additionally, TSP had higher net benefits than automated roadway de-icing. Tri-Met can use this information when deciding which ITS projects to fund.

Metropolitan, state, and federal policy makers setting long-range plans, and determining funding policies can also use the CBA results to set policy. Available

TABLE 21.19
Net Benefits for Transportation Studies

Study Title	Author	Method	Year	D Rate	Sector	ITS Investment	Net Benefit	B/C Ratio
Benefit Cost Assessment of the Commercial Vehicle Information Systems and Network	Bapna, S. Zaveri, J. Farkas, A.Z.	Cost–benefit Assessment	1999	6% and 8%	Commercial Vehicle	Electronic Credentialing & Roadside Enforcement	$112 million to 133 million	3.38 to 4.83
Twin Cities Ramp Meter Evaluation	Cambridge Systematics	Cost–benefit Assessment	2001	n/a	Highway Traffic MGMT	Electronic Ramp Metering	$32 to $37 million	n/a
Intelligent Transportation Systems Benefits and Costs 2003 Update	Mitretek Systems for DOT	Cost–benefit	2003	n/a	Highway Traffic MGMT	Automated roadway de-icing	$1,179,274	2.36
Benefits Assessment of Advanced Public Transportation System Technologies	Goeddel, D.	Cost–benefit Assessment	2002	7%	Transit Transit Transit Transit	Fleet Management System Computer Aided Dispatch Advanced Traveler Information Systems Electronic Fare Payment	$6,282,723[18] $26,905,829 $10,596,026 $13,259,668	n/a n/a n/a n/a
This Study	Morrow, M.	Cost–benefit Analysis	2004	2.5%	Transit	Traffic Signal Priority	$2 to $6.5 million	1.44 to 2.44

CBA studies demonstrate the true social cost of transportation in comparison to the projects listed in Table 21.19 and personal vehicle travel (Victoria Transport Policy Institute 2004).

Approximately $635 million is spent on transportation in the Portland metropolitan region each year through a combination of federal, state, regional, and local sources. This includes spending on maintenance and operation of existing roads and transit as well as the construction of new roads, sidewalks and bike facilities, and implementation of programs to manage or reduce demand on the region's transportation system. The Regional Transportation Plan (RTP) identifies a twenty-year list of future transportation projects based on regional transportation and land-use policies (http://www.metro-region.org/article.cfm?articleID=139, 2004). CBA empowers policy makers to make decisions based on knowing their true social value as opposed to political pressure.

In addition to knowing the social value of other public transportation options, The Victoria Transport Policy Institute found that motor vehicle use is significantly underpriced. Their study included external costs that normally do nt show up such as higher prices for commercial goods (for parking costs), increased local taxes (for road services), higher insurance premiums (from automobile accidents), illnesses (from pollution), and lower residential property values (from urban traffic) (Victoria Transport Policy Institute 2004). When policy makers look at the external as well as the internal costs, the public benefits.

Because of the potential to benefit the public, policy makers on all levels may require a CBA prior to investing in transportation projects. The data to determine costs and benefits for ITS projects is available, and ITS projects for which a social benefit has been calculated are comparable to other transit investments. Although the data to determine costs and benefits is available from transit agencies, skill is required to obtain, prepare, and analyze this data. However, the cost of hiring skilled analysts is minimal in comparison to the cost of not performing a CBA for major ITS investments.

To address this issue, the Federal Department of Transportation's Joint Program Office, has established a cost–benefits database, which is available at the following Web site (http://www.benefitcost.its.dot.gov). Despite this effort, a recent report indicated that there are not enough evaluation data to make an assessment of the system's impact on many of the relevant performance measures (http://www.mitretek.org/its/benecost/BC_Update_2003/index.html). This study has indicated otherwise.

The CBA study demonstrated that the barriers to performing a CBA of an ITS project can be surmounted. Tri-Met's data was accessible for the study, and analysis of Tri-Met's TSP system indicated significant benefits, especially for certain schedule types and routes. Aside from knowing which routes and schedule types are complemented by TSP, Tri-Met knows, and can further investigate routes and schedule types that do not work well with TSP.

Because a net social benefit value was arrived at, Tri-Met can compare the TSP investment in light of other investments. In this case, CBA methods have indicated a benefit for investing in ITS; they have also provided a means of justifying future ITS investments.

NOTES

1. This cost represents the total system cost which was funded jointly by Tri-Met, the City of Portland, and the U.S. government. Tri-Met's portion of the cost was $1,500,000.
2. Each day Tri-Met's AVL system captures information at approximately 600,000 bus stop visits.
3. Agencies include this figure in their annual budget reports. It is derived a per-dollar vehicle maintenance expense cost (fuel, oil, transmission fluid, etc.), then dividing it by the total vehicle miles. In 2001 it was $0.48 (NTD, 2001), expressed in 2003 dollars $0.50.
4. The average operator wage rate for a bus driver in Portland is $19.68 (Jarigese 2003).
5. An annual annuity value is calculated with the following variables: the cost of a new bus $b = \$300,000$ (Turner, 2002) expressed in 2003 dollars $306,837, n = the lifespan of a bus (15 years), (NTD, 2001), i = discount rate of 2.5 percent (OMB, 2003), and s = average bus salvage value of $1,500 (Jarigese, 2003). Two calculations were made: (1) $PV = b - s/(1+i)^n$, and (2) $AV = PV * i/ (1+i)^n - 1$. The results of the calculations were $PV = \$298,964, AV = \$16,672$.
6. Agencies report this figure to the Bureau of Transportation Statistics. It is derived by dividing "Vehicle Revenue hours Operated in Max Service" by "Vehicles Needed to Meet Peak Service." It represents the number of hours a vehicle is expected to operate annually. For Tri-Met this factor was $1,856,166/568 = 3,268$ (NDT 2001).
7. The Hausman test indicated that a random effects model was not an appropriate fit. Consequently, fixed effects models were employed.
8. An alternative specification, c^s would have assumed that each route had the same effect on miles traveled.
9. Schedule Type 1 = the AM rush.
10. Schedule Type 3 = the PM rush.
11. The 1994 Apogee Research estimate of $2.37 per gallon for the Portland Metropolitan area was used in the calculation, as EPA did not respond to a request to provide information (expressed in 2003 dollars $2.94) (Krupnick et al. 1997).
12. An average MPG figure can be derived from agency figures for fuel consumed and miles traveled. For FY 2002 it was 4.5 mpg (Turner 2002).
13. The wait time value equals Portland Metro's average value of time * 2.
14. The travel time value equals Portland Metro's average value of travel time.
15. A random number generator was used to select the 200 stops. A small number of stops were dropped because their data was only for the before TSP timeframe. Finally, stop IDs that were situated on more than one route were only estimated once.
16. When TSP goes into effect on a given route, $Z(b,t)$ will change from 0 to 1 for *every stop on that route*. TSP will only be installed on the portions of the route that cross through downtown Portland. However, wait time for passengers at suburban stops will be impacted by the system, as the travel time out to the suburbs will change.
17. The number presented equals Goeddel's net benefit divided by the total systems in the study (191).
18. The number presented equals Goeddel's net benefit divided by the total systems in the study (191).

BIBLIOGRAPHY

Alexiadis, V. (1998) *Metropolitan Model Deployment Initiative National Evaluation Strategy.* Washington, D.C.: ITS Joint Program Office, U.S. Department of Transportation.

Beesley, M.E. (1976). *Urban Transport: Studies in Economic Policy.* London: The Butterworth Group.

Beesley, M.E., and Foster, C.D. (1963). "Estimating the Social Benefit of Constructing an Underground Railway in London." *Journal of the Royal Statistical Society.* Series A, vol. 126, no.1.

Black, A. (1995) *Urban Mass Transportation Planning.* New York: McGraw-Hill.

Black, K., Collura, J., and Spring, G. (1997)."Evaluation of Automatic Vehicle Location Technologies for Paratransit in Small and Medium-Sized Urban Areas." *Journal of Public Transportation,* vol. 1, no. 4.

Boardman, A., Greenberg, D., Vining, A., and Weimer, D. (1997). "Plug-in Shadow Price Estimates For Policy Analysis." *The Annals of Regional Science.* New York: Springer-Verlag, 345.

Brandwein, R., and Sheldon, N. (1973). *The Economic and Social Impact of Investments in Public Transit.* Lexington Books. Lexington, MA. 1973.

Cambridge Systematics. (1996). *Measuring and Valuing Transit Benefits and Disbenefits Transit Cooperative Research Program Report 20.* Washington D.C.: Transportation Research Board.

Campbell, D.T., and Stanley, J.C. (1969). *Experimental and Quasi Experimental Designs For Research* (4th ed.). Chicago: Rand McNally.

Carruthers, R.C. (1977). *Behavioural Travel Modelling.* D.A. Hensher and P.R. Stopher, eds. London: Croom Helm Ltd.

Casey, R.F., Labell, L., Carpenter, E., LoVecchio, J., Moniz, L., Ow, R., Royal, J., and Schwenk, J. (1998). *Advanced Public Transportation Systems: State of the Art Update 98.* Washington D.C.: Volpe National Transportation Systems Center, Federal Transit Administration, U.S. Department of Transportation.

City of Portland. (2002). Setting Detection Ranges for Transit Priority Wapiti HC11 Software with Opticom Equipment. Unpublished.

Crout, D. (2001). Tri-Metropolitan Area Transit Authority. Portland, OR. Unpublished.

Crout, D. (2005). Personal conversation.

DeBlasio, A., Jackson, D., Tallon, A., McEwan, A., and O'Donnel, A. (1996). *Intelligent Transportation Systems Assessment of ITS Deployment: Review of Metropolitan Areas Discussions of Crosscutting Issues.* Washington, D.C.: Volpe National Transportation Systems Center, Research and Special Programs Administration, U.S. Department of Transportation.

Fowkes, T., and Wardman, M. (1988). "Design of Stated Preference Travel Choice Experiments With Special Reference to Inter-Personal Taste Variations." *Journal of Transport Economics and Policy,* XXII(1), January, 27–44.

P.J. Mackie, Fowkes, A.S., Wardman, M., Whelan, G., Nellthorp, J., and Bates, J. (2003). Value of Travel Time Savings in the U.K. Available at http://www.dft.gov.uk/stellent/groups/dft_econappr/documents/source/dft_econappr_source_022708.doc (accessed September 2001).

Frost, W. (1988). "Costs and Benefits of Toronto's Communications & Information System. International Conference on Automatic Vehicle Location. Canadian Urban Transit Association, 1988.

Government Accounting Office. (1997). "Urban Transportation: Challenges to Widespread

Deployment of Intelligent Transportation Systems." *RCED-97-74*. Washington, D.C.: Author.

Goeddel, D. (1996). *Benefits Assessment of Advanced Public Transportation Systems*. John A. Washington D.C.: Volpe National Transportation Systems Center, U.S. Department of Transportation.

Goeddel, D. (1999). Personal communication.

Greenberg, Dr. D. (1997). Class notes.

Government Accounting Office.(1997) "Urban Transportation: Challenges to Widespread Deployment of Intelligent Transportation Systems." *RCED-97-74*. Washington, D.C.: Author.

Hensher, D.A. (1988). "The Role of Stated Preference Methods in Studies of Travel Choice." *Journal of Transport Economics and Policy*, XXII(1), January: 45–48.

Hensher, D.A. (1997). "Transport Economics Selected Readings." T.H. Oum, J.S. Dodgson, D.A. Hensher, S.A. Morrison, C.A. Nash, K.A. Small, and W.G. Waters, eds. Netherlands: Harwood Academic Publishers.

Hill, C., Griffiths, W., and Judge, G. (1997). *Undergraduate Econometrics*. New York: John Wiley.

Holland, A. (1990). The Impact of Automatic Vehicle Monitoring Systems on Transit Operations: Master Thesis. University of Calgary. Department of Geography. Calgary: Canada.

Hounsell, N., and Mcleod, F. (1998)." Automatic Vehicle Location. Implementation, Application, and Benefits in the United Kingdom." *Transportation Research Record 1618*. Transportation Research Board.

ITS America. (1998). The National Architecture for ITS. CD-Rom.

Jones, W. S. (1995). *ITS Technologies in Public Transit: Deployment and Benefits*. Washington, D.C.: ITS Joint Program Office, Department of Transportation.

Kim, K.W. (2003) Personal communication.

Krupnik, A., Rowe, R., and Lang, C. (1997). "Transportation and Air Pollution: The Environmental Damages." *The Full Costs and Benefits of Transportation*. New York: Springer-Verlag.

Lee, D. (1999). Volpe National Transportation Center. Lead Investigator for MMDI Initiative. Personal conversation.

Levine, N., and Wachs, M. (1986). "Bus Crime in Los Angeles: Measuring the Incidence." *Transportation Research* A. vol. 20, no. 4. Washington, D.C.

Levine, N., and Wachs, M. (1986). "Tracking Crime on Buses." *TR News*. November–December. Washington, D.C.

Long D.A, Mallar C.D., and Thornton, C.V. (1981). "Evaluating the Benefits and Costs of the Jobs Corps." *Journal Of Policy Analysis and Management,* 1(1):55–76.

Lutterman, J. (2002). Personal communication.

Mandell, M. (1998). Statistical Applications in Evaluation Research. Class notes.

Metro (2002). Metro Travel Forecasting Trip Model Methodology Report. Unpublished.

Miller, T.R., Cohen, M.A., and Rossman, S.B. (1994). "The Costs and Consequences of Violent Behavior in The United States." *Understanding and Preventing Violence*. National Academy Press, vol. 4.

Miller, T. (1997). "Societal Cost of Transportation Crashes." *The Full Costs and Benefits of Transportation*. New York: Springer-Verlag.

Mohring, H., Schroeter, J., and Wiboonchutikula, P. (1987). "The Values of Waiting Tmie, Travel Time, and a Seat on a Bus." *Rand Journal of Economics*, vol 18. no. 1.

Mohring, H., and Anderson, D. (1997). "Congestion Costs and Congestion Pricing." *The Full Costs and Benefits of Transportation*. New York: Springer-Verlag.

Mohring, H. (1999). "Congestion." *Essays in Transportation Economics and Policy.* J. Gomez-Ibanez, W. Tye, and C. Winston, eds. Washington D.C.: Brookings Institute.

Morlok, E., Bruun, E.C., and Battle-Blackmon, K. (1993). *Advanced Vehicle Monitoring and Communication Systems for Bus Transit: Benefits and Economic Feasibility.* Washington D.C.: Department of Transportation, Federal Transit Administration.

Morrow, M. (2005) Evaluating the Effectiveness of Intelligent Vehicle Systems For Bus Transit Management: A Cost–Benefit Approach. Diss. University of Maryland, Baltimore, MD.

Nash, C.A. (1997). "Transport Economics Selected Readings." T.H. Oum, J.S. Dodgson, D.A. Hensher, S.A. Morrison, C.A. Nash, K.A. Small, and W.G. Waters, eds. Netherlands: Harwood Academic.

National Research Council. (1997). *The Bureau of Transportation Statistics: Priorities for the Future.* J. Norwood and C. Citro, eds. Washington, D.C.: National Academy Press.

National Transit Library. Operation TimeSaver—ITI Transit Components. Available at http://www.fta.dot.gov/ntl/index.html (accessed September 2001).

NTD (2001). National Transit Database. Available at http://www.ntdprogram.com (accessed September 2001).

Okunieff, P. (1997). *Synthesis of Transit Practice 24: AVL Systems for Bus Transit.* Washington D.C.: Cambridge Systematics, Transportation Research Board, National Academy Press.

Peng, Z., Octaria, S. Zygowicz, R., and Beimborn, E. (1999). "Evaluation of the Benefits of Automated Vehicle Locator Systems for Small and Medium Sized Transit Agencies." Unpublished.

Peters, J. (1997). *ITS Benefits: Continuing Successes and Operational Test Results.* Washington, D.C.: Intelligent Transportation Systems, Federal Highway Administration, Department of Transportation.

Peters, J. (1999). Federal Highway Administration. Joint Program Office. Model Deployment Initiative Evaluation Program Assessment Specialist. Personal conversation.

Quarmby, D.A. (1967). "Choice of Travel Mode For The Journey to Work; Some Findings." *Journal of Transport Economics and Policy,* 1: 273–314.

Ridker, R.G. (1967). *Economic Costs Of Air Pollution.* New York: Frederick A. Praeger.

Russell, B.G. (1995). The Values of Waiting Time and A Seat On The Bus. University of Minnesota. Dissertation Database.

Small, K.A. (1975). "Air Pollution and Property Values: Further Comment." *The Review of Economics and Statistics,* vol. 57, no. 1, February.

Small, K.A. (1999). *Essays in Transportation Economics and Policy.* J. Gomez-Ibanez, W. Tye, and C. Winston, eds. Washington D.C.: Brookings Institute.

Smith, K.V. (1976). *The Economic Consequences Of Air Pollution.* Cambridge, MA: Ballenger Publishing.

Smith, K.V., and Huang J.C. (1995). "Can Markets Value Air Quality? A Meta-Analysis of Hedonic Property Value Models." *Journal Of Political Economy,* vol. 103, no. 11.

Stopher, P.R., and Meyburg, A. (1976). *Transportation Systems Evaluation.* Lexington MA: Lexington Books.

Strathman, J., Dueker, K., and Kimipel, T. (1999) Automated Bus Dispatching, Operations Control, and Service Reliability: Baseline Analysis. Transportation Research Board 78th Annual Meeting.

Symes, D. (1998). Personal conversation.

Transit Cooperative Research Program (1999). *Report 46—Transit Design Game Workbook.* Washington, D.C.: National Academies of Science.

Tri-County Metropolitan Transportation District. (2001). *5 Year ITS Plan*. Portland, OR: Author

Tri-County Metropolitan Transportation District. (2001). *Rider Alert: 4-Division/Fessenden —Transit Signal Priority*. Portland, OR: Author.

Tri-County Metropolitan Transportation District (2003). *Improving Transit—Streamline Program*. Portland, OR: Author.

Turner, Ken. (2002). Personal conversation.

Victoria Transport Policy Institute. (2004). *Transportation Cost and Benefit Analysis*—Transportation Cost Implications. Available at http://www.vtpi.org (accessed September 2004).

Viscusi. W.K. "The Value of Risks to Life and Health." *Journal of Economic Literature*, 31.

Waters, W. (1994). "Variations in the Value of Travel Time Savings: Empirical Studies and the Values for Road Project Evaluation." *International Journal of Transport Economics*.

Watson, P. (1974). *The Value of Time; Behavioral Models of Modal Choice*. Lexington MA: Lexington Books.

Weimer, D., and Vining, A. (1999). *Policy Analysis Concepts and Practice,* 3rd ed. Saddle River, NJ: Prentice Hall.

Wooldridge, J. (2000). *Introductory Econometrics*. South-Western College Publishing.

22 The Disadvantaged Business Enterprise Program and Transportation Policy

John A. Anderson, Michael T. Behney, and Joanne L. Lubart

The federal Disadvantaged Business Enterprise Program, referred to as the DBE Program, has been a focal point of debate at the national, state, and local level for over two decades. Authorized and administered under federal law and regulations, the program exists due to the government's recognition of longstanding discrimination by private contractors and lenders who have repeatedly refused to employ women-owned and minority-owned businesses in federal transportation subcontracting. Since its inception, the DBE Program has never failed to trigger extreme reactions in those compelled to adhere to it (prime contractors required to include DBE commitments in their bid submissions on federally assisted contracts); those who stand to benefit from it (small for-profit firms that are at least 51 percent owned and controlled by socially and economically disadvantaged individuals and that have obtained DBE certification by a state or local entity charged with certification eligibility determinations for DBEs); and, those required to implement it (state and local transportation entities).

Highly charged reactions resonate, in large part, due to misinformation about the DBE Program; misinterpretation of the federal regulation, which sets forth the DBE Program's guidelines and standards; confusion over program duality with state and local disadvantaged programs; and the fact that federal transportation contracting accounts for more than $25 billion a year.[1] This chapter attempts to forge a better understanding of the DBE Program by focusing on nine key elements that make it the most viable tool for creating economic opportunity in federal transportation contracting.

BACKGROUND

The DBE Program began under several federal executive orders in the early 1980s that focused on the contract barriers encountered by minorities and women.[2] However, when the United States Congress enacted the Surface Transportation Assistance Act (STAA) in 1982, it incorporated the first DBE statutory provision.[3] This provision focused primarily on small business firms owned and controlled by minorities in the United States Department of Transportation's (USDOT) highway and transit programs.

431

Women-owned firms and airport programs looked to the executive orders for application until 1987. The parameters of the program were contained in a federal regulation set forth in Title 49 Code of Federal Regulations (C.F.R.) Part 23. Part 23 emphasized the need to "maximize opportunities" for DBE firms in federally assisted contracts. USDOT assumed the role of the overseer charged with ensuring that firms competing for its federally-assisted contracts at the state and local level were not disadvantaged by unlawful discrimination.

Under the federal statute and Part 23, USDOT was required to ensure that at least 10 percent of the funds authorized for highway and federal assistance programs were expended through the use of DBE subcontractors. DBE participation resulted from subcontracting opportunities available on projects funded by the Federal Highway Administration (FHWA) and the Federal Transit Administration (FTA) and, later, the Federal Aviation Administration (FAA).[4]

In 1987, Congress enacted, and President Reagan signed, statutes expanding the program to airports and to women-owned small businesses.[5] The program was further expanded by reauthorization statutes enacted by Congress and signed by President George Herbert Walker Bush in 1991 (for highway and transit programs) and in 1992 (for airport programs).[6] While the program continued to be reauthorized in successive federal transportation reauthorization bills, Part 23 was revised on several occasions to make needed programmatic changes.

Prior to 1999, one constant in the program was the imposition of a single DBE contracting goal of 10 percent nationwide. If a USDOT recipient was unable to achieve the goal, it was required to offer a justification to the secretary of USDOT.

Inevitably, the continuing imposition of the 10 percent goal in federal transportation contracting provided the catalyst for lawsuits. Plaintiffs in federal court argued that the imposition of a 10 percent contract goal without any frame of reference represented unconstitutional affirmative action and served as the functional equivalent of a *de facto quota* or *set-aside* program.[7] Contractors took issue with the use of DBE goals in general and with the nationwide 10 percent goal in particular. As long as Part 23 remained in effect, they vehemently argued that the 10 percent national goal created a skewed picture of reality and wrought reverse discrimination, since USDOT failed to proffer any evidentiary documentation to support it.

The most significant legal challenge to the program commenced in 1995 when the United States Supreme Court decided the landmark decision in *Adarand Constructors Inc. v. Pena*, 515 U.S. 200 (1995), a 5 to 4 decision, referred to as *Adarand I* (several additional cases were brought later by the same contractor). The Supreme Court firmly established that a heightened standard of judicial review, the strict scrutiny standard, would apply to federal programs that focus on race or ethnicity as factors including federal highway construction programs. Using a two-pronged test, the Court held that these programs must be "narrowly tailored" to serve a "compelling governmental interest."[8]

The test for "narrow tailoring" was set forth in the Supreme Court's decision in *United States v. Paradise*, 480 U.S. 149 (1987). It requires that programs for the disadvantaged limit the following: the duration of relief; the availability of waiver provisions; the nexus between goals and the relevant labor market; the impact on third parties, and that it not last longer than the discrimination it is intended to eliminate.[9]

The "compelling governmental interest" was and continues to be the preexisting and longstanding discrimination and disadvantage relative to minorities and women in federal transportation contracting. Even opponents of the program have conceded that such discrimination persists and have remained silent about the existence of discrimination in the transportation marketplace.

While the Court set a high standard of review for all governmental race-conscious remedies, it did not prohibit Congress from crafting remedies for past societal discrimination. Consistent with its pre-*Adarand* holding in *City of Richmond v. J.A. Croson Co.,* 488 U.S. 469 (1989), the Court recognized that since Congress legislates on a nationwide basis, it has inherently broader powers to remedy discrimination and is accorded greater deference than state and local governments. The Court refused to reject properly designed disadvantaged or discrimination programs.

The annals of program history reveal that, contrary to public expectations, *Adarand* did not prove to be the death knell for the program. The program was retained by the 1998 Transportation Equity Act for the 21st Century (TEA-21). TEA-21 authorized USDOT to expend funds for federal surface transportation programs during fiscal years 1998 to 2003; and, again, two years later when Congress extended this Act by passing the Surface Transportation Extension Act of 2005.[10] Through the most recent transportation reauthorization in the Safe, Accountable, Flexible, Efficient, Transportation Equity Act: A Legacy for Users (SAFETEA-LU), the program was recently reauthorized for an additional six years.

Following the Supreme Court decision, USDOT and the Congress recognized the need to reexamine Part 23 in light of the new strict scrutiny standard. This led to the issuance of a new regulation intended to replace Part 23 and to meet the "narrow-tailoring" test established by the Supreme Court. The new regulation resulted from the *Adarand* decision, nine hundred sets of public comments, and the most heated Congressional debate and thorough analysis of DBE legislation since the program's inception.

During the 1998 Congressional debate, several prominent U.S. Senators offered testimony in support of the program. Senator Baucus noted that while minorities then made up 20 percent of the population, they owned 9 percent of construction businesses and received only 4 percent of construction receipts.[11] Senator Kerry added that while women owned 9.2 percent of the nation's construction firms, their companies earned half of that earned by males.[12] And Senator Robb noted that construction firms owned by white males received fifty times as many loan dollars as African-American owned firms with identical equity.[13]

The congressional testimony and debate memorialized the need for significant change in program implementation. Ample evidence existed demonstrating that access to federally-assisted transportation contracts remained a problem for women and minorities and other disadvantaged individuals; and, that, without the program, the federal government would become a willing participant in continuing discrimination. In revamping the program through the promulgation of a new DBE regulation, Congress examined a record that included a range of studies, factual material, and extensive evidence of federal transportation discrimination and statistical disparity between the availablilty and utilization of women-owned and minority-owned businesses in federal transportation contracting.[14]

In 1999, Part 23 was replaced by the newly revamped DBE regulation, set forth in 49 C.F.R. Part 26 (Part 26).[15] Part 26 attempts to "mend, not end" the program.[16] Noticeably absent from Part 26 is Part 23's former focus on "maximum participation" by DBEs. The new focus is on the creation of a "race neutral" environment in which all small businesses benefit, not just DBEs. Nonetheless, Part 26 emphasizes the continuing need to remedy the effects of current and past discrimination against small businesses owned and controlled by socially and economically disadvantaged individuals.

Part 26 scrupulously adheres to the points raised by the Supreme Court, public comments, and issues raised in the 1998 Congressional debate. The law that led to its promulgation was passed with solid bipartisan majorities in Congress.[17]

Part 26 bears witness to the congressional finding that there is a "compelling governmental interest" in remedying invidious discrimination and its effects in federally-assisted transportation contracts. It also establishes a "narrowly- tailored" program by meeting the factors described above for narrow tailoring and by limiting its applicability to those parts of the nation where discriminatory practices exist. The program's longevity and *raison d'etre* can be attributed to the nine keys (discussed below) that distinguish the DBE Program from any other federal and/or state disadvantaged or affirmative action program.

THE FIRST KEY

The focus on disadvantage serves as the first key to promoting better understanding of the DBE Program and Part 26. In the last decade, the mettle of the DBE Program has been severely tested by non-DBE contractors and opponents of affirmative action. Historically, one of the fundamental flaws in the thinking of opponents of the program has been their persistent reluctance to acknowledge the disadvantage basis which includes individuals others than women and minorities. Program opponents have underplayed the disadvantage basis of the federal DBE regulations and overfocused on the inclusion of DBE contract goals in federally assisted, transportation-related contracts. Part 26 clearly evinces the disadvantage premise upon which the program is built. Section 26.1 outlines the most important objectives of Part 26 including that of remedying the effects of current and past discrimination against small businesses owned and controlled by disadvantaged individuals and fostering equal opportunity in federal transportation contracting.

Part 26 significantly alters the DBE Program, but retains the focus on eliminating discrimination. In a report issued by the United States General Accounting Office (GAO) in 2001, the GAO stated: "Studies finding statistical disparities between the availability and utilization of minority-and women-owned firms in transportation-related contracting are recognized as a potential source of evidence of discrimination."[18] The GAO report also noted that the federal courts have concluded that discrimination adversely affects DBEs as evidenced by studies of business practices affecting DBE formation and competition, and disparity studies.

The preamble to Part 26 reinforces the notion that the program continues to endure due to well-documented history of race and gender exclusion in the transportation industry. Source material includes relevant court cases, studies of lending, bonding, and business practices (affecting the ability of DBEs to compete in the marketplace), state and local disparity studies, and discrimination complaints. There is an unwritten rule in the transportation contracting sector that favors the "Old Boys" network and closes the door to certain groups within American culture including women and minorities.

Part 26 continues to recognize the disadvantage of minorities and women by including the Part 23 rebuttable presumption of disadvantage for women and certain designated groups. Women and members of the designated groups are presumed to be socially and economically disadvantaged unless proven otherwise.[19] Part 26 states that Black Americans, Hispanic Americans, Native Americans, Asian Pacific Americans, Subcontinent Asian Americans, women, and any additional groups whose members are designated as socially and economically disadvantaged (disadvantaged) by the Small Business Administration (SBA) are presumed to be disadvantaged.[20]

The net effect of the presumption is the elimination of the need for group members to prove individually that they have been the subject of discrimination or disadvantage. However, in order to narrowly tailor this provision, Part 26 requires that applicants who are members of the designated groups sign an affidavit in which they aver that they are, in fact, disadvantaged.[21]

Part 26 also contains a specific provision used in federally assisted, transportation contracts that emphasizes the disadvantage basis for the DBE Program. Section 26.13 contains a DBE assurance clause that functions as a non-discrimination clause and must be used in all contracts involving federal highway, transit, and aviation funds. Every contract that a recipient or subrecipient enters into with a contractor or consultant must contain this provision which includes a commitment not to discriminate on the basis of race, color, national origin, or sex in the performance of the contract. This provision firmly establishes the first key to understanding the DBE Program as a disadvantaged-based program.

THE SECOND KEY

Historically, the most vigorous opponents of former Part 23 and current Part 26, white prime contractors and other non-DBE subcontractors, have been minimally affected by the program. This is the second key to understanding the program.

The DBE Program is designed to replicate a transportation marketplace in which there is no discrimination. Since the program only affects a relatively small percentage of total federal-aid dollars, non-minority prime contractors are not impacted in any significant manner. In fiscal year 2000, less than 10 percent of prime contracts were awarded to DBEs; and, from 1993 through 2002, $37 billion of federal funds expended by highway contracts went to DBEs while $277 billion was spend on federal highway contracting projects.[22]

Under Part 26, USDOT recipients choose their own method for goal-setting, and have broad discretion relative to whether or not to use a goal on every project.[23] They are no longer bound by a uniform national percentage. When they include a DBE goal, they are free to set it at any level that is deemed appropriate for the type of work and the location of the work.

Part 26 goal-setting is based upon local market conditions supported by data rather than the former nationwide goal, and, therefore, the transportation contracting community finds a tighter fit between DBE contract goals and market realities.

Moreover, since eligibility is based upon social and economic disadvantage, white males are eligible for the program if they demonstrate that they are disadvantaged on an individual basis. Appendix E of Part 26 provides detailed guidance for individual determinations of disadvantage and is based on SBA regulations. To date, businesses owned by white males have qualified for DBE status.

In addition, all certified DBEs are limited by the new Part 26 personal net worth threshold for disadvantaged owners and business size caps related to the DBE firm. To the extent that these thresholds are exceeded, DBEs are no longer eligible for the program. Therefore, Part 26 contains a narrowly-tailored mechanism that compels firms to leave the Program when they grow too large. This was not the case under Part 23.[24]

White and non-DBE contractors are further insulated by Section 26.31, a new provision in Part 26 that requires that a recipient take steps to address over-concentration of DBEs in certain types of work. The inclusion of this provision ensures that a recipient will take measures to address any situation in which he or she learns that DBEs are overrepresented in an area of work and that non-DBEs are being deprived of economic opportunity. Recipients can take definitive action such as varying the use of contract goals to lessen the burden on non-DBE specialty contractors.

Finally, Part 26 adheres to a *good faith effort* frame of reference. A contractor no longer loses a contract if it can be documented that a good faith effort to meet a DBE goal was made but was unable to be reached. Appendix A of Part 26 sets forth examples of factors to take into account in making good faith effort determinations. In the final analysis, each case turns on its own facts, but a recipient's failure to accept a valid showing of a good faith effort is inconsistent with the spirit and intention of Part 26.

THE THIRD KEY

Part 26 has been able to withstand the strict scrutiny standard established by the litigation that preceded it because it serves as a narrowly tailored, disadvantaged-based tool used to remedy the compelling governmental interest in breaking down barriers and level the playing field for qualified female- and minority-owned firms in the marketplace. Throughout the 1998 debate that preceded the promulgation of a new DBE regulation, both houses of Congress repeatedly described the continuing need for the program due to the need to remedy the effects of discrimination in federally assisted contracting. The most relevant evidence cited was the drop in DBE participation in state contracting when goal-oriented programs end, compared to participation rates in the federal DBE Program. Significantly, a 1997 Urban Institute Study found that when the State of Michigan terminated its state-funded program, minority participation plummeted to zero; the state's federal DBE Program achieved 12.7 percent participation.[25]

Part 26 ensures narrow-tailoring in all areas of the DBE Program by introducing a new mechanism for calculation of DBE goals based upon the local marketplace, giving priority to race neutral measures (that benefit all small firms, not just DBEs), placing greater emphasis on good faith efforts submitted by contractors, placing a cap on economic disadvantage through the use of a personal net worth cap, and by limiting the DBE Program's duration by requiring that the program be reauthorized rather than automatically renewed in each successive transportation authorization bill. All of these forces work together to ensure economic opportunity for those who would otherwise not have access to projects involving the construction of new highways, public transportation enhancements, improvements, and highway maintenance.

THE FOURTH KEY

Part 26 shares one problem in common with the former DBE regulation. The public often fails to recognize that the DBE regulation only applies to federally funded, transportation contracts let by state and local entities and is separate and distinct from other minority business enterprise programs. Across the nation, state and local minority and women disadvantaged programs operate under executive orders, local ordinances, or state statutes and apply when contracts involve the use of state and/or local funds. These programs have their own certification standards and requirements.

Since some of USDOT's recipients or subrecipients run dual programs within the same office, applicants are frequently uncertain about the type of certification that would best serve their needs.[26] Certification applicants focus less on the source of the funding stream and more on the nexus between the work being solicited and the work that they can perform.

State and local government programs fall more closely in line with traditional affirmative action programs and have also been revamped due to constitutional challenges and lawsuits of their own. However, these programs continue to be confused with the DBE Program, and better communication and lines of demarcation are necessary. Former Part 23 and current Part 26 were never intended to apply to entities other than recipients of federal highway, aviation, and transit funds. If one federal dollar originates from these funds, the DBE Program applies. If 100 percent state funding or a mix of state and local funding is involved, then the DBE Program does not apply.

THE FIFTH KEY

DBE certification is narrowly tailored by using more focused eligibility standards and a checks and balances approach that allows for close monitoring of a DBE firm's continuing eligibility to participate in the DBE Program. Like Part 23, Part 26 imposes the certification obligation on USDOT recipients, principally, the state transportation agencies and other local agencies or authorities that have been assigned this responsibility.

Part 26's certification guidelines contemplate an intensive scrutiny that begins with the use of a uniform, nationwide application.[27] Once an application is deemed complete, an investigatory process is used to determine whether the applicant firm is a small, for-profit firm at least 51 percent owned and controlled by bona fide disadvantaged individuals. These individuals must be American citizens or lawfully admitted permanent residents of the United States.[28] Business size is measured by the SBA's regulations. To qualify as a small business, a firm must have average annual gross receipts over a three-year period that do not exceed either the SBA size standards or the DBE Program size cap of $19,570,000.[29]

The certification process itself requires an assessment of the firm's eligibility by examination of licenses, stock ownership, equipment, bonding capacity, resumes of principal owners, the firm's gross receipts for the previous three years, cancelled checks, bank signature cards, articles of incorporation and bylaws, stock transfer ledgers, visits to the principal office of the firm, and job site visits.

Part 26 imposes a new narrowly tailored personal net worth threshold for disadvantaged owners. Each disadvantaged owner whose ownership and control is relied upon for DBE certification must have a personal net worth (PNW) that does not exceed $750,000 (termed the "hard cap").[30] Therefore, even though the rebuttable presumption of disadvantage remains intact, the disadvantaged owner(s) of the applicant firm must complete a notarized PNW Statement to ensure that only genuinely disadvantaged individuals participate in the DBE Program. If a presumptively disadvantaged owner's PNW exceeds the threshold, then he or she is no longer considered disadvantaged.

Part 26 requires that every DBE firm submit a "no change" affidavit sworn to be the owners of the firm each year on the anniversary of the firm's certification. This affidavit must be accompanied by updated financial information and tax returns that ensure that the firm continues to be eligible to participate in the Program. A DBE firm must also submit a "notice of change" within thirty days of any change that might impact its continuing eligibility.[31] These new provisions ensure that the DBE Program is not overinclusive and comport with narrow tailoring.

Part 26 also includes provisions that allow the certification of any firm to be challenged by recipients, USDOT, and third parties. Where any of these entities initiate an ineligibility complaint, the recipient must determine whether there is reasonable cause to conclude that the currently certified firm is no longer qualified for the program.[32] In addition, DBE firms must apply for recertification after an initial certification of three years or longer.[33]

The benefits of DBE certification are well-documented. Certified DBEs are listed in a unified, statewide DBE directory available in hard copy, electronic form, and on the Internet. Only those firms that are certified at the time of bid submission can receive credit toward achievement of a DBE goal.

THE SIXTH KEY

Goal-setting, considered the heart of the DBE Program, is also placed squarely on the shoulders of USDOT recipients. The 10 percent goal is now considered an aspirational goal, and is used solely as a means of evaluating the overall performance of the program nationally. Part 26 overhauls the entire DBE goal process, and state and local USDOT recipients are no longer required to use a 10 percent goal or justify goals lower than 10 percent. It is not tied to individual state highway, transit, and aviation authorities

Part 26 goals result from a methodology created by recipients using Part 26 guidelines. USDOT recipients must collect, analyze, and use data relative to local market conditions and account for other factors that impact on discrimination in federal transportation contracting marketplace.[34] This market-based approach is the sixth key to understanding the program.

Under Part 26, USDOT recipients must establish goals for the participation of DBE entrepreneurs before the start of each federal fiscal year. Section 26.5 defines recipients as "any entity, public or private, to which DOT financial assistance is extended, whether directly or through another recipient, through the programs of the FAA, FHWA, or FTA, or who has applied for such assistance."

In a major change from former Part 23, Part 26 calls for a two-step goal-setting process.[35] Under step one, the recipient must establish a base figure representing its best estimate of the relative availability of DBEs. The recipient must use the best available data available for its relevant marketplace including Census Bureau data, bidders' lists, disparity studies and other demonstrable evidence of local market conditions. Once the recipient has identified its base figure, it is compelled, under step two, to examine all available evidence in the jurisdiction including the capacity of DBEs to perform work in federally assisted contracts and findings from disparity studies and then adjust the goal downward or upward accordingly to arrive at the overall goal. This step relies on data relative to past discrimination and directs the recipient to determine where the DBE availability figures are artificially low due to the effects of past discrimination, or whether DBE availability would be higher "but for" past discrimination.[36]

Once overall goals are established, they must be sent to the appropriate operating administration within USDOT for approval on an annual basis. In practice, the actual subcontracting goals vary due to the need to take into account other factors such as the type of work and the location of the work. However, at the end of the fiscal year, the amount of contracts or subcontracts awarded to DBEs should measure up to the overall goal.[37] The net effect is that recipients set narrowly-tailored goals based upon their own methodology which must be approved by the appropriate USDOT operating administration that administers the federal funds being utilized.

Part 26 effectively shifts the focus of the DBE Program from achieving "the maximum feasible extent" of DBE participation in federally assisted contracts to achieving a "level playing field," defined as the amount of participation DBEs would be expected to achieve absent discrimination. Moreover, as noted below, USDOT recipients must meet the maximum feasible portion of their overall DBE goals using race-neutral measures (designed to benefit all small businesses) rather than race-conscious measures or traditional DBE contract goals.

As part of narrow tailoring, Part 26 requires that DBE goals be monitored throughout the year to ensure that DBE contract goals are used only to the extent necessary to achieve a level playing field. USDOT recipients are now required to use contract goals to meet only that portion of their overall goals that they do not anticipate meeting through race neutral measures.[38] When the GAO surveyed a number of the states for fiscal year 2000, it found that, on average, they used race-neutral measures to achieve slightly over one-third of their overall DBE participation goals.[39]

THE SEVENTH KEY

To further ensure a narrowly tailored program, Part 26 requires public participation in the goal-setting process. In the past, the public voice resonated in the federal courts. Part 26 now affords the actual stakeholders, as well as any member of the general public, the opportunity to participate in the annual goal-setting process. Recipients are required to consult with minority, women's, and general contractors' groups while preparing the DBE goal. Recipients can hold public hearings, town meetings, and seminars to solicit public input and participation in the goal-setting process.

Recipients must also announce their proposed goals in a public notice and make their goal(s) and methodology available for inspection during normal business hours at their principal place of business for thirty days following the dates of the notice. They must also conduct a forty-five-day public comment period commencing on the date of the public notice. Since public input could require adjustments to an overall goal, the public participation component is meaningful and opens the door to better communications between and among recipients and stakeholders.

THE EIGHTH KEY

Part 26 goal-setting opens the door to a whole new "race-neutral" world. This represents a significant change in the manner in which federal transportation contracting is addressed. Part 23 did not require the use of race-neutral measures so Part 26's emphasis on them represents a major departure from the traditional race-conscious or DBE contract goals that once served as the mainstay of the program.

As noted, Part 26 mandates that recipients meet the "maximum feasible" portion of their overall goals by using "race-neutral" measures. These are means or measures designed to increase contracting opportunities for all small businesses, not just DBEs and include outreach and technical assistance.[40] Other race neutral measures include bonding assistance, business development, and unbundling contracts (breaking contracts into smaller components that lend themselves to performance by small firms). Supportive services programs (funded by FHWA) serve as race-neutral measures designed to help certified firms gain technical expertise as well as assistance with bid preparation that allows them to compete in the marketplace.

Race neutral DBE participation includes any time a DBE wins a prime contract through traditional competitive procurement procedures or is awarded a subcontract on a prime contract that does not carry a DBE goal. It also transpires when a DBE wins a subcontract from a prime contractor that did not consider its DBE status in making the award.

Part 26 also includes a waiver mechanism in the goal-setting arena. Recipients have the option of applying for a Program waiver if they propose to administer their individual DBE programs in an innovative way.[41] This is another aspect of the DBE Program that makes it separate and distinct from traditional affirmative action.

THE NINTH KEY

The ninth key is easily misunderstood or ignored by members from all ranks of the transportation contracting sector. The factor most overlooked is that the program was never intended to serve as a permanent resting place for small and disadvantaged businesses. The duration of relief for individuals and firms is limited by the PNW component, the overall business size cap, and SBA size standards.

A DBE is no longer eligible for the program if it exceeds the small business cap or if the firm's owner exceeds the personal net worth threshold (and the remaining disadvantaged owners do not own and control 51% of the business) set forth in the certification eligibility standards. Firms must leave the program if they grow too large or if their owners become too wealthy.

Moreover, DBE firms can never rest on their laurels or be complacent about the DBE program, since the duration of the program lies in the hands of Congress and reauthorization decisions take place in Washington. In each successive reauthorization bill for the surface and airport programs, Congress has the opportunity to examine the current state of federal transportation contracting and determine whether the program statute is still necessary to remedy a compelling governmental interest in eliminating discrimination in federally assisted contracting. Reauthorization is never a guarantee.

CONCLUSION

The DBE Program provides a viable tool to remedy the effects of past and current discrimination in federal transportation contracting. The data and the case law amply detail the continuing problem of invidious discrimination in the federal transportation marketplace. The program meshes with the economic and social climate of the nation in the new millennium.

Five American presidents have supported the DBE Program. In the final analysis, unless and until such time as all stakeholders come together and willingly partner to make federal transportation contracts a seamless, integrated, and diverse workforce, the DBE Program will continue to operate as the best tool to level the playing field so that the doors of federal transportation contracting remain open to small and disadvantaged businesses.

NOTES

1. See preamble to Title 49 Code of Federal Regulations (C.F.R.) Part 26.
2. Present day programs focusing on assisting minorities and women in federal contracting originated in Section 8(a) of the Small Business Act of 1958. The Small Business Administration (SBA) used its statutory authority to obtain contracts from federal agencies and

subcontract them on a noncompetitive basis to firms located in socially and economically distressed areas.

3. P.L. 97-424, § 105(f), 96 Stat. 2097 (1982). This took effect in 1983 and represented the first DBE statutory provision.

4. See Disadvantaged Business Enterprise (DBE) Program information at the Office of Small and Disadvantaged Business Utilization at Web site: http://osdbu.dot.gov/.

5. Ibid.

6. Ibid, at 2. The Surface Transportation and Uniform Relocation Assistance Act of 1987 continued the program and included nonminority women in the statutory definition of disadvantaged individuals. The Intermodal Surface Transportation Efficiency Act of 1991 and the Transportation Equity Act for the 21st Century (TEA-21) reauthorized the program and continued the combined 10 percent provision for participation by women and minorities.

7. A set-aside permits no one but DBEs to compete for a contract. The program has never required the use of set-asides. While books about affirmative action abound, little or no mention is made about the DBE Program. Affirmative action involves measures designed to correct or compensate for past or present discrimination or to prevent discrimination from recurring in the future.

8. The Supreme Court did not pass judgment on the constitutionality of the program. It only settled the debate over the standard of strict scrutiny.

9. See 480 U.S. at 171.

10. Pub.L. No. 105-178, Section 1101(b)(1), 112 Stat. 107, 113.

11. See Disadvantaged Business Enterprise (DBE) Program information at the Office of Small and Disadvantaged Business Utilization at Web site: http://osdbu.dot.gov/.

12. Ibid.

13. Ibid.

14. See United States General Accounting Office, *Disadvantaged Business Enterprises: Critical Information is Needed to Understand Program Impact,* GAO- 01-586 at 6 (June 2001).

15. A new airport concessionaire regulation is now set forth in former Part 23, and Part 23 remains in effect only in this area.

16. See preamble to Part 26.

17. Ibid.

18. General Accounting Office, *Disadvantaged Business Enterprises: Critical Information is Needed to Understand Program Impact,* GAO-01-586 at 6 (June 2001).

19. See preamble to Part 26. The presumptive groups were included in the 1983 DBE statutes and were adopted from the SBA regulations. However, Subcontinent Asians were added later. Hispanic Americans include those of Mexican, Puerto Rican, Cuban, Dominican, Central or South American, or others of Spanish or Portuguese origin. Native Americans include American Indians, Eskimos, Aleuts, or Native Hawaiians. Asian Pacific Americans include those whose origins are from Japan, China, Taiwan, Korea, Burma, Vietnam, Laos, Cambodia, Thailand, Malaysia, Indonesia, the Philippines, Brunei, Samoa, Guam, the U.S. Trust Territories of the Pacific Islands, the Commonwealth of the Northern Marianas Islands, Macao, Fiji, Tonga, Kirbati, Juvalu, Nauru, Federated States of Micronesia, or Hong Kong. Subcontinent Asian Americans include those whose origins are from India, Pakistan, Bangladesh, the Maldives Islands, Nepal, or Sri Lanka.

20. 49 C.F.R. Part 26, Section 26.67.

21. Section 26.67(a).

22. Information provided by Charles Klemstine, Federal Highway Administration.

23. Note that the latest reauthorization statute, SAFETEA-LU also includes the National Highway Traffic Safety Administration (NHTSA) under the Program.
24. Part 26 is narrowly tailored to address only those individuals who are impeded by barriers in transportation contracting. The new eligibility standards prevent over-inclusiveness by ensuring that these with too great a net worth are no longer eligible for the program.
25. Urban Institute, *Do Minorities Get a Fair Share of Government Contracts?* (1997).
26. For example, the City of Philadelphia runs a city program for local funds and the federal program for federal funds. Both are administered by the City's Minority Business Enterprise Council.
27. Prior to the formation of a Unified Certification Program (UCP) mandated under Part 26 recipients used their own applications.
28. Many state and local programs mandate that participants be American citizens.
29. The overall program size cap is adjusted periodically for inflation by USDOT's Secretary. This is the second adjustment that has taken place since 1999.
30. Spirited, lively congressional debate focused on the fact that absent a PNW, outrageously wealthy individuals could participate in the program (the preamble cites the Sultan of Brunei as an example).
31. When an individual owner exceeds the threshold and loses his or her disadvantage status, the question remains whether where there are other disadvantaged owners whose combined ownership if 51 percent or greater.
32. Part 26, Section 26.87(b). An administrative due process hearing must be offered to the firm where a reasonable cause determination is made.
33. Part 26 requires that initial certification last for a minimum of three years.
34. Part 26, Section 26.45.
35. Ibid.
36. Ibid.
37. USDOT has never penalized a recipient for failure to meet an overall goal. Under Part 26, a recipient is not required to set a DBE contact goal on every contract.
38. To the extent that race-conscious or contract goals are no longer needed to achieve overall goals, USDOT recipients must discontinue their use.
39. See GAO report at 15.
40. See Sections 26.5 and 26.51 which contain a definition and examples of race neutral measures.
41. The certification component of Part 26 cannot be waived. However, waivers can be sought for alternative means of setting goals. All waivers must be approved by the USDOT Secretary.

Part IV

Managing Transportation Systems

23 From Transportation to Logistics to Supply Chain: Evolution in How Industry Thinks about Moving Goods

Richard R. Young

INTRODUCTION

While many first think of passenger movement when considering the topic of transportation, there nevertheless remains an even more significant need for developing an understanding of how freight transportation fits into the overall theme. In order to accomplish this, consideration must first be given to the larger themes of physical distribution, materials management, logistics and supply chain management, each of which has an increasingly expansive role for transportation.

In the latter part of the last century many firms began to combine business functions in order that they avoid suboptimal behavior. Specifically, transportation decision making was a key variable in the creation of both physical distribution and materials management as aggregated functions. In the case of the former, it was the combining of finished goods inventory, warehousing and outbound transportation; for the latter, it was procurement, raw materials inventory and inbound transportation. Towards the mid-1980s physical distribution and materials management were combined at many firms to establish integrated logistics where control of the movement and storage of all materials would fall under a single organization. For the purpose of this discussion it is instructive that transportation decision-making now became just one variable that could be traded-off against others in the drive to manage costs and customer service (Coyle 38).

Although many may attribute the term *supply chain* to Chrysler Corporation in the early 1980s, it was not until the mid-1990s that the term *supply chain management* came into fashion. A group of industry and academic representatives, who ultimately would go on to form the nucleus of what would become the Supply Chain Council developed the Supply Chain Operational Reference (SCOR Model). The SCOR Model essentially took the concept of integrated logistics as an activity within the boundaries of a single firm and established a paradigm where the control of materials spanned the boundaries to one's customers and suppliers (Supply Chain Council). Again, transportation was but one variable within an even larger scheme.

DEVELOPING THE ANALYTICAL FRAMEWORK

Economists view the transportation of goods as having two principal means of adding value. Specifically, value is added through spatial utility, but also through temporal utility. Spatial essentially means that a good has more value in the hands of its potential consumer than in possession of its producer. This is the *ceteris paribus* explanation, but transportation also provides temporal utility, hence the ongoing discussions on modal choice. Temporal utility can be achieved through two means: faster transportation or by maintaining inventories closer to the points of consumption. This presents the first important tradeoff: whether to invest in inventories or to incur a greater expense for transportation. If the former, the holding of inventory represents a range of costs, each of which must be evaluated (Coyle 65).

The holding of inventory represents significantly more than the opportunity cost of the investment. Additional concerns include a facility to physically house the goods, obsolescence factors, insurance, and potential shrinkage—otherwise attributed to loss and damage. Physical housing is normally thought of as a building, but in the case of bulk materials may be a tank for liquids or a piece of vacant land for dry materials. In the case of building structures, specific accommodations may be made such as cooling for temperature sensitive items, extra security provisions for high-value and highly theft prone ones, or special safeguards when goods possess hazardous qualities such as poisons, flammables, oxidizers, and corrosives. Obsolescence is a particular issue with high tech items such as computers where a steady flow of innovation is constantly added to products (see Figure 23.1).

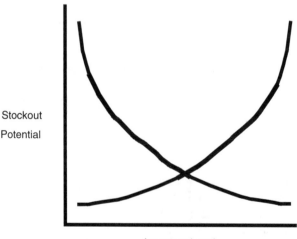

FIGURE 23.1   Inventory vs. stockout tradeoff.

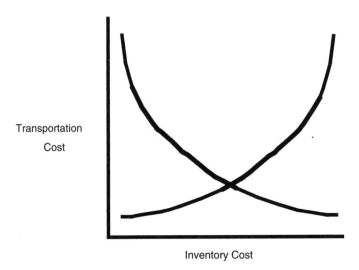

FIGURE 23.2 Transportation-inventory tradeoff.

Similarly, dated goods, such as pharmaceuticals and food items, experience similar phenomena. Loss and damage is a considerable factor when goods are either easily rendered unsalable due to poor handling or may be stolen. Inventory tax is typically levied by the state where the inventory is housed and is based on the acquisition value or manufacturing cost rather than its selling price averaged over an entire year. Most believe that the inventory carrying costs as a percentage of value can be estimated at somewhere between double to triple the cost of capital. In current terms, this means that inventory costs somewhere between 12 to 15 percent of its value to carry, annually.

Herein lies a basic tradeoff in logistics management: inventory investment may be reduced in exchange for faster transportation and vice versa. In solving this tradeoff problem, one only needs to ask if the cost of the faster transportation is greater to or less than the cost of holding inventory for the difference in transit times for two modes of transportation given a specific customer service standard. Interestingly, these tradeoffs can be loosely plotted on a graph as shown in Figure 23.2 that largely mimics that of the tradeoffs discussed in Figure 23.1 (Coyle 65).

Freight transportation is referred to, again by economists, as demand derived. Specifically, there is no demand for freight transportation unless there is demand for the underlying goods to be transported. Significant recognition needs to be given to William Baumol who was able to derive his inventory theoretic as a valuable tool for evaluating transportation and inventory tradeoffs. Evaluating the tradeoffs possible, Baumol (1970) considered inventory holding costs, ordering costs, the cost of owning inventory while in transit and the transportation costs to be the building blocks of any logistics tradeoff analysis.

This work was an extension of the economic order quantity (EOQ) equation that has been found in the literature since the early 1900s, including a well-known text by Buffa and Miller (1979, 176). Specifically, this is:

$$EOQ = \sqrt{\frac{2RA}{VW}}$$

Where
    EOQ = economic order quantity
    R = annual requirements
    A = ordering costs
    V = unit cost of the item
    W = inventory holding cost as a percentage

The EOQ equation, however, is based upon the tradeoff between ordering costs and inventory holding. As such it is the derivative of a total annual cost that would appear as follows using the same variable values. Effectively, these calculations are most frequently carried out on an annual basis, hence, total annual cost, or TAC, is the preferred quotient.

$$TAC = \frac{1}{2} QVW + A\frac{R}{Q}$$

Inventory carrying costs are calculated on the basis of one half the quantity using the assumption that inventory is consumed at a constant rate and that the minimum quantity on hand is set at zero while the maximum on hand will be that established by the EOQ formula. To this Baumol added the cost of owning the inventory during the period of transportation as well as the cost of the transportation itself. While in the equation the cost of carrying inventory is based on the average quantity on hand, the ownership during transportation equation calculates the cost of owning every unit that is to be transported. Therefore, the full equation becomes:

$$TAC = \frac{1}{2} QVW + A\frac{R}{Q} + \frac{t}{365} RVW + TR$$

Where
    t = average number of days that each unit is in transit
    T = unit cost of transporting each item

Tradeoffs now become readily apparent with perhaps one of the most common being that of modal selection. While conventional wisdom would suggest that a firm make every attempt to avoid airfreight, one can easily make a case for airfreight being the low cost alternative from a total cost perspective once the value of the inventory, both in terms of cycle stock in the warehouse and inventory in transit are concerned. Clearly, the more valuable the material or product being transported, the better the case for utilizing a faster mode. While airfreight will always handle the occasional low-value cargo because it is urgently needed, these are one-time events and fall outside of the scope of this analysis (Young 1996).

This is to say that until the current time, inventory decisions have largely driven transportation decisions. Consider, for example, that when industry has been canvassed regarding what is important relative to the selection of transportation firms that the rate or price paid is secondary to timely and consistent service. Bardi, Bagchi, and Raghurathan (1989) provide a list of factors in Figure 23.3 that highlights rates, or pricing, as one of only many factors worthy of consideration.

The "key impacts" column has been added for the purpose of providing the non-logistician reader with some context. Note that better than half of these factors address

Rank	Factor	Key Impacts
1	Transit time reliability or consistency	Inventory level
2	Door-to-door transportation cost or rate	Transportation
3	Total door-to-door transit time	Inventory level
4	Willingness to negotiate rates	Transportation
5	Financial stability of carrier	Administrative, inventory
6	Equipment availability	Customer service
7	Frequency of service	Inventory level
8	Pickup and delivery service	Transportation
9	Shipment expediting	Inventory level
10	Quality of operating personnel	Inventory level

FIGURE 23.3   Importance ranking of carrier selection determinants.

the problem of how much inventory needs to be carried. Inventory, in many situations, represents nothing more than an insurance policy protecting firms from unforeseen variation in either demand for product or supply. While variation in quantity may be an issue here, so is variation from a temporal standpoint.

A MACRO VIEW OF LOGISTICS COSTS IN THE U.S. ECONOMY

Since 1980, the year that most consider to be the watershed of economic deregulation of the transport sector in the United States, the logistics costs as a percentage of the gross domestic product has steadily declined as shown in Figure 23.4.

Particularly instructive is the methodology that is used to derive this information is credited to Heskett, Ivie, and Glaskowsky (1973, 26) and has a strong resemblance to those factors encompassed by Baumol only three years prior and was previously discussed. Whereas Baumol sought to build cycle inventory, in-transit inventory, ordering cost, and transportation cost into his total cost model, Hestkett aggregated the

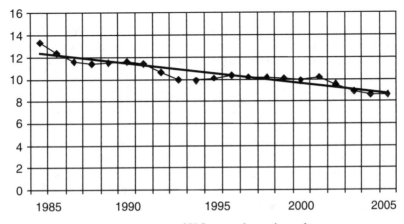

FIGURE 23.4   Logistics cost as percent of U.S. gross domestic product.

	2000	**2004**
Inventory Carrying Costs		
Interest	93	23
Taxes, Obsolescence, Depreciation	206	227
Warehousing	75	82
TOTAL	374	332
Transportation Costs		
Truck	481	509
Rail	36	42
Pipeline	9	9
Air	27	31
Water	26	27
Forwarders	10	18
TOTAL	608	636
Administrative Costs	39	39
Other	5	8
GRAND TOTAL	1,025	1,015

FIGURE 23.5   Annual state of logistics cost model.

two inventory statistics, accounted for transportation, and expanded ordering costs to include all logistically- related administrative costs. Although the least significant cost category, it is intended to include all of those activities that are required to execute the commitment, delivery, and payment for goods from a systems or cyclical standpoint.

Using the Heskett methodology, Wilson, makes an annual assessment of logistics costs and their constituents and presents these as an annual event on behalf of the Council of Supply Chain Management Professionals (formerly the Council of Logistics Management), as in Figure 23.5.

During the period shown, overall logistics costs in the U.S. economy remained at a relatively flat 8.6 percent, while inventory costs actually dropped a greater amount than transportation costs increased. Historically, increases in inventory costs would be expected to positively correlate with growth in GDP, but that has not been happening. Instead improved transportation that has shorter transit times as well as more consistent transit times has increasingly replaced inventory investment. Competition and productivity improvements in transportation have also accounted for transportation steadily declining as a percentage of GDP as well, as is shown in Figure 23.6, below (Eno 2005).

Administrative costs have remained relatively flat for as long as the annual logistics report has been published. Modest increases, although still insignificant given the magnitude of the other costs, are accounted for by the greater number of transactions as well as an increase in the complexity of those transactions as supply chains, even their domestic counterparts, have continued to lengthen. Substantially offsetting those increases is the greatly expanded use of technology in managing transactions whether it is web-based applications, radio frequency identification (RFID), or integrated planning mechanisms between buyers and sellers.

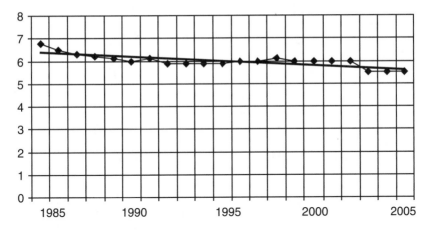

FIGURE 23.6 Inventory as a percentage of U.S. gross domestic product.

APPLYING THE MODEL TO LOGISTICS DEVELOPMENTS

The value of tradeoffs, however, does not end with the modal decision. Many of the events and technology developments of recent years need to be considered as well, not only for their economic consequences on supply chain management, but also for the manner in which they have affected the market for transportation.

Perhaps the greatest impetus to lower supply chain costs was economic deregulation[1] where government shackles over the pricing of transportation services, entry and exit of firms from the industry, geographic coverage, and the adoption of multimodal services. The result was more supply relative to the demand for transport service with the expected drop in rates. Railroads were free to abandon or sell off unprofitable branches and to contract with shippers. Truckers were free to enter into new and often more profitable traffic lanes. Soon, however, competition was not just price-based, but service-based, as well. Deregulation, as a seminal event, drove down the values of the *T variable* in Baumol's equation, but increasingly the *t variable* thereby affected the amount of inventory that firms needed to keep on hand.

Effective communications plus the willingness of buyers and sellers to enter into closer relationships served to reduce administrative costs, or the *A variable*, specifically of transactions. Even among those firms employing the economic order quantity formula for setting inventories, this reduction drove downward the *Q variable* and with it the *V variable* as well as firms soon realized that the actions taken by a buyer can impact the costs of the sellers of goods. Process re-engineering became a major factor in cost reductions.

Technology, specifically, electronic data interchange (EDI), E-commerce, and radio frequency identification (RFID) enabled expensive inventory to be replaced by ever less costly information. Smaller lot sizes worked hand-in-hand with such initiatives as just-in-time (JIT) with the result being smaller shipment sizes that would need to occur on a much more frequent basis. Where truckloads were once the norm,

| Mode | 1993 | | 1997 | | |
	$ Bil.	Share	$ Bil.	Share	% Change
Truck	870	338.2	1023	40.6	17.7
Rail	943	41.4	1022	40.6	8.5
Water	271	11.9	261	10.4	-3.8
Air	4	6	6	0.3	55.5
Pipeline	NA	NA	NA	NA	NA
Multimodal	191	8.4	204	8.1	6.8
Total	2279		2516		10.4

FIGURE 23.7   Model distribution of ton-miles. U.S. Census Bureau.

less than truckload (LTL) and small shipments increased in frequency. The steady downward spiral of transportation on a per pound basis only further accelerated the process. As speed and consistency became the critical success factors of supply chain management, those modes of transportation that could provide both were rewarded in the marketplace, as is illustrated in Figure 23.7.

Finally, in more recent years lower interest rates have served to further reduce the cost of holding inventory as well as investing in the infrastructure to house it. Those noneconomic issues that have driven supply chain management as the emerging leading business process would have to include an accelerating variety of products and number of product extensions, globalization, and a product life cycle that continues to compress for many of the higher technology products and materials. The complexity represented by the number and variety of products has meant that many items now must be both stored and moved in smaller quantities. Similarly, goods with shorter life cycles dictates that no one wants to hold large quantities that have the potential for becoming obsolete. For example, no one would want to hold large inventories of personal computers with Pentium I processors once the next generation became available.

APPLYING THE MODEL LOOKING FORWARD

Just as the total cost model is useful for considering the past impacts on total logistics costs, it is equally well suited for evaluating the potential impacts when examining current events. Although it has already been stated that inventory has been largely the driver of transportation decisions, the capacity constraints facing all modes of transportation are beginning to appear to invert this situation whereby transportation will begin to drive inventory decisions (Biondo 2005).

Firms that have been accustomed to paying ever-lower transportation rates may already be experiencing a change as the paradigm that has been in place for the past twenty-five years has changed. The paring back of capacities of the railroads coupled with capacity problems for each of the other modes appears to be the driving force for this phenomenon; however, there are other factors that need to be considered.

Nearly fifteen years ago, the U.S. Department of Transportation (1990, 52) warned of a need to add to capacities for all of the modes and only six years ago the U.S. Depart-

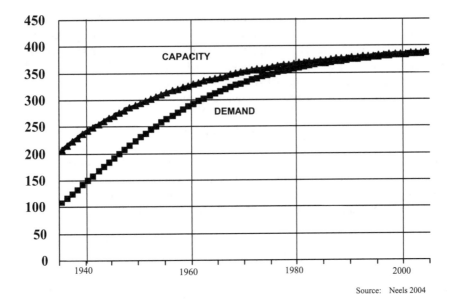

Source: Neels 2004

FIGURE 23.8 Railroad capacity—demand vs. supply.

ment of Agriculture (Brennan) warned of constrained railroad capacity and the threat that it presented to the distribution of basic materials in the food chain. At the same time, railroad congestion became legendary in the post-merger integration of the Class Is including the Southern Pacific into the Union Pacific, and the breakup of Conrail with parts acquired by both CSX and Norfolk Southern (Saunders 2003, 329). Figure 23.8 depicts the supply and demand situation as pertains to railroad capacity. Note that equilibrium appears to be approached in the period between the years 1995 and 2000.

Railroads, perhaps, pose an even more compelling issue with the number of private car operators, or those firms who require specialized equipment that the railroads refuse to invest in. Private car fleet sizing algorithms are driven in part by the number of annual turns a firm can get from each car. When congestion occurs, the number of turns drops thereby prompting the equations to add cars. Added cars to the system further chokes the network with the ultimate result being gridlock (Young, Swan, and Burn 2002). The railroads will need to double track routes where single track has existed and potentially triple track that which has been double tracked. Such projects are subject to long lead times and potential legal battles.

Inland water transportation is also threatened by capacity constraints as, for example, the Ohio River system's locks need both maintenance and upgrading. Built in the early part of the twentieth century, much of the infrastructure was designed around smaller barges as well as smaller tows due to less powerful motive power. Not unrelated are the ocean ports where the advent of the ever-larger container vessels now stresses container terminals with regard to both berthing space and container yard acreage. While firms such as Maersk-Sealand have continued to add larger vessels to their fleets, many only see delays waiting for berthing space before they can unload. Alternative solutions to this problem in the short-term include rerouting vessels from West Coast to East Coast ports; in the long-term, adding significant new port capacity such as that in progress at Prince Rupert, British Columbia (Constantineau 2004). As an alternative to the congestion at Los Angeles and Long Beach, development of a major port in the Baja is being considered (Lindquist 2005). These alternatives, while also having long lead times, still may be achieved more quickly than expanding existing ports where land may not be available.

Airlines continue to get much press coverage, especially when they abandon long-established markets, but also when they file for Chapter 11 bankruptcy. Not quite so obvious is the fact that historically some 60 percent of airfreight has moved as belly cargo in passenger aircraft and not carried by all freight carriers such as FedEx, UPS, and DHL. As the passenger carriers struggle for profitability, many of the new aircraft assigned to routes are regional jets, such as those produced by Brazil's Embraier and Canadair, a unit of Canada's Bombardier. Clearly, these are efficient aircraft, but unfortunately have little cargo capacities with their absence of any pallet positions.

Finally, trucking may complete the scenario for transportation's "perfect storm" as the hours of service regulations imposed in early 2004 confounded an already troublesome driver shortage, especially for the long haul firms. Those problems stemmed from relatively low wages and poor lifestyle, and early on many of the leading firms in that sector of the industry sought to use intermodal for long hauls (Min and Lambert 2002). Ten years ago J.B. Hunt, a leading truckload carrier, endeavored to switch much of its business to the rails when it made a conscious decision to purchase containers, chassis, and tractors without sleepers. Today, some firms are looking to make acquisitions, not so much to gain customers or geographic coverage, but to obtain drivers.

At this juncture the reader is directed back to the Baumol total cost equation. Not only will the T *variable* increase as transportation rates climb, a natural function of capacity constrained supply in the face of increasing demand, but so will the inventory investment increase as a function to the t *variable* (transit time) and the s *variable* (safety stock) as a constrained transportation network become significantly less predictable with regard to its service (Kuhn 1970, 62).

Where the title of this chapter addressed how industry thinks about transportation, it is suggested that shippers will need to rethink their inventory-transportation relationships. In many cases inventory will once again become the in-vogue insurance policy against variations in the system—variations that are caused by constrained capacities that have resulted from a lack of investment both as private and public. Nevertheless, we are in the midst of a paradigm change. Moreover, history has proven that such changes are extremely difficult for most to recognize in mid-change, but can amply recognize after the fact.

NOTE

1. Deregulation is the collective term applied to several acts of Congress including the Staggers Rail Act of 1980, Motor Carrier Act of 1980, Shipping Act of 1984, and the Airline Deregulation Act of 1977.

REFERENCES

Bardi, Edward J., Bagchi Prabir, and T.S. Raghurathan (1989), "Motor Carrier Selection in a Deregulated Environment." *Transportation Journal*, 29:1, pp. 4–11.

Baumol, William J., and H. D. Vinod (1970), "An Inventory Theoretic Model of Transportation Demand." *Management Science*, 16:7, pp. 413–421.

Biondo, Keith (2005), "Tipping Point, Again." *Inbound Logistics*, 25:1, p. 12.

Brennan, William (1998), "Long-term Capacity Constraints in the U.S. Rail System," *Agricultural Transportation Challenges for the 21st Century*. Washington, DC: Agricultural Marketing Services, U.S. Department of Agriculture.

Buffa, Elwood S., and Jeffrey G. Miller (1979), *Production and Inventory Systems: Planning and Control*, 3rd ed. Homewood, IL: Richard D. Irwin.

Constantineau, Bruce (2004), "Price Rupert Plans $500m Port Expansion." *Vancouver Sun*, July 27.

Coyle, John J., Edward J. Bardi, and C. John Langley (2003), *The Management of Business Logistics*. Mason, OH: South-western.

Heskett, James E., J. Ivie, and W. Glaskowsky (1973), *Business Logistics*, 2nd ed. New York: The Ronald Press.

Kuhn, Thomas S. (1970), *The Structure of Scientific Revolutions*. Chicago: University of Chicago Press.

Lingquist, Diane (2005), "New Port on Horizon: Mexico Plans an Alternative to the Jammed Docks in L.A., Long Beach." *San Diego Union-Tribune*, August 14, http://www.singonsandiego.com/uniiontrib/20050814/news_1n14port.html.

Min, Hokey and Thomas Lambert (2002), "Truck Driver Shortage Revisited." *Transportation Journal*, 42:2, pp. 5–16.

Neels, Kevin (2005), "Railroading in an Era of Tight Capacity: Where is the Equilibrium?" Presentation to the Transportation Research Forum, Annual Meeting, Washington, DC, January 10.

Saunders, Richard (2003), *Main Lines: Rebirth of the North American Railroads, 1970–2002*. Dekalb, IL: University of Northern Illinois Press.

Supply Chain Council (2005), *Supply Chain Operational Reference Model Guide*, version 6.0. Washington, DC.

U.S. Census Bureau (1999), Commodity Flow Survey, 9.

U.S. Department of Transportation (1990), *Moving America: New Directions, New Opportunities*.

Wilson, Rosalyn (2002), *Transportation in America, 19th ed*. Washington, DC: Eno Transportation Foundation.

Wilson, Rosalyn (2005), "16th Annual State of Logistics Report: Security Report Card—Not Making the Grade." Oak Brook, IL: Council of Supply Chain Management Professionals.

Young, Richard R., (1996), "Atlantic Pharmaceuticals Case," appearing in Joseph L. Cavinato, *Business Logistics Casebook*. University Park, PA: Center for Logistics Research and Division of Research, Smeal College of Business Administration.

Young, Richard R., Peter F. Swan, and Richard Burn (2002), "The Problem of Excessive Holding Time of Private Railcar Fleet Operators in the North American Chemical and Plastics Industries." *Transportation Journal*, 42:1, pp. 51–61.

24 Transportation Asset Management

Pannapa Herabat, Sue McNeil, and
Aileen Switzer

INTRODUCTION

HISTORICAL BACKGROUND

Infrastructure network expansion was initiated after World War II. Highway agencies focused on the construction of infrastructure networks. Road and rail networks were developed to provide mobility and efficiency in different modes of transportation to users. The infrastructure network expansion slowed down after the late 1970s because of shifts in focus from expansion to preservation. Figure 24.1 captures the historical timeline from infrastructure network expansion to the present. Shifts in federal, state, and local policies relative to infrastructure management and expansion, budgeting decisions, and staff resource allocations over the last twenty to thirty years have impacted transportation investment decisions and are likely to play a key role in the future. Highway agencies continue to face tough challenges in simultaneously expanding and maintaining the infrastructure network. To assist, different technologies have been incorporated to maintain the infrastructure network to prevent catastrophic failure while providing a safe network for users. Among the technologies introduced were the concepts of single-asset-type management systems such as the pavement management system and bridge management system in the late 1970s to 1990s as shown in Figure 24.1.

Federal transportation policy and legislation have seen significant shifts in response to constrained budgets and shifting priorities at all levels. Specifically, the Intermodal Surface Transportation Efficiency Act (ISTEA), adopted in 1991, implemented a national intermodal transportation systems approach intended to "link highway, rail, air, and marine transportation. Prior to ISTEA, the Federal-Aid Highway Program had been directed primarily toward the construction and improvement of four federal-aid systems: the Interstate, primary, secondary, and urban highways" (Schweppe 2002). ISTEA required public sector agencies to shift their focus away from capacity expansion and emphasize the preservation and operation of the country's $1 trillion investment in its highways and bridges (US DOT 1999).

The Transportation Equity Act of the 21st Century (TEA-21) continued to build on the policies of ISTEA and offered greater spending flexibility to fund highway safety and transit programs. In response to shifting priorities and the need to assess tradeoff

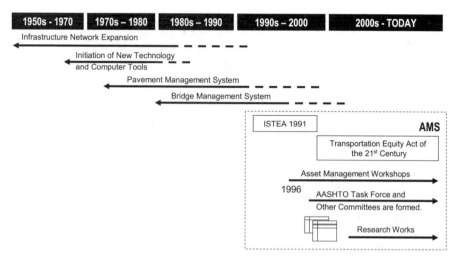

FIGURE 24.1   Historical timeline of asset management.

analyses using constrained funding sources, the principles of asset management began gaining acceptance in the transportation industry. Prior to 1995, asset management in the United States was something private sector companies did; transportation agencies in Australia and New Zealand said they practiced (Norwell and Youdale 1997), and state departments of transportation (DOTs) thought they should be practicing. In September 1996, the American Association of State Highway and Transportation Officials (AASHTO) and the Federal Highway Administration (FHWA) held the first asset management workshop focused on sharing experiences in both the public and private sectors (US DOT 1996). Since 1996, a series of activities has helped to advance the state of the art and state of the practice of asset management including (Oberman et al. 2002):

- 21st Century Asset Management, a second workshop (US DOT 1997),
- AASHTO Transportation Asset Management Task Force formed (AASHTO 1998), which became the Subcommittee on Transportation Asset Management in 2004,
- FHWA Office of Asset Management formed to provide technical support,
- Survey of state agencies conducted (McNeil et al. 2000),
- Asset Management Peer Exchange: Using Past Experiences to Shape Future Practice, a third workshop (AASHTO 2000),
- Transportation Research Board Asset Management Task Force formed, which became a committee in 2004,
- Community of Practice Web site Transportation Asset Management Today (TAMT) launched by FHWA and AASHTO (Winsor et al. 2004),
- Multiple National Cooperative Highway Research Program (NCHRP) studies,
  - Project 20-24(11), Asset Management Guidance for Transportation Agencies— completed in 2002 (http://www4.trb.org/trb/crp.nsf/All+Projects/NCHRP+20-24(11)),

- Project 20-57, Analytic Tools to Support Transportation Asset Management—completed in 2005 (http://www4.trb.org/trb/crp.nsf/All+Projects/NCHRP+20-57),
- Project 20-60, Performance Measures and Targets for Transportation Asset Management completed in 2005 (http://www4.trb.org/trb/crp.nsf/All+Projects/NCHRP+20-60),
- Project 19-04, A Review of DOT Compliance with GASB 34 Requirements—completed in 2003 (http://www4.trb.org/trb/crp.nsf/All+Projects/NCHRP+19-04),
- Taking the Next Step, a fourth workshop (Wittwer et al. 2002),
- Moving from Theory to Practice, a fifth workshop (Wittwer et al. 2004).
- Making Asset Management Work in Your Organization, a sixth workshop (http://www.trb.org/publications/circulars/ec093.pdf).

Asset management has long been an important component of the the private sector. Recently, asset management has been receiving significant interest in the public sector around the world. Many agencies are implementing asset management concepts as a way to expand their infrastructure management practices. Examples can be found in the United States, Australia, and Canada. Several factors motivated the different agencies to include asset management strategies in their agency's objectives. The following are objectives defined by several agencies (US DOT 1999; and US DOT 2002):

- To improve the highway management efficiency and capability,
- To support the paradigm shift from new construction to maintenance management,
- To reinforce budget demands by providing rational justification for investment in infrastructure when competing with other publicly supported programs,
- To increase public acceptance and accountability,
- To support tradeoff decisions as demand continues to grow causing increased congestion and wear and tear on the system,
- To overcome personnel constraints due to downsizing problems and competition in the employment market, and,
- To improve communication with customers, owners, and elected officials.

DEFINITION OF ASSET MANAGEMENT

Highway assets are economic resources that provide services to the public (McNeil et al. 2000). Highway assets can be divided into two types: physical highway assets and other operational types (US DOT 1999). Physical highway assets include pavement, structures, tunnels, and hardware (i.e., guardrail, signs, lighting, barriers, impact attenuators, electronic surveillance and monitoring equipment, and operating facilities). Other operational highway assets include construction and maintenance equipment, vehicles, real estate, materials, human resources, and corporate data.

Public highway assets are generally under the responsibility of public agencies or government-owned agencies, such as, municipalities, and departments of transportation. Whether funds are received from a national level government or local streams of revenue, agencies rarely receive sufficient capital funds to build new and enhance existing public assets. Ongoing significant investments are required to maintain the physical and operational quality of the public highway assets to ensure public safety and to maintain an overall condition above the minimum acceptable level. Private highway assets are managed by the private sector. In most cases, the private sector is more business-oriented since it generally has to be self-sustaining. The management activities of the private sector are similar to those of the public sector: management and maintenance.

Asset management is a tool that can be used for managing transportation assets. The Federal Highway Administration (FHWA) has promoted asset management since the mid-1990s to assist transportation agencies in managing different types of assets. In 1999, the FHWA formed the Office of Asset Management. Also in the United States, professional organizations have formed taskforces and committees to promote the concept of transportation asset management. These include the AASHTO Task Force on Asset Management formed in 1997, the American Public Works Association (APWA) task force on asset management formed in 1998, and the Transportation Research Board (TRB) task force on asset management established in 2000 (McNeil et al. 2000).

Asset management is described as a strategic enterprise that combines engineering practices and analysis with sound business practices and economic theory (US DOT 1999). The transportation community is continually refining the definition of asset management to meet the needs of specific organizations. As a result, various definitions have been developed. With each definition, the overall concepts remain the same. The following definitions illustrate this point:

- "A systematic process of maintaining, upgrading, and operating physical assets cost-effectively" (US DOT 1999).
- "A methodology needed by those who are responsible for efficiently allocating generally insufficient funds amongst valid and competing needs" (Danylo and Lemer 1998).
- "A comprehensive and structured approach to the long-termed management of assets as tools for the efficient and effective delivery of community benefits" (Austroads 1997).
- "A comprehensive business strategy employing people, information, and technology to improve the allocation of available funds amongst valid and competing asset needs" (TAC 1996).
- "Asset Management...goes beyond the traditional management practice of examining singular systems within the road networks, i.e., pavements, bridges, etc. and looks at the universal system of a network of roads and all of its components to allow comprehensive management of limited resources" (OECD 1999).
- "Asset management...a set of concepts, principles, and techniques leading to a strategic approach to managing transportation infrastructure. Transportation asset management enables more effective resource allocation and utilization, based upon quality information and analyses, to address facility preservation, operation, and improvement." (Cambridge Systematics 2002).

- "The combination of management, financial, economic, engineering, operation and other practices applied to physical assets with the objective of providing the required level of service in the most cost-effective manner" (Federation of Canadian Municipalities 2003).
- "A dynamic management system that combines and integrates engineering, business, and technological aspects to optimize infrastructure management under budget constraints. The system collects asset inventory and condition, analyzes the impacts and the asset deterioration process to further establish alternative maintenance strategies, estimates costs and benefits received from maintenance actions, determines the trade-offs among investments in different infrastructure assets, and establishes the prioritization and optimization programs for asset maintenance planning" (Herabat and McNeil 2005).

FRAMEWORK OF ASSET MANAGEMENT

The overall framework of asset management suggested by the US DOT (1999) consists of an asset inventory assessment, condition assessment and performance modeling, maintenance alternative selection and evaluation, methods of evaluating the effectiveness of each strategy, project implementation, and performance monitoring as shown in Figure 24.1. System complexity substantially depends on the types of assets that are being managed and the available budgets or resources.

The general concept of transportation asset management is designed to be policy

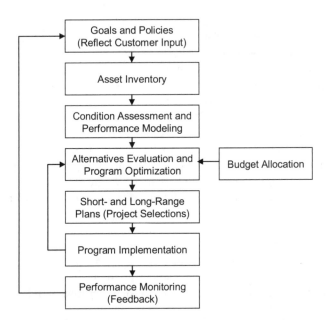

FIGURE 24.2 Generic asset managment system components (modified from US DOT 1999).

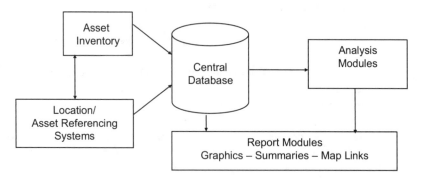

FIGURE 24.3   Basic components of an asset management system.

or goal-driven. Goals and performance indicators are the key elements that drive the decision-making process of the asset management system and help establish different investment levels (US DOT 1999). Asset inventory is composed on the basic data of the asset and their referencing systems as illustrated in Figure 24.3. A central database can be utilized to store, manipulate and retrieve data from different sources, including but not limited to field inspection and special testing. Condition assessment is used to assess the performance of an asset, which can be represented in many forms. Examples of asset condition assessment are safety index, overall structural condition, user cost distance, user satisfaction index, and consumption of road transport, freight and fuel indicators.

This information is then used in performance modeling that relates the changes in the performance of an asset with the contributing factor(s) that affect(s) the degradation process of such asset or the change in the level of service of an asset. The analysis module shown in Figure 24.3 is related to the short- and long-term plans, which involve optimizing the management planning in the most cost-effective manner that is subjected to a budget constraint. The optimization module of highway asset management is a decision support tool that balances the objective function, (i.e., minimizes maintenance costs or maximizes the overall benefits), and selects the optimum set of Maintenance, Rehabilitation, and Replacement (MR&R) actions for the entire highway network as illustrated in Figure 24.4. Its determination is subject to user-defined budget constraints and other considerations. Optimization provides a bundle of projects that satisfies a set of criteria including budget and other constraints over an analysis period. Once the short- and long-term management plans are determined, the overall performance of the developed management plans is monitored before program implementation is executed.

Highway asset management systems are designed to support and enhance different decision-making processes ranging from the detailed technical aspects of each maintenance project to the administrative level. Figure 24.5 presents the levels of decision making (Haas et al. 1994) and the relationship to the managed business process by (US DOT 1999). The linkage between the business process and decision-making levels emphasizes the following points (US DOT 1999):

• Interdisciplinary decisions should be coordinated among agency divisions, and

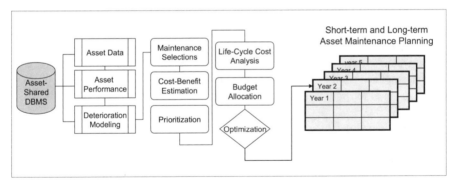

FIGURE 24.4   Elements of AMS analysis module.

- Strong top-down and bottom-up communication ensures that strategic decisions are well-informed by tactical information and that tactical information are aligned with strategic direction.

Higher level management requires extensive calculation based on the data analysis module to determine the optimal maintenance planning. Network-level maintenance planning is prepared for administration and politicians for budget allocation as illustrated in Figure 24.5. Oftentimes, highway maintenance budgets have to compete with other publicly supported programs such as education and healthcare. Therefore, reliable reports for the needs of asset maintenance are essential. Quantifying the benefits received from maintenance actions and the improvement of the overall asset performance can help convince administrators and politicians to allocate the maintenance budget to transportation agencies.

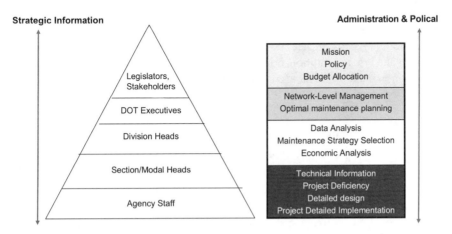

FIGURE 24.5   Levels of decision making. Adapted from US DOT (1999) and Haas et al. (1994).

Customizing the asset management framework to a particular organization is essential to the successful implementation and application of an asset management system, there are many ways to look at the key components or elements of an asset management system. For comparison purposes, the components of an asset management system are briefly reviewed as identified by Figure 24.5 (Austroads 2002). The components of the comprehensive planning framework are:

- Policy development,
- Planning,
- Planned execution, and
- Verification.

TOOLS USED IN ASSET MANAGEMENT

Asset management is a complex process that relies on data and information to support decision making. A variety of tools are available to support this process and many agencies have developed custom systems to support their specific needs. This section begins with an overview of the various types of tools and then provides two examples. The tools described here are not intended to be mutually exclusive but, building blocks that can be used either together or in isolation or in integrated into stand-alone systems.

Types of Tools

Databases

Databases are basic tools for organizing, compiling, accessing and reporting information on particular topics such as the asset inventory or highway performance standards by functional classification. Some state DOTs have a number of databases designed to collect inventory, performance and historical information such as construction history, pavement and bridge condition, bridge inventory, traffic, and accident data. Steps have been taken to make this data user friendly with outputs delivered in text and graphic formats.

Management Systems

In response to ISTEA mandates that were later rescinded, many agencies built asset specific management systems, for pavements and bridges (AASHTO 2001; Robert et al. 2003). These concepts have been generalized to other types of assets such as signals, slopes, grade crossing, and right of way. In addition, congestion, safety, public transit and intermodal management systems have also been developed by some state DOTs to assess tradeoff analyses, investment options, and identify system needs.

Management systems are used to inform agencies of the status, needs and trends of infrastructure assets. They also enable staff to evaluate infrastructure deterioration to generate and rank candidate projects for action. As the AASHTO Asset Management Guide states: "Effective management systems and complete, current and accurate information on transportation infrastructure are practical necessities in meeting the policy and process requirements of asset management" (Cambridge Systematics 2002). Central to these management systems are an inventory of the assets and some assessment of their condition and performance. These systems and data are fundamental building blocks for other types of assets.

Simulation Models

Simulation models provide detailed analyses of performance, costs, and impacts of decisions regarding transportation systems. While useful for analyzing complex problems with many interactive elements, they require considerable data input and either a well-structured set of decision rules or repetitive runs to analyze different options.

Sketch Planning Tools

Sketch planning tools while less detailed than simulation models, provide "analyses of performance, costs, and impacts of transportation decisions" allowing the user to explore a range of options quickly and effectively (Cambridge Systematics 2005).

What-If Tools

What-if Tools offer simple and easy to use analytic procedures that may be used to explore the impact of specific scenarios. What-if tools might be developed in a simple spreadsheet or a more complex application. Using this approach, existing simulations or sketch-planning tools are applied repetitiously to solve a particular problem.

Mapping and Visualization Tools

Asset management also serves as an important communication tool. Geographic Information Systems (GIS) play an important role, as they preserve the spatial relationships among different assets and provide a visual representation in the form of maps of the location of assets and related maintenance, rehabilitation, and improvement activities.

INVESTMENT LEVEL AND TRADEOFF ANALYSIS TOOLS

A number of investment and tradeoff analysis tools have been developed that aid transportation officials to assess infrastructure needs and measures of effectiveness over a multiple years for a range of budget levels within and across investment categories. For example, the National Bridge Investment Analysis System (NBIAS) allows users to analyze impacts to the national bridge network while applying different budget levels (Cambridge Systematics 2005). Similarly, the Highway Economic Requirements System (HERS) reports on the condition and performance of the nation's transportation system (Cambridge Systematics 2005).

Highway Economic Requirements System (HERS-ST)

The Highway Economic Requirements System (HERS) is a simulation tool developed by FHWA to provide an estimated highway budget or develop an understanding of the impact on performance of a specific budget level. HERS-ST is a modified version of HERS for use by state DOTs. It is designed to analyze tradeoffs between preservation and mobility programs for state DOTs (Cambridge Systematics 2005). The tool includes capacity analysis, condition assessment and safety analyses to evaluate the cost of expanding, upgrading and maintaining the highway system (US DOT 2005).

The questions addressed using the HERS-ST model are:

- What is the impact of a change in budget over a specified time frame?
- What investment is required to maintain current conditions?
- What are the budgetary requirements to improve the network to a specified level?

The HERS-ST model functions by simulating network segments relative to the cost to implement a specific strategy and its impact in travel time, safety, vehicle operating costs, emissions and improvement costs. Using an incremental benefit-cost analysis in HERS-ST users can assemble a series of projects that address overall policy goals.

Oregon Department of Transportation (ODOT) began using a customized version of HERS to supports its investment decision-making process in the late 1990s. Since 1991 ODOT had been using the Highway Performance Monitoring System Analytical Process that focuses on engineering criteria. HERS provided the tools to recognize the impact of investments on highway users. HERS now supports needs analyses, the development of the State Transportation Improvement Program (STIP) and special studies such value of time (US DOT 2003).

TOOLS THAT EVALUATE AND COMPARE OPTIONS

There are a number of benefit-cost analysis tools that can be applied at the project level. The wide range enable the user to evaluate the benefits and costs associated with specific highway and bridge projects ranging from adding capacity, new alignment, to rehabilitation and maintenance activities. Among the benefit-cost analysis tools available are MicroBENCOST (analyzes highway projects ranging from added capacity, to rehabilitation work, to bridge projects), Strategic Decision Support Tool for Highway Planning and Budgeting (StratBENCOST—a highway improvement analysis tool that compares several projects during concept development), Surface Tranportation Efficiency Analysis Model (STEAM—analyzes the costs, benefits, and impacts of multi-modal investments), and Intelligent Transportation Systems Deployment System (IDAS—analyzes the benefits and costs of Intelligent Transportation System investments).

Asset Manager NT

AssetManager NT was recently developed under National Cooperative Highway Research Project 20-57 "Analytical Tools for Asset Management." The prototype Asset Manager NT focuses on network-level tradeoffs between different types of assets. It uses the outputs from individual management systems such as the Pavement Management System (PMS) and the Bridge Management System (BMS) as inputs to the tradeoff analysis. The tool provides graphical analysis of the tradeoffs. Asset Manager NT is designed to assist users in understanding how "different patterns of investment in transportation assets will affect the performance of the system over the long term...pavement versus bridge, geographic areas, or system sub-networks" (Cambridge Systematics 2005).

ASSET MANAGEMENT STRATEGIES

PERFORMANCE MEASUREMENT

Performance measures are a mechanism for monitoring progress towards some goal. Measures related to preservation, mobility, and safety are commonly associated with asset management although measures reflecting environmental and societal impacts are also considered. These performance measures are useful in assisting decision makers in setting priorities, identifying potential financial resources, and allocating funds. They may be used to assess needs, evaluate system performance, and communicate actions and results with customers. Consistent evaluation of the performance of transportation assets requires the use of performance measures. "Performance measures allow decision makers to compare actual performance with desired performance as well as to provide the basis for making investment decisions to improve performance of the transportation system" (Falcocchio 2004).

Performance measures also serve as a common language between planning and programming (Barolsky 2005), and asset management and strategic decision making (Pagano et al. 2005). They are widely used in many countries to enhance accountability to the general public and improve communications with decision makers and management (International Scanning Study Team 2004).

INNOVATIVE CONTRACTING APPROACHES

The focus on asset management increases as resources become more constrained. Integral to asset management is the exploration of opportunities for innovative contracting practices to deliver transportation services in the most efficient way possible. Asset management, however, does not require innovative contracting practices and innovating contracting practices do not require asset management. The following sections focus on four innovative practices.

Design-Build

Under this contracting approach, a general contractor assumes responsibility for the project from design through construction. The benefits of this approach are generally improved project quality with savings measured in terms of cost and time. In order to implement this approach, agencies need statutory authority (Stidger 2002). This is necessary to address the dramatic shift in procurement procedures typically handled in state agencies in which contractors and designers are retained separately through different bid and competitive processes.

Performance Specifications

Under traditional or conventional construction contracts, agencies generally specify materials and methods for project delivery. Implementing performance specifications as part of a project places the risk on the contractor or supplier as to how to produce a particular result (Stidger 2002). This approach gives the contractor the greatest latitude in the selection of materials or procedures and eliminates the need for extensive inspection or sampling.

Partnering

As a growing standard practice among many state agencies, partnering is used to set the tone for the project, but does not alter the terms or risk allocation identified in the contract. Partnering brings together interested parties to develop an atmosphere of cooperation, dedication, and dispute resolution with all involved agreeing to work through problems and maintain communication (Stidger 2002).

Outsourcing

"Outsourcing is defined as the management and/or day-to-day execution of an entire business function by a third party service provider" (Wikipedia 2005). Common tasks outsourced by transportation agencies including information technology services and maintenance (Eger et al. 2002).

LEGISLATION TO SUPPORT ASSET MANAGEMENT

Four states, Michigan, Vermont, Montana, and Florida have asset management related legislation in place. The legislation in Michigan and Vermont explicitly addresses asset management. The legislation in Montana and Florida addresses the performance of the transportation infrastructure.

Asset management is increasingly becoming an integral part of any state transportation plan. This is the reason institutionalization of asset management is seen as an obvious step towards making it a part of the planning process. This assumes more significance as many states are actually practicing asset management without calling it such.

The Transportation Asset Management Guide (Cambridge Systematics 2002) identifies some of the key elements necessary to institutionalize asset management:

- Creation of a technical advisory panel for overseeing asset management efforts,
- Development of performance measures,
- Establishing a GIS database,
- Inclusion of life-cycle cost analysis as part of the asset management plan,
- Maintaining a base level of funds for maintenance activities to sustain infrastructure,
- Maintenance of statutory formulas for distribution of state and federal transportation funds.

The following two states have institutionalized asset management in the transportation decision-making process.

MICHIGAN

As part of House Bill No. 5396, Michigan's state legislature created a transportation asset management council within the state transportation commission, to provide a unified effort by various roadway agencies within the state. The council is responsible for developing a statewide asset management strategy. The council includes ten voting members appointed by the state transportation commission. The procedures and requirements set by the council as part of the asset management strategy include areas of training, data storage and collection, reporting, development of a multiyear program, budgeting and finance and other issues related to asset management. A technical advisory panel was also created to support the council, but its recommendations may be considered advisory only. Necessary funding is provided by an annual appropriation from the Michigan transportation fund to the state transportation commission (Michigan Department of Transportation 2005).

VERMONT

The General Assembly of Vermont passed sections 24 and 25 of Act no. 64 in July 2001 (VTrans 2002). The sections require the Vermont Transportation Agency (VTrans) to submit information on its assets to the House and Senate committees on transportation. As part of this effort, the agency is required to develop an asset management system, which is a systematic goal setting, performance-driven management and decision-making process of maintaining, upgrading and operating the state's transportation assets cost effectively. The system identifies all assets and their condition related to pavements, structures, facilities, maintenance equipment, vehicles, materials, and data. In addition, it was recommended that it also includes deterioration rates for all infrastructure assets. The resulting asset management plan includes the costs of implemention activities to be undertaken by the plan and comparative cost differentials between maintaining the infrastructure and utilizing the maintenance program versus deferring maintenance.

VTrans presented the asset management plan as the Fiscal Year Budget Narrative to the House and Senate Transportation Committees and it was well received. If, however, the Committees do not accept the plan as is, VTrans will have to submit a revised plan for approval.

MONTANA

Montana has a statutory requirement for the distribution of Primary Highway Funds (MCA 60-3-205) and the allocation of funds to the Interstate and National Highway Systems. Montana's Performance Planning Process (P³) supports the legislation (Montana DOT 2009). The "Performance Programming Process" links ongoing annual and multiyear activities to plan program and deliver highway improvements. P³ is a project nomination process that is closely linked to the evaluation of performance measures. The inputs include:

- **Vision**—Statewide Long Range Transportation Plan; updated on a five-year cycle and includes customer input, technical analysis and policy direction.
- **Performance Goals**—Funding distribution plan, on a one-year cycle this plan involves trade-off analysis and performance measures that are derived from the management systems.
- **Performance Measures**—Construction Program Delivery and System Monitoring; these are ongoing efforts that provide system through existing systems and public involvement.
- **Investment Decisions**—Statewide Transportation Improvement Program; the project nominations and customer input are updated annually.

FLORIDA

The Florida Department of Transportation (FDOT) and the Florida legislature have a close statutory and working relationship through three mechanisms (Florida DOT 2005):

- Transportation Code. The purpose of the Florida Transportation Code, developed by the administration, establishes the importance of preservation of all transportation facilities in the state.
- Performance Measures. The legislature has charged the Florida Transportation Commission to develop and adopt measures for evaluating the performance and productivity of the DOT. FDOT is responsible for carrying out the planning and maintenance of Florida's infrastructure.
- Management Systems. The legislature also mandated that FDOT, in cooperation with Metropolitan Planning Organizations (MPOs) and other affected entities, develop and implement a separate and distinct system for managing each of the following programs:

- Highway pavement
- Bridges
- Highway safety
- Traffic congestion
- Public transportation facilities and equipment
- Intermodal transportation facilities and equipment

The established FDOT management system is intended to provide adequate information for FDOT to make informed decisions regarding the proper allocation of transportation resources.

RELATED REQUIREMENTS

ASSET REPORTING

Federal reporting requirements apply to several classes of assets including all bridges over twenty feet in length on public roads and a sample of roadway sections that make up the Highway Performance Monitoring System (HPMS).

The requirement to inspect all bridges over twenty feet in length on public roads was instituted after the collapse of the Silver Bridge in Ohio in 1967 (FHWA 1986). The failure resulted in loss of life and property in addition to several major lawsuits. This legal action prompted Congress to institute the National Bridge Inspection Standards (NBIS). The resulting laws require the inspection of all U.S. bridges at least every two years. The data is recorded in the National Bridge Inventory (NBI) (FHWA 1995). Updated procedures went into effect in January 2005 to remove ambiguities in the NBIS procedures (Federal Register 2004).

The HMPS was initiated in 1978 to reflect the condition, performance, use, and operating characteristics of the national highway system. The database includes data for a sample of all public roads and was originally intended to support the biennial Condition and Performance Reports to Congress. These reports provide a comprehensive, factual background to support development and evaluation of the Administration's legislative, program, and budget options. They also support the strategic planning process and asset management initiatives by states, Metropolitan Planning Organizations (MPOs) and local government. States are required to provide HPMS data to FHWA under 23 CFR 420.105(b) (US DOT 2003).

GOVERNMENT ACCOUNTING STANDARDS BOARD STATEMENT 34

In June 1999, the Government Accounting Standards Bureau (GASB) (GASB 1999) issued reporting guidelines (Statement 34) that state and local governments in the United States report the value of the infrastructure assets they own. While reporting asset value is not a requirement, most state statutes for state and local agencies require the agencies to follow the GASB guidelines. Similar accounting practices are in place in Canada, Australia, and New Zealand and agencies privatizing their assets also need to understand the value of those assets.

Valuing assets requires that an agency maintain inventories of their infrastructures. The guidelines also provide the option for agencies to either depreciate their assets over time or use an asset management system to demonstrate that they have maintained their assets in some specified acceptable level of condition.

The guidelines, although controversial, have increased the visibility of assets in the accounting systems. NCHRP Report 522 documents experiences in state DOTs with GASB 34 (PB Consult 2004).

BENEFITS

The benefits from asset management include (Austroads 2002, US DOT 1996):

- More clearly defined objectives,
- More consistent approach to prioritization,
- More transparency in decision-making,
- More efficient and effective use of funding,
- Improved communication between stakeholder expectations and asset performance,
- Improved understanding of trade-offs,
- Better information to support investment decisions, and
- Increased benefits to system users.

The benefits realized from implementing asset management can also be classified in terms of nine categories, created by the Organization for Economic Cooperation and Development[1] (OECD 2000), and four different stakeholders' perspectives, identified by Haas et al. (1994). These benefits are summarized in Table 24.1 (Mizusawa and McNeil 2005). As Table 24.1 shows, each level has different benefits depending on the objectives of the stakeholder groups.

Several efforts have been made to quantify the benefits of implementing a pavement management system (PMS), an important element of asset management. For example, Cowe Falls and Tighe (2004) found that the value of pavement assets in Alberta increased $550 million and the Pavement Quality Index (PQI) increased by 0.5 for the network when Alberta used the PMS to support decisions.

ASSET MANAGEMENT APPLICATIONS

All public sector agencies practice asset management. The real question is whether these agencies are systematically and cost-effectively maintaining, upgrading, and

---

1. The Organization for Economic Cooperation and Development (OECD) is composed of industrialized nations of North America, Europe, Asia, and Australia. It provides a forum for its members to share, discuss, and develop economic policies (Cambridge Systematics Inc. 2002).

TABLE 24.1
Benefits by Stakeholder Group

Category	Stakeholder	Benefit
Budget allocation process	Elected Representatives (Strategic Level)	Assurance of best expenditure of funds
	Top Management (Tactical Level)	Improved allocation process within a program area
		Assurance of best use of available budget
		Providing a basis for allocating funds among different districts or agencies
		Justifying capital spending and maintenance programs to the elected council or legislature
		Use of standard accounting concepts and terms to provide understandable information to the decision makers
Asset Inventory	Technical Level People (Operational Level)	Defining the "management fee" as a percentage of the spending on capital and maintenance work
	Public (User & Non-user Level)	Ability to build more accurate information
		Ability to track the performance of treatment strategies
		Ability of a wide range of staff to query database
		Integrated harmonized database (consistent data)
		Provision of up-to-date accurate information on the condition
Road performance	Elected Representatives (Strategic Level)	Improved road performance
	Top Management (Tactical Level)	Improved road performance
		Savings in agency costs (construction and M&R)
	Technical Level People (Operational Level)	Improved road performance
	Public (User & Non-user Level)	Satisfaction of using improved assets
		Improved road serviceability
		Savings in user costs (travel time, vehicle operation, and safety)
		Reduction of environmental impacts (air, noise, and annoyance)
Management Tools	Elected Representatives (Strategic Level)	Actual operation of the system being able to defend/justify programs of maintenance and rehabilitation
		Reduction of pressure (from constituents) to make arbitrary program modifications
		Objective answers to the implications of lower levels of funding, and lower standards
	Top Management (Tactical Level)	Common definitions and standards
		Economic modeling
		Comprehensive, comparative assessment of: • current status of the network • expected future status Objectively based answers to: • what level of funding is required to keep the current status • the implications of greater or lesser budgets • the implications of deferred work • the implications of lower standards

(Continued)

TABLE 24.1 *Continued*

Category	Stakeholder	Benefit
	Technical Level People (Operational Level)	Common definitions and standards Economic modeling Satisfaction of providing best value for available funds Capability of assessing the implications of less funds/lower standards Capability of making the case for higher standards Capability of quantifying the assessment of the condition Improved credibility of decision-making process when dealing with top management
Staff development	Elected Representatives (Strategic Level)	Improved knowledge of pavement conditions and needs
	Top Management (Tactical Level)	Improved knowledge of pavement conditions and needs
	Technical Level People (Operational Level)	Improved recognition of various administrative and operating elements of the organization Broad multi-disciplinary knowledge Provision of access to accurate data, state-of-art IT, and analysis tools needed for cost-effective management Improved knowledge of pavement conditions and needs Upgrade skills
Communication	Top Management (Tactical Level)	Improved communication Common benchmarks Improved internal and external communications Adoption of accounting practices Ability to defer lobbying pressures from special interest groups
	Technical Level People (Operational Level)	Improved communication Common benchmarks Improved internal and external communications Adoption of accounting practices Improved communication with design, construction, maintenance, planning, and research Enabling front line staff to become more involved in the decision making process
	Public	Understanding of agencies business via performance monitoring reports
Application of Technology	Technical Level People (Operational Level)	Increased awareness of available technology and how to use it Better utilization of manpower Time saving in evaluating development alternatives

Modified from Mizusawa and McNeil (2005).

operating their transportation assets. Experiences in agencies in the Unites States are documented in conference papers and presentations, a series of case studies developed by the Federal Highway Administration's Office of Asset Management and material on the Transportation Asset Management Today (TAMT) Web site (http://assetmanagement.transportation.org). This section describes a cross section of these experiences.

In April 2005, an International Scanning Tour comprised of representatives from federal, state, and local government and academia completed a tour of Canada, Australia, New Zealand, and England to review asset management practices and applications (Bugas-Schramm 2005). Given the breadth and depth of that effort, this chapter will focus on national applications.

REVIEW OF STATE EXPERIENCES WITH ASSET MANAGEMENT

Several states that have applied asset management principles indicated their prior investment decisions were based upon a worst first approach toward maintenance and improvement decisions. Over the years, as asset management has grown in application and understanding, these same states either through voluntary effort or in response to state level legislative mandates are moving toward asset management to better address system level needs. A handful of states have passed legislative mandates requiring greater accountability and implementation of asset management principles and practices into decision-making processes—among these are Florida, Michigan, Montana, and Vermont. In addition, the District of Columbian DOT and the Virginia DOT have begun using performance based contracting for asset management including repair, maintenance, and rehabilitation of assets.

MICHIGAN DOT

Michigan DOT applies a comprehensive transportation management system that supports integrated views of pavement, bridge, congestion, and safety information (Cambridge Systematics Inc. 2005). The five-step resource allocation and utilization process integrates department policy goals and objectives, planning, programming, project delivery, quality information analysis, system monitoring, and performance results analyses to manage the network. In 2002 the state legislature passed Act 499 requiring transportation agencies at the state and local levels to conduct "an on going asset management process" (Michigan DOT 2005). Key to this legislative mandate was the formation of the Transportation Asset Management Council assembled to "enhance the productivity of investing in Michigan's roads and bridges through coordination and collaboration among state and local transportation agencies" (Transportation Asset Management Goal Statement 2002).

Montana DOT

In 2002, the Montana DOT developed the Performance Programming Process (P^3) to provide the state's Transportation Commission with information and guidance on the allocation of transportation funds. P^3 is a performance based analytical tool that distributes funds for systems, by geographic areas, and types of work. The system integrates performance measures for pavement and bridge infrastructure and safety to compare investment levels against performance outcomes to obtain the best overall investment.

New York State DOT

New York State DOT (NYSDOT) has implemented a capital program update asset management process designed to cross-reference the various database programs including pavement, bridge, congestion/mobility, and safety (Cambridge Systematics 2005). Improved accountability was one of the motivating factors driving NYSDOT's efforts to implement an asset management effort in the late 1990s. The state's legislature increasingly mandated reporting requirements "to ensure that the legislature's transportation objectives are achieved" (Clash and Delaney 2000). As a decentralized agency with a large number of staff in regional offices, the department's primary focus was on the clarification of roles and responsibilities among the various offices. Strategic program direction and policy are developed by senior management and the commissioner in the central office who are accountable to the legislature and governor; the region offices are responsible for selection of most projects and the delivery of their respective regional programs. Regional programs are submitted to the central office for review and approval to ensure consistency between regional and statewide strategic directions (Clash and Delaney 2000).

Virginia DOT

In 2002, the Virginia DOT launched *Dashboard* a Web-based performance measuring tool designed to improve accountability through real-time reporting of each highway project's status in terms of schedule and budget. Users are able to examine the status of individual projects, review construction performance across the entire state, or review certain types of projects within the region. "By using easily distinguished categories that are universally recognized, performance attributes can be quickly reviewed and communicated...one of the biggest achievements...was the development of a common language for VDOT to discuss performance" (Gifford and Carlisle 2004).

The next step in its effort to further implement asset management is VDOT's emphasis on instilling an asset management culture; turning measurements into project accountability. "One of the new procedures is a monthly statewide videoconference in which Dashboard data are reviewed by the commissioner before district managers and staff. The meetings are at the heart of VDOT's efforts to move the agency toward a culture of performance" (Gifford and Carlisle 2004).

Washington, D.C.

In July 2000, the District of Columbia DOT (DDOT) established D.C. Streets, the first urban, outcome- performance-based asset management project (Sheldahl 2005). The five-year effort's objective was to preserve and maintain about seventy-five miles of National Highway System within D.C.'s jurisdiction. Prior to establishing this program, maintenance of the street system fell to the City, which had an inadequate budget to cover the range of needs. Under D.C. Streets, the system qualified for federal aid allowing it to apply a cost share to project, as well as take advantage of innovative solutions to address the range of maintenance needs.

CHALLENGES FACING IMPLEMENTATION

As a paradigm shift for most public agencies, asset management implementation is a challenge. For example, limited staff and fund resources offers significant challenges to both management and agency staff working to reflect the needs based analysis while promoting economic development activities. Asset management says that agencies need to make resource allocations among programs and across geographic regions based on performance expectations not by historical splits or formulas that do not correlate to objective indications of system condition (AASHTO 2000).

The 2004 Transportation Research Board Asset Management Peer Exchange Meeting identified six barriers to asset management implementation:

- Lack of integration using more sophisticated analytical tools to evaluate and prioritize maintenance and rehabilitation (M&R) projects;
- Database issues such as the inability of existing legacy systems to conduct predictive analyses and related costs associated with data collection;
- Lack of adequate communication tools and methods to relate to different audiences;
- Jurisdictional issues such as gaps in asset management approaches between agencies at different levels of government (in some states, the majority of roadway infrastructure is under local or county jurisdiction);
- Institutional issues such as lack of coordinated and consistent asset management implementation; and
- Costs. (Hendren 2005)

The accompanying report *Asset Management in Planning and Operations: A Peer Exchange* summarized the interviews with a range of state DOTs and found that oftentimes "challenges will vary according to agency size and jurisdiction. For example, smaller agencies struggle with the initial steps of establishing an AM system and collecting data, while larger agencies may have data but struggle with how to analyze and use the data" (Hendren 2005).

In addition to the findings of the TRB peer exchange, the *Asset Management Guide* included a synthesis of asset management practice. The synthesis grouped challenges facing state DOTs into two groups: technical and institutional (which was identified as more significant and difficult to overcome). Specifically, institutional challenges include integrating decision making and resource allocations across asset classes; combining traditional business areas such as financial, engineering and operations within the decision making-process; securing senior management support for the implementation of asset management typically a long-term effort; defining performance measures effectively representing customer perspective and user costs; and developing appropriate public and private sector roles to address change and implement roles effectively. Technical challenges identified in the report include overcoming the stovepipe approach toward data management for different asset classes; developing GIS compatible enterprise-wide databases that reflect concepts of asset management; development of management systems that address "what if" scenarios for a range of assumptions; improving life cycle analyses; and strengthening system monitoring capabilities to conduct program evaluation and policy formation (Cambridge Systematics Inc. 2002).

RESOURCES TO SUPPORT ASSET MANAGEMENT

Although there are many barriers to asset management implementation, there are also resources to help support agencies and professional staff. The Transportation Research Board (TRB) and the American Association of State Highway and Transportation Officials (AASHTO) have an active Asset Management technical committee and subcommittee respectively. The Federal Highway Administration Office of Asset Management works in partnership with these committees to develop research statements, put on conferences and support a Community of Practice Web site (Winsor 2003). The Web site can be accessed at http://assetmanagement.transportation.org. The American Public Works Association, and the National Highway Institute also offer training as needed. In addition, several University Transportation Centers (UTCs) have asset management as their theme and offer training and undertake research projects.

REFERENCES

American Association of State Highway & Transportation Officials (AASHTO), *Pavement Management Guide,* American Association of State Highway & Transportation Officials, Washington, D.C., 2001.

American Association of State Highway and Transportation Officials (AASHTO), AASHTO Asset Management Task Force Strategic Plan, American Association of State Highway & Transportation Officials, Washington, D.C., 1998.

American Association of State Highway and Transportation Officials (AASHTO), *Asset Management Peer Exchange: Using Past Experiences to Shape Future Practice,* Proceedings of a Workshop held in Scottsdale, Arizona, American Association of State Highway & Transportation Officials, Washington, D.C., 2000.

Austroads, "Integrated Asset Management Guidelines for Road Networks," (AP-R202/02), Association of Australian and New Zealand Road Authorities, New South Wales, Australia, 2002.

Austroads, "Strategy for Improving Asset Management Practices," Association of Australian and New Zealand Road Transport and Traffic Authorities, New South Wales, Australia, 1997.

Barolsky, R. Performance Measures to Improve Transportation Planning Practice: A Peer Exchange, Transportation Research Board E-Circular, E-C073, May 2005. http://trb. org/publications/circulars/ec073.pdf (accessed October 13, 2005).

Bugas-Schramm, P. The Tipping Point? Trip Summary on the International Scan on Transportation Asset Management, *APWA Reporter*, American Public Works Association, September 2005. http://www.apwa.net/Publications/Reporter/ReporterOnline/index. asp?DISPLAY=ISSUE&ISSUE_DATE=092005&ARTICLE_NUMBER=1113 (accessed October 13, 2005).

Cambridge Systematics, Incorporated, Analytical Tools for Asset Management, NCHRP Report 545, T*ransportation Research Record*, Washington, 2005.

Cambridge Systematics, Incorporated, Transportation Asset Management Guide, American Association of State Highway & Transportation Officials, Washington, D.C, and Federal Highway Administration, Washington, D.C., 2002. http://downloads.transportation. org/amguide.pdf (accessed October 2, 2005).

Clash, Thomas W., and John B. Delaney. New York State's Approach to Asset Management; A Case Study. *Transportation Research Record*, 2000, 1729, pp 35–41.

Cowe Falls, L., and Susan Tighe. Analyzing Longitudinal Data to Demonstrate the Costs and Benefits of Pavement Management. *Journal of Public Works Management and Policy*, 8 (3), 2004, pp. 176–191.

Danylo, N. H., and Lemer, A., "Asset Management for the Public Work Manager Challenges and Strategies," Findings of the APWA Task Force on Asset Management, American Public Works Association, Kansas City, MO, 1998.

Eger, R.J. II, Knudson, D.; Marlowe, J., and Ogard, E. "Evaluation of Transportation Organization Outsourcing: Decision Making Criteria for Outsourcing Opportunities," Final Report to the Midwest Regional University Transportation Center, Madison, Wisconsin, October 2002. http://www.mrutc.org/research/0103/report0103.pdf (accessed October 13, 2005).

Falcocchio, J.C. Performance Measures for Evaluating Transportation Systems: Stakeholder Perspective. *Transportation Research Record*, 2004, 1895, pp. 220–227.

Federal Highway Administration (FHWA), "Inspection of Fracture Critical Bridge Members: Supplement to the Bridge Inspector's Training," FHWA-IP-86-26, Federal Highway Administration, Washington D.C., September 1986.

Federal Highway Administration (FHWA), "Asset Management, Advancing the State of the Art into the 21st Century through Public-Private Dialogue," FHWA-RD-97-046, Federal Highway Administration, Washington D.C., September 1996.

Federal Highway Administration (FHWA), *Bridge Inspector's Training Manual/90*, Washington, D.C., Rev. March 1995.

Federal Highway Administration (FHWA), "Highway Economic Requirements System: The Oregon Experience, Transportation Asset Management Case Studies," Federal Highway Administration, Washington D.C., FHWA-IF-03-037, 2003.

Federal Register, National Bridge Inspection Standards, Federal Register, 23 CFR Part 350, F69 FR 74436, Federal Highway Administration, Washington D.C., Dec. 14, 2004

Federation of Canadian Municipalities, *Municipal Infrastructure Asset Management: A Best Practice by the National Guide to Sustainable Municipal Infrastructure*, Issue No. 1, November 2003.

Florida Department of Transportation, "The Asset Management Process," Available: http://www. dot.state.fl.us/planning/statistics/assetmgt/default.htm (accessed October 14, 2005).

Gifford, Jonathan L., and Carlisle, W.H. *Virginia Department of Transportation's Dashboard Performance Measurement and Reporting System; Going the Full Monty. Transportation Research Record,* 2004, 1895, pp. 207–219.

Government Accounting Standard Board (GASB) Statement No. 34, Basic Financial Statements and Management's Discussion and Analysis for State and Local Government, Government Accounting Standards Board, Norwalk, Connecticut, June 1999.

Haas, R., Hudson, W. R., and Zaniewski, J. *Modern Pavement Management.* Kreiger Publishing, Malabar, FL,1994.

Hendren, P. Transportation Research Board. Asset Management in Planning and Operations: A Peer Exchange. *Transportation Research Circular,* No. E-C076, 2005. http://trb. org/publications/circulars/ec076.pdf (accessed October 13, 2005).

International Scanning Study Team, Transportation Performance Measures in Australia, Canada, Japan and New Zealand, Federal Highway Administration, December 2004.http://assetmanagement.transportation.org/tam/aashto.nsf/All+Documents/ 38F1D8E2D429FBD985257042003F764C/$FILE/2004%20-%20Transportation%20 Performance%20Measure.pdf (accessed October 13, 2005).

Herabat, P., and McNeil, S. Highway Asset Management System, *The Handbook of Highway Engineering*, T.F. Fwa, ed., chapter 23, Boca Raton, FL, CRC Press, 2005.

McNeil, S., Tischer, M. L., and DeBlasio, A. "Asset Management: What is the Fuss?" *Transportation Research Record,* 2000, No. 1729, pp. 21–25.

Michigan Department of Transportation 2005. http://www.michigan.gov/mdot/ (accessed October 13, 2005).

Mizusawa, D., and McNeil, S. Quantifying the Benefits of Implementing Asset Management, Proceedings of the 1st Annual Inter-university Symposium on Infrastructure Management, Waterloo, Canada, August 2005.

Montana Department of Transportation, (2000). "Performance Planning Process, A Tool for Making Transportation Investment Decisions." Available at http://www.mdt.mt.gov/ publications/docs/brochures/tranplanp3.pdf (accessed October 1, 2005).

Norwell, G., and Youdale, G. "Managing the Road Asset," Association Mondiale de la (PIARC), Special Report on Concessions 1997.

Oberman, W.; Bittner, J.; and Wittwer, E. "Synthesis of National Efforts in Transportation Asset Management," Midwest Regional University Transportation Center, May 2002, Available at http://www.mrutc.org/research/0101/report0101.pdf (accessed December 20, 2003).

Organisation for Economic Co-operation and Development. *Asset Management for the Roads Sector.* Publication DSTI/DOT/RTR/IM1(2000)1, Paris, France, 2000.

Organization for European Cooperation and Development (OECD), "Asset Management System," Project Description, Paris, France 1999.

Pagano, Anthony M., McNeil, S., and Ogard, E. "Linking Asset Management to Strategic Planning Processes: Best Practices from State DOT's," *Transportation Research Record* No. 1924, 2005. pp. 184–191.

PB Consult, Incorporated, A Review of DOT Compliance with GASB 34 Requirements, NCHRP Report No. 522, Transportation Research Board, Washington, D.C., 2004. http://gulliver. trb.org/publications/nchrp/nchrp_rpt_522.pdf (accessed October 3, 2005).

Robert, W.E., Marshall, A.R., Shepard, R.W., & Aldayuz, J, Pontis Bridge Management System: State of the Practice in Implementation and Development, Transportation Research Board E-Circular, 9th International Bridge Management Conference, Orlando, Florida, 2003, *Transportation Research Board;* Washington D.C., pp. 49–60. http://gulliver.trb. org/publications/circulars/ec049.pdf (accessed October 13, 2005).

Schweppe, E., "Do Better Roads Mean More Jobs?" *Public Roads*, 2000, 65(6), pp. 19–22.

Sheldahl, Edward. "Along the Road; Innovative Contract Improves Maintenance in Washington D.C.," *Public Roads,* 2005**,** 68(6), p. 4.

Stidnger, Ruth W., March 2002. "Agencies and Contractors—Working Together" *Better Roads*, 2002, 72(3), pp 52-55. Available at http://www.betterroads.com.

Transportation Association of Canada (TAC), *Primer on Highway Asset Management Systems*, Transportation Association of Canada, Ottawa 1996.

U.S. Department of Transportation (US DOT), Federal Highway Administration (FHWA), Highway Performance Monitoring System Field Manual, OMB No. 21250028, Washington, D.C., December 2000.

U.S. Department of Transportation (US DOT), Federal Highway Administration, Highway Economic Requirements System—State Version, HERS-ST, http://www.fhwa.dot.gov/infrastructure/asstmgmt/hersindex.htm (accessed October 2, 2005).

U.S. Department of Transportation (US DOT), Federal Highway Administration (FHWA), *Asset Management, Advancing the State of the Art into the 21st Century through Public-Private Dialogue*, FHWA-RD-97-046, Washington D.C., September 1996.

U.S. Department of Transportation (US DOT), Federal Highway Administration (FHWA), *21ˢᵗ Century Asset Management, Executive Summary*, Prepared by the Center for Infrastructure and Transportation Studies at Rensselaer Polytechnic Institute, Troy, New York, October 1997.

U.S. Department of Transportation (US DOT), Federal Highway Administration (FHWA), Asset Management Primer, Washington, D.C., 1999.

U.S. Department of Transportation (US DOT), Federal Highway Administration, Life-Cycle Cost Analysis Primer, U.S. Department of Transportation, Washington, D.C., August 2002.

US DOT, Overview of Highway Performance Monitoring System (HPMS) for FHWA Field Offices, Federal Highway Administration, April 2003. http://www.fhwa.dot.gov/policy/ohpi/hpms/hpmsprimer.htm (accessed October 2, 2005).

Vermont Agency of Transportation (VTrans), "VTrans Asset management Vision and Work Plan," final report prepared by Cambridge Systematics, Inc. January 15, 2002.

Wikipadia, "Outsourcing," http://en.wikipedia.org/wiki/Outsourcing (accessed October 13, 2005).

Winsor, J., Adams, L., Ramasubramanian, L., and McNeil, S., "Transportation Asset Management Today: An Application of Community of Practice Collaboration in the Transportation Industry," *Transportation Research Record*, 1885, 2005, pp. 88–95.

Wittwer, E., Bittner, J., and Switzer, A., "The Fourth National Transportation Asset Management Workshop," *International Journal of Transport Management,* 2002, 1(2), pp. 87–99.

Wittwer, Ernie, Katie Zimmerman, Sue McNeil, Jason Bittner, and The Workshop Planning Committee, "Key Findings from the Fifth National Workshop on Transportation Asset Management," Midwest Regional University Transportation Center, July 2004. http://www.mrutc.org/outreach/FinalReport5thNTAM.pdf (accessed March 9, 2005).

25 Performance Measurement in Transportation Agencies: State of the Practice

Theodore H. Poister

Transportation agencies in the United States and elsewhere have dramatically transformed the way they do business over the past ten to fifteen years, and performance measurement is an essential ingredient in their quest for managing effectively to produce results. This general movement toward managing for results has been driven by (1) increased demands for accountability and improved performance from the public, elected officials, and the media, (2) strong leadership and the desire to strive for excellence within agencies, and (3) recognition that sea changes in the environment in which transportation agencies function require strategic thinking to plot new courses of action and then measure success in implementing them (Lockwood 1998, 2000).

The commitment to increased accountability and performance has led to a plethora of approaches to improved management and decision making, typically initiated first by a few leading edge agencies and than adopted by the mainstream, that have radically transformed, or have the potential to transform, the way these agencies operate on a day-to-day basis. These tools include strategic planning and management, performance-based transportation systems planning, stakeholder engagement processes, asset management, performance management, performance budgeting, process reengineering, and quality/productivity improvement processes. Transportation agencies have also widely adopted performance measurement systems, which are results oriented management tools in their own right but are also critically important for linking and aligning these other planning and management processes.

PERFORMANCE MEASUREMENT IN TRANSPORTATION

Local public transit agencies have been monitoring comprehensive sets of performance measures regarding operational efficiency, ridership, and revenue versus expense for more than two decades in an effort to management strategically in a competitive industry (Fielding 1987). State departments of transportation (DOTs) have been experimenting with, refining, expanding, and enhancing their performance measurement systems over that same period. While the DOTs have always been "data rich" agencies in some respects, though, early measurement systems were oriented internally, focusing principally on production and cost efficiency.

However, the field continued to evolve, and a TRB synthesis report published in 1997 found that the "new" generation of performance measures tracked by DOTs were significantly more outcome oriented, tied to strategic goals and objectives, and focused more on service quality and customer service (Poister 1997). Other articles published around the same time illustrated such developments in a number of states including New York (Albertin et al. 1995), Wisconsin (Etmanczyk 1995), Washington (Ziegler 1996), Delaware (Abbott et al. 1998), Virginia (Sorrell and Lewis 1998), and Texas (Doyle 1998).

Most of the managerially oriented work cited above focuses more on measuring organizational performance than on transportation systems performance. However, other transportation professionals have been working to incorporate performance measurement more centrally in transportation planning processes (Halvorson et al. 2000, Newman and Markow 2004). A few years ago a guidebook on performance-based planning was published to help agencies improve the development, implementation, and management of their transportation plans and programs by adding the element of performance measurement to existing planning processes in order to be able to evaluate alternative programs, projects, and services against overall transportation plan goals and objectives (Cambridge Systematics 2000).

Growing out of a workshop for state DOT chief executive officers on managing change, a recent report addresses the need for transportation agencies to tie performance measures to strategic planning processes (TransTech 2003). This report makes a distinction between externally and internally driven performance measures and summarizes the kinds of measures used by DOTs in such areas as mobility and congestion, safety, community quality of life, environment, economic development, system preservation and maintenance, project delivery, and human resources.

In the fall of 2000, a national conference focused on the use of performance measures to improve the performance of both transportation systems and transportation agencies (*Performance Measures to Improve Transportation Systems and Agency Operations* 2001). The general sense of the conference was that performance measurement was becoming a permanent way of doing business in transportation agencies and that a number of lessons had been learned concerning the development of measurement systems, data collection, effective utilization of performance data, and maintaining measurement programs over the long run. In a second national conference on performance measurement in transportation in 2004, it was apparent that although many issues remain, measurement systems are continuing to mature, with many agencies moving into second and third generation systems, and state DOTs are using performance data proactively in many ways to improve decision making and transportation system performance (*Performance Measures to Improve Transportation Systems* 2005).

This chapter tracks recent trends in the development and use of performance measures in transportation, assesses the current state-of-the practice, and points out further issues that must be addressed in order to use measurement systems most advantageously. Focusing primarily on state departments of transportation, it addresses the questions of what is measured, how performance is measured, how performance data are reported, and how performance measures are used. The chapter concludes with a summary of recent trends in the field and outlines continuing challenges that need to be addressed.

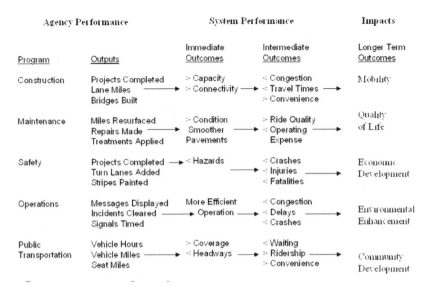

FIGURE 25.1 Transportation program logic.

WHAT IS BEING MEASURED?

Transportation agencies have become more holistic in the coverage of their measurement systems, focusing on the full range of performance as illustrated in the program logic model shown in Figure 25.1. The major focus areas are agency performance, system performance, and broader impacts. While agency performance concerns service delivery, projects completed, improvements made, and so forth, system performance focuses on the capacity and condition of transportation systems and their performance in terms of travel time, cost, convenience, and safety. Increasingly, transportation agencies are also concerned with the broader impacts of transportation initiatives regarding community quality of life, economic development, and the environment.

The kinds of performance measures monitored by transportation agencies span the entire model. Some focus on resources, primarily human and financial resources, while others measure outputs and agencies' operating efficiency in producing them. Effectiveness measures are tied to outcomes oriented objectives for improving transportation system performance and generating positive impacts. Quality measures relate both to service outputs as well as outcomes, and customer satisfaction measures similarly reflect satisfaction with outputs but even more so with transportation outcomes. Finally, cost-effectiveness measures and benefit–cost measures relate transportation outcomes and broader impacts to resources consumed and other costs.

BALANCED SCORECARD MODELS

Many transportation agencies have employed the balanced scorecard model (Kaplan and Norton 1996) to ensure both an internal and external perspective, and a process as

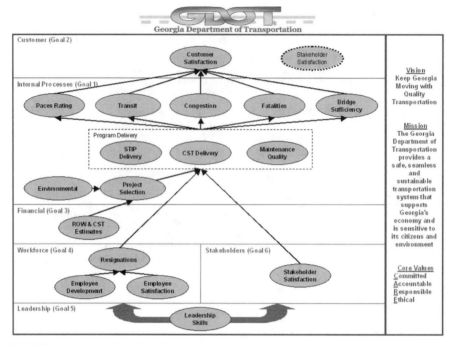

FIGURE 25.2 Georgia DOT FY2005 strategy map.

well as results orientation, in defining goals and performance measures. The City of Charlotte, North Carolina, Department of Transportation pioneered the use of this approach in the field of transportation, developing measures for each of the four original quadrants of performance including the customer, financial, internal business practices, and learning and growth perspectives. Other DOTs have customized the model. The Illinois DOT, for example, has identified customer satisfaction and partnerships, business practices, delivery of programs and services, and learning and growth as the focal points of its strategic objectives and performance measures. The Georgia DOT organizes its strategic goals and performance measures in the six domains related in its strategy map shown in Figure 25.2.

PROGRAM DELIVERY

Many states now are especially concerned with getting more effective control over program delivery and implementing their annual state transportation improvement programs (STIPs). This concerns the entire process from planning, preliminary engineering, design, and letting, through actual construction. This is an important core business of all state DOTs and consumes a substantial proportion of their financial resources and professional workforce on an ongoing basis. In this age of accountability, governors, legislatures, and transportation commissions have mounted substantial pressure on DOTs to deliver on the projects to which funds have been committed.

Thus, the top priority of many state DOTs around the country now focuses on delivering the projects that have been promised to their customers. The Virginia DOT (VDOT), for example, in the wake of serious financial mismanagement issues in a previous administration, "jumpstarted" its renewed strategic planning process in 2002 with the central objective of getting its program delivery process back on track. Thus, time and budget related measures focusing on project completion, as shown in Figure 25.3, predominate in all of VDOT's internally and externally focused performance reporting systems.

In addition, several states (Washington, Oregon, Georgia, Ohio, and New Mexico) have received quantum jumps in funding through additional revenue sources or expanded revenues from traditional sources and will now be responsible for delivering

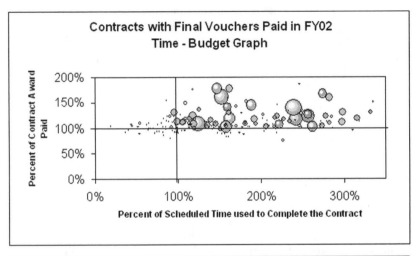

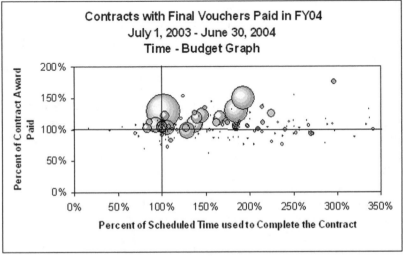

FIGURE 25.3 VDOT time-budget graphs: FY2002 and FY2004.

significantly larger programs. Given the pressure to make good on their commitments to the public, and in some cases the added challenge of moving significantly more projects through the process, most DOTs are increasingly concerned with tracking measures of program delivery, usually focusing on bringing in projects on time and within budgets. In taking a closer look at these measures, some DOTs have been particularly surprised to find that their performance in bringing projects to contract letting in the year programmed for letting is significantly lower than previously assumed. This has led to substantial efforts to streamline their processes, but it has also led to recognition that in some cases STIPs have been dramatically overprogrammed and that programs need to be "right sized" to afford more reasonable expectations of what they can actually accomplish.

Working to improve program delivery through a highly structured process improvement effort, PennDOT has ten working groups focusing on specific issues such as planning and preliminary engineering, funding and programming, environmental clearance, right-of-way acquisition, utilities, permitting, design and development, consulting agreements, contract management and construction, and bridge design and construction. The performance measures PennDOT is developing to track the efficiency of its program delivery focus on cycle times for completing overall projects as well as the individual elements of the process. However, at this point it is encountering difficulties in operationalizing some of these indicators because it needs better reporting mechanisms to provide the data input.

INCIDENT MANAGEMENT

Over the past several years, operating the highway system has been increasingly recognized as a central component of DOT's highway program responsibilities. In addition to utilities and work zone management, this includes coordination of signals and other traffic controls, pavement markings, use of HOV lanes, signage, and the use of Intelligent Transportation Systems (ITS) technology to provide motorists with current traffic information via on-site variable message signs, Web sites, and the media.

A major thrust in this emphasis on system operations concerns incident management, in particular coordinating effective responses to incidents that disrupt traffic on highways due to crashes, debris in the road or spills of hazardous materials, vehicle repairs, repair work zones and construction lane closures and so forth. As DOTs have discovered that effective management of such incidents can have major impact on both subsequent traffic congestion and secondary crashes, they have developed proactive programs to respond to them, particularly in large urbanized areas.

Thus, DOTs are now monitoring the occurrence of such incidents and tracking their performance in coping with them. For example, the Maryland State Highway Administration tracks such indicators as incident duration, initial response time, and overall recovery time in terms of service quality and initial outcomes. In annual evaluations of its Coordinated Highway Accident Response Team or CHART program, MDSHA also computes measures of the reduction in vehicle operating hours, total traffic delay time, fuel consumption, total emissions, and secondary accidents avoided due to its incident management efforts, as well as an overall benefit–cost ratio (Chang et al. 2003).

CUSTOMER SATISFACTION

Complementing the focus on service delivery and operations, transportation agencies increasingly have also been monitoring quality and effectiveness from the customer perspective (Stein and Sloane 2003). Public transit agencies have a long history of using customer surveys, not only to obtain information on trip origins and destinations, but also to solicit feedback on customers' perceptions of the reliability, safety, convenience, and overall quality of the services they provide.

State DOTs that conduct regular surveys of the public at large, motorists, or other stakeholder groups include those in Minnesota, New Mexico, Illinois, Kentucky, Pennsylvania, Ohio, and Georgia among others. The Pennsylvania DOT, for example, conducts an annual Highway Administration Customer Survey (HACS) mailed out to one thousand randomly selected licensed drivers in each of Pennsylvania's sixty-seven counties. This survey tracks changes in customer satisfaction with a number of specific performance attributes related to ride quality, traffic flow, and safety separately for interstate highways, numbered traffic routes, and secondary roads on the state system. In addition to statewide results, illustrated in Figure 25.4, HACS provides statistically reliable measures at the district and county maintenance unit levels.

The Florida DOT uses a mix of telephone surveys, mail surveys, and response cards to monitor feedback from six customer segments including resident travelers, visitor travelers, commercial travelers, special needs travelers, property owners, and elected government officials. These data indicate the percentages of these groups who are satisfied versus dissatisfied with Florida highways, transit services, and other modes as well as FDOT's communications and interaction with external stakeholders. They

	INTERSTATE HIGHWAYS (I)				TRAFFIC ROUTES (T)				SECONDARY ROADS (S)			
	Grade/ Mean	% of As & Bs	% of Ds & Fs	# of Resp.	Grade/ Mean	% of As & Bs	% of Ds & Fs	# of Resp.	Grade/ Mean	% of As & Bs	% of Ds & Fs	# of Resp.
1 - SAFETY (Safer)												
1. Prompt removal of snow and ice	B/3.04	79.5%	5.7%	7,602	B-/2.75	66.8%	10.8%	12,772	C/2.21	43.3%	25.0%	12,134
2. Effective removal of snow and ice	B/3.03	79.3%	5.3%	7,766	B-/2.77	67.6%	9.7%	12,946	C+/2.36	49.2%	20.0%	12,161
3a. Removal of debris	B-/2.61	60.0%	12.5%	7,649	C+/2.47	53.6%	15.1%	12,770	C/2.23	42.6%	22.2%	11,810
3b. Removal of dead deer	C/2.23	45.4%	25.2%	7,419	C/2	36.9%	32.3%	12,471	C/1.86	31.8%	37.1%	11,513
4. Sufficiently wide travel lanes	B/3	77.0%	5.4%	7,567	B-/2.64	60.6%	10.7%	12,795	C/2.07	34.6%	27.2%	11,870
5. Appropriate traffic signs	B/3.12	81.8%	2.9%	7,647	B/2.92	73.9%	5.1%	12,850	B-/2.7	62.9%	9.0%	12,145
6. Clearly readable traffic signs	B/3.17	83.5%	2.9%	7,891	B/2.99	76.3%	4.8%	12,883	B/2.79	66.5%	8.5%	12,127
7. Clearly visible traffic lines	B/2.84	69.5%	9.1%	7,765	C+/2.47	53.1%	17.0%	12,945	C/1.95	32.3%	33.7%	11,889
8. Clear sight lines	B/3.15	82.4%	4.0%	7,623	B-/2.68	62.4%	10.0%	12,756	C/2.15	38.3%	24.9%	11,820
9. Safe alignments	B/3.11	80.7%	3.6%	7,466	B-/2.6	58.5%	10.0%	12,576	C/2.01	31.4%	28.3%	11,846
10. Smooth transitions from road to shoulders	B/3.01	78.0%	4.7%	7,662	C+/2.47	53.7%	14.9%	12,822	C/1.86	29.3%	35.8%	11,728
11. Sufficient safety barriers and guiderails	B/3.12	81.5%	3.3%	7,764	B-/2.72	64.8%	8.9%	12,940	C/2.19	41.7%	23.9%	11,982
12. Safe on and off ramps and intersections	B/2.87	71.4%	9.1%	7,642	B-/2.85	61.4%	10.0%	12,705	C+/2.24	47.5%	14.3%	11,841
Overall Safety Grade	B/2.96	77.0%	3.9%	7,009	B-/2.82	60.5%	7.8%	11,544	C/2.16	36.9%	20.6%	10,776
2 - TRAFFIC FLOW (Swifter)												
21. Sufficient travel lanes to handle peak periods	C+/2.43	53.6%	19.4%	7,573	C/2.24	44.3%	23.3%	12,832	C+/2.31	46.0%	19.5%	12,557
22. Sufficient travel lanes to handle other times	B/2.89	71.3%	6.9%	7,679	B-/2.66	61.4%	10.1%	12,890	B-/2.62	59.1%	10.6%	12,757
23. Clearly identified travel lanes at work zones	B/2.98	75.5%	6.0%	7,823	B/2.81	68.3%	8.2%	13,007	B/2.69	62.4%	10.6%	12,808
24. Effective warning signs at work zones	B/3.17	82.9%	3.3%	7,683	B/3.01	76.7%	5.4%	13,115	B/2.83	68.7%	8.8%	12,900
25. Minimal travel delays at work zones	C+/2.34	48.4%	19.1%	7,824	C+/2.42	50.7%	15.8%	13,051	C+/2.43	50.8%	15.1%	12,876
Overall Traffic Flow Grade	B-/2.66	62.2%	9.6%	7,732	B-/2.55	56.3%	10.8%	12,517	B/2.53	54.9%	11.1%	12,432
3 - RIDE QUALITY (Smoother)												
31. Smooth road surfaces	C/2.25	43.7%	20.8%	7,872	C/2.04	33.8%	26.1%	13,030	C-/1.53	16.2%	47.5%	12,826
32. Durable pavements	C/2.02	35.7%	29.6%	7,804	C/1.87	27.9%	33.4%	13,014	C-/1.5	15.9%	48.9%	12,832
33. Sufficient shoulders	B-/2.75	67.1%	10.2%	7,851	C/2.2	42.6%	23.0%	13,036	C-/1.5	18.1%	50.2%	12,898
34. Road repairs when needed	C/2.14	40.0%	25.2%	7,869	C/1.9	29.4%	32.5%	13,007	D+/1.48	16.7%	50.2%	12,955
35. Timely completion of road repairs	C/2.2	42.9%	23.7%	7,849	C/2.24	43.9%	21.2%	13,055	C/2.06	36.5%	26.9%	12,873
36. Effective road repairs	C+/2.31	47.4%	19.0%	7,847	C/2.13	37.9%	23.8%	13,098	C/1.8	26.0%	35.0%	12,957
37. Attractive landscaping	C+/2.37	49.1%	19.4%	7,716	C/2.04	34.7%	28.1%	12,771	C-/1.69	22.8%	41.1%	12,465
Overall Ride Quality Grade	C+/2.29	45.0%	18.6%	7,018	C/2.08	34.4%	23.9%	11,619	C-/1.64	18.1%	42.0%	11,531
OVERALL GRADE FOR ROADWAYS	B/2.8	69.7%	7.4%	7,359	C+/2.46	52.2%	12.9%	12,550	C/1.97	30.3%	29.1%	11,921

 2005 HACS Results

 DiagnosticsPlus

FIGURE 25.4 PennDOTs highway administration customer survey results.

are reported as individual performance measures but are also aggregated into an overall index of customer satisfaction.

How Is Performance Measured?

Transportation agencies are increasingly careful about how they specify particular measures of performance, and this can be critically important in driving decisions and actions. In the area of highway safety, for example, trying to reduce fatalities as measured by the number of traffic fatalities per one million vehicle miles focuses attention on safety improvement projects, improved operations, and more effective enforcement activities—making the roads safer—while tracking the number of traffic fatalities per one hundred thousand resident population might prompt the same kinds of policies but also emphasizes the use of alternative modes, promote telecommuting, and, in the long run, changing land use patterns to reduce highway usage—basically a strategy of getting people off the roads. The National Highway & Traffic Safety Administration and some state DOTs track data on both these measures.

Highway System Safety and Condition

All state DOTs track measures of highway safety and measures of highway and bridge condition on a regular basis. The standard safety measures concern the number of crashes, injuries, and fatalities per million vehicle miles traveled on an aggregate basis, but some states also measure numbers of crashes occurring at high accident locations after safety improvement projects have been completed as compared with those same numbers before the projects were undertaken. Other outcome oriented safety measures include the number of crashes at at-grade railroad crossings, the number of pedestrian or bicycle injuries or fatalities on state highways, and the number of crashes at highway repair work zones.

   State DOTs monitor the condition of their highway systems in terms of ride quality, measured chiefly by the International Roughness Index (IRI), and pavement condition, as monitored in Georgia for instance with the Pavement Condition Evaluation System (PACES). The Ohio DOT, for example, measures system condition every year with pavement condition ratings based on visual inspections of 100 percent of its pavements. Similarly, the Pennsylvania DOT conducts annual windshield surveys of its roads to track pavement deficiencies, shoulder conditions, drainage problems, guiderails, signs, and other appurtenances. PennDOT also places heavy emphasis on ride quality data, running 100 percent of its interstate highways and 50 percent of its other NHS highways for IRI data every year. States also monitor the number of deficient or weight-limited bridges.

Traffic Flow and Congestion

Tracking good measures relating to traffic flow and congestion on state highways has been a more challenging enterprise. Traditional volume/capacity ratios have been the mainstay in this area, but they may be problematic in terms of knowing what the traffic handling capacity of particular segments of highway really is. The Ohio DOT runs computer models applied to highway capacity measures to compute volume/capacity ratios on the entire network over a twenty-four-hour period. From the results ODOT develops annual estimates of the percent lane miles congested, the percent VMT in areas exceeding congestion limits, and the percent peak hour VMT exceeding congestion limits.

The Annual Urban Mobility Report produced by the Texas Transportation Institute tracks traffic congestion in the largest seventy-five urban areas in the United States (Shrank and Lomax 2003). This method uses data from the Highway Performance Monitoring System, maintained by the Federal Highway Administration, with supporting data from state and local agencies. The resulting measures are computer modeled estimates based on roadway characteristics and traffic volume counts because high quality actual speed data are not available for many cities. The measures include:

- Travel Time Index—ratio of peak period travel time to free-flow travel time,
- Delay per Person—hours of extra travel time divided by number of residents,
- Cost of Congestion—value of extra time and fuel consumed due to congestion,
- Percent VMT congested—amount of traffic occurring on congested roads during peak periods,
- Percent congested lane miles—number of lane miles congested during peak periods,
- Percent Congested Time—percent of time travelers expected to encounter congestion.

Methodologies exists or are being developed to estimate the impact on reducing congestion of a range of solutions including additional highway construction, demand reduction, freeway entrance ramp metering, freeway incident management, traffic signal coordination, use of high occupancy lanes, and public transportation improvements.

Urban Congestion Measures

Mitretek reports travel time trends on a monthly basis for ten metropolitan areas where public or private sector organizations provide suitable point-to-point travel time data (Jung et al. 2004). This approach involves the automated acquisition of roadway travel times posted to traveler information Web sites, such as Georgia Navigator.com in Atlanta or Smartraveler.com in Miami, for five minute intervals for times of the day and days of the week when information is monitored. The measures reported out include:

- Travel Time Index—congested travel duration in ratio to free-flow duration for all congested trips (those over 130% of free-flow travel times);
- Buffer Index—average time a traveler would have to reserve during the day for a trip in order to be on-time 95 percent of the time;
- Average Duration of Congested Travel per Day—hours network is designated as congested, when 20 percent or more of all trips are congested (> 130% of free-flow);
- Percent Contested Travel—hours of congested travel as percent of fourteen hours.

The urban congestion measures reported by MitreTech sometimes differ substantially from the urban mobility measures reported by TTI because they are derived from travel time data rather than estimates based on traffic volume counts.

Washington

The Washington DOT uses archived loop detector data to track travel times between specific pairs of origins and destinations on twelve of the most heavily traveled corridors in the Puget Sound region. These real-time data are used to report current travel times in each of these corridors for each five minute interval throughout the day and are posted on a Web site (www.wsdot.wa.gov/pugetsoundtraffic/traveltimes) along with the average travel times for the same trips. WSDOT recognizes the limitations of loop technology for monitoring travel times and is beginning to experiment with other emerging technologies that may provide more accurate data and be more cost-effective than loop detectors. WSDOT has begun to use roadside speed cameras to estimate travel speeds, and the data is processed and reported the same way as the loop detector data. In addition, WSDOT is considering the possibility of using automatic vehicle locators (AVL) for this purpose at some point in the future. Many public transit systems use this GIS satellite-based technology at present, which is feasible because they are operating relatively few vehicles.

Travel time reliability is another important indicator of the quality of transportation. WSDOT also uses its travel time data to compute estimated 95 percent reliable travel times, within which trips in particular corridors can be completed 95 percent of the time. Interestingly, the Minnesota DOT (MnDOT) has measured perceived travel time reliability for numerous pairs of origins and destinations around the state from motorist survey data.

USE OF ALTERNATIVE MODES

Most DOTs track the volumes of passenger trips on their urban and rural public transit systems, and at least one, the Georgia DOT, measures the annual growth in transit ridership as compared with the growth in VMT on highways. Occasional surveys can provide measures of the percentage of work trips, or total trips, made by transit, bicycles, or walking, but this requires heavy sampling fractions. A desirable measure of comparable service quality might focus on average transit travel times in an urban area in ratio to average driving times for the same trips, but that is difficult to operationalize. Other indicators of the efficient utilization of urban area transportation systems focus on numbers of vehicles or individuals using transit park & ride lots, and the percent of vehicular traffic on highways that does not consist of single occupied vehicles.

ENVIRONMENTAL AND ECONOMIC IMPACT

The kinds of performance measures typically used on an aggregate basis to track the environmental impacts of transportation projects focus on outputs in environmental compliance such as the number of wetlands impacted and preserved or the number of sites mitigated. The Maryland DOT, for example, tracks the number of acres of wetlands created and reforestation planted as percent of acres required, and the number of storm water management enhancements completed compared to the number targeted. The Washington DOT uses the following measures of environmental compliance:

- Number of noncompliance events concerning fish habitats, wetlands, water quality, or other issues;
- Total acreage of replacement wetlands through creation, enhancement, buffers, or restoration;
- Number of replacement wetland projects meeting all standards, some standards, or no standards.

With respect to the economic development impact of transportation improvements, one of the most important performance measures may be the number of jobs that are created, or retained, in a state through initiatives in which transportation commitments or projects are a contributing factor. Generally speaking, while ongoing research, program and project evaluations, and case studies continue to illuminate our understanding of the real impacts of transportation facilities and services, quantitatively and qualitatively, on environmental quality and economic development (Meyer 2001), few practical measures exist at present in this area that can be incorporated into performance monitoring systems on a regular basis.

BENEFIT–COST RATIOS

Benefit–cost ratios have long been used by transportation agencies to evaluate and prioritize proposed projects and to prioritize projects competing for funding commitments. In addition, benefit–cost ratios have been used on a selective basis after the fact to measure the effectiveness of projects that have been completed. For example, the Illinois DOT routinely computes benefit–cost ratios for all safety improvement projects three years after completion. However, a few agencies are now starting to use them to monitor the overall economic efficiency of their programs on an annual basis. For example, in the state of Victoria, Australia, VicRoads tracks the aggregate benefit–cost ratios for all projects completed in a given year. In addition, ViCRoads monitors the "achievement index" of all projects, which compares post project benefit–cost ratios computed two years after project completion in ratio to benefit–cost ratios projected before project implementation.

USE OF INDEXES

As the number of measures incorporated in some monitoring systems proliferate to a point where minutiae tend to overwhelm a central overall focus, some agencies have developed indexes which combine multiple measures in order to summarize performance with fewer numbers. The Florida DOT, for example, focuses on eleven key performance measures to monitor progress in accomplishing its strategic objectives and executive board initiatives ranging from employee satisfaction and work program delivery to system performance and customer satisfaction. While a few of these measures are captured by single indicators, others are indexes in which a number of indicators are combined to provide an overall assessment of performance.

For instance, one of FDOT's key performance measures focuses on system condition, which is an index of maintenance ratings, bridge condition, and bridge replacement measures. In turn, the maintenance rating program includes eighty-four separate indicators of various specific aspects of highway condition. Where the data indicate some degree of slippage, executives can then drill down to find which components of system condition are the source of the problem. At the program management and operating levels, the individual measures are more meaningful because they are more directly actionable in terms of resource allocation, treatments, and managerial initiatives.

The Ohio DOT uses its Organizational Performance Index (OPI), created in 1997, to evaluate performance in various areas and combine dozens of performance measures into a single index of overall departmental performance. ODOT has decentralized decision making and operational responsibilities, and the OPI focuses on the performance of the department's twelve districts, and by extension the eighty-eight county level maintenance units, in the following eight functional or "topical" areas:

- Construction management,
- Contract administration,
- Equipment and facilities,
- Finance,
- Information Technology,
- Plan Delivery,
- Quality and Human Resources,
- System Condition.

These eight indexes are further combined into a single index of overall departmental performance on the same percentage format. All the individual measures and the eight indexes are monitored in monthly reports for each district. As illustrated in Figure 25.5, they are also combined into total index values for each district and ODOT as a whole. While the system has the capability of setting differential weights for the measures and sub-indexes, at present all of most of them are weighted evenly. The measures in each of the eight topic reports are "owned" by a deputy director or other senior managers in ODOT's four central office functional divisions, who review the monthly OPI reports and work with district engineers to take corrective actions in areas where performance might be slipping.

HOW ARE PERFORMANCE MEASURES USED?

State DOTs use performance measures for a number of purposes, and systems are being designed more intentionally to support particular uses. These uses range from

Index Summary

District	Total Index Value	Construction Management	Contract Administration	Equipment and Facilities	Finance	Information Technology	Plan Delivery	Quality and Human Resources	System Conditions
1	95.8333	83.3333	100.0	72.0238	100.0	98.8889	100.0	75.0	100.0
2	91.6667	79.1667	100.0	82.7381	100.0	100.0	50.0	87.5	95.0
3	97.9167	91.6667	100.0	85.119	100.0	100.0	80.0	93.75	91.6667
4	97.9167	91.6667	100.0	83.9286	100.0	100.0	95.0	68.75	100.0
5	100.0	91.6667	100.0	91.6667	100.0	100.0	95.0	93.75	100.0
6	100.0	83.3333	100.0	86.3095	100.0	88.8889	83.3333	93.75	93.3333
7	95.8333	91.6667	100.0	88.6905	100.0	100.0	65.0	87.5	100.0
8	100.0	91.6667	100.0	87.5	100.0	100.0	95.0	87.5	98.3333
9	89.5833	87.5	100.0	66.6667	100.0	100.0	50.0	75.0	100.0
10	95.8333	100.0	100.0	90.4762	100.0	100.0	90.0	56.25	93.3333
11	93.75	79.1667	100.0	95.8333	100.0	100.0	65.0	87.5	100.0
12	91.6667	79.1667	100.0	82.7381	100.0	100.0	70.0	81.25	93.3333
ODOT INDEX	93.2192	91.6667	100.0	90.4762	100.0	94.4444	83.3333	87.5	98.3333

Total Index Value Historical Trend — Statewide

FIGURE 25.5 ODOT organizational performance index: executive summary.

reporting performance to governor's offices, legislatures, oversight bodies, and funding agencies to communicating with the public at large as well as planning, budgeting, and performance management.

COMMUNICATING WITH THE PUBLIC AND OTHER EXTERNAL STAKEHOLDERS

The Virginia DOT publishes a quarterly report card for public consumption on its Web site and makes hard copies available to groups of external stakeholders. Consistent with VDOT's top priority, the report card focuses solely on project delivery, keying on the number of construction contracts actually completed versus scheduled for completion, the number of maintenance contracts completed versus scheduled, the percentage of construction projects completed that were within budget, and the percent of maintenance contracts completed within budget. In addition, a real innovation at VDOT is its Project Dashboard, also published on the web (http://dashboard.virginiadot.org). The Dashboard indicates the status of all VDOT engineering, construction, and maintenance projects, allowing the user to select projects by district, local government jurisdiction, road system, or route, in addition to tacking performance data on safety, finances, and environmental impacts, as shown in Figure 25.6.

WSDOT produces a quarterly report, called *Measures, Markers and Mileposts*, for the Washington State Transportation Commission and also makes it available to the public on its Web site at www.wsdot.wa.gov/accountability. Often referred to as the *Gray Notebook*, this report uses "performance journalism" to provide brief narrative explanations and illustrations along with a mix of tables, charts, and graphs conveying

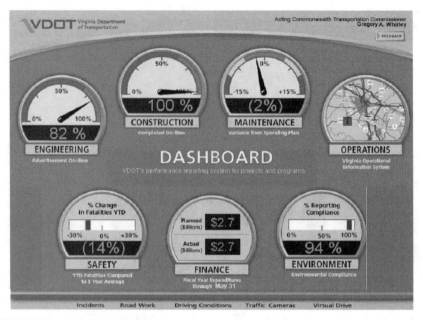

FIGURE 25.6   VDOT dashboard.

a wide range of performance data. In addition to a major section on project delivery, the *Gray Notebook* also serves to monitor performance in such areas as worker safety, employment levels and training, highway safety, asset management, highway maintenance, environmental programs, incident response, use of vanpools and park and ride lots, Washington state ferries, and state supported Amtrak service. This report simultaneously provides accountability and makes a WSDOT "case statement" to a variety of external stakeholders.

Transportation Planning

Performance measures are being used increasingly to establish the criteria for transportation systems plans, as well as for subsequent decisions about preserving existing assets and programming projects to advance those plans. The Ohio DOT (ODOT) recently completed work on its statewide multimodal transportation plan called *Access Ohio*. This project specific plan is keyed to a number of performance-based objectives for the next ten years, including the following:

- Reduce the frequency of crashes from current levels by 10 percent,
- Reduce the crash fatality rate from the current 1.31 fatalities per 100 million vehicle miles traveled to not exceed 1 fatality per 100 million vmt,
- Maintain an average level of service of D on the urban state freeway system and an average level of service B on the rural freeway system,
- Reduce the growth in vehicle hours of delay on the state's multi-lane divided highway system to 8 percent per year from the current 12 percent per year,

- Sustain Ohio's pavements so that at least 93 percent of all state maintained lane miles meet pavement condition rating standards.

Planners at ODOT ran separate sufficiency ratings for safety, condition, and congestion over the entire network to identify locations that fell below standards that had been established in each area for each functional class of highway. The projects contained in the plan were selected to remedy these deficiencies and meet other objectives established by *Access Ohio*. ODOT will monitor progress in moving toward these performance targets and will alter programming or adjust funding between programs and districts as necessary to achieve these objectives.

Mn/DOT updated it statewide transportation systems plan in August 2003 in an effort that completed its conversion to a performance-based planning process. This statewide plan is guided by Mn/DOT's three strategic objectives and ten strategic policies, which then led to identifying outcomes, performance measures, and twenty-year targets. One or more performance measurement sets have been identified for each of the ten strategic policies, with specific performance measures defined within each category, separately for each modal group as appropriate. While Mn/DOT's statewide transportation plan specifies transportation outcomes, measures, and targets, it does not quantify needs on a statewide basis. However, the eight districts are now in the process of developing district plans that will represent the first attempt to quantify needs in order to fulfill the performance based on a twenty-year plan.

STRATEGIC PLANNING AND MANAGEMENT

Many state DOTs have well-established strategic planning processes at this point, and performance measurement systems are a critical element as these agencies are focusing more attention on implementing their strategic agendas and accomplishing strategic goals and objectives (Poister 2004). VDOT's strategic planning process illustrates the central role of performance measures in this regard. Strategic goals are defined to address critical issues, and then performance measures are identified for tracking the intended results. Strategies are developed for achieving the goals, and the measures are monitored to evaluate success in implementing them.

In past years, the New Mexico DOT's *Compass* has been the prototypical example of a performance measurement system used proactively as a management tool. Initiated under a previous administration to help the organization stay focused on its "true north" values, the *Compass* incorporated sixteen customer-focused key results monitored through a total of eighty performance measures. Because it grew out of a quality improvement tradition, NMDOT executives looked for continuous improvement on these measures rather than setting annual targets for them. Through detailed quarterly reviews involving some fifty to seventy managers, the *Compass* became the driving force behind all management and decision making at NMDOT. In effect, for several years the *Compass* served as a de facto strategic agenda for the department, even though it had never conducted a formal strategic planning effort.

Recently, however, the new administration at NMDOT has developed a strategic plan for the department based on an assessment that, though useful as a performance management tool, the *Compass* lacked a big-picture strategic orientation, included too many measures, and was limited by its total reliance on available data. Thus, NMDOT's strategic plan for 2004–2005 includes strategic objectives and approximately forty high-level performance measures with ambitious targets, some of which have had to be operationalized with new data collection procedures. Plans are for the top management team to review these strategic performance measures on a monthly basis. While some of the *Compass* measures have been incorporated in the new strategic plan, the *Compass* itself is being aligned with the strategic agenda and redirected to the operating level where it will continue to be used as a principal performance management tool.

PERFORMANCE BUDGETING

As transportation agencies are more committed to results-based allocation of funds to programs and organizational units, performance data are used to project differential levels of outputs and/or outcomes associated with alternative funding levels. The performance measures provide the linkage between plans and budgets, sometimes between strategic plans and budgets, and in other cases, between strategic plans and business plans and then between business plans and budgets.

The Minnesota DOT's budget is organized along product and service lines using an activity-based budgeting structure. The department has established four product and service lines including multi-modal systems, state roads, local roads, and general support and services. Within each product and service line, Mn/DOT's budget is formatted in a hierarchy consisting of budget activities, products and services, core activities, and specific work activities. Parenthetically, with respect to the lowest level in this budget structure, Mn/DOT has established sets of approved activity codes, and each individual employee's time sheet records the time spent on each activity, allowing actual costs to be assigned to programmatic activities.

Mn/DOT's biennial budget allocates resources to these product and services, and each product and service is tracked in the budget with performance measures which are linked to the department's strategic plan, the twenty-year statewide transportation plan, supporting district and metropolitan area plans, modal plans, and the business plans prepared by the districts and functional divisions. The business plans are developed to advance Mn/DOT's strategic agenda and twenty-year transportation plan, and because funds are being allocated to products and services, core activities, and specific activities, Mn/DOT is building the capability to track the dollar investment in each of its strategic policies and evaluate the results by cumulating the corresponding sets of performance measures.

The New Mexico DOT began transitioning to a performance budgeting process in 2001 as required by New Mexico's Government Accountability Act. This entails budgeting funds to programs rather than organizational divisions and relating budgets to outputs and outcomes with performance measures. Thus, NMDOT has developed a program structure that overlays the organizational structure. The major program areas consist of construction, maintenance, program support, aviation, traffic safety, and public transportation, and each of these is divided into various programs.

For example, the overall maintenance program comprises three separate but related programs: preservation, scheduled maintenance, and routine maintenance. Responsibility for these programs crosses organizational lines. For instance, the engineering design division, the transportation planning division, the field operations division, and the road betterments division all share responsibility for the construction program, and the overall budget for the construction program therefore is allocated among these units, as shown in Figure 25.5. The performance measures related to this budget include project profilograph numbers for construction projects, the percent of final cost increase over bid amounts, the number of calendar days between the date of physical completion of a project and the date of final payment notification, and the number of combined system wide miles in deficient condition.

COMPARATIVE PERFORMANCE MEASURES

There are many examples of comparative performance measurement across transportation agencies in the United States, including the U.S. DOT's Conditions and Needs Report, the National Bridge Inventory, and the National Transit Database in addition to the urban mobility and urban congestion reports discussed above. In addition, many state DOTs in the United States benchmark performance data against DOTs in neighboring states or those with similar size systems or programs in order to see where they stand in the field and where they might get ideas for improving their own programs and operations.

One university-based research report annually compares the fifty states on a wide range of performance measures relating to their highway programs in terms of condition, congestion, safety, and expenditures (Hartgen 2004). The ongoing controversy surrounding the rankings produced by this report illustrates the complex issues involved in trying to secure uniform measures from different agencies as well as specifying and standardizing measures that afford "fair" and useful comparisons.

A project being conducted for the Transportation Research Board (NCHRP Project 20-24-37) is currently exploring possibilities for systematic comparative performance measurement within peer groupings of state DOTs, with voluntary participation, which might be configured differently for different focus areas. The use of "adjusted" performance measures, the percentage of miles of good pavement statistically adjusted for average number of freeze/thaw cycles or maintenance expenditures per lane mile, for example, might also help make comparative performance data more palatable and more meaningful to transportation agencies.

CONCLUSIONS

This review of performance measurement in transportation indicates that the state of the practice continues to advance. Obviously, there is wide variation among agencies with respect to the evolution of their performance measures, the kinds of measurement systems they have, and how and the extent to which they are using performance data in planning, management, and decision making. A few agencies have mature systems at this point, characterized by (1) a range of sophisticated measurement systems in place, (2) alignment of measures with performance oriented goals, objectives, standards, and targets, (3) useful performance reporting processes tailored for various audiences and management needs, and (4) systematic procedures for reviewing performance data and using the information to strengthen planning and decision making.

SUMMARY OF RECENT TRENDS

Some of the more notable currents over the past few years include the following:

- More states committed to using performance measures. Some are just starting out, but leading edge agencies are implementing second and third generation systems that are more sophisticated;
- Continuing trend emphasizing more strategic performance measures, more outcomes, and more customer oriented measures;
- Current emphasis on measures to track performance in program and project delivery, but also advances in implementing better measures of transportation system performance;
- Increased use of customer satisfaction measures;
- More holistic approaches in terms of coverage, relating different performance measurement systems, and tracking data at different levels ("rollup, drill down" systems);
- More disciplined efforts to align measures with goals and objectives and to use them as tools for integrating systems;
- More sophisticated software applications, system support, and data displays;
- Great proliferation of performance measures, but also recognition of the need to focus more selectively on the "vital few" strategic objectives;
- More intentional use of measurement systems to support other management, planning, and decision-making processes;
- Increased reporting of performance data directly to the public, especially in online report cards, to promote transparency in government.

CONTINUING CHALLENGES

Transportation agencies are investing increased resources in performance measurement and finding innovative ways of measuring the performance of transportation systems and programs. The real objective here has to be the development and implementation of measurement systems that are cost-effective tools whose contribution to improved planning and decision making is worth the effort. Some of the issues that still need to be addressed include the following:

- Improving measures concerning travel times, congestion, and delay, especially on non-instrumented roads;

- Developing measures that allow cross-modal comparisons regarding service levels, quality, travel times, and costs;
- Developing improved measures for freight transportation;
- Obtaining systematic feedback from other external stakeholders beyond motorists and the public at large (e.g., other user groups, local governments, legislators, the media);
- Interpreting the implications of customer satisfaction measures in relationship to engineering and professional planning performance criteria;
- Using objectives and performance measures relating to system performance to articulate the relationship between strategic plans and transportation system plans more clearly;
- Implementing workable comparative performance measurement systems that provide information that is useful for benchmarking and process improvement.

REFERENCES

Abbott, E.E., J. Cantalupo, and L.B. Dixon. (1998). "Performance Measures: Linking Outputs and Outcomes to Achieve Goals," *Transportation Research Record 1617*. Washington, D.C.: Transportation Research Board, National Research Council, pp. 90–95.

Albertin, R.J.; Romeo, LJ; Weiskopf, L.; Prochera, J. and J. Rowen. (1995). "Facilitating Transportatin Agency Management Through Performance Measurement: The NYSDOT Experience with the 'Management Performance Indicators Report'." *Transportation Research Record 1498*, Washington, D.C.: Transportation Research Board, National Research Council, pp. 44–50.

Cambridge Systematics. (2000). *A Guidebook for Performance Based Transportation Planning*. NCHRP Report 446. Washington, D.C.: Transportation Research Board, National Research Council.

Chang, G. et al. (2003). *Performance Evaluation of CHART: The Real-Time Incident Management System*. Baltimore: Maryland State Highway System, Office of Traffic and Safety.

Doyle, D. (1998). "Performance Measure Initiative at the Texas Department of Transportation," *Transportation Research Record 1649*. Washington, D.C.: Transportation Research Board, National Research Council, pp. 124–128.

Etmanczyk, J.S. (1995). "Wisconsin DOT Measures Quality from Top to Bottom: *Journal of Management in Engineering*, Vol. 11, no. 4, July/Aug., pp. 19–23.

Fielding, G.J. (1987). "Measuring and Monitoring Transit Performance," Chapter 4 in *Managing Public Transit Strategically*. San Francisco: Jossey-Bass.

Hartgen, D.T. (2004). *The Looming Highway Condition Crisis: Performance of State Highway Systems, 1984–2002*. Charlotte: University of North Carolina at Charlotte.

Halvorson, R., T. Hatata, M.L. Tischer, and P. Kolakowski. (2000). "Performance-Based Planning, Asset Management, and Management Systems," Chapter 5 in *Transportation Research E-Circular Number E-C015: Statewide Transportation Planning*. http://gulliver.trb.org/publications/circulars/ec015/contents.pdf.

Jung, S. et al. (2004). *Urban Congestion Reporting (URC)*. Falls Church, VA: Mitretek.

Kaplan, R.S. and D.P. Norton. (1996). *The Balanced Scorecard: Translating Strategy into Action*. Cambridge, MA: Harvard Business School Press.

Lockwood, S. (1998). *The Changing State DOT*. Washington, D.C.: American Association of State Highway and Transportation Officials.

Lockwood, S. (2000). *Factors Affecting the Future of State DOTs as Institutions.* Washington, D.C.: Transportation Research Board.

Mallory, Bradley L. (2002). *Managing the Strategic Plan with Measures.* Presented to the Transportation Research Board Annual Meeting, Washington, D.C., January.

Meyer, M. (2001). "Measuring That Which Cannot Be Measured — At Least According to Conventional Wisdom," in *Performance Measures to Improve Transportation Systems and Agencies,* Washington, D.C.: National Academy Press.

Newman, L.A. and M.J. Markow. (2004). "Performance-Based Planning and Asset Management," *Journal of Public Works Management & Policy,* Vol. 8, no. 3, pp. 156–161.

Performance Measures to Improve Transportation Systems and Agency Operations: Report of a Conference. (2001). Washington, D.C.: National Academy Press.

Performance Measures to Improve Transportation Systems. (2005). Washington, D.C.: Transportation Research Board.

Poister, T.H. (1997). *NCHRP Synthesis of Highway Practice 238: Performance Measurement in State Departments of Transportation.* Washington, D.C.: Transportation Research Board, National Research Council.

Poister, T.H. (2004). *NCHRP Synthesis of Highway Practice326: Strategic Planning and Decision Making in State Departments of Transportation.* Washington, D.C.: Transportation Research Board, National Research Council.

Poister, T.H., Van Slyke, D. (2002). Strategic Management Innovations in State Transportation Departments. *Public Performance & Management Review,* Vol. 26, no. 1, pp. 58–74.

Schrank, D. and T. Lomax. (2003). *The 2003 Annual Urban Mobility Report.* College Station: Texas Transportation Institute.

Sorrell, C.S. and J.F. Lewis. (1998). "VDOT Is Moving in a New Direction" How Virginia's Department of Transportation is Using Strategic Management to Revamp its Entire Operation," *Transportation Research Record 1649.* Washington, D.C.: Transportation Research Board, National Research Council, pp. 115–123.

Stein, K.E. and R.K. Sloane. (2003). *Using Customer Needs to Drive Transportation Decisions.* NCHRP Report 487. Transportation Research Board, National Research Council.

Transtech Management, Inc. (2003). *Strategic Performance Measures for State Departments of Transportation: A Handbook for CEOs and Executives.* Washington, D.C.: American Association of State Highway and Transportation Officials.

Ziegler, B.J. (1996). *Transportation Research Circular 465: Transportation Planning and Performance Measurement in Washington State.* Washington, D.C.: Transportation Research Board, National Research Council, pp. 14–16.

26 Public–Private Partnerships in Urban Rail Transit: Recent International Experience

Sock-Yong Phang

INTRODUCTION

The wave of privatization that has swept the infrastructure, utilities, and transportation sectors in the past three decades appears to have found fewer converts in the urban rail transit sectors of the developed world. While there has been greater success with regard to the privatization of commuter rail, intercity rail services as well as the deregulation of urban bus transit, private sector involvement in urban rail transit remains more of a rarity in the developed world.

That urban rail transit has historically been a sector that cannot be run profitably, whether publicly or privately owned, is often cited as one of the obstacles to successful private sector involvement (Due 2003; Gomez-Ibanez 1993). The difficulties arise from a number of sources: (1) expensive construction, operating and maintenance costs, (2) the inadequacy of fare revenue resulting in the need for direct and/or indirect public subsidies such as land development rights, and (3) the complexities of forming and sustaining coalitions and partnerships necessary in rail transit privatization. The average fare box recovery ratio was 27 percent for United States metros and 25 percent for United States light rail transit systems (1997 data from Babalik-Sutcliffe 2002).

According to Due (2003), "government-owned urban transit systems remain largely intact in the U.S., even more so in continental Europe, and less so in the developing world." A recent study to identify the factors behind the success of new urban rail systems was based on eight government-owned and operated systems: four in the United States, three in the United Kingdom, and one in Canada (Babalik-Sutcliffe 2002). The issue of private sector involvement was not considered at all. Often cited as a reason for urban rail's failure to attract private capital is that the venture is perceived as risky in light of the diffusion of benefits and difficulties in recapturing value.

Outside of the United States, however, there has been a wave of urban rail projects involving the private sector in the last fifteen years. Cities that have competitively contracted out services for its urban rail lines include cities of Buenos Aires and Rio de Janeiro. London Underground in 2002 began a process of transferring rail infrastructure (track, signaling, bridges, tunnels, lifts, escalators, stations, and trains) to three private infrastructure companies, in order to secure long-term sustained funding for the tube through public–private partnership. Train and station services, however, remain in the public sector.

The record for East Asia has also not been as dismal as that of the United States. Japanese railway conglomerates have led the way for rail and land use development for most of the last century. While this was also true for the United States a century ago, the co-investment in railways and new town development is still commonly practiced in Japan. Many other East Asian cities, with incomes and land use density levels that are more favorable to higher levels of transit ridership, have looked to Tokyo as a model for rail and land development. Large cities in Europe, North America, and Japan built their rail transit systems before World War II when cars were not as common as today. Most Asian cities, however, could not afford to build urban railways in prewar days and with the growth in motorization after the war, it was not easy for them to build urban rail systems. However, rising incomes and car ownership rates, with the attendant urban congestion and pollution problems, have resulted in the need to seriously consider urban rail as a solution. The governments of Bangkok, Jakarta, Kuala Lumpur, and Manila have utilized urban rail concessions to build new rail transit systems, while previously state-owned operators in Hong Kong and Singapore have become publicly listed companies.

Grimsey and Lewis (2004) make the following distinction between privatization and Public–Private Partnerships (PPP):

> within a PPP the public sector acquires and pays for services from the private sector on behalf of the community and retains ultimate responsibility for the delivery of the services, albeit that they are being provided by the private sector over an extended period of time (i.e., twenty-five years or longer). By contrast, when a government entity is privatized the private firm that takes over the business also assumes the responsibility for service delivery…A PPP is a formal business arrangement between the public and private sectors.… regulation through contract and the lack of government disengagement define much that is distinctive about a PPP.

Based on the above distinction, most recent efforts at involving the private sector in the provision of public transport services come under the category of PPP. As recent international experience has demonstrated, different strategies have been used to involve the private sector in the urban rail transit business. This chapter provides a review of four alternative PPP strategies adopted by various governments in the past fifteen years. The four strategies reviewed here are:

1. The development of new systems through super turnkey procurements
2. The concessioning of rail and subway services
3. The sale of state-owned operators through share issue privatization
4. PPP for infrastructure maintenance and upgrading

DEVELOPMENT OF NEW TRANSIT LINES THROUGH SUPER TURNKEY PROCUREMENTS

The involvement of the private sector in the implementation of new urban rail projects can take many forms. In what has become known as the "traditional design-bid-build" strategy, the transit authority's engineering team is responsible for the detailed designs and solicits bids and awards contracts to the private sector to build the system. Under a design-build procurement strategy, the authority solicits bids at typically 30 percent of design with detailed designs prepared by the successful contractor (Zweighaft 2001). Variations of the design-build strategy include turnkey, design-build-operate-maintain (DBOM), and super turnkey. In a turnkey procurement, a single contractor takes entire responsibility for the project allowing for the owner to simply "turn the key" to begin operations. In DBOM, the contractor has operational maintenance responsibilities upon project completion.

In design-build-finance-operate (DBFO)[1] or super turnkey[2] projects, the contractor also brings its own financing for the construction program. These contracts are usually long term (twenty-five to thirty years being common), have detailed provisions on payment, service standards and performance measures, provide an objective means to vary payment depending on performance, and with the concessionaire usually having to assume substantial risk.

While design-build allows transportation agencies to gain access to technologies beyond their current organizational capabilities thus saving time and money, DBOM can help assure the development of a system that could be economically maintained and operated. Super turnkey can turn initially financially nonviable projects into viable ones by bringing private investors into the transit industry as partners. Many of the risks and much of the project management responsibility are also transferred from the authority to the private contractor.

In a survey of the organization models for fifteen recent major transit projects in the United States, Zweighaft (2001) cites two instances of DBOM (the JFK Airport Access Project rail system and Puerto Rico's Tren Urbano), and one instance of super turnkey, the Hudson-Bergen LRT project (see Middleton 1997 for details). Most of the remaining projects fell under the traditional design-bid-build categories. Private financing for new rail transit projects is thus rarely used in the United States. Gomez-Ibanez (1993) cites two examples: monorails in Disney amusement parks, and a short rail line for internal circulation in a major office and retail center at Las Colinas near Dallas, Texas. However, super turnkey has been extensively used in infrastructure projects in other countries, particularly the United Kingdom, France, Thailand, Malaysia, Hong Kong, Indonesia, and the Philippines (Gomez-Ibanez 1993; Halcrow 2004).

London remains an important testing ground for a range of private sector involvement in urban rail development. The extension of the Docklands Light Railway into the city's financial center was part funded by the major private developer in

---

1. DBFO is a term coined by the United Kingdom Highways Agency to describe their concession-based road schemes under the Private Finance Initiative (Grimsey and Lewis 2004).
2. The Unted States Federal Transit Authority refers to DBFO projects as super turnkey projects.

Docklands. In the 1990s, a decision was taken to extend it across the river Thames to Lewisham, and to turn the operation of the entire system over to a private concession. This involved awarding the design and build concession for the 4 km (£200m)[3] cross river concession and a seven-year operating concession in 1997 to the SERCO group (which was subsequently extended to run until 2006). London's Croydon Tramlink, a new suburban light rail system which opened in 2000, was procured through a de-sign-bid-built-operate-maintain strategy where the bids were assessed on the lowest capital subsidy required to construct the system, on the basis of no on-going revenue support and operation within the London Transport integrated fares and service regime (Halcrow 2004). London Transport funded £125 million of the £200 million capital costs. However, as revenues were lower than expected by the concessionaire, financing arrangements have had to be restructured.

In this section, we review the experiences of Kuala Lumpur, Bangkok, and Manila all of which have acquired new rail systems in the past decade. In all three cases, private investors proposed significant funding for new rail transit systems. These cases offer a variety of insights into the possibilities and problems of super-turnkey procurement in urban rail transit.

KUALA LUMPUR

Kuala Lumpur (KL), the capital of Malaysia, has an area of 243 square kilometers with a population of 1.4 million and employment of 838,000. Up until the late 1980s, public transport was mainly performed by buses. In the early 1990s, proposals for urban rail transit took root and developed rapidly, with the government first approving the BOT proposal from the foreign Taylor/Woodrow/AEG consortium to build the STAR LRT. After KL was awarded the 1998 Commonwealth Games in 1994, the government ex-tended the route length of STAR and approved the PUTRA LRT (Halcrow 2004).

The STAR system started as the first urban rail BOT project in Malaysia with a sixty-year lease in November 1991. The 1998 Commonwealth Games precipitated the government to request a southern extension of the line to serve the games stadium. As a compensation for the low density extension, STAR was given a three kilometer northern extension into a high-density residential area. Operations began in December of 1996 for Phase I (12 kilometers) with completion of the line in 1998 with a total route length of twenty-seven kilometers.

PUTRA was incorporated in 1994 with a sixty-year concession to design, con-struct, and operate a twenty-nine kilometer LRT. PUTRA was wholly owned by Renong Berhad—a major Malaysian conglomerate that was asked to start work before signing a concession to meet the Commonwealth Games deadline. The fully automated driver-less system began operations in September 1998.

After a few years of operation at less than one third of forecast demand, and under difficult conditions brought on by the Asian economic crisis, both STAR and PUTRA faced serious financial difficulties in servicing their debts and were subsequently bailed out in 2002 by the government. Phase I of the takeover involved the government

---

3. £1 is approximately US$1.87 (as of October 9, 2006).

converting overdue loans into bonds in the nation's largest corporate restructuring through a government-owned company Syarikat Prasarana Negara Berhad (SPNB) established to manage "critical public infrastructure" in the Klang Valley. In 2001, the SPNB purchased all the rights to the outstanding debts of STAR and PUTRA via the issue of RM 5.5 billion[4] of fixed rate guaranteed bonds to the two companies' creditors. In 2002, the government effectively took over the assets and operations of the two LRT systems following their inability to meet their debt obligations after being served winding-up petitions.

The takeover of the LRT systems was considered by many to be a failure of the privatization program (Wong et al. 2005) and was justified by the government as necessary and unavoidable as public interest was involved, and affordable public transport services were considered ultimately to be the responsibility of the government. As PUTRA was also a subsidiary of Renong, the biggest conglomerate with the largest debt in the country (over RM25 billion), a government takeover also helped reduce its debt as well as the amount of non performing loans in the banking system. Critics however viewed sums involved to save STAR and PUTRA as excessive, with actual construction costs believed to be much less. Moreover, SPNB subsequently leased back the LRT operations to the management of PUTRA and STAR at discounts after nationalization and Wong et al. (2005) has described the saga as "tantamount to socializing losses and liabilities while allowing profits and profitable assets to be privatized."

Other than the two LRT systems, the KL is also served by the state-owned KTM commuter rail, an express rail link to the KL International Airport (constructed under a thirty-year concession with services starting in 2002), and a 8.6 km Monorail, a BOT project which serves the central area and helps to connect the various rail lines serving KL. The monorail concession contract was signed in 2000 and the project company KL Investment Group Berhad was listed on the KL Stock Exchange in 2003 when operations began.

BANGKOK

As the capital city of Thailand, the population of Bangkok is in excess of ten10 million with notorious peak hour traffic speeds at 10 kilometers per hour throughout much of the metropolitan area. There were a number of failed attempts at attracting investors to build a much needed transit system in the 1980s (Perez 2004). Half a dozen megatransport infrastructure projects, all involving the private sector, were finally initiated in the late 1980s and 1990s, and comprised expressways and three transit lines: Blue, Red, and Green. A new agency, the Metropolitan Rapid Transit Authority (MRTA), was established to coordinate the rail projects.

In 1990, the Hong Kong based Hopewell Holdings signed a concession agreement with the State Railway of Thailand for the sixty kilometers US$3.2 billion Red Line cum expressway system. In 1993, the Blue Line concession was awarded to a group led by Bangkok Land, a large Thai real estate company. Both the Red and Blue Lines were designed as above ground elevated transit systems. In 1994, however, the

---

4. RM 1 is approximately US$0.271 (as of October 9, 2006).

government made a decision to require the MRT lines to be built underground within a twenty-five square kilometer. zone in central Bangkok. The decision was to cause Bangkok Land to withdraw from the Blue Line project, which subsequently became an MRTA project. Construction began in 1997 on the fully underground system. A concession to equip and operate the Blue Line was put out to bid in 1999 and the line opened for service in 2004.

The Red Line was exempted from the requirement to go underground as it was already under construction. However, Hopewell stopped construction in August 1997 in the midst of the Asian economic crisis. The concession was then unilaterally terminated by the government in December 1997, with further development delayed by Hopewell's claims for reimbursement for the US$600 million it had spent on the project (Gomez-Ibanez 2000).

The fifteen kilometers Green Line or Skytrain was conceived to serve downtown Bangkok and its alignment included two routes that cross in downtown Siam Square. The line was to be financed from fare revenues with the Bangkok Metropolitan Authority providing all the right-of-way for free by allowing the line to be built over important arterial streets. When the thirty-year concession was put out to bid in 1991, Tanayong Corporation, a Thai real estate company, was selected from three short-listed bidders partly because it had offered the lowest fare to users—12 baht.[5] With a price tag of over US$1.5 billion, all of which was to be privately financed, the project attracted much international attention.[6] Tanayong subsequently created a separate company, the Bangkok Transit System Company (BTS), to build and own the concession. The concession contract provided for fare increases every eighteen months thereafter with the increase in consumer price index, with provisions for increases also in the event of exceptional circumstances including major changes in foreign exchange rates.

Project implementation was far from smooth: there were lengthy disputes over the site of the train depot, going underground or remaining elevated, as well as location of support pillars. Financiers for the projects, other than Tanayong and a large Thai construction company (Italian-Thai), also grew to include Siemens, the German government's international development bank, a syndicate of Thai banks, as well as the International Finance Corporation, the World Bank's private sector lending arm. The Asian financial crisis and the devaluation of the Thai baht hit the BTS hard as many foreign loans, construction, and equipment costs were in foreign currency, while Tanayong's revenues were primarily in baht. A controversy over fares that BTS could charge had to be brought before the seven-person arbitration panel. And all these were before Skytrain opened for service in December 1999 (at fares ranging from 10 to 40 baht), some three years later than stipulated in the 1992 concession contract (Gomez-Ibanez 2000).

Since opening, ridership has been below the forecasted 570,000 level: year one ridership was just one-quarter of the forecast; the system, at present, carries an average of 350,000 passengers/day (Halcrow 2004). While fare box revenue has been sufficient to cover operating costs, the ability of BTS to service its substantial debt remains a

---

5. This was increased to 15 baht in 1992 after negotiations began. One Thai baht is approximately US$0.0267 (as of October 9, 2006).

6. Perez (2004) contains a seventy-three-page case study of the BTS project.

source of great concern. BTS today continues to face the challenges of increasing ridership, restructuring its debt, and the threat of nationalization.

MANILA

Manila, another mega-city with a population of approximately eleven million, built a MRT line through a build-lease-transfer concession in the 1990s. Under the concession contract signed in 1993, the concessionaire (MRTC) finances, constructs, and maintains the project for twenty-five years and implements commercial developments for fifty years. In return, it receives a fixed revenue stream and annual rental payments for property. The government takes foreign exchange and revenue risks and provides sovereign guarantee for all debt. MRTC takes construction and maintenance risks in return for a guaranteed 15 percent return on equity on the basis of lease payments for the railway, with property upside. Operations are run by the government, which bears the commercial risk and shares in the property upside. The MRTC opened for service in phases beginning in 1999 and carries an average 375,000 passengers per day (Halcrow 2004).

CONCESSIONING RAIL AND SUBWAY SERVICES

Since the 1980s, competitive tendering for bus services has been implemented in numerous cities where services were formerly operated by the state. Competitive tendering slowly spread to urban rail in the 1990s, starting with Argentina and Brazil (to be discussed in greater detail in this section). Concessioning of rail lines often depend on the fact that public sector investments in rail lines have been largely written off by the government with no need to be recovered by new private owners/operators. Stockholm Transport has awarded five-to-ten year contracts for operating its three metro rail lines, its light rail system, the suburban railway service, and commuter rail services. It normally leases vehicles to contractors and owns the tracks and facilities. In some instances, station staffing is also contracted out. In 1999, Singapore's Land Transport Authority awarded a concession to run the brand new twenty kilometer Northeast Line and two adjoining LRT systems in a close tender exercise involving the two major local bus operators, conspicuously keeping the incumbent rail operator out. The line commenced operations in 2003 and is operated by publicly listed SBS Transit.

BUENOS AIRES

In the mid-1990s, as part of an overall privatization program, Argentina launched an ambitious plan to privatize its entire transport sector. Gomez-Ibanez, in 1997, described Argentina as "the only country outside Japan that had private urban commuter railways and the only country in the world that had granted a private concession to operate its subway." This certainly reflects how privatization of urban rail has spread in the past decade.

The Argentine concession model, used in the concession of the Buenos Aires urban rail systems, required interested private sector parties to submit bids to execute an investment plan defined and funded by the state and to be implemented by the concessionaire. The urban commuter railroad services are centered around Buenos Aires and include a network of 899 kilometers, 267 stations, and 1,800 trains carrying over one million passengers daily. These services, which were previously operated by the state-owned railway company, were divided into seven separate lines and offered as twenty year concessions to the private sector. The municipally-owned subway system (36.5 kilometers and one LRT of 7.4 kilometers) was included in one of the commuter concessions.

The bids required the submission of a schedule of declining operating subsidies to be paid by the state and of fees to be paid by the concessionaire to the state for the concession rights (Robelo, 1999b), given stipulated level of service provisions and tariff set by the government. The schedule of subsidies must decline to zero by a certain date, after which the concessionaire starts paying the government an annual concession fee. The winner of the concession would be the bidder with the lowest net present value for the cost of the investment plan plus the subsidy to be paid by the government minus the concession fee to be paid by the concessionaire.

The concessions attracted a large number of bids and winners were selected in January 1993; by May 1995, all seven lines had been transferred to the concession winners. The operation of Subte, Buenos Aires' subway system was taken over by Metro Vias on January 1, 1994 with a commitment to US$394.8 million in improvements to the antiquated system by 2012. Metro Vias' performance according to Perez (2004), has "won plaudits from observers around the world, encouraging the Argentines to pursue additional rail transit projects in the capital and British transport officials to consider the privatization of London Underground." Overall, Gomez-Ibanez (1997) cited three concerns over the concession program: delays between award and transfer leading to service deterioration, ambiguities in the concession contracts that required renegotiation of bids, and concessionaires' worries over unexpectedly high ridership since the awards were based on smallest subsidy to complete the required investment program.

RIO DE JANEIRO

The Rio de Janeiro metropolitan area comprises 546,865 hectares and has a population of ten million. The mostly private bus system is the backbone of the public transport system, with only 4 percent of the 8.7 million public transport trips daily made by suburban train (Flumitrens, 264 kilometer network) and 3 percent by subway (Metro, twenty-three kilometers long). While bus services were provided by private operators without direct subsidies, in 1995–1996, Flumitrens received US$180 million in subsidies and the Metro US$109 million (Robelo 1999a). To help address a budget crisis in the mid 1990s, the government implemented reforms to sell or concession loss making state-owned enterprises to the private sector. As part of the reform program, the Metro was concession in December 1997 and Flumitrens in July 1998.

The Rio concessions differed from the Buenos Aires concessions in that the concessionaires were not required to fund the investment plans given that the state had already secured loans from Brazil's National Development Bank for the Metro and was in the process of negotiating with the World Bank in the case of Flumitrens. Although initial financial projections suggested that the Metro would require an operating subsidy for one or two years and the Flumitrens over the first four years, the state decided against a negative concession (subsidy) for a number of reasons. The concessionaires would have no major investment funding obligations; ongoing extensions continue to be state financed and rolling stock already ordered would be taken over by the concessionaire; tariffs were increased to account for inflation and the concessionaire was expected to move more boldly to rationalized staff than the projections have assumed. Moreover, federal law apparently did not allow "negative concessions"; the government was also facing criticism from the opposition party that it was giving away state property as well (Robelo 1999b). In the case of the Flumitrens concession, the government got round the problem by specifying that the concession fees paid by the Metro concessionaire would be used to subsidize the Flumitrens concession.

The state government commissioned two major studies each for the Metro and Flumitrens to help with the design of the concession and the bidding process (see Robelo, 1999a for details). Table 26.1 summarizes the main features of the Rio de Janeiro urban rail concession contracts. The Metro concession attracted a large number of bidders, with sizeable number of foreign bidders participating. The prequalification and bidding processes were handled in a transparent manner by a special commission of the Rio de Janeiro stock exchange. The winning bid was submitted by a consortium led by an Argentine company and a local investment bank, with the bid about ten times the minimum price set in the bidding documents.

In the case of Flumitrens, the prequalification process attracted only one consortium. The state, suspecting a cartel, delayed the bidding and revised the documents to make the concession more attractive and to provide time for other bidders to enter (Robelo 1999b). The Metro operator was also prevented from bidding in the Flumitrens concession. Five bids were received with the winning bid submitted by a Spanish-Brazilian consortium at six times the minimum price set. The concessionaire however was required to make out-of-pocket payment equivalent to the minimum price and the materials in the inventory. The rest of the payment would be in terms of rehabilitating the train fleet and civil works to be completed, through discounted loans made available by the state. The concessionaire would benefit if it is able to deliver the specified outputs at less than the cost quoted.

SALE OF STATE-OWNED OPERATORS THROUGH SHARE ISSUE PRIVATIZATION

Share issue privatization (SIP) is a method of privatization in which some or all of a government's stake in a state-owned enterprise (SOE) is sold to investors through a public share offering. Jones et al. (1999) analyzed a large sample of 630 SIPs from fifty-nine countries over the period 1977 to 1997. The large sample indicates that

TABLE 26.1
Rio de Janeiro Metropolitan Region Urban Rail Concessions

	Metro Concession (1997)	Flumitrens Concession (1998)
Package size	41 km right-of-way extension.	200 km right-of-way extension.
Term	20 years, renewable once for 20 more years.	25 years, renewable once for 25 more years.
Ownership of equipment and tracks	Rio de Janeiro state government.	As for the Metro.
Service quality specifications	Based on performance targets for frequency, reliability, safety, and comfort established in the concession contract.	As for the Metro.
Payments by the government	None.	None. But proceeds of the Metro concession fee will be made available to the concessionaire for investments.
Award criterion	Net present value of best offer above the minimum price (US$25 million) plus materials in stock (US$3.56 million).	Net present value of best offer above the minimum price (US$28 million) plus materials in stock (US$8.25 million), plus the discount on capital made available by the state, plus the cost of optional investments assumed by the bidder.
Tariff renegotiation conditions	The flat tariff for a one-way trip was set by the state in the bidding documents and can be updated only for inflation, according to a formula. For expansion and new investments under the present contract, the concession must submit a plan for approval by the state government.	As for the Metro. The concessionaire will be allowed to increase the tariff by 50 percent if it installs air conditioning in the trains.
Performance assurance	Concession contract monitoring by the Public Services Regulatory Agency of Rio de Janeiro State.	As for the Metro.
Network planning	The state will establish the conditions for operation of new lines.	As for the Metro.
Access to facilities		The concessionaire of the freight railway system has access to Flumitrens lines and pays a track access fee.

Source: Robelo (1999b), with minor modifications.

this was a commonly used method of privatization in many sectors. However, when Singapore's Mass Rapid Transit operator (SMRT) went public in July 2000, it was the world's first urban rail operator to do so. This was followed a few months later (in October) by Hong Kong's MTR Corporation's SIP (Ho 2001a), and these two cases have remained the only instances of urban rail SIP since.

In SIP, the government has to make three sets of interrelated decisions: how to transfer control, how to price the offer and how to allocate shares (Megginson and Netter 2001). The control transfer decision includes how large a fraction of the company's share to issue in initial versus subsequent offers, as well as whether there would be any post-privatization restrictions on corporate control. The most common technique used is government retention of a "golden share," which gives it power to veto certain actions such as foreign takeovers. The pricing decision requires the government to decide whether the offer price should be set by tender, a book-building exercise, or at a fixed price. If the latter, the amount of underpricing, and whether the price should be set immediately prior to the offer or many weeks in advance must be decided. The share allocation decision requires the government to choose whether to favor one group of potential investors (such as individual or domestic investors or SOE employees over another (for example foreign and institutional investors). The decisions in these areas that were taken for the Hong Kong and Singapore rail transit SIPs are reviewed here.

HONG KONG

Hong Kong has one of the highest population densities in the world with a population of seven million living in a mountainous land area of 1,099 square kilometers, where only 17 percent of the land is built upon. More than 2.2 million passengers travel daily over the Mass Transit Railway (MTR) network which is a network of six lines totaling eighty-eight kilometers and fifty stations. The basic network of Hong Kong's MTR, comprising three lines, was designed in the early 1970s. The government established the Mass Transit Railway Corporation (MTRC) in 1975 as a statutory corporation wholly owned by the Hong Kong government and gave it full responsibility for financing, constructing and operating the subway system. The MTRC did not receive any government subsidies except in the form of land grants as it was not required to buy land in the open market (Tiry 2003). The first lines began operations in 1979. The system was expanded during the 1990s when a new airport was built thirty kilometers west on Lantau Island.

To remain financially viable, the MTRC adopted an aggressive business strategy involving pursuit of substantial income from real estate constructed over its stations. These projects were undertaken either by the MTRC itself or in joint ventures with other developers. The opening of MTR subway lines since 1979 has therefore been accompanied by numerous real estate projects promoted by the MTRC. These real estate projects both financed construction of transit infrastructure and also attracted more users to the nearby facilities and services. Ho (2001a) described the MTRC's property development unit as the "jewel in the MTRC's crown." Tiry (2003) views the Hong Kong experience as showing that "cities can be redeveloped and renewed through mass transit if the transit system is given supports, such as combined functions, denser use at interconnecting nodes, intermodality, and appealing open spaces."

In 1999, when the government decided to privatize the MTRC, the state-owned enterprise recorded HK$2.1 billion in profits for the year and was considered one of the world's most successful metro. The decision was to privatize the MTRC on an as-is basis (Ho 2001a), with the setting up of a limited company known as Mass Transit Railway Corporation Limited (MTRCL). All the assets (including tracks, tunnels, stations, and properties) and liabilities of MTRC were vested in MTRCL following approval by legislators in February of 2000 of the Hong Kong Mass Transit Railway Bill, which was passed by an easy majority of 34 votes to 22.

Under the plan, the government would enter into an Operating Agreement with the MTRCL that would specify detailed terms of franchise, including performance monitoring and fare setting mechanisms. The exclusive franchise was for an initial term of fifty years. The government intended to remain the majority shareholder, and would sell off less than 50 percent of the MTRCL and retain the majority shares over the next twenty years. The offering in October 2000 was for one billion shares (200 million retail investors and 800 million institutional investors) or 20 percent of the issued share capital of the MTRCL. The offer price per share had been set at the top end of an HK$8 to HK$9.38 price range, with retail investors in Hong Kong enjoying a 5.25 percent discount at HK$8.88.[7] Eligible retail investors could get loyalty bonus shares of one for every twenty shares purchased in the offer and held continuously for one year, and one for every fifteen shares purchased held continuously for two years (Ho 2001a).

Over subscription of more than 20 times by retail investors and 15.25 times by institutional investors caused the government to change the ratio of retail to institutional allocation from 2:8 to 6:4 as one of the objectives of the exercise was to encourage participation by retail investors in Hong Kong. Sixty percent of the shares available were eventually allocated to the approximately 618,000 applicants received in the Hong Kong public offer. On October 5, 2000, MTRC shares soared to a high of HK$13, closing at HK13.65 on December 29, 2000 (Ho 2001b). Through the sale of 20 percent of the company, the government managed to raise more than HK$10 billion while retaining majority control of MTRCL.

SINGAPORE

Singapore is a densely populated high income city state with 4.2 million people and a land area of only 697 square kilometers. The idea to build a rail transit system, eventually called the MRT, was first discussed in the early 1970s. While the government wanted Singapore to have a healthy and vibrant public transport system, it did not wish public transport to be a continual drain on government funds. After ten years of studies and still faced with conflicting advice, the government finally made the decision to build a sixty-seven kilometer MRT system in 1982. It was felt that the MRT system would improve competitiveness in attracting the kind of higher value added investments desired by Singapore, especially in the financial and business sectors (Phang 2003).

Other than Cost Benefit Analysis, the financial viability of the proposed rail system was the other key element of the MRT studies. The government insisted that the revenue generated from MRT fares had to cover operating and maintenance costs, including the replacement of operating assets like rolling stock. Consistent with this philosophy, the government funded the construction cost of the long-term MRT infrastructure—tunnels, viaducts, and stations. The government also funded the first set of operating assets, including trains and signalling systems, which would be expected to wear out and require replacement after about thirty years of operation. Commuter fares were set to cover the day-to-day operating cost of the MRT and, under the License

---

7. HK$1 is approximately US$0.128 (as of October 9, 2006).

and Operating Agreement (LOA), the operator was required to make annual deposits to an Assets Replacement Reserve that would accumulate funds to replace the original equipment with a second set in due course (Phang 2003).

By 1983, the Mass Rapid Transit Corporation (MRTC) was established as a statutory board and construction began in October 1983. Part of the system began operations in November 1987 and the full first-stage project, comprising forty-two stations and a route length of sixty-seven kilometers, was completed in July 1990. In 1987, MRTC leased the running of the rail system to a new company, the Singapore MRT Limited, which is commercially run, although wholly government-owned. Temasek Holdings Private Limited, a government holding company, held all but one share of the SMRT. The MRTC and subsequently from 1995, the Land Transport Authority (LTA) held a single Special Share which provided it with veto rights to fundamental issues.

The conditions of the first ten-year lease stated that SMRT must pay an annual rental for the lease of the train fleet and upon expiration of the lease term may be required to purchase the rolling stock at its book value. As a pioneer company, SMRT enjoyed tax exempt status. The SMRT had also to set aside funds for the replacement or overhaul of major capital assets required to operate the MRT system. Fares were set to cover operating costs and equipment depreciation but not the capital costs of the infrastructure. In 1999, the year before it was listed on Singapore's stock exchange, SMRT reported an annual ridership of 346 million passengers, turnover of S$353 million and a profit before tax of S$121 million.[8]

Prior to the SIP of SMRT, the government had in a 1996 White Paper, changed its financing policy in favor of rail transit as follows: "The Government to continue funding infrastructure and the first set of operating assets, and commuters to continue paying fares which cover operating costs including depreciation. However, the second set of operating assets will be financed by fare revenue covering only the historical cost of the first set of operating assets, while Government co-finances the balance." This change paved the way for Cabinet approval of rail transit proposals that have almost doubled the size of the rail system in the past decade (Phang 2003).

With the push toward more rail lines, the government decided on a multi-modal duopoly model for the public transport industry. The concession for the new Northeast Line was awarded to the largest bus operator Singapore Bus Services (now SBS Transit) in 1999. The SMRT's ten-year licence and operating contract with the LTA to operate the MRT system expired on August 26, 1997, and was extended by the LTA to March 31, 1998. LTA signed a new thirty-year license and operating agreement with SMRT which commenced on April 1, 1998. Under the new LOA, which would be reviewed every five years, SMRT leases rolling stock from the LTA and pays license fees to the LTA each year for the use of track and stations. As part of the agreement, other operating assets for the MRT system were sold at net book value to the SMRT, with the proceeds from the sale of $1.2 billion payable in five equal installments from 1998 to 2002. At the same time, the LTA provided the SMRT with a grant amounting to $480 million to help SMRT purchase the assets (1999 Annual Reports of LTA and SMRT). This second LOA transformed SMRT's financial structure with the objective of paving the way for its eventual listing on the stock exchange (Phang and Walder

8. S$1 is approximately US$0.629 (as of October 29, 2006).

2000). LTAs new agreement with the rail operators dispensed with the golden share arrangement and the requirement for an asset replacement reserve.

When the SMRT was listed on the Singapore Exchange on July 26, 2000, it was the world's first urban rail transit operator to go public. The government investment holding company, Temasek Holdings, sold 33 percent of SMRT Corporation or 492 million shares for S$300 million (S$0.61 per share), thus retaining majority owner-ship and control. The SIP attracted international attention as the SMRT had shown steady growth in passenger volume, and had a steady and above-par dividend policy promised by the management. The government grant had also effectively padded the SMRT's bottom-line, and had enabled the company to derive strong recurrent income in the future (Ho 2001). On December 11, 2001, SMRT became a multi-modal trans-port operator through its acquisition of TIBS, Singapore's second licensed public bus operator, thus completing the public transport industry restructuring process initiated by the government in 1998. In August 2005, Temasek Holdings announced a reduction of its stake in SMRT Corp to 55 percent through a further placement of 110 million shares at S$1.11 per share.

PPP FOR INFRASTRUCTURE MAINTENANCE AND UPGRADING

LONDON

The London Underground dates back to the late nineteenth century when two techno-logical breakthroughs—electrification and underground tube railways—changed the face of London's transport system. The system was built by privately owned companies that obtained charters from Parliament to build seven electric tube underground lines. Much of the funding for constructing the London tubes came from Americans who had electrified urban transit earlier than the British and had made great profits (Armstrong and Gourvish 2000). By the early twentieth century, the lines faced competition from two sources—buses and electric trams, neither of which had been anticipated in busi-ness forecasts. The underground rail companies were effectively nationalized, with compensation, in July 1933. Today, the extensive system is a major business, with a 408 kilometer metro network, over 3 million passenger journeys a day, some 500 peak trains, 275 stations, over 12,000 staff, and vast engineering assets (http://tfl.gov.uk/tube/company, accessed in October 2006).

Public provision and financing was dominant for most of the twentieth century, however, in the last two decades, private financing has returned to the top of the agenda (Grimsey and Lewis 2004). The UK government cited the Underground's inability to cover operation and maintenance costs as the reason for an investment backlog of £1.2 billion. This substantial backlog provided justification for its decision in 1998 to em-bark on a radical change to secure long term sustained funding, through Public–Private Partnership. Under the PPP scheme, the core of the Underground—the track, signaling, bridges, tunnels, lifts, escalators, stations, and trains would be transferred in three parts to private infrastructure companies (Infracos). The contracts would last thirty years, but with prices agreed for only the first seven and one-half years, and enable £8 billion to be invested in the Underground's infrastructure over fifteen years. The train services continue to be run by London Underground Limited. The preferred bidders for the publicly run and privately built investment program for the Tube were announced in 2001 (National Audit Office 2004).

These PPP contracts with the Tube Lines (Infraco JNP) and Metronet consortia (Infraco BCV and Infraco SSL) to modernize the London Underground, signed in 2002 and 2003, represent the largest Private Finance Initiative (PFI) contracts by capital value (Grimsey and Lewis 2004). The net present value of the scheme was estimated to be about £16 billion and the cost of setting it up £455 million. Given the scale and change provisions in the PPP contracts, a Greater London Authority Act 1999 provided for the appointment of a PPP Arbiter who can be asked to determine the key financial terms periodically, and to give guidance on any aspect of the agreements at any time (http://www.ppparbiter.org.uk accessed in October 2006).

Administratively, the appointment of the Infracos was followed by the transfer of control of the London Underground Ltd. (LUL) from the control of the government and Secretary of State for Transport to the Mayor of London and Transport for London (TfL) on July 15, 2003. The PPP scheme has attracted a great deal of controversy[9] and was imposed on TfL against its will by the government TfL in fact opposed the PPPs and made a number of interventions, including two applications for judicial review, in its efforts to change the deals (National Audit Office 2004).

Other areas where the private sector is involved in financing the development of the London Underground include rolling stock leasing as well as renewal of power supplies and communication systems. These PFIs typically involve the private sector making specified investments in the Underground or reducing its debt and then leasing the rolling stock or facilities back to the LUL. For example, half a billion pound's worth of new cars required for the Northern Line was procured from GEC Alsthom through a twenty-year PFI concession. GEC Alsthom took over two depots, funding, constructing, commissioning, and maintaining the new trains and providing these for LUL to operate (Halcrow 2004).

The efforts that have been taken by London Underground to involve the private sector in financing its investment backlog involved complex institutional arrangements and sophisticated financial institutions, leading Halcrow (2004) to warn that care must be taken when attempting to apply London's experience to other cities.

CONCLUSION

The above review of recent international experience involving the private sector in the delivery of urban rail transit infrastructure and services has been encouraging. While significant political and popular opposition to outright privatization remains, governments worldwide have found Public–Private Partnerships to be viable solutions in the infrastructure sector, with the urban rail sector no longer the exception. The often

---

9. "TSSA cross examines Derek Smith's 10 Tube PPP myths" provides an overview of the areas of disagreements (Transport Salaried Staff's Association website at http://www.tesa.org.uk accessed in October 2006).

cited challenges inherent in urban rail privatization (high costs, long payback period, and complex partnerships) have been overcome in many instances through innovative solutions. There is no simple paradigm and choice of solution appropriate for local requirements requires great care. Halcrow (2004) does warn that the consequences of the wrong choice can be costly and long lasting.

The high costs inherent in developing new transit systems provided strong motivation in Southeast Asia for governments to seek private sector financing. While it is recognized that financial self-sufficiency is an important aid to privatization, and that very few metros can be self-financing, the experiences of Buenos Aires and Rio de Janeiro suggest that even in systems experiencing high deficits, concessions can be designed in such a way as to attract the private sector.

Competition for service concessions is, however, limited for small economies that desire operations to remain within the control of domestic firms. Singapore and Hong Kong, therefore, chose the share issue privatization model, under which the operator becomes subject to capital market discipline while remaining under government control. The public share offerings in Singapore and Hong Kong demonstrate that profitability of the firm remains the prerequisite for successful privatization via share offering.

London, with its extensive rail system, substantial investment backlog, and strong government inclination toward involving the private sector despite the complexities of PPP arrangements, continues to provide a testing ground for a range of types of private sector involvement in urban rail development and operations (Halcrow 2004).

As rightly pointed out by Grimsey and Lewis (2004), "PPPs are not, and probably never will be, the dominant method of infrastructure acquisition. They are too complex, and costly, for many small projects, and constitute 'using a sledgehammer to crack a nut.' In some cases, they may be beyond the capacity of the public sector agency to implement and manage. For other projects the tight specification of the outputs required may be difficult to detail for an extended period." Nonetheless, the varied international experiences of the past decade serve to demonstrate that PPPs can be an important instrument in urban rail transit policy.

REFERENCES

Armstrong, J., Gourvish, T. London's Railways—Their Contribution to Solving the Problem of Growth and Expansion. *Japan Railway and Transport Review*, 2000, 23, 4–13.

Babalik-Sutcliffe, E. Urban Rail Systems: Analysis of the Factors Behind Success. *Transport Reviews*, 2002, 22, 415–447.

Due, J.F. A New Look at Urban Transit: Control vs. Market Approaches. University of Illinois, Urbana-Champaign Economics Department Working Paper, 2003.

Gomez-Ibanez, J.A. Privatizing Transport in Argentina. CR1-96-1363.0. Cambridge, MA: Harvard University Kennedy School of Government Case Program, 1997.

Gomez-Ibanez, J.A. Bangkok's Skytrain (A): Opening the System. CR14-00-1591.0. Harvard University Kennedy School of Government Case Program, 2000.

Gomez-Ibanez, J.A., and Meyer, J.R. *Going Private: The International Experience with Transport Privatization.* The Brookings Institution, Washington, D.C., 1993.

Grimsey, D., Lewis, M.K. *Public–Private Partnerships: The Worldwide Revolution in Infrastructure Provision and Project Finance.* Edward Elgar, UK, 2004.

Halcrow Group Limited. A Tale of Three Cities: Urban Rail Concessions in Bangkok, Kuala Lumpur and Manila. Report commissioned for the ADB-JBIC-World Bank East Asia and Pacific Infrastructure Flagship Study; Halcrow Group Limited, London, 2004.

Ho, M. Privatization of the MTR Corporation. Hong Kong University Centre for Asian Business Cases, HKU139, 08/15/01, 2001a.

Ho, M. Privatization of the MTR Corporation: Teaching Note. Hong Kong University Centre for Asian Business Cases, HKU140, 08/15/01, 2001b.

Jones, S.L., Megginson, W.L., Nash, R.C., and Netter, J.M. Share Issue Privatizations as Financial Means to Political and Economic Ends. *Journal of Financial Economics*, 1999, 53, 217–253.

Megginson, W.L., Netter, J.M. From State to Market: A Survey of Empirical Studies on Privatization. *Journal of Economic Literature*, 2001, XXXIX, 321–389.

Middleton, W.D. NJ Transit Chooses Super-Turnkey. *Railway Age*, February 1997.

National Audit Office. London Underground PPP: Were They Good Deals? Report by the Comptroller and Auditor General HC 645 Session 2003–2004; The Stationery Office, London, 2004.

Perez, B.G. *Achieving Public–Private Partnership in the Transport Sector.* iUniverse, Inc., New York, 2004.

Phang, S.Y. Strategic Development of Airport and Rail Infrastructure: The Case of Singapore. *Transport Policy*, 2003, 10, 27–33.

Phang, S.Y., Walder, J.H. Singapore's Public Transport. Harvard University Kennedy School of Government and National University of Singapore Public Policy Program Teaching Case, 2000.

Rebelo, J.M. Reforming the Urban Transport Sector in the Rio de Janeiro Metropolitan Region: A Case Study of Concessions. Policy Research Working Paper 2096, World Bank, Latin America and the Caribbean Region, Finance, Private Sector and Infrastructure Department, Washington D.C., 1999a.

Robelo, J.M. Rail and Subway Concessions in Rio de Janeiro: Designing Contracts and Bidding Processes. Public Policy of the Private Sector, Note No. 183. The World Bank Group Finance, Private Sector and Infrastructure Network, Washington D.C., 1999b.

Tiry, C. Hong Kong's Future is Guided by Transit Infrastructure. *Japan Railway and Transport Review,* 2003, 33, 28–35.

Wong, S.C., Jomo, K.S., and Chin K.F. *Malaysian "Bailouts"? Capital Controls, Restructuring and Recovery.* Singapore University Press, Singapore, 2005.

Zweighaft, S. Dividing the Pie: Organization Models for Major Rail Projects. Paper presented at APTA Rail Conference, Seattle, WA, 2001.

Part V

Securing and Protecting Transportation

27 Transportation Security Policy

Van R. Johnston, Paul Seidenstat, and Erik W. Johnston

INTRODUCTION

A congressional committee formally defined terrorism, in 2002, as it seriously and proactively began to evaluate and engage the terrorism and security situation confronting the United States after September 11, 2001.

> Terrorism is the illegitimate, premeditated use of politically motivated violence or the threat of violence by a sub-national group against persons or property with the intent to coerce a government by instilling fear amongst its populace. (Johnston 2004a, 271)

Transportation security measures are a subset of overall homeland security activities. The objective of strong, long-term policy initiatives is to minimize overall security losses and to match overall security benefits with security costs in allocating resources while conveying a true sense of security to the population. Achieving the optimal expenditure on transportation security has to be related to securing the optimal overall homeland security level.

In the post-September 11 world, transportation security has emerged as a key component in the overall mission of protecting the homeland against terrorist attacks. Achieving acceptable levels of security is the goal. To achieve that goal requires an understanding of the concept of security, the current production methodology, the history of recent policies for achieving security, the dimensions of the task, and the prospects of new technology.

To secure our transportation network involves difficult decisions relating to the allocation of resources. It is important to continually evaluate how to reach the optimal level of security since we have neither the technology nor the resources to reduce potential damages to zero. Decisions are being made based on conditions of constant threat from terrorists who intend to inflict damages.

TABLE 27.1
Productivity = Efficiency + Effectiveness

Productivity	= Efficiency	+ Effectiveness
	= Output	Output
	Input	+ Standards
	= Products/Goods	+ Services
	= Quantitative Measures	+ Qualitative
Measures		
	= Market Systems	+ Political Systems
	= Private Industry	+ Public Organizations
	= Private Firms	+ Nonprofit
Organizations	= %	+ %

Source: Van R. Johnston

TRANSPORTATION SECURITY POLICY

For over two decades now, transportation security policy in the United States has been primarily focused on efficiency. Efficiency is the market model's measurement formula for success. It features output over input, and has products and goods as its products. It uses quantitative measures and is firm and industry oriented (see Table 27.1).

Government policy and management have traditionally been more effectiveness oriented. Here, we witness output over standards, like security and safety. Services and qualitative measures are featured. And, political systems are more predominant than the market systems of the private sector (Johnston 2004a). The term "security" in the context of transportation security includes the deterrence and/or interception of acts of terrorism against all forms of transportation: air, ground, and water.

Prior to September 11, government had been lured away from the traditional effectiveness formula emphasizing security and safety in general; but also for our purposes here, for transportation. The avoidance of terrorist acts requires the allocation of resources. This manifested as airport security being contracted out to private firms like Argenbright and Wackenhut. This followed the evolution toward privatization and reinventing government that had been going on for a couple of decades. Neither government nor the private sector, e.g., airlines and other transportation providers, wanted to invest in transportation security (Schiavo 2001). Security was viewed as a burden to the bottom line more than as responsibility to the people they served. Argenbright became known for providing almost meaningless airport security (Johnston and Seidenstat 2003). These recent examples demonstrate that there is a security production function.

Figure 27.1 shows the characteristics of the functional relationship between resource expenditures and the levels of security (avoidance of damages) expressed in dollars. Given technology and the efficient allocation of resources, as more resources are expended, more damages are avoided. In the short run, diminishing returns will

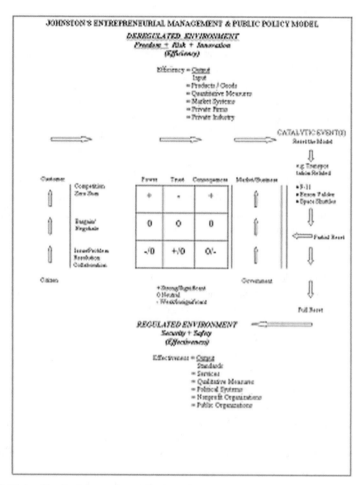

FIGURE 27.1   Van R. Johnston's productivity formulas.

be encountered such that to achieve a higher equal increment of security will require larger and larger increments in expenditures. Thus, after major targets are hardened and stricter screenings of passengers are achieved, it becomes increasingly expensive to achieve higher levels of damage avoidance.

While efficiency can be increased in many ways by utilizing private sector quantitative formulas, the risk of not having overall effectiveness values based on security and safety standards also increases. So Argenbright, for instance, hired minimally qualified employees, many of whom were reportedly basically illiterate, but were easy on the budget. At times, it appears, they were giving only the illusion of providing security. Wackenhut, known for its private prison guard business, was developed from the same mold. Needless to say, when the events of September 11 unfolded, knowledgeable transportation security experts were not very surprised by the lack of effective security by those private sector security personnel.

SECURITY AS A PUBLIC GOOD

Most of transportation security is provided by the public sector rather than left simply to the decision calculus of transportation providers. Transportation security typically has the characteristics associated with a public good. Once produced, everyone in the community, even the entire nation, potentially benefits. A hijacked airplane can crash into almost any structure or group of people, or a bomb planted on a train can blow up the train station. However, the damages go beyond the loss of life or injuries on the airplane or train and the value of the plane or the train itself, but there may be substantial collateral damage to bystanders and property.

The broader community benefits from the security measures whether or not it pays for these services. Moreover, there is no effective way for airlines or other transportation producers to collect from most of the community. Consequently, collective action is necessary to undertake an optimal level of security services. Government has the responsibility of providing for security services either by regulatory action or by direct government production. Active cooperation by businesses with security oriented government procurement needs, regulations, and business processes in defense and security areas, is a high expression of national citizenship (Holcomb 2003).

A few decades ago, U.S. transportation security policy was treated similar to other public goods and flowed from a fairly regulated environment, emphasizing effectiveness, security and safety. This was prior to President Carter's deregulation of air transportation in 1978. At the time, transportation policy emphasized citizenship and was covered by the Civil Aeronautics Board for rates and routes, and by the FAA for air traffic control and safety, though it had a built in conflict of interest in being mandated to support the industry as well as to monitor its safety.

In a model built by Van R. Johnston, it can be seen that as we moved from a regulated environment (at the bottom) toward a deregulated environment (at the top), security and safety (effectiveness) were replaced by freedom, risk, and innovation (efficiency). Along the way, citizens are treated more as customers, and government contracts out more as it works more like business and the marketplace. From the conflict management literature, we can also see that issue/problem resolution and collaboration of the past undergoes a change through bargaining and negotiating, toward the competition and zero sum emphasis of modern business and industry. The net result is that power and consequences are prominent while trust virtually disappears. When this happens, as it certainly did in air transportation security policy, a catalytic event or crisis can occur. In this case it turned out to be September 11 (Johnston 2004a).

As the model demonstrates, it is possible to reset the model down the right side to reestablish a more regulated, secure, and safe (effectiveness) environment for transportation security policy. Forming the new 40,000 federal employee Transportation Security Administration and the new 170,000 federal employee Department of Homeland Security (Haynes 2004) are major efforts to reset Johnston's Emerging Entrepreneurial Management and Public Policy model for transformed and improved viability in Transportation Security Policy.

PROGRESS IN AIR TRANSPORTATION SECURITY

Prior to September 11, air transportation security was characterized by primary reliance on airlines with only limited federal government oversight. Since most of the benefits of security accrued to the broader society, airlines opted for a modest level of security, as they were required to finance the screening and related security operations. Private firms were employed for the screening operation and they sought to minimize costs. The defects of this security system were examined, but little action was taken until the catastrophic events of September 11.

Congress acted rapidly after the catalytic terrorist attack to federalize the airline security system almost entirely. The Transportation Security Agency (TSA) was created and took over passenger and baggage screening and greatly expanded the tiny air marshal force. Congress also mandated an aggressive program to control airport access by employees and contractors. The FAA continues to perform some oversight of airlines and airports.

The tightened security efforts have shown mixed results. Strict airport security still appears to be lacking in terms of access and in screening employees and contractors with screeners failing to detect weapons at roughly the same rate as shortly after the attacks (Harris and O'Reilly 2005). The tightened security, however, has come at very large increases in expenditures as well as passenger inconvenience. In less than a year the airport passenger screeners contract grew more than seven times, to $741 million (Harris and O'Reilly 2005) and the FY2005 budget for TSA alone is $5.3 billion (Rugy 2004).

INTERMODAL TRANSPORTATION SECURITY

So far, air transportation has been highlighted. This is primarily due to its prominence in the attacks of September 11, the catalytic events that focused attention, money, and effort toward securing our transportation systems from terrorist acts with improved transportation security policy. Using Johnston's Emerging Entrepreneurial Management and Public Policy Model, we can see how transportation security policy is being reset down the right hand side of the model to a more secure and safer environment that is more effectiveness based, for all the major transportation modes. A terrorist example of not resetting the model sufficiently would be the failure to reset the model adequately for increased security after the terrorist attacks on the world trade center in 1993, leaving it vulnerable to the tragedy of the repeat attack and destruction of September 11.

Progress in intermodal transportation security systems will be explored below, based significantly upon the work of intermodal transportation security experts who contributed to a symposium on Terrorism and Transportation Security in a professional journal in 2004 (Johnston 2004b).

Air transportation recently received model reset assistance primarily from the establishment of the Transportation Security Administration and the Department of

Homeland Security. The General Accounting Office reviewed the Federal Aviation Administration which led to security related improvements in this agency overall, including more effective screening procedures, security technology, and personnel training (Seidenstat 2004).

Railroad security was improved, thus resetting the model, by forming expert teams working with the American Association of Railroads and the private sector. The strategies emphasized operational security, hazardous materials, military liaison, and technology; and were primarily industry based. Numerous government agencies were also involved, including: The Federal Railroad Administration, the US Department of Transportation, the Department of Homeland Security, the Federal Bureau of Investigation, Amtrak, and the Federal Transit Administration (Plant 2004).

Efforts to reset the model for increased mass transit security are being led by the American Public Transit Association and the US Department of Transportation. Primary work is being done researching security initiatives and commuter rail system threats. Building more effective communication and cooperation between transit agencies and industry is also a priority. Among the other significant organizations working to reset the model for increased security are: the Transportation Security Administration, the Federal Emergency Management Association, the Department of Homeland Security, the Immigration and Naturalization Service, the General Services Administration, and others.

Some of the major local transit systems, like those in Atlanta and Washington, D.C., are also contributing. This is an area where police departments at various levels of government can and are providing support as well (Waugh 2004).

A primary concern of highway security and terrorism, which includes bridges and tunnels etc., is the hazardous materials threat. Among the stakeholders working to reset the model in this highway and hazmat arena are: the US Department of Transportation, the Federal Motor Carrier Safety Administration, the Office of Hazardous Materials, the Federal Bureau of Investigation, and the General Accounting Office. Many state agencies and police departments are also involved, providing better highway security. In the private sector, assistance is being provided by the Commercial Vehicle Safety Alliance, and the Teamsters Union. The American Association of State Highway and Transport Officials is also proactively involved (Field 2004).

Insuring America's seaports from terrorism requires attention toward prevention, detection, response and recovery. Seaports are high on the list of terrorist targets, and are central to intermodal transportation. Primary stakeholders dealing with local, state, and federal seaports include: the US Coast Guard, the Maritime Administration, the Customs Service, the Corps of Engineers, the Commerce Department and the US Department of Transportation, among others. Seaports are critical because they are links to other major intermodal transportation systems, such as: highways, railroads, waterways, and pipelines (Price 2004).

In their second report, "America Still Unprepared—America Still in Danger," Gary Hart and Warren Rudman (Hart and Rudman 2002) warn that the country is not only still in danger, but that the agenda for intermodal transportation security needs to be adjusted. They argue that the sea and land modes are more vulnerable to terrorist attack than air transportation. Noting the potential catastrophic impact on commerce, they also point out the unique vulnerability and low security involved in our intense utilization of containers (over 100 million a year globally). Their position is supported by Robert Bonner, Commissioner of the US Customs Service, who admonishes that the impact on global trade and the global economy would be devastating (Hart and Rudman 2002).

The Hart–Rudman Task Force recommended the following for intermodal transportation. A layered security system needs to be developed for intermodal transportation, focusing primarily on our transportation system security vulnerabilities. Build a more secure system infrastructure for intermodal containers. Develop tracking devices and sensors. Put together a viable database and communication system for transportation security. And work with the appropriate U.S. and international agencies and organizations to reset the model by providing increased intermodal transportation security (Hart and Rudman 2002).

Now that the model is being reset, priorities have shifted back toward effectiveness, and public safety is at the forefront of public policy. The challenge, under such circumstances becomes how to optimize the effectiveness of new policy measures during this unique opportunity available during this critical transition period.

ACHIEVING OPTIMALITY

Looked at from a transportation perspective only, in Figure 27.2, the optimal level of security is where the marginal benefits of security are matched with the marginal costs of security production at the point where the lines intersect. In any case, getting the most security possible for whatever expenditure undertaken is essential. If there are excessive numbers of airline passenger screeners relative to the number required to effectively screen, then the overall level of protection would be less than if some screening personnel were diverted to protecting airport access or screening rail passengers.

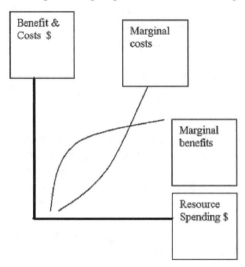

FIGURE 27.2   Optimizing security spending.

Moreover, even if all resources devoted to transportation security are being used efficiently, allocating resources among the various transportation security modes is important to achieve maximum output. For example, funds spent on additional air marshals might have a higher payoff if those marshals were used to inspect cargo containers. Expensive equipment expenditures might yield more protection in railroad protective devices, and so on.

However, optimizing transportation security expenditures as shown in Figure 27.2 may be suboptimal from the broader view of homeland security. Since higher levels of public security are possible up to some likely maximum point, decisions have to be made as to the optimal cost-effective level since there are competing uses for the resources involved. For example, first responder actions to attacks require resources. Do we spend more for response to attacks in the form of emergency medical facilities, storing of vaccines, or paying for more fire department equipment or for transportation security in the form of such things as more baggage or container screening equipment and air marshals? Thus, comparison between the various resource uses is necessary in light of the objective of minimizing total damages including loss of life.

OBSTACLES TO ACHIEVING OPTIMALITY

The obstacles to getting to the optimal position include bureaucratic and political constraints, imperfect knowledge, and the consequences of the limited vision of complex organizations.

A recent article in the *National Review*, for instance, shows the current formula for that budget allocations are not based on maximizing spending in the most effective means:

> A substantial portion of new homeland-security spending is being used for grants to state and local governments that are unlikely to have any impact on terrorism. The formula used by DHS to spread federal funds provides every state with a guaranteed minimum amount, regardless of risk or need. As a result, states in rural, less-populated areas receive a disproportionate amount of grant money. Incredibly, among the top ten money-receiving states and districts, only the District of Columbia also appeared on a list of the top ten most at-risk places. (Rugy 2004)

Experience has taught us some lessons about protecting airplanes from hijacking or ports from bombing, but knowledge is lacking as to the most efficient resource mix to achieve various levels of protection. For example, in the case of air transportation security, what is the most effective mix of airport screeners, air marshals, reinforced cockpits, airport personnel access control, and so on, and how do we measure the results?

Overall transportation security also requires deciding upon the optimal mix of resources among the various modes of transportation. Policy makers have to decide how much to spend for airport, port, rail, and trucking security measures. They also have to decide whether the best way to allocate their budgets is on modes of transportation first, or if allocation decisions should first be on meeting global transportation objectives. Regardless, rendering a decision about the overall expenditure level, given all the other budgetary priorities, is exceptionally difficult.

Most of all, designing an overall transportation security policy is complicated by a variety of organizational complexities, such as:

1. Multiple levels of government in the U.S. federal system that provide funding; and
2. Multiple layers of security suppliers that include various agencies in the new Department of Homeland Security, state and local law enforcement agencies, and private or public transportation suppliers (airports, railroads, ports).

TOWARD RESETTING THE MODEL

The 9/11 Commission Report "Final Report of the National Commission on Terrorist Attacks Upon the United States" was released July 22, 2004. The Commission's Chair, Thomas Kean, said at the release of this report: "We do believe that we are safer today than we were on 9/11. But we are not safe." The report calls for an overhaul of intelligence operations in the United States. This includes a strong recommendation to focus on counterterrorism (9/11 Commission Report 2004).

Specifically, the commission proposes that we put a National Intelligence Director in place who would report to the president, and who would be in charge of a new National Counterterrorism Center. The deputy directors would be the: CIA director, for foreign intelligence; the FBI director, for homeland intelligence; and the under secretary for defense intelligence. National Intelligence Centers would also be put in place and report to the National Counterterrorism Center. They would include: WMD proliferation, international crime and narcotics, Middle East, Russia Eurasia, and China East Asia.

The intelligence director would oversee the fifteen intelligence agencies and would be in charge of their budgets. The director would also control top deputies from the following agencies: Homeland Security, Department of Defense, the Central Intelligence Agency, and the Federal Bureau of Investigation. The Intelligence "czar" would need to be confirmed by the Senate, and would report directly to the president.

The mission of the new National Counterterrorism Center would be to improve data analysis regarding the work of the: CIA, FBI, DoD, Homeland Security, and the other intelligence agencies. It would be built upon the framework and infrastructure already under way which is now known as the Terrorist Threat Integration Center. The center would also work on developing national standards to build data bases, and improve technology to identify terrorists at transportation hubs, national borders, and so forth.

The present security system in the various modes of transportation features a layered system. For example, some airline systems screen passengers, others systems screen those with access to the airplane or the airport, and luggage; but also use air marshals, secure cockpit doors, and have pilots carrying weapons. The concept is to require an intruder to get through multiple barriers. Similarly, port security can screen containers both at the port of debarkation and the U.S. port of entry as well as placing some responsibility on the shipping company.

Congress would become more involved and be more accountable. Its oversight function would be enhanced. Its committees would be more focused on the terrorism threat. And its fiscal responsibility would be more aligned with security purposes (9/11 Commission Report 2004). Toward that aim, there have been efforts to align security spending with the utility it provides:

> Republicans are moving toward a consensus that the allocation of homeland-security spending needs to be based on more rational, cost-benefit analysis. House Homeland Security Committee Chairman Chris Cox (R., Calif.) has been fighting to change the criteria used to allocate these funds so that they are based exclusively on the risk of terrorist attacks and the magnitude of potential damages. (Rugy 2004)

The continuation of the 9/11 Commission itself, at least through the initial phases of the model reset mentioned above, is another means of taking advantage of the unique knowledge that the commission has accrued since its formation.

New technology and procedures are being researched and developed to shift the production function in order to be able to reduce the potential damages due to terrorism for the resources being expended. Most of the development is in the area of electronic screening and the development of computerized databases and recognition systems. To screen individuals, applying finger or iris recognition systems are being contemplated. Efforts to develop databases of fliers or the ability to tap other national databases to screen passengers, employees, and contractors are underway. To detect dangerous material in luggage and in containers new Pulsed Fast Neutron Analysis (PFNA)—similar to MRI technology—and Thermal Neutron Analysis (TNA) systems are being developed.

Whether these systems will offer larger reduction in potential damages compared to their costs, remains to be seen. Moreover, side effects via privacy issues will have be addressed. The existence and purchase of the latest technologies does not insure security. All technologies are fallible in one capacity or another. However, the responsible deployment, training, and use of these systems have the potential to significantly improve security.

Many of the 9/11 Commission recommendations would significantly assist in furthering the policy and goals of transportation security. In order for them to be highly successful, there must be proactive political support.

PERSPECTIVES

The events of September 11 have reshaped our thinking and our emphasis on transportation security issues. Significant damages in the form of: death and injury to passengers, to our transportation infrastructure, and to collateral persons and property, threaten to undermine transportation and to engender fear of traveling.

By clearly and effectively communicating the goals and requirements to the affected organizations, businesses, and other stakeholders, the resistance to adoption and implementation of these measures is reduced. Businesses can only be realistically expected to enroll in efforts when the advantage of doing so is transparent.

Investing in security is in the interest of individuals, businesses, and organizations. Investment follows many forms including the adherence to government regulations, taxation, or ensuring that organizational actions are consistent with homeland security measures. Security is not a project with an endpoint but a continual part of everyday operations. Long- and short-term goals must always be reevaluated. The government should invest in future technology in the areas of information, analysis, prediction, coordination, and other areas that can improve security. This investment should be in academic institutions, the private sector, and various governmental units as well. A multi-factored approach is necessary with a combination of individual, methodological, technology, organizational, political, and business approaches.

The U.S. economy is vulnerable and can be being badly wounded. It is important to bear in mind that transportation security policy cannot be constructed in a way that accomplishes two of the objectives of terrorism itself—to spread fear and cause economic instability.

REFERENCES

Counterterrorism Intelligence Capabilities and Performance Prior to 9/11. Report of the Subcommittee on Terrorism and Homeland Security, House Permanent Select Committee on Intelligence, US House of Representatives, Saxby Chambliss, Chairman of the Subcommittee on Terrorism and Homeland Security (July, 2002). Washington, D.C.: Government Printing Office.

Esterbrook, Gregg. (2004). *In an Age of Terror, Safety is Relative. New York Times*, June 27, "Week in Review."

Field, Mary A. (2004). Highway security and terrorism. *Review of Policy Research*, 21 (3), 317–328.

General Accounting Office (GAO). (2004). *Aviation Security: Improvement Still Needed in Federal Aviation Security Efforts.* Testimony before the Subcommittee on Aviation, Committee on Commerce, Science, and Transportation. U.S. Senate. GAO-04-592T, March 30. Washington, D.C.: Author.

General Accounting Office (GAO). (2004). *Summary of Challenge Faced in Targeting Oceangoing Cargo Containers for Inspection.* GAO-04-557T, March 31. Washington, D.C.: Author.

General Accounting Office (GAO). (2004). *Rail Security: Some Actions Taken to Enhance Passenger and Freight Rail Security but Significant Challenges Remain.* GAO-04-598T, March 23. Washington, D.C.: Author.

Hart, G., & Rudman, W.B. (2002). *America Still Unprepared — America Still in Danger. Report of the Independent Task Force, US Commission on National Security.* New York: The Council on Foreign relations.

Haynes, Wendy. (2004). Seeing around corners: Crafting the new department of homeland security. *Review of Policy Research, 21* (3), 369–395.

Hingham, S., & O'Harrow Jr., Robert (2005). Contracting rush for security led to waste, abuse. *Washington Post.* Retrieved December 2, 2005, from http://www.washingtonpost. com/wp-dyn/content/article/2005/05/21/AR2005052100778.html.

Holcomb, John M. (2003). Corporate Global Citizenship: Conflicts between human rights and power politics. *Business and Professional Ethics Journal*, 22 (2), 21–49.

Johnston, Van R. (2004a). Terrorism and transportation policy and administration: Balancing the model and equations for optimal security. *Review of Policy Research*, 21 (3), 263—274.

Johnston, Van R., ed. (2004b). Symposium on terrorism and transportation security. *Review of Policy Research*, 21 (3), 255–402.

Johnston, Van R., & Nath, Amala. (2004) Introduction: Terrorism and transportation security. *Review of Policy Research*, 21 (3), 255–361.

Plant, Jeremy F. (2004). Terrorism and the railroads: Redefining security in the wake of 9/11. *Review of Policy Research*, 21 (3), 293–305.

Price, Willard. (2004). Reducing the risk of terrorism at seaports. *Review of Policy Research*, 21 (3), 329–49.

Rugy, V. D. (2004, Oct 15). Homeland-security scuffle. *National Review Online*, Retrieved December 2, 2005, from http://www.nationalreview.com/comment/rugy200410150840. asp.

Schiavo, Mary F. (2001). Homeland defense and crisis management. Executive summary report, 9–10. Retrieved March 12, 2004 from http://www.e-gov.com/events/2002/hls2/downloads/hlsdec18report.pdf.

Seidenstat, Paul. (2004). Terrorism, airport security, and the private sector. *Review of Policy Research*, 21 (3), 275–291.

The 9/11 commission report. (2004). *Final Report of the National Commission on Terrorist Attacks on the United States.* Thomas H. Keane, Chairman of the Commission. New York: Norton.

Waugh, William L., Jr. (2004). Securing mass transit: A challenge for homeland security. *Review of Policy Research*, 21 (3), 307–316.

28 Globalization and Transportation Security

Joseph S. Szyliowicz

INTRODUCTION

Transportation has always had been an international activity. From earliest times, merchants and traders were dealing across state boundaries. The ancient Egyptian, Chinese, and Persian empires were all engaged in international trade. Subsequently, as Europe expanded outwards and created the colonial system, trade assumed a truly global dimension. In recent decades, however, this dimension has accelerated greatly. The level of international trade continues to increase as does the numbers of people who travel to other countries.

Transportation security must thus be viewed from an international perspective. It requires attention to the modes that are involved in international activities, notably aviation and shipping as well as to the borders through which millions of people enter the United States annually. Among them have been terrorists. Domestic terrorists can not be overlooked, as demonstrated only too tragically by Timothy McVeigh's attack on the federal building in Oklahoma City in 1995 and the more recent mailing of envelopes containing anthrax to various members of Congress. Nevertheless, the most devastating attack on the United States, the destruction of the World Trade Center was carried out by foreign nationals and it is obvious that the main threat to homeland security comes from overseas, especially the Islamic World, not only in the form of direct attacks but also through their ability to persuade native Muslims to engage in terrorism. The recent bombings of the London underground system highlight this danger.

Safeguarding transportation facilities is essential for many reasons. First, they are attractive targets because of their functional economic importance. All countries are dependent upon transportation. Every day tons of goods are carried by water, air, road, or rail and millions of people use private or public transport for business and leisure trips. Millions of people work in transportation or transport related industries. In the United States, it is estimated that the transportation sector employs almost twelve million people, generates over \$1 trillion annually, and accounts for over 10 percent of the Gross Domestic Product. Disrupting this sector imposes heavy losses on any economy. Nor can one overlook the symbolic appeal of destroying what are generally recognized as national and international icons such as the Golden Gate Bridge or a major airport, especially since mass casualties would likely be involved. Second, transportation vehicles make powerful and effective weapons. Truck bombs have become commonplace and the potential of airplanes was tragically revealed by the September

2001 attacks on the Pentagon and the World Trade Center. Finally, in order to attack a target, terrorists must travel to their destination and convey their weapons to the target. Thus borders have to be safeguarded yet it is essential to do so in a manner that does not place undue burdens on innocent travelers and on the flow of goods. The tradeoffs between security and commerce are complex yet they cannot be ignored.

TRANSPORTATION AND GLOBALIZATION

Although globalization is recognized as a major factor shaping the contemporary world, there is a considerable debate about its novelty and consequences. Its principal characteristic is increased mobility—of capital, goods, technology, labor, ideas and knowledge. Its dimensions include accelerating scope and breadth of trade and financial flows, the elimination of barriers that limit free markets, and increased cross border activities and linkages of all kinds. Many argue that these developments are increasing the gap between the poor and the advanced countries and that it creates anger and frustration among those who fear its economic impacts and view it as a destroyer of traditional cultures. Such feelings readily fuel extremism in the Islamic world and elsewhere which provides fertile ground for the recruitment and training of terrorists who regard the United States as the primary force behind globalization. Furthermore, it is much easier today for terrorists to travel and to ship weapons across borders.

These changes in the international economy can be attributed to developments such as the end of the cold war, the liberalization of economies, and the impact of technology. Advances in transportation and communications technology have made for greater and easier movement of both goods and people. Of particular significance has been the widespread adoption of the use of containers for transporting goods rather than loading and unloading individual items of cargo which caused costs to decrease exponentially. Today, an estimated 200 million containers travel around the world annually. The increase in the overall transportation of goods has been paralleled by other international trends such as the rise in outsourcing and "Just in Time" manufacturing techniques, both of which require a well developed transportation and communication infrastructure. The impact of these developments can be seen in U.S. trade figures. U.S. imports have grown from $22 billion in 1960 to $1263.9 billion in 2004, exports from $25.1 billion to $1146.1 (ITA 2005). Imports now account for over 15 percent of the U.S. economy as compared to 3 percent in 1960, exports for 17 percent as compared to 5 percent in 1970 (Hodges 2005). These technological changes also impact the manner in which people conduct their daily lives as the number of people who travel for pleasure and business continues to grow with millions of Americans flying to foreign destinations and millions of foreigners entering the United States. For example, almost 100 million people have entered the United States from Canada, while 325 million came in from Mexico (BTS 2005).

Such a volume of traffic obviously greatly complicates the task of homeland security. First, it is impossible to seal the borders in such a way as to prevent unwanted persons or undesirable goods from entering the United States. Efforts to prevent illegal immigration, primarily from Mexico, for example, have failed to prevent a steady flow across the border. Similarly, the amount of drugs being smuggled into the country does not seem to have decreased despite strenuous efforts and lavish expenditures. Furthermore, any effort to seal the borders would necessarily entail extensive screening of people and containers. Doing so, however, would have serious consequences since it would inevitably slow down the pace of international commerce. Such a slowdown would have very serious consequences for both U.S. imports and exports and, indeed for global trade with repercussions that would negatively affect growth in the United States and throughout the world.

Globalization has also led to increased linkages between U.S. infrastructure and that of other countries such as Canada, especially in the area of energy. Thus it is conceivable that terrorists could strike a deadly blow against the United States by an attack outside the homeland. The great blackout of August 2003 which left millions without electricity originated in Canada. Hence, U.S. security is inextricably linked to the degree of security that obtains in other states. Of particular concern is the global freight system which is vulnerable to attack at many points outside the United States. The consequences of closing down the aviation system after the events of September 11 that stranded thousands of people for several days were relatively trivial in comparison to what would happen if a terrorist, for example, placed a nuclear device into a container in some foreign port and it exploded in the United States. The impact would not only seriously affect this country but the entire global economy. As the Commissioner of the U.S. Customs Service, Robert Bonner, has noted:

> The consequence of a terrorist incident using a container would be pro-found...If terrorists used a sea container to conceal a weapon of mass destruction and detonated it on arrival at a port, the impact on global trade and the global economy could be immediate and devastating—all nations would be affected. No container ships would be allowed to unload at U.S. ports after such an event. (Bonner 2002, p. 8)

The economic costs alone would be immense. How devastating these would be can be deduced from the fact that the closure of the West Coast ports for eight days when dock workers went on strike is estimated to have cost about $60 billion. National economies would receive a major shock as international trade would not return to its, pre attack, normal state for months. As a result, economic growth throughout the globe would slow, imposing a heavy burden on all states, especially upon those least able to bear it.

The nature of the contemporary world complicates efforts to deal with such issues since there is no central international body with power and authority to impose rules and regulations. National governments continue to cherish the sovereignty of their states so it is often necessary to engage in long and difficult negotiations. As we shall see below, the United States has actively pursued a strategy of negotiating for the right to place customs agents at foreign ports. Some transportation modes do have international organizations which have been assigned safety and security responsibilities. Especially noteworthy are the International Civil Aviation Organization (ICAO) and the International Maritime Organization (IMO). Nor can one overlook such agencies as Asia Pacific

Economic Cooperation (APEC) which has undertaken various initiatives to strengthen transportation security in its member states. Nevertheless the fragmented nature of the system with its numerous private and public, national and international actors greatly complicate the achievement of transportation security in the United States

INTERMODALISM

The container revolution that has fueled the trend towards integrated supply chains and globalization has also contributed to another development with important implications for transportation security. Global freight now moves along a system that links the individual modes, highway, rail, and shipping and that system is becoming ever more integrated as a result of technological change. This development is due to the nature of modern economic systems which are characterized by constant pressures to reduce costs by increasing productivity and reducing inefficiencies and by increasing customer expectations on both freight and passenger systems. Such expectations extend beyond economic efficiency. Today, policy makers are concerned with minimizing environmental impacts and the use of energy, promoting safety and security, and providing more mobility choices. Intermodalism promotes such goals because it integrates the different modes into a seamless system and uses each mode for the purpose for which it is best suited and is a rapidly growing characteristic of transportation systems everywhere.

This development has important implications for security since, traditionally, the focus has been upon enhancing the security of individual modes, especially aviation. Such an orientation, while necessary, is no longer adequate. Not only must attention be paid to the protection of the modes but the intermodal dimension also requires attention. And, its very characteristics such as the increased number of stakeholders, the terminals, which are critical elements in the infrastructure, and the increasing reliance of information technology further complicate the task of dealing with terrorism.

A successful cyber attack on transportation systems can originate anywhere in the world and cause massive disruptions. Yet the sites and networks that are operated by both the private and the public sector concerning trucks, planes, and containers are by no means secure. In a recent national study of three hundred large companies in October 2004, for example, 80 percent reported that they felt that cyber attacks were increasing. Furthermore, 20 percent revealed that the company's computers had been successfully hacked (Security 2004). Nor are government databases secure. The inspector general of the USDOT has been conducting annual audits of the department's cyber security since 2001. In 2004 he reported that a serious effort was being made to remedy the numerous weaknesses that had been identified. However, many of them were never fixed. This year's audit concluded that "much remains to be done and new challenges have also emerged." It identified over three thousand problems, some of which involved the critical air control system that remained to be fixed. Some "clearly require immediate action." Among these was the fact that the Federal Railroad Administration's server was taken over during the study (USDOT 2005).

THE HISTORICAL BACKGROUND

Transportation security emerged as an issue when airplane hijackings began in the 1960s. Hence, the focus was upon aviation, little attention was paid to other modes. Yet even in regard to aviation, no systematic and effective set of policies were ever put into effect. A successful attack would focus attention and demands for action would be more or less heeded and resources allocated. However, the key issue was always how to prevent another successful attack so the concern was always with trying to prevent a repetition of the previous attack. In other words, the FAA and the other relevant agencies tended to be reactive rather than proactive Hence, when planes were hijacked, the policy of screening passengers to prevent terrorists from bringing guns on board was implemented. When a suitcase bomb destroyed Pan Am 103, bomb detection devices became the center of attention.

Although various experts and officials occasionally called for enhanced security measures in other areas (in 1995, for example, the USDOT suggested that the shipping industry should evaluate its vulnerabilities) little was done. Some attention was paid to the borders, especially the one with Mexico since the Canadian border was considered safe. As a result relatively few resources were allocated to it and it remained thinly patrolled—three hundred agents were responsible for the four thousand-mile-long border. Twenty agents were in charge of four states. Staffing was an issue at the ports of entry; even at important ones like the Detroit Bridge and Tunnel, a major entry point for freight, which had less than half of the 102 inspectors that were needed. In the words of one immigration inspector, "inadequate staffing, facilities and equipment have made incomplete and/or poor inspections the rule at many busy ports" (Smith 2000, p. 2). These problems extended to the border with Mexico which, because of concern with illegal immigration, received greater attention. In 1994, a comprehensive plan was implemented whereby a system of lights, sensors, and fences was put in place and the number of agents increased to eight thousand for the two thousand-mile border. That effective border security is essential was vividly demonstrated in 1999 when Ahmed Ressam, a known bomb maker, was caught trying to enter the United States on a ferry boat from Canada. In this case, luck and a perceptive official prevented what might have culminated in a major terrorist incident. A heightened state of alert followed for a brief period and the Bush administration proposed, in its FY2001 budget, to recruit an additional 430 border patrol agents—less than half of the one thouand agents that had been mandated by Congress. And, this increase still left 164 unfilled positions since there were 594 vacancies at the time. The new administration's measure can be viewed, as indicative of its general lack of concern with terrorism until September 11.

Although the Clinton administration never developed a systematic approach to homeland security, it demonstrated an awareness of the seriousness of the problem of homeland security and did enact various measures, as noted above. It also appointed, with the consent of the Republican Congress, the bipartisan U.S. Commission on National Security/21st Century, co-chaired by Gary Hart and Warren Rudman which produced three reports arguing that new global trends were creating new threats, the most serious of which was a potentially devastating attack on American soil that would result in thousands of casualties. To deal with such a likelihood, the commission called for major changes in the organization of national security institutions and the creation of a cabinet level agency (U.S. Commission 2001)

Whether September 11 could have been prevented is a controversial issue. Certainly, despite numerous warnings, reports, and studies, serious deficiencies characterized the anti-terrorism effort put forth by the new administration and the transportation security system remained highly vulnerable. Tragically, the shortcomings were relatively easy to identify. In a co-authored article (Szyliowicz and Viotti 1997), we identified the following:

1. The lack of inter governmental coordination, especially in regard to intelligence, perhaps the most critical area for the prevention of terrorist attacks;
2. The relationship between state action and the private sector, especially given the latter's tendency to minimize expenditures on security and the need to answer the key public policy question of how much security at what price is required;
3. The only unit concerned with coordinating security across modes possessed inadequate powers and resources and was vulnerable to the actions of congressional budget cutters;
4. The focus remained on technology and law enforcement with little attention to the context of terrorism or the social causes or to coordinating policy with security issues; and,
5. The need to supplement the focus on transportation modes as targets with a sound paradigm based on a systems approach.

THE CONTEMPORARY SCENE

September 11 tragically vindicated all the Cassandras in government, academia, and elsewhere who had been warning of the need to accord a high priority to terrorism, including infrastructure security. It also unleashed a torrent of policy responses ranging from wars in Afghanistan and Iraq to the decision to accept the recommendation of the Hart-Rudman Commission and to integrate all the agencies concerned with homeland security. The new Department of Homeland Security which involves twenty-two agencies and 170,000 employees (including critical transportation related agencies such as the Transportation Security Administration) represents the largest governmental reorganization in decades. It incorporates the United States Customs Service (currently part of the Department of Treasury), the Immigration and Naturalization Service and Border Patrol (Department of Justice), the Animal and Plant Health Inspection Service (Department of Agriculture), the Transportation Security Administration (Department of Transportation), as well as the Federal Protective Service (General Services Administration). The Coast Guard also comes under its jurisdiction. This reform is designed to replace an inchoate structure characterized by a lack of clearly defined lines of authority, overlapping jurisdictions, limited coordination between independent agencies, and gaps in coverage with an organization that possesses unambiguous jurisdictions and responsibilities.

Creating such an organization is never an easy matter given the massiveness of the bureaucratic reorganization, the need to change organizational cultures, and the many traditional obstacles that have to be overcome. Indeed, one knowledgeable observer, a former staff director for the White House Commission on Aviation Safety and Security, has written "...the strategic role...propose(d) for the TSA cannot be accomplished by the current organization with the current staff and under the existing legislation" because lobbyists influence departmental R & D programs and policymakers override the conclusions of the researchers. Nor will the new Department of Homeland Security be able to carry out the analytical tasks suggested above, given the immediate needs that it must deal with (Kauvar 2002, p. 6). Furthermore, the reorganization is being carried out at the same time that efforts are being made to develop and implement policies to enhance the security of the homeland, thus complicating the achievement of each goal. As one expert has noted, FEMA's response to Hurricane Katrina "hardly seemed to have been facilitated by its incorporation within a larger, new organization" (O'Hanlon 2005, p. 4).

Not surprisingly the ambitious goals assigned to DHS and TSA are far from being met. Such factors as inexperienced personnel and leadership, turf battles (many involving transportation), funding disputes, personality conflicts, a conservative administrative culture, and managerial failures, have so severely limited its ability to achieve its mission that it has been frequently labeled "dysfunctional." The former approach to transportation security remains in place, despite the many changes that have been implemented. Essentially, DHS has not yet emerged as an integrated cohesive entity with a developed policy vision based on strategic thinking so that such key infrastructural elements as chemical plants, nuclear power plants, and the rail transport of hazardous chemicals remain highly vulnerable, secure containers have not been developed, and people and cargo at the borders are not tracked. Hence, when one knowledgeable critic, its former inspector general, was asked about its weaknesses, he responded "I don't know where to start....I've never seen anything like it" (Mintz 2005, p. A01). Inadequate planning processes are a major reason—stakeholders are not adequately involved, the relationship between annual and long-range plans has never been identified with the obvious result that DHS cannot assess the degree to which its goals are being achieved, and strategic planning is inadequate (GAO March 2005c). Change, however, may at last be forthcoming. The new Homeland Security Secretary, Michael Chertoff, who replaced Tom Ridge in 2005, has promised to focus on high security targets rather than spread resources across the nation (Lipton 2005b). The importance of such an approach was recently highlighted by a study which revealed the vulnerability of the more than one hundred sites located in New Jersey that pose a threat to twelve million people in the New York metropolitan area and to air, rail, pipeline, and highways systems (Kocieniewski 2005).

The lack of strategic planning is but one of the problems confronting the new secretary. These have been identified as follows (Wermuth 2005, p. 2):

> The first challenge is the lack of robust strategic planning and analysis capabilities.... This deficiency is clearly revealed in the context of border and transportation security and in other areas as well. The second major challenge is the lack of performance metrics and the inability to tell what works and

what doesn't.... The third challenge is the structure of the organization, both internally and as it relates to other organizations.... The fourth problem is intelligence as it relates to the fulfillment of the DHS operational mission.

These weaknesses have influenced all aspects of transportation security including the one area that has received priority attention—aviation. Many security measures, costing billions of dollars, have been adopted to safeguard this mode. These include: replacing the much criticized system of having private poorly trained and paid personnel with a force of over forty-five thousand federal workers, installing new machines to check all baggage for explosives (an expensive and controversial policy given the level of technological development), random baggage searches, reinforcing cockpit doors, placing air marshals on many flights, and naming federal security directors at 440 major airports.

Yet the degree to which these measures safeguard aviation remains questionable. Particularly troublesome is the heavy and costly reliance on screening whose effectiveness continues to be seriously questioned by many observers including, most recently, the Department's acting Inspector General. In 2003 comprehensive tests were conducted at fifteen airports whereby investigators attempted to smuggle weapons and explosives through the screening process. The classified results were called "extremely disappointing" by Representative John Mica (R), Chair of a House aviation subcommittee. Since then, little if any progress has been made (Lipton 2005). As the Inspector General of the DHS stated in his report (DHS 2005, p. 2),

> Improvements are still needed in the screening process to ensure that dangerous prohibited items are not being carried into the sterile areas of airports or do not enter the checked baggage system.... The lack of improvements since our last audit [2004] indicates that significant improvement in performance may not be possible without greater use of new technology.

Such efforts are now underway. New technologies, including fingerprint scanning and other biometric tools, are now being tested at various airports in an effort to improve passenger screening and access control to various airport areas including cargo (Leib 2005).

Nevertheless, this is merely a pilot program and other measures are also appropriate. Although the IG's report suggested that the screening personnel were functioning as effectively and efficiently as could be expected, a GAO report criticized the TSA's training efforts as needing updating and additional staff, better intranet and internet connections, and internal controls including monitoring and evaluation mechanisms. Furthermore, screening remained focused on passengers and baggage did not receive the attention that is required (GAO May 2005a).

Passenger and baggage screening operations are supposed to be supervised by Federal Security Directors who are also responsible for working with airport authorities, airlines, and other stakeholders to prepare a plan to deal with a potential terrorist attack. Their roles and responsibilities have been defined by the TSA but the GAO found serious gaps in the system: "TSA's guidance to FSD's authority is outdated and lacks clarity regarding FSD authority relative to other airport stakeholders. TSA's document...gives them authority to supervise and deploy a TSA law enforcement force *that was never established* (my emphasis). Also, it does not clearly address FSD authority during a security incident...." (GAO September 2005, p. 5).

In short, even in regards to this mode into which billions of dollars have been poured, serious problems of security remain. As a panel of experts noted in 2002, in the absence of coherent strategy, the response to September 11 could be neither systematic nor comprehensive:

> ...after the attacks, federal policymakers, seeking to secure commercial aviation and regain public confidence in air travel, did not have a well-designed security system in place that could be assessed methodically to identify gaps that needed to be filled. (TRB 2002, p. 15)

Such a system has not yet been implemented. Hence, it is not surprising that, in addition to the concerns cited above, other risks such as the degree to which access to planes is secured and especially the serious vulnerabilities of general aviation and air cargo require far more attention than they have hitherto received (Szyliowicz 2004). Nor can the threat posed by shoulder fired missiles be minimized though it is now receiving serious attention and tests are underway to determine the effectiveness of a high tech defensive system (Lipton 2005c). However, in the absence of a holistic risk management approach, it is difficult to determine whether it is cost effective to deploy such a system. The Rand Corporation has estimated that it would cost $11 billion to arm each commercial passenger plane plus annual operating costs of $2.1 billion. The total expenditure would amount to $40 billion over twenty years. At present, $4.4 billion is being spent annually to safeguard the transportation system (Wermuth 2005).

The emphasis on aviation security inevitably led to the neglect of other areas of concern that pose an even greater threat. As the new Hart-Rudman commission report noted (p. 2):

> While 50,000 federal screeners are being hired at the nation's airports to check passengers, only the tiniest percentage of containers, ships, trucks and trains that enter the United States each day are subject to examination—and a weapon of mass destruction could well be hidden among this cargo.

Accordingly, the commission emphasized the need to "recalibrate the agenda for transportation security; the vulnerabilities are greater and the stakes are higher in the sea and land modes than in commercial aviation"

The need to enhance the security of the sea mode is widely accepted especially since Al Qaeda has mounted some successful operations and is believed to own over twenty vessels that it can utilize for smuggling nuclear and other weapons and as means of attack (Sinai 2004). Accordingly, in 2002, Congress passed the Maritime Transportation Security Act (MTSA) that called for various initiatives to safeguard U.S. ships and ports. These include the establishment of a multi agency Container Working Group (sixteen government agencies are involved) that also includes a large number of private sector organizations. Its goal is to enhance the security of the process through which cargoes are packed, loaded, and shipped to the United States To do so, it has established four subgroups. They deal with: information technology, the acquisition and dissemination of cargo information; security technologies, physical security, detection of weapons of mass destruction, and tracking of containers; business practices, identify commercially viable "best practices"; and international affairs, interacting with relevant foreign actors and organizations. The goal is to establish criteria to identify high risk containers and trucks, implement a pre-screening process at foreign points of origin, develop and deploy technologies to prescreen high risk cargoes and secure containers and trucks en route to U.S. ports, and improve the security of containers as they are transported to their domestic destinations (Bemis 2002). That this group faces serious problems of coordination should not be surprising.

The key agency is the Custom and Border Protection agency (CBP) that oversees the Customs-Trade Partnership Against Terrorism (C-TPAT) program. Since supply chain and border security requires the cooperation of the private sector, this initiative is designed to safeguard supply chains by having private sector participants agree to meet certain standards and to ensure that all their suppliers, importers and shippers meet the same standards. Firms that cooperate and meet the standards along their entire supply chain benefit because their products are subjected to fewer inspections and thus encounter fewer delays.

Closely related is the Container Security Initiative (CSI), which was launched in January 2002 and places U.S. Customs inspectors at the top foreign ports (from which most America-bound containers originate) so that they can check the containers before they leave for a U.S. port. To prescreen high risk containers, the CSI utilizes various technologies and computerized information data bases. By November 2002, eleven of the top twenty ports (Le Havre, Rotterdam, Singapore, Vancouver, Halifax, Montreal, Antwerp, Hamburg, Bremerhaven, Hong Kong, Yokohama, Tokyo, Kobe, and Nagoya) were participating in the CSI. By mid-2005, thirty-four governments were participating; by the end of the year the number was scheduled to increase to forty-five. Given the huge number of containers that are involved, it is essential to identify those which pose the highest risk. That is the responsibility of the National Targeting Center, staffed by a dozen Customs officials who seek to identify potential terrorists trying to enter the United States as well as the high risk containers on the basis of the advanced information that they have received from the shippers and U.S. intelligence agencies. Each container receives a grade ranging from 0 (no risk) to 300 (highest risk). Those with a grade above 190 are the ones that are checked before being loaded onto a ship.

However, the effectiveness of this effort remains in doubt given the magnitude of the task and the prevalence of cargo theft at various ports throughout the world as well as the degree to which piracy continues to thrive. Moving the inspection overseas inevitably raises questions about the integrity, reliability, and honesty of the local officials checking suspected containers. Indeed, a recent GAO study found that about 30 percent "potentially dangerous" containers were not screened in foreign ports due to diplomatic consideration and inadequate staffing (GAO April 2005).

The greatest danger involves nuclear materials. In 2003, ABC news successfully smuggled depleted uranium into the United States, once from Europe, once from

Indonesia. The CBP subsequently "enhanced its ability to screen targeted containers for radioactive emissions by deploying more sensitive technology at its seaports, revising protocols and procedures, and improving training of CBP personnel" (Skinner 2005, p. 2). In early 2004, four importers agreed to incorporate a Container Security Device (CSD) into their regular sealing process so as to create a "smart box". This phase of the project led to the development of an improved CSD which his now being tested in sixteen trade routes. The CBP is also evaluating other technologies (X-ray and gamma-imaging systems) designed to provide non-intrusive inspection (NII) of containers. Large scale NII systems are operational at 166 ports of entry, 59 of which are at seaports. To minimize the threat of a nuclear weapon or radiological dispersion device, radiation detection technologies are being deployed so as to achieve the goal of screening every container for radiation (Jacksta 2005). Hopefully, all these new measures will prevent a terrible scenario from ever being realized.

Each of these projects has clearly yielded some positive results but the lack of clear guidance and unclear roles for port owners and operators has delayed adequate implementation of appropriate solutions at the nation's seaports. The Coast Guard, the lead agency under the MTSA, is responsible for developing new regulations and conducting port and harbor security assessments. Though it has implemented a number of important measures in this and other areas, much remains to be done and it is not obvious that they possess the manpower or the expertise to carry out its new functions. Three areas are of particular concern. To increase security, the Coast Guard is developing an Automatic Identification System (AIS) to track vessels but apparently lacks adequate resources. Second, the port security assessments are not based on a "defined management strategy, specific cost estimates, and a clear implementation schedule" so that this vital activity is not as effective as is necessary. Third, the Coast Guard's efforts to ensure that security measures are implemented appropriately are not adequate in such areas as staffing, training, and managing inspectors and carrying out inspections (GAO March 2005b).

In a subsequent study, the GAO noted that important steps had been taken to safeguard seaports but that "Assessing the progress made in securing seaports is difficult, as these efforts lack clear goals defining what they are to achieve and measures that track progress toward these goals." Nevertheless, it identified the following major challenges: "failure to develop necessary planning components to carry out the programs; difficulty in coordinating the activities of federal agencies and port stakeholders to implement programs; and difficulty in maintaining the financial support to continue implementation of security enhancement" (Wrightson 2005, p. 2).

The funding issue is one that has handicapped efforts to achieve port security for some time. The Maritime Security Act (2002) which was designed to improve port security provided no funding mechanism. Since its passage, Congress has allocated a total of $491 million but the Coast Guard has estimated that $7.3 billion will be required to safeguard the ports by 2012. At present, funding levels, the goal will not be achieved until the middle of the century—probably after a Mars landing is achieved. However, the Bush administration continues to maintain that the private sector should assume most of the costs (Zeltech 2005).

Ports of entry are not limited to airports or seaports. Many are located along the borders with Mexico and Canada. In this area too, geographic and other factors—the tremendous length (over 5,500 miles of border with Canada and almost 2,000 miles with Mexico) as well as the tremendous flow of goods and people (over 500 million people enter the United States annually, including 330 million noncitizens)—pose formidable and complex challenges. It is obviously impossible, and undesirable even if possible, to check every vehicle that enters the United States The only way of dealing with border security is to develop and implement a system that identifies the high risk travelers and containers. In this effort, technology is being utilized to seal cargoes at their production sites and to monitor shipments so as to maintain "in transit visibility." Thus, when the cargo reaches the border, seals and codes can be quickly checked. To what degree such a system has already been implemented at the Mexican and Canadian borders is unclear, especially since the needed equipment is expensive and costs have always been an obstacle to deploying new technologies at the borders, especially given their length. Customs is also developing an ambitious Automated Commercial Environment Program (ACE) designed to identify high risk trade activity and to facilitate the reporting required by actors in the supply chain. This program, estimated to cost over $3 billion over its nine-year implementation, has, however, encountered significant delays, cost overruns, and performance issues since its inception (GAO 2005a).

Similar problems plague another ambitious and expensive ($10 billion) program designed to safeguard the borders. The need for such a program was recently highlighted by the results of a test by government officials equipped with false birth licenses and driver's licenses that they had created using standard computer software. Claiming to be U.S. citizens, they successfully passed the INS inspection at Miami International Airport (Chardy 2003). US-VISIT, launched in 2003 and intended to cover the land borders as well as all the major ports of entry, is designed to accurately screen all foreign visitors. This effort involves establishing a modern visa system based on biometric information that is shared between various federal databases as well as a computerized entry—exit system that would ensure that visitors comply with their entry conditions. Whether this ambitious goal will ever be realized is increasingly being questioned since "government officials are betting on speculative technology while neglecting basic procedures to ensure that taxpayers get full value from government contractors" (O'Harrow and Higham 2005, p. D04).

Developing effective border security requires coordination among many agencies though primary responsibility rests with the DHS's Border and Transportation Security Directorate (BTS) and incorporates many heretofore independent units such as the Customs Service, the Border Patrol, the Immigration and Naturalization Service. In addition the Coast Guard, the TSA, the Department of State and the Department of Justice are also key players in the effort to secure the borders. All these agencies have to struggle with issues of breadth (what persons and cargo should be examined), depth (how thoroughly and how), coverage (how frequently and for what objective), and jurisdiction (which agency) (CRS 2005). Thus many difficult issues remain unresolved and it is not at all clear when the overall goal which has been described as follows will be realized:

> ...a border of the future that provides greater security through better intelligence, coordinated national efforts, and unprecedented international coop-

eration against terrorists, the instruments of terrorism, and other international threats. At the same time, it would help ensure that this border of the future better serves the needs of legitimate travelers and industry through improved efficiency. (p. 22)

Even with secure borders, attacks can take place as the recent attacks on the Madrid train stations and the London underground illustrate only too clearly. Securing these passenger systems is perhaps even a greater challenge in light of their extent, openness, accessibility, and complexity. Millions of passengers use light rail, subways, buses, intercity rail, and commuter rail daily so passenger and baggage screening is difficult if not impossible, thus enhancing their attractiveness to terrorists. Important measures have been taken by the Federal Transit Association to improve the security of these systems including vulnerability assessments, deploying technologies, especially a chemical detection system to prevent bio chemical attacks and training and awareness programs. Local transit agencies are urged to establish integrated security programs (FTA 2005). However, funding is a major issue for transit has received very little help from the government which allocated a mere $250 million between 2002–2005 to mass transit, compared to over $15 billion for aviation security (Millar 2005). Furthermore, security planning for all passenger systems suffers from serious weaknesses as a 2004 GAO report noted.

Implementation of risk management principles and improved coordination could help enhance rail security. Using risk management principles can help guide federal programs and responses to better prepare against terrorism and other threats and to better direct finite national resources to areas of highest priority. In addition, improved coordination among federal entities could help enhance security efforts across all modes, including passenger and freight rail systems. We reported in June 2003 that the roles and responsibilities of the Transportation Security Administration (TSA) and the Department of Transportation (DOT) in transportation security, including rail security, have yet to be clearly delineated, which creates the potential for duplicating or conflicting efforts as both entities work to enhance security. (Abstract, p. 1)

Recognizing the importance of greater emphasis upon surface systems, Congress has called for improved security planning and authorized vastly increased expenditures for rail security (CSO 2005).

THE FUTURE

That terrorism continues to pose a deadly threat to the United States and its allies is obvious. When and where and how a future attack will come cannot be identified but recent coordinated attacks on the London underground and the hotels in Amman, Jordan, reflect the continuing ability of al-Qaeda and its supporters to carryout deadly strikes. Today the United States is more secure that it was before September 11 but, despite all the measures that have been implemented and the billions that have been spent, it is clear that the transportation system retains important vulnerabilities. Furthermore, the inadequacies and shortcomings of the DHS in regards to planning for responding to a massive attack were tragically and dramatically highlighted by the response to hurricane Katrina. The manner in which the relief effort was bungled led Newt Gingrich, former Speaker of the House to remark: "I think it puts into question all the Homeland Security and Northern Command planning for the last four years, because if we can't respond faster that this to an even we saw coming across the Gulf for days, then why do we think we're prepared to respond to a nuclear or biological attack?" (Philpott 2005). This is a serious indictment of the policies that have been implemented to date, especially since the "lessons learned" from the disaster have been identified as: Better Planning and Preparedness at all levels, Better Command at the federal level, Faster response, Better Communications, Better Equipment, and More Cooperation (Philpott 2005). Such elementary "lessons learned" highlight the bureaucratic weaknesses that still remain and the magnitude of the challenge that remains in regards to effective crisis response.

But response is only one, albeit a critical one in any strategy to safeguard the transportation system. Successfully managing the consequences of an attack means that other dimensions of the anti terrorism strategy have failed. These can be summarized as follows:

- Prevention—the use of various state instruments ranging from military to economic aid to foreign policy interventions to eliminate the conditions that breed and support terrorists.
- Border security—ensuring that terrorists and their weapons, especially nuclear devices and biochemical agents not enter the country.
- Internal security—domestic intelligence and related activities to identify and capture terrorists who have managed to cross our borders as well as sleeper cells.
- Strengthening critical infrastructure—actions ranging from the design to police patrols to minimize the risk of an attack and the damage that would result from a successful attack.
- Consequence management—the ability of local, state, and federal officials to react quickly and effectively when confronted with a terrorist attack.

Technology plays an important role in many of these dimensions and many different ones have already been deployed ranging from radiation detectors to biometric devices. On its Web site, the TSA proudly proclaims that it "is delivering on its commitment to leverage new technology to secure the nation's airports and other modes of transportation." Yet more is needed. Transportation security officials have identified several areas where further development would be helpful. Of particular concern are technologies that improve intelligence, communication, and decision making in high-volume environments. The Coast Guard, for example, would like to acquire better tools to provide it with accurate information concerning every vessel and cargo that enters U.S. waters and the ability to track each continuously just as the FAA is able to identify the name and position of every plane in the air. The ability to provide law enforcement personnel with real time biometric data on every person seeking entry into the United

States would enhance border security. Systems that would permit all ports of entry to exchange information and to communicate with each other are also desired. (Arnone 2005). The IEEE has also identified various gaps and, in 2004 adopted issued a position paper recommending increased funding for the following areas:

- Establishment of transportation security standards
- Surveillance and sensors, including hazardous material detection
- Promising emerging technologies, such as robotics and automated response systems
- Geographic location and identification
- Data gathering and analysis
- Communications and dissemination of information
- Physical security controls employing techniques, such as biometrics

Despite the urgent need for such new technologies, the GAO found that the TSA and DHS have apparently not yet developed an effective R and D program. Although they funded more than 200 projects in FY 2003 and 2004, most projects were related to the aviation sector. Furthermore, despite the importance of basic research in this area, neither the TSA nor the DHS have funded any such projects. Nor have they estimated when the new technologies would be deployed. The GAO in its report on Transportation Security R&D concluded:

> ...neither agency has fully complied with the laws or implemented the best practices. For example, neither agency has prepared a strategic plan for R&D that contains measurable objectives. In addition, although TSA has completed threat assessments for all modes, it has not completed vulnerability and criticality assessments. DHS also has not completed risk assessments of the infrastructure sectors. Furthermore, both TSA and DHS lack complete, consolidated data for managing their R&D projects. Finally... their outreach to consider the concerns of the transportation industry have been limited. (GAO September 2004, p. 1)

Even if an effective technology development program is developed, its output, though a major asset, will not provide a "fix" to the problem of counter terrorism. New technologies do not always meet expectations, deploying technologies is a long and expensive process and, for some threats, no promising technologies are evident. Moreover technologies also have social and economic consequences, and it is essential to include these in any calculation of risks and benefits before making a decision to deploy a particular technology. Such calculations are essential (as indicated by the case of the surface to air missiles discussed above) otherwise, as has happened in the past, technologies will be hurriedly deployed despite high financial and other costs and prove to be of limited effectiveness. Nor can one ignore the human element as the events of September 11 demonstrated so tragically.

Education and training thus require particular attention at all levels. Every person concerned with any aspect of transportation—planning, design, operation, and maintenance—requires new skills and awareness. Nor can one overlook the importance of public awareness. The enormity of this task should not be underestimated for, traditionally, few transportation professionals in either the public or the private sector received any systematic exposure to security issues. A wide range of people are involved—truck drivers, engineers, logistics managers, freight forwarders, terminal operators, to name a few—and all require training. Although various programs are being implemented, developing an integrated and coherent strategy to tackle such educational and training needs is a matter that requires urgent attention,

The most effective way to deal with the terrorist threat is to prevent an attack. That requires effective intelligence which, in today's globalized world must be based on trust and cooperation with the intelligence services of other states. Trust and cooperation can be gained primarily through the "soft power" of the United States. However, since the United States is viewed very unfavorably by many throughout the globe, because of its power, historic willingness to pursue strategic interests at the expense of proclaimed values and ethical goals, and its new security policy of preemption and suspicion of international treaties and multilaterism, it is essential to develop and implement policies that will enhance its "soft power" so that it can more easily gain support for its anti terrorism efforts. These must become an integral part of its foreign policy. Such an approach must be nuanced. With many countries it will involve close consultation and cooperation, with others, such as state sponsors, it may be appropriate to use economic and other instruments of force to persuade them to change their policies.

This approach is consonant with the recommendations that have been advanced by a former senior CIA officials who has persuasively argued that U.S. foreign policy should be based on the following concepts (Pillar 2001):

- Inject the counterterrorist perspective into foreign policy decision making.
- Pay attention to the full range of terrorist threats.
- Disrupt terrorist infrastructure worldwide.
- Use all available methods to counter terrorism, while not relying heavily on any one of them.
- Tailor different policies to meet different terrorist challenges.
- Give peace a chance.
- Legislate sparingly.
- Keep terrorist lists honest.
- Encourage reforming state sponsors to reform even more by engaging them, not just punishing them.
- Help other governments to help with counter-terrorism.
- Work with, not against, allies.
- Use public diplomacy to elucidate Terrorism without glamorizing terrorists.
- Level with the American people.
- Remember that more is not necessarily better.

An era marked by globalization, however, requires another dimension. Globalization has produced not only winners but also losers and many who worry about the implications of the accelerated flow of new ideas, technology and knowledge for traditional cultures and values. This is especially true in the Islamic world where many consider that a new crusade has been launched against their religion. Not surprisingly anti-American feelings are especially strong in this region. Accordingly, the effort to increase America's "soft power" through public diplomacy must be complemented by a serious attempt to deal with the factors that breed terrorists and win them support. As I have suggested previously (Szyliowicz and Viotti 1997, p. 92):

> To rely only on law enforcement and enhanced security measures is, at best, a partial remedy that only addresses the symptoms (or effects) of the underlying social and social- psychological causes. No amount of law enforcement or enhanced security measures can fortify or protect every carrier or terminal, much less every passenger.... Grievances—real or imagined, just or unjust, legitimate or illegitimate—are still grievances; and terrorism provides the weak or frustrated with a means for gaining attention, if not for achieving ultimate ends. To identify these motivations, of course, is not to sanction or apologize for what is still illegal, organized violence. It is only to recognize that a comprehensive approach to the transportation-security challenges has to go beyond law enforcement and enhanced security measures to grapple with the more difficult social causes. Addressing social causes requires great patience, which is often lacking in policy makers who habitually focus on short-term measures with more immediate, hopefully positive effects.

There are signs that such a policy may be emerging. In domestic security policy, too, change is evident in regards to many aspects of homeland security including greater cooperation among intelligence agencies and a decision to base future security funding on the basis of risk assessments and prioritization rather than on the basis of political criteria. Moreover the draft of a detailed, comprehensive and specific New National Infrastructure Protection Plan is being circulated to a wide variety of public and private stakeholders for their input. These are promising developments but much remains to be done. Hopefully a strategy that can meet the difficult challenges posed by transportation security will emerge. Terrorism may well be a fact of life for decades to come but appropriate foreign and domestic policies can reduce its significance and potential danger and lead to a safer and more secure transportation system.

REFERENCES

Arnone, Michael. (2005). "Better Intell, Info Sharing Top Transportation Security Wish Lists," http://www.fcw.com/article91277 (accessed November 1,2005).

Bemis, R. (November 18, 2002). Statement Before the Committee on Government Reform Subcommittee on National Security Affairs, and International Relations.

Bonner, R. (August 26, 2002). Presentation Before the Center for Strategic and International Studies.

Bureau of Transportation Statistics. (BTS, 2005). *Pocket Guide to Transportation*, pp. 24–25.

Chardy, A. (January 31, 2003). "Lax Security at MIA," *Miami Herald*.

Congressional Research Service. (2005). "Border and Transportation Security: Overview of Congressional Issues."

CSO. (2005) "Rail-Thin Security," http://www.csoonline.com/read/080105/wonk_wonk.html.

Dacey, R. F. (November 19, 2002). "Computer Security: Progress made, but critical Federal Operations and Assets remain at risk," Statement Before the Subcommittee on Government Efficiency, Financial Management and Intergovernmental Relations, Committee on Government Reform, House of Representatives, U. S. General Accounting Office.

FTA. (2005). "Five Point Security Initiative," http://transit-safety.volpe.dot.gov/Security/Default. asp#FTA's 5-POINT SECURITY INITIATIVE.

GAO. (August 13, 2001, 01-751). "Information Security: Weaknesses Place Commerce Data and Operations at Serious Risk."

GAO. (March 23, 2004, 04-598T). "Rail Security: Some Actions Taken to Enhance Passenger and Freight Rail Security, but Significant Challenges Remain" and Abstract.

GAO. (March 14, 2005a, 05-267). Report to Congressional Committees. Information Technology: Customs Automated Commercial Environment Program Progressing but Need for Management Improvements Continue.

GAO. (September 30, 2004, 04-890). "Transportation Security R&D."

GAO. (March 17, 2005b, 05-364T). "Coast Guard. Observations on Agency Priorities in Fiscal Year 2006 Budget Request."

GAO. (March 31, 2005c, 05-300). "Improvements to DHS's Planning Process Would Enhance Usefulness and Accountability."

GAO. (April 26, 2005, 05-557). "Container Security: A Flexible Staffing Model and Minimum Equipment Requirements Would Improve Overseas Targeting and Inspection Efforts.

GAO. (May 2, 2005a, 05-451). "Aviation Security: Screener Training and Performance Measurement Strengthened, but More Work Remains."

GAO. (May 26, 2005b, 05-434). "Critical Infrastructure Protection. Department of Homeland Security Faces Challenges in Fulfilling Cybersecurity Responsibilities."

GAO. (September 25, 2005, 05-851). "More Clarity on the Authority of Federal Security Directors is Needed."

Hart, Gary and Rudman, Warren B. (October, 2002). *America Still Unprepared — America Still in Danger*. Report of the Independent Task Force, New York, Sponsored by the Council on Foreign Relations.

Hodges, Michael. (2005). Foreign Trade and International Debt Report, http://mwhodges.home. att.net/reserves.htm.

Hosenball, M. and E. Thomas. (December 23, 2002). "High Seas Hunting." *Newsweek*.

IEEE. (2004). Surface Transportation Security, http://www.ieeeusa.org/policy/positions/surfacetransportation.html.

International Trade Administration. (ITA, 2005). http://www.ita.doc.gov/td/industry/otea/usfth/ aggregate/H04t01.html.

Jackstra, Robert. (May 17, 2005). Testimony Given at a Full Committee Hearing, U.S. Senate Committee on Commerce, Science and Transportation.

Kauvar, G. B. (Fall 2002). "Transportation Security," *Issues in Science and Technology*, p. 6.

Kocieniewski, David. (May 9, 2005). "Row of Loosely Guarded Targets Lie Just Outside New York City," *New York Times*.

Leib. J (April 26, 2005). "Fingerprints of DIA Workers to be Scanned," *Denver Post*.

Lee, J. (February 7, 2003). "Progress Seen in Border Tests of ID System," *New York Times*.

Lipton, Eric. (April 20, 2005a). "Transportation Security Agency Criticized." *New York Times*.

Lipton, Eric. (March 3, 2005b). "Security Chief Vows to Spend Based on Risk." *New York Times*.

Lipton, Eric. (May 29, 2005c). "Jetliners to Test Defense Mechanism." *New York Times*.

McIntyre, Dave. (July 23, 2002). "Finding the Path Among the Trees," *ANSER Institute for Homeland Security*.

Millar, Bill. (2005). "Comments," http://www.apta.com/media/releases/050620senate_cuts.cfm.

Mintz, John. (February 2, 2005). "Infighting Cited at Homeland Security," www.WashingtonPost.com.

National Memorial Institute for the Prevention of Terrorism (MIPT). http://www.tkb.org/Incident-TargetModule.jsp?startDate=01%2F01%2F1968&endDate=12%2F31%2F2004&imageField.x=0&imageField.y=0&imageField=filter+results&pagemode=target

O'Hanlon,Michael. (October 26, 2005). Testimony before the Senate Subcommittee on Terrorism, Technology and Homeland Security of the Committee of the Judiciary.

O'Harrow Jr, R. and Higham, Scott. (May 23, 2005). "U.S. Border Security at a Crossroads," *Washington Post*.

Perl, A. and J. Szyliowicz. (December, 2001). "Transportation Security: The Energy Dimension," *Journal of Urban Technology*, pp. 134–136.

Philpott, Don. (September 2005). "Hurricane Katrina," *Homeland Defense Journal*, pp. 22–26.

"Post Attack Economy is Less Global, as Trade Falters" (October 17, 2001). *Christian Science Monitor*.

Prince, T. (January, 2003). "Sneak Preview," *American Shipper Magazine*.

Sinbai, J. (March 2004). "Future Trends in Worldwide Maritime Terrorism," *The Quarterly Journal*.

Slater, R. E. (October, 2000). "Transportation: The Key to Globalization," *Economic Perspectives*, Electronic Journal of the U.S. Department of State, vol. 5, no.3, pp. 7–10. Available: http://usinfo.state.gov/journals/ites/1000/ijee/ijee1000.htm.

Pillar, Paul. (2001). *Terrorism and U.S. Foreign Policy*. Washington, D.C.: The Brookings Institution Press.

SecurityProNews. (2004). "Cyber Attacks and Breaches on the Increase," http://securitypronews.com/news/securitynews/spn-45-20041108CyberAttacksandBreachesontheIncrease.html.

Skinner, Richard L. (2005). Testimony Before the Committee on Commerce, Science, and Transportation, Unites States Senate.

Smith, O. A. (February 10, 2000). "Enhancing Border Security," Statement Before the U.S. Senate Subcommittee on Immigration Committee on the Judiciary.

Szyliowicz, J. and P. Viotti. (1997). "Transportation Security," *Transportation Quarterly*.

The White House. (June, 2002). "Border and Transportation Security," The Department of Homeland Security, http://www.whitehouse.gov/deptofhomeland/sect3.html.

Transportation Research Board. (2002). "Deterrence, Protection and Preparation: The New Transportation Security Imperative," Transportation Research Board, Special Report 270.

U.S. Commission on National Security/21st Century. (February 15, 2001). "Road Map for National Security: Imperative for Change," Phase III Report, http://www.nssg.gov/PhaseIIIFR.pdf.

USDOT. Information Security Program. Report # FI-0006-002, October 7, 2005, http://www.oig.dot.gov/StreamFile?file=/data/pdfdocs/DOT_FISMA.pdf.

Wermuth, Michael A. (2005). Testimony Before the Committee on Homeland Security and Government Affairs, Unites States Senate.

Wrightson, Margaret. (2005). Testimony Before the Committee on Commerce, Science and Transportation, United States Senate." GAO-05-448T.

Zeltech. (September 11, 2004). Port Security Faces a Funding Abyss. http://www/zeltech.com?News/News_Sept_11_04_Portsecurityfacesfundingabyss.asp.

U.S. Customs. (November, 2002). "U. S. Customs Container Security Initiative Guards America, Global Commerce From Terrorist Threat," press release, http://www.customs.ustreas. gov/.

U.S. General Accounting Office. (November 2002). "Using Biometrics for Border Security."

Winner, L. (October 22, 2002). "Complexity, Trust and Terror," *Tech Knowledge Revue*, vol. 3, no. 1.

29 Seaport Security from Terror: Risk and Responsibility

Willard Price

Security at seaports used to be manageable even if the impacts could be high. In a recent article, the author offered this explanation of seaport security before and after September 11 (Price 2004):

> The risk of natural or human disasters at seaports has been common…with hazardous cargo, complex technology and many climatic and geological happenings…safety efforts to protect workers and local neighborhoods from accidents and toxic releases were the principal concern before 9/11…It was desirable to remove concentrations of people from the "footprint" of port disasters.
>
> Acts of terror now appear more likely than these previous disasters. Since seaports are part of the nation's borders, they appear to be one of the weaker barriers to entry and a valuable opportunity for destruction.

Now seaport security is more difficult because terror has become a possible event, even likely in some opinion, and the implications are much more potentially damaging to people, property and the economy. National policy creates local port risk, for the port can not be considered as the cause of terror, rather it is the opportunity. Terror is alive and well, with attacks on airplanes, buildings, rail and mass transit, embassies, U.S. Navy ships, and other facilities where large populations, national symbols, and economic havoc are ripe fruit, apparently easy for the picking.

Seaports have been lucky in the past. Considering they are without a deliberate security barrier, there are limited cases of known terror events or evidence of terrorists prevented or apprehended before striking. Now it is perceived as more important to protect port assets from being used or damaged. Any attempt to disarm or disable terrorists before they reach the harbor can only be the responsibility of the federal government, although U.S. Coast Guard, local law enforcement. and port security forces might apprehend terrorists as they approach port infrastructure. The U.S. Department of Homeland Security (DHS) screens and inspects cargo. Security strategy and financing is debatably a joint responsibility of all levels of government and private companies engaged in port operations. Port owners, mostly public agencies, shippers, and terminal operators view is likely less to be aggressive, but none the less must consider how to respond to this threat. Their security strategy and prevention initiatives are influenced by federal and state forecasts, strategies, and support of security investments.

A main theme of this exploration is the sharing of risk and responsibility for predicting, addressing and reducing terror events and human and economics impacts among the public and private sector participants in maritime cargo movements. Further, this discussion is intended to view seaport security from the port's perspective, including the actors dependent on this transportation transfer point for their livelihoods and the material flows for their economic viability. Specifically, this chapter will examine (1) terror behavior at ports, (2) a life cycle of security activities, (3) risk or terror and barriers to prevent terror, (4) strategic plans for securing ports, (5) roles for federalism in requiring and financing security initiatives at seaports and ends with (6) hypotheses for further study about questions still unanswered.

Port systems include breakwater barriers, harbors and channels, inland waterways and locks, bulkheads, quay walls and piers, cargo storage spaces and buildings, intermodal transportation highways, rail lines and pipelines, all with several avenues of entrance where terrorists and threatening materials can pass through the port from sea to land and then more freely move throughout the country. With much greater consequence for the port and its operators, terrorists can choose to destroy people and property and to cause significant disruption of economic activity at the port, in the country and across the global supply chain.

TERRORIST BEHAVIOR: ACCESS AND DESTRUCTION

Terrorists may plan to use the seaports as *paths of terror* for (1) accessing the United States to cause destruction elsewhere in the nation, simply using the port to "get materials or weapons through the borders," or (2) entering the harbor and causing destruction to port resources and adjacent property and people, to cause the personal and economic damage they so revere (Price 2004).

To visually demonstrate these paths of terror, two diagrams have been included from the article referenced above. Figure 29.1 and Figure 29.2 present simple diagrams of seaports, labeled as Paths of Terror with descriptions of both Avenues of Entry and the Points of Destruction.

Terrorists are likely driven by their hatred of the United States and its international policies, manifested by their desire to accomplish these goals:

1. Destroy national symbols, attempting to injure national pride, and create fear
2. Damage concentrations of people and property, causing human injury, and death
3. Disrupt economic activity, both locally and throughout the country to create chaos

Ports seem to be a less likely target, given less symbolism and less density of people, but the terrorists reward will come from economic disruption locally, nationally and globally. Cutting an important part of the global supply chain network seems desirable

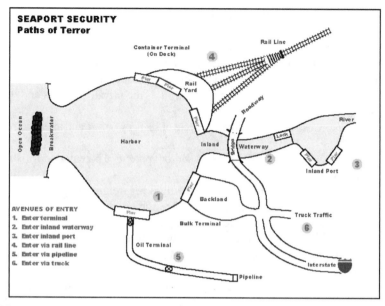

FIGURE 29.1

but it has not been accomplished to date. Does this indicate ports are a lower priority for terror; does this explain the nation's hesitancy to have fully secured seaports?

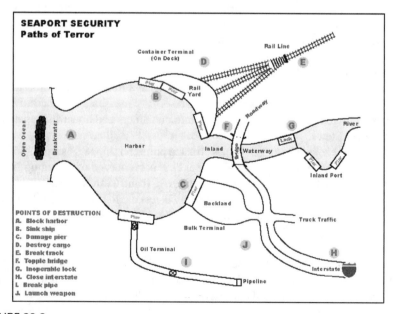

FIGURE 29.2

LIFE CYCLE OF SECURITY ACTIVITY

A logical order of terrorist and security seems obvious, but this frame allows a clearer description of the various activities planned and conducted by security resources. This cycle model also focuses the possible responsibility for each initiative, separating the involvement of all levels of government as well as the private partners and operators at ports.

Six stages are established for the life cycle of security before and after a terror event:

1. Prevent terror plans and resources and/or apprehend potential terrorists around the globe
2. Prevent and/or detect events at their origin in foreign countries
3. Protect with barriers at the port entrance and boundaries
4. Screen cargo and detect threats at the port during transfer
5. Respond to successful events, rescue and apprehend terrorists
6. Recover with removal, rebuilding, and reimbursement

The listing below identifies principal activities and actors across these stages:

Security Stages

1. Prevent Terror Globally
Federal intelligence and security agencies pursue, deny safe haven and resources, and capture or kill terrorists before an attempt to conduct an event. This effort is a continuing battle, yet may not be totally successful as terror continues to reign in other parts of the world, if not the United States since the September 11 terror success. Most will not bet against another terror attack on U.S. soil sometime soon.

2. Prevent/Detect at Origin
Federal security and law enforcement agencies make agreements with foreign governments, their ports, and shippers to provide security measures intended to prevent terrorists from getting people or materials into containers and aboard ships destined for the United States.

The federal government establishes "trusted ports and shippers" so as to minimize the chance that dangerous cargo will arrive at U.S. ports in need of screening. This effort operates as the Container Security Initiative (SCI) and Customs-Trade Partnership against Terrorism (C-TPAT) programs and may detect cargo from sources that are not trusted, requiring further inspection upon arrival at U.S. ports.

3. Provide Barriers at Port Entrance and Boundaries
Once arriving at the U.S. port, ships are subject to Coast Guard patrol and boarding if doubt exists about the cargo. The DHS massive information technology titled Operation Safe Commerce (OSC) demands information about all movements across the oceans and allows DHS to signal its Coast Guard vessels and seaports to pursue suspicious ships and their cargo at arrival.

The seaport also is a border and requires fences, gates, and patrols to ensure individuals are restrained from entering the United States by small boat or maritime ship from the ocean as well as those who threaten the port from inside the United States. Human and automated detection methods are contrasted in the technology below.

4. Screen Cargo during Transfer

If the trusted strategy fails or if suspicious cargo is identified earlier, a second level of screening is possible as the cargo moves from the vessel to its intermodal transfer out of the port of entry. This stage is a visible and debated point of security at U.S. ports. The obvious opportunity is to inspect every container or other cargo that enters the port to ensure no unwanted people or materials are present.

This is easier to demand than to conduct, as any complete search would cause serious and unacceptable disruption of cargo movements and denial of port productivity. Instead the alternative DHS policy is to predetermine suspicious cargo and then complete a scan or inspection as the container leaves the port. This creates less total delay and, coupled with rapid screening technology, can make additional security measures much more acceptable to the port and shippers.

5. Response to a Terror Event

In the case ports are not secure from terror and an event is successfully conducted entering or destroying facilities and causing humans suffering, immediate and capable first responses are essential to minimize destruction and death and to apprehend perpetrators. Yet it is regrettable that so much attention and adulation is paid to responders when their response is an indication of security failure.

State, local, and port resources are considered essential to this response, but as September11 and hurricane Katrina recoveries demonstrate, the federal government through Federal Emergency Management Agency (FEMA) and the military increasingly share the responsibility for response. A slow or inadequate response is unacceptable and politically risky, further showing that the federal financial burden of disaster will be huge if they fail to prevent terror.

6. Recovery from Terror

No doubt the further burden of terror events is the recovery of life, infrastructure, and economy. Removal of debris, rebuilding of facilities, roads, rails, and utilities are necessary for people to return and maritime economic activity to resume at this place. Additional capital must be provided to ensure health and survival and to compensate financial losses beyond the fault of the victims.

The most interesting challenge for our national leadership regarding the burden of response and recovery is that these likely costs could be avoided if all actors can commit to a prevention strategy and minimize the probability of successful terror.

RISK OF TERROR EVENTS

The comprehensive risk of the results of a successful terror event depends on a logical chain of probabilities. The general representation of this risk for the port and the nation is described by an adaptation of Yacov Haimes' description of the risk of terrorism (Haimes 2002).

Risk of Terror = Probability of a type of attack (threat) X
                   Probability of access to port (vulnerability) X
                   Consequences of this type of terror (impact)

The result of this calculation is the *expected impact of terror* at any port at any time. Such analysis tells us the likelihood of these losses and may cause us to act differently depending on this risk. That is, public and private actors may choose to neglect security investments if the probability of terrible outcomes appears small because the threat and/or the vulnerability is low. The absence of any significant terror to date at U.S. ports suggests an explanation of the present hesitancy to provide full barriers to terror.

Yet the lack of information to allow the determination of these probabilities and calculation of the ultimate risk certainly indicates we need a different strategy to be prudent and protect our citizens and economy. Concepts of decision theory state when the possible outcomes of random variables are known without their probabilities, this decision situation is uncertainty and not risk. Without prior probabilities available under risk, security investments cannot be compared to the future cost savings without terror. In essence, a calculation of the expected net payoff or benefit cost ratio for security initiatives v. response and recovery cost savings can not be determined (Price 2004, 335).

The implication of uncertainty is that some decision rule other than expected values based on prior probabilities must be used. The most commonly accepted decision rule in this situation is to avoid risk or take the action that will minimize the worst outcome. To do this, ports must realize a serious decrease in the probability of either the threat or the vulnerability; if not they must decrease the potential consequences of terror. Considering that the nation can not seriously decrease the threat immediately, the probability of vulnerability is a more desirable target for reduction by security initiatives. It is also desirable, but less likely, that ports will reduce the consequences by hardening facilities, equipment and ships, removing personnel, and keeping local populations away from port operations.

The goal of risk avoidance is therefore to create *full barriers* to vessels, terrorists, or materials so nothing will pass through the port or be used to destroy the harbor, port or community. Much of the following discussion will identify those barriers, question their effectiveness, and suggest who could be responsible for decreasing the risk.

FULL BARRIERS TO TERROR

A full barrier would obviously never allow a successful terror event; all attempts would be intercepted or prevented before cargo reached the United States or before it could do its damage in the port or elsewhere. Complete barriers must overcome the uncertainly of many conditions and is truly difficult to achieve. This challenge is so complex, but actions can be chosen to get as close as comprehensible. Again, if risk knowledge is weak, uncertainly demands we definitely close the gates, set barriers for which no weakness can be found. To achieve the barrier, every effort must be made to meet the following conditions:

1. No terrorist, bent on accessing the country, is able to enter via walking off the ship or moving inland via a cargo container or vehicle. Containers must be secure and security guards must be thorough. Yet it is so difficult to know if anyone has been or will be successful at such entry, so the closure of this barrier can not be completely assured.
2. All dangerous cargoes are kept from being loaded on exporting ships via arrangements with foreign ports and shipping companies who truly are trustworthy. The United States should not make such arrangements if there is any doubt that such ports and companies cannot be trusted, therefore requiring their cargoes to be fully inspected at destination.
3. Any cargo, containers in particular, must be confidently trusted, or must be screened with total assurance that no nuclear, biological, or chemical materials are allowed to do their damage at the port or pass through to destroy elsewhere. If there is sufficient doubt about the effectiveness of scanning devices, then an increased number of containers must be opened and inspected to ensure the barrier.
4. Security forces and surveillance equipment at the border or perimeter of the port, including water and land patrols must be able to detect and prevent attacks on the port assets via rockets, aircraft, or submarine/surface vessels. Creating barriers to ships and their cargo gets much attention, but anyone who can get in proximity to maritime terminals can launch a military type threat that is difficult for the port to fully prevent without the help of local law enforcement or military forces.

One challenge for every port is to build a model to determine the extent of protection or the extent to which they achieve full barriers to terror attempts. This would allow a more credible measurement of vulnerability, instead of using the number of security methods and technologies in place as suggested by DHS. The effectiveness of security initiatives should provide the same protection against terror consequences as that described by full barriers.

STRATEGIC PLANNING FOR SECURITY

Preparing a plan to decrease the risk of the consequences of terror is certainly a prudent management action by ports, whether they are coerced by government or not. Seaport actors should know the possible financial and human consequences of a successful terror event and publicly announce their strategy to minimize the likelihood that terror accomplishes their objective. The port and operator strategies may seek to get others to pay for the security investment or may inform the local constituents and private owners that they intent to take the risks, accepting the impacts and expecting response and recovery assistance from others. Does this hesitancy to accept responsibility for protection represent rational local public and private planning? Maybe in financial terms, but in human terms local employees and communities may have a different view.

Planning for security involves both physical and electronic barriers to people, human biometric IDs, personnel on patrol to survey, detect and apprehend as well as technology to identify nefarious items in maritime cargoes. These security initiatives or systems must pass several tests to be effective at creating barriers:

1. Technology and methods must be invented to ensure the potential terrorist means or avenues into the port are imagined and resisted.
2. Each technology or method must show near perfect effectiveness at preventing access, in terms of minimizing false positives and false negatives.
3. The ultimate vulnerability of security systems must be logically explained so that statements about barriers are defensible.
4. Investments must be forthcoming to satisfy the logical needs for these plans and implementation of the systems can not be delayed while risk continues.

In this brief history of seaport security from terror, the greatest battle is over which actor will pay for the necessary funding of security. Typically, the Federal Government finds it easy to mandate security initiatives, but without a corresponding and prompt federal payment. Commonly yelling "unfunded mandates," the locals always present the argument against federal demands without support. Kurt Nagle, president of the American Association of Port Authorities (AAPA), recently spoke about the underfunding of seaport security to the National Press Club (Nagle 2005):

> ...funding for seaport security in the federal budget proposed earlier this year (2005) was far below what U.S. public ports need for implementing new, federally-mandated seaport security programs

During this long debate as to responsibility, terror risks go on and some day all may be embarrassed and criticized loudly for letting terror at a seaport happen. Why be required to say, "we must not let this happen again," when we can prevent the event in the first case.

FEDERALISM AND SECURITY INVESTMENTS

Given the risk discussion above, it is clear the understanding of terror probabilities is weak at best. Absent a history of seaport terror and with the inability to accurately know terrorist plans, all actors in seaport operations should strive to imagine the means and sites terrorist might choose. After comprehensive *imagineering* and with a strategy for barriers, each public and private actor has to decide the type of security initiative they need. Then a decision is required on whether to develop and implement security infrastructure and technology in their own interest. It would be rational to pay for security yourself if it will sufficiently prevent actual losses later and reduce total life cycle costs. Yet, it is possible others will pay for prevention and detection initiatives and/or provide response and recovery reimbursement, changing each actor's decision calculus and providing fewer defenses for proceeding with security initiatives on their own.

All levels of government in the federalism structure as well as public, private, and joint enterprises are engaged in maritime commerce. So for seaports, security is not simple or obvious for it is not clear as to who is responsible for securing ports and protecting communities in proximity to the waterfront. Here is a model of these several actors with an indication of their potential responsibility for securing seaports from terror:

Government Levels	Potential Responsibility for Security Initiatives
1. Federal Government/ Homeland Security	• Conduct intelligence and develop policy on national security • Gather information and observe/inspect cargo movements • Invest in security research, provide grants to investigators • Conduct Coast Guard and Customs Service operations • Fund security initiatives at transportation terminals
2. State Government	• Support regional and statewide planning of security activities • Develop adjacent infrastructure to ease transportation security • Provide emergency responders, including National Guard forces • Invest in security initiatives for their own port facilities
3. Local/Regional Government	• Build and maintain infrastructure for seaports, with federal, state, or regional funding • Deliver law enforcement and other emergency services • Invest in support services to ports they own
Port Enterprises	• Potential Responsibilities for Security Initiatives
4. Public Port Authority	• Develop a security strategy and plans • Invest in security infrastructure and conduct security operations
5. Public-Private Partnership For Port Terminal	• Develop a joint strategy and share investment risk for security development and operation
6. Private Shipper/ Terminal Operator	• Develop strategic plans for terminal security • Provide security investments consistent with the plan • Conduct security operations and cooperate with DHS agencies

Each of these responsibilities is not separable by actor, for all may be involved in the same security response. Both federalism and the partnerships between public ports and private maritime businesses are now common. Reality suggests all actors behave in their self interest and are expected to pass these responsibilities and related financial obligations to any other actor who will take up the burden. Will these other actors be willing to invest in absence of or ahead of a significant seaport terror event? A U.S. Navy ship has been attacked in a foreign port, showing the cleverness of terrorists and the naiveté of those under attack. Prevention has no glory; heroes are only born with responses to terror.

What follows are predictions of the most likely scenario for each actor in this model. These scenarios are the author's expectations of behaviors surrounding seaport security. They become the bases for more research and represent preliminary recommendations for security managers.

Federal/Homeland Security Responsibilities

Terror is not created because of port or shipper behavior, its origin is certainly in international public policies. Therefore, some responsibility, if not the major responsibility, must rest with the U.S. government. Of course, the federal establishment has taken on many aspects of national security, particularly the search for and elimination of terrorists as well as the comprehensive research tasks to develop prevention and detection technology and methods. Yet terror events occur locally and human and physical assets of ports and commercial companies are at risk. Congress often clamors for funding from the DHS or other federal agencies because senators and representatives have been spoiled over the years with a national system of spending, partially because it satisfied a theory of federalism and partially because the pork barrel payoff was too good to resist.

No doubt confidence in the theory of federal funding is waning and local agencies will increasingly be required to find local innovations to finance infrastructure. These innovations include increased service fees, public-private partnerships and private contributions to public works that serve their own economic activity (Price 2001). While this federal government is not in the same budget position to provide state and local subsidies, the political pressure is massive. Federal agencies apparently will continue to provide limited funding below the demand from ports and their commercial partners.[1]

Federal politics may not know the actual risk and do not appear to be overly concerned. They are not anxious to spend all that is prudent; certainly they are not afraid of being embarrassed by successful terror with their slow pace of investment. This may be cynical, but they are either betting on the ports getting lucky or they are quite willing to wait for an event and reap the political payoff of their response. It may not be financially rational, but possibly politically sensible, for the federal government to avoid prevention, a position that may lose its acceptance given the Gulf Coast debacle. Proposals for the investment decision for each of the six actors are presented as a simple decision calculus or benefit cost result.

Federal Decision Calculus:

They face a positive benefit cost ratio since their expenditures on prevention and security barriers are surely less than their cost of response, recovery, economic losses, and political anger.

Federal agencies are providing support for security initiatives, but are not currently contributing the full share, risking terror events. With military demands and other needs, the national government has significant competition for its funds. In spite of the political payoff of seaport grants, the DHS and other agencies appears hesitant to provide the funds requested by the ports themselves. Do they believe the ports are being greedy or do they feel they have given enough and the remaining responsibility belongs to states and their local authorities?

State Responsibility

In this case state rights does not imply the national government should stay out of the game of security, in fact most states are in some degree of financial stress and would not, at this time, begin to argue they are financially responsible for seaport security. In this country, several states are the port authority in their region and should be more directly concerned with security. In fact, some states provide substantial subsidy to port operations and are acting like investors, seeking an economic return to their region.[2]

Terror events would cost states severely in terms of infrastructure and human loss, for they will contribute to response and rebuilding. Even this reality will not help states put security initiatives in place; they prefer to or need to push such responsibility up to federal agencies or down to commercial operators at ports. Yet state assets are at risk for those more directly involved with their seaports.

State Decision Calculus:

While several states own ports and may reap in their revenues, their share of response and recovery is smaller. They are not big investors in terror prevention; spoiled by the Federal Government largesse and port operators' ability to pay. Their benefit cost ratio is less than one.

Local or Regional Government Responsibilities

Local and regional public agencies are certainly at the site of port operations and their neighborhoods will be damaged the most. While they often own port authorities and appoint commissioners, cities or regional governments do not often integrate port finances with their own. No doubt they hunger to take some port "profit" in addition to the fees and overhead payments they often charge port operations. As a more distant owner, sometimes even a silent player, local communities can not afford and do not seek to take on the security burden of their ports. Yet should they be so silent about terror events that will disrupt their regional economy, demand local first responders and require local support for recovery and rebuilding?

Of course, the probability of an attempt and/or success of such events still will not cause local entities to take financial risks, for they expect prevention and recovery help from others. They still should support strong local emergency planning and preparation as the Gulf Coast's recent hurricane event surely demonstrates. Such planning is an opportunity to enhance security and ease response that local agencies should not avoid. These costs do not include the task of ship/cargo screening and inspection as well as security of the port boundaries (borders). Security initiatives to reduce the risk of terror events are more appropriately the responsibility of the nation and those conducting business at the waterfront.

Local Decision Calculus:

The local benefit cost ratio is less than one because they do not reap large cost avoidance since these governments are not obligated to the big costs of terror, emergency response and reimbursement for losses in the economy.

Port Authority Responsibilities

In the United States, most ports are political subdivisions or authorities of the local or regional entity. They operate to a very large extent as public enterprises and are expected to survive and prosper without subsidy (Price 1981). Their local partners, shipping companies, and terminal operators are surely not expecting large subsidies from the public sector, but they do expect the port enterprise to protect port assets and make investments consistent with the return they get from service fees and revenue sharing.

Seaports receive much less funding for their own development, let alone security, than airports. This situation is supported by the reality that seaports are able to raise the revenues necessary due to the large economic activity associated with substantial cargo movements. In effect, seaports are a more viable financial entity than many airports, with the biggest ports clearly producing positive net revenues in more significant amounts. Otherwise the sea side should receive more Federal funding than they do at this time. There is little disagreement that airports have received the bulk of security funding to date, no doubt because massive populations are present and they have historically been the target of terrorists. Are terrorists so clever that they will surprise us with attacks on new infrastructure as they did with Spanish trains and English subways and buses?

Yet, while these ports are public enterprises and accumulate net revenues from their operations, their constituents may not be risk takers. This public does not want to put up the capital (taxes) to seek a return. Ports normally raise capital by retained earnings and they too are hesitant to take excessive risk and would need funds other than earnings in the event of financial failure. Instead, they share or pass this risk entirely on to private tenants.

Ports are caught between big government and private risk takers. If federal or state governments do not invest in security, ports will want to shift the burden to the private sector. Most likely, the port will share some of the investment risk for security, particularly for assets which they control, those not built or owned by their tenants. It is not certain that seaports will be willing or able to finance security initiatives without grants from federal agencies, choosing not to make the investments in absence of subsidy. They resist recouping this investment with higher user fees since this may drive some operators to other ports, resulting in inadequate security investment.

Port Decision Calculus:

Any port will resist investments, letting either the Federal agency or the shipper/operators commit to security. For them the benefit cost ratio is likely less than one without passing investment costs to users. If no one else steps up, these local actors will accept the risk.

Partnership Shared Responsibilities

Most seaport developments and delivery of cargo services are joint ventures between public ports, private investors, and maritime operators. Some shipping companies with ocean vessels make an arrangement with the port to have dockside space available solely for their shipping line. They want the space open whenever their ships arrive since queuing or delay in the harbor is very costly. They err on the side of excess capacity that they pay for by capital investments and/or fees to the seaport.

Terminal operators may be separate companies whose expertise is cargo transfer and they too may engage in partnerships with the port authority to develop and conduct operations. If a private company invests in infrastructure and uses their own equipment to handle cargo and to make intermodal freight transfers, it is their responsibility to protect their assets with security measures. If we knew more about the risk of terror and their demand sensitivity to price, it may be financially rational for private operators to invest in security measures. Private operators are probably willing to take the risk.

Partnerships are intended to make it more feasible for both parties to participate (i.e., to invest). Ports take some risk but rely on service fees to recover their capital and shippers/operators recover their investment with shipment charges.

Partnership Decision Calculus:

Partnerships should create the ability for both partners to realize a benefit cost ratio above one, allowing local security barriers without Federal help. Fees will rise without harming the commercial viability of any supply chain member, particularly without the burden of response and recovery.

Shipper/Terminal Operator Responsibilities

The shipping terminal is the point where the cargo enters the United States, where the entry of people or hazardous cargo occurs, and where destruction of facilities will harm workers and those in proximity to terminal operations and certainly disrupt economic activity and community life. Much of the damage and disruption is felt by these private companies. It is rational to insure their assets, operations and revenues against terror by paying for security barriers and screening as well as buying traditional insurance.

The private sector is in business to take risks, so insurance providers may well make them produce the barriers as a condition of insurance. The economic burden is the cost of doing business and such methods of insurance should save private companies from financial distress in the event of a terror attack.

Of course, any business is sensible if they shift the financial investment to the port authority, possibly in the partnership agreement, and/or to other governments. Again, they can argue that private business operations have not stimulated terror, albeit they do provide a fairly rich target. When does the burden stay with port operators or when does it shift to governments? Even if it is perceived as rational by the private entity to invest in port security, it is still perceived by the public that this is a federal responsibility. If the national actors are hesitant or slow to provide the security resources demanded by the ports or the government's policy, can the private sector proceed on their own to implement security barriers or will they wait for federal or state payment?

Private Decision Calculus:

Terminal operators will not pay for security investments themselves, relying on contributions from the port or other governments. Without investing in security, private companies assume the risk of terror attacks, but their benefit cost ratio is less than one because they too do not assume the full cost of response and recovery.

TECHNOLOGY'S OPPORTUNITY TO SECURE PORTS

There are "low tech" approaches to enhancing security that can work in tandem with sophisticated "high tech" methods so that both complement each other. For gathering intelligence with people on the ground, talking personally to key members of the supply chain, placing human security patrols about the landside, riding boats in the harbor, boarding ships, manually inspecting cargo and demonstrating a leadership presence is a necessary complement to technology.

Yet, many would argue that the big security gains will only come from productive, responsive, and effective "high tech" solutions. In many cases accomplishing tasks with technology may be the only viable alternative because of the remarkable functionality and productivity associated with technology. At the same time, reliability, cost, and flexibility are weaknesses that diminish the value of technology and must be overcome by the payoffs demonstrated by an advancing security industry.

For this author, technology is divided in to two categories. *Automation technology* replaces human motion and allows speed and consistency. *Information technology* replaces paper records and ensures accuracy and access. Both may be needed at any work station, but automation is often a second choice because of the omnipresent information technology. The goal of automation is to reduce the numbers of workers, avoiding the challenges of employment. Yet automation requires more sophisticated development and is more capital intensive to accomplish the same task. Variable cost savings must recover the large fixed costs and not be diminished by downtime, maintenance, or complexity.

Technology is not only popular because of creative solutions, but also because the industry has been able to be more effective and productive over time. If ports are hesitant to use technology now because of cost or ineffectiveness, its value will become more convincing and its price will decline with time and volume produced. Waiting to create barriers does continue the danger.

Following the security life cycle, a spectrum of technologies is introduced, explaining their functionality. While defensible, particularly when someone else is paying, seaport security technology is in an early development stage and its cost and effectiveness are still suspect. For the moment, it is desirable for ports to be part of initial experiments with technology since we can imagine the terrorists are scheming as the door remains open. Terrorists appear more aware and clever than our political will to create barriers.

1. Shippers and Cargo Data Bases

An international information system, administered by DHS, receives and digests massive data on each cargo movement and container. Origins, contents, shipper/handlers and destinations are analyzed to predict those movements that require more extensive screening at their origin or destination. The effectiveness of this stage totally depends on the reliability of the input data and the federal security system's ability to correctly select "suspicious" cargo. Valid analysis is crucial to accurately reducing the need for extensive inspection of containers at U.S. ports.

Selecting suspicious cargo is based on the expectation that U.S. and foreign ports develop strategies and actions that reduce their vulnerability to terror under CSI guidance. C-TPAT pursues security achievements of supply chain actors, including importers, brokers, sea and rail carriers and seaport terminal operators (Price 2004, 337–338). C-TPAT establishes "trusted shippers" who prevent terrorists and dangerous cargo from entering the supply chain and U.S. ports. These are data heavy initiatives, requiring accurate information technology and rapid telecommunication to all who need to know.

2. Border Barriers

Physical or technical and human barriers at the harbor's edge and on the port's perimeter are essential. These include fences, secure portals or gates, and detection equipment in the harbor and at the perimeter are intended to close off access to terrorists while letting necessary cargo movements occur. Some human observers and inspectors complement automatic technology of motion detectors, cameras and biometric ID systems at entrance points to increase total effectiveness. Coast Guard vessels, security patrols, and cargo inspections by humans will be necessary until automatic patrol and detection technology are very effective. Once high technology systems suggest a violation of the barrier, human investigation, inspection, and apprehension are required.

3. Smart Buoys

Smart Buoys at harbor entrances are being tested to passively scan ships to detect nuclear radiation. This technology was developed at Lawrence Livermore National Laboratory (LLNL). An article in their journal, *Science and Technology Review,* offers this testimonial (Heller 2004):

...buoys outfitted with commercially available radiation detectors could... play an important role by warning of the presence of nuclear materials in maritime environments...[Designed to] protect military bases...if the new detection devices are successful, they could also be installed in civilian areas such as busy ports.

Once radiation is detected, further screening and human inspection are necessary to apprehend and dispose of the material or turn the vessel around. Effectiveness of smart buoys remains to be determined. A passive scan at that distance from the material seems uncertain.

4. Container Security

Two devices provide another layer of security for container cargo. First, radio frequency identification (RFID) chips can be installed in each container to ensure the container location is constantly known and can be communicated to all who want to know the status of cargo movements. Further, selected container movements can be anticipated as they approach U.S. ports (Greenemeier 2004).

Second, access to containers must be controlled to ensure cargo is trusted. Smart e-seals can ensure containers have not been "tampered with while en route" and these seals can track information on the history of the container and its contents. (McCrea 2004) These technologies intend to increase the reliability of trusted movements and enhance the selection of suspicious cargo.

5. Cargo Scanning

Specific screening of any cargo or container is the most significant issue facing DHS and ports. The federal government has chosen a security strategy that selects certain cargo for further review, based on information channels and software credibility. This is a different strategy from using technology to scan all containers. The distinction is remarkable and demonstrated so well by the Hong Kong system currently being tested (Figure 29.3), with the encouragement of the United States. Ortolani and Block (2005) presented a description of the alternative technologies and arguments for each strategy:

Using scanning machines supplied by Science Applications International Corporation of San Diego, Hong Kong's method sends all containers on their chasses through three scans:

1. Gamma Ray scan looks at images and densities of content and identifies suspicious objects;

2. Optical character scan compares this container with data base on suspect shippers;

3. Radiation scan for emissions from nuclear material that can be withdrawn from the supply chain (with care).

The comparative effectiveness of these two strategies is still to be tested (Ortolani and Block 2005):

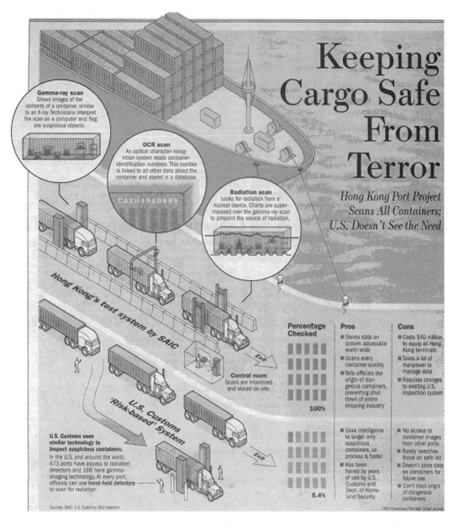

FIGURE 29.3

...the effectiveness of the systems has been called into question...suggesting that random inspections of ships are better at uncovering smuggling activities than Automatic Targeting System (ATS, or the current U.S. screening strategy).

Screening all containers seems preferable, especially if the scanning technology is highly effective. But the effectiveness of these new scanning technologies requires more testing as suggested by LLNL. A researcher at the Lab commented (Slaughter 2005):

Testing at the DHS test site is the best place to determine how well any of these technologies work...We are preparing to build a prototype field system to be evaluated in a realistic cargo setting at the DHS test facility in Nevada...A variety of technologies will be tested there including ours.

Until effectiveness is well understood, DHS or ports are not likely to shift to the multiple scan process in Hong Kong. The lack of knowledge about technology performance definitely encumbers investment decisions.

6. Securing Other WMDs

Besides nuclear devices, chemical and biological threats are another matter. If these weapons of mass destruction are desirable and easier choices for terrorists, as seen in prior attacks, then technologies must be developed to detect these threats. Invasive Technologies is a company that has developed an explosive detection system "intended to be a full-fledged supplier for seaports" (Pimentel 2002).

There is much less conversation about securing ports from weapons other than nuclear materials. If alternative chemical and biological weapons are more likely to enter the country, effective detection technologies must be available without the technology requiring cargo delays while minimizing human inspection.

Hand held devices chosen to provide an additional screen for maritime cargo for radiation and pathogens have been demonstrated at LLNL (Brewer 2005; Rennie 2003). They require a human to conduct the test, but provide the flexibility often required by security needs. They certainly are cheaper, but as hand held equipment demand human presence and provide limited functionality.

All scans, be they passive or active, will always require further manual inspection. Containers detected with questionable materials must be opened by inspectors or denied entrance and returned to sea. Such human screening does create risks for inspectors, so robotic equipment can be used to provide additional safety for security workers. Additionally, these materials must remain contained to protect the port and the community. Technology will undoubtedly get more effective and take more of the burden off humans. Whether technology will make ports more secure by decreasing the risk of terror success remains unanswered.

RESEARCH HYPOTHESES FOR FURTHER STUDY

After completing the research and interviews for this chapter, there is no doubt that several questions remain unaddressed. An extensive and specific study of terror vulnerability at any one port, as described above, has not been pursued here or discovered in the work of others. Of course, a comprehensive and analytical security plan by each port could provide some answers. Such a case study would not only provide some clarity to the port but also offer a model for others to pursue, assuming the demonstration port is unwilling to accept the risk of terror. Researchers and consultants identified with this research are listed later in the chapter.[3]

Based on this research experience, including interviews with port practitioners, the following hypotheses are offered for subsequent study. These proposals are predictions of the most likely behaviors, even if some hypotheses postulate outcomes not consistent with security from terror. Rejecting those outcomes provides useful information and makes the desirable result more likely.

Hypothesis 1: Increases in security or decreases in vulnerability relate inversely to cargo productivity

The suggestion is that any barriers, screening, or inspection will decrease throughput rates and impose additional time and cost burdens on the port and private operators (Price 2004, 341). Technology and screening methods can be designed to reduce delay, since very little negative impacts on cargo movements will be tolerated by shippers. This may mean that ports and their tenants are not willing to accept security initiatives that impede cargo movements and, therefore, are willing to accept higher risk to ensure cargo productivity.

Hypothesis 2: Given an unknown threat risk, ports and private operators will not invest in security

Making an argument that security from terror is a federal responsibility, local actors wait for financial aid from governments. Rather than accepting the absence of such support as serious risk for their assets; taking financial responsibility themselves will not be considered prudent or necessary to keep the enterprise from failure. Insurance policies may minimize the risk or the actual risk of terror may be considered overblown. Private businesses are risk takers, maybe public ports are not. Yet ports do not seem anxious to invest in security even with the slow response to prevention by federal or state agencies.

Hypothesis 3: Screening cargo with technology will not provide a full barrier to terror

The effectiveness of scanning and detection technology surely needs a meaningful test to determine is value in creating security barriers. Some percentage of false positives and false negatives are expected or demonstrated in early design testing. Most technical systems and tests present some degree of error given the several random variables that may be involved. What level of accuracy is possible to achieve; how close to perfect barriers will cargo screening technology deliver?

Hypothesis 4: Federal funding of port security will never be complete, demanding local contributions

Rather than just being slow to fund port security, the federal government will eventually expect state and local governments as well as ports and their shippers to pay some share of investments in prevention. The expected distribution of responsibility could involve as much as 50 percent federal share and the remaining 50 percent split among public and private local entities. This does not mean that federal agencies will apply the same theory for response and recovery. For seaports, the Gulf Coast disaster demonstrates how much the citizenry will demand a near complete federal bailout of local infrastructure, business, and individuals. The deep pockets of ports and private business may alter those politics, but big business got help after September 11 and may get benefits on the Gulf.

Hypothesis 5: Ports will resist paying for security, choosing not to pass on these costs with higher fees

Seaports, while conducted as public enterprises, will not get political support from their constituencies to absorb security investments and risk their financial viability. They fear increasing fees for their tenants because these operators do have option at other ports. While all U.S. ports are faced with the same dilemma, they do complete with foreign ports that may not have the same danger with terrorism. For instance, Mexican ports could receive cargo from the Pacific and land bridge to the Gulf or distribute cargo throughout the United States, thereby competing with the ports of Southern California.[4] Ports are always willing to claim high security investment needs as long as the expectation is that federal agencies will pay. How will they view the terror threat if no subsidy is forthcoming? Local obligations to pay for security will surely change the competitive strength of seaports and impact the cost of the supply chain for all of us. What a trap for our national government, either their budget or the economy loses.

CONCLUDING SECURITY FROM TERROR

It seems appropriate to speak to the status of seaport security or conclude how close ports are to being secure. There appears to be general apathy, or at least a hesitancy, to complete the security challenge. The causes of this hesitancy probably include the lack of knowledge about the threat and an inability to understand the relationship between investment and vulnerability. This surely makes it more difficult for all actors to commit. Given the cost of technology, more certainty is needed to make it financially obvious to invest. Since technology is in an early stage of development, its performance must be assured to justify usage. There is plenty to observe in the near term, for both the ports and the public to know.

Further, the perception is that the risk is less for seaports than other targets since they have not been seriously attacked to date. While there is much political talk about port vulnerability, this debate does not seem to move anyone to action. The theory of full prevention is not how yet ports are winning the terrorism war, although the current attempts at detection may be intimidating terror attempts. Current investments appear sufficient as long a significant terror event does not occur.

In reality, no one wants to accept the burden to pay for security, even the federal establishment. Everyone may be bluffing hoping to entice others will pay, although the expected losses could eventually make local governments more willing to engage security investment. The eventual cost of sharing the burden is surely worth watching.

A favorite question of this author is whether screening technologies and methods will impact cargo productivity to the extent that it will cause ports to avoid security. The evidence uncovered is that no technology can be developed that delays cargo to any significant extent. It may cost more to develop rapid screening and inspection, but surely it is the only solution that will be accepted. The United States suffers from a competitive disadvantage in cargo efficiency and does not need another impediment to productivity improvement.

Some expect it is seaports' turn to receive an attack, possibly because of the richness of the targets, but mostly because not enough supply chain actors are troubled if ports are chosen by terrorists. With so much political and press attention to port vulnerability, are terrorists discouraged from pursuing ports or do they see ports as an easier target?

On the fourth anniversary of the September11 events, Sandalow (2005) presented arguments on disasters and federal responses, examining both the September 11 terror events and Gulf Coast natural event. Director of Foreign Policy Studies at the Brooking Institution, James Steinberg, argued:

> …we really need to put more resources on prevention…No matter how well we plan, you can't plan for everything. The big lesson is that there are limits to our response.

Richard Falkenrath, former homeland security advisor to the White House, suggests:

> Our country is not so ready to respond to the 'uber-disasters' as we'd like to be, four years after 9/11.

For seaports *first preventers* are more valuable than *first responders*, especially if this nation wants to avoid the trauma of addressing the victims of disaster.

NOTES

1. As this chapter goes to print, the Congress has passed and the President has signed the Security and Accountability for Every (SAFE) Port Act of 2006 (HF4954). This statute does provide new funding for port security, but still does not assume the full financial burden that the Feds and the ports have identified. Increased tests of security technology are proposed at both overseas and U.S. port facilities. Time will determine whether seaport security is enhanced by this legislation.
2. Some examples of state ports include Oregon, Massachusetts, Maryland and the bi-state compact for the Port of New York and New Jersey.
3. The following individuals should be contacted by scholars or practitioners who are pursuing the topic of seaport security:
   Steven Flynn: Security Consultant, Council of Foreign Affairs and author of the book, *America the Vulnerable*.

Michael Nacht: Dean of the Goldman School of Public Policy, University of California, Berkeley.

Dennis Slaughter: Researcher, Lawrence Livermore National Laboratory.

David Waters: Product Manager, Transportation Security, Science Applications International Cooperation, San Diego, California.

Lawrence Wein: Professor of Management Science, Stanford University.

4. The author is beginning a study with Universidad Anahuac Xalapa in Mexico to conduct joint investigations about supply chain operations between Mexico and the United States. One study will examine maritime cargo "land bridging" across the Mexican peninsula from the west coast to the east coast. Terror risk and security obligations will be contrasted between the two nations' seaports.

REFERENCES

Brewer, Rick, "Homeland Chief Praises Lab's Effort," *The Record*, July 28, 2005, pp. A1 and A9.

Greenemeier, Larry, "Step Up in Security: Inroads Have Been Made in Securing the Nation's Seaports, but More Work Needs To Be Done," *Information Week*, Issue 1011, October 25, 2004, pp. 53–56.

Haimes, Yacov, "Risk of Terrorism to Cyber-Physical and Organizational-Societal Infrastructures," *Public Works Management and Policy*, Vol. 6, no. 4, April 2002, pp. 231–240.

Heller, Arnie, "Smart Buoys Help Protect Submarine Base," *Science and Technology Review*, January/February, 2004, pp. 19–22.

McCrea, Bridget, "Total Tracking and Visibility Star in Port Security," *Logistics Management*, Vol. 43, Issue 3, pp. S69–S74.

Nagle, Kurt, President, *Security*, Vol. 42, Issue 4, April 2005, p. 10.

Ortolani and Block, "Keeping Cargo Safe from Terror," *Wall Street Journal*, July 29, 2005, pp. B1–B2.

Pimentel, Benjamin, "What's Next in Security Technology: Government Seeks New Ways to Protect Transportation System," *San Francisco Chronicle*, September 5, 2002, pp. E1–E3.

Price, Willard, "Reducing the Risk of Terror Events at Seaports," *Review of Policy Research*, Vol. 21, No. 3, 2004.

Price, Willard, "An Odyssey of Privatizing Highways: The Evolving Case of SR 91," *Public Works Management and Policy*, Vol. 5, No. 4, April 2001.

Price, Willard, "Seaports as Public Enterprise: Some Policy Implications," in Hoole, Friedheim, and Hennesey, eds., *Making Ocean Policy: The Politics of Government Organization and Management*, Boulder, CO: Westview Press, 1981.

Rennie, Gabriele, "Portable Radiation Detector Provided Laboratory Scale Precision in the Field," *Science and Technology Review*, September 2003, pp. 24–26.

Sandalow, Marc, "The Quest for National Security," *San Francisco Chronicle*, September 11, 2005, pp. A1 and A15.

Slaughter, Dennis, e-mail communication with the author, August 29, 2005.

30 The Evolving Role of the Department of Defense in Homeland and Transportation Security

Kurt A. Heppard and Steve G. Green

INTRODUCTION

> FAA: Hi. Boston Center TMU (Traffic Management Unit), we have a problem here. We have a hijacked aircraft headed towards New York, and we need you guys to, we need someone to scramble some F-16s or something up there, help us out.
>
> Boston Center TMU: Is this real-world or exercise?
>
> FAA: No, this is not an exercise, not a test.

With this simple chilling exchange between Federal Aviation Administration (FAA) air traffic controllers in Boston and the North American Aerospace Defense Command's (NORAD) Northeast American Defense Sector in Rome, New York, a new era in Department of Defense (DOD) involvement in Homeland and Transportation Security was born (*The 9/11 Commission Report* 2004, p. 20). While most Americans probably assume that the DOD will be available during a homeland crisis, in all likelihood few understand the complexities of military involvement at the local level, or the evolving role of the DOD's capabilities in Homeland and Transportation Security.

Perhaps this expectation that the full capabilities of the federal government, including the DOD, would be available when and where they are needed was best expressed by New Orleans Mayor Ray Nagin. On September 2, 2005, in an interview with a local radio station after Hurricane Katrina devastated the region, Mayor Nagin declared (CNN 2005):

> Don't tell me 40,000 people are coming here. They're not here. It's too doggone late. Now get off your asses and do something, and let's fix the biggest goddamn crisis in the history of this country.

Like most Americans, Mayor Nagin could not comprehend how the vast resources and capabilities of the federal government were not immediately mobilized to address a national crisis on the order of magnitude that his city had experienced. In this brief emotional exchange, Mayor Nagin captured the essence of responding to any emergency, whether it be natural or man-made (i.e., terrorist attacks). The questions that will stoke the fires of future policy debates for years to come will most likely involve the dual elements of determining what capabilities are required, and then determining how to get these capabilities to where they are needed as quickly as possible.

This chapter examines evolving DOD capabilities and responsibilities vis-à-vis Homeland and Transportation Security. In many respects, the DOD has a unique set of qualifications and capabilities that are typically needed in just about any type of crisis situation. For example, the DOD is one of the few organizations that possess the intelligence systems, command and control structures, communication capabilities, and sheer manpower required to predict, prevent, and respond to real and potential disruptions in Homeland and Transportation Security.

In several recent national-level crises, there has been an unprecedented amount of direct DOD involvement. But this level of interaction is not commonplace for the DOD. In fact, not only policy, but public law allows only minimal military involvement at the state level and only in exceptional cases (Washington University 1997). But, when local capabilities are overwhelmed, which was the case with Hurricane Katrina, for example, federal help including DOD involvement was not only requested, but demanded by local authorities. The traditional reluctance to have federal troops react to local crisis situations also seems to be mitigated somewhat by their successful engagement. There is every indication that the magnitude of major natural disasters and an ever-present dynamic terrorist threat will only encourage future DOD involvement in crisis situations. Mayor Nagin provided an excellent example of a local authority embracing DOD involvement during his crisis (CNN 2005):

Now, I will tell you this—and I give the president some credit on this—he sent one John Wayne dude down here that can get some stuff done, and his name is [Lt.] Gen. [Russel] Honore. And he came off the doggone chopper, and he started cussing and people started moving. And he's getting some stuff done. They ought to give that guy—if they don't want to give it to me, give him full authority to get the job done, and we can save some people.

This chapter also discusses this evolving role of DOD capabilities, in the context of Homeland and Transportation Security, by examining the primary capabilities that are expected to be utilized, and how these evolving capabilities are executed in the context of the DOD's operational structure. By presenting several examples of operations that have utilized DOD capabilities, and by discussing the existing limitations imposed by the *Posse Comitatus* Act of 1878, the Homeland and Transportation Security landscape is described. Potential implications for Homeland and Transportation Security are discussed and conclusions are provided.

EVOLVING DOD CAPABILITIES

Immediately following the attacks of September 11, President Bush and Congress responded to protect the nation. President Bush issued Executive Order 13228 establishing the cabinet-level Department of Homeland Security (DHS) and signed into law the USA Patriot Act (Public Law 107-56), which enhanced law enforcement agencies' ability to fight terrorism (GAO-03-260 2002, p. 9). Soon after, the Congress enacted the Transportation Security Act (Public Law 107-56), which created the Transportation Security Administration (TSA) (GAO-03-260 2002, p. 9). The creation of the DHS empowered a single cabinet official whose primary mission is to protect the American homeland from terrorism by preventing terrorist attacks within the United States, reducing the nation's vulnerability to terrorism, and minimizing the damage and recovery from attacks that do occur (Ridge 2002).

Following the enactment of these laws, there has been an increased emphasis on Homeland and Transportation Security that has resulted in many federal agencies reallocating equipment and personnel from their traditional missions. For example, U.S. Coast Guard cutters and aircraft that were mainly used to patrol the high seas off the nation's coasts, were relocated closer to major harbors to guard potential terrorist targets such as oil refineries and port facilities, and the National Guard mobilized approximately 7,200 guardsmen to protect travelers at 444 commercial airports nationwide (GAO-03-260 2002, p. 15). This type of unprecedented interactions between federal agencies and local authorities in response to the new expanded limits of the law, often blurred the distinction between the two authorities.

The role of the U.S. Army in homeland defense has also been thoroughly studied. In the context of Homeland and Transportation Security specifically, a study by the Rand Corporation discusses several capabilities that will be critical in response to unpredictable terror threats. The Army's capabilities fall into several general categories. However, the primary capability provided by the Army is modular ground forces and medical teams that can be tailored to specific environmental conditions and constraints. The Army has a large pool of trained and organized "labor" that can be deployed in response to a myriad of Homeland and Transportation Security threats (Davis 2004).

More specialized capabilities include chemical, biological, radiological, nuclear, or high explosive (CBRNE) detection, defense, and mitigation. This capability to respond rapidly to CBRNE threats to Homeland and Transportation Security clearly must be carefully integrated with response from civil authorities. An illustration of this is the deployment of military personnel in Operation Noble Eagle discussed later in this chapter. In Operation Noble Eagle, Army personnel were deployed to help guard and maintain security at airports, tunnels, and rail stations, Navy and Coast Guard seamen provided seaport defense, and Air Force pilots patrolled the skies.

The role of the U.S. Navy and the importance of its capabilities in securing American transportation systems is often underestimated. However, when policy makers confront the fact that more than 95 percent of overseas trade enters the United States through its 361 seaports and that over 9 million shipping containers enter the nation each year across 26,000 miles of commercially navigable waterways, the importance of Navy capabilities becomes evident (Sherman 2005). However, the Navy has seldom found its primary mission in homeland harbor and seaport defense (Swartz 2003).

As the Navy works with other agencies in Homeland and Transportation Security, such as the Coast Guard, to develop maritime transportation security, several capabilities emerge as most critical. These capabilities include seaborne intelligence, identification, tracking, and intercepting threats to Homeland and Transportation Security. The overall collaborative effort between the Navy, Coast Guard, and other security entities has been called "maritime domain awareness." This emerging capability means getting the right information to the appropriate place in sufficient time to stop the terrorists before they threaten transportation security.

Recent proposals have been made to create what is being called a "Maritime NORAD" (Matthews 2005). These proposals seek to secure ports and transportation infrastructure with an organization that focuses on detection and the interception of threats before they reach the United States. The model for this organization would be NORAD which currently monitors the air space over the United States and Canada. The proposed organization would enlarge the role of the Navy and the Coast Guard in a layered defense of North American ports. The idea has been submitted to the Quadrennial Defense Review (QDR) for analysis and consideration (Matthews 2005).

CAPABILITIES-BASED ORIENTATION

While the DOD has a long history of providing assistance and support to state, local, and other federal agencies in times of national emergencies, utilization has not necessarily been strategically applied based on a current assessment of capabilities available. They appear to be more reactionary and *ad hoc* at best. But over the years, agencies within the DOD have developed or acquired significant capabilities that are now considered homeland defense related. As threats to Homeland and Transportation Security have evolved since September 11, some of these capabilities have become critically important to national security. For example, the almost unthinkable threats of the use of CBRNE weapons have accelerated DOD involvement in supporting civil authorities in Homeland and Transportation Security (BAST 2003).

It is also obvious that DOD capabilities in intelligence and communication have, and will continue, to be of critical important during any major crisis. Some authors advocate the utilization of DOD capabilities so strongly, in terms of both public sector effectiveness and efficiency in response to terror threats, that they see this military support and cooperation with Homeland and Transportation Security as imperative (Johnston 2004).

DOD capabilities such as those associated with response to potential terror threats can be considered essentially "strategic asset stocks" that have developed over many years (Dierickx and Cool 1989). These Homeland and Transportation Security related DOD capabilities can be thought of in terms of the bathtub metaphor used by strategic management theorists to explain long term competitive advantage of particular firms. The organization, like a bathtub, collects a wide range of strategic assets and capabilities over the years. These assets and capabilities are typically developed slowly, like the flow of water into a tub.

This metaphor is also helpful in considering how Homeland and Transportation Security officials can tap into existing capabilities in order to counter the emerging and, to a large extent, unpredictable threats to transportation security in general. As Homeland and Transportation Security officials plan for possible terrorist attacks, it is logical that they would adopt a capabilities-based mindset in developing concepts of operations and to enhance responses to emerging threats.

Capabilities-based planning is an approach to resource allocation and planning that focuses on developing or acquiring capabilities that support the overall mission of an agency and its performance outcomes. This approach differs from a threat-based approach which allocates resources and develops plans based on specific threats in the external environment. Secretary of Defense Donald Rumsfeld, in his February 2004 testimony to the House Armed Services Committee, explained the new planning approach:

> We have moved from a "threat-based" to a "capabilities-based" approach to defense planning, focusing not only on who might threaten us, or where, or when—but more on how we might be threatened, and what portfolio of capabilities we will need to deter and defend against those new threats.

In an attempt to determine which capabilities could be leveraged, an extensive survey of capabilities related to Homeland and Transportation Security as well as civil support has been conducted. The survey found that these capabilities include; command and control, search and rescue, crisis and deliberate planning, fire-fighting assistance, rapid, flexible airlift, security-police assistance, intelligence, surveillance, and reconnaissance, crowd control, computer network defense, decontamination, medical operations, explosive ordnance disposal (EOD) teams, engineering support, and mortuary affairs (Rinaldi 2002).

IMPLEMENTING CAPABILITIES: THE ROLE OF NORTHERN COMMAND (USNORTHCOM)

By any measure, a large national investment in critical capabilities related to Homeland and Transportation Security has been made within the framework of national defense. However, the DOD deploys its capabilities and "goes to war" in unified commands. There are five geographically focused commands (Southern Command, Pacific Command, European Command, Central Command, and Pacific Command) and four non-geographically oriented unified commands (Strategic Command, Joint Forces Command, Special Operations Command, and Transportation Command).

For example, most Americans are familiar with ongoing U.S. operations in Iraq. While most people can see the DOD capabilities in action, they are not aware of how the capabilities are executed and how forces are commanded. In the case of Iraq, DOD capabilities are executed by Central Command and its Combatant Commander. This geographically focused unified or warfighting command is charged with the actual command and control of U.S. forces in the region. While each of the military services organizes, trains, and equips forces related to its mission, the National Command

Authority (NCA) exercises control and deployment of these forces through unified or geographically oriented commands. In other words, if the DOD is involved in any activity that includes other federal agencies, the DOD needs to utilize its command structure.

For this reason, following September 11, it became clear that an additional unified command dedicated to commanding, controlling, and executing DOD capabilities in North America was needed. Therefore, to enable the DOD to effectively deploy this cumulative investment and resulting capabilities toward the goals of homeland and transportation security, structural change was needed. U.S. Northern Command (USNORTHCOM), the newest unified command in the DOD was formed. This change has been characterized as the most significant reform of the nation's military command structure since the first command plan was issued shortly after World War II (GAO-03-260 2002, p.12). However time and again, history has provided us with examples of skepticism related to the benefits of major organizational change (Reese and Pohlman 2005):

> We trained hard ... but it seemed that every time we were beginning to form up into teams we would be reorganized. I was to learn later in life that we tend to meet any new situation by reorganizing; and a wonderful method it can be for creating the illusion of progress while producing confusion, inefficiency, and demoralization. (Petronius Arbiter, ca. 210 B.C.)

But the benefits of the structural change associated with the creation of USNORTH-COM was not an illusion. The formation of this unified command is important in the context of Homeland and Transportation Security because the DOD executes or utilizes its capabilities through these unified "combatant" commands.

While individual armed forces develop capabilities through service specific or joint acquisition and training programs, the capabilities are used or deployed by the unified commands. Secretary Rumsfeld summarized the formation for the new unified command (USNORTHCOM 2005):

> The creation of USNORTHCOM means that we now have a command assigned to defend the American people where they live and work... US-NORTHCOM complements the other nine regional and functional commands dedicated to defending the United States and our interests abroad, as well as our allies and friends.

The creation of this command and a new orientation toward Homeland and Transportation Security provides an example of the national adjustments from "efficiency to effectiveness" described by Johnston (2004, p. 269). Given that the DOD has high levels of capability related to potential threats to transportation security, the deployment of these capabilities through USNORTHCOM is primarily focused on effective response to emerging threats rather than market or fiscal efficiencies (Johnston 2004).

USNORTHCOM was formally established in April 2002 and has a relatively small number of personnel permanently assigned to it. There are approximately twelve hundred civil servants and active duty members from all of the armed forces currently on staff at Peterson Air Force Base in Colorado Springs, Colorado (USNORTHCOM 2005). This small group provides an organizational infrastructure which can be expanded and made operational whenever directed by the President and the NCA. As the need arises and threats emerge, USNORTHCOM can mobilize massive DOD assets and capabilities against these threats.

The USNORTHCOM Commander is responsible for fulfilling the homeland defense mission in addition to serving as the leader of NORAD. USNORTHCOM's area of operations includes the United States, Canada, Mexico, parts of the Caribbean, and the contiguous waters in the Atlantic and Pacific oceans. The USNORTHCOM Commander is responsible for commanding and managing DOD assets that operate in support of civil authorities. The command structure responds to both attacks and natural disasters that impact its area of responsibility.

Within USNORTHCOM, there is an inter-armed force structure that enables the Commander to deploy DOD capabilities jointly against potential threats. The Joint Force Structure includes both Joint Force Headquarters (JFH) and Joint Force Task Forces (JFTF). Typically, the JFH transitions to JFTF when they actually execute DOD capabilities during national incidents. Like the combatant commands within the DOD, these JFH and JFTF have been arranged geographically to respond to specific geographic threats as well as strategically to respond coherently to threats from weapons of mass destruction (WMD). These organizations include Joint Task Force-Civil Support (JTF-CS), Standing Joint Force Headquarters North, Joint Task Force-North, Joint Force Headquarters-Capital Region, and Joint Force Headquarters-Alaska (Joint Task Force Civil Support Fact Sheet 2005).

Joint Task Force Civil Support (JTF-CS) ensures that DOD assets are prepared to respond to requests from the NCA, or other designated federal agencies, in the aftermath of an attack or incident related to WMDs (Joint Task Force Civil Support Fact Sheet 2005). The mission of JTF-CS is to protect lives, prevent injury and provide temporary critical life support during time of national crisis. The specific types of missions resulting from this mission range from command and control functions to responding to CBRNE. Other anticipated operations include providing medical requirements, transportation, and other logistics tasks.

Standing Joint Force Headquarters North is located at Peterson Air Force Base in Colorado (Standing Joint Task Headquarters North Fact Sheet 2005). The mission of this headquarters unit is to constantly monitor and report on developments within USNORTHCOM's area of responsibility. Their goal is to maintain an ongoing focus on constant assessment of trouble spots and potential areas where planning is required to implement Joint Task Force initiatives. The headquarters is divided into a Joint Operations Team, a Joint Planning Team, Information Synchronization Team, and a Joint Support Team (Joint Task Force Civil Support Fact Sheet 2005).

Joint Task Force North (JTF-N), formally known as Joint Task Force Six, is based at Fort Bliss, Texas. It primarily provides DOD support to federal law enforcement officials in detecting and intercepting transnational threats along approaches and borders to the United States (Joint Task Force North Fact Sheet 2005). In the past, the clear threats in this area have been from drug infiltration and the potential for the unlawful movement of weapons, particularly WMDs, across U.S. borders. The DOD capabilities provided by JTF-N include support for civil operations, training, and intelligence.

Joint Force Headquarters-National Capital Region (JFHQ-NCR) is headquartered at Fort McNair in Washington, DC. The mission JFHQ-NCR is to support civil authorities and to employ DOD capabilities for incident management in the National Capital Region. This area is particularly vital for DOD capabilities to support because of the high concentration of political and military activities that are essential for Homeland and Transportation Security.

Joint Task Force Alaska (JTF-A) has its headquarters at Elmendorf Air Force Base in Alaska (Joint Task Force Alaska Fact Sheet, 2005). JTF-A is responsible for coordinating DOD land and maritime resources and capabilities in support of civil authorities. It is responsible for the planning and coordination of all federal resources including those from other agencies such as the Federal Emergency Management Agency (FEMA). JTF-A has a civil support mission that includes hurricanes, fires, floods, earthquakes and volcanoes as well as responding to the consequences of the use of WMDs (Joint Task Force Alaska Fact Sheet 2005).

However, it is important to note that currently USNORTHCOM is a military organization and is therefore prohibited from direct involvement in law enforcement activities. Instead, the mission of USNORTHCOM is to mobilize DOD capabilities for military homeland defense and for civil support of other federal agencies. It is expected that this differentiation between military and law enforcement functions will emerge as a difficult challenge for military agencies involved in homeland defense.

Given this geographically and strategically oriented structure for USNORTH-COM, the following examples of on-going operations or task force related activities provide insight into how DOD capabilities are actually employed in times of crisis or increased threat.

OPERATION NOBLE EAGLE

Operation Noble Eagle is one of the longest running and best know examples of how USNORTHCOM integrates DOD capabilities to support Homeland and Transportation Security. Operation Noble Eagle formally began on September 14, 2001, in direct response to the attacks of September 11. The operation was coordinated and commanded by USNORTHCOM but includes capabilities from organizations and components throughout the DOD.

The operation utilizes the capabilities of NORAD, the Air National Guard, Air Force Reserve and active Air Force units to maintain and control air space that is the responsibility of USNORTHCOM. The DOD currently tracks approximately seven thousand aircraft approaching U.S. airspace and monitors about ten thousand aircraft making eighty thousand departures and landings on a daily basis (Herbert 2005).

The operation includes a network of sensors, aircraft, and Air Force personnel that maintain aerospace security for the homeland (Hebert 2005). The operation has evolved since the basic combat air patrols were initiated after September 11 and is now a $1.2 billon per year program. Interestingly, currently there are no supplemental budget authorizations so the funding comes directly from the Air Force budget (Colarusso 2005). This means that operations and maintenance costs will need to be found elsewhere in the Air Force. In this respect, USNORTHCOM's "efficient" deployment of needed resources may impact "effectiveness" elsewhere in the Air Force.

Operation Noble Eagle illustrates the classic efficiency and effectiveness tradeoffs inherent in a capabilities-based approach to Homeland and Transportation Security. There is likely to be continued debate about the most effective use of DOD capabilities and how they can be best employed given the organizational structures in place. Because the DOD organizations supporting Homeland and Transportation Security are in many ways competing with other DOD organizations for how DOD capabilities will be utilized, it can be expected that the debate will mirror the current discussions related to Operation Noble Eagle. Given the expectation of tighter budgets and diminishing resources, there may also be rivalry between warfighting commands such as USNORTH-COM and Central Command regarding how best to deploy DOD capabilities.

JOINT TASK FORCE CIVIL SUPPORT (HURRICANES KATRINA AND RITA)

Another example of the implementation of DOD capabilities came in response to Hurricanes Katrina and Rita in 2005. The efforts related to these two natural disasters demonstrate perhaps the best and worst examples of how the JTF process works. In the immediate aftermath of Hurricane Katrina and in preparation for Hurricane Rita, USNORTHCOM organized and deployed DOD capabilities into Task Force Katrina and Task Force Rita. These task forces' organizational structures and activities provide examples of how the considerable capabilities of the DOD are executed in the event of a Homeland or Transportation Security emergency. USNORTHCOM, through the JTF, provided and/or coordinated the following DOD capabilities (USNORTHCOM 2005):

- Defense Coordinating Officers (DCOs) and Defense Coordinating Elements (DCEs) in Clanton, Alabama, Baton Rouge, Louisiana, Jackson, Mississippi, Tallahassee, Florida, to liaison between USNORCOM, FEMA and the DOD.
- Maxwell Air Force Base, Alabama, Naval Air Station Meridian, Mississippi, Barksdale Air Force Base, Alexandria, Louisiana, Keesler AFB, Biloxi, Mississippi, and Ft. Polk, Louisiana, as federal operational staging areas to expedite the movement of relief supplies and emergency personnel to affected areas.
- US Transportation Command flew eight swift water rescue teams from California to Lafayette, Louisiana. These teams provided approximately fourteen personnel with vehicles and small rigid hulled boats who were highly trained and capable of rescuing stranded citizens from flooded areas.
- *USS Bataan* (LHD 5) and HSV Swift from the Naval Station Ingleside, Texas, sailed to the waters off Louisiana to provide support. The four MH-53s and two HH-60s helicopters off the *Bataan* flew medical evacuation and search and rescue missions in Louisiana. *Bataan*'s hospital was also available for medical support.

- The Iwo Jima Amphibious Readiness Group sailed from Norfolk, Virginia, loaded with disaster response equipment. The ARG consisted of *USS Iwo Jima* (LHD 7), *USS Shreveport* (LPD 12), *USS Tortuga* (LSD 46), and *USNS Arctic* (T-AOE 8).
- The hospital ship, *USNS Comfort* (T-AH 20), brought DOD medical capabilities to the Gulf region.
- The *USS Grapple* (ARS 53) brought DOD capabilities to assist with maritime and underwater survey and salvage operations.
- Three Army Helicopters from III Corps in Fort Hood, Texas, were in Baton Rouge, Louisiana, and two others were in Mississippi to assist with search and rescue and damage assessment.
- Five Air Force helicopters from the 920th Rescue Wing (RQW) at Patrick AFB, Florida, and the 347th RQW at Moody AFB, Georgia, were in Mississippi for search and rescue missions. These aircraft provided the much needed capability of nighttime search and rescue.
- USNORTHCOM established Joint Task Force Katrina to be the military's on-scene commander in support of FEMA. Lt. Gen. Russel Honore, Commander of the First Army in Fort Gillem, Georgia, is the JTF-Commander. JTF-Katrina was based out of Camp Shelby, Mississippi.
- Standing Joint Forces Headquarters-North provided an augmentation cell and its command and control vehicle to JTF-Katrina.
- JTF-Civil Support provided a joint planning augmentation cell.
- USNORTHCOM's Joint Operations Center was on twenty-four-hour duty in Colorado Springs, Colorado, to facilitate any additional requests for assistance that may come from FEMA representatives.

Clearly, much will be written in the next several years on the successes and failures of the JTF efforts implemented to respond to Hurricanes Katrina and Rita. Preliminary indications are that the two events have dramatically shown that in some extreme situations, only DOD resources are capable of responding to massive disasters. While the unique role of the DOD has been well established for supporting response to WMDs, these huge storms and the JTF responses to them, have pointed out to many, the need for a greater DOD role in Homeland and Transportation Security.

DETECTING AND PREVENTING HOMELAND AND TRANSPORTATION SECURITY THREATS

In order to prevent terrorist attacks within America's borders, perhaps one of the most important and controversial roles for the DOD in Homeland and Transportation Security is in the area of intelligence gathering. Intelligence gathering can be accomplished in many ways; some utilizing cutting-edge technology and some related to more basic technologies and intelligence gathering techniques including human intelligence programs.

With regard to high technology and national intelligence systems, much of the DOD capabilities in space are critical for several Homeland and Transportation Security missions (Kuo 2003). For example, DOD space assets are central for communication, intelligence, and weather predictions. Some applications like the Global Positioning Satellite (GPS) System are so commonly used that they are no longer thought of as DOD capabilities. However, space assets like overhead signal and image intelligence collection are consistently listed as among the most important DOD capabilities for detecting and defeating emerging Homeland and Transportation Security threats.

One of the evolving DOD capabilities of particular interest to Homeland and Transportation Security is remote sensing (Kuo 2003). Remote sensing is key in providing regions, cities, and transportation centers with high resolution images and data. These images, along with geographic and geospatial information, will be vital in assisting local and regional civil authorities in determining where their greatest vulnerabilities lie. In this way, the civil support provided by DOD intelligence capabilities will serve much the same function as it does with military organizations. It will provide information on transportation choke points, key logistical information regarding distribution of supplies, and real time information on disruptions to the transportation system (Kuo 2003).

Currently, the role of DOD intelligence systems in domestic law enforcement and security roles is among the most highly visible and controversial with regard to maintaining distinctions between national defense and local civil enforcement roles required by federal law. Federal officials are confronting very difficult questions regarding how and when intelligence data, that was generated and interpreted by the DOD, can be used by law enforcement officials.

Perhaps the most well known and controversial case regarding how and when DOD intelligence can be shared with local authorities relates to a more low technology, human intelligence program. In the summer of 2005, Congressman Curt Weldon made claims on the floor of the House of Representatives regarding critical intelligence information from the Army's "Able Danger" intelligence collection program.

> Mr. Speaker, I rise because information has come to my attention over the past several months that is very disturbing. I have learned that, in fact, one of our Federal agencies had, in fact, identified the major New York cell of Mohamed Atta prior to 9/11; and I have learned, Mr. Speaker, that in September of 2000, that Federal agency actually was prepared to bring the FBI in and prepared to work with the FBI to take down the cell that Mohamed Atta was involved in in New York City, along with two of the other terrorists. I have also learned, Mr. Speaker, that when that recommendation was discussed within that Federal agency, the lawyers in the administration at that time said, you cannot pursue contact with the FBI against that cell. Mohamed Atta is in the U.S. on a green card, and we are fearful of the fallout from the Waco incident. So we did not allow that Federal agency to proceed.

While there is still widespread skepticism regarding the specific allegation in Congressman Weldon's statement (Bennett, Burger, and Waller 2005), the high level of interest and emotion regarding the claims illustrate how deeply divisive and potentially critical the debate is regarding the role of DOD intelligence capabilities in Homeland and Transportation Security.

UNDERSTANDING LEGAL LIMITATIONS ON IMPLEMENTING DOD CAPABILITIES

The primary limitation on DOD involvement with civil authorities in Homeland and Transportation Security is the *Posse Comitatus* Act of 1878. The law was originally written following the Civil War during the Reconstruction Period and was passed in order to prohibit the military from enforcing civilian laws. The law sought to codify the traditional aversion of American citizens to a standing army that would be an instrument of governmental tyranny and control (Washington University 1997). It established clear boundaries regarding the role the military could play in civil law enforcement.

The law has been amended over the past several decades to allow the military to play a more active and long-term role in first the drug war and then to threats of WMD (Washington University 1997). For example, in the 1980s specific laws were passed to allow the DOD to a greater role in drug interdiction and border security. In the 1990s, in response to the domestic terror attack in Oklahoma City and growing fears about global terrorism, the military was given an expanded role in responding to attacks that may use WMDs.

In the aftermath of the attacks of September 11 and more recently the Hurricane Katrina disaster, many Americans, were stunned by the amount of time it took the government to respond to the disaster. Many felt that only the DOD had the capabilities and competencies required to provide adequate and timely response. The considerable assets, capabilities and competencies available from the DOD make it the logical and efficient choice to provide such assets. But much debate remains as to the best manner to utilize these federal assets at the local level.

Recently, President Bush publicly advocated amending the *Posse Comitatus* Act even further by allowing the military to become involved immediately and automatically following natural disasters (Senger 2005).

> I want there to be a robust discussion about the best way for the federal government, in certain extreme circumstances, to be able to rally assets for the good of the people.

During his September 15, 2005, address to the nation following Hurricane Katrina, President Bush stated directly that he felt the capabilities of the military would play a greater role in future disasters (Peters and Vest 2005):

> It is now clear that a challenge on this scale requires greater federal authority and a broader role for the armed forces—the institution of our government most capable of massive logistical operations on a moment's notice.

Some analysts feel that extending the DOD role beyond the limitations of the current *Posse Comitatus* Act will enhance funding and public support for the military. However, many from the military express concerns about diluting and distracting the DOD mission (Colarusso 2005; Center for Defense Information 2003). These mission related issues, in addition to concerns about military infringement on civil liberties, will shape future discussions about the evolving role of DOD capabilities in Homeland and Transportation Security for years to come.

CONCLUSION

Until the attacks of September 11, there was not widespread expectation for high levels of continuing DOD support for Homeland and Transportation Security missions. It was expected that DOD capabilities would be used on an occasional or case by case basis where civil authorities requested such help or where WMDs were employed. Today, however, there is a widespread realization that DOD resources and capabilities will play a major and continuing role in responding to threats to transportation and the homeland. In fact, the DOD has established USNORTHCOM to execute DOD capabilities in a unified combatant command specifically for the homeland.

This structural change in the DOD in response to the evolving Homeland and Transportation Security missions is one example of how far-reaching the changes in our national defense institutions have gone to best support Homeland Security. It can be reasonably expected that debates about how these changes will impact overall DOD readiness for its traditional mission will be ongoing and spirited. There will also be debates and discussions regarding how extensively DOD resources and capabilities can be used in Homeland and Transportation Security without negatively impacting civil authorities and civil liberties.

Unfortunately, when the next national crisis occurs, there are major policy issues that remain unresolved and many questions that remain unanswered. For example, can the specific support required by a particular national crisis be orchestrated to meet the needs in a timely manner using the existing command structure? Further, will cooperation between federal and local authorities continue, and will they embrace lessons learned form recent incidents? Also, if each operating agencies trains, equips, and deploys its own personnel, will competition for scare budget authority create undesirable and nonproductive competition for scarce resources, encourage duplication of effort, and will interoperability continue to be an issue? If the nation intends to train the way they fight, as the slogan suggests, then America must ensure that its agencies can put its training and resources to use in a cogent, orchestrated, and timely manner leveraging its capabilities to their full extent.

Only by examining and exploring evolving DOD capabilities, and through discussing and debating the increased involvement of federal assets at the local level, will America be able to supply the degree of Homeland and Transportation Security it needs. With proper planning, coordination, and execution, when terrorist next attempt to attack America's homeland, they will not again be met with interagency chatter; they will face the full synchronized fury of the nation's might and will.

NOTE

Opinions, conclusions, and recommendations expressed or implied within are solely those of the authors and do not necessarily represent the views of USAFA, USAF, the DOD, or any other government agency.

REFERENCES

BAST (Board on Army Science and Technology). (2003). Science and Technology for army Homeland Security. Washington D.C.: National Academies Press.

Bennett, B., Burger, T.J., & Waller, W. (2005, August 14). Was Mohammed Atta Overlooked? *Time.* Retrieved October 20, 2005, from http://www.time.com/time/nation/printout/0,8816,1093694,00.html.

Center for Defense Information. (2003). Security After 9/11: Strategy Choices and Budget Tradeoffs. Washington D.C.: Author.

CNN (2005, September 2). Mayor to Feds: Get Off Your Asses. Retrieved September 2, 2005, from http://www.cnn.com/2005/US/09/02/nagin.transcript/index.html.

Colarusso, L.M. (2005, February 7). Air Force Told to Pick Up Noble Eagle Costs. *Air Force Times*, 1.

Davis, L.E., Mosher, D.E., Brennan, R.R., Greenberg, M.D., McMahon, K.S., & Yost, C.W. (2004). *Army Forces for Homeland Security.* Santa Monica, CA: Rand Corporation.

Dierickx, I & Cool, K., (1989). Asset Stock Accumulation and Sustainability of Competitive Advantage. *Management Science*, 35(12), 1504–1514.

Hebert, A. J. (2005). Noble Eagle without End. *Air Force Magazine*, 88(2), 42–47.

Johnston, V. R. (2004). Terrorism and Transportation Policy and Administration: Balancing the Model and Equations for Optimal Security. *Review of Policy Reseach*, 21(3), 263–274.

Joint Task Force Alaska Fact Sheet. (2005). Joint Task Alaska. Retrieved October 15, 2005, from http://www.northcom.mil/index.cfm?fuseaction=news.factsheets&factsheet=6# Alaska.

Joint Task Force Civil Support Fact Sheet. (2005). Joint Task Force Civil Support. Retrieved October 15, 2005, from http://www.northcom.mil/index.cfm?fuseaction=news.factshe ets&factsheet=3#civilsupport.

Joint Task Force North Fact Sheet. (2005). Joint Task Force North. Retrieved October 15, 2005, from http://www.northcom.mil/index.cfm?fuseaction=news.factsheets&factsheet=2# taskforcesix.

Kuo, S.D. (2003). High Ground Over the Homeland: Issues in the Use of Space Assets for Homeland Security. *Air and Space Journal*, Spring, 2003, 47–56.

Matthews, W. (2005). Maritime NORAD. *Armed Forces Journal.* July, 14.

Peters, K.M. & Vest, J. (2005). Calling in the Cavalry. *Government Executive.* Retrieved October 15, 2005, from http://www.govexec.com/features/1005-01/1005-01s1.htm.

Reese, D.L. and Pohlman, D.W. (2005). Centralized Purchasing Power: Why Air Force Leadership Should Care. *Air Force Journal of Logistics*, XXVIV (1), Spring, 10.

Ridge, T. (2002). The Department of Homeland Security: Making Americans Safer. Statement for the Committee on Governmental Affairs, U.S. Senate, June 20, 2002.

Rinaldi, S. M. (2002). Protecting the Homeland: Air Force Roles in Homeland Security. *Aerospace Power Journal*, Spring, 1–10.

Rumsfeld, D.H. (2004). Before the Committee on Armed Services, United States House of Representatives Regarding the President's 2005 Budget Request for the Department of Defense. February 4.

Senger, D. E. (2005, September 27). Bush Wants to Consider Broadening of Military's Powers During Natural Disasters. *New York Times.* Retrieved October 15, 2005, from http://www.nytimes.com/2005/09/27/national/nationalspecial/27military.html.

Sherman, J. (2005). Navy, Coast Guard Seek National Strategy for Maritime Security. *Seapower*, May, 48(5): 20.

Standing Joint Headquarters North Fact Sheet. (2005). Joint Task Force North. Retrieved October 15, 2005, from http://www.northcom.mil/index.cfm?fuseaction=news.factsheets&fact sheet=7#Standing.

Swartz, P.M. (2003). Forward from the Start: The U.S. Navy and Homeland Defense. Alexandria, VA: Center for Naval Analyses, Center for Strategic Studies.

The 9/11 Commission Report. (2004). New York: W.W. Norton.

United States General Accounting Office. (2002). "Homeland Security: Management Challenges Facing Federal Leadership." Report to the Chairman, Committee on Governmental Affairs, U.S. Senate. GAO-03-260. December, 2002.

USNORTHCOM. (2005). Joint Task Force Civil Support Joins Katrina Relief Effort. Retrieved October 15, 2005, from http://www.jtfcs.northcom.mil/pages/news20050901.html.

Washington University. (1997). The *Posse Comitatus* Act: A Principle in Need of Renewal. *Washington University Law Quarterly*, 75(20).

Weldon, C. (2005). Before the United States House of Representatives Regarding U.S. Army's "Able Danger" Intelligence Collection Program. September 21.

31 Enhancing Railroad Security

Jeremy F. Plant

INTRODUCTION

Protecting the nation's railway system from threats posed by terrorism has become a major consideration for the nation's railroads and government agencies concerned with railroad safety and homeland security. Since the September 11 attacks growing attention has been given to the vulnerability of the vast and complicated network of railway lines in the US and other nations concerned with terrorism. The reasons for this concern are not hard to identify. Railway lines are critical to the nation's economy, moving large numbers of commuters, a large portion of the nation's freight, and form a critical part of the evolving intermodal system critical to global commerce. Because railroads are by virtue of their basic technology able to move heavy bulk cargoes efficiently, they dominate the movement of such vital cargoes as coal and other minerals, automobiles and auto parts, grain, chemicals, and agricultural products. They are the preferred surface mode to move hazardous and dangerous materials safely. (Imagine such cargoes as nuclear waste or nerve gas moving along the nation's roadways by truck instead of train.) In larger cities, they are the means of moving large numbers of commuters from suburbs to central business districts. They move more people and more tonnage per gallon of fuel than other modes, due to the inherent efficiency of the steel wheel on the almost frictionless steel rail. They are, in short, critical to the functioning of our society, and that alone might suffice to make them a logical target for terrorists.

In addition to the value they represent, rail systems form likely terrorist targets for more specific reasons. The vastness of the rail system makes simple policing and surveillance approaches infeasible—think of how many security cameras would need to be employed to scan the over three hundred thousand miles of trackage in the United States alone, much of it far from population centers and civilian police.

Railroads have reduced the size and deployment of crews in recent decades, with most freight trains operating with a crew of two, both riding in the lead locomotive, leaving the remaining mile or so of equipment unmanned. Cost savings extend to the physical plant of railways also. Many formerly double or multiple tracked lines have been reduced to a single set of tracks, leaving an adjacent access road that provides a convenient means for terrorists or other trespassers to access remote locations along the lines. Signals, once controlled on many roads by operators in towers along the right-of-way, are controlled centrally by dispatchers often states away from the location of the trains they are guiding. The efficiency and effectiveness of such cost-saving measures, however, may be an indication of the problem that Johnston (2004) finds indicative for transportation as a whole and the airline industry in particular before September 11; that "the forces of efficiency (output over input) were winning the battles over effectiveness (output over standards—like security and safety). Across the country, pressures mounted for trimming organizational fat and launching improved performance" (Johnston 2004, p. 266).

While following many of the same cost-saving motives as other modes, railroads are unique among modes of transportation in the ownership as well as operation of the key facilities they need to function. In this regard, it is not simply the trains that may be targets but also the bridges, tunnels, stations, tracks, signals, computer programs, and other infrastructure that need security.

Railways may also be the means of delivering weapons of mass destruction to their intended target, rather than serving as the major target. In this regard, three major threats have consistently been identified. In the first, a weapon of mass destruction moves from a foreign destination by container and then is loaded for delivery on a train of intermodal cars, with the unsuspecting railroad the deliverer of a bomb or biological device. In the second, the railroad's role of moving such hazardous materials as chlorine gas provides a way for terrorists to avoid having to move the material themselves into a crowded urban region, but instead merely puncture by bullet or rocket a chemical car as a train passes, leading to mass destruction. In the third scenario, a passenger places a bomb or other WMD on a commuter train, which to be efficiently run provides little opportunity for the sort of screening of passengers and luggage that is characteristic of air travel. This was the scenario that led to the bombing of commuter trains in Madrid, Spain in March 2004 by Islamic terrorists, an event that showed the vulnerability of commuter rail systems to attack, and which had serious political ramifications immediately for the Spanish government.

Railways are thus a logical and established target for terrorist attack. The General Accountability Office, using information provided by the Mineta Institute at San Jose State University, estimates that close to two thousand such attacks were mounted on transportation targets worldwide between 1997 and 2000. The Rand Institute documented 181 attacks on trains and rail facilities between 1998 and 2003 that led to 431 deaths, the majority of these, 275, in a brutal bombing and gunfire attack by rebels in Mozambique in 2001. Buses, however, are by far the favored mode of transportation for terrorists to attack. The General Accountabililty Office has estimated that 41 percent of terrorist attacks on public surface transportation systems between 1997 and 2000 were on buses (Plant 2005).

RAILROAD SECURITY: DEFINING THE PROBLEM

The September 11, 2001, attack on the World Trade Center towers was without question a turning point for consideration of security needs for all modes of transportation. Although the attacks used aircraft as the means of attack, in the aftermath of the event rail security became a subject of intense interest, by scholars, government officials, rail operators, and the media. In part, it was the realization that passenger rail service in the heavily populated Northeast was the only feasible public transportation alternative to air travel; Amtrak, which operates the Northeast Corridor rail system between Washington, D.C., and Boston, saw a 3.8 percent increase in traffic in the weeks following September 11.

Passenger rail, however, is only one aspect of rail transportation. Freight movements constitute the bulk of rail activity, and the industry is organized in such a way that its component parts are organizationally separate: seven major freight railroads; larger numbers of regional, short-line and terminal freight railroads; Amtrak, a national passenger rail operator; and publicly operated passenger commuter rail systems in large metropolitan areas. Deregulation of the industry since 1980 has allowed the major railroads to compete against one another (and against other modes) with much less openness and accountability to the public compared to the regulatory regime that preceded deregulation.

Rail security, then, is a complicated matter. Assuming that railroad operations are both vulnerable to terrorist acts and necessary for the maintenance of our economy and society, public policy must address a number of critical issues:

- What are the proper roles of private sector rail operators, states and local governments, and the federal government in securing rail facilities and operations? Better yet, how can we facilitate the exchange of information and a partnering of activities to provide enhanced levels of security at reasonable costs to the public?
- What are the likely targets and means to be employed by terrorists, and how can we develop a system of risk assessment to counter their efforts in a timely and proactive manner?
- What are the policy options to provide security to the nation's railways in the post September 11 era? Each of these major issues is discussed below.

GUARDING THE RAILS: PUBLIC AND PRIVATE RESPONSIBILITIES

Prior to September 11, rail security thinking was dominated by two basic assumptions: first, that conventional attacks using bombs or armed incursions on trains was the most likely sort of hostile act; and second that private rail operators, by virtue of their ownership of the rights-of-way as well as equipment, needed to secure their properties by their own internal police units. (Unlike other transportation modes, railroads have historically employed large and professionally trained private police units, most of whose members are deputized as peace officers, carry weapons, and work closely with public police forces.) During World War II, the critical role played by the nation's railroads—moving around 90 percent of the freight and intercity passenger demand at its peak—coupled with actual attempts by enemy soldiers to infiltrate rail infrastructure led to a partnership between the government and the private operators to quarantine rail properties and arrest and detain those trespassing on or near rail facilities. The rail network of the 1940s, with much more mileage and more separate rail operators than today, managed to operate without serious impediment throughout the war.

In peacetime circumstances, attention shifted from protection against enemy attack to securing the rail property from vandals, criminals, trespassers, and vagrants. Much of the concern was the legal liability of the railroad companies for damages related to injuries sustained by trespassers on rail rights-of-way. Rail rights-of-way are tempting locations for users of all-terrain vehicles and dirt bikes. Tunnels and bridges are special risks, with trespassers often misjudging the danger of finding oneself alongside a train with nowhere safe to flee. Vandalism is a serious problem, ranging from the all-too-common defacing of rail equipment with spray paint to theft and damage of cargoes, railcars, and other railroad properties. Rocks are often thrown from bridges onto moving trains, and in many urban locations the fear of physical attack or even shooting is a problem for railroad employees.

In other words, the concern before September 11 for rail operators was security against trespassing, broadly defined, and not the threat of terrorist attack (Savage 1998). Federal and state public policy recognized this guiding assumption also. Groups such as the American Association of Railroads, the leading industry trade association, and state-based rail associations pushed for anti-trespass legislation that would criminalize trespassing on private rail rights-of-way and sanction tougher penalties, ranging from fines of $200 or more to jail sentences. These efforts led to the passage in 1994 of the Federal Railroad Safety Authorization Act (49 U.S.C. 20151). This act required the Secretary of Transportation to develop a Model State Railroad Trespass bill, in collaboration with industry and state and local governments. Several states had either adopted such laws or were actively considering them when the September 11 attacks shifted the focus of rail security from criminal trespass to terrorist threats.

Shifting gears after the attacks, the rail industry was quick to respond to the challenge of terrorist attack that followed the World Trade Center attacks. The industry, working through its trade association, the American Association of Railroads (AAR), quickly put together a network of teams of experts to deal with presumed threats to the rails. Five major areas of concern were identified: hazardous materials shipments; protection of physical infrastructure; liaison with the military; securing vital operations; and securing information and communications systems (Fronczek 2001). Given the continental nature of rail operations since the passage of the North American Free Trade Agreement (NAFTA), the railroads also worked to coordinate with the Canadian government's efforts to deal with security issues.

As it did during World War II, the AAR provided an organizational center around which industry-wide efforts could be based and managed. Activities directed or coordinated by AAR included a center for risk analysis; a 24/7 operations control center; enhanced tracking of hazardous cargo shipments; cross-checking employee records with FBI files to prevent infiltration of terrorists posing as rail employees; and a clearinghouse approach to reports of suspicious individuals or activities on or near major rail facilities (Plant 2004).

It is less clear what the organizational center of the government is regarding rail security. The Transportation Security Administration of the Department of Homeland Security has focused its work, until recently, on the commercial aviation industry and the screening of air passengers (Frederickson and LaPorte 2002). The Federal Railroad Administration (FRA) retains its role in rail safety, and has worked to assess the network approach of the private rail industry (Rutter 2002). The Federal Bureau of Investigation shares terror warnings with the railroads, as it did in October 24 when evidence suggested that Al-Qaeda was preparing to mount attacks on rail facilities and movements (Brinkley 2002). The General Accountability Office (GAO) has studied the problem of fragmented governmental responsibility for rail security, in particular the need for the FRA and DHS to agree upon their respective responsibilities and means of coordination.

How well this network approach is working is difficult to measure. Has it prevented terrorist attacks? Does it provide a comprehensive framework for disaster mitigation as well as prevention? Lacking any empirical evidence to go on, it remains open to question what the threats are to the railways and how best to provide security. It is to the issue of possible threats that we turn our attention next.

WHAT IS THE NATURE OF THE THREAT?

The historical record of terrorism directed against railroads strongly suggests conventional attacks on passenger trains. However, other sorts of terrorist targets or strategies may present greater payoffs and present greater risks. In this section we examine the role played by railroads to identify ways in which they are essential to the functioning of society.

- The transport of coal for electric production and industrial use, as well as export to other nations. Coal has been historically one of the most important cargoes for the rail industry, with inland waterways the only major modal competitor. Since the 1980s, the locus of coal mining and rail operations has shifted from traditional mining centers in the East to the Powder River Basin of Montana and Wyoming, where the two major western U.S. rail systems, BNSF and Union Pacific, have invested heavily in new rail infrastructure to meet growing demand, mostly from the electric utility industry.
- Intermodal shipments related to domestic and global commerce have been increasing as a percentage of freight traffic since the 1980s. Intermodal traffic includes several different technologies, including truck trailers on flatcars or "TOFC" shipments; single or double-stack containers of standard size, which can be transferred to and from most transportation modes, including maritime shipping, trucking, air transport, and rail; and the least common technology, the use of trailers that can either be used as stand-alone freight cars on the rails or rubber-tired truck trailers. Rail intermodal traffic has more than tripled since 1980. In 2003, for the first time ever, intermodal overtook coal as the primary source of revenue for the U.S. carriers, with rail intermodal revenue at $7.7 billion, compared with coal revenue of $7.6 billion.
- Commodities using specialized freight cars and moved in freight trains; the most important to the economy are heavy or bulky materials unsuitable for trucking, such as grain, automobiles and automobile parts, lumber, chemicals, animal feed, and so on; and oversized or hazardous materials, due to limits on roadway

clearances or weights and the reduced likelihood of dangerous mishaps compared to trucking. Commodities may move either in unitized trains (grain is a good example) or in mixed-freight movements.

CRIPPLE THE GLOBAL ECONOMY

Just as terrorists targeted the World Trade Center in the 1990s as a symbol of a world economy dominated by the West, by the United States, and by globally interdependent businesses, so might they see the railroads and the port and intermodal facilities they serve as a key element in the so-called global economy. In this regard, the logic of the global economy—to create seamless movement between modes and over great distances, to enforce rigorous requirements on efficient and low-cost operations, to coordinate efforts of participating organizations through sophisticated information-management technology—has created types and levels of vulnerability that go far beyond the historically limited disruptions caused by bombing a train, tunnel, or bridge (Flynn 2002). The global commerce moves through a limited number of portals; concentrates train movements over a limited number of high-speed arteries; and allows for great distances between points of production (in recent years, concentrated heavily in East Asia) and distribution and consumption (largely the developed nations of Europe and North America).

CRIPPLE A MAJOR CITY

Terrorists have shown a proclivity toward attacks on major urban areas. Large cities provide opportunities for clandestine activity, through the concentration and diversity of the population and the many ways in which groups can meet and operate. Cities are important symbols of modern society, centers of government and business, and have the potential for major casualties resulting from attacks. As mentioned above, several of the largest U.S. cities are largely dependant on rail systems and would be immobilized if such systems were taken out of operation for any period of time.

CAUSE MAJOR CIVILIAN CASUALTIES

As the means of moving weapons of mass destruction, the railroad system may invite terrorist attack either through the destructive potential of a train loaded with dangerous materials (such as the chloride gas released in the non-terrorist related South Carolina derailment) that might be sabotaged, or by the use of a train to move a clandestinely loaded weapon, perhaps in an intermodal shipment or aboard a freight car. Given the enormity of the rail freight system, remote points along a right-of-way might be chosen over more heavily guarded ports or major rail yards. The large size of rail containers and cars means virtually any sort of explosive, chemical or biological weapon, or even nuclear device could easily be added to a rail movement, most likely on a freight train but also on commuter and passenger trains.

Disrupt the U.S. Economy

If the global economy were not the target, terrorism against rail targets might be seen as a way of crippling the U.S. economy, possibly by targeting critical movements such as coal to power plants. This goal, however, seems to have less appeal than the ones listed above, both because the industry maintains a level of redundancy (although today, little or no excess capacity as was true before deregulation) that allows different routing of trains, and because the effects of such attacks might take some time to show their effect.

Create Fear Among the Civilian Population

The railroad system might be seen as a target to show the American population how impossible it is to protect them from attacks that might come anywhere in the nation at anytime. The ubiquitous nature of railroads, even with some cutbacks in the size of the system in the past quarter-century, their presence in almost every community, might be seen as a way of convincing the public that nothing the government does to protect them can guard against potential disaster. Unlike other types of physical infrastructure, transportation is mobile—and nothing that moves created by man comes close to the size, and hence destructive potential, of a moving train, which may be a mile long, weigh 10,000 tons, and be moving at 60 miles per hour. Michael Chertoff, the Secretary of Homeland Security, expressed this point in remarks at the George Washington University Homeland Security Policy Institute on March 16, 2005:

> Think of last month's train derailment in California. It was evidently caused by a man contemplating suicide. Suppose he had been a terrorist? It would not have changed the event and unfortunate outcome. But would it have changed how we reacted psychologically? It might have—and that psychological difference is important. Terrorists seek to exploit psychological vulnerability in order to leverage their force, to control and manipulate our behavior. (Chertoff 2005, p. 6)

What Are the Policy and Administrative Options?

However complex the problem of rail security may be, there is no lack of theorizing on what we should be doing to prevent and prepare for terrorist acts. Distilled down to their essentials, we can identify four solutions that have been advanced for the problem of rail security:

Policing Strategy

This is the most traditional approach, building on the fact that, compared to other modes, the rail industry had in existence prior to September 11 highly competent professional police operations to monitor activities on rail rights-of-way, prevent unlawful trespassing on private property, and to secure important centers of activity such as rail yards, engine terminals, and stations. Advocates of the policing strategy point to the ease with which terrorists now may have access to trains and rail facilities, and the historical success of the policing approach in preventing sabotage during World War II. A downside of this approach is the enormity of the rail system in the United States, with over one hundred thousand miles of track, and its interconnectivity with other modes and economic activities. It is difficult to police the entire network, which has led to the passage of legislation in many states to criminalize trespass on rail property and to enlist the assistance of federal, state, and local policing agencies to work with rail operators to prevent unwarranted access to rail facilities and trains. Another drawback is the need to employ ethnic profiling to identify likely terrorists.

Cordoning Strategy

This strategy is modeled after the approach employed by airports and airlines after September 11. It differs from the policing approach by concentrating efforts on tight screening of entry to rail facilities and trains, employing a "search and screen" approach to individuals, baggage, and freight at points of entry to the rail system: for passenger rail, boarding of trains and perhaps entry to stations; for freight and intermodal operations, entry to terminals and transfer points. The advantages of this approach are assumed to be similar to those for air travel: interception of terrorists and weapons, and deterrence due to the high likelihood of disclosure. The disadvantages lie in the highly decentralized nature of passenger rail travel. Unlike air travel, rail stations are often not easily separated from their immediate environment, especially in downtown areas; and trains, unlike planes, make frequent stops to take on passengers, often at unmanned locations. For example, it is common for individuals to board commuter trains and Amtrak trains without showing or even obtaining tickets beforehand; little screening is done prior to boarding (although there is experimentation with pre-boarding screening at selected rail stations). Stations themselves are usually open to the public and relatively unguarded. It is hard to imagine how commuter rail and mass transit systems could operate as they do today with the costs of screeners and screening machinery and the delays in boarding they represent. Many of the same problems are confronted in making rail terminals and intermodal ports tightly quarantined, although it is feasible to do more than is now being done.

Network Management Approach

The network management approach is predicated on the understanding that no one organization or intervention approach can adequately deal with the complexity, fluidity, and uncertainty posed by the need to secure the rails against terrorist acts. The network approach holds that any successful effort to avoid terrorism or mitigate the effects of terrorist acts requires the collaboration of a multitude of players sharing information, planning for contingencies, and continually learning from empirical evidence and models of potential risk and attack. An example of this in action is the continuing effort to plan for catastrophic events by simulating terrorist acts, involving the network of players—rail service providers, other transportation modes, police, emergency medical personnel, counter-terrorism experts, government agencies, and the like—that must work together to deal with the problem of rail security.

Developing an approach to network management that creates not just quick responses to events, but also shares information, learns from past events and adjusts its measures to reduce risk, and enhances security while allowing railroads to operate efficiently and productively is the challenge not just for the Department of Homeland Security and the Department of Transportation, but for everyone involved in rail operations. Although the formation of DHS was seen by many as a retreat to a bureaucratic, single-agency approach to the problem of homeland security, realistically it has had to think in network terms to develop cooperation both within the department itself, and with the state and local agencies and private sector organizations involved in various homeland security efforts. How well it has done this, how much it has been guided by coherent theory and policy, is open to question, and in fact we are seeing significant changes in policy in the transition of leadership at DHS from Tom Ridge to Michael Chertoff.

Network management is the new frontier of organization and management theory, so the efforts to make the rails secure from terrorism may become a model for others to follow, not just in homeland security, but in moving away from reliance upon outdated ideas of bureaucratic structure and single-organization management. As the lead agency empowered to act on transportation security, the actions of DHS and the philosophy of its leadership is crucial to making the network approach work. In his March 16 remarks, Secretary Chertoff expressed the need for partnerships between government and key industries, and also the need to extend the partnership or network concept to international partners as well as domestic ones (Chertoff 2005, p. 5).

Risk Management Strategy

Risk management is predicated on realistic projections of finite resources and the need to make decisions on where best to place them. As explained by the General Accountability Office, an advocate of the approach in regard to antiterrorism efforts, risk management seeks to classify risk in three areas: vulnerability of the system; likelihood of threat; and criticality of asset. As represented by three interconnected circles, the area in which the three factors are conjoined represents the highest risk and so the best investment of limited resources. Risk management has been adopted by the Transportation Security Administration of DHS as its planning and decision making approach, but as GAO's report GAO-04-598T, "Rail Security: Some Actions Taken to Enhance Passenger and Freight Rail Security, but Significant Challenges Remain" notes, much work remains to be done to coordinate efforts among the many public and private entities involved in rail security. Risk management, as defined by GAO, "entails a continuous process of managing, through a series of mitigating actions, the likelihood of an adverse event happening with a negative impact." The last four words of the preceding sentence are critical to understanding the approach. Risk management hopes to mitigate impacts, but is realistic in accepting the impossibility of preventing the range of terrorist attacks on the rail system that are conceivable. Its goal is not so much prevention as intelligent investment in those areas that combine vulnerability, likelihood, and criticality of asset.

There are at least two problems with relying upon the risk management approach. One is the lack of historical data to guide managers in determining the likelihood of threats and system vulnerability, or the types of threats we need most to guard against. Although there is a considerable history of terrorist attacks on rail operations, most are not relevant to the sort of major event orchestrated by Al Qaeda that causes sleepless nights for the rail industry and experts in terrorism. The second is the arbitrary character of assigning weights to values for the other factor, criticality of assets. This is essentially a value judgment. For example, how should we weight economic losses versus loss of life? Perhaps by disruption of home-to-work commuting versus disruption of the movement of freight? Or the particular importance of some locations, such as the nation's capital, versus others? Rational assessment using standardized approaches such as cost-benefit ratios versus political decision making?

ANALYSIS AND CONCLUSION: FINDING A PROPER BLEND

Isolating the four approaches, as is done in the previous section of the paper, is not to suggest that we choose one pure type of action over the others. Rather, by assessing the relative strengths and weaknesses of each ideal type, we can come up with the necessary blend of the four approaches to provide as much security as is possible in the uncertain period in which we live. The link between a policy based on risk assessment and an organization built around network principles seems to be fundamental to the approach envisioned by the new leadership at DHS. Risk management is now the guiding policy approach at DHS, with the allocation of resources changing from one based on widespread sharing of resources (some say a pork-barrel or political approach) with a great deal of autonomy given to state and local officials on how the money will be spent, to one that says, in the Secretary's words, "we have to put the resources where the highest risks are" (*Aviation Week* 2005). The department still plans to involve the network organization in developing the National Preparedness Plan, but the goal will be a more disciplined way of putting resources where risks appear to be greatest, or have the potential for the greatest physical, economic, and psychological impact. The allocation of resource will give each state only a small fraction of the total funding, with the rest based on the risk assessment exercise (de Rugy 2005).

While risk assessment combined with flexible, network-oriented organizational approaches appears to be the favored approach, it does not rule out the benefits of the policing and cordoning approaches. The first may provide additional information on actual behavior to add to the highly speculative nature of risk assessment without a body of data to support analysis. The second is useful in providing a sense of security or trust to the public that visible measures are being taken to protect against terrorist attack.

What are the implications of the move to a risk-assessment approach, as is unquestionably the direction now being taken by DHS? First, railroad security is an important element in the two areas of DHS programming, the Urban Area Security Initiative and the Targeted Infrastructure Protection Program, which together would receive an increase of $462 milllion in the proposed presidential budget. Second, the network of organizations involved in homeland security programs may evolve in a way that stresses partnerships among a smaller number of cities and industries with high risk levels, compared to one that tries to fold in first responders and communities regardless of risk. Railroads, through the industry-wide approach facilitated by the American Association of Railroads, appear to be the sort of industry partner envisioned by Secretary Chertoff to figure prominently in such efforts (Plant 2004). Factoring in the role that the industry's well-trained private policing and security staff can play in the coordinated approach to policing, cordoning, and risk assessment, the rail industry may find itself one of the partners most valuable in the homeland security effort.

However, the logic of partnership has to be tempered with a sense of history and industry culture. Compared to other transportation modes, the railroad industry has favored a hands-off approach to its industry, preferring isolation to partnership with the public sector. Part of this may be explained by the early and pervasive nature of regulation beginning with the Interstate Commerce Act of 1883; by negative public attitudes toward the industry, the largest and most powerful sector of the economy for many decades when it held a virtual monopoly on modern transport in the country; by virtue of the need for railroads to own large amounts of real property; and by the transformation of the industry after deregulation in the 1980s and 1990s. In recent years, this traditional antithesis toward government has been changing, with greater involvement by the rail industry in state and regional transportation planning efforts, increased public support for rail infrastructure projects to ease highway congestion and stimulate economic development, and a sense among industry leaders that homeland security can also provide a logic for the public sector to work with them to limit trespass and ease liability claims for events on railroad property.

Despite some real changes, there is still a long way to go before it is likely that railroads and the public will be true partners in a network approach. Railroads still resist efforts at public accountability, even in regard to facilities envisioned to be paid for by public dollars, and are not often willing to put forth the funds needed to deal with obvious security problems, such as the vulnerability of major cities to hazardous materials now routed through such cities as Baltimore and Washington, D.C., a problem that could be eased by building bypass lines for freight that now moves through the center of cities. Seen in light of Johnston's balance between private and public values (2004), the rail industry and its public sector partners in homeland security have not yet had to move significantly away from the private sector/efficiency side of the equation to the public sector/effectiveness side. Or, the development of a network approach that seems to satisfy demands for increased vigilance, information sharing, and planning without a loss of independence by the private sector organizations may be seen as a way of achieving public sector values through partnering, perhaps requiring less of a shift in control than experienced by the airlines after September 11.

Of course, all that we know about railroad-directed terrorism is conjecture, or based on examples drawn from other national settings. Should the rails be used for an actual terrorist attack, especially one of the magnitude of the World Trade Center attacks or greater, or perhaps a coordinated attack on multiple rail targets in a short period of time, the risk-based network approach will be put to its greatest test, as will the public's willingness to tolerate any level of risk in an area of demonstrated vulnerability, and perhaps the will of government and the public to provide funding needed to insure that the industry's economic losses are covered so that it can continue to serve as the safest and most efficient way to move people and freight.

NOTE

(This chapter is a revised version of an article entitled "Competing Models for Enhancing Railroad Security" that appeared in *The Public Manager*, Fall 2005, pp. 13–19. Reprinted with permission of the copyright holder.)

REFERENCES

Chertoff, Michael 2005. Remarks to the George Washington University Homeland Security Policy Institute, March 16, 2005.

Comfort, Louise K. 2002. Rethinking security: organizational fragility in extreme events. *Public Administration Review*, 62, Special Issue, September: 98–107.

De Rugy, Veronique 2005. Homeland Preparedness. Web site of the American Enterprise Institute, http://www.aei.org/about, March 18, 2005, posting.

Dobbins, J. 2004. The Effect of Terrorist Attacks on Spain on Transatlantic Cooperation in the War on Terror. Testimony presented to the Senate Committee on Foreign Relations Subcommittee on European Affairs on March 31, 2004.

Flynn, Stephen E. 2002. America the vulnerable. *Foreign Affairs*, 81, 1: 60–74.

Frederickson, H. George, and Todd R. LaPorte 2002. Airport security, high reliability, and the problem of rationality. *Public Administration Review*, 62, Special issue, September: 33–43.

Johnston, V. R. 2004. Terrorism and Transportation Policy and Administration: Balancing the Model and Equation for Optimal Security. *Review of Policy Research*, 21, 3: 263–274.

Plant, J. F. 2004. Terrorism and the Railroads: Redefining Security in the Wake of 9/11. *Review of Policy Research*, 21, 3: 293–306.

Plant, J. F. 2005. Competing Models for Enhancing Railroad Security. *The Public Manager*, 34, 3: 13–19.

Riley, J. 2004. Terrorism and Rail Security: Testimony presented to the Senate Commerce, Science, and Transportation Committee on March 23, 2004.

Savage, Ian 1998. *The Economics of Railroad Safety*. Kluwer Academic Publishers.

U.S. General Accountability Office 2004. Rail Security: Some Actions Taken to Enhance Passenger and Freight Rail Security, but Significant Challenges Remain. GAO-04-598T.

32 Securing Mass Transit after the Madrid and London Bombings

William L. Waugh, Jr.

The security of the nation's mass transit systems became a concern for Americans after the World Trade Center and Pentagon attacks in September 2001. But, while New York City's subway and train systems were affected by the attacks and transportation links in south Manhattan have had to be rebuilt, neither system was a direct target. However, intelligence gathered as the nation launched its "war on terrorism" has indicated that the nation's subway systems and perhaps its interstate bus systems might become targets of terrorist violence. Nonetheless, little was done to secure the systems until the Madrid train bombings in March 2004 and much remains to be done if the systems are to be reasonably secure.

Following the London and Madrid bombings, alerts were issued and transit systems in much of Europe and North America mobilized their security forces. The bombings were not the first indication that terrorists might choose railway and subway systems as targets, but the scale of the attacks focused attention on the vulnerability of rail systems and on the political repercussions that might befall a government that failed to deal with similar attacks effectively. The response of the British government was quick. Years of experience with Irish Republican Army bombings served to guide the British response and the transit system was back in operation within days. The response of the Spanish government to the Madrid attacks was slow. Officials initially blamed domestic terrorists and, when their error became clear, they lost the national election and were replaced by a new government. Still, little federal investment in securing America's mass transit systems followed. Following the Madrid bombings, the U.S. Department of Homeland Security raised the national alert to level orange (high) and the largest systems were enjoined to step up their security measures accordingly. But the raised alert level did not bring extra dollars. Mass transit systems in the United States are still largely left to their own devices to protect facilities, vehicles, staff, and passengers and many do not respond at all when alert levels are raised (Weiss 2004).

How vulnerable are the nation's transit systems and how likely is it that they will be targeted by terrorists? Transit systems in the United States have largely been spared to date. The attacks that have occurred have been relatively minor. Elsewhere in the world the situation has been very different. The common wisdom used to be that terrorists wanted a lot of people watching and not a lot of people dead, but that has changed since the 1980s. Terrorists have attempted to kill hundreds, even thousands, of people and there is some fear that terrorists might attempt to kill millions of people.

Any locations where thousands of people might gather have become targets. Therefore, transit systems, particularly buses and trains, have become attractive targets. While transit systems in the United States have not experienced mass casualty attacks, transit systems in other parts of the world have. Between July 1997 and December 2000, terrorists and criminals attacked or attempted to attack transit systems in forty-eight different countries. The largest numbers of attacks on buses and trains were in India, Israel, Georgia, Russia, Egypt, Germany, Japan, Pakistan, the United Kingdom, China, Sri Lanka, Nigeria, and the Philippines (Jenkins and Gersten 2001).

After the Madrid and London bombings, should we expect that the United States will suffer similar attacks? Will al Qaeda or another international or domestic terrorist group target American subway or bus systems? Certainly alerts have been issued and transit security forces have been mobilized, but will the threats become reality? The potential loss of life from mass transit attacks in the United States is not hard to imagine. Transit systems are part of the nation's critical infrastructure. The potential loss of service, in addition to any loss of life, could severely damage local economies and cause considerable fear among those who use mass transit and even those who do not. The economic repercussions could be widespread if commuters, tourists, and other riders could not or would not use the systems and businesses dependent upon the systems were closed. The potential economic impact alone might draw terrorists to transit systems, as they are drawn to tourist resorts, hotels, and other sites (Richter and Waugh 1991). Attacks on tourists in Egypt in the early 1990s, for example, caused substantial financial losses for hotel and resort owners and for tour operators and it took years to lure tourists back. The U.K. suffered similar reductions in tourism when the IRA bombed the Tower of London in the 1980s and New York City suffered similar losses after September 11.

Following the September 11 attacks, there was some concern voiced about the vulnerability of mass transit systems in the United States and transit officials were asked to increase their security. Counter-terrorist and anti-terrorist programs also were stepped up after the sniper attacks in the Washington, D.C., area when it was discovered that the snipers had ridden on the METRO system. Nonetheless, most of the federal government's attention has remained on the security of aircraft and airport facilities. Both the US Department of Transportation and the Department of Homeland Security have invested most of their efforts in securing civil aviation (see, e.g., Office of Homeland Security 2002; GAO 2003). Given that the September 11 attacks involved aircraft and given that there has been a long history of skyjackings and other aviation-related violence, that focus is understandable. But, it clearly does not address the full range of risks to the nation's transportation systems.

There are lessons that can be learned from aviation security that can help reduce the vulnerabilities of transit systems. The crash of PanAm Flight 103 over Lockerbie, Scotland in 1988 lead to the creation of the Presidential Commission on Aviation Safety and Terrorism in 1990 and the adoption of baggage screening measures to prevent similar attacks. Airport security measures helped prevent hijackings and armed attacks. International conventions against attacks against civil aviation discouraged nations from providing sanctuary to hijackers. Changing air routes to avoid airports with lax security and discouraging tourists from using such airports also had an impact. And, the fact that terrorist organizations themselves chose to use other means of carrying out their attacks greatly reduced the incidence of hijackings and other attacks on aircraft and airport facilities (see, e.g., Waugh 1990). No such international consensus against attacks on mass transit systems yet exists. Attacks on mass transit systems are still viewed as largely a national, rather than an international, problem. But, it may be possible to develop international conventions against attacks involving rail systems that cross international boundaries or simply to increase information sharing about terrorist organizations. Securing facilities and screening passengers and baggage would seem to be the most effective approaches. This is the approach used in securing aircraft and airport facilities and appears to be the best model for securing mass transit systems, but there are significant differences between air and land transportation and the systems themselves.

It is problematic that policy makers seldom address vulnerabilities until a crisis forces them to act. Passage of the Defense Against Weapons of Mass Destruction (Nunn-Lugar-Domenici) Act of 1996 was in response to the growing number of mass casualty attacks, including the 1995 attack on the Tokyo subway system. The Tokyo attack drew attention to the vulnerability of the nation's infrastructure and the potential lethality of chemical weapons. Presidential Decision Directive 63 followed in 1998 to protect the nation's critical infrastructure. The bombing of the *USS Cole* in 2000 and an attack on a French freighter in 2002 also drew attention to the vulnerability of shipping. The creation of the Office of Homeland Security, the creation of the Transportation Security Administration in the U.S. Department of Transportation, and the Aviation and Transportation Security Act of 2001 followed the World Trade Center and Pentagon attacks (Rubin et al. 2004). The point is that policy initiatives follow major attacks and tend to focus on those kinds of events. The pattern in Homeland Security policy making has been very much like it has been in natural disaster policy making Policy makers address specific crises with little attention to future crises. That is the principal reason why the White House and Congress have been so slow to recognize and deal with the threat to mass transit systems. Border and aviation security, the two vulnerabilities revealed by the September 11 attacks, are clearly the priorities of the Department of Homeland Security.

It is also problematic that the level of risk to mass transit systems in the United States is still unknown. Attacks on transit systems have been threatened, according to Homeland Security officials. The national alert level has been elevated with particular mention of the threat to transit systems. However, similar warnings have been issued for possible attacks on airports and aircraft, ships and port facilities, bridges and tunnels, pipelines, high rise buildings, public buildings, water systems, power stations, gasoline and other hazardous materials storage sites, and other potential targets. Warnings were issued about possible attacks on subways and rail systems in May 2002 (Salant 2002) and against passenger trains in October 2002. A specific warning about possible attacks on transit systems was issued in 2005. But, no such attacks have taken place as yet and transit system security measures have yet to be tested.

Despite the Madrid and London bombings, the adoption of nationwide mass transit security programs has been very slow. Security measures have been implemented in those systems that have already been involved indirectly in terrorist attacks (such as New York City, Boston, and Washington, D.C.) and those that have been involved in special events that might make them targets of terrorists (such as Atlanta and Salt Lake City, which have hosted Olympic Games). The vulnerability of transit systems has also been a concern in cities that have hosted World Series, Super Bowl, and other major cultural and sporting events—so-called events of national significance. However, the federal government has not made an investment in transit security comparable to the investments in other potential terrorist targets, even after the Madrid and London bombings. Even with adequate funding and state-of-the-art security technologies, it is extremely difficult to protect people, equipment, and infrastructure in transit systems while, at the same time, protecting the financial viability of the systems (Waugh 2004). In other words, fortifying the systems is possible, but it might ultimately lead to the destruction of the systems.

THE SECURITY PROBLEM IN TRANSIT SYSTEMS

Transit systems are defined as "all multiple-occupancy-vehicle services designed to transport customers on local and regional routes, such as bus, trolley bus, commuter rail, van pool, ferry boat, and light rail services..." (GAO 2002, 4). In 2000, transit systems in the United States provided over 9 billion passenger trips and employed approximately 350,000 people. The American Public Transportation Association has estimated that 61 percent of the ridership is by bus, 28 percent by heavy rail (including subways), 4 percent by commuter rail, 3 percent by light rail, 2 percent by other (e.g., ferry boats, vans, etc.), and 1 percent by trolley bus (GAO 2002, 5). Four percent of operating expenses are provided by the federal government, 21 percent by state governments, and 22 percent by local governments. Thirty-six percent of operating expenses are covered by fares. In short, public transit systems are heavily dependent upon ridership for their operating funds. Fares account for over one-third of their operating budgets while 47 percent of their capital funding is provided by the federal government (GAO 2002, 7). Security measures are largely operating expenses, therefore they are primarily paid for by state and local taxpayers and by riders. Given state and local financial problems in recent years, mass transit funding has seldom kept up with basic system needs. Transferring the costs of security to riders would not be as easy as it has been for air passengers. Security costs an estimated $7.50 per passenger trip for air travelers (Petersen 2005). Mass transit riders would not pay that much per passenger trip. Indeed, transit fares are usually well under that amount. Moreover, transit riders frequently have other transportation options. Many would use private automobiles rather than subways or buses if the fare was much higher than they are paying now.

In a 2002 U.S. General Accounting Office (now the Government Accountability Office) report, it was found that transit systems in the United States were assessing vulnerabilities, developing emergency plans, and preparing for attacks. Financing security was the biggest challenge. The transit systems serving populations over two hundred thousand are prohibited under federal law from using federal funds designated for building and maintaining systems for security. Securing facilities and routes is very expensive and systems have little internal funding for such activities. Much the same is true of the local law enforcement, fire and medical services, and emergency management agencies upon which the transit systems have to rely. While some limited investment of transit system monies and state and local monies has been made, the transit systems need federal funds to support security measures.

The American Public Transportation Association (APTA) has supported voluntary audits of rail, commuter rail, and bus system safety. APTA created a task force on security initiatives and identified areas needing research (*Passenger Transport* 2001a, 6) and entered into a partnership with the Department of Transportation in 2003 to help protect the nation's transportation infrastructure. The partnership's foci have been on communication and cooperation among federal agencies and the transit industry, threat awareness workshops for transit officials, and strategies to reduce the risk of attack (USDOT 2003). Still, the implementation of those efforts has been slowed by lack of funding.

In addition to financial challenges, securing transit systems also presents political and logistical challenges. Cooperation among jurisdictions is a political challenge. Agreement on security objectives and measures requires considerable political and administrative effort. Transit systems often cross many jurisdictional boundaries and coordination is necessary to assure that all rails and roads, tunnels, bridges, and other infrastructure are secured. Private firms, community organizations, and federal agencies, as well as local and state governments, are stakeholders. An anti-terrorism exercise, for example, may involve dozens of agencies. A terrorist event would further expand the roster of participants as more federal and state representatives become involved.

However, the biggest challenge is maintaining public access while securing facilities and equipment. That access can also afford opportunity for terrorist access. Fortifying rail and bus stations is relatively easy. Guarding dozens to hundreds of miles of rails and roads is not. The experience with aviation security measures provides some guidance, but it is not the same. Anything that reduces convenience and speed of transit for riders may cause a significant loss in ridership. Even metal detectors may slow access and reduce convenience enough to dissuade travelers from using the system. A loss of riders will reduce fare revenue and affect the financial viability of the transit system. Intrusive security measures can cause riders to feel that the system is unsafe. For air travelers, there are few alternative means of travel for long distances but, for transit passengers, there generally are alternatives. There is evidence that some travelers are choosing to drive rather than to fly shorter distances, because the additional time it takes to deal with baggage and security makes up for or nearly makes up for the increase in travel time. While some riders will choose to use mass transit even with delays going through security gates and having bags checked, many others will choose to drive if security measures slow travel time by more than a few minutes.

THREATS TO MASS TRANSIT

Perceptions of the vulnerability of transit systems have certainly changed since the Madrid and London bombings, although those perceptions have not lead to more security. The Madrid bombings were relatively complex operations in terms of the timing of the bombs and the London bombings were all the more frightening because they were suicide attacks and involved British residents who were not readily discernible in the diverse population. Israeli authorities have been frustrated by their inability to prevent suicide attacks and Western European and North American authorities had been warning that suicide attacks might occur in their nations. Prior to the Madrid and London attacks, the sarin gas attack on the Tokyo subway in 1995 was the most disturbing attack on mass transit. The subway attack caused a dozen deaths and over five hundred serious casualties, but it could have been much worse had the terrorists been able to disperse the chemical better. Despite the fact that the group, Aum Shinrikyo, had considerable financial and technical resources, the delivery system for the chemical was very crude. Had they been able to disperse the chemical more widely, the moving trains might have distributed the agent within the system and the ventilation system might have blown it out onto sidewalks and streets. More passengers and pedestrians might have been exposed and many more people may have been killed. Thousands might have been killed.

The lessons of the Tokyo subway bombing were that (1) some terrorists are willing to kill hundreds or even thousands of people and (2) some terrorists have the wherewithal to create "weapons of mass destruction." But, while terrorists have access to toxic agents, they may not have the delivery systems necessary to expose thousands of people. Aum Shinrikyo had very large financial resources, members with scientific training and skills, and operated in an open society, but it still could not produce a sophisticated delivery system for its weapon. That is not to say that other groups do not have the same kinds of resources and skills, but it does suggest that delivering chemical, biological, and radiological weapons is not as easy as some might assume. Nonetheless, some U.S. transit systems have chemical and radiological monitors and effective biological agent monitors is a priority. More conventional bombs, including homemade bombs, are still the weapons of choice for most terrorist organizations (see, e.g., Smithson and Levy 2000; Waugh 2003) and are the most likely threat to transit systems..

Crowded stations, trains, and buses are very difficult to monitor. Backpacks, suitcases, briefcases, shopping bags, bulky clothing, and all manner of boxes and bags present serious difficulties for security. Freight, vendor stock, and parcel deliveries may be used to transport bombs. Passengers may carry bombs into stations and on board trains. Workers may carry in bombs. Israel's experience with suicide bombers is instructive and similar attacks may be carried out in our transit systems, as they were in London's Underground and bus systems. The point is that the systems are vulnerable and that vulnerability is difficult to address. Armed guards may not be an effective deterrent. The most effective defenses, as the Israelis have discovered, are trained drivers and police who can identify suspicious persons and an aware public that can keep watch for suspicious persons. Low-tech tactics may be the easiest for terrorists to use and low-tech security measures may be the most effective defense for the public and for authorities.

HOMELAND SECURITY AND MASS TRANSIT

How is the U.S. government dealing with the threat posed by terrorists to our mass transit systems? One month after the September 11 attacks, Senator John McCain introduced a bill, the Rail Transportation Safety and Security Act, to increase the penalties for attacking or threatening to attack freight and passenger trains. The bill included funds for security upgrades ranging from more guards to surveillance equipment. The bill did not pass. Another bill, the Rail Security Act of 2001, was reported out of the Senate Commerce, Science, and Transportation Committee a week later, but it did not make it to the floor of the Senate for a vote. The FY02 Defense appropriation included some limited funding for rail safety and security, including funds to increase security for tunnels, bridges, and other rail infrastructure, and to study of economic impact of security investments (NGA 2002). Other congressional attempts to increase funding for mass transit security have also failed (see, e.g., *National Journal* 2004; Sharn 2004).

With the signing of the Aviation and Transportation Security Act of 2001, a little over a month after the September 11 attacks, the Transportation Security Administration (TSA) was created. Along with the Federal Transit Administration and the Federal Aviation Administration, TSA was charged with responsibility for securing America's transportation systems. TSA was created because of the threat to civil aviation, but its responsibilities include other transportation modes, including mass transit systems. Up until this time, airlines, railroads, subway systems, and other transit systems were largely responsible for their own security and relied on their own security forces and on mutual aid agreements with local and state law enforcement agencies.

The Federal Transit Administration has been collaborating with transit authorities in London, Paris, Tokyo, and Israel to identify "best practice" security measures. As of 2002, the FTA administrator assisted with thirty-seven threat and vulnerability assessments, provided eighty-three security training grants, helped implement chemical detection programs in the Washington, D.C. and Boston subway systems, developed an information sharing center to provide intelligence information to transit officials, and assisted in the implementation of "transit watch" systems in which employees and passengers are trained to watch for and report suspicious activity. The agency has been working on national standards for transit systems, as well as civil aviation (GAO 2002). TSA provided $148 million in grants to beef up security, although only $15 million was provided to the interstate bus systems for "vehicle tracking and driver protection" (Dunn 2003). Attacks on bus drivers provided impetus for that funding.

Most of the security on the nation's transit systems has been provided by the systems themselves. Track walkers, armed security guards, transit police, and other measures have been used to reduce the likelihood of attacks. Trash bins, newspaper vending machines, luggage lockers, and bicycle storage lockers have been removed from public areas so that they cannot be used to conceal bombs. Soon after the September 11 attacks, the Washington METRO sought funding for closed circuit television cameras, a fiber optic network to support CCTV cameras, intrusion monitoring equipment, employee ID equipment, personal protective equipment and training for five thousand employees, cameras and a locator system for system buses, an expanded chemical sensor program, and personnel to provide a high visibility patrols (*Passenger Transport* 2001b, 9). In 2003, CSX Transportation, one of the nation's major rail companies, adopted an identification system for its employees so that access to its facilities could be better controlled (CSX 2003). A credentialing system for transportation workers was one of the priorities identified by TSA, as well (White House 2003).

The U.S. Department of Transportation did issue a planning and emergency preparedness guide for transit systems in 2003, but funding of security programs has been slow in coming. Notwithstanding the scarcity of federal funding, some transit systems have recently implemented programs to involve passengers in security, such has having periodic announcements that passengers should report suspicious behavior and packages, and in emergency procedures, such as training some passengers to assist with evacuation and posting information on evacuation procedures. New technologies to identify bomb residue on passengers boarding commuter trains have been tested (CNN 2004), but they have not been deployed nationally. Chemical, radiological, and biological monitors are being placed in the systems considered to be at the greatest risk, but they have not been deployed widely. The systems are still relying on more traditional security technologies. For example, New York's Metropolitan Transportation Authority is implementing a more sophisticated system of closed circuit television cameras and motion detectors for its subway, bus, and commuter train network, but the new system is the first major investment ($200 million) since the September 11 attacks (CNN 2005).

Mass transit may benefit from its connection to the nation's critical infrastructure. According to *The National Strategy for the Physical Protection of Critical Infrastructures and Key Assets* (2003), mass transit is an area of concern and it recommends (1) the identification of critical planning areas and the development of standards, (2) the identification of "impediments" to security enhancements, and (3) working with public, private, and other groups to develop priorities and plans (61–62). Nonetheless, mass transit still seems an afterthought in the national strategy and it seems much less important to policymakers than the nation's rail, aviation, and maritime infrastructure. However, the potential losses from attacks on transit systems should encourage greater attention and greater funding to mitigate risks.

CONCLUSIONS

One would expect that the Madrid and London bombings would have given much greater impetus for major investments in security for the nation's mass transit systems. But, funding and other resources are still going to other Homeland Security priorities. It may well take a major mass casualty attack in the United States to encourage close attention to the threat. The challenge of securing mass transit systems from terrorist attack is also a daunting one, not because the systems cannot be made much more secure but because of the trade-off between security and access. Any measures that delay travelers for more than a few minutes will lower fare revenue. Travelers may have more patience if there is a major attack, but that patience may lessen as the perception of the threat lessens. It is part of the common wisdom in disaster management that the memories of disaster fade rather rapidly and, as the memories go, the willingness to remain prepared for disaster also goes. It has taken the airline industry years to overcome the drop in air travel after September 11 and the effects are still being felt. For small transit systems with relatively few passengers and few alternative means of transportation, passengers may be willing to trade convenience for security. But, for large systems, the crowds will be difficult to surveil. For systems heavily subsidized by the government or able to transfer the costs of security to consumers, the costs of security may be acceptable. However, for most mass transit systems in populous areas, the large numbers of passengers and resultant costs of comprehensive screening processes are likely to be prohibitive. Delays of even a few minutes may encourage riders to seek alternative means of transportation.

The cost of transit security may also be too high for systems and riders to bear. While securing stations and platforms may be relatively easy because there are familiar technologies for doing so, securing entire systems is not possible. Adequate investments in security technologies, training, and personnel will require federal funding. Mutual assistance agreements can expand capabilities, but they also increase the need for joint training and communications. The most cost effective approach will be to maximize the use of "dual use" technologies and "all hazards" plans. Building the security system on the existent disaster management and crime control systems will increase local capacities and assure that investments are efficient. The same programs that are in place for hazardous materials spills and fires, not to mention transportation accidents, can be made adaptable for terrorist-sponsored disasters (Waugh forthcoming).

Federal funding and basic capacity building are the answers. First, however, transit system security needs much greater national attention. Unfortunately, that is not likely to happen until there is a major terrorist attack. Emergency managers had to wait for a major natural disaster to remind public officials, including Homeland Security officials, that terrorism is not the only threat to life and property in the United States. Transit officials may have to wait for a similar reminder.

REFERENCES

CNN (2005), "New York's MTA Orders $200 Mission Security System," http://www.cnn.com/2005/US/08/23/transit.security.ap/index.html. Accessed September 8, 2005.

CNN (2004), "Government to Test New Rail Security System," http://www.cnn.com, Accessed May 4, 2004.

Government Executive Magazine (2003), "Port, Bus Security Grants Total $148 Million," GovExec.com, January 14. http://www.govexec.com/dailyfed/0103/011403td1.htm. Accessed January 15, 2003.

Jenkins, Brian Michael, and Larry N. Gersten (2001), *Protecting Public Surface Transportation Against Terrorism and Serious Crime: Continuing Research on Best Security Practices*, Mineta Transportation Institute, College of Business, San Jose State University, San Jose, CA, MTI Report 01-07, September.

National Governors' Association (2002), "Homeland Security—Transportation Security," Homeland Security Web site, http://www.nga.org/legislativeUpdate/1,1169,C_IS-SUE_BRIEF^D_3261,00.html. Accessed November 9, 2002.

National Journal (2004), "House Bill Would Provide Money to Protect Public Transportation," GovExec.com, May 13. http://www.GovExec.com. Accessed May 13, 2004.

Office of Homeland Security (2002), *National Strategy for Homeland Security*, Washington, D.C., July.

Passenger Transport (2001a), "APTA at Forefront of Industry's Response to Security Threats," *America Under Threat: Transit Responds to Terrorism,* Supplement to *Passenger Transport*, December 10, p. 6.

Passenger Transport (2001b). "WMATA Stays the Course and Rises to the Occasion," *America Under Threat: Transit Responds to Terrorism,* Supplement to *Passenger Transport*, December 10, p. 9–10.

Petersen, John E. (2005), "Costing Out Security," *Governing*, September, p. 66.

Richter, Linda K., and Waugh, William L., Jr. (1991). "Terrorism and Tourism as Logical Companions," in *Managing Tourism*, ed. by S. Medlik (Oxford, U.K.: Butterworth Heinemann), pp. 318–326.

Rubin, Claire B., Cumming, William R, and Tanali, Irmak R. (2002). *Terrorism Time Line: Major Milestone Events and Their U.S. Outcomes (1988–2001)*, Arlington, VA: Claire B. Rubin & Associates, May.

Salant, Jonathan D. (2002). "Nation: Transportation Department Warns of Terrorism by Rail, Sea," *The Nando Times*, May 24. Http://www.nandotimes.com/nation/story/413085p-3290348c.html. Accessed June 3, 2002.

Sharn, Lori (2004),."Senate Panel OKs $4.5 Billion to Ramp Up Transit Security," GovExec. com, May 6. http://www.GovExec.com. Accessed on on May 13, 2004.

Smithson, Amy, and Levy, Leslie-Anne (2000), *Ataxia: The Chemical and Biological Terrorism Threat and U.S. Response* (Washington, D.C.: Stimson Center, Report No. 35, October).

U.S. Department of Transportation, Federal Transit Administration (2003), *The Public Transportation System: Security and Emergency Preparedness Planning Guide* (Washington, D.C.: USDOT, FTA, January).

U.S. Department of Transportation (2003), "DOT, American Public Transit Association Form Partnership to Protect Public Transportation Infrastructure," Washington, D.C.: USDOT Office of Public Affairs, January 23.

U.S. General Accounting Office (2002), *Mass Transit: Federal Action Could Help Transit Agencies Address Security Challenges*, Washington, D.C.: GAO, GAO-03-263, December.

U.S. General Accounting Office (2003), *Major Management Challenges and Program Risks: Department of Homeland Security*, Washington, D.C.: GAO, GAO-03-102, January.

Waugh, William L., Jr. (forthcoming), "Reducing Risk to Rail and Transit Systems After the Madrid Bombings: An All-Hazards Approach," *Public Performance and Management Review.*

Waugh, William L., Jr. (2004), "Securing Mass Transit: A Challenge for Homeland Security," *Review of Policy Research* 21 (3): 307–316.

Waugh, William L., Jr. (2003), "The Global Challenge of the New Terrorism," *Journal of Emergency Management* 1 (Spring): 27–38.

Weiss, Jack (2004). "Orange Crunch." *New York Times* (January 14).

The White House (2003). *The National Strategy for the Physical Protection of Critical Infrastructures and Key Assets*, Washington, D.C., February.

Index

Page numbers in italic refer to figures or tables.